Imperialism and After

Imperialism and After
Continuities and Discontinuities

Edited by
WOLFGANG J. MOMMSEN and
JÜRGEN OSTERHAMMEL

THE GERMAN HISTORICAL INSTITUTE

ALLEN & UNWIN
London
Boston   Sydney

© The German Historical Institute, 1986
This book is copyright under the Berne Convention.
No reproduction without permission. All rights reserved.

**Allen & Unwin (Publishers) Ltd,
40 Museum Street, London WC1A 1LU, UK**

Allen & Unwin (Publishers) Ltd,
Park Lane, Hemel Hempstead, Herts HP2 4TE, UK

Allen & Unwin, Inc.,
8 Winchester Place, Winchester, Mass. 01890, USA

Allen & Unwin (Australia) Ltd,
8 Napier Street, North Sydney, NSW 2060, Australia

First published in 1986

British Library Cataloguing in Publication Data

Imperialism and after: continuities and discontinuities.
1. Imperialism – History
I. Mommsen, Wolfgang J.   2. Osterhammel, Jürgen
3. German Historical Institute
325'.32'0904   JC359
ISBN 0-04-909018-6

Library of Congress Cataloging in Publication Data

Main entry under title:
   Imperialism and after
Includes index.
1. Imperialism – Addresses, essays, lectures.
I. Mommsen, Wolfgang J., 1930- . II. Osterhammel, Jürgen.
JC359.I47 1985   325'.32   85-6142
ISBN 0-04-909018-6 (alk. paper)

Set in 10 on 11 point Times by Computape (Pickering) Ltd,
North Yorkshire
and printed in Great Britain by Mackays of Chatham

Contents

Preface *Wolfgang J. Mommsen*		*page* ix
1	Imperialism and Empire: An Introduction *H. L. Wesseling*	1

PART ONE The New Imperial Powers

2	The Global Role of the United States and its Imperial Consequences, 1898–1973 *Klaus Schwabe*	13
3	The Paradox of Imperialism: The American Case *A. E. Campbell*	34
4	American Imperialism is Anti-Communism *Tony Smith*	41
5	Modern Imperialism? The Tsarist and the Soviet Examples *Dietrich Geyer*	49
6	The Politics of Expansion of the Japanese Empire: Imperialism or Pan-Asiatic Mission? *Bernd Martin*	63
7	Some Thoughts on Japanese Expansion *Ian H. Nish*	83
8	Imperialism and Revisionism in Interwar Germany *Hartmut Pogge von Strandmann*	90

PART TWO The Legacy of Empire: Some Regional Studies

9	Imperialism and State Formation in Africa: Nigeria and Chad *Albert Wirz*	123
10	The Legacy of the British-Indian Empire in Independent India *Dietmar Rothermund*	139
11	Continuities and Discontinuities in Indo-British Economic Relations: British Multinational Corporations in India, 1920–1970 *B. R. Tomlinson*	154
12	Imperialist Domination in Vietnam and Cambodia: A Long-Term View *Dieter Brötel*	167

PART THREE Imperialism and the World Economy

13	Historical Roots of Economic Underdevelopment: Myths and Realities *Paul Bairoch*	191

viii *Contents*

14	The Third World in the International Economy *J. Forbes Munro*	217
15	'A New Imperial System'? The Role of the Multinational Corporations Reconsidered *David Fieldhouse*	225
16	Multinational Corporations in World System Perspective *Volker Bornschier*	241
17	The Newly Industrializing Countries of East Asia: Imperialist Continuity or a Case of Catching Up? *Ulrich Menzel*	247

PART FOUR   Towards a General Theory of Imperialism

18	The Excentric Idea of Imperialism, with or without Empire *Ronald Robinson*	267
19	Semi-Colonialism and Informal Empire in Twentieth-Century China: Towards a Framework of Analysis *Jürgen Osterhammel*	290
20	Conflict and Convergence in Development Theory *Colin Leys*	315
21	Theories of Imperialism in Perspective *Anthony Brewer*	325
22	The End of Empire and the Continuity of Imperialism *Wolfgang J. Mommsen*	333

Notes on Contributors   359

Index   363

Preface

More than forty years ago Sir Keith Hancock, the great British Empire and Commonwealth historian, complained bitterly that research into the history of empire was being impeded by a variety of inconsistent and ideological notions of imperialism which had little to do with reality: 'Imperialism is no word for scholars. The emotional echoes which it arouses are too violent and too contradictory. It does not convey a precise meaning.'[1] However, this term cannot be abandoned easily, given the fact that imperialism still figures prominently as a concept in the present controversies on the relationship between the West and the Third World, in the past and in our own day. Historians cannot opt out of contemporary debates if they want to bring the message of history across to their audience. They should be conscious of the political implications of historical reasoning, rather than shy away from them. If they refuse to tackle the problems more or less directly associated with the term 'imperialism', they miss an opportunity to exercise a rationalizing and enlightening influence on the passionate debate about imperialism, neo-colonialism and *dependencia*, still being carried on with great force at the present time. When Sir Keith Hancock wrote his indictment of the terminology of imperialism, partly a result of his reluctance to give any credit to the Marxist–Leninist theories of colonialism and imperialism, the British Commonwealth of Nations was moving fairly smoothly towards the gradual emancipation of the colonial peoples, although it was presumed that this would take a long time. Imperialism appeared to have lost its nasty character to a certain degree, and colonial rule in trust for the colonial peoples seemed to be a truly respectable policy.

After the end of the Second World War, however, there was a sudden acceleration in the process of decolonization, making nonsense of earlier notions of a careful preparation for independence, however slow, by paternalistic colonial administrations. Only a few years earlier the transfer of power had appeared to many to be a still distant affair, but during the 1950s the strengthening of the nationalist movements forced the imperial powers to agree to hand over control to indigenous élites within a very short time. Two decades later most of the colonial dependencies of the imperial powers had been granted independence. It must be added, however, that in the majority of cases the new states decided to maintain a special relationship with the former mother country by joining associations such as the British Commonwealth or the Union Française, which retained at least the semblance, if not the substance, of imperial paramountcy for the former metropolitan power in the foreseeable future. However, optimistic expectations that the new nations would closely follow the developmental path of the former metropolitan countries, and that they would be able to catch up in the competitive struggle for modernization and industrial development were sorely disappointed. The same was true of the assumption that democratic government could successfully be transplanted to the former colonies. While some of the former dependent territories did manage to catch up with the advanced industrial countries, albeit with considerable delay, most of them found it increasingly difficult to break the mould of dependency and backwardness. On the whole, the gap between the advanced industrial countries of the West and their former colonial dependencies did not narrow at all; on the contrary, it widened further and, indeed, it appears to be still widening today.

For this reason, among others, the debate about imperialism and its aftermath did not die away with the granting of independence, as might have been expected during the 1950s and 1960s when Western modernization theories had their heyday. From the point of view of the Third World, imperialism was, and is, seen as a continuing reality even after independence. Indeed, for the former colonial peoples, the transfer of power was only the starting-point for an attempt gradually to overcome the state of dependency in which they found themselves, economically, politically and culturally.

For many years historical research concentrated on the period of classical imperialism and on the driving forces behind imperialist expansion inside European societies. The field was left largely to the social scientists who concentrated on modernization and developmental theory. Only during the last two decades have the history of decolonization and the development of the new nations after independence received more attention from historical scholarship. The social scientists working in this field did not care to devote much of their energy to studying the history of empire or to analysing the historical conditions which gave rise to a policy of modernization. They were convinced that the problems could be solved with the instruments of modern technology and modern social science. Therefore they cared little about the history of these territories or, indeed, imperialism in general. Consequently, the field was by and large left to the ideologists who invoked the allegedly dirty word 'imperialism' for a great variety of political purposes. As a result, historians and social scientists have been working alongside each other for many years without taking much notice of each other. A huge body of literature on underdevelopment and *dependencia* was produced which took almost no account of the work of the historians; only the classic theoreticians, such as Hobson, Lenin and Schumpeter, for example, were given a prominent position in the debate. Conversely, in historical scholarship the discussion about the rights and wrongs of the economic interpretation of imperialism was the main topic of interest for a long time. It is only recently that the gap which was allowed to develop after 1945 between social science and history in the fields of imperialism and post-imperialism has begun to close, if only to a limited degree. Some years ago W. H. Morris-Jones and Georges Fischer convened a conference on 'Decolonisation and After: The British and French Experience';[2] its proceedings were published in 1980. In the same year the Centre for the

Preface xi

History of European Expansion in Leiden published a collection of essays on the subject of history and underdevelopment.[3] More recently a considerable number of area studies have appeared, dealing with the problems of post-imperialism and neo-colonialism and underdevelopment, such as Colin Leys's *Underdevelopment in Kenya*,[4] and Giovanni Arrighi's *The Political Economy of Rhodesia*.[5] These studies go beyond the mere theoretical reasoning which was dominant for two decades.

This book is intended to contribute to this debate. It has emerged from an international conference on 'Imperialism after Empire' which was arranged by the German Historical Institute, London, and took place from 27 to 29 September 1982 at the Werner-Reimers-Stiftung in Bad Homburg.[6] The initial idea for the conference came from Professor Ronald Robinson, Dr Hartmut Pogge von Strandmann and Professor David Fieldhouse. It would not have been possible to convene the conference without their advice and assistance. The conference itself depended to a large extent on the intellectual orientation provided by Ronald Robinson's introductory paper, which now opens Part Four of this book.

The objective of the conference was to look into the continuities and discontinuities of imperialism from the 1880s to the present day. It focused on the questions of whether the granting of independence was a definite cæsura, whether imperialist relationships survived informally, and whether it makes sense to speak of a re-emergence of imperialism after 1945.

The ambiguities in the concept of imperialism, which Hancock found so irritating, have to be accepted as a fact of life from which historical analysis must begin. There are not only different forms of imperialism, but also widely deviating interpretations of imperialist policies. The chapters in this book look at the issues afresh, rather than reiterating the traditional formulæ on this controversial subject. Representatives of different schools of thought and of different political persuasions were asked to present their views, no matter how controversial they might be. Furthermore, an attempt was made to balance, as far as possible, the theoretical contributions with empirical, regionally oriented studies, in order to present a rich and informative assessment of the issues in question. The regional studies could easily have been multiplied, but constraints of space required a limitation to case studies concerning Africa and South and East Asia. It is regrettable that, contrary to initial plans, the Middle East and South America did not receive special coverage. Similarly, economic issues could only be dealt with selectively. The discussion concentrates on three key questions: the roots of underdevelopment, the role of the multinationals and the economic consequences of colonial rule for indigenous economies. On the whole, however, prominence is given to conceptual and theoretical issues, that is, the question of whether it makes sense to talk of imperialism and imperialist dependency after the end of formal empire and if so, why. The answers to this question vary according to different vantage points, but they are none the less not incompatible with each other. In this respect, the imperialist policies of the superpowers, in the past as well as the present, are being examined anew.

The arrangement of the book into four parts corresponds to these themes. Part One is devoted to the new imperial powers, and Part Two to the legacies of empire, which are discussed in a number of regional cases. Part Three looks at problems of development and underdevelopment respectively, while in Part Four, an attempt is made to formulate, in more general terms, observations towards a modern theory of imperialism which encompasses not only the various forms of imperialist rule in the past, but also more recent reverberations of imperialist policy, in whatever ideological guise it may appear. Needless to say, it proved impossible to arrive at unanimous conclusions and, indeed, this was never the intention. In our opinion, it is preferable to record the controversial results of an intensive and frank exchange of ideas by scholars who approach the problems of imperialism and its aftermath from altogether different points of view.

This book could not have been prepared without the help and advice of many people. Thanks are above all due to Dr Konrad von Krosigk for allowing us to use the magnificent premises of the Werner-Reimers-Stiftung in Bad Homburg for the original conference, even though this meant hard work for the staff who do not usually have to accommodate such a large number of guests. The friendly atmosphere and the remarkable hospitality of the Werner-Reimers-Stiftung did much to make the conference a success. Thanks are also due to all those participants who contributed to the discussions; many of their arguments have been indirectly incorporated into these essays. Furthermore, I should like to thank Dr Wolfgang Mock, who helped to organize the original conference. We are also obliged to Professor H. L. Wesseling for numerous helpful suggestions and for kindly agreeing to write an introductory essay to this book. Thanks are also due to Dr Angela Davies, who has devoted considerable effort to the stylistic improvement of the translations from German. Last but not least, I should like to thank the staff of the German Historical Institute London, who have helped to make the publication of this book possible.

London, June 1985   Wolfgang J. Mommsen

Notes: Preface

1 Sir Keith Hancock, *Survey of British Commonwealth Affairs*, Vol. 2: *Problems of Economic Policy*, pt 1 (London, 1940), pp. 1–2.
2 W. H. Morris-Jones and G. Fischer (eds), *Decolonisation and After: The British and French Experience* (London, 1980).
3 L. Blussé, H. L. Wesseling and G. D. Winius (eds), *History and Underdevelopment. Essays on Underdevelopment and European Expansion in Asia and Africa* (Leiden, 1980).
4 C. Leys, *Underdevelopment in Kenya. The Political Economy of Neo-Colonialism* (London, 1975).
5 G. Arrighi, *The Political Economy of Rhodesia* (The Hague, 1967).
6 See the reports on this conference by H. L. Wesseling, in *Itinerario*, vol. 6 (1982), pt 2, pp. 19–22, and J. Osterhammel, in *German Historical Institute Bulletin*, no. 12 (Spring 1983), pp. 5–12.

1 Imperialism and Empire: An Introduction

H. L. WESSELING

I

This book is about imperialism and empire. It tries to explain the differences as well as the relationship between the two: not an easy thing to do. Obviously the problem does not lie in the word 'empire'. We know what empire is and we know it is over. The problem lies with the word 'imperialism'. After about a century of use, its meaning seems to have become more confused than ever. 'Imperialism is not a word for scholars', Sir Keith Hancock remarked quite correctly, and some time ago. But what choice do scholars have? Either they can give up the word entirely, which is unrealistic as it will be used anyway, or they can agree on a specific meaning, which is even less realistic because with every debate the concept has become less rather than more clear.

The whole problem with the term 'imperialism' started with Hobson. Not that Hobson invented the word – it had already been in use as a political term for quite some time – but he was the first to develop something like a theory of imperialism, and to believe that this was a useful thing to do. As is well known Hobson, a radical, was deeply impressed by the South African War. What he had in mind when he wrote about imperialism was 'the recent expansion of Great Britain and the chief continental Powers',[1] and, for him, 'expansion' meant the fact that over 'the last thirty years ... a number of European nations, Great Britain being first and foremost, have annexed or otherwise asserted political sway over vast portions of Africa and Asia, and over numerous islands in the Pacific and elsewhere'.[2] Thus Hobson was not vague at all about the meaning of imperialism: it was the establishment of political control. Nor was he vague about where imperialism came from: from the financial milieu in the mother country. Other people such as statesmen, soldiers and missionaries might play some role, 'but the final determination rests with the financial power'.[3] Thus with Hobson, we have a definition, a periodization and an explanation.

Unfortunately it can hardly be said that the many authors after Hobson who used the word and took over part of his argument were equally clear. In fact a great conceptual confusion came into being, above all under Marxist influence. However, in the historical literature before the Second World War a certain consensus existed about the principal facts. Imperialism was the extension of empire. At the end of the nineteenth century a great and sudden extension of empire took place as a consequence of certain developments in European economy and society.

2 Imperialism and After

This consensus broke down after 1945 under the influence of two major political developments: decolonization or the end of empire and the rise of two new empires, those of the United States and the Soviet Union. That the United States and the Soviet Union were the new superpowers of the postwar era – and that of the two the United States was the more powerful – was not a matter of debate. But were they imperialist? On this there was some hesitation because their political conduct did not fit in with traditional patterns of imperialism. The Soviet Union bullied its neighbour states into a client position, it extended its territory, it sent its army to all places it wanted to control. Clearly here was the extension of empire, but was it imperialism? Hugh Seton-Watson thought so and called it *The New Imperialism*.[4] Others hesitated. Did not imperialism presuppose the extension of the economy and society?

With the United States the process was the reverse. The United States demobilized its army. It had no territorial ambitions of its own. It pressed for the dissolution of the British and French empires, it gave up the Philippines and forced the Netherlands to give up Indonesia. On the other hand, the economic and financial hegemony of the United States was unique in world history. After the Second World War the United States alone produced more than 50 per cent of the world's GNP. The Marshall Plan was the symbol of its unbelievable economic power as well as of the enlightened way in which it used it. The American struggle for free trade was successful. The United States dominated the world in a way even Britain had never done. It was clearly an imperial power, but was it imperialistic?

The new world political situation had an impact on the theory of imperialism. The rise of American hegemony inspired the Cambridge historians, J. Gallagher and R. Robinson, to rethink nineteenth-century British imperialism. In their well-known article, 'The imperialism of free trade' they developed the concept of 'informal empire'.[5] They argued that the real heyday of British imperialism was not during the spectacular scrambles of the late nineteenth century but rather during the mid-Victorian period of economic and commercial hegemony. What mattered was not the struggle for political control but the quiet exercise of economic power: not formal but informal empire. For Gallagher and Robinson informal empire was not so much another type of expansion as a certain stage in imperialism. It was imperialism before empire.

At the same time other theorists discovered imperialism after empire. This resulted not so much from reflections on the rise of the United States but from a reassessment of decolonization. The hope that the end of empire had opened up a new stage in the development of the overseas world had not been fulfilled. Independence had brought an end neither to economic problems nor to economic dependency. Some of the new states had become more involved in, and dependent on, the Western-dominated world system than they had been under colonial rule. Neo-colonialism was the new word and dependency the new theory. For many people it became increasingly clear that the end of empire was not the end of imperialism. The days of Hobson's definition and periodization were over. Imperialism was not only the extension of political control, nor was it limited to a certain period. Other forms of dominance were also labelled imperialist. Empire was only one form of imperialism, one stage in the history of Western dominance, sandwiched between informal empire before and neo-colonialism after empire. The distinction between an anti-imperialist, mid-Victorian and an imperialist, late-Victorian period was abandoned. It did not make sense within the new conceptual framework of imperialism.

However, the question of why one form of imperialism was replaced by another remained. Hobson's – and thus the traditional – answer to this question had been in terms of economic changes in the mother country. This answer was also to be questioned and it was again Gallagher and Robinson who put forward a new theory. In various studies they argued that changes in the periphery, in the overseas world, rather than in the mother countries were responsible for changes in the forms of imperialist control. Imperialism is to be considered as a system of collaboration between European and non-European forces.[6] The imperialist form of collaboration is one between unequals because one partner, the European one, is the more powerful. But even so there is always a price to be paid to the collaborators, and therefore imperialism is essentially a question of bargaining. The changing forms of imperialism are changing forms of collaboration that result from changes in the bargaining positions of the two parties.

These ideas have greatly improved our understanding of the workings of nineteenth- and twentieth-century imperialism. What is much less clear is to what extent they are also useful in reaching a better understanding of modern imperialism, of the current world situation. Is imperialism continuing in different forms or has its character essentially changed? Are the former imperial powers continuing to exercise their influence in some way or other – informal rather than formal – or have they been replaced completely by the two superpowers? Was imperialism something entirely new for the two superpowers, something that began abruptly at the end of the Second World War or was there a certain continuity? Could they fall back on imperialist traditions? If imperialism is a system of collaboration, to what extent has independence changed the terms in favour of the overseas countries? If political control is only one form of imperialism – among others – does not the losing and regaining of political independence, at least from the colonized people's point of view, make a qualitative difference in their position? Is there not an essential difference between the bipolar heterogeneous world of today, a world split up into two ideologically hostile blocks that do not even recognize each other's existence, and the multipolar, homogeneous world of the Concert of Europe that presided over the partition and exploitation of the overseas world in the nineteenth and twentieth centuries?

II

When Professor Mommsen convened the conference on 'Imperialism after Empire', he formulated its aim as follows: 'to take a fresh look at the continuation of various forms of imperialist intervention, imperialist influence or imperialist control, formal and informal, after colonial rule had ended, from about 1880 to the present day.' And he continued: 'The legacy of classical imperialism both in political and in economic terms deserves a fresh assessment, regardless of whether one adheres to the current arguments of the *dependencia* school or not.' Even though this to a certain extent limited the enormous subject of imperialism, and of imperialism after empire, it was still a very ambitious programme. Obviously the chapters included here could not deal with it comprehensively. There are numerous lacunae. As far as the great powers are concerned the book deals only with today's superpowers, the United States and the Soviet Union, and with Japan, an economic giant that in the fairly recent past tried to set up a formal empire of its own before turning to the more peaceful imperialism of cameras, cars and computers. It does not cover the post-colonial experience of Britain and France, the two great imperial powers of the last century, or of smaller countries, such as Portugal and Holland which both had huge colonial empires. As far as the periphery is concerned the accent lies on the Asian countries, whether they were once colonies or not, while the African countries get less attention. The relations between France and Francophone Africa would most certainly make a very interesting case of imperialism after empire, well worth studying not only from the metropolitan but also from the African point of view. The evolution of Latin America after independence would also be interesting from a comparative point of view. The fact that most of the authors are from Britain and Germany is, of course, not without some influence on the questions that were asked, the approaches that were presented and the answers that were given. Within these limitations and restrictions what is offered here is a many-sided approach to the problem of imperialism.

In Part One the focus is on the superpowers. Is their behaviour imperialistic in a way that is comparable with classical imperialism? To what extent is there continuity in their imperialism? This problem of continuity and discontinuity is also looked at from the standpoint of the periphery. In Part Two a few case studies try to answer the question of whether the end of empire was a watershed in the history of these countries or whether to some extent the imperialist situation continued. In both these parts political as well as economic aspects are considered. The approach in Part Three, however, is a purely economic one. The various forms of economic relations between centre and periphery are considered while, at the same time, an attempt is made to assess the influence of those relations on the (under-)development of the Third World. Finally, the chapters in Part Four try to reformulate, or at least to contribute to, the theory of imperialism.

The concept of American imperialism is a very ambiguous one. As Schwabe points out, according to New Left authors American imperialism is nothing but the participation of the United States in world politics. Imperialism is thus the alternative to isolationism. The world political role of the United States only really began with the Second World War, although Wilson's interventionism in the First World War could be seen as a prefiguration of it. American foreign policy after 1945 could be labelled as 'informal imperialism' in so far as American power is obviously used. But then at least two observations should be made: (1) there is very little continuity between the traditional imperialistic activities of the United States in the Pacific and the Caribbean at the end of the nineteenth century and its imperial role in world politics after 1945; (2) to speak about an informal empire of the United States is to confuse rather than to illuminate the issue. In the first place, as Campbell points out, informal empire supposes at least the possibility of formal empire. In the second place, as Tony Smith argues, American global politics are essentially a power struggle with the Soviet Union and its ideological system. Imperialism would thus become synonymous with power politics *tout court* and lose any meaning. In the third place, at least *vis-à-vis* Europe, it is based on consensus. When American and Russian imperialism in Europe are compared it is remarkable that, while the instrument of Russian imperialism is the Red Army, the instrument of American imperialism is the threat to withdraw the American army.

In the chapter on the Soviet Union by Dietrich Geyer the interesting question is not so much the imperialist element in the Soviet Union's international behaviour – which is rather obvious – but the fact that it is only expressed in formal, that is, political ways. The Soviet Union traditionally did not develop techniques of informal empire. Its only form of imperialism is the expansion of the state. After 1945 we could speak of an informal empire in Eastern Europe because it was put under Soviet control without being formally annexed; but even here the instruments are essentially political and military, not economic. If this is indeed an element of continuity we should not overestimate the continuity between tsarist and Communist Russia. Before the Revolution Russia itself was expanding in Asia, but was at the same time an object of informal, that is, financial, imperialism. It belonged to the periphery of the world economic system. In practically all respects the Revolution brought a complete break with the past while also changing the international system. To consider Soviet expansionism as a continuation of tsarist imperialism with a different ideology would be a misunderstanding of the situation.

The case of Japan is very interesting. Martin underlines strongly the continuity, and indeed almost the necessity, of Japan's expansionism. He relates this to internal tensions in Japanese society and the struggle to protect the existing social order. While stressing continuity he distinguishes four different periods, all with their own individual characteristics but also all in one way or another imperialist. For Japan, the Second World War was not much of a break. The élite was kept in power and expansion continued within the old sphere of influence, albeit by different means. Ian Nish questions this emphasis on Japan's continuity after 1945. After all, Japan's expansion stopped with the end of the war and, when in the 1960s its economic expansion began once again, it followed a different geographical pattern. It was not oriented towards China; it was not directed towards its former sphere of influence (Taiwan, Korea, Manchuria); and its entry into the American market was something new. Moreover, the difference between, on the one hand, military conquest and domination of East

Asia and, on the other, the peaceful promotion of competitive commodities on a world scale seems so large that it makes little sense to consider the latter as an informal form of the former.

Germany seems to be a somewhat comparable case but here the break of 1945 is even more evident. Nazism led to a social revolution and we certainly cannot speak of a continuity within the German élite after 1945. Moreover, the traditional German sphere of influence, east and south-east Europe, was blocked by the advance of the Soviet Empire. And, finally, if Japan's place was on the periphery of the Cold War, where it did not have any military obligations, Germany was right at its centre, and, indeed, became the symbol of it, while it also re-emerged as a major military force.

Obviously the retreat of the European powers from the main scene of world politics where they had played a dominant role for several centuries and the emergence of the two new super states was a major event in world history. What did the retreat from empire mean as seen from the periphery? The authors on this subject seem to agree that the end of empire did not automatically and immediately mean a great change in economic affairs and relations. Thus Tomlinson demonstrates that, in the history of the economic relations between Britain and India, 1947 was not a turning-point. Rather there was continuity in economic terms from the 1920s to the 1960s, when the economic link between Britain and India was finally cut.

If independence was not very important from an economic standpoint – no more than the transition from informal to formal empire had been – it did have a great political impact and it is here that the real meaning of empire seems to lie. Many authors refer to the political aspects of empire. Wirz underlines the importance of state formation and nation building. Under colonialism the nation-state became the one and only form of political organization. Other forms, including stateless societies, empires and chiefdoms, disappeared. Rothermund mentions the imperial legacy in India: the civil service, law, the apolitical army, the idea of federalism, and so on. The political impact of formal colonial rule remained even after the economic relations had disappeared. Brötel explains the French struggle for the reconstruction of empire in Indochina and the later involvement of the United States in this area in terms of political motives. For the French, after the sad story of the Second World War, the essential motive in Vietnam was *grandeur*, prestige and military success. For the Americans, Vietnam became a test case of the Cold War. Clearly, in both cases economic motives do not explain imperialist ambitions.

However important the political consequences and factors have been, it is also worth looking at imperialism from a purely economic point of view, as is done in Part Three. Bairoch, writing from a long-term perspective, refutes some myths about the effects of colonialism on development and underdevelopment, many of them due to an overestimation of the amount of exploitation by the colonial powers. His general conclusion is that colonialism has had a negative influence on the Third World, without, however, having had a strong, positive influence on the development of Europe. The Industrial Revolution in Britain brought about the de-industrialization of India, but the reverse is not true: the Third World did not play a major role in creating or maintaining the industrialization of Europe. Here again we see the interconnection of political and economic factors. That British industrial textiles could destroy Indian textiles was, of course, due to the productivity of British industry. After the Industrial Revolution a British labourer was 300 to 400 times more efficient than the traditional Indian producer. This advantage existed also *vis-à-vis* European and Latin American producers, but they were politically independent and protected themselves with tariffs. In this respect, independence had important economic effects in the long run because thereafter the new states developed their own industry and the Third World acquired a more important place in the world economy. It is, however, difficult to measure exactly the importance of this factor. Forbes Munro warns us that this improvement in the position of the Third World perhaps had less to do with independence than with the emergence of China and the general economic boom of the 1950s and 1960s. Another remarkable phenomenon is that after independence the terms of trade of the Third World deteriorated whereas they had improved under colonial rule when the colonial powers had felt some responsibility for the social situation in the colonies.

Why economic growth was particularly spectacular in one part of the Third World, that is, East Asia, is not very clear. The success stories of Hong Kong and Singapore are *sui generis* and a result of the exceptional position of these two city-states. But the fact that South Korea and Taiwan – the other two success stories – are both former Japanese colonies is too remarkable not to be examined. Menzel recalls that Japanese imperialism had a strong tendency to develop its colonies by investing in infrastructure and schooling. It would seem that this has benefited the subsequent development of its former colonies.

The multinational corporation (MNC) is often seen as the agent of imperialism after empire. What the administrator and officer were in colonial days, the pin-striped MNC executive with his attaché case is today. Both Fieldhouse and Bornschier, despite their differences on the role of the MNCs, reject this comparison. The absence of political control is an essential difference in comparison with colonial days and the power of the MNC should not be overestimated. The MNC of today is essentially a manufacturing corporation and much less powerful than the big mining and extracting companies of the old days. The power of the state has considerably increased.

The relationship between imperialism and development is a complicated one with a long intellectual history. Classical Marxist theorists considered capitalist imperialism to be an objective progressive force. As Colin Leys reminds us, their criticism of *dependencia*-theorists would be that the cause of underdevelopment is not capitalist exploitation, but the lack of it! Orthodox Marxists would argue that the causes of China's stagnation were not external but internal. As Osterhammel demonstrates, China was certainly a country that was influenced by imperialist activities without ever becoming a colony. Here informal empire was not a stage in the process of transition from independence to colonial rule but a system in itself. Here imperialism never became colonialism. As such it demonstrates very clearly the collaborationist character of imperialism.

8 Imperialism and After

As Brewer argues, it was the willingness or the refusal of the élites at the periphery to collaborate that was decisive in the transition from colonial rule to independence. When this élite – bureaucracy, commercial circles – ceased to be willing to collaborate, decolonization became inevitable. It was not necessarily impossible to force them back into co-operation but invariably the price was too high. Some powers realized this beforehand; others had to learn it the hard way.

III

What does this book tell us about the power politics of the classical colonial powers of the nineteenth century or the superpowers of the twentieth century? What do we learn about imperialism and empire? Does it amount to a new 'theory of imperialism'?

The first thing that we are reminded of is the old saying that there is nothing new under the sun. According to Professor Martin, Kōtoku Shūsui, a Japanese author, had published a theory of imperialism even before Hobson. Chinese authors had their collaborationist theory of imperialism in the 1920s and as early as 1946 the Chinese scholar Wang Yanan developed a kind of *dependencia* theory of his own.

After many case studies and nearly as many theories of imperialism the problem of imperialism and empire seems to be as complicated and as intractable as ever. On the one hand, the mere fact that the Third World depends on the economic situation in the West does not make the West 'guilty' of imperialism. On the other hand, reducing imperialism exclusively to colonial rule would be taking too formal a position, one that would obstruct historical insights. There are many variations. In some cases forms of informal imperialism clearly existed which the imperial power preferred to creating a formal empire. That was the case of Britain in the nineteenth century and certainly of the United States after the Second World War. Here there seems to be a historical parallel but it should not be exaggerated. The United States with its huge domestic market is much less dependent on foreign trade than Britain was in the nineteenth century, and plays a smaller role as a clearing house for Third World products. There were also the opposite cases of colonial empires, such as the Portuguese and the Dutch, that were empires without imperialism, at least until the twentieth century, or cases like France and Japan where imperialism followed empire. These last two created considerable empires by military means, while trade and investment – if at all – followed the flag and not vice versa. Finally, we have countries such as Germany and the United States that have been two of the most expanding and dominating nations of the twentieth century. Their economic imperialism was grandiose, their formal colonial empires were as ridiculous as they were short-lived.

For all these reasons we have to accept that empire is one, but not the only, form of imperialism, that there was imperialism before and after and even instead of empire. However, this is not to deny that colonialism was a very typical form of imperialism with such unique characteristics that, at least from the colonized people's point of view, it is practically *sui generis*. The changes in the political structure, the loss of sovereignty, the submission to a foreign people, are too important to be considered as only gradual changes in an essentially continuous process of economic transformation. Inversely, independence had such an enormous political impact – and in the long run also an economic one – that it should be considered as a major historical change. Therefore a theory of imperialism should not only explain the transition from informal to formal empire but also the end of empire. In this, the interplay of three variables has been decisive: the colonizing power (its policy and its political power); the colony itself (its character as a settlement, trading or administrative colony); and the international situation (the conjuncture of anti-colonialism and anti-communism). It is clear that imperialism continued after empire but it is also clear that the homogeneous system of the Concert of Europe was fundamentally different from the heterogeneous system of the Cold War, that a bipolar system has replaced a balance-of-power system, that powers which had dominated the world for centuries have abdicated and that the terms of collaboration have drastically changed in favour of the former colonized countries. For all these reasons the world after the end of empire seems to be very different from the world of the old colonial days.

As far as the theory of imperialism is concerned this leaves us with two possibilities. We can either consider it as a historical concept applying to a specific period in the history of the expansion of Europe. Or we can define it in such a way that it becomes an analytical tool in the study of international relations or of power politics in general. The Robinson model Mark IV, the excentric theory of imperialism as presented in this book (see Chapter 18), belongs to the last category. In this model, imperialism is conceived of in 'terms of the play of international economic and political markets in which degrees of monopoly and competition in relations at world, metropolitan and local levels decide its necessity and profitability'. While older Robinson models, like the 'imperialism of free trade', the 'periphery' and the 'collaborationist' theories, explained several aspects of the transition from imperialism to empire, then to independence, the new model is a convertible: it can be used both for specific situations and as a universal theory. It analyses imperialism in terms of a struggle between big and little brothers, of asymmetry of power and of changing terms of collaboration. Thus formulated, history becomes a rather abstract thing. All power relations have some asymmetry and all history is the history of collaboration between human beings. Perhaps it would be better to reserve the terms of imperialism and empire to a specific period in world history, that of the expansion of Europe. But then again a question arises: is it a specific period? The expansion of Europe is over – or is it? The answer is a complicated one.

In 1945 the days of empire were over and Europe was politically and militarily overwhelmed by the United States and the Soviet Union. The economic centre of gravity of the world has moved to the West, away from Europe and even away from the Atlantic. But in some respects the expansion of Europe seems to continue. The United States may be a 'new world', but it is also to a very large extent a child of Europe, of the optimistic Europe of the Enlightenment. Likewise, Russia, even renamed the Soviet Union – with all the singularities this rebaptism has brought with it – belongs to Europe, and its social and political system is based on European ideas and values. Islamic and other forms of fundamentalism and revivalism notwithstanding, many peoples of the Third World seem to adopt 'Western' forms of material civilization and to articulate traditional European values. In this way there is a very real 'imperialism after empire'.

Notes: Chapter 1

1 J. A. Hobson, *Imperialism: A Study* (London, 1902), p. 25.
2 ibid., p. 15.
3 ibid., p. 65.
4 H. Seton-Watson, *The New Imperialism: A Background Book* (London, 1961).
5 J. Gallagher and R. Robinson, 'The imperialism of free trade', *Economic History Review*, vol. 6 (1953), pp. 1–15.
6 See R. Robinson, 'Non-European foundations of European imperialism: sketch for a theory of collaboration', in R. Owen and B. Sutcliffe (eds), *Studies in the Theory of Imperialism* (London, 1972), pp. 117–40; R. Robinson, 'European imperialism and indigenous reactions in British West Africa, 1880–1914', in H. L. Wesseling (ed.), *Expansion and Reaction* (Leiden, 1978), pp. 141–63.

Part One

The New Imperial Powers

2 The Global Role of the United States and its Imperial Consequences, 1898–1973

KLAUS SCHWABE

The theme of 'American imperialism' is as boundless as it is controversial. Whoever takes it up not only immediately confronts the communist definition of this phenomenon,[1] but is also drawn into the great debate in and outside the United States which has accompanied the Vietnam War, and has inflated the concept of imperialism beyond all recognition.[2]

In order to gain some ground in this difficult situation, the historian needs to arrive at a conceptual clarification beyond his faithfulness to empirically ascertainable facts. The first step taken here is to look at the historiography of American imperialism. This chapter will therefore begin by glancing at some of the relevant interpretations provided by history and political science. This will be followed by a preliminary conceptual definition. The more descriptive and empirical section that follows will first concentrate on the period from 1898 to 1912 in which there is general agreement that American foreign policy was imperialist. Next, it will be necessary to compare this early imperialist phase with American global policies from 1912 until the end of the Second World War. To what extent the imperialist stage influenced American foreign policy after 1945 must also be determined. In the context of this final period, the question of continuity will arise.

American Foreign Policy and Interpretations of Imperialism

The issue of imperialism in the history of American foreign policy has met with the response of two schools of American historiography.[3] The first considers American imperialism as a passing experiment which followed the Spanish-American War of 1898. It was an experiment which was in fact abandoned a few years after its inception, and one whose last remains were buried with the Second World War.[4]

The notion that empire was no more than a fleeting moment in American history was opposed by a second school of thought which claimed to discern imperialist tendencies in American foreign policy as a whole.[5] An early advocate of this view was the left-liberal historian Charles Beard. During the past three decades the most influential representative of this school has been William A. Williams, one of the most outspoken exponents of the New Left in American historiography.[6] For Williams, the United States is the classical example of an imperial power – from the conquest and settlement of the North American continent, through the Cold War, and into the present day.[7] Williams recognizes three major patterns in the foreign policy of imperial America: (1) the striving towards markets open for American exports, known as the open-door policy;[8] (2) the preference for informal, and especially economic, means of domination;[9] (3) the more or less hypocritical legitimation of American imperialism under the pretence of an altruistic desire for a new order in international relations which would be guided by progressive principles. Here, Williams speaks of an 'imperialism of idealism'.[10] All the differences which may have existed in the actual practice of twentieth-century American foreign policy are, according to Williams, merely of a tactical nature.[11] For him, most of the domestic debates about the part the United States has played in international relations are merely superficial babble, while the basic consensus among the American public concerning imperialism has never been questioned.[12] Williams's critique of American foreign policy, which he describes as a 'tragedy',[13] seemed to have been confirmed by the war in Vietnam. His verdict against the imperialist tendencies of the United States as a world power achieved almost canonical status among the ranks of the New Left.[14] His arguments also found their way into numerous general accounts of American foreign policy and into university textbooks.[15] During the Watergate crisis they took on an added dimension in domestic policies: the perpetrators of an imperialist foreign policy were also held to be advocates of an 'imperial presidency' in so far as they tended to expand presidential powers at the expense of Congress during the Vietnam War. Congress itself attempted to curb the 'imperial' policies of President Nixon by limiting the executive power's scope for action through legislation and especially by the War Powers Act of 1973.[16] This self-criticism of American foreign policy, having become fashionable among the American public, found an echo in the press and among European allies of the United States.[17]

It cannot be said that this wave of self-criticism which swept across the United States during the early 1970s, and which occasionally bordered on national masochism, always contributed to a sounder understanding of the phenomenon of American imperialism. On the contrary, nuances were often lost in the turmoil of political debate. The American imperialism against which the New Left mounted a campaign often came to stand merely for American participation in world politics as such. Increasingly, anti-imperialism and isolationism tended to signify the same thing. The call for a break with the imperial past of the United States culminated in the dream of it withdrawing completely from world politics and returning to the idyllic condition that it was believed to have enjoyed before the achievement of full nationhood.[18]

Yet there were certain basic elements of the imperialist phenomenon which were accepted by both critics and defenders of American foreign policy. These elements of consensus can be used as the point of departure from which to develop a more detached concept of imperialism. This concept would have to be broad enough to include some of the constituent parts of American international relations in this century; at the same time it would have to remain sufficiently precise to illuminate American imperialism with its unique and characteristic features.

As our starting-point for this discussion let us examine the relatively general definition given by A. P. Thornton:

> An imperial policy is one that enables a metropolis to create and maintain an external system of effective control. The control may be exerted by political, economic, strategic, cultural, religious, or ideological means, or by a combination of some or all of these.[19]

A look at some further American studies on the theme of imperialism will allow the application of this definition to the case of the United States. Thus we read in George Liska's examination of 'imperial America'[20] that the metropolis of an empire must be considerably more extensive than its constituent parts – in terms of size, population, and especially economic and military capability. The interests of the metropolis, according to Liska, are aimed not merely at its own preservation, but primarily at the continued existence of the outward-facing system of control as a whole; hence the interests of the empire tend to spread in many directions, in some circumstances assuming a world-wide orientation. Initially, of course, the system of control serves the interests of the metropolis. But it also reflects the desire on the part of the metropolis for a durable order in international relations. To Liska's ideas we may add that control obviously means not so much a short-term or one-off opportunity to bring influence to bear on foreign policy, but a system of domination extended over a longer period.

There is an additional feature of imperialist control which distinguishes it from normal power politics. This is the requirement that imperial control should be effective.[21] In the recent discussion concerned with imperialism, however, there has been some uncertainty as to where the term 'effective' can be applied. Effectiveness is apparently not primarily dependent on what means are employed to impose imperialist control. Thornton, for example, lists various different means of exercising power ranging from the political to the ideological. Here he shows himself to be a follower of the expanded conception of imperialism as it was first put forward by Gallagher and Robinson. It is well known that this conception seeks to include not merely direct and formal political domination, but also indirect and informal control which can dispense with overt political pressure.[22] Of course, this does not answer the question of whether these are the conditions under which imperial control is effectively exercised. This presents a very difficult problem especially whenever the identification of a system of informal control as either 'imperialist' or 'non-imperialist' is at issue.

The question of the effectiveness of imperial control must first of all be directed towards the dominating metropolis. It should be formulated as follows: Is the imperial power willing to exercise effective control over the controlled without consideration of their political aspirations? Is it willing to carry out this control with all means at its disposal? If this is the case, a further question is whether the dominating power possesses an ideology which justifies its domination with arguments more high-minded than those merely of brute strength.

But we can also look at the effectiveness of imperialist control from the viewpoint of the dominated, as does Raymond Aron.[23] We can ask whether it is possible for the dominating power to assert its will at all among those dominated; that is to say, whether it can force the latter completely to renounce their claims to self-determination and to adopt the aims of the dominating power. But is it always possible to answer this question? Is it possible to know the true direction which the desires of the dominated power may take? Can we even be sure that every subject member of an imperial system is capable of articulating its own political, social and ideological ideas? If this were so, it would be possible that some of the self-determined aims of a member would be those of the imperial power while others would not. To be more specific, it is quite possible that one social stratum of a given people would view the aims of the ruling power as their own and another stratum would not. In other words, the dividing line between self-determination and alien rule in an imperialist system could be blurred, and in some extreme cases, self-determination may be realized to such a degree that it would be out of place to identify the role of the stronger power with imperialist domination.

In order to find out whether American influence in international relations is imperialist or not, the scholar thus has to study both the effectiveness of American imperial control and to discern how far the professed aims of the United States coincide with the aspirations of peoples which are subjected to its influence or domination. Imperial aims are likely to reveal something about the motivations which govern an imperialist policy. With the exception of orthodox Marxists most scholars are in agreement, in that they assume the coexistence of a plurality of motivations whether political, economic, strategic, or of another nature. This variety of motivating forces includes what is called 'preclusive imperialism', that is, the effort to pre-empt a potential rival by assuming a position of domination in a given area.[24] Racial prejudices, of course, could motivate an imperialist policy, and yet current American scholarship tends to view imperialism not only as an effective control exercised by whites over Third World countries but also in terms of the domination of 'whites' by 'whites'.[25]

Relying on contemporary interpretations of the phenomenon of imperialism the following sketch tries to steer a middle course between an over-restrictive and an over-extensive definition of the nature of imperialism. Thus imperialism, for the purposes of this chapter, will mean something more general than just direct colonial rule; it will encompass informal domination as well, including relations of domination within the industrially advanced world. At the same time, it will mean something more specific than mere inequality of power between different nations and the effects of that inequality.[26] Effective control will remain an essential quality of the notion of imperialism as used in this chapter.

From Imperialism to the Good-Neighbour Policy

American imperialism, in particular, requires a broader definition in order to be recognized as such, because it was not limited to coloured peoples. This is apparent from its very beginnings. The first time that the United States reached out beyond its original power base on the continent was during the war with Spain in 1898. As victors, the Americans became heirs to the last remains of the Spanish Empire in the Caribbean and the Far East. Populations that were at least partially of Spanish origin were the objects of this transfer of power. And yet, President McKinley's administration did not hesitate to bring these areas – including the Philippines, Cuba and Puerto Rico – under American sovereignty. Many American contemporaries welcomed these acquisitions which seemed to furnish the basis for an enlarged colonial empire in the future. Various factors can account for this colonialist enthusiasm: hopes for an increased American export market, strategic objectives in Central America and, finally, the need to preclude other parties interested in inheriting Spain's colonies.[27] It was still uncertain whether this would lead to a colonial empire on the European model. This depended, in part, on whether the American people – or its congressional representatives – would be willing to engage in a long-term policy of classical imperialism. Initially it seemed that they were.[28] Yet the long-term success of this move towards colonialism depended on reconciling the fashionable imperialism with the older American tradition of republicanism.

In subsequent years this proved to be more difficult than had been anticipated in 1898. From the start, there had been opposition by some anti-imperialist Boston brahmins and left-wing politicians. They recalled the revolutionary origins of the United States, with its ideal of democratic self-determination, and this certainly ran counter to the domination of one country by another.[29] This anti-imperialist ideology became a permanent part of the Democratic Party's platform.[30] But even Republicans, including Theodore Roosevelt, increasingly came to have misgivings about the expansionist policies begun in 1898. The earlier colonial enthusiasm turned out to have been no more than a passing fancy. This was not so much due to the anti-imperialists whose influence should not be exaggerated. Rather, it can be attributed to the simple fact that the conditions which had bred the imperialist atmosphere of 1898 no longer existed. The awareness of a social and economic crisis, the hope of being seen as liberators from the Spanish colonial yoke, and speculations about fantastic profits from trade with China – all these factors had disappeared a few years later. Perhaps the main reason for this change of mood was the violent guerrilla war in the Philippines, where the United States had become engaged in the oppression of a native liberation movement. This was almost a dress rehearsal for the war in Vietnam. Many an American had not forgotten that the United States had actually entered the war against Spain as liberators from Spanish colonialism – with the slogan 'Cuba libre'. Now the liberator had turned oppressor, adding grist to the mill of those who wished to discontinue the American colonial experiment.[31]

18 Imperialism and After

When Woodrow Wilson became Democratic President in 1912, anti-imperialism was laid down as the official policy of the administration. Wilson accepted, as did his later antagonist Lenin, the basic outline of Hobson's famous critique of imperialism.[32] Throughout his further political career, he steadfastly remained convinced of the virtue of an essentially anti-imperialist policy.[33]

The administrations after Wilson never returned to a policy of traditional imperialism. Since 1913 the American government's conception of its international role and the stated intentions of its foreign policies have been as non-imperialistic as those of the Soviet government since the October Revolution.[34] Hence the following sketch no longer deals with American imperialism as an official programme, but only with the imperial consequences of American foreign policy.

Wilson wanted not only to put an end to the imperialist policies of his predecessors, but also to undo what they had achieved. This aim was served, for example, by the Jones Act of 1916, which granted home rule to the Philippines, making its full independence only a matter of time.[35] The United States clearly entered the First World War with an anti-imperialist purpose. It was the Central Powers, and especially Imperial Germany, which were seen as the imperialistic aggressors.[36] During that conflict the United States became a world power. But this had, at most, only indirectly to do with its previous imperial expansion in the Caribbean and the Pacific. It is also well known that Wilson opposed the traditional colonialism of his associates at the Paris Peace Conference.[37]

And yet, if we turn away from Wilson's foreign policy conceptions and look at what he actually did, we are face to face with the imperial consequences of great power diplomacy. The numerous occasions on which the United States intervened militarily in Central America during his presidency cannot be overlooked. Was he, after all, intent on replacing the unpopular American colonial empire with a zone of *informal domination*?

There had already been moves in this direction by his predecessors. Secretary of State Hay's famous notes of 1899/1900 advocating an open-door policy for China are one example. His aim was to establish equal trade opportunities for all the industrial powers, and to prevent China from being split up into zones of interest. Much more important in this respect was the Roosevelt Corollary to the Monroe Doctrine, with which the United States in 1905 claimed the right of 'international policing' in Central America. The United States was to have the right, for example, of intervening in its small neighbouring states in order to collect their debts with foreign creditors.[38] Of course, this was basically meant to prevent European creditor nations from attempting the same sort of intervention in its backyard. In practice, the Roosevelt Corollary amounted to the right, at least temporarily, of the United States to turn its neighbours into a protectorate. Thus, in a sense, Central America became its 'informal empire'.

Pointedly harking back to the Roosevelt Corollary, Wilson intervened in the Caribbean on several occasions. So, for example, American troops occupied Haiti after a bloody domestic coup in 1915. When in 1916 the United States rounded out its sphere of influence with the purchase of the

The Global Role of the United States 19

Danish Virgin Islands, this was mainly aimed at keeping Germany out of the region and also at protecting access to the Panama Canal. None the less, these strategic considerations arising from the First World War should not obscure the fact that Wilson's interventionist policies in the Caribbean mainly sprang from anti-imperialistic motives. For the most part, his administration was not concerned with protecting American business interests in that region, but rather with the realization of a specific conception of international order. Wilson, in fact, hoped that an American presence in some of Central America's smaller states would guarantee their continuous, stable and peaceful domestic development, thus making any further interventions to secure the interests of creditors unnecessary.[39]

Wilson's decisive motive becomes even more apparent in his policies towards Mexico, which underwent a period of revolutionary upheavals starting in 1910. Wilson's opposite number in Mexico was the dictator Huerta. He had come to power by means of a coup, and was supported by foreign business interests. By opposing Huerta and even intervening militarily, Wilson intentionally turned against the (partially American) foreign business interests in Mexico. The aim of intervention was the reinstatement of a constitutional government in Mexico. Wilson saw himself as the champion of a 'progressive' foreign policy, and was genuinely surprised by the fact that this almost led to war with Mexico. Only in 1917 did the United States pull out of Mexico's domestic affairs. By this time a constitutional administration (led by President Carranza) firmly held the reins. Judged by its own purposes, Wilson's intervention had ended successfully.[40] Can the underlying ideological motivation be described as imperialistic, perhaps in the sense of W. A. Williams's 'imperialism of idealism'?[41] The United States had undoubtedly employed the means of an expansionist policy – including the use of American troops in northern Mexico. But was Wilson really interested in domination? Certainly not in domination by certain American business interests, nor in the subjugation of Mexico as an American protectorate after the fashion of Cuba. What he really wanted to assert in Mexico was a certain conception of political order. This conception was, of course, American in origin. There were also realistic and practical considerations in favour of having stable political conditions on the southern border of the United States. And yet Wilson himself sincerely believed that his intervention helped the Mexicans to gain an independent political identity. He sought neither domination nor effective control, but hoped instead for the domestic stabilization of a Mexican republic. Certainly this can not be described as imperialism in the sense defined above.

Again, Wilson sought neither formal nor informal domination when he dispatched 35,000 American troops to Russian ports in the summer of 1918. As was later recognized even by the Soviets, his aim was not to topple the Bolshevist regime, but to prevent the Japanese from maintaining a stronghold in Siberia – thus creating the conditions for Russia's eventual return to parliamentary democracy.[42]

American intervention in Mexico and in a Russia torn by civil war were both part of Wilson's efforts to assert his conception of political order, that is, they were intended precisely to do away with imperialistic caprice. This was also the aim of the League of Nations in wanting to limit the sovereignty of member nations – as was plain for Wilson's domestic opponents to see.

By reaching for military means to defend its conceptions of political order against Germany, Wilson's United States was inevitably cast in the role of an interventionist power. This role seemed barely distinguishable from conventional imperialism in the eyes of some contemporary and later critics. Thus it created a paradox with which American global policies have continually had to deal.

Wilson's successors were aware only of the military consequences of his *Weltpolitik*, that is, the Americans' seemingly permanent entanglement in Europe. Hence they rejected his view of American global co-responsibility for maintaining peace and constitutional government, and thus allowed radical anti-imperialism to gain the upper hand in the United States. However, even they would not forego all means of influencing global politics. They believed that they held these means in the form of the economic and financial trump cards that the United States had gained in the First World War. Playing out these cards (along with the Far East disarmament talks) now took the place of military intervention – the acceptability of which steadily declined, and which was no longer resorted to even when American economic interests were at stake. Both American withdrawal from the conflict with Mexico, which had nationalized its partly American-controlled oil deposits, and the purely verbal protests by the United States against the Japanese invasion of Manchuria in 1931 can serve to demonstrate this point.[43] President Hoover, a Quaker, came to be seen as representing an essentially non-imperialist stance in foreign policy. At the same time, it could no longer be overlooked that during his term of office Europe, which for a time seemed to have become a kind of informal American empire, turned out to be ignoring American economic influence and going its own way. The United States had to stand idly by while precisely those forces which it had fought in the First World War regained the upper hand in Germany. Europe in the 1930s, under Hitler's impact, was anything but a sphere of informal American influence – much less one of domination.

In some respects this even applies to South America. The series of American interventions was broken off with F. D. Roosevelt's inauguration of a good neighbour policy. Even before this, the State Department had explicitly declared the Roosevelt Corollary of 1905 as void,[44] and with it were gone the times in which the great powers had cashed in their financial demands with the aid of gunboats. The status of *de facto* protectorate imposed on Cuba after the Spanish–American War was lifted in 1934, leaving only the military base at Guantánamo in American hands.[45] The question of Mexico's nationalized oil deposits was finally and peacefully settled.[46] Entering the Second World War in 1941, the United States was an anti-imperialist power – both consciously and in fact. Again it was Germany as the major aggressor which seemed to embody imperialist ideals, while the United States renewed its military and political role as a world power under the banner of anti-imperialism. Although one area formally subject to American administration, the Philippines, was in the theatre of war, the important military operations took place in Europe where American influence had been almost extinguished during the 1930s.

American policies from 1941 to 1945 were not designed to prepare for a future American empire. The Anglo–American expansion of power, from the occupation of Iceland to the conquest of North Africa, mainly served short-term military aims. Only twice did the American administration reveal how it conceived of the role of empires after the defeat of the Axis: first, in the debate concerning the future of the colonies of all the imperial powers and, secondly, in the ideas it put forward for a postwar international order.

The hopes expressed by F. D. Roosevelt and his colleagues – and especially Secretary of State Hull – were unambiguous as far as the future of the colonies was concerned: generally they sought the dismantling of colonial rule, which included giving complete national independence to colonial peoples. The United Nations was supposed to become the trustee of the colonies during the interim period. There were tense debates on this point between Britain, on the one hand, and Roosevelt and the State Department representatives on the other. This matter is as well known as the American President's opposition to France's return to Indo-China.[47] Although shortly before his death Roosevelt toned down this attitude in view of possible strains with the Alliance, his standpoint in principle continued to guide the American government, not least as far as the remnants of its own colonial empire were concerned. The best example of this attitude can be found in the American preparations for the final independence of the Philippines, which took place on 4 July 1946. As in Cuba, the United States retained a few military bases, but the first agreements concerning these bases ensured that they would only be used for military purposes, and not for a future political penetration of the islands.[48] Apart from a few bases, only Puerto Rico remained of its previous formal empire. Here the population had become citizens with the same rights, if not the same obligations, as Americans. Apart from a small minority, they apparently did not want national independence.[49] By its attitude towards colonialism, the United States prevented its return to the status of an imperial power with colonial dependencies in the classical sense.

As far as the postwar period is concerned, the Roosevelt administration's conceptions regarding the future influence of the United States as a world power remained indecisive and ambivalent. Roosevelt's much-debated concept of a regional division of the world, with each region being subordinate to a 'world policeman', could have had consequences in the Western hemisphere – envisaged as an American 'zone of control' – which might have been similar to those of the Roosevelt Corollary of 1905. It could have established the basis for the exercise of effective informal domination by the United States over Latin America.[50] None the less, Roosevelt did not intend this scheme to be imperialistic in the traditional sense. According to him, rivalling empires were to be replaced by a collective and co-operative hegemony of superpowers.

Although this conception of a 'co-operative imperialism' may have been realistic, Roosevelt did not consistently stick to it. Under the influence of the State Department and the American public, both of which took the Atlantic Charter of 1941 more seriously than did Roosevelt himself, the President increasingly returned to the vision of an undivided world, in which principles of order jointly established by the victorious powers would prevail. This was to be a world governed by the United Nations in conjunction with the victorious powers, and no longer riddled by spheres of influence. This fundamentally anti-imperialist notion guided the American attitude at the Yalta Conference (and not, as is often believed today, a desire to carve up the world). Germany was to be a testing ground in the midst of this undivided world, demonstrating the level of co-operation that would be possible between the major victorious powers.[51] Roosevelt wanted his country to participate in a direct control of the defeated German empire; but only on a short-term basis. In fact, he anticipated the withdrawal of American troops within two years of VE Day.[52] Roosevelt thus hoped to avoid the imperial consequences of the new role of the United States as a world power.

Only by recalling these facts does Roosevelt's distance from the 'classical' tradition of American imperialism become apparent. This alone can make clear why its actual role as global opponent of the Soviet Union after the Second World War did not live up to Roosevelt's hopes for the future – but confirmed his fears instead. For American foreign policy, 1945 is thus a turning-point, and in some respects a new start.

Anti-Imperialism as Containment

The period after the Second World War saw the third attempt by the United States in the course of this century to promote a conception of order in international relations, one which, at least in theory, claimed world-wide applicability. First, in 1918, Wilson had laid down the principles of a 'new diplomacy' which was to counter the danger of what was believed to be a Russo-German hegemony in Eurasia. Then, Roosevelt had seen the Atlantic Charter of 1941 as an answer to the allegedly closely co-ordinated imperial policies of the Axis powers. Finally, the policy of containment which was gradually implemented between 1946 and 1948 was turned against another allegedly solid block – the 'camp' of the communist countries from Red China to Yugoslavia, a solid block which seemed to threaten the independence of the Western world.[53] Thus on three occasions in this century the United States has been under the impression that it has had to counter a hostile conspiracy on a global scale: in 1918 against the so-called Russo-German conspiracy, in 1941 against the Axis, and in 1946 and thereafter against world Bolshevism.

To what degree have the American administrations since 1945 been acting with the conviction that they had to meet a global challenge by trying militarily, economically and politically to *control* those parts of the world they wanted to protect from Bolshevism? Has the United States actually been capable of effectively exercising this type of control, and can it therefore be described as an authentic imperial power? I shall attempt to answer these questions successively with regard to Europe, Asia and South America.

If conditions for the creation of an American empire existed anywhere in the world (with the exception of Japan), then it was surely in those parts of *Europe* not occupied by the Red Army. Here in 1945 there was not only economic, but also complete military dependence on the United States. Europe sought American protection and aid of its own accord, and it should not be forgotten that this originally meant protection from the Soviet bloc. The centre of potential American hegemonial power in Europe was in Germany. This was due not only to geographical factors but particularly to the fact that here its control as a victorious power was not only effective but total – at least in its own occupation zone. In line with Wilsonian aspirations, the United States initially made the fullest possible use of its control of Germany in order to create a new political order – one only has to think of de-Nazification or the reinstatement of a parliamentary system of government. By making use of its economic and financial leverage, the United States also wielded its influence *vis-à-vis* the other European states. This, however, took a direction that can hardly be described as imperialist in the traditional sense. On the other hand, the United States put pressure on the Europeans to abandon their colonies. This led to tensions with the Netherlands, a permanent conflict with France (over Algeria), and even to a confrontation with Britain during the Suez Crisis of 1956. Suez was possibly the most drastic American involvement in Europe – hegemonial policies under an anti-imperialist banner! Here, as elsewhere, the United States was not primarily intent on inheriting the position of a colonial power from the Europeans, but rather on making sure that the Soviet Union would not be given a chance to exploit the nationalism of colonial peoples for its own purposes.

On the other hand, the United States encouraged West European unification at all levels. The aim of this policy was the gradual acquisition of independence by what was hoped would be a European great power. One aspect of this would be West Germany's entry into this federation of states. The American administration pulled its whole weight to achieve this goal, even against the misgivings of a number of Western European countries. Western Europe was to be built up as a largely independent source of power *vis-à-vis* the Soviet Union. The fact that Western Europe might develop interests (and not least economic ones) that could collide with those of the United States was a risk that was consciously accepted, given the overriding importance of strategic and political necessities.[54]

Indeed, this type of conflict was soon to arise with the creation of the Common Market. Initially these conflicts concerned the issue of tariffs alone. The most serious challenge to American hegemony, however, came when France left the integrated defence structure of NATO. At first, this involved the creation of an independent atomic *force de frappe*, followed by France's withdrawal from NATO's defence system in 1966. Washington acquiesced to both moves, partly because it could no longer exert the sort of economic and financial pressures that it had been able to do after 1945, partly because its hands were tied in Vietnam. More importantly, however, President Johnson did not conceive the American role in relation to Europe as being hegemonial or even imperial to such a degree that he would seriously consider blocking off France's special path by force. Contrary to the expectations of the theoreticians of informal empire during the days of the Marshall Plan, Western Europe in the late 1960s ceased to be part of an American informal empire.[55] At the same time it also became apparent that there were limits to the willingness and ability of the United States 'effectively' to control Western Europe as part of an empire. During the oil crisis which followed the Yom Kippur War of 1973, when Western Europeans once again went their own way diplomatically and economically, the Americans did not attempt to bring them back into the fold. Similarly, the United States supported Willy Brandt's *Ostpolitik*, despite growing misgivings. In this case as in others 'effective' control of European diplomacy on Washington's part was certainly not achieved, nor was it intended.[56]

The relationship between the United States and Western Europe has been a unique one. On the one hand, the military inferiority of Western Europe *vis-à-vis* the Soviet Union means that the former has remained a *de facto* military protectorate of the United States. On the other, the longer this has been the case, the less the United States has made use of this military dependency to exercise political or economic control. Thus the United States occupies a hegemonial but not an imperial position. As regards Eastern Europe, the United States, despite election rhetoric, has never seriously threatened that area dominated by the Soviet Union. This self-restraint amounts to an additional limitation of American hegemony in Europe.[57] That the United States conceives its role in Europe as one of protection – rather than domination – is confirmed by the fact that it regards the threat to abandon this role, in the form of withdrawing American troops from Western Europe, as its most effective trump card *vis-à-vis* the Europeans.

After Chiang Kai-shek had been driven off the Chinese mainland, the situation of the United States in *Asia* was rather different from its situation in Europe. There were no previous war allies of the importance of the French or the British whose sensibilities might have to be catered to. Furthermore, in contrast to Europe, here the American engagement twice led to prolonged military confrontations in which American troops were directly involved – the Korean and Vietnam wars.

The role of the United States as a Far Eastern world power also differed from its role in Western Europe because until the outbreak of the Korean War, no clear line of demarcation delimiting its sphere of security and interests had been established. This left uncertainties as to whether parts of the Far Eastern mainland were part of this sphere.[58]

All this was changed by the Korean War. The United States became a power protecting and controlling South Korea, and took responsibility for a system of alliances designed by Dulles to protect strategically important parts of Asia. The armistice that finally ended the Korean War was possible only because of the American administration's dominating influence over the Korean government. It forced South Korea to forego the continuation of the war, and thus to refrain from the immediate re-establishment of national unity.[59]

The critical instance in which the question of American 'imperialism' arises is, of course, Vietnam. Some authors go so far as to claim that the Vietnam War was the first and only American imperial war.[60] In actuality, this conflict had its precedents. Both the Korean War and the Truman administration's aid to Greece during the Greek Civil War can be taken as examples.[61] If anything, these military engagements come under the heading of 'preclusive imperialism'. In Indo-China, Korea and Greece, the United States did not have the slightest intention of establishing direct domination, nor did it have overriding economic interests which it might have wanted to defend. The desire to keep these countries from falling under communist control was the only important motive in these cases.

After the Korean War, the United States succeeded (with British assistance) in delimiting the sphere of direct communist influence fairly sharply. The only exception was Indo-China, its previous French colonial rulers having been unable to prevent the further spread of communist (Vietminh) influence, even after the Geneva Conference on Indo-China in 1954. The American government blamed France's alleged relapses into the role of a colonialist and its sweeping aside of the Vietnamese people's national aspirations for the success of nationalist communism in that country. From 1954 onwards, the United States increasingly took over the reins of Western Indo-China policies.[62] Without doubt, one of them was 'preclusive imperialism' in so far as a communist takeover of the whole of Vietnam was to be avoided. But another aim pointed towards alliance policies on a global level: American administrations from Eisenhower to Nixon had made continuing support of their Vietnamese protégés into a global litmus test of the loyalty of the United States to its allies, and of its steadfastness in the Cold War. Finally, its aim was also to establish Western-style political order, an aim which was reminiscent of Wilson's intervention in the Mexican Civil War. Particularly in the early days of the American quasi-protectorate, it was hoped that the South Vietnamese would be educated towards democratic nationhood, so that they would one day be strong enough to provide for their own security and could eventually dispense with American support. Thus the long-term goal of the United States was to extricate itself from this arena within the foreseeable future. In Vietnam it acted as but a temporary 'imperial power'.[63]

One of the paradoxes of the Vietnamese tragedy is that the United States became deeply entangled in domestic Vietnamese politics, precisely when it thought it was pursuing the emancipation of the country. The events surrounding the elimination of the South Vietnamese President, Ngo Dinh Diem, in 1963 offer a telling example. The Americans had supported him initially but then increasingly considered him incompetent and ultimately aquiesced in his political and physical liquidation by some of his officers. Admittedly, the American government wanted to give the new Saigon government more popular support, which would also strengthen South Vietnam's position in its struggle against the communist underground.[64]

But the partial responsibility of the United States for the Diem administration's débâcle, combined with the domestic and military failure of successive South Vietnamese governments, undoubtedly reduced its capacity to exercise effective control in South-East Asia.

Washington never intended to make South Vietnam the centre of an American empire in South-East Asia by a continued occupation with American troops. On the contrary, the various American administrations wanted nothing more than to relinquish control over the non-communist part of the country to the South Vietnamese.[65] Nixon's policy of the Vietnamization of the Vietnam conflict in the end served only to confirm a policy that had already been in operation.[66] This was also true of the doctrine put forward by Nixon in 1969 to the effect that the United States would henceforth lend assistance only to peoples who requested it, and ones who would themselves contribute towards their defence against communist subversion. In the final analysis, the Nixon doctrine and the American policy in Vietnam were attempts to harmonize the security interests of the United States as a world power with the principle of national self-determination.

American policies towards *Latin America* after 1945 similarly reflect these concerns of security and self-determination. Relations between the United States and the Western hemisphere were coloured by the fact that Americans had invested relatively large amounts of capital in individual Latin American economies. Nationalizations without compensation of American property carried out by revolutionary regimes in these countries have led to a constant strain in relations between the United States and its southern neighbours. If the United States after 1945 in some respects exercised effective control in Central America, and the consequences showed it to be an imperial power, this was still not primarily due to the investments made in the economies of these countries. They accounted for only a small part of the total foreign investments of the United States, which still flowed mostly into developed countries (while still playing an important role in the weak Central American economies).[67] American administrations after 1945 (by contrast to their predecessors) always hesitated to intervene when it was merely a matter of protecting American property in Latin America. Washington, too, took the principle of mutual non-interference agreed by the countries in the Organization of American States (OAS) seriously.[68]

If the United States none the less made at least three exceptions to this principle between 1945 and 1965, and got involved in the domestic development of Latin American states, this was primarily due to considerations of security and ideology. To the outside world, it seemed that in these interventions the United States was exercising a kind of watch-dog function over its Caribbean neighbours. In each case, the main concern of the United States was to prevent the establishment of a communist regime on its own doorstep. This was the aim of the mutiny of Guatemalan officers in 1945, which was aided by the CIA and toppled the elected administration of President Jacobo Arbenz, a regime known to be friendly to communists.[69]

There was, of course, one important instance in which this anti-communist policy of containment failed: Castro's Cuba. One reason for the failure was that initially after the overthrow of the dictator Batistá by Castro's revolutionary movement, the new Cuban leader enjoyed a great deal of sympathy in the United States. Only Castro's increasingly anti-American course provoked the Eisenhower administration's willingness to have Castro removed by his own opponents.[70] This was attempted by his successor Kennedy in April 1961. Contrary to Washington's hopes, the landing of Cuban emigrants at the Bay of Pigs did not turn out to be the signal for a general uprising against Castro's regime. The insurgents were defeated and Castro emerged more powerful than ever from this test of strength. He now drew even closer to the Soviet Union. But Cuba became a military protectorate of the Soviet Union in a qualified sense only. This came about as a result of the Cuban missile crisis in 1962, which ended in the Soviet Union bowing to American pressures, and refraining from the planned stationing of offensive missiles on the island. This outcome could be construed as a restriction of Cuba's sovereign right to defend itself militarily. On the other hand, the American administration reciprocated by promising not to intervene against Castro, and in this sense restricted the freedom of its own decision-making.[71]

While Cuba has been subject to American control only in an extremely limited military sense, the American administration for its part was determined to prevent the emergence of further Cubas in the Caribbean. This explains the American intervention in the Dominican Republic in 1965. Superficially, it seemed to resemble the numerous American interventions in the Caribbean early in the century. But, at the same time, it shows clearly a new type of control that was exercised by the United States in Central America. This incident will therefore be examined in more detail.

The United States was given the opportunity to step in when a civil war broke out in Santo Domingo in 1965. The antagonists were followers of the ruling military junta headed by Reid, a civilian politician, on the one hand, and followers of President Juan Bosch, who had been toppled by this junta in 1963, on the other. Bosch, initially held in high esteem as a liberal by the United States, and particularly by Kennedy, lived in exile in Puerto Rico at the time of the disturbances. The United States had reacted to his removal from office by the junta by withholding diplomatic recognition from the rebel regime. This sanction was lifted only when the junta promised to hold elections. At the time of the disturbances in 1965, these elections were imminent. One might have expected the Johnson administration to back Bosch's followers, if indeed it had wanted to get involved in the civil war in Santo Domingo at all. This, however, was not to be the case, for American observers on the scene reported to Washington that Bosch's following was infiltrated by communists. Under these circumstances, their victory in the civil war could possibly lead to a communist takeover in Santo Domingo – a second Cuba. This alleged danger became the rationale for the landing of more than 20,000 marines in Santo Domingo at the end of April 1965. Meanwhile, Washington's official explanation for military intervention was the need for the protection of American citizens.[72]

The inhabitants of the island republic thus found themselves in a position in which they had in fact been until shortly after the First World War: namely, under the effective control of the United States as an occupying power. By its sheer presence, this power made the hostilities between the civil war factions cease for the time being. This amounted to the military junta remaining in power unchallenged. But it could not provide a solution to Santo Domingo's domestic problems – even in the view of the United States. In order to re-establish a stable and legitimate democratic order in the occupied country, the United States called in the OAS as a first step. Three Latin American nations then took part in the occupation of Santo Domingo on behalf of the OAS, and later in supervising its elections. These took place in June 1966. The winner, Joaquin Balaguer, became the new President of the Dominican Republic. He was a moderately conservative politician who was also favoured by the Americans: Juan Bosch, who had returned from exile, lost as a candidate against Balaguer.[73] After Santo Domingo's domestic situation had been stabilized, the occupying troops were withdrawn in September 1966. Previously, the United States had sought to speed up the process of stabilization by giving massive economic aid.[74] The American administration interpreted the events in Santo Domingo in a wider sense by declaring, in the Johnson doctrine, that the United States would not stand idly by while communist regimes were created in the Western hemisphere.[75] This type of language was somewhat reminiscent of the Roosevelt Corollary. The Johnson doctrine reserved the right to limited – but effective – control by the United States over the domestic development of Latin American republics. This doctrine would also be applied to the Allende regime in Chile in 1973, although in a hesitant manner and with limited means.[76]

The American intervention in Santo Domingo was significant in several respects. First, in contrast with Wilson's involvement in Mexico's internal affairs, it had taken place to protect a government that had come to power by means of a coup. The only motivation had been genuine apprehension about the communist takeover in the Dominican Republic. Secondly, the United States directly took control over its Caribbean neighbour. At the same time, however, it tried to get other Latin American countries to share its responsibilities and generally to get its policies sanctioned by the OAS. And thirdly, the goal of intervention was to create the preconditions for a democratic approval of the new regime. In the course of these efforts, the United States had run the risk of having Juan Bosch elected. This, as far as Washington was concerned, was the same as risking communist influence on the island republic. The United States took this risk because it wanted to reconcile its temporary control over Santo Domingo with the right to self-determination – if only after the event.

Despite the Cold War climate of the 1960s, and in contrast to its behaviour around the turn of the century, the United States in Central America shied away from appearing as an outright imperialist power. Even in its immediate backyard, the United States had not followed the Soviet example of 1956 in Hungary. At best it had retained informal control.

'Imperial' Consequences of Containment: Conclusions

This view can be applied to American foreign policy after the Second World War in general. After 1945 the United States had unprecedented opportunities to expand imperial control – perhaps even to attain global hegemony, but this possibility was deliberately rejected.[77] None the less, on several occasions, it seized the chance to take temporary control in specific cases in order to successfully implement its policy of containment. The motivation behind this policy was a defensive one. It operated by very carefully selected means, and used indirect means of control wherever possible. American control was not going to appear as imperial domination – domestically or internationally. Throughout the heat of battle, American administrations have never lost sight of the fact that containment was oriented against the communist bloc's claims for imperial domination – in practice as well as in principle. This policy would have to be justified before the world on the basis of its principle of anti-imperialism. Hence the constant efforts on the part of the United States to obtain, wherever possible, democratically legitimized mandates from the population in cases where military intervention had come to be seen as inevitable.

The aims of intervention were generally defined by reference to the notion of political stability. In other words, American administrations have justified it with the wish to re-establish stable and democratically sanctioned conditions in the countries concerned. Woodrow Wilson had been able to afford this aim as a kind of luxury for the purposes of political education. Even at that time, however, the United States was playing a greater part in the economies of its neighbours, and thus had some interest in orderly government in them. After 1945, the domestic development of nations outside the communist orbit became the direct and primary concern of the United States. The survival of non-communist political systems, even those whose democratic credentials have been somewhat dubious, has been – and still is – the major concern of the United States in the Cold War.[78]

In conclusion it may be said that empire has remained a mere episode in American foreign policy. The acquisition of colonies and permanent informal control were the goals of American foreign policy only from 1898 to 1912. Only in this period did the ideology of classical imperialism exert a dominant influence on the American public. What came after this time must be seen as a problem of the imperial consequences, stemming from the actual exercise of American foreign policy. These consequences were sanctioned neither by the anti-imperialist self-conception of all American administrations after Wilson, nor by a majority of the American public.

The United States rose to the level of a global power in the course of its two struggles with what it considered as German imperialism, and after 1945 in the wake of the 'containment' of what was officially perceived as 'Soviet imperialism'. With the assumption of this leadership role, the United States had to face the question of control. At stake was not only control in the interests of a joint system of defence, but also in the sense of maintaining certain values which the Western world deemed worth defending. Particularly 'progressive' American administrations, such as Kennedy's, were willing to use all available means of control in order to attain that goal. With these means they sought to influence the domestic development of their allies, in order to guarantee the preservation of human rights and the maintenance of democratic fair play. Whether motivated by considerations of security, or guided by the notion of stability and orderly political growth, American interventions, judged by their consequences, could not always avoid giving the impression that they were the result of quasi-imperialistic global policies. These instances of intervention were, however, short-term and sporadic. This was the case even in the Caribbean, its immediate backyard. Basically, American global policies after Wilson had less and less to do with the concept of imperialism, at least as it has come to be understood since the turn of the century. Whoever refers to American foreign policy in general simply as American imperialism is moved by motives of political denunciation, and not by the pursuit of historical truth.

This is not to deny certain continuities between American foreign policy before and after 1912. One type of continuity is manifest in American interests in security. The United States has always put store by an unendangered flank in the south, and has had a desire to keep the coasts facing the Atlantic and Pacific oceans free from the controlling influence of an inimical great power, be it Germany or the Soviet Union. A second type of continuity lies in the fact that every American administration is obliged to justify its foreign policy before a voting public and its representatives. For American presidents, imperialist policies were tenable only as long as they had extensive public support. This was the case only until 1912. Since then, the foreign policy of every American administration has been bound by the principle of self-determination which pervades the political tradition of the American republic. Since Wilson, no administration has been able to allow itself a wholesale contravention of this principle without risking its credibility among the voters, even when national security was said to be at stake. Wherever the United States acts as a global power, wherever it pursues policies which suit its own interests, it is at the same time obliged to conform to the principles which are the unalterable foundation of its political tradition.

Notes: Chapter 2

This chapter was translated by Ralph Schroeder.

1 See also a pamphlet written by the secretary-general of the Communist Party of the USA: G. Hall, *Imperialism Today* (New York, 1972), p. 7.
2 See R. W. Tucker, *The Radical Left and American Foreign Policy* (Baltimore, Md, 1971).
3 See J. Slater, 'Is the United States foreign policy "imperialist" or "imperial"?', *Political Science Quarterly*, vol. 91 (1976), pp. 63–87; H.-U. Wehler, *Der Aufstieg des amerikanischen Imperialismus* (Göttingen, 1974), pp. 354–7.
4 S. F. Bemis, *A Diplomatic History of the United States* (New York, 1955), ch. 26; J. W. Pratt, *America's Colonial Experiment: How the United States Gained, Governed, and in Part Gave Away a Colonial Empire* (New York, 1950); E. R. May, *American Imperialism: A Speculative Essay* (New York, 1968), pp. 207 ff.

5 R. Hofstadter, *The Progressive Historians: Turner, Beard, Parrington* (New York, 1970), pp. 171, 325, 334.
6 On Williams see R. J. Maddox, *The New Left and the Origins of the Cold War* (Princeton, NJ, 1973), pp. 13 ff.
7 See his latest work: W. A. Williams, *Empire as a Way of Life: An Essay on the Causes and Character of America's Present Predicament along with a Few Thoughts about an Alternative* (New York, 1980).
8 W. A. Williams, *The Tragedy of American Diplomacy* (New York, 1962), p. 45 and *passim*; idem, *The Roots of the Modern American Empire: A Study of the Growth and Shaping of Social Consciousness in a Marketplace Society* (New York, 1969).
9 Williams, *Tragedy*, p. 39 and *passim*.
10 Thus the subtitle of chapter 2 in Williams, *Tragedy*, pp. 52 ff.
11 ibid., pp. 106 ff.; W. A. Williams, *America Confronts a Revolutionary World: 1776–1976* (New York, 1976), pp. 199–200.
12 Williams, *Tragedy*, p. 44.
13 cf. the title of Williams's most important book: *The Tragedy of American Diplomacy*.
14 Tucker, *Radical Left*, pp. 46 ff., 55–6, 63 ff., 146 ff.
15 For example, S. E. Ambrose, *Rise to Globalism: American Foreign Policy 1938–1980* (New York, 1980); L. C. Gardner *et al.*, *Creation of the American Empire*, Vol. 2 (Chicago, 1976), pp. 513 ff.; G. Liska, *Imperial America: The International Politics of Primacy* (Baltimore, Md, 1976); J. Spanier, *American Foreign Policy since World War II* (New York, 1975), pp. 234 ff.; T. Smith, *The Pattern of Imperialism: The United States, Great Britain, and the Late-Industrializing World since 1815* (Cambridge, 1981).
16 G. C. Herring, *America's Longest War: The United States and Vietnam, 1950–1975* (New York, 1979), p. 256; Gardner *et al.*, *Creation*, Vol. 2, pp. 521–2; A. M. Schlesinger, Jr, *The Imperial Presidency* (New York, 1974), pp. 177 ff.
17 R. Aron, *The Imperial Republic: the United States and the World, 1945–1973* (Englewood Cliffs, NJ, 1974); C. Julien, *L'Empire américain* (Paris, 1968); U. Küntzel, *Der nordamerikanische Imperialismus* (Darmstadt, 1974).
18 Williams, *America Confronts a Revolutionary World*, pp. 183 ff.; R. W. Tucker, *A New Isolationism* (New York, 1972); K. Schwabe, *Der amerikanische Isolationismus im 20. Jahrhundert. Legende und Wirklichkeit* (Wiesbaden, 1975), pp. 15–16.
19 A. P. Thornton, *Imperialism in the Twentieth Century* (London, 1978), p. 3.
20 Liska, *Imperial America*, pp. 9–10.
21 See also Smith, *Pattern of Imperialism*, p. 6; Slater, 'Is the United States', p. 85; Aron, *Imperial Republic*, p. 253.
22 Thornton, *Imperialism*, pp. 3–4; Aron, *Imperial Republic*, p. 255; Smith, *Pattern of Imperialism*, pp. 6–7.
23 Aron, *Imperial Republic*, pp. 258 ff.
24 Smith, *Pattern of Imperialism*, p. 3; Aron, *Imperial Republic*, pp. 257–8, 280; Liska, *Imperial America*, pp. 99–100.
25 Smith, *Pattern of Imperialism*, *passim*; Spanier, *American Foreign Policy*, p. 235; G. Liska, *Career of Empire: America and Imperial Expansion over Land and Sea* (Baltimore, Md, 1978), p. 156.
26 R. Girault, 'Les Impérialismes de la première moitié du XXe siècle', *Relations Internationales*, vol. 3 (1976), p. 195. Girault introduces the term of 'super-impérialisme' or 'ultra-impérialisme' without, however, clearly defining it (pp. 208–9).
27 May, *American Imperialism*, p. 209.
28 ibid., pp. 248 ff.; P. Coletta, 'Bryan, McKinley and the Treaty of Paris', *Pacific Historical Review*, vol. 26 (1957), pp. 131–46; G. Rystad, *Ambiguous Imperialism: American Foreign Policy and Domestic Politics at the Turn of the Century* (Lund, 1975).
29 E. B. Tompkins, *Anti-Imperialism in the United States* (Philadelphia, Pa, 1970); May, *American Imperialism*, pp. 95 ff.
30 ibid., p. 210; Thornton, *Imperialism*, p. 106.
31 Rystad, *Ambiguous Imperialism*, pp. 234 ff.
32 L. C. Gardner, 'Woodrow Wilson and the Mexican Revolution', in A. S. Link (ed.), *Woodrow Wilson and a Revolutionary World, 1913–1921* (Chapel Hill, NC, 1982), p. 14.
33 W. Johnston, 'Reflections on Wilson and the problems of world peace', in ibid., pp. 202–3.

34 See Chapter 5 by Dietrich Geyer in this volume.
35 Pratt, *America's Colonial Experiment*, pp. 203–4; A. S. Link et al. (eds), *The Papers of Woodrow Wilson*, Vol. 28, pp. 323–4; ibid., Vol. 36, p. 555.
36 R. Koebner and H. Schmidt, *Imperialism* (Cambridge, 1965), p. 242.
37 A. S. Link, *Woodrow Wilson: Revolution, War, and Peace* (Arlington Heights, Va, 1979), p. 10; *Papers relating to the Foreign Relations of the United States: The Paris Peace Conference 1919*, Vol. 3 (Washington DC, 1943), p. 766.
38 L. D. Langley, *The United States and the Caribbean, 1900–1970* (Athens, Ohio, 1980), pp. 29, 127; D. Perkins, *A History of the Monroe Doctrine* (Boston, Mass., 1963), pp. 238 ff.
39 Perkins, *A History of the Monroe Doctrine*, pp. 257 ff., 268; A. S. Link and W. B. Catton, *The American Epoch*, Vol. 1 (New York, 1973), pp. 149 ff.
40 Link, *Woodrow Wilson*, pp. 9 ff; idem, *Wilson: The New Freedom* (Princeton, NJ, 1956), pp. 347 ff.; Gardner, 'Woodrow Wilson and the Mexican Revolution', pp. 3–48. For a misrepresentation of Wilson's policy towards Mexico see Julien, *L'Empire américain*, pp. 121 ff.
41 Williams, *Tragedy*, pp. 52 ff.
42 B. M. Unterberger, 'Woodrow Wilson and the Russian Revolution', in Link (ed.), *Woodrow Wilson and a Revolutionary World*, pp. 49–104, espec. p. 87; N. G. Levin, *Woodrow Wilson and World Politics* (New York, 1968), pp. 183 ff.; G. F. Kennan, *Soviet-American Relations, 1917–1920*, Vol. 1: *The Decision to Intervene* (Princeton, NJ, 1958); P. Trani, 'Woodrow Wilson and the decision to intervene in Russia: a reconsideration', *Journal of Modern History*, vol. 48 (1976), pp. 440–61.
43 On Europe: M. P. Leffler, *The Elusive Quest: America's Pursuit of European Stability and French Security, 1919–1933* (Chapel Hill, NC, 1979). On Mexico: R. F. Smith, *The United States and Revolutionary Nationalism in Mexico* (Chicago, 1972). On the Far East: M. D. Reagan, 'The Far Eastern Crisis of 1931–32: Stimson, Hoover, and the armed services', in H. Stein (ed.), *American Civil-Military Decisions* (Birmingham, Al., 1963), pp. 27–42.
44 Pratt, *America's Colonial Experiment*, pp. 320 ff.
45 R. F. Smith, 'Republican policy and the Pax Americana, 1921–1932', in W. A. Williams (ed.), *From Colony to Empire: Essays in the History of American Foreign Relations* (New York, 1972), p. 266, quoting the banker, Thomas W. Lamont: 'The theory of collecting debts by gunboat is unrighteous, unworkable and obsolete. While I have, of course, no mandate to speak for my colleagues of the investment banking community, I think I may safely say that they share this view with Mr. Morrow and myself...' (letter of 9 January 1928).
46 H. F. Cline, *The United States and Mexico* (New York, 1963), pp. 239 ff.
47 Wm R. Louis, *Imperialism at Bay, 1941–1945: The United States and the Decolonization of the British Empire* (Oxford, 1977); R. von Albertini, 'Die USA und die Kolonialfrage', *Vierteljahreshefte für Zeitgeschichte*, vol. 13 (1965), pp. 18–31; Herring, *America's Longest War*, pp. 5 ff.
48 Pratt, *America's Colonial Experiment*, pp. 360 ff.
49 This applied primarily to the period after 1945 when the economies of Puerto Rico and the United States were interconnected to such an extent that severing ties would have meant economic suicide for the Puerto Ricans. Moreover, the poverty on the neighbouring independent islands was unlikely to have stimulated Puerto Rican demands for independence. See Langley, *The United States and the Caribbean*, pp. 157 ff., 260 ff.
50 R. A. Dallek, *Franklin D. Roosevelt and American Foreign Policy, 1932–1945* (Oxford, 1979).
51 ibid., pp. 482–3; R. A. Divine, *Second Chance: The Triumph of Internationalism in America during World War II* (New York, 1967); K. Schwabe, 'Die Vereinigten Staaten und der Frieden in Europa 1919 und –945', in *Historia Integra. Festschrift für Erich Hassinger* (Berlin, 1977), pp. 399 ff.; H. Gollwitzer, *Geschichte des weltpolitischen Denkens*, Vol. 2 (Göttingen, 1982), pp. 379, 395–400.
52 Dallek, *Franklin D. Roosevelt*, p. 510.
53 J. L. Gaddis, *Strategies of Containment: A Critical Appraisal of Postwar American National Security Policy* (Oxford, 1982).
54 Smith, *Pattern of Imperialism*, pp. 101 ff., 160 ff.; Spanier, *American Foreign Policy*, pp. 45 ff.; W. Link, 'Die Rolle der USA im westeuropäischen Integrationsprozess', *Aus*

Politik und Zeitgeschichte. Beilage zu Das Parlament, 1 April 1972, pp. 3–13; idem, 'Zum Problem der Kontinuität der amerikanischen Deutschlandpolitik im 20. Jahrhundert', in M. Knapp (ed.), *Die deutsch-amerikanischen Beziehungen nach 1945* (Frankfurt-on-Main, 1975), pp. 86–131; L. S. Kaplan, 'Western Europe in the "American Century": a retrospective view', *Diplomatic History*, vol. 6 (1982), pp. 111 ff.
55 Communication from Professor Ronald Robinson to the author. As far as France is concerned see the President's own testimony: L. B. Johnson, *The Vantage Point: Perspectives of the Presidency 1963–1969* (London, 1971), pp. 305 ff. The weakening of the American financial position was partly caused by the fact that France no longer recognized the US dollar as a world reserve currency as had been the case since Bretton Woods. France's criticism of the international financial system went hand in hand with its dissociation from NATO. See D. Calleo, *The Imperious Economy* (Cambridge, Mass., 1982), pp. 45–61.
56 H. Kissinger, *Years of Upheaval* (London, 1982), pp. 143 ff.
57 Liska, *Career of Empire*, p. 153.
58 W. LaFeber, *America, Russia, and the Cold War* (New York, 1972), pp. 88–9.
59 R. A. Divine, *Eisenhower and the Cold War* (New York, 1981), p. 30.
60 Liska, *Career of Empire*, pp. 143, 286, 321; Smith, *Pattern of Imperialism*, p. 178.
61 D. Yergin, *Shattered Peace: The Origins of the Cold War and the National Security State* (Boston, Mass., 1977), pp. 293–4. However, American troops were never involved in combat in Greece.
62 Herring, *America's Longest War*, pp. 39 ff., 49 ff.
63 ibid., pp. 55 ff.; Smith, *Pattern of Imperialism*, pp. 163, 178.
64 Herring, *America's Longest War*, pp. 94, 105–6.
65 A. E. Goodman, *The Lost Peace: America's Search for a Negotiated Settlement of the Vietnam War* (Stanford, Calif., 1978), pp. 73, 86 ff., 102–3.
66 R. Osgood, *Retreat from Empire?*, Vol. 2 (Baltimore, Md, 1973), pp. 1–27; Smith, *Pattern of Imperialism*, p. 172.
67 Aron, *Imperial Republic*, pp. 240 ff.; Link and Catton, *American Epoch*, Vol. 3, pp. 134, 245.
68 Slater, 'Is the United States', pp. 82–3.
69 Langley, *The United States and the Caribbean*, pp. 205 ff.
70 L. D. Langley, *The Cuban Policy of the United States* (New York, 1968), pp. 160 ff.; idem, *The United States and the Caribbean*, pp. 211 ff.; R. E. Welch, 'Lippmann, Berle, and the US response to the Cuban Revolution', *Diplomatic History*, vol. 6 (1982), pp. 125–43.
71 Langley, *The United States and the Caribbean*, pp. 226 ff.
72 J. Slater, *Intervention and Negotiation: The United States and the Dominican Revolution* (New York, 1970); A. Lowenthal, *The Dominican Intervention* (Cambridge, Mass., 1972); Langley, *The United States and the Caribbean*, pp. 239 ff.
73 Link and Catton, *American Epoch*, Vol. 3, p. 298.
74 R. J. Barnet, *Intervention and Revolution* (New York, 1972), p. 207.
75 L. C. Gardner, 'Cold War counterrevolution', in Williams (ed.), *From Colony to Empire*, p. 471; Johnson, *The Vantage Point*, pp. 187 ff.
76 Kissinger, *Years of Upheaval*, pp. 374 ff. Kissinger confirms American interference in Chilean domestic politics, but rates its significance lower than was done by a committee of the Senate.
77 Liska, *Career of Empire*, p. 153. This attitude reflected recommendations made by the Joint Chiefs of Staff.
78 Spanier, *American Foreign Policy*, pp. 261 ff.; Liska, *Career of Empire*, pp. 349 ff.; Smith, *Pattern of Imperialism*, p. 174. Smith tends to underestimate the importance of control and equates globalization with imperialism.

3 The Paradox of Imperialism: The American Case

A. E. CAMPBELL

All students of imperialism today must begin by pointing to some of the many ambiguities in the term. Those ambiguities are there even within the last period of serious imperial expansion – the late nineteenth and early twentieth centuries – but they become more pronounced when we try to draw analogies between that period and our own times.

For students of the United States formal imperialism presents, as it presented almost from the outset, two obvious difficulties. First, a nation with a strong tradition of anti-imperialism, which had won its own independence from an earlier empire in battle and which had insisted that the maintenance of European empires in the Americas was unnatural, now seemed to be making imperialist claims indistinguishable from those of European powers. Secondly, however, the American interest in formal empire was short-lived and apparently superficial. Well before the First World War most Americans had lost such interest in the Philippines as they had ever had. It is hard to argue that the possession of empire had the evil consequences for American society which anti-imperialists foresaw.

Aware of such difficulties – and also of the course of later events – Professor Schwabe draws a distinction, for the United States at least, between an 'imperialist' policy – a systematic attempt to establish an empire – and an 'imperial' policy – the policy of a major power which claims some responsibility for the ordering of the world.[1] The distinction is a valid one, and it at once suggests parallels with the work of Professors Gallagher and Robinson, the leading theorists of imperialism in our day.[2] The distinction between 'imperialist' and 'imperial' has much in common with their distinction between 'formal' and 'informal' empire. For both formulations, however, the central problem is not one of distinguishing between two related conditions but of defining the relationship properly.

Professor Robinson has recently advanced a revised definition of informal imperialism.[3] It exists when an expenditure by a metropolitan state – of money, or energy, or even armed force – which is small to the metropolitan state has an effect which is large in an outlying region. If there is merit in such a formulation, there must surely be merit in it when applied to the United States, by far the richest and most powerful of modern states. If any state can avoid the necessity of turning informal into formal imperialism, surely the United States can.

Important though Professor Robinson's insight is, however, it is not precise enough to carry us much further forward. Most obviously, it offers no guidance as to how great the discrepancy in wealth or power between two related political units must be before we can properly call the relationship imperialistic. If *all* unequal relationships are imperialistic – an idea which would certainly give joy to some egalitarian thinkers – the term is simply empty. Unequal is unequal, and that is all. Beyond that, we are given no reason for considering a relationship between two units only. A relationship among a complex of political units, some powerful and cohesive, others weaker both externally and internally, is easy to envisage. Indeed, it corresponds to the real world. But it complicates the Robinson model to the point at which its usefulness is in question.

The complexity of the international order reminds us of one possible function of imperialism which Gallagher and Robinson were among the first to notice – its function as a means of bringing order out of confusion and simplifying complexity. That is not an economic function, although of course it has economic implications. It is not even, in the ordinary sense, a political function. It is a cultural function. The main purpose of this chapter is to suggest that that cultural function has been too much neglected in most studies of imperialism, and that its restoration to a central place will lead towards a definition of imperialism both wide enough and limited enough to be useful.

If we return, then, to Schwabe's question – When is it advisable to term a system of informal control imperialistic? – some limitations suggest themselves at once, and they apply to the United States as well as to other powers. First, in the period which this volume has under consideration, that from the late nineteenth century onwards, mere exploitation was no longer possible. We may doubt whether it was ever possible. Even in the days of the *conquistadores*, or the early Anglo-Dutch-French rivalry, some ideological defence of expansion had to be offered. It was not by accident that the first wave of European expansion coincided with the development of the idea of 'Europe' as a replacement for the idea of 'Christendom'. There was still life in that idea at the end of the nineteenth century, but it had already been much weakened. The imperialism with which we are concerned is an attenuated form, and many difficulties derive from the failure to give adequate weight to that fact.

The first anti-imperialist movements, let us remind ourselves, arose among Europeans. For our purposes the rebellion of Britain's American colonies, followed by those of Spain and Portugal, is not immediately relevant: they were political rebellions. It was the movement for Italian independence from Austrian rule – stronger than any movement for Italian unification – which foreshadowed the future. Hardly had that succeeded than the subject peoples of eastern Europe began to press similar claims. Once such claims were admitted for European peoples, they could be denied for others only by insisting on some shared European (or Western) moral and intellectual superiority. The imperialism of the late nineteenth century was the last statement of that felt superiority.

An imperialistic policy requires an ideology of imperialism. But we can go further than that. The powers of the late nineteenth century – including, briefly, the United States – all claimed essentially the *same* ideological justification. They were rivals claiming to pursue a common, even a shared, purpose. The moral position on which the empire of each was based required recognition of the same position when claimed by rivals. That made the resolution of rivalries not only possible but relatively straightforward. In our period colonial rivalries did not lead to war. In earlier periods they sometimes did – but never to total war. The ideology of empire contains its own limitations.

So attenuated was empire in our period that those limitations were a necessary condition of its survival. But how can we tell with assurance when domination is being exercised? If people live more or less quietly under imperial rule, are we not entitled to conclude that, in some sense, they accept it, or at least prefer it to any alternative they can envisage? There is a paradox here in Professor Robinson's formulation. If the expenditure of *small* resources by the metropolitan power is sufficient to maintain control, can we distinguish imperialism – other than formal imperialism – from other types of political control? The solidarity of the Western powers over their imperial claims was a large part of the reason why those claims survived for so long.

Nevertheless, they could not survive for ever. The thrust of romantic anti-imperialism was too strong, and it was felt by imperialists as well as by their subjects. It is the romantic, the cultural, aspect of modern anti-imperialism which left-wing criticism most neglects; yet it is this aspect which, in other contexts, is increasingly coming to the fore. The great weakness of the communist formulation is its exclusive emphasis on economic exploitation. Cultural exploitation is more important, and it works, so to say, in reverse. The capitalist is accused, rightly or wrongly, of the fault of the Dutch – of offering too little and asking too much. In cultural terms the imperialist insists on offering too much and asking too little. The 'native' who adopts Western ways is becoming civilized; the Westerner who adopts native ways is 'going native'. Yet the cultural difference is the core of the problem. If the imperialist tries to reform, he is quickly disillusioned; if he decides to leave an alien culture alone, it is only out of pessimism. Professor Robinson is persuasive in insisting that imperialism is cheap for the imperialist, and is abandoned when it is not. He is surely less persuasive in suggesting that imperialism brings about large changes in the subject areas. Students of modernization, who study much of the same evidence from a different standpoint, would commonly argue that the changes brought about are not large enough.

The conflict between cultural and economic interests is the essence of imperialism, and it manifests itself as a political problem. An empire, whether formal or informal, is a political system, and there must therefore be within it chains of political authority or patronage in one direction, and chains of loyalty or support in the other. The characteristic of an empire is that such chains are broken, or at best much weakened, at the point where they link metropolitan and client states. It is at that point that force must be called in to strengthen a weak link, and it is *that* use of force – by no means the only political use of force – which defines imperialism.

The Paradox of Imperialism 37

All modern political theory derives authority from the consent of the governed. Dominant modern theory bases representation on a geographical constituency. Any aspiring leader establishes his base in Wales, or Bavaria, or California, and then hopes to enlarge it, to cover Great Britain or Germany or the United States. In empire that possibility is denied. In formal empire the idea that a leader from the client state can ever exert control at the centre has been explicitly rejected; in informal empire it has been implicitly rejected. The knowledge, their own and that of everyone else affected, that there is a clear limit to their political aspirations weakens the local position of local leaders. They are being invited to undertake an impossible job. The more effective their control over their own peoples, the clearer it becomes that they cannot advance towards real power in the larger system. If they try to adapt to the political practices of that system, the likely outcome is that they will lose control at home while coming no closer to imperial power.

There is, of course, a whole spectrum of political possibilities, influenced by such various factors as the sheer size of the client area – in an extreme case, China was so large that the only possible agreement was to leave it alone – and the width of the cultural gap between the metropolitan and client regions. As we have seen, it proved possible for a time to argue that imperialism was inappropriate within Europe while still maintaining it outside Europe. Imperialism, therefore, has more to do with culture than with class, and with politics than with economics; and therein lie its contradictions. Subject peoples can be made more prosperous, even if in practice they usually are not. They cannot be made more civilized, and therefore fitter for self-government, if civilization is defined in alien terms.

It would be a mistake, however, to put too much weight on racialism as the central defect of imperialism. Probably Anglo-Saxon imperialism – and German, so far as it ever developed – is more racialist than most. That has the advantage that when imperialism becomes expensive or wearisome the emotional commitment to it proves to be weak. Racialist arguments can be used, and were used, for anti-imperialist as well as for imperialist purposes. Americans readily concluded that the task of trying to uplift peoples naturally inferior was futile and unrewarding. Among modern imperialists it was the French who worked most strenuously towards the incorporation of chosen colonies into France, and were pained to discover that Vietnamese or Algerians rejected the privilege of becoming Frenchmen.

What subject peoples did want, naturally enough, was the chance of advancing, absolutely and relatively, towards prosperity of the sort enjoyed by their masters. Much of the animus against imperialism derives from the belief that it prevented such advance. Yet anti-imperialist movements, or the successor governments to the rulers of empire, have, with few exceptions, still to prove that they can do better. If ordered stagnation rather than development was characteristic of empire, it does not follow that the disorder attending its decay has necessarily been seminal.

As the most recent age of empire recedes into the past, it may loom less enormous, whether for good or for ill, than its exponents once hoped and its critics once charged. That may enable us to move, if not towards a satisfactory definition, at least towards the statement of some conditions without which we cannot usefully use the term, except as a stick with which to beat political opponents. Some of those conditions are:

(1) There must be the possibility of formal empire, even though we may agree with Professor Robinson that the imperialists themselves prefer informal empire. It is essential to imperialism that the metropolitan power should have the option of taking over formal control, although in practice that degree of choice implies a possible decision not to do so, for whatever reason.
(2) That option requires, in turn, a deferential world order, domestic as well as international. Unless colonial peoples acquiesce, in some sense, in an alien rule which they perceive as no more alien than that of other possible rulers, imperialism quickly becomes expensive – and, even more damaging, frustrating.
(3) A deferential world order requires, in turn, that all imperialist powers, actual or potential, should share the same basic ideology and agree in regarding it as setting them apart from potentially subject states or regions. An ideological conflict among the powers renders imperialism excessively expensive, by destroying the deference on which it relies. If such conditions are met it matters little whether empire is formal or informal, or whether it is more or less economically exploitative.

In the imperialist world order of the late nineteenth century the United States participated briefly and hesitantly. That order passed away, partly at least, because Americans took the lead in criticizing it even while they were still participating in it. But, more importantly, it passed away because colonial peoples declined to accept it any longer, and they did so principally because they no longer accepted the Western vision of a desirable and inevitable future. When the European powers hammered each other into ruin in the First World War young colonials such as Ho Chi Minh were there to watch. The Second World War was still more damaging. Yellow men humiliated the lords of human kind and yielded, when they yielded, only to overwhelming force. Because the victors were already ideologically divided, that force could not be transmuted into authority.

Attempts to retain empire were expensive failures. Attempts to withdraw in good order, leaving good order behind, failed also. Post-imperial attempts to use development as an anti-communist weapon have been indifferently successful. But that does not justify describing them as a new variant of imperialism. By every test the circumstances of our time are new ones, and nothing shows that more clearly than the position of the United States. The contrast between the late and half-hearted imperialist power, easily able to withdraw, on the one hand, and the vehement spokesman for an ideology, the more vehement because withdrawal is impossible, on the other, could hardly be sharper.

Few episodes point the contrast like the Vietnam War. There was no possibility of formal empire. Vietnamese independence was never for a moment in question – what was in question was which Vietnamese should rule from which capital and over how much of the country. So far from being deferential, American clients in Vietnam were obstreperous and unreliable (and in this, we may note in passing, they were like other American clients from Israel to Honduras). One American weakness, though not the only one, was that neither Americans nor South Vietnamese ever had full control of the conduct of the war. Most important, far from the case being one in which small expenditure on the part of the United States made a large impact on Vietnam, almost the reverse is true. Whatever the damage done to Vietnam by massive bombing, the damage to the economy and society of the United States was as great. If the North Vietnamese had not received formidable support from the ideological rivals of the United States, the war would probably not have begun and, if it had, the United States could either have won it or have withdrawn from it at much less cost.

At almost every point, then, there is contrast with the classic pattern of late nineteenth-century imperialism. If there is an element of continuity, it is surely to be found in the appeal to economic science, just as the important split comes over the question of what economic science prescribes. It is too easily forgotten that imperialists believed that an important part of their duty was to protect their subjects from economic exploitation, at the hands of corrupt local rulers in collusion with irresponsible financiers; and that none took that duty more seriously than Americans. When the United States took over the administration of customs collection in Caribbean states, foreign creditors, European and American, benefited – but so did the treasuries of the countries concerned. The losers were local embezzlers, and Americans believed that they were exercising the same sort of control abroad that they were coming to think necessary at home.

The ideological split in the modern world is essentially a split among economists. The sort of economic control that imperialists once exercised is no longer tolerable. That role has had to be handed over to a new international bureaucracy – the International Monetary Fund, the World Bank, and the like – who are less effective in controlling borrowers because they have so little control over lenders. They are most effective with countries like Britain which in some residual sense are both. Imperialists and their successors are alike only in this, that both try to depoliticize issues by making some appeal to the science of the day. The first offered positive leadership. The second offer a choice between the discipline of international bankers and domestic *dirigisme*.

The case of Poland perhaps focuses the problem most sharply. Here is a European nation whose partitioning was an international scandal in the late eighteenth century, which regained its identity only in the aftermath of imperialism, on whose account Britain went to war in 1939, and whose people have a substantial constituency in the United States. Is Poland today a victim of Soviet imperialism because it lives under the shadow of the Russian army? Or is it a victim of Western imperialism because it is almost hopelessly in debt to Western bankers? Communists have their answer, of course, but there is no reason for non-communists to accept it. The better course is to recognize that there were certain limiting conditions which rendered 'imperialism' appropriate, for the United States as for any other power; that they no longer exist; and that, while exploitation, international rivalry and the struggle for power are with us still and always will be, they operate for the time being in a context which calls for a different terminology.

Notes: Chapter 3

1 See Chapter 2 by Klaus Schwabe in this volume.
2 See especially R. Robinson and J. Gallagher, with A. Denny, *Africa and the Victorians: The Official Mind of Imperialism* (London, 1961); J. Gallagher, *The Decline, Revival and Fall of the British Empire* (Cambridge, 1982); R. Robinson, 'Non-European foundations of European imperialism: sketch for a theory of collaboration', in R. Owen and B. Sutcliffe (eds), *Studies in the Theory of Imperialism* (London, 1972), pp. 117–40.
3 See Chapter 18 by Ronald Robinson in this volume.

4 American Imperialism is Anti-Communism

TONY SMITH

The essence of American imperialism since 1945 has been anti-communism. No other aspect of American foreign policy has been maintained so consistently and so determinedly as this: that the influence of the Soviet Union in global affairs should be limited as far as possible, and that the coming to power of communist parties locally the world around should be strongly resisted. In pursuit of this policy, Washington has acted in a *hegemonic* fashion towards allies with relatively strong domestic political systems that have insulated them from the threat of civil wars or overwhelming foreign influence, while it has acted in an *imperialist* manner with respect to regimes more weakly constituted and more pliable. Imperialism is thus a function of the determination of the strong and the vulnerability of the weak. In the case of American policy since 1945, this degree of determination has only been attained in the effort to block communist expansion. In circumstances where this has involved massive intervention in the internal life of other peoples (the threshold of what constitutes 'massive' being sometimes difficult to establish), the United States has been imperialist.

Why, then, the anti-communism?

The Marxist Explanation

If we ask the communists themselves, or their sympathizers, why the essence of American policy has been anti-communism, their answer is instructive, and an exploration of its terms serves as a useful foil to set off what I believe is a far better explanation of American conduct. Put briefly, their analysis would run something as follows. At the end of the Second World War, the United States found itself the undisputed economic and military power of the world. The economic interests of its ruling capitalist class called for international free trade, as such an international division of labour corresponded to its concerns for securing an optimum market position and accumulating profit.[1]

In order to achieve a world order based on a non-discriminatory, multilateral economic system (or free trade) the United States was anti-colonialist as well as anti-communist. It is true that Secretary of State Cordell Hull later wrote, 'At no time did we press Britain, France, or the Netherlands for an immediate grant of self-government to their colonies. Our thought was that it would come after an adequate period of years, short or long, depending on the state of development of respective colonial peoples, during which these peoples would be trained to govern themselves.'[2] We have the Secretary's word for it, however, that American pressure was nevertheless considerable. So, as he recounts, every effort was made, beginning early in the war, to have the British rally India to the Allied side by guaranteeing the country's speedy independence in the aftermath of the fighting. And this call for Indian self-determination was accompanied by reiterated demands that the United States be extended an open door economically in India, in disregard of the imperial preference system. Or again, with respect to South-East Asia, Hull reports that in September 1944, he sent a memorandum to Roosevelt that the President 'warmly approved'. The document suggested the value of

> early, dramatic, and concerted announcements by the nations concerned making definite commitments as to the future of the regions of Southeast Asia ... It would be especially helpful if such concerted announcements could include 1) specific dates when independence or complete (dominion) self-government will be accorded, 2) specific steps to be taken to develop native capacity for self-rule, and 3) a pledge of economic autonomy and equality of economic treatment toward other nations ... In addition to their great value as psychological warfare [against the Japanese] such announcements would appear to be directly in line with American postwar interests.[3]

From the Marxist perspective, just as the Americans were anti-colonial so they were anti-communist. For just as protected colonial markets blocked American capitalism's ambitions to have the entire world as its oyster, so communists with their national development strategies and their loyalty to the interests of workers and peasants could not be expected to be docile subordinate members of a global American economic empire. Communists would stand independent of the host of mechanisms whereby international capitalism had yoked other Third World leaders to do its bidding. The argument deserves special consideration.

The Marxist interpretation of the character of Third World governing élites links their conduct to the actions of the international economic system run by the United States (and earlier by Great Britain). The result is a unified theory of imperialism, one that explains events in the 'South' or on the 'periphery', as well as in the 'North' or in the 'core'. As the account runs, most Third World élites have been made hostage to the international economic system thanks to the logic of the international division of labour. Nineteenth-century colonialism and informal, free-trade imperialism created 'dual economies' in much of Africa, Asia and Latin America. Here modern export sectors tied directly into the global economic order have been run under the dynamic of the industrial revolution in Europe and the United States, while local subsistence sectors have become sites of destruction as their artisanry was destroyed, their growing peasant populations pushed on to poorer land, and their capital appropriated – all by the undertakings of the modern sector. Moreover, the situation became self-perpetuating. Its native artisanry destroyed and its peasantry impoverished, a southern country lacked the necessary preconditions for industrial development, a circumstance made all the more hopeless by the conduct of the ruling élites in the modern sector, ever more committed to preserving things as they were despite the terrible misery this caused.[4]

Communist liberation efforts in the Third World thus have as their goal the rescue of the mass of the population in the subsistence sector from its enslavement to the modern sector. Given the logic of the development of these circumstances historically, such a project necessarily entails struggling against the forces of imperialism as well, since the modern sector can count on its friends abroad to come to its aid. For the fate of what may be called these collaborating élites on the periphery has to be considered important to capitalists in the core, since collectively they have markets and resources of real value. Of course here and there an outpost of international capital might be lost without any real consequence. But the wretched of the earth might be emboldened by successes in one place to rise up again in another. Hence the importance of being on guard everywhere against communism. In short, Marxists can explain the fact that American imperialism is anti-communism for the simple reason that communism alone has the vision and the strength to root out capitalism locally and in the process to endanger it globally. Washington may talk in moral and political terms about the danger of international communism, but its real concern is to block the spread of communism so as to safeguard the interests of the economic forces it represents. Only when the socio-economic order in the United States is changed can we have any reason to expect that an American government will act differently.[5]

The strength of the Marxist approach should be apparent. Not only does it explain Washington's policy in terms of a consistent, long-term set of interests, but it does this within an even wider historical perspective that sets the Third World as a whole within an on-going international division of labour. Such a comprehensive and unified viewpoint is bound to receive an enthusiastic reception. A theory at once as complex and as clear as this is certain to have an appeal to those who seek formula-like explanations for historical processes. Such 'vulgar Marxism', as it is commonly known, operates, in effect, by having a predetermined answer for every question, a prefabricated interpretation for every event. And how difficult to dispute it! With so many actors working over such a long period of time, it requires considerable expertise to raise problems with the analysis, thus allowing those who subscribe to it to possess their ideas in undisturbed equanimity. Moreover, such thinking has a natural political constituency among southern nationalists across a wide spectrum of opinion, for it assigns responsibility for the manifold problems plaguing the Third World to the acts of predatory capitalist imperialism: yesterday the European colonial powers, today the United States — one and the same struggle. Of course, there may be decided differences among these nationalists. Those who belong to a rising local bourgeoisie may be seeking to expand their own power under the camouflage of nationalist rhetoric, while those who represent the working class and peasantry may be planning to turn on the local bourgeoisie once they have joined a united front with it to gain power. Whatever the case, Marxism of the variety we have been reviewing here (known as 'world system analysis' when it concerns the international scene and as the 'dependency school' when it deals with change in the south) has turned out to be a potent ingredient in Third World nationalism.

Theoretically coherent this Marxist explanation may well be; but that is not the issue. The question is whether it is an accurate reading of events and to what extent. In the next two sections, let us look in turn first at the problems of explanation on which the Marxist analysis founders, and second at an alternative, and I think stronger, account of how and why American anti-communism became imperialism.

Problems with the Marxist Explanation

In order to illustrate the proposition that Marxism reveals more about the biases of its analytical categories than about the way history runs, let us consider two of the most important challenges to American policy in the Third World since 1945, the war in Vietnam and the rise of the Organization of Petroleum Exporting Countries (OPEC).

The obvious difficulty in understanding American involvement in Vietnam from a Marxist point of view is that there was nothing whatsoever of economic value there to corporate America. True, Indochina had been a source of profit to the French; but then we have to deal with the troublesome fact that Presidents Roosevelt and Truman had initially opposed a French return to South-East Asia, knowing that Ho Chi Minh would set up a communist government there. One might, of course, maintain that South Vietnam had to be kept 'free' in order to demonstrate Washington's resolve to other countries in the region, such as Indonesia and the Philippines, that might otherwise be menaced in turn by communist insurrections and where the economic stakes were far greater. In order to sustain such a position, however, several propositions would have to be defended: (1) that policymakers in Washington had a clear sense of American (and Japanese) economic interests in the area and saw them as vital to the business and financial community; (2) that these rich lands were, in fact, menaced by a communist takeover if the insurgency in Vietnam succeeded and that such struggles could be avoided should Washington prove victorious in Indo-China; and (3) that a communist victory in any of these countries would indeed lead to a form of economic nationalism fundamentally more hostile to the interests of the capitalist world than business as usual with the regimes in place.

In fact, none of these contentions can be sustained. Today, twelve years after a communist victory in Vietnam, we can see that whatever the fate of Indo-China, the future of the Philippines and Indonesia was not engaged. Nor has there been information forthcoming to establish that economic considerations were a significant, or even secondary, reason for Washington committing itself to the struggle there. Nor is there any particular reason to think that a communist regime will be automatically hostile to mutually beneficial economic relations with the capitalist world, as we can see from current relations between the United States and the People's Republic of China. In short, an explanation of the American involvement in Vietnam that rests on a Marxist foundation is more interesting as a chapter in the sociology of knowledge than it is as an insightful analysis of American policy.

Or consider what a Marxist explanation of the rise of OPEC might produce. Here was an act of economic nationalism *par excellence*, just the kind of blow to the international economic system that we are told communism might deliver and that Washington is mobilizing its forces to prevent. And yet OPEC emerged from its historically unprecedented act of economic extortion quite unscathed by American actions. Certainly, it can be argued that in certain respects OPEC actually served American interests: American oil companies reaped record wind-fall profits; economic competitors of the United States in Japan and Western Europe found their production costs rising faster than those in the United States (as they were far more dependent on foreign supplies of energy); and some of the newly enriched countries (Iran especially) could be counted on to spend their added income on military procurements from the United States and thereupon become 'surrogates' for American power in their regions. Washington's passivity in the face of OPEC might, then, be explained by its belief that, on balance, its interests might actually be being served.

Once again, the case is difficult to make. A decade after the October War, it is clear that the sudden and steep price increases engineered by OPEC in 1973–4 and again in 1979–80 have dealt a serious blow to the economies of the Organization for Economic Co-operation and Development (OECD), and have made political stability in the Third World – of the oil-rich countries as well as those unfortunate in not having domestic energy supplies – increasingly difficult to maintain, with generally negative consequences for American concerns. Moreover, this has been basically apparent since 1973. There is no reason to doubt Henry Kissinger when he writes of the early days of the crisis, 'The United States never saw [the price rise] as anything but a disaster . . .'[6] The conclusion is thus difficult to avoid that a Marxist analysis would have predicted a stern reaction on the part of the Western Alliance to the serious economic challenges posed by OPEC, yet despite a few vague threats and some ineffectual motions towards putting together a consumer bloc to thwart OPEC's power precious little was done to deal with the matter.

Other serious problems for a Marxist analysis of American policy could be cited. Why was a country like China or a region like Eastern Europe – both economic prizes – allowed to 'go communist' with such relatively little opposition? How do we explain American support for Israel when corporate interests might plausibly be argued to be far better served by a policy more pro-Arab? Why do statistical analyses show American trade and investment in the Third World to be a relatively small and declining concern so far as the United States' GNP is concerned (including even petroleum)? In other words, it is not only in attempting to explain the American involvement in Vietnam or its reaction to OPEC that Marxist analysis encounters serious difficulties.

46 *Imperialism and After*

Theoretically unified and comprehensive Marxism may well be, but evidently that is not sufficient to guarantee its accuracy in historical analysis. It certainly is not helpful in allowing us to understand why American imperialism has been so consistently and determinedly anti-communist. For the proposition that in being anti-communist Washington is representing the best interests of corporate America founders on the evidence that, on the one hand (as in Vietnam), major initiatives have been undertaken where no economic interest is perceptible while, on the other (as with OPEC), Washington has been relatively passive in the face of acts of economic nationalism by non-communists that have seriously threatened the well-being of the United States, its allies and clients the world over. In the face of these objections, it would seem to be better to understand the Marxist perspective not as a contribution to the comprehension of American policy but as an expression of Third World nationalism, and important for that reason alone.

Explaining American Anti-Communism

Why, then, has American imperialism been anti-communism? The reasons would seem to be essentially political. The struggle against fascism had instructed American leaders to think globally and to see the failings of an isolationist policy. Moreover, just as their lack of a socialist tradition made Americans blind to the socio-economic conditions that fostered communist successes in the late-industrializing world, so the strength of their own fervent religious convictions made many Americans particularly sensitive to the crusading tone of Moscow's communism with its early calls for 'world revolution' and its later manoeuvring under Stalin's ruthless leadership to expand its control wherever this appeared feasible.

It was a particular turn of historical events, however, that consolidated the anti-communist bias in Washington and made it the capstone of its global policy. For in the immediate aftermath of the war, the United States speedily withdrew its troops from Europe, opposed the return of France to Indo-china, and after an initial attempt to aid Chiang Kai-shek in his efforts to secure control of China, ultimately proposed to leave him to his own devices on the island of Taiwan. Where the United States intervened to stop communist advances this was linked either to a sense of historical obligation (the Philippines), or to the view that Moscow was planning its own deliberate expansion (as in parts of Turkey and Iran and with respect to Greece). In other words, anti-communism was neither as central nor as deep-felt a policy immediately after 1945 as it was later to become.

Here the decisive event was Korea. The attack by North Korea on the South in June 1950 was followed by heavy fighting between American and Chinese soldiers in November. Now it could be tenably argued that China and the Soviet Union were in league with one another – and that they were on the march. The American commitment to the French in Indo-China thus was handsomely increased and when Eisenhower came into office in January 1953, Washington began to explore other ways to keep the Vietnamese communists at bay, ultimately setting up the South-East Asian Treaty Organization (SEATO) as the institutional vehicle for increased American involvement. With his CIA-sponsored coups in Guatemala and Iran against governments there deemed too close to communists, Eisenhower completed setting a series of traps which would be sprung on his successors.

Once the character of American policy was set it became difficult to change. On the one hand, there was the argument about 'credibility' and warnings that should the United States default on its obligations to one party the entire structure of political commitments of which it was a part would be put in doubt. On the other hand, there was the domestic constituency for being 'tough on communism', so that each President had to weigh what it meant for him and his party should he be in office when another country was 'lost' to communism.[7] (This explains in good measure, I believe, the difference in American policy towards Cuba and Vietnam. In terms of objective interests there can be no doubt that a communist Cuba represented a far greater risk to the United States than a communist Vietnam. But since Castro had insisted he was not a communist prior to taking power, the question of an American commitment to his predecessor Batistá was never an issue.)

While the Kennedy and Johnson administrations were locked in by this process of reasoning, the terrible cost of the war in Vietnam allowed Kissinger to break out in a new direction once Nixon had taken office. Certainly, the new team made opposition to Soviet expansion the centrepiece of its policy, but it saw the danger of overcommitment to lost causes and realized with the opening to China that differences among communists could be exploited in American interest. Moves against Allende in Chile and Neto in Angola were thus seen more as anti-Soviet than as anti-communist. None the less, by focusing so exclusively on the Soviet Union, events in countries as disparate as Iran, Libya, Nicaragua, El Salvador and Guatemala were ignored and OPEC was able to work its will unchallenged.

With the Carter administration came a break in policy, a frank admission that the United States should not have 'an inordinate fear of communism', and a considered effort to form an American policy towards the South based on its own merits and so far as possible decoupled from relations with the Soviet Union. The problem was that the policy did not meet with success. Neither the Sandinistas in Nicaragua nor Khomeini in Iran viewed Washington with other than the greatest suspicion when they came to power, while Soviet activities in the Horn of Africa, Afghanistan, and Poland indicated that Moscow was not imitating American moves.

The antidote came with the Reagan administration in 1981. In line with the Nixon-Kissinger initiative, American relations with China continue to be distinguished clearly from those with the Soviet Union. But a confrontational approach towards Moscow once again dominates policy, and with Moscow its non-communist clients such as Gaddafi's Libya. More, the deep-felt demands for change in so much of the South as the subsistence sectors there find themselves ever more squeezed by demographic and economic pressures go unaddressed. A case in point: Reagan's Caribbean

Basin Initiative. Designed to stimulate trade and investment in the region, the Initiative ignores the fact that Central America grew at an annual rate of 8 per cent for some two decades without the plight of the poor being eased. In short, the civil war close to the surface in so many Third World countries will be joined by the United States on the part of the ruling classes there and in the name of anti-communism.

There can be legitimate dispute as to what kinds of activities ought rightly to be labelled imperialist. The thresholds of control (or the effort to secure it) that distinguish relations of 'influence' from those that are 'hegemonic', and these, in turn, from those that are 'imperialist' are impossible to specify precisely. As we have seen, there are two parties to an imperialist relationship: a people capable of being politically penetrated to such a point that foreign actors become important players in domestic affairs, and an outside power eager to exercise the power at its disposal in this respect. The contemporary Third World with its terrible class and ethnic tensions and its shallowly rooted governments based on military might and shifting social coalitions are obvious targets of imperialist design – either as turf to be protected or as low-risk stakes to be picked up as so many prizes in the tournaments of the strong. In periods of increased rivalry between major powers the weak are especially liable to become counters in the greater struggle of which they become unwillingly a part. That the United States has consistently seen the civil conflicts in the Third World geopolitically, that is as aspects of its struggle with the Soviet Union (partial exception made for the Carter administration), is the key to understanding its policy. The root causes are political, not economic.[8] That the policy has been pursued so vigorously in areas so exposed to foreign penetration has made the policy imperialistic. American imperialism is anti-communism.

Notes: Chapter 4

1. The most important writers in the United States advancing this point of view are probably William Appleman Williams and Gabriel Kolko.
2. C. Hull, *The Memoirs of Cordell Hull*, Vol. 2 (London, 1948), p. 1599.
3. ibid., pp. 1600–1.
4. The literature of this 'dependency school' is voluminous. A very readable presentation of this viewpoint (by a man who was not, however, central to its genesis) is W. J. Murdoch, *The Poverty of Nations* (Baltimore, Md, 1980), chs 8 and 9. For a criticism of this perspective see T. Smith, *The Pattern of Imperialism: The United States, Great Britain, and the Late-Industrializing World since 1815* (Cambridge, 1981), ch. 3, and idem, 'The logic of dependency theory writing revisited', *International Organization*, vol. 35 (1981), pp. 755–61.
5. An author who presents this viewpoint well, though none of the ideas are original, is A. Szymanski, *The Logic of Imperialism* (New York, 1981).
6. H. Kissinger, *Years of Upheaval* (Boston, Mass., 1982), p. 888.
7. D. Ellsberg, *Papers on the War* (New York, 1972); L. H. Gelb and R. K. Betts, *The Irony of Vietnam: The System Worked* (Washington DC, 1979).
8. Additional evidence for this point of view may be found in Smith, *Pattern of Imperialism*, chs 4 and 5.

5 Modern Imperialism? The Tsarist and the Soviet Examples

DIETRICH GEYER

Historians might be self-assured, even influential people, but they are not yet powerful enough simply to do away with historical terms of which they are weary. Imperialism is one such term. Although it is threadbare and has deteriorated into an empty catchphrase, it is unlikely that even a solemn resolution of the entire history fraternity would be sufficient to invalidate it. Above all, it is still an indispensable part of the public language of politics, mostly used as a polemical metaphor, but also as a label for many different things: for expansion of a military, economic and political nature, for unequal associations, unequal treaties, unequal terms of trade, for hangovers from former colonial relationships, including cultural colonialism, for forms of exploitation, oppression and penetration, for the international policies of the great powers, and of some of the lesser powers, too. The very popularity of the term 'imperialism' guarantees its continued survival, but also indicates that it gives expression to some aspects of an existing reality for which everyday political discourse obviously cannot find a more appropriate word. If we decided to liquidate the term, it would return to us from outside.

It will come as no surprise to discover that there is little agreement among historians as to precisely how imperialism is to be defined. The vast range of explanatory hypotheses which have been put forward will not be discussed here. There is a great temptation to avoid the problem altogether by declaring all the traditional and newly invented theories of imperialism obsolete, and keeping to the general, colloquial usage of the word. One could argue in general terms that, after all, imperialism has always been with us: from classical antiquity to the present day empires have existed and expanded, politically and militarily, or economically; there have always been forms of direct and indirect, formal and informal rule over foreign populations and territories by superior, stronger, more 'advanced' powers; there are, and always have been, oppression and exploitation of 'peripheries' by 'centres' or by 'metropolises'.

However, those who demand of historical terms more than that they serve to describe different or even timeless circumstances will not be satisfied with such a wide field of reference. Such loosely defined terms have almost no explanatory value; in any case, it is no greater than that of the label itself. It is therefore to be welcomed that historians have recently arrived at more precise definitions. They have not resolved differences and controversies, but have laid sufficient foundations for a minimal consensus to emerge. This was made possible by the remarkable concentration of interest on imperialism before 1914, the last decades before the First World War, a period which has long been described in our school books and reference works as the 'Age of Imperialism'.

When attempts were made to define conceptually what in recent literature is called modern imperialism, or sometimes classical imperialism (in view of the restricted period to which it refers), existing theories, both old and new, were resorted to. The majority of authors use a combination of the classical theories of imperialism, mostly economic and of Marxist and social-liberal provenance, and explanatory models from the arsenal of the contemporary social sciences. General and specific theories of modernization and development head the list.[1]

From this perspective, modern imperialism means direct or indirect rule by developed industrial nations over less developed territories and populations. Modern imperialism, imperialism before 1914, appears as a product of capitalist modernization, of industrialization in particular; as a product of economic cycles and the tensions caused by economic growth; as a result of rapid social change with all its consequences for the stability or instability of political regimes. Social and ideological mobilization, especially of a nationalistic variety, should also be mentioned in this context. Some historians even see modern imperialism functioning as a particular form of anti-cyclical management of economic crises, as a strategy for diverting attention from social conflicts to allow their suppression, as a defensive reaction on the part of the traditional élites when they found their privileges threatened by the pressure and speed of the changes taking place.

It can be seen that these definitions cover a wide field. But there is enough overlapping for a considerable area of agreement to emerge. Thus recent research, including that undertaken in the Federal Republic of Germany, has been concentrated mainly on the endogenous aspects of imperialism. Interest is (or has been) focused, above all, on domestic factors, on the preconditions and results of imperialism in the metropolises, and less on its consequences for the conditions under which development takes place in the colonies or the penetrated peripheries.

I shall take up the discussion at this point. The central issues include to what extent the term modern imperialism, coined specifically for the prewar period, can be applied to history since the First World War, and to what extent it can be transformed into a term which has reference to contemporary history. In discussing this problem of continuity and discontinuity, I shall focus on the Tsarist Empire and the Soviet Union. This undertaking, however, presents several difficulties.

First, it is questionable whether Russian imperialism of the tsarist period can be called 'modern' at all, that is, can be associated with a concept derived from highly developed capitalist modernization, from 'advanced capitalism', 'organized capitalism', 'state monopoly capitalism' – or whatever we like to call this stage. There is no escaping from the fact that modern imperialism is a term which relates to historical stages or periods.

According to both Marxist and non-Marxist theories of development, the Russian Empire before 1914–17 was underdeveloped in comparison with Europe. It belonged to the periphery of the industrial world; its main feature was not modernity, but backwardness. We have only to think of the economic underdevelopment of this predominantly agrarian country, its chronic lack of capital and financial dependence on Western markets and powers, and the few opportunities available to the Russians for developing foreign-trade strategies and for practising *pénétration pacifique* by dominating markets or exporting capital. In addition, we must remember the comparatively low degree of modern class formation in Russia, the autocracy's as yet undiminished monopoly of power, the ideological and cultural penetration of Russian society from the West, and the role of Russia as an object or target of modern imperialism – conditions which at times made it possible to speak of the Tsarist Empire's 'semi-colonial' status. These observations suffice to show that in the case of pre-revolutionary Russia, the term 'imperialism' needs to be defined more precisely.[2] I think that historians of the future will try to loosen, if not to dissolve altogether, the rigid link between this term and Western criteria of modernization and traditional thinking in 'stages'.

Second, the concept of modern imperialism fits the Soviet Union even less easily than tsarist Russia, even if the reasons are different. The fit is inexact, not because the heirs of the Revolution would like the Soviet Union's activities as a world power to be seen as the antithesis rather than as a special form of imperialism, but because as long as fully developed capitalism, with all that it implies, remains one of the basic assumptions underlying the concept of modern imperialism, it cannot be applied to the Soviet Union. Whatever Soviet power structures, Soviet economy and Soviet society may be called, they are not 'capitalist'. Although Chinese, Albanians and others have argued that a 'restoration of capitalism' has taken place in the Soviet Union, these theories have rapidly been abandoned and, in any case, have not found general acceptance. Consequently, to speak of 'Soviet imperialism' means modifying what is normally understood by modern imperialism, if not abandoning the term altogether. The feasibility of a concept of 'non-capitalist' or 'post-capitalist' imperialism which can be used for comparative studies has still to be investigated. In any case, a revision of terms which produces nothing more than a reversion to an unexplained, timeless, or simply polemical usage of the word does not take us any further.

A third difficulty is connected with the fact that the problem of continuity cannot be ignored. The continuity of Russian imperialism over the caesura of the Revolution is one of those perennial questions which, together with the controversies accompanying it, have a long history of their own – in this case, a mostly unpleasant and unproductive one extending to the dispute-ridden milieu of the most recent Soviet emigration. The passions aroused by this polemical issue are no less strong than those produced by discussions of continuity in other countries. The debates still raging about the continuity of German history from Luther or Bismarck down to Hitler could be cited. Another example is the indignation unleashed by the American New

Left with their allegation that global expansion is the fundamental principle of American capitalism, or with their argument that capitalist America's military intervention in Vietnam has deep historical roots reaching as far back as the bloody destruction of the Indian tribes, or at least to the opendoor policy of Secretary of State John Hay. Similarly, again and again, Russian tsars, Ivan the Terrible or Nicholas I, were, and still are, held responsible for Joseph Stalin and Russian expansionism, and this mostly by people who vigorously oppose continuity stereotypes as soon as they are applied to their own country, to the United States, for example. The astonishing popularity of referring to the tsarist period and of drawing analogies and parallels, even among professional historians, is a cause for scepticism and critical restraint. It would be easy to demonstrate how such references to the tsarist period turn into imprecise clichés, often in their learned authors' own unwitting hands, and then have to take the place of an analysis which is not forthcoming.[3] Stereotypes suggest historical erudition where there is nothing more than a superficial profundity. Only seldom is an answer provided to questions about the substance of continuity, and about how its relationship to historical change, to continuing history, can be ascertained.

Space does not permit all three issues raised here to be discussed successively: the particular nature of tsarist imperialism, the preconditions of Soviet imperialism and, finally, the problem of continuity between both. I shall therefore attempt to establish links between them by using the third issue as a starting-point for the following reflections.

The most trenchant argument *against* the continuity of Russian imperialism is provided by the Russian Revolution. No serious discussion will be able to play down or disregard the significance of this upheaval for the history of Russia, and therefore also for the problem of imperialism. The October Revolution was so firmly anti-imperialist both as a *coup d'état* and as a mass movement that it would be absurd to see Lenin's declaration of war on imperialism as nothing more than the revolutionary rhetoric of a clique of leaders who were as cynical as they were power-mad. The Bolsheviks' message was that the Revolution, the Russian as well as the international one, could only be victorious in a civil war *against* imperialism. The theory of imperialism and the theory of revolution were one.

Revolutionary theory naturally involved a radical break with the previous history of the Russian Empire; the end of all except revolutionary continuity was an axiom of the Bolshevik Revolution. The Bolsheviks saw the history of Russia in the same way that, according to de Tocqueville, the generation of 1789 saw the history of France: split, as it were, into two halves. The Bolsheviks were deeply stirred by the thought that there had been a complete break between the old Russia, the Russia of landowners and capitalists, and what was to become the new socialist Russia. Solemn declarations by the Soviet government seemed to justify this claim. It promised to cancel all 'unequal treaties' which tsarism had forced other nations to accept, to recognize rights of national self-determination in their most radical form, to allow the empire to fall apart into its national constituent parts, and systematically to destroy what, in the eyes of the world, had been Russian imperialism.

It is well known that this leave-taking from the past was based on self-deception, and that the revolutionaries failed in many respects. There were several reasons for this. Undoubtedly one of the most important was that the Bolsheviks remained alone: the international revolution which was to absorb the Russian Revolution did not take place. Instead, the new rulers found themselves thrown on to their own resources, isolated in a hostile world, facing the problems of backwardness, poverty and lack of culture in an exhausted and disorganized country. Under these circumstances, it was of the greatest importance that right from the beginning and without much hesitation, the new rulers declared the primary importance of retaining their position of power.

Priority was given to tasks and problems which faced the Bolshevik dictatorship in the peasant regions of Russia, and also to the recovery of those parts of the old empire's territory which had been lost during the civil war. All efforts were concentrated on a strategy of socio-economic development committed to overcoming Russia's backwardness, to industrializing, to 'catching up with and outstripping capitalism'. What was really achieved in this respect under the slogans 'state capitalism', 'war communism' and 'new economic policy' can be read in the books of economic and social historians.[4] Foreign policy was soon allotted the task of shielding the process of economic modernization and recovery in a period of 'temporary coexistence'. As Stalin's 'construction of socialism in one country' proceeded with the help of the first Five-Year Plans, the need for international security and a preservation of peace increased. The Soviet Union was declared the 'fatherland of the international proletariat', the darling and centre of the world revolution; henceforth, increasing the power and strength of the Soviet Union was to be understood as the most important condition of future victories 'on a global scale'. This applied particularly to the parties of the Communist International. The Comintern's most noble task was to serve the Soviet fatherland, and to protect this fatherland against all its enemies.

If we look ahead as far as the Second World War, three factors emerge which make it possible to speak of a continuity between pre-revolutionary and post-revolutionary times, and which also relate to the problem of imperialism. The first is based on the physical continuity of the empire itself, which covers almost identical territory. The second is closely related to this and is based on the comparatively rapid recovery of Russia's traditional great power status within the international system. The third factor points – in spite of the change of élites and all the social upheavals that have taken place – to the continuity of nationalist and imperialist attitudes and behaviour, to the regeneration of power politics which may have a Soviet flavour, but are undoubtedly of Russian origin.[5] I should now like to make some remarks about all three aspects of the problem.

On the Constancy of the Empire's Geographical Extent

It is well known that the phase during which the old empire was disintegrating and Bolshevik Russia was temporarily reduced to the central territories of the Grand Duchy of Moscow lasted only a few years. When the Union of Soviet Socialist Republics was created in 1922, it lacked, in comparison with the pre-revolutionary empire, those western border states which had become independent: Finland, the Baltic republics and Poland. But such important colonial peripheries of the Tsarist Empire as the Caucasus, Central Asia, Siberia and the Far East were firmly integrated into the Union. This meant, of course, that the multinational structure of the empire was retained, and that unlike other multinational empires under the old order, such as Austria-Hungary and the Ottoman Empire, Russia under the Bolsheviks did not fall apart into its national constituent parts. There is no doubt that this was due in large measure to the social-revolutionary nature of the civil war. It was not the bayonets of the Red Army alone that checked the process of disintegration within a few years. The relatively underdeveloped state of nationalism among the 'alien peoples' and its lack of a firm social basis also helped to conserve the old empire.

By the end of the Second World War, Stalin had regained for the 'Soviet fatherland' most of the territories which had not initially been recovered, including Lithuania, Latvia and Estonia which, like Bessarabia (temporarily part of Romania), were annexed under the Hitler–Stalin Pact. The eastern Polish provinces were annexed under the slogan of the 'reunification' of the Ukrainian and White Russian peoples: language strikingly reminiscent of National Socialist vocabulary. In 1945 only an independent, though territorially reduced Finland remained outside Soviet borders towards the west and, in addition, the territory of the Kingdom of Poland (obliterated from 1863 onwards) which now formed the core of postwar Poland, transferred westwards to the Oder–Neisse line. Moreover, in northern East Prussia, the area around Lemberg, the Carpatho-Ukraine and Bukovina, the Soviet Union gained strategically important territories which had never belonged to the Tsarist Empire. In the Far East, too, the borders of the old empire were maintained. After the victory over Japan whose troops had been in Vladivostok until 1922, South Sakhalin and the Kuril Islands were returned in the autumn of 1945, together with several islands which had never been Russian, even in the nineteenth century. The 'black mark' of Russia's defeat in the war of 1905 was, as Stalin said, finally wiped out.

If one wanted to make suggestive comparisons, it would be only a slight exaggeration to say that the Soviet Union achieved within twenty-five years a repetition of the expansion for which the tsarist state required several centuries, a period extending from the Livonian Wars of Ivan the Terrible to the annexations in Central Asia and the Far East under Emperor Alexander II, and including the conquests of remarkable rulers such as Peter the Great and Catherine II. This picture fits in with the patriotic Soviet view, according to which the Soviet present represents the provisional culmination of Russian imperial history. It sees every tsarist annexation as a progressive act because it elevated the annexed peoples to the historical level of their more advanced Russian brothers and eventually allowed them to share the blessings of the Revolution.

Statistics show that the borders of the Soviet Union enclose, as did those of the Tsarist Empire before it, the *Lebensraum* of many large, small and tiny nations, nationalities and peoples. In 1926, during a period of vigorously promoted national development (*korenizacija*), 194 ethnic units were officially recognized; in 1979 the official figure was still 91. Although the federal constitution, unlike the tsars, guarantees them equal rights and cultural autonomy, in practice, the Russian element enjoys a clearly dominant position, as it has always done. This is true in a quantitative sense, as roughly half of the total population are Russians, or appear in the statistics as Soviet citizens of Russian nationality. But it is also true in many other respects: politically, economically and socially. Under Stalin, the regime even officially claimed the role of leader for 'the great Russian people'. Today, the term 'Soviet people' (*sovetskij narod*) is meant to express the inviolable unity of the Soviet family of nations in the stage of 'developed socialism' or 'transition to communism'. In fact, of course, this newly created people is little more than an ideological construct, a metaphor for what should be, rather than a description of what is.[6]

The path of Soviet advancement still leads from the provinces and national peripheries into a Russian milieu. The nature of 'political culture' is stamped by the Russians. Russian is the *lingua franca* of the Soviet Union. Industrialization (however uneven it may be) and continuing modernization have strengthened the trend towards Russification, without the other national cultures having begun to disintegrate. Where an international level is aspired to, in the fields of scientific and technological achievement, the Russian element dominates, as it does in the military. The nurturing of tradition, as far as it relates to the state as a whole, is also predominantly Russian. Every presentation of the History of the USSR, in its formal construction, in the organization of its contents and the way in which space is allocated, illustrates how accidental and peripheral in comparison with the mainstream of imperial history the 'history of the (non-Russian) peoples of Russia' is considered to be.[7]

Does all this indicate the return of old conditions, or their continued existence, in fact, the continuity of tsarist imperialism? It seems to me that such a limited perspective remains superficial and is unable to expose the realities of Soviet existence. In spite of the indisputable dominance of the Russian element, the most decisive changes have also taken place in the national republics of the Soviet Union. Even the most impressive illustrations of continuity cannot detract from their significance. Partial modernization of the economy and of society has also transformed what was passed on, and has not allowed it to survive unchanged within the old framework. For this reason alone it would be inappropriate and totally unproductive to describe the Soviet Union as a multinational federation of states, using concepts and categories derived from the tsarist internal colonial system. Even before 1914, the 'prison of the nationalities' was little more than a polemical phrase which could express something only vaguely approximating to the real conditions of those nationalities prevented from undergoing a national development. Stereotyped ideas about the past provide a bad basis for an analysis of what has become of it.

On the Continuity of the Great Power Position

Undoubtedly, the retention of the old imperial framework was an important precondition of Bolshevik Russia's recovery within a comparatively short time of the great power status traditionally enjoyed by the Tsarist Empire. Other factors also played a part in releasing the Soviet state from its position of marginal isolation and 'capitalist encirclement', and allowing it to emerge, within a short time, as an independent power in the international forum, adhering to the standards of international law and, in spite of its revolutionary rhetoric, less and less intent on overthrowing the international order. Of these factors the following should be mentioned: (1) the relative stability of the Bolshevik system of power which faced no serious competition within Russia from any other political force; (2) the measurable successes achieved under the Stalinist policy of 'revolution from above', which involved forced industrialization, total mobilization of the workforce even in the villages, and a build-up of the military power of the Soviet Union; (3) continuing changes in the international system, crises in the peace system imposed at Versailles and in the world economy – with the result that the Soviet Union soon became a coveted partner of the other great powers.

By the 1930s at the latest, the Soviet Union was generally recognized as a potential ally. This applied to those countries supporting the status quo and the League of Nations which, like Britain and France, vacillated between ideas of appeasement, collective security and containment when confronted with Hitler's Germany. And it also applied, even earlier, to those countries working for change in international relations, such as the Weimar Republic, which could build on a special German-Soviet relationship created in Rapallo in 1922. Later, Hitler's military planning in the period leading up to the Second World War, and in its first phase, also took the Soviet Union into account. The competition among the powers for an alliance with Moscow into which both German and Anglo-French politics were drawn in the summer of 1939 illustrates the Soviet Union's international importance as a great power. It is superfluous to mention the extent to which this importance increased after 1941 within the framework of the anti-Hitler coalition.

Examining the continuity of the empire's coherence and its great power position frequently draws attention to 'objective' constants, interests which bridge the revolutionary period and continue to operate: power-political objectives and ambitions, and a continuing need for security and partners. It is easy to provide evidence for this. Policies towards Poland and the Baltic, for example, offer impressive illustrations of such constants, as do maritime interests, especially in the matter of access to the Mediterranean, and policies towards the Near and Far East.[8] A few brief references may suffice to indicate the fascination of this sort of backward-looking perspective. The frequently mentioned 'Russian drive to the Straits', to Constantinople (the old Tsargrad), is one example. It was spiritually interwoven with the beliefs of Moscow Orthodoxy; transposed, in modern times, into innumerable wars and projects against Turkey; put into effect ideologically in

Pan-Slavic programmes; proclaimed as an official war aim in the First World War and approved by the Allies. Then, finally, and almost without a break there was Lenin's attachment to the new Turkey of Kemal Atatürk as an expression of continuing interest; carried on in the efforts undertaken by Soviet diplomats in Lausanne and Montreux to introduce a new statute governing the Straits; and coming to a head in the demand for bases made in Molotov's Berlin talks in 1940. Less than five years later, in a changed international climate, interest was renewed as massive pressure was brought to bear against Ankara, and since the 1960s it has been extended in the constant Mediterranean presence of the Soviet fleet, and in the Soviet strategy of concluding alliances in the Arab world.

Poland is another example which seems to support the view that Soviet policy has not moved away from the traditional patterns by which tsarist diplomacy operated. Ever since the partitions of Poland, Prussian-German and Russian interests have co-operated over this issue. Poland was the connection which guaranteed good relations between Petersburg/Moscow and Berlin: Catherine II and Frederick the Great, Alexander I and Frederick William III, Gorchakov and Bismarck, the Red Army and the Reichswehr, the era of Rapallo, Stalin and Hitler – names and dates which show that Poland continued to be a function of Russo-German relations beyond the upheavals of 1917. Even today, fears remain in Poland, feeding on the trauma of the German-Soviet partition treaty of 1939.

A similar pattern of power politics can be observed in Russo-French relations. Alliances between these two powers were generally a reaction to symptoms of crisis in relations between Russia and Germany: the alliance of 1891-3 a result of the non-renewal of the Re-Insurance Treaty; the Mutual Assistance Pact of 1935 a reply to the threat to the status quo emanating from Germany; Soviet courting of de Gaulle and the general's ceremonious handling of Moscow reflections of barely perceptible tensions in the relationship with Bonn. The history of the alliances between Russia and Prussia/Germany also seems to follow this rule: in 1813-14 the war of liberation against Napoleon; conservative solidarity between monarchs against the danger of revolution during the *Vormärz* period; the common front established in 1863 against Napoleon III's nationality principle spreading to Poland; later, in 1922, Rapallo and resistance to the Versailles system which was supported by France; then in 1939 the German-Soviet settlement as compensation for the policy of collective security destroyed at Munich.

The interrelationship between Russia's policies in Europe and in Asia also reveals a causal nexus extending beyond the October Revolution: the Tsarist Empire's defeat in the Crimean War released Russian expansionism in Central Asia; the defeat by Japan in 1905 was followed by a revival of Russian ambitions in the Balkans and relative restraint in the Far East; confrontation with the victors of Versailles was matched by the solidarity established with the 'nations of the East', and by co-operation with the Chinese Guomindang; after 1931-2 the threat to the Soviet Union's Far Eastern borders posed by Japan stimulated Soviet efforts to establish a European security system; during the German-Soviet war there was a standstill agreement with Japan based on the Non-Aggression Treaty of 1941; for the 1960s and 1970s, the connection between the Sino-Soviet conflict and attempts to ease tension in Europe can be considered established. Policy in Europe and policy in Asia have thus always been closely interconnected.

I shall stop here, but not without issuing a warning against the widely held view that an analysis of contemporary Soviet policy can be based on a series of historical constants, and illustrated more or less empirically by examples from history. The explanatory value of such vertical comparisons and circular arguments is highly overrated. Although these methods draw their evidence from history they, in fact, largely ignore the actual historical conditions surrounding each political constellation. This sort of analysis lacks a sense of change, the essentially historical element; only if this is taken into account, can references to tradition and continuity become more than an erudite intellectual game. Any attempt to explain foreign policy which does not give sufficient weight to changes in the international system, as well as to internal determinants, is not worthy of consideration. If we examine, for example, one single factor, the international role of the United States and its significance for the Soviet Union's foreign policy since 1945, it is clear that continuity stereotypes drawing on the tsarist period are extremely dubious as aids to interpretation.

On the Continuity of Nationalist and Imperialist Attitudes and Behaviour

Because of the nature of the sources, only the behaviour and conditions of the ruling élites can be discussed under this heading. The process itself, the regeneration of a powerful, predominantly Russian nationalism which is called 'Soviet patriotism', is not in question and requires no detailed exemplification here. It is more difficult, but none the less imperative, to explain plausibly the revolutionary élites' return to pre-revolutionary imperial traditions and value patterns, and the nationalistic historicism of Soviet political culture with its well-known manifestations: glorification of Russian imperial history and its prominent rulers; military tradition, including the Alexander Nevskij Medal, the Kutuzov Medal, the Suvorov Cadets and officers' epaulettes; stories of battles and heroes; the blurring of Marxist class categories by emotional references to home, earth, people and fatherland. The reversion of an international revolutionary consciousness, within a generation, to an imperial, nationalistic power-consciousness is naturally connected with the factors described above: the continuity of the empire and its role as a great power in the international system.

But the social upheavals since 1929 resulting from the Five-Year Plans and collectivization are equally significant for this process. The rural population, which had lived largely on the periphery of the Soviet system, was drawn into the centrally controlled organization of labour by the destruction of the traditional agrarian order. The Soviet leadership was faced with the task of the ideological re-education and integration of these people, who had been forcibly mobilized and deprived of their traditional way of life. It soon became apparent that Bolshevism's concepts of proletarian revolution were hardly suitable for the ideological training of the majority of the population. Neither did Stalin's codification of Marxism–Leninism have great emotive power. Thus taking recourse to elements of pre-revolutionary imperial patriotism and nationalism made good political sense. They also accommodated the petty-bourgeois value patterns which, in the new Soviet industrial society, increasingly overlaid both the old peasant and the proletarian norms.[9]

The Second World War, the Great Patriotic War, contributed greatly to the social consolidation of Soviet patriotism. After the war, this strange amalgam of Great Russian nationalism and a Stalinist version of Marxism–Leninism made an impact outside the borders of the Soviet Union. As an imperialist ideology of domination, it had a strangely ambiguous message for the rest of the world, but especially for those nations within the Soviet Union's sphere of influence. On the one hand, it promised that the socialist Soviet Union was showing the rest of mankind what their own future would be like because, thanks to its social order, the Soviet Union was an entire historical epoch ahead of everyone else. On the other hand, it insisted that the achievement of being at the forefront of humanity's progress was not due to chance, but was the logical result of the whole history of the 'heroic Russian nation'.

Under Stalin, the Soviet Union claimed the role of a leader and teacher of nations. This claim manifestly accompanied the Soviet policy of hegemony in the socialist camp. After Stalin's death, it was only slightly refined and modified by the slogan of 'socialist internationalism'. Nevertheless, the idea of the Soviet Union's priority as guaranteed by world history and the laws of history has still not been abandoned in principle. But the falseness of these ideological claims is obvious to all: the gap between theory and reality cannot be bridged.

Soviet development aims have always been set by 'capitalist' standards. With the exception of armaments and the military sector, the Soviet Union is being left further and further behind the highly developed parts of the Western world. The world economy continues to be dominated by capitalism, and the Soviet economic system is not capable of playing a global role. The Soviet Union, together with the countries in its sphere of hegemony (which can only be preserved by military means), are increasingly resembling a system penetrated from the West: economic development is dependent on the transfer of technology and on loans; the system is incapable of feeding its own population; fashions, youth culture and leisure activities are all imitations of the West. At the same time, the Soviet Union is as unwilling as it is unable to allow its own citizens freedom of movement and free access to information.

Under these circumstances, the Soviet Union can exercise its position as a world power in confrontation with the United States essentially only in the military sector. So-called 'competition between systems' boils down to mutual military deterrence. But here, too, the Soviet world power behaves rather defensively in view of the growing costs occasioned by the continuing arms race, the preservation of the Soviet sphere of hegemony and the rising expectations of its own population. At the same time, however, the desire for militarily secured equality with the United States as a world power seems to be one of the few driving forces still capable of arousing some dynamism in a rigid regime which has got stuck in its own contradictions and has become incapable of reforming itself.[10]

Can we therefore speak of continuity with regard to tsarist imperialism? A final comparison with conditions before 1917 once again points to the enormous differences which exist, and to the limited usefulness of the question of continuity. Compared with the differences, the common factors are rather insignificant and, in any case, do not determine our understanding of pre-revolutionary or post-revolutionary conditions. Changes in the domestic context of foreign policy have been immense, as have the violent upheavals affecting the structure of international relations since the First World War. Not least, revolutionary developments in arms technology have rendered older strategies obsolete. Sand table reconstructions of past battles as they are fought out in Soviet headquarters and military academies can serve today, at most, to awaken patriotic memories, glorify military virtues and warm old soldiers' hearts.

The conditions of the political decision-making process have also changed so radically that even establishing functional equivalents is not fruitful for the analysis of contemporary history. Under the last tsars, there was a critical public opinion of great influence, which undertook to articulate the interests of the nation and the empire, even in opposition to the government, and to prescribe to this government standards of political behaviour.[11] Compared with Soviet conditions, tsarist Russia was an open society. Unlike the Soviet Party leadership, the old regime made extremely inadequate use of national ideologies. Nationalism and Pan-Slavism were not the products of autocracy or any particular government, but of autonomous social movements. The tsarist regime was frequently put on the defensive by the political mobilization of public opinion. Under Soviet domination, there were no longer comparable forces of social opposition after the civil war. There is also no parallel in Soviet times to the constitutional order of the Tsarist Empire after 1906. To compare the functions of the Russian Duma's committees – for example, in the handling of government bills on naval armament – with those of the Supreme Soviets of the USSR would be absurd. It would be equally misleading to see the interest groups which American researchers, in particular, regard as influencing decision-making processes in the Soviet Union today as successors to tsarist pressure groups.[12]

What remains comparable in substance is the continental character of Russian imperialism in its tsarist and Soviet varieties. Until the Second World War, power was increased by expanding national territory, and this expansion was always strategic and justified by the needs of the empire's security. Even the territorial gains made as a result of the Hitler–Stalin Pact were incorporated into the multinational Soviet Union by annexation, rather than being subjected to Soviet interests by forms of indirect rule.

Tsarism had used these forms before 1914 in northern Persia, in Mongolia and in the three northern provinces of Manchuria, and also in central Asia in the emirates of Khiva and Bukhara. After the Revolution, this method of securing spheres of influence could initially be revived only in Outer Mongolia – in 1921, by the establishment of a Mongolian People's Republic as a protectorate of the Soviet Union. It is common knowledge that the creation of an informal empire on a large scale took place only as a result of the Second World War. It was initially concentrated in the Soviet Union's zone of hegemony in Eastern Europe, and later spread to Asia, with varying – and in China, retrograde – results.[13] In Eastern Europe, it took place, militarily secured, on the basis of ideologically 'aligned' political systems, and within the bipolar framework of the Cold War period. If any conclusion can be drawn, it is that the Soviet sphere of hegemony cannot in any sensible way be compared with the Tsarist Empire's protectorates and spheres of interest.

Aspects of historical continuity of some importance, however, are revealed in the precedence of military and power-political over economic interests. In the declining Tsarist Empire, economic factors played only a secondary role as a driving force for imperial expansion. Finance Minister Witte's attempt to link forced construction of industries with economic expansion in the Far East, so that each could be used to stimulate the other, was rapidly overtaken by military ambitions. The idea of the 'peaceful penetration' of China ended in the débâcle of the Russo-Japanese War. In Persia, power-political interests of protecting and securing spheres of influence were dominant. Subsidized trade did not have a stimulating effect – it was only a prop. In the Ottoman Empire, which with the Straits and its European possessions had always been a traditional object of Russian expansionist interests, the Tsarist Empire had no sphere of influence, nor did it dominate the market. Russia's relative backwardness never allowed tsarist imperialism to become economically competitive.

The same applies to the Soviet Union. Because catching up with and overtaking advanced capitalist powers has remained the firm aim of the Soviet Union's élites, economic backwardness has continued to be the fundamental condition of Soviet politics. Forms of economic dependence on the Soviet Union have developed and been put to use in relations with other nations only since the Second World War, and they have essentially been limited to its Eastern European and East German sphere of hegemony. Even here, within its own sphere of influence, the superiority of the West has remained much in evidence. Especially in global competition with the United States, the Soviet Union has no adequate economic means to deploy. Its development aid to the Third World is only really impressive when it comes to the export of weapons. Cuba and individual 'socialist orientated' countries in Africa and Asia are expensive, subsidized undertakings by the Soviet Union. It is not economic, but military and maritime power which qualifies the Soviet leadership to take part in world politics.

Notes: Chapter 5

This chapter was translated by Angela Davies.
1. W. J. Mommsen, *Theories of Imperialism* (London, 1981).
2. cf. D. Geyer, *Der russische Imperialismus. Studien über den Zusammenhang von innerer und auswärtiger Politik, 1860–1914* (Göttingen, 1977).
3. Apart from the works of R. Pipes, see as the most blatant examples of recent years: A. Yanov, *The Origins of Autocracy. Ivan the Terrible in Russian History* (Berkeley, Calif., 1981); L. Ruehl, *Russlands Aufstieg zur Weltmacht* (Düsseldorf, 1981).
4. Brief introductions are A. Nove, *An Economic History of the U.S.S.R.*, rev. edn (Harmondsworth, Middx., 1982) and R. Lorenz, *Sozialgeschichte der Sowjetunion*, Vol. 1: *1917–1945* (Frankfurt-on-Main, 1976).
5. The problem of continuity in Russian/Soviet foreign policy has rarely been examined seriously. cf. recently A. Dallin, 'The domestic sources of Soviet foreign policy', in S. Bialer (ed.), *The Domestic Context of Soviet Foreign Policy* (Boulder, Col., 1981), pp. 335–408.
6. H. Carrère d'Encausse, *L'Empire éclate. La révolte des nations en U.R.S.S.* (Paris, 1978).
7. In this respect the latest edition of *Istorija SSSR* (Vols 1–11, Moscow, 1966–80), published by the Academy of Sciences, is most instructive. The topic is discussed in A. Martiny, 'Das Verhältnis von Politik und Geschichtsschreibung in der Historiographie der sowjetischen Nationalitäten seit den 60er Jahren', *Jahrbücher für Geschichte Osteuropas*, vol. 27 (1979), pp. 238–73.
8. On the following see the contributions in I. J. Lederer (ed.), *Russian Foreign Policy. Essays in Historical Perspective* (New Haven, Conn. and London, 1962).
9. cf. R. C. Tucker (ed.), *Stalinism. Essays In Historical Interpretation* (New York, 1977); G. Erler and W. Süss (eds), *Stalinismus. Probleme der Sowjetgesellschaft zwischen Kolletktivierung und Weltkrieg* (Frankfurt-on-Main, 1982).
10. The latest survey of the problem, including Russian interpretations, is K. von Beyme, *Die Aussenpolitik der Sowjetunion* (Munich, 1983).
11. C. Ferenczi, *Aussenpolitik und Öffentlichkeit in Russland 1906–1912* (Husum, 1982); M. Hagen, *Die Entfaltung politischer Öffentlichkeit in Russland 1904–1914* (Wiesbaden, 1982).
12. H.-H. Nolte, *Gruppeninteressen und Aussenpolitik. Die Sowjetunion in der Geschichte internationaler Beziehungen* (Göttingen, 1979).
13. As a comparative analysis of this process the classical work by Z. Brzezinski, *The Soviet Bloc. Unity and Conflict* (Cambridge, Mass., 1960), is still indispensable.

6 The Politics of Expansion of the Japanese Empire: Imperialism or Pan-Asiatic Mission?

BERND MARTIN

Japan's politics of expansion from the emergence of modern Japan during the Meiji Restoration to the present time have produced highly conflicting interpretations. One of the major works on international relations in the Far East after 1918 – Akira Iriye's *After Imperialism: The Search for a New Order in the Far East*[1] – suggests that the era of imperialism came to an end with the First World War. This point of view has many advocates among revisionist historians of modern Asia, especially in the United States. They interpret the period leading up to the Pacific War mainly in terms of a political antagonism between the United States and Imperial Japan. This view lacks an awareness of the increasing radicalization in both socialist and fascist directions that characterized Japan's domestic politics during the interwar years. What also tends to be neglected is the fact that the European powers, including Germany, maintained their strong positions in the Far East throughout the 1920s and 1930s. Although as early as 1901 the Japanese socialist, Kōtoku Shūsui, published a fundamental treatise on imperialism anticipating J. A. Hobson's theory which appeared the following year,[2] the specific origins and effects of Japanese imperialism have received scant attention in the West. Europe continued to be seen as the sole source of territorial expansionism, and neither the realities of modern East Asian history, nor the debates among champions and opponents of imperialism in Japan were fully taken into account. Japan was regarded as an altogether peculiar country to which the concepts of Western social science, including that of imperialism, could by no means be applied. At best, Japanese expansionism was explained as the retarded stirrings of a 'late-comer' on the international scene, in other words, as a kind of derivative imperialism in a nation prone to imitating foreign models in all conceivable respects. This view is still almost as widespread today as it was several decades ago.

This chapter will attempt to survey 'imperialist' tendencies in Japanese society and foreign policy over a period of more than a hundred years, paying special attention to connections between the various sources and external manifestations of Japanese 'imperialism'. After a few remarks concerning the particular preconditions of Japanese imperialist policies, a four-stage model of their evolution will be suggested. Finally, each of the four stages will be discussed in terms of current Western theories of imperialism.

National Determinants of Japanese Imperialism

The expansionist policies of Imperial Japan, which culminated in the occupation of South-East Asia and collapsed with the empire's unconditional surrender in September 1945, were primarily determined by endogenous factors, the impact of the international system taking second place. Japan's social order[3] was rigid even by Asian standards, its small and atavistic élite totally committed to defending the system and obstinately opposed to reform of any kind. Unless Japan could somehow integrate itself into the capitalist world order, the situation could only lead to a war with the West. After more than two hundred years of hermetic seclusion from the outside world, the static order of the Tokugawa shogunate – a kind of centralistic military dictatorship – was challenged by the superior American navy in 1853 and confronted with the consequences of an unequal commercial treaty forced upon the *shōgun*'s government. The European powers quickly followed suit with similar treaties. As a result, the Japanese market was exposed virtually unprotected to industrial imports from the West. Japan, like China at the same time, seemed to be wide open for the more advanced 'white' nations to make political inroads.[4] But, in contrast to the lofty caste of Chinese literati who despised Western progress and Western material achievements, the traditional Japanese warrior-élite, the *samurai*, rose to the challenge. Determined to defend Japan's national identity and their own long-established right to privilege and leadership, this group engineered an internal shift of power in 1868: the *shōgun* system was eliminated, and the godlike emperor was reinstated as the central political authority endowed with absolute power. The so-called 'renewal of the Meiji period', sometimes even referred to as the 'Meiji Revolution', was, in reality, a restoration, stemming from a will to preserve the existing social order.[5]

The social system of vertically stratified small groups, the hierarchical principle of loyalty embedded in the system of childlike devotion of inferiors towards the paternal benevolence of their superiors (*oyabun-kobun*),[6] and hence the harmony of a village-centred social order were to be protected against the divisive and corrupting influence of the Western 'barbarians'. At the same time, traditional values and norms of behaviour were to be preserved in order to guarantee the position of power and the claim to leadership of a pre-modern élite. During and after 1868 a body of dictatorial leaders emerged, hiding behind the sacred shield of the allegedly omnipotent and god-like emperor. It recruited its members from the three focuses of power which were alternately to dominate the country up to 1945: the military, the court circles and the civil politicians (later to evolve into party politicians) who were closely tied up with the big merchants.

The oligarchy committed itself to a programme of modernization that was basically nationalistic and defensive. From the very beginning, its principal aim was the establishment of an efficient heavy industry along with the necessary infrastructure. Only thus, was it thought, could a military force be created that would rank equally with that of the West. Foreign experts were hired to help the government in building model factories and initiating pilot projects, which were later sold to the *zaibatsu* (literally, money cliques) already in existence, thus strengthening their hold on the market. From the start, there was a dual economy in Japan. Alongside a few large modern enterprises, there were a multitude of small family workshops which continued the pre-industrial tradition of highly developed craftsmanship. They soon found themselves in a position of semi-feudal dependence on the modern corporations which were able to dictate prices and terms of delivery to them. The family firm of medium size which played such a decisive role in the industrial development of the West was absent in Japan and, with it, the politically assertive bourgeois entrepreneur. Neither a bourgeois stratum nor a horizontally integrated working class developed in Japan during the period of industrialization.

Two main problems had to be overcome for the ambitious programmes of industrialization and militarization to succeed: a scarcity of natural resources and a lack of capital. Those raw materials required for establishing heavy industry (minerals, coal and, later, oil) were often available only in insufficient quantities or not at all, and were also of inferior quality. Since most of these raw materials and essential machinery had to be imported from Western countries, increasing exports had to take top priority in economic policy. After the First World War, textiles and other products of light industry made up the bulk of exports. During the preceding period, agriculture not only had to supply most of the goods which Japan sold abroad; it also bore the burden of financing almost the entire economic development. Peasants had to pay a fixed tax in cash which amounted to 18 per cent of the value of their crops.[7] The revenue derived from this tax, together with the proceeds from the export of silk, contributed decisively to financing early industrialization. There were only two foreign loans during the early Meiji period,[8] because the Japanese government wanted to minimize opportunities for Western interference in the domestic economy.

Although enforced modernization transformed the country into a great power within one generation, the social costs were considerable. Above all, agriculture was ruined, a sector which, as late as during the Pacific War, provided employment for more than half the population. Serfdom had been abolished in 1871. Even so, a small stratum of big landlords kept the peasants in a position of quasi-feudal tenancy. As a result, social disaffection and unrest were smouldering among the impoverished peasants. In the cities, the small artisans, totally dependent on the large enterprises, formed a potentially restless element. Industrialization dictated from above endangered the village community, which had always been seen as the hub of Japanese society; it threatened to reduce the mass of the people to a materially and politically deprived proletariat. It was therefore inevitable that, as industrialization proceeded, Japan sank deeper and deeper into a dichotomy between traditional concepts of legitimacy and traditional social norms, on the one hand, and the reality of a conflict-ridden society on the other. Most of the social and political conflicts in modern Japan can be traced back to this fundamental separation between traditional social and moral values and the harsh world of incipient and superficial industrialization. For the people and the leadership alike, the only way to bridge this gap was to escape into a mythical nationalism, which was rooted in the peasant masses, but could also be manipulated from above.

Classical (Competitive) Imperialism

The Japanese ruling élite never abandoned the battle-cry of the Restoration: 'rich country – strong army'. Politics of all kinds were governed by the supreme goal of attaining parity with the Western powers. The strengthening of the nation was to be achieved by a build-up of heavy industry which, in turn, would supply an army based on compulsory military service.

The beginning of Japan's policy of expansion and thus of Japanese imperialism date back to the pre-industrial period. In the early 1870s, the pros and cons of territorial expansion had been fiercely debated within the small circle of the Meiji 'founding fathers'. The compromise reached at that time led to the first, albeit cautious, steps being taken on the path of imperialism. While the majority of the government were on their first official mission abroad (Iwakura mission) to negotiate a revision of the unequal treaties, their colleagues in Tokyo were planning the invasion of Korea. The rationale for their plan was twofold. First, Japan was to share in the partition of China (which claimed suzerainty over Korea) on an equal footing with the Western powers. Secondly, the energies of the restless *samurai* class were to be deflected abroad in a war of conquest. In numerical terms, the strength of the *samurai* class was considerable. Together with their families, the *samurai* comprised about 4 to 5 per cent of the population: a total of approximately 2 million people. After the abolition of the feudal fiefs in 1871 this class lost its social functions, and ways had to be found to fit it into the new order.

Having hastily returned from Europe, the members of the Iwakura mission, impressed by what they had seen abroad, vehemently opposed all military adventures.[9] In their view, which eventually prevailed, Japan should concentrate its energies on domestic development before territorial annexations could be contemplated. The *samurai* class would be of greater use to the country if its virtues and abilities could be made to serve administrative and economic reform at home rather than being wasted in a bloody military gamble.

Japan's activities abroad were, therefore, limited to the annexation of the Ryūkyū Islands (Okinawa) in 1872, a punitive expedition against Formosa in 1874 and the forcing open of the Korean port of Pusan two years later. Although not very significant in themselves, these moves foreshadowed the double thrust that was to characterize Imperial Japan's expansion in the following decades: first, via the Korean peninsula to the Asian mainland and, secondly, over the chain of islands extending to Formosa towards South-East Asia. The two leading clans of the Meiji Restoration, Choshu and Satsuma, favoured the northern and the southern strategy respectively. Henceforth, the rivalry between these two clans shaped the conflict over the direction of imperial expansion. It later turned into an antagonism between army (Choshu) and navy (Satsuma) that continued right up to the Pacific War.

The constitution of 1889, which largely followed the Prussian model,[10] marked the outward culmination of the Meiji reform and seemed to set Japan on the track towards a Western-style constitutional state. However, the Imperial Rescript on Education[11] of the following year represented an ideological retreat from this position, demanding a return to Confucian values and emphasizing the idea of the Japanese as the chosen people, thus indicating that Japan was again turning its back on the West. All the prerequisites for a belligerent foreign policy were now present: military power, an indigenous ideology and the end of domestic reform. Japan was prepared to join the imperialist struggle for China and to strive for equality with the Western powers. The Japanese systematically enhanced their influence at the Korean court and, having secured British diplomatic backing,[12] went to war with China over Korea. When in 1895 Japan imposed harsh peace terms on the defeated Chinese Empire, it unwittingly furthered the interests of Western imperialism. The acquisition of Formosa and the Pescadores as well as the lease of the Liaodong Peninsula encouraged the European powers to fulfil their own ambitions. Even the Americans arrived on the scene as guarantors of free trade with China – a role which they had arrogated to themselves. The huge 'indemnity' of 230 million taels[13] – almost twice the amount of the Japanese state budget at that time – ruined China's public finances and increased its financial dependence on the Western powers. Nevertheless, Japan failed to gain the equality it desired in the international arena. The emptiness of Japan's claim to be a major power was exposed when the Triple Intervention of France, Russia and Germany forced it to give up the leased territory in Southern Manchuria.

It was the victory over tsarist Russia in 1905[14] that finally established Japan's hegemony in Southern Manchuria and paved the way for the annexation of Korea five years later. Imperial Japan now assumed a new role as leader of the Asian peoples' anticolonial struggle against their white masters. On the other hand, the Western powers could no longer deny Japan recognition as a great power in its own right. In 1911 tariff autonomy was finally attained and a protectionist foreign-trade policy implemented forthwith.[15] At the time of the Emperor Meiji's death in 1912, Japan seemed to be at the peak of its domestic strength and international standing.

Agrarian Socialism versus Capitalist Expansion: Ideological and Economic Motives behind Japan's 'Manifest Destiny'

It was not until the First World War that Japanese imperialism acquired unequivocally aggressive features. The military victory over the Germans at Qingdao, in conjunction with the unexpected wartime boom in domestic industry, induced the leaders in Tokyo to launch a diplomatic surprise attack on China. The Twenty-One Demands of January 1915 are remarkable in that for the first time in the history of Japanese expansion, economic concerns were paramount. Japan demanded control over China's raw materials, its infrastructure and its administrative apparatus.[16] As the Western powers were involved in the European war and therefore could not provide the support requested by China, the weak government of Yuan Shikai gave in to Tokyo's ultimatum and conceded most of Japan's demands. Even the United States, which was to acknowledge Japan's special position on the Asian mainland in the Lansing–Ishii Agreement of November 1917,[17] offered no help.

At home, an unprecedented economic upturn stimulated the concentration of industry and doubled the industrial labour force from 1 to 2 million.[18] At the same time, social unrest increased, especially in urban areas, where it erupted in the rice riots of the summer of 1918.[19] Influenced by the Russian Revolution, the Japanese proletariat gained political self-confidence and shifted to the left, demanding higher wages, social benefits and, last but not least, more political rights. One way out for the oligarchy would have been to channel social and political discontent into expansionist adventures. This failed, however, because the Western powers were determined to restrict Japan's position to that of an imperialist junior partner. At the Versailles Conference, the Japanese demand for racial equality was rejected by the colonial powers. At the Washington Conference of 1921–2,[20] Japan had to abandon its privileges in Shandong province (the former German sphere of interest) and, furthermore, to agree to a limitation of its naval armaments to maintain a ratio of 3:5:5 in relation to the United States and Britain. In addition, the alliance with Britain[21] was abandoned in favour of collective treaties reaffirming the status quo in the Pacific and the 'open door' in China. In both nationalist and socialist circles in Japan these agreements were denounced as the 'Japanese Versailles'. The exclusion of the Japanese from immigration into the United States which came into force at the same time added to this sense of national humiliation. The social-imperialist policy of distracting attention from internal tensions by imperialist adventures abroad was thus sabotaged by the Western powers.

The domestic crisis deepened after the collapse of the wartime boom in the spring of 1920, and the government found itself compelled to introduce reforms. Moreover, the shift to party Cabinets in 1918 and the introduction of universal male suffrage in 1925 resulted in a corrupt symbiosis of party politicians and business leaders rather than in a genuine democratization of the country.[22] The Peace Preservation Laws of the same year[23] put heavy penalties on all political activities that were deemed dangerous to the imperial system (*kokutai*); in effect, they amounted to a ban on socialist and even liberal political parties. 'Taishō democracy' meant little more than a shift of power from the Meiji founding fathers who had been close to the court, many of whom were now dead, to professional politicians and business circles.

An unstable economy with widely fluctuating prices and stagnant real incomes was the hallmark of the 1920s. The population continued to grow, and the increase had to be absorbed by the agrarian sector. Agriculture suffered heavily after the government, anxious to pacify the restless urban masses, opened the market to cheap imports of rice. The Ministry of Commerce and Industry which was founded in 1925,[24] was looking for foreign models: American rationalization of production and Germany's state-controlled economy of the First World War were those recommended by Kishi Nobusuke, a young ministry official who had undertaken a series of study trips abroad.[25] Even before the onset of the Great Depression, the state was called upon to manage the economy and to curb the allegedly selfish activities of big business. Demands of this kind were chiefly voiced by military and social-revolutionary groups. However, they went unheeded in Parliament, where 55 per cent of the members of the lower house (in 1930)[26] were known to be closely affiliated with powerful economic interests.

The military, which prided itself on being the creator and guardian of the nation's greatness, had been affected by budget cuts, and attacked the capitalist alliance of politicians and industrial magnates. Since the majority of the conscripts and about half of the officers came from the impoverished peasantry, they were easily won over by nationalist agitation clamouring for anti-capitalist revolution and imperialist expansion.[27] The 'General outline of measures for the reorganization of Japan', written by the socialist Kita Ikki in 1923,[28] envisaged an uprising from below and the creation of a Great Asian Empire comprising India, Australia and Eastern Siberia. Parallels to fascist movements in Europe are obvious, although Kita was not influenced by them. The various nationalist groups were united by the call for the restoration of direct imperial rule. Under the impact of the Great Depression, this turned into something of a religious creed.

The mismanagement of monetary policy by the *zaibatsu* led to an acute depression as early as 1927. Whereas the big industrial corporations weathered the crisis fairly comfortably (if only at the expense of the small suppliers), the slump had disastrous effects on agriculture, especially from 1929 onwards when the American market could no longer absorb Japanese agrarian exports. Rural Japan suffered unparalleled impoverishment; only a third of all peasant households earned a modest income from agriculture. Most farmers had to try and find other means for eking out a living; a considerable number rented out their daughters in the flourishing red-light districts of the cities. Since the government was closely allied to the *zaibatsu*, it did nothing to counter the growing misery, thus providing an opening for the anti-capitalist and social-revolutionary opposition movement that was led by the army.

The occupation of Manchuria had long been prepared for by army circles and was finally carried out in September 1931. It was an openly imperialistic act of aggression, fuelled by nationalistic motives and initiated against the wishes of government and industry. The army or, more precisely, the officers of middle rank, transformed Manchuria into their territorial power-base and used it as a laboratory for testing their ideas about state socialism and economic planning. Just as the pauperized classes within any society resist material deprivation, Japan as a 'have-not' nation claimed its share of the world's natural resources. In 1931, Imperial Japan threw off its role as a junior partner of the old-established imperialist powers and openly challenged the Western nations as well as Republican China, which was gaining strength under the government of the Guomindang. The Manchurian Crisis dealt a heavy blow to the international order created at Versailles; it presaged a military showdown with the West.

Having eliminated the party Cabinets and having reduced the influence of the *zaibatsu* (in several ways, including by political assassination), the army dominated the various leadership factions between 1932 and 1936. Yet it was unable to implement its aim of a planned economy. The *zaibatsu* kept aloof from acts of political violence at home and abroad, and refused to co-operate with the military in Manchuria; court and navy circles, too, shrank back from openly antagonizing the Western powers and attacking Soviet Russia. They preferred peaceful penetration of South-East Asia, where those raw materials which were not available in Manchuria could be found: oil, bauxite, rubber and certain kinds of minerals.[29]

From 1932 onwards, the government resorted to a policy of deficit spending, thus bringing army and industry once again closer together in Japan. The military benefited from a programme of large-scale armaments: between 1932 and 1936 the military budget increased two and a half times.[30] During the same period, heavy industry overtook light industry as the focal point of Japan's industrial structure. Within four years, the production index rose by 60 per cent.[31] By 1935 Japan had overcome the depression, but the growing demand for raw materials could only be met by an increase in exports. Beginning in 1934 Japan infiltrated Britain's traditional markets for consumer goods (above all, cotton textiles) in South-East Asia and Latin America using methods of underselling that were widely denounced as dumping. Britain retaliated by raising its tariffs, as did the United States. Japan was forced to fall back on markets at home, limited as they were, and in its colonies. So, in 1935 the government had to choose between two options: to expand the domestic market for consumer goods by implementing a programme of social reform, or to go ahead with plans for further social-imperialist expansion overseas.

The final decision was strongly influenced by a *putsch* of young officers on 26 February 1936. It was Emperor Hirohito himself who helped to defeat the coup, when he sided with industry and the navy, declared himself against any attempt to install a fascist-authoritarian system from below and insisted on Draconian punishment for the insurgents. Seizing the opportunity, navy and industry tried to have their plan of a southward expansion adopted as government policy. The attempt failed, and in the Cabinet decision on the 'Fundamental principles of national policy'[32] of 7 August 1936, the southern thrust was only referred to as one of two alternatives, the other being an army attack against the Soviet Union.

The issue was resolved when war broke out with China in July 1937. The army seized upon one of the almost routine skirmishes with Chinese troops on the outskirts of Peking and expanded it into a full-scale military action. The intention was to push for a speedy and spectacular victory so as to unite the battered nation as one large family behind the Tennō, and then to put into effect the army's ideas of revitalizing the economic and political order. The government of Prime Minister Count Konoe Fumimaro, however, representing as it did the traditional upper class, grasped the opportunity of keeping the unruly army busy in the field of honour. The army's thrust was deflected southwards, towards central China, and the army's hopes for an early peace were disappointed.[33] The war in China was escalated not by the army, but by the traditional oligarchy acting together with the court, the navy and industry.

Since the First World War a fundamental antagonism had become apparent between, on the one hand, the army which held anti-capitalist views and spoke out for the disadvantaged masses and, on the other, the traditional élite with its close ties to big business. This contrast was now submerged by a wave of belligerence and chauvinism. Within the alliance between the army and the wealthy ruling class that was forged during the war against China, the army played a subservient role; the true masters were the *zaibatsu*. From 1937 onwards, two modes of imperialism that had initially been opposed to each other formed a strange symbiosis: a mythical and vainglorious brand of nationalism and a carefully calculated policy of using overseas expansion as a safety valve for domestic tensions. The traditional oligarchy never deviated from the rational pursuit of their own interests. In the final analysis, it was they who kept the upper hand over the idealistic military men.

Illusions of Liberation and Realities of War: the Greater East Asia Co-prosperity Sphere

The War Mobilization Laws of 1 April 1938 gave the state absolute control over both entrepreneurs and workers, at least in theory. But, in reality, official regulation only strengthened the dominant role of big business, whose representatives held all the key positions in cartels and other industrial associations. They and their allies from the traditional oligarchy sabotaged any attempt made by reformist officials, such as Kishi Nobusuke, the Deputy-Minister of Commerce and Industry, to subordinate the egotistical and profit-oriented behaviour of the *zaibatsu* to the imperatives of national armament, and to put state commissioners in charge of industrial production.[34] The government instead accommodated the *zaibatsu* by promulgating the Major Industries Association Ordinance of September 1941.[35] It gave the chairmen of the various industrial control committees, most of them *zaibatsu* representatives, the final say in matters concerning compulsory mergers, pricing and raw-material quotas. Although this vertical organization of arms production corresponded to Japan's social structure, it was to prove a fatal and irreversible mistake. It allowed the *zaibatsu* full scope to further their own selfish interests, which were opposed to the requirements of warfare. By the end of the war, they owned more than 70 per cent of all bank deposits and controlled more than 50 per cent of industrial production; during the war years they had been able to increase their capital more than fourfold.[36]

72 Imperialism and After

The process of economic concentration and the aggrandizement of the *zaibatsu* had a decisive influence on Japan's internal development and also on its foreign relations, in particular on policy towards the territories which were occupied during the war. Japanese propaganda was fond of hailing China as an Asian brother nation, but from its very beginning, the military campaign was conceived and conducted as a war of annihilation. The aim was ruthlessly to destroy China's society and culture and to reduce the country to the status of a colony. Political control of the conquered territories was taken out of civilian hands and given to the military whose only way of achieving 'pacification' was by brutal force. The *zaibatsu* and the government were partners in the Central China Development Company and the North China Development Company which took over the entire economy of the occupied areas and, within a short time, ruined it completely.[37] The realities of Japanese rule in China made all slogans of Pan-Asiatic liberation sound utterly cynical. The Japanese were even unable to develop a political concept for China that would have gained them the collaboration of the weak Chinese ruling class.

At home, remodelling the nation along national socialist lines was a much-debated topic. Since 1938 vigorous efforts had been made to form a party of national unity. It finally materialized in October 1940 after Japan had joined Nazi Germany and Fascist Italy in the Tripartite Pact of 27 September 1940.[38] The Imperial Rule Assistance Association and its numerous branches such as the Greater Japan Patriotic Industrial Movement that included both workers and employers, were used as instruments to bring about national unity in view of the anticipated war with the Western powers. Central to the ideological war effort was the Showa Research Institute which was mainly staffed by former socialists and which had served as a think tank for Konoe.[39] It moulded the various nationalist currents into a coherent ideology of Greater Japan, centring on domestic social reforms and the creation of a self-sufficient empire in East and South-East Asia. The very eclecticism of Japanese nationalist and expansionist socialism, this strange amalgam of totalitarian and fascist views with ideals of socialist reform, can also be interpreted as a strained attempt to harmonize social tensions. Socialists, even communists, militant farmers, small craftsmen, big capitalists, traditional court circles and former party politicians could all come together under the same ideological roof which was hardly more than a camouflage designed to glorify imperialist aggression.

The Greater East Asia Co-prosperity Sphere was officially proclaimed in August 1940. Its envisaged borders were delineated in negotiations with Germany in the following month. The new *Lebensraum*, anticipated in the writings of Kita Ikki, was to include India, Australia, New Zealand and the Pacific Islands as far east as New Caledonia.[40] This programme of conquest reflected the views of industry, but also of court circles and the navy. The army's northern strategy – a direct strike at the Soviet Union – was finally laid to rest as a result of Japan's defeat in border clashes with the Red Army, and because of the supposedly friendly relations between Hitler's Germany and Stalin's Russia. The southern strategy was expected to lead to the carving out of an unassailable and autarkic regional base which could be used as a stepping-stone towards the status of a world power. Little heed was paid by the self-deluded strategists of empire to the fact that Japan's industrial capacity amounted to only 10 per cent of that of the United States.

After successful operations, the originally limited military plans were modified in the spring of 1942 to include India and Australia as well.[41] Euphoric about their easy victories during the opening months of the Pacific War, the military overruled the diplomats' plans for consolidating Japanese rule in the occupied countries. Projects for an economic transformation of the former European colonies came to nothing. Conquest and occupation soon gained a momentum of their own, all the more so since the Japanese troops had to live off the subjugated areas. Raw materials of military significance were seized immediately, but a bottleneck in shipping capacities allowed only a fraction of them to be sent to Japan. The goods shipped from South-East Asia to Japan in 1942, that is, before American submarines controlled the sea routes, amounted to a mere 15 per cent of overall Japanese imports and were thus decidedly below prewar levels.[42]

The new masters proved unable to fill the gap left by the 'whites' who had been expelled or interned. Instead of elevating Japan to the 'light of Asia', as the official commentary on the outbreak of war would have it,[43] an ignorant occupation force caused economic havoc in the 'liberated' territories. Famine raged in South-East Asia; the entire economic life of the region regressed to the level of subsistence production and barter trade.[44] Even if Japan did not succeed during the Pacific War in becoming the hub of East Asian trade, the occupation had profound and long-lasting consequences in the region. Of particular importance was the destruction of the plantation economy which put an end to the traditional trade between the colonies and their mother countries. After the war, this almost inevitably led to a new economic orientation towards the former occupying power. The war thus laid the foundation for today's system of trade in East Asia with Tokyo at its centre.

As the war dragged on, it became more and more apparent that the Japanese economy needed a thoroughgoing refurbishment if it were to stand up to the economic and military might of the West. The performance of the arms industry was disappointing; basic supplies for the civilian population were totally inadequate; the administration disintegrated into utter chaos. Put on the defensive, in 1943 the leadership changed both its occupation strategy and economic organization at home. The Philippines, Burma and the government of Free India were granted independence in 1943, and Indonesia during the last days of the war. Yet, this was all too obviously dictated by the hopeless military situation and did not win over the Asian peoples to the Japanese cause. Economic reform, masterminded at the newly created Munitions Ministry by Kishi Nobusuke, the Japanese counterpart to Albert Speer, met with greater success.[45] The *zaibatsu* were deprived of their influence and production was organized horizontally rather than in the traditional vertical manner. Factories in certain branches of industry were placed under government supervision and their output was limited to one type of product only. Owing to modern management methods, Japan was remarkably successful in manufacturing tankers, aircraft and the necessary electronic equipment. Arms production finally peaked in September 1944. Much of the economic revival in postwar Japan was based on these wartime reforms and especially on those branches that had reached a high level of technological sophistication during the war. After Kishi had eventually become Prime Minister in 1957, he successfully continued the reconstruction of the economy, relying on the Ministry of International Trade and Industry (MITI), which developed directly from the Munitions Ministry. Kishi's economic policy culminated, between 1957 and 1960, in 'the most rapid development since the foundation of the state'.[46]

Japan's Hegemony in East Asia: the Continuity of Economic Expansion in the Postwar Period

The capitulation of Imperial Japan on 2 September 1945 was an act of military surrender, but not of political and social self-denigration. Government, administration and even the institution of the Tennō remained in existence, even though the American High Command insisted on its authority to issue orders to the 'Son of Heaven'. The victors came to Japan with a carefully prepared programme of reform and re-education: those responsible for the war were to be put on trial, the country was to be liberated from feudal relics and a democratic order was to be introduced. The American administrators, many of whom had a New Deal background, regarded the eight leading *zaibatsu*, the court and a few thousand big landowners as the forces behind Japan's aggressive war policy.[47] In fact, despite devastating bombardment of their factories, the *zaibatsu* had survived the war as its true winners. Striking evidence of their purely profit-seeking behaviour and their close involvement with the traditional leadership is provided by the fact that the *zaibatsu* and the government divided among themselves the remaining supplies during the interregnum between the armistice (15 August) and the arrival of the Americans (2 September). Within two weeks, stores of iron, steel, aluminium, food, machine tools and raw materials valued at approximately $US4,000 million vanished without trace.[48] Civilian and military authorities destroyed a large number of files that might have proved incriminating;[49] many people simply disappeared or, with official connivance, acquired new names to avoid persecution. Thus, the Japanese prepared to undermine over-zealous American reforms.

In the event, only those reforms were carried out which were either imposed by the occupation authorities – the new constitution being the chief example – or which had already proved to be overdue during the war. The original American plan involving a radical purge of the ruling élite, the dissolution of the *zaibatsu* and a reorganization of the economy according to Western principles of industrial relations, was foiled by the tenacious obstruction of those potentially affected. In general, the Japanese ruling élite remained intact beyond 1945 to a much larger extent than that of the

'Third Reich'. In the main trial of war criminals, held in Tokyo from 1946 to 1948, seven of the twenty-eight defendants received death sentences and were executed; former Foreign Minister Hirota Kōki was the only civilian among them. In further military trials some 920 people were condemned to death and executed.[50] The political purges, by contrast, were relatively harmless: of a total of 210,288 people removed from their positions, 80 per cent belonged to the military and only 16·5 per cent were civilian politicians. The all-powerful bureaucracy, where only 1,809 people (0·9 per cent) of all personnel temporarily lost their jobs, escaped virtually unscathed. The same was true for industry where 1,898 people (0·9 per cent) were purged.[51]

Nevertheless, the occupation brought about a significant shift in the composition of the ruling élite. The court was deprived of its political function, the big landowners were expropriated during the land reform and the alleged villains – the military – were singled out for punishment. The locus of power now shifted to industry and the bureaucracy. This new and numerically larger élite, however, remained committed to the same conservative and nationalistic values that had guided the traditional oligarchy.[52] What was new after the war was that the leadership now managed to reconcile these traditional norms with Western pragmatism. As in the Meiji period, Japan after 1945 opened itself to the West only as far as was deemed necessary to achieve equality with the advanced industrial nations. Now, however, the competition was economic rather than military.

The moving spirit behind this policy of covert restoration, and its foremost representative, was Yoshida Shigeru, a leading politician in postwar Japan who had once, as a diplomat, pushed for the Japanese takeover in Manchuria.[53] Now his policy was to reject all reforms initiated by the Americans, or, if this could not be done, to distort them into a Japanized form. His chosen instrument was the loyal and omnipotent bureaucracy. The dissolution of the *zaibatsu*, decreed by the Americans in 1947, was abandoned only a year later.[54] In the meantime, however, the old family-owners had been replaced by experienced industrial managers. In a way, this meant that the *zaibatsu* were nationalized and put under direct state supervision. In 1949, the MITI was put in charge of the economic reconstruction programme. A protectionist foreign-trade policy and underhand bureaucratic manœuvres were used to shield economic reconstruction. Import restrictions were lifted as late as 1971, under direct pressure from other countries.[55] By then, Japanese industry had a firm grip on the domestic market and was penetrating foreign markets all over the world and Japan had developed into the second strongest industrial power behind the United States. Today Mitsubishi, the former armaments *zaibatsu*, is the world's largest corporation. The six largest enterprises in Japan effectively control 21 per cent of the turnover in the private sector, and 23 per cent of total share capital; they employ 10 per cent of the permanent workforce.[56]

The political corner-stone of the alignment between industry and bureaucracy was laid with the founding of the Liberal Democratic Party (LDP) in October 1955.[57] Neither liberal nor democratic, the ruling party is a loose coalition of all kinds of conservative groups. It could well be described as an authoritarian alliance of corrupt parliamentary factions. More than 54 per cent of LDP members of the Diet are themselves employers or closely connected with business interests.[58] Just as in the interwar period, the conservatives today reinforce their position with an anti-socialist ideology that gives overriding importance to the nation's greatness and to what is seen as the welfare of the people. Since socialists and communists are even more divided among themselves than the LDP, and since they lack financial support from big business which would enable them to buy votes, as is customary in Japan, they are unlikely to assume political power unless the entire system undergoes fundamental change. The present government tends to glorify the country's imperialist past rather than to maintain a critical distance from it. The Tennō myth is being revived and there are moves to give greater power to the emperor in a revised constitution. History books used in schools blatantly falsify the recent past and monuments are being erected for leaders who were condemned as war criminals.

While the national unity of the Japanese is often admired in the West, the former victims of Japanese nationalism are highly suspicious of Japan's re-emergence as a major power. Tokyo's foreign and economic policy towards the countries of East and South-East Asia has strengthened rather than dispelled distrust of the deeds and intentions of that 'chosen' nation. Today Japan regards the former Greater East Asia Co-prosperity Sphere as a source of raw materials and as a market for industrial exports. Neither the Japanese government nor the big private corporations have undertaken long-term and costly development projects which might have contributed to autonomous economic development in those countries. The question of reparations had not been settled in the peace treaty of San Francisco and was left to bilateral agreements; Japanese businessmen were able to influence them so as to secure maximum advantage for the domestic economy. Loans were extended on conditions that were more beneficial to the Japanese economy than to the recipients. South-East Asian countries have run up growing deficits in their trade with Japan; the gulf has widened between developed Japan and underdeveloped South-East Asia.

Japan gives practically no economic aid for the training of professionals and skilled labourers. The number of students from the poorer Asian countries who are studying at Japanese universities is negligible, partly because of a shortage of grants, partly on account of latent racial discrimination that keeps away undesired foreigners.[59] Vice versa, there are hardly any Japanese experts engaged in aid projects in South-East Asia, as the people in those countries have shown themselves to be persistently hostile to the Japanese. Japan's contribution to international development aid does not reflect its economic strength; contributing only 0·26 per cent of its GNP (in 1980), Japan was well below the average of 0·34 per cent.[60] The South-East Asian countries today merely serve as a peripheral area for Japan's expansionist capitalism; they are kept in their present state of underdevelopment by means of 'structural violence'. This state of affairs goes virtually unchallenged in Japan. Even the socialists, who like to regard themselves as the Asiatic conscience of the nation, tolerate this kind of informal imperialism,[61] just as in the past they gave their open support to formal militarist expansion. Then, as now, the honour and greatness of the nation seemed to be at stake.

The economic and social system of contemporary Japan appears to be somewhat unstable.[62] The economy could not withstand a drastic recession because the capital market would collapse instantly. Japan has managed to build up and maintain its economic hegemony only at the expense of its international environment: of the dependent Third World countries, of the Americans who are still suffering from a guilt complex towards Japan, and also of the Europeans who have so far taken little notice of the working of the Japanese system.

Japanese Imperialism: a Theoretical Perspective

Neither classical theories of imperialism nor those derived from the contemporary social sciences can do full justice to the unique prerequisites of Japanese imperialism and to its historical development. In particular, those theories have to be ruled out which focus too strongly on Europe as the source of imperialist expansionism. Japan's building of formal and informal empires was largely initiated and sustained by internal forces. While this process is characterized by a strong underlying continuity, it has passed through four stages.

The period from 1868 to 1915, when the Twenty-One Demands were presented to China, was marked by pre-industrial capitalism which proceeded cautiously and was careful to seek British cover. Its aim was to elevate Japan to equal rank with the West. Disorientation and discontent among the people in the course of precipitate modernization converged with the inclinations of the ruling oligarchy, resulting in a desire for a strong and united nation, inspired by time-honoured values and virtues.

In the second stage, lasting from 1915 until the outbreak of the war with China in 1937, nationalism spread among the people as economic conditions took an unfavourable turn, especially in the agrarian sector. The leadership was put under mounting pressure. During the Great Depression nationalist attitudes and sentiments were infused with elements of social-revolutionary Utopianism which were particularly popular among the middle ranks of the army. The occupation of Manchuria was an early attempt to put these ideas into practice. Reacting against popular pressure, the traditional élites and the representatives of big business drew closer together in an effort to channel the nationalism fermenting among the people into a programme of southward expansion. Nationalism from below and manipulative social-imperialism from above jointly resulted in the war with China.

During the third stage, from the beginning of hostilities with China in 1937 to the end of the Pacific War, an aggressive military expansionism was unleashed which soon was no longer amenable to rational control from above. It resulted in plunder and fierce repression of the occupied areas. The idea of the Greater East Asian Co-prosperity Sphere lost its original idealistic and anti-colonialist overtones and degenerated into cynical propaganda. Several factors combined to defeat Japan's self-proclaimed mission: the inability of a backward-looking élite to introduce reforms; the 'unpatriotic' behaviour of the *zaibatsu* which totally failed to contribute to the war effort; and the military set-backs of the war.

The fourth stage began in 1952. Elements inherent in all of the three earlier forms of imperialism can be traced as constituents of the informal trade imperialism that has come to characterize the postwar era. Again, control is exercised from the top and the masses give their tacit support. This sort of informal imperialism is part and parcel of the present social and economic system and is likely to continue as long as prosperity can be maintained.

Of the classical theories of imperialism, Joseph A. Schumpeter's ideas about imperialism being an 'atavism of ruling aristocracies' and serving the 'preservation of feudal structures'[63] appears to fit the Japanese case most closely. The postwar period can also be analysed in terms of the theory of state monopolistic capitalism.[64] Japan surpasses all other Western nations in the degree to which the state manipulates the economy. If there is one continuous thread which links the Meiji founding fathers to the oligarchs of the first half of the twentieth century and these, in turn, to today's élite of bureaucrats and business leaders, it is the desire to preserve the traditional social structure and defend a political system that has constantly denied real participation to the majority of the people.

The 'excentric approach', as advocated by Ronald Robinson,[65] does not really explain the characteristics of Japanese expansion. In the Japanese case, there was no transition from formal and colonialist imperialism to informal economic penetration. Apart from Korea and Taiwan, the empire did not possess colonies. Since its colonial policies aimed at repeating the process of modernization that had taken place in the mother country,[66] they cannot be compared with those of the Western powers. Moreover, the brutality that accompanied Japan's expansion and the claim to cultural leadership *vis-à-vis* the people in occupied China ruled out the emergence of collaborationist élites. As far as allegiance was pledged to the Greater Asian Co-prosperity Sphere by nationalist circles in the conquered areas, they did it from pragmatic motives and in expectation of Japan's ultimate defeat which would allow them to get rid of their 'yellow' colonial masters who had already replaced the 'white' ones.

In postwar Japan itself, the debate about imperialism has been dominated by the official views of the communist and socialist parties. Little progress has been made in these circles since the communist analyses of the interwar period. As early as 1927 the Comintern labelled Japan 'the most threatening imperialist power in East Asia' and described the Pacific region as 'a central battleground for the imperialist powers'. In 1932 the term 'absolutist military and feudal imperialism'[67] was coined to account for the characteristics of Japanese society.

Japan's defeat seemed to have destroyed imperialist tendencies. The debate now focused on American imperialism. Japan's economic imperialism as it is displayed in South-East Asia is usually ignored by socialist and

Imperialism or Pan-Asiatic Mission? 79

communist theorists, or minimized by regarding it as a result of Japan's dependence on the United States. Attempts made by some economists to develop Marxist explanations in the tradition of Lenin and Hilferding[68] met with as little response as did liberal efforts to build upon the ideas of Max Weber.[69] Given the overwhelming influence of American economic theory, those approaches remained limited to circles outside the academic mainstream.

As before the war, the conservative ruling groups prefer to see Japan's expansion on the Asian mainland neither as aggression nor as imperialism, but rather as a gradual 'advance'.[70] As one Japanese Foreign Minister said, when confronted with the accusation that Japan had in the past behaved as an imperialist power: 'If that was "imperialism", then it was glorious imperialism.'[71]

Notes: Chapter 6

This chapter was translated by Christian Sonntag and Jürgen Osterhammel.
    Parts of the present chapter are based on some of the author's previous publications on modern Japanese history: 'Restauration – Die "Bewältigung der Vergangenheit" in Japan', *Zeitschrift für Politik*, vol. 17 (1970), pp. 155–70; 'Aggressionspolitik als Mobilisierungsfaktor: Der militärische und wirtschaftliche Imperialismus Japans 1931–1941', in F. Forstmeier and H.-E. Volkmann (eds), *Wirtschaft und Rüstung am Vorabend des Zweiten Weltkrieges* (Düsseldorf, 1975), pp. 222–44; 'Japans Kriegswirtschaft 1941–1945', in F. Forstmeier and H.-E. Volkmann (eds), *Kriegswirtschaft und Rüstung 1939–1945* (Düsseldorf, 1977), pp. 256–86; 'Sozialer Wandel in Japan während des Zweiten Weltkrieges und seine Folgen für die Nachkriegszeit', in W. Długoborski (ed.), *Zweiter Weltkrieg und sozialer Wandel* (Göttingen, 1981), pp. 364–84; 'Die Weltwirtschaftskrise in Japan: Wirtschaftliche Konzentration und soziale Konflikte', in D. Rothermund (ed.), *Die Peripherie in der Weltwirtschaftskrise: Afrika, Asien und Lateinamerika 1929–1939* (Paderborn, 1982), pp. 197–223. For a survey of recent research see 'Japans Weg in den Krieg. Bemerkungen über Forschungsstand und Literatur zur japanischen Zeitgeschichte', *Militärgeschichtliche Mitteilungen*, vol. 23 (1978), pp. 183–209, and 'Japan und der Krieg in Ostasien. Kommentierender Bericht über das Schrifttum', *Historische Zeitschrift*, special issue no. 8 (1980), pp. 79–220.

1 Cambridge, Mass., 1965. See also his recent study: A. Iriye, *Power and Culture: The Japanese-American War, 1941–1945* (Cambridge, Mass., 1981).
2 *Imperialism: The Specter of the Twentieth Century*. The book was first published in Japanese in 1901. See F. G. Nothelfer, *Kotoku Shusui: Portrait of a Japanese Radical* (Cambridge, 1971), pp. 82–7. J. A. Hobson, *Imperialism: A Study*, was published in London in 1902.
3 For the peculiarities of Japanese society see: Chie Nakane, *Japanese Society* (Berkeley, Calif.: 1970); T. Doi, *The Anatomy of Dependence* (New York, 1973).
4 See the stimulating, but not always convincing, book by F. V. Moulder, *Japan, China, and the Modern World Economy. Toward a Reinterpretation of East Asian Development, ca. 1600 to ca. 1918* (Cambridge, 1977).
5 The standard account is W. G. Beasley, *The Meiji Restoration* (Stanford, Calif.: 1972). See also E. H. Norman, *Origins of the Modern Japanese State*, ed. J. W. Dower (New York, 1975).
6 J. W. Bennett and I. Ishino, *Paternalism in the Japanese Economy: Anthropological Studies of oyabun-kobun Patterns* (Minneapolis, Minn., 1963).
7 W. W. Lockwood, *The Economic Development of Japan: Growth and Structural Change, 1868–1938* (Princeton, NJ, 1954), p. 98. On the agrarian order see A. Waswo, *Japanese Landlords: The Decline of a Rural Elite* (Berkeley, Calif. and Los Angeles, Calif., 1977).
8 The first loan of 3·5 million yen was originally granted to the shogunate with the purpose

80 Imperialism and After

of building Japan's first railway line (Tokyo–Yokohama); it was actually paid to the Meiji government. The second loan of over 10·7 million yen was used for paying the pensions of the *samurai* from 1872 onwards. cf. G. C. Allen, *A Short Economic History of Modern Japan, 1867–1937*, 3rd edn (London, 1972), p. 41.

9. See the memorandum by T. Okubo, 'Reasons for opposing the Korean expedition', in R. Tsunoda *et al.* (eds), *Sources of Japanese Tradition* (New York, 1958), pp. 658–62. For the debate see I. H. Nish, *Japanese Foreign Policy, 1869–1942: From Kasumigaseki to Miyakezaka* (London, 1977), pp. 21–5.
10. So far there is no comprehensive study on Prussia-Germany's influence on the modernization of Japan. For the legal system see N. Toshitani, 'Japan's modern legal system: its formation and structure', *Annals of the Institute of Social Science, University of Tokyo*, vol. 17 (1976), pp. 1–50. For the German impact on Japanese military organization see E. L. Presseisen, *Before Aggression: Europeans Prepare the Japanese Army* (Tucson, Ariz., 1965). For German influence on the constitution of 1889 see J. Siemens, *Hermann Roesler and the Making of the Meiji State* (Tokyo, 1968).
11. Extracts from both documents in D. Lu (ed.), *Sources of Japanese History*, Vol. 2 (New York, 1974), pp. 66–71.
12. H. Conroy, *The Japanese Seizure of Korea* (Stanford, Calif., 1974).
13. 200 million taels in the original peace treaty of Shimonoseki, a further 30 million taels indemnity payment for Japan's retrocession of the Liadong Peninsula after the Triple Intervention. cf. Nish, *Japanese Foreign Policy*, pp. 39–41.
14. S. Okamoto, *The Japanese Oligarchy and the Russo–Japanese War* (New York, 1970).
15. F. C. Jones, *Extraterritoriality in Japan and the Diplomatic Relations Resulting in its Abolition, 1853–1898* (New Haven, Conn., 1931); Nish, *Japanese Foreign Policy*, pp. 46–50.
16. Reprinted in Lu (ed.), *Sources of Japanese History*, Vol. 2, pp. 107–9.
17. See Nish, *Japanese Foreign Policy*, pp. 111–18.
18. Lockwood, *The Economic Development*, pp. 38–9.
19. J. Halliday, *A Political History of Japanese Capitalism* (New York, 1975), pp. 70–2.
20. T. H. Buckley, *The United States and the Washington Conference, 1921–1922* (Knoxville, Tenn., 1970).
21. I. H. Nish, *Alliance in Decline: A Study in Anglo-Japanese Relations, 1908–1923* (London, 1972).
22. P. Duus, *Party Rivalry and Political Change in Taishō Japan* (Cambridge, Mass., 1968).
23. R. H. Mitchell, *Thought Control in Prewar Japan* (Ithaca, NY, 1976).
24. C. Johnson, *MITI and the Japanese Miracle: The Growth of Identical Policy, 1925–1975* (Stanford, Calif., 1982), pp. 83–4.
25. ibid., p. 103. For a biography of Japan's leading industrial bureaucrat see D. Kurzman, *Kishi and Japan: The Search for the Sun* (New York, 1960).
26. A. E. Tiedeman, 'Big business and politics in prewar Japan', in J. W. Morley (ed.), *Dilemmas of Growth in Prewar Japan* (Princeton, NJ, 1971), pp. 267–316.
27. B.-A. Shillony, *Revolt in Japan: The Young Officers and the February 26, 1936 Incident* (Princeton, NJ, 1973), p. 20. See also T. R. H. Havens, *Farm and Nation in Modern Japan: Agrarian Nationalism, 1870–1940* (Princeton, NJ, 1974).
28. Extracts in Lu (ed.), *Sources of Japanese History*, Vol. 2, pp. 131–6.
29. Only 6 per cent of total Japanese imports of iron-ore originated from Manchuria. cf. Lockwood, *The Economic Development*, p. 524.
30. H. T. Patrick, 'The economic muddle of the 1920s', in Morley (ed.), *Dilemmas of Growth*, p. 250.
31. Allen, *Short Economic History*, p. 139.
32. J. B. Crowley, *Japan's Quest for Autonomy: National Security and Foreign Policy, 1930–1938* (Princeton, NJ, 1966), p. 190.
33. ibid., p. 358.
34. Hoshino Naoki, president of the Cabinet Planning Board, and Kishi, Deputy-Minister of Commerce and Industry, both drew up plans for a state-controlled economy. Both were charged with 'red thinking' and forced to resign at the beginning of 1941. See Johnson, *MITI and the Japanese Miracle*, pp. 150–2.
35. E. B. Schumpeter, *The Industrialization of Japan and Manchukuo, 1930–1940* (New York, 1940), pp. 686, 793, 820; J. B. Cohen, *Japan's Economy in War and Reconstruction* (Minneapolis, Minn., 1949), p. 32.

36 K. Ikeda, *Die industrielle Entwicklung in Japan unter besonderer Berücksichtigung seiner Finanz- und Wirtschaftspolitik* (Berlin, 1970), p. 129; T. A. Bisson, 'The zaibatsu's wartime role', *Pacific Affairs*, vol. 18 (1945), pp. 355–68.
37 Cohen, *Japan's Economy*, p. 42. For the Japanese occupation of North China see L. Li, *The Japanese Army in North China, 1937–1941: Problems of Political and Economic Control* (London, 1975). From the Japanese point of view: J. W. Morley (ed.), *The China Quagmire: Japan's Expansion on the Asian Continent, 1933–1941* (New York, 1983), pp. 292–3, 326–7, 428 ff.
38 For an analysis, based on Japanese sources, of Japan's orientation towards Germany see G. Krebs, *Japans Deutschlandpolitik. Eine Studie zur Vorgeschichte des Pazifischen Krieges* (Hamburg, 1984).
39 M. Fletcher, *The Search for a New Order: Intellectuals and Fascism in Prewar Japan* (Chapel Hill, NC, 1982).
40 For the full English text of the decision taken by the Inner Cabinet and reconfirmed by the Liaison Conference of 19 September 1940 see T. Sommer, *Deutschland und Japan zwischen den Mächten 1935–1940* (Tübingen, 1962), pp. 509–24.
41 B. Martin, *Deutschland und Japan im Zweiten Weltkrieg* (Göttingen, 1969).
42 Cohen, *Japan's Economy*, p. 69.
43 'Commentary on the imperial declaration of war', in Tsunoda *et al.* (eds), *Sources of Japanese Tradition*, pp. 799–801.
44 J. C. Scott, 'An approach to the problems of food supply in Southeast Asia during World War II', in B. Martin and A. Milward (eds), *Agriculture and Food Supply in World War II* (Stuttgart, 1985), pp. 269–82.
45 Johnson, *MITI and the Japanese Miracle*, pp. 157–97.
46 'Jimmu Keiki'. Between 1956 and 1961 industrial production and mining increased 2·7 fold. Big business finally re-established its dominance. See H. Hammitzsch (ed.), *Japan-Handbuch* (Wiesbaden, 1981), cols 2077–8.
47 T. A. Bisson, *Japan's War Economy* (New York, 1945), p. 7. (Bisson served on the US Government Committee on Economic Warfare.)
48 Halliday, *A Political History*, p. 162.
49 Interview with Colonel S. Nishiura by the author, Tokyo, 13 August 1969. Nishiura was in charge of burning the files of the War (Army) Ministry in August 1945. After the war, being an expert on the lost material, he became head of the Historical Division of the Ministry of Self-Defence.
50 R. H. Minear, *Victors' Justice: The Tokyo War Crimes Trial* (Princeton, NJ, 1971); P. R. Piccigallo, *The Japanese on Trial: Allied War Crimes Operations in the East, 1945–1951* (London, 1979).
51 H. H. Baerwald, *The Purge of the Japanese Leaders under the Occupation* (Berkeley, Calif., 1959), pp. 80ff.
52 An excellent study on the continuity of the political élite in Japan was written by the former secretary of the German Embassy in Tokyo, K. F. Zahl: *Die politische Elite Japans nach dem Zweiten Weltkrieg* (Wiesbaden, 1973).
53 J. W. Dower, *Empire and Aftermath: Yoshida Shigeru and the Japanese Experience, 1878–1954* (Cambridge, Mass., 1979).
54 Halliday, *A Political History* pp. 175 ff.; J. G. Roberts, 'The "Japanese Crowd" and the zaibatsu restoration', *Japan Interpreter*, vol. 12 (1979), pp. 384–415.
55 Johnson, *MITI and the Japanese Miracle*, pp. 275–304.
56 R. Gaul *et al.*, *Japan-Report. Wirtschaftsriese Nippon – die sieben Geheimnisse des Erfolgs* (Munich, 1981), pp. 190–3.
57 N. Thayer, *How the Conservatives Rule Japan* (Princeton, NJ, 1969).
58 ibid., pp. 323–32: A. Dettloff and H. Kirchmann, *Arbeitsstaat Japan – Exportdrohung gegen die Gewerkschaften* (Reinbek, 1981), p. 108.
59 J. Halliday and G. McCormack, *Japanese Imperialism Today: 'Co-Prosperity in Great East Asia'* (New York, 1973), p. 69; Hammitzsch (ed.), *Japan Handbuch*, col. 86. In 1969 there were only 563 students from underdeveloped countries enrolled at Japanese universities, most of them from Africa and the Near East. In 1974 the majority of the 2,000 foreign students in Japan came from Europe and the United States.
60 E. Wilkinson, *Japan ist ganz anders. Geschichte eines grossen Missverständnisses* (Königstein, 1982), p. 195.

82 Imperialism and After

61 Hammitzsch (ed.), *Japan-Handbuch*, p. 421.
62 Halliday, *A Political History*, p. 297: 'bicycle-economy' (if it slows down, it collapses). See also Z. Brzezinski, *The Fragile Blossom: Crisis and Change in Japan* (New York, 1973); F. Gibney, *Japan: The Fragile Superpower* (New York, 1975).
63 J. A. Schumpeter, 'Zur Soziologie der Imperialismen', *Archiv für Sozialwissenschaft und Sozialpolitik*, vol. 46 (1918/19), pp. 1–39, 275–310.
64 See M. Dobb, *Organisierter Kapitalismus. Fünf Beiträge zur politischen Ökonomie* (Frankfurt-on-Main, 1966).
65 See Chapter 18 by Ronald Robinson in this volume.
66 E. Chen, 'Japanese colonialism in Korea and Formosa: a comparison of the system of political control', *Harvard Journal of Asiatic Studies*, vol. 30 (1970), pp. 126–58; G. H. Kerr, *Formosa: Licensed Revolution and the Home Rule Movement, 1895–1945* (Honolulu, 1974); G. Wontroba and U. Menzel, *Stagnation und Unterentwicklung in Korea: Von der Yi-Dynastie zur Peripherisierung unter japanischer Kolonialherrschaft* (Meisenheim, 1978). R. H. Myers and M. R. Peattie (eds), *The Japanese Colonial Empire, 1895–1945* (Princeton, NJ, 1984).
67 Hammitzsch (ed.), *Japan-Handbuch*, pp. 419–20.
68 T. Sekine, 'Uno-Riron: a Japanese contribution to Marxian political economy', *Journal of Economic Literature*, vol. 13 (1975), pp. 847–77.
69 Hammitzsch (ed.), *Japan-Handbuch*, col. 2374.
70 This propaganda term was used at the time of the Sino-Japanese War of 1937–1945. It was revived in 1982 in officially licensed textbooks for schools. The Chinese vehemently protested against this falsification of history.
71 Foreign Minister Shiina Etsusaburo in 1966, quoted in A. Axelbank, *Black Star over Japan: Rising Forces of Militarism* (New York, 1977), p. 123.

7 Some Thoughts on Japanese Expansion

IAN H. NISH

That there was Japanese expansion in the three-quarters of a century down to 1945 no one could deny. My own view of Japan's expansion is that there was neither a single-minded and uninterrupted pursuit of expansionist goals nor was there a grand pattern of continuity in Japanese imperialism. On the contrary, there was a sort of stop-go effect, a cycle of peaks and troughs, in much of Japan's expansion. There were expansionist groups which were nationalistic in their appeal and other groups which were opposed to expansion, very often on the ground that it would incur international opposition. For much of Japan's history from 1870 onwards the ruling élite was divided over expansion. This led to serious disagreements, delays, indecision and sometimes even contradictions in policy-making.

These features changed over time. The closer we get to the 1930s, the more pronounced the zeal for expansion is and the more popular it is as a cause. In the earlier years of the new Japan, the element of caution is more evident. In 1872 while the Iwakura mission was on a tour of inspection overseas, the members of the government left in Tokyo planned an expedition to Korea. When Iwakura and his colleagues returned to Tokyo in the following year, they made clear their opposition to the military expedition which was called off. It was not until 1910 – and after many changes of fortune had taken place – that Korea was finally annexed by Japan. But by the mid-1930s voices of caution were very rare. From his retirement the former Foreign Minister, Shidehara, wrote in 1935: 'The army has this time really asserted itself at the Foreign Ministry over China policy. It looks as though not only the foreign minister but also the prime minister are busy waving white flags.'[1] As this quotation indicates, power was passing in the 1930s from the civilian, internationalist and liberal elements in Japan to the army and navy which were more or less insensitive and unsympathetic to influences from other countries. The brake on expansion was applied much less freely from 1930 onwards.

In the historical period down to 1945, there was, of course, an underlying economic factor. Japan was dependent on imported raw materials and looked zealously for sources of them from 1870 onwards. This search became more urgent as the population grew and industrialization developed in the present century. Since Japan had to pursue a raw-materials strategy, it may have been pushed into trying to establish control over lands which offered it the raw materials it needed and into drawing up guidelines for the Greater East Asia Co-prosperity Sphere in the early 1940s.

There were equally strong strategic considerations. The main agent of

Japan's imperialism was the military, either acting directly or indirectly, by subverting, or manipulating, or circumventing the apparatus of the Japanese state. This is indeed the conventional view, generally accepted by Japan's postwar historians. I incorporated this idea in the subtitle of my book on Japanese foreign policy, *Kasumigaseki to Miyakezaka*, in which I tried to suggest that between 1870 and 1942 power in Japan passed gradually from the civilians, as represented by the Foreign Ministry, into the hands of the Japanese military, as represented by the General Staff.[2] The power of the General Staff derived partly from the Meiji Constitution of 1890 whereby the commanders of the army and navy had the right of direct access to the emperor without going through the Prime Minister and Cabinet. This gave them leverage within the Japanese state and enabled them to climb the ladder to a position of unassailable strength.

Certainly the military were in the van of Japanese expansion. Japan, being a maritime country, could not expand without the co-operation of both the army and the navy. The engine of its expansion tended to be the military factions within the Japanese state or even factions within the army-navy. There were occasions when the military discouraged further territorial advances; but these were exceptional. There were times, too, when the army and navy disagreed about objectives but these cannot be elaborated on here. The activities of the military over expansion were sometimes contested by civilians. There were, therefore, policy options or alternatives which were open to Japanese leaders at times of crisis. There were also discontinuities when a wave of expansion was followed by a period of cooling off. By the 1930s these cooling off periods became fewer.

Let me start in the area of my current researches: the approach of the Russo-Japanese War of 1904–5. My studies have indicated that there was a war party in existence among the Japanese military as early as 1901. Russia was then in military occupation of Manchuria, the name given to the three eastern provinces of China, while it also had effective political control over the Korean court. The Japanese decision-makers were divided over whether to do a deal with the Russians whom they did not really trust or to go to war with them, even though Russia had a much larger army worldwide than the Japanese. The elder statesman, Itō Hirobumi, went to St Petersburg in November 1901 in order to discuss with the Russian statesmen means for keeping the peace. He failed to persuade them to make a conciliatory offer to Japan; and, while he was naturally disappointed, he returned home to keep up the pressure for pursuing negotiations with Russia.[3] These were eventually held between August 1903 and January 1904 and resulted in a stalemate. Only then did Itō drop his opposition to the course of making war on Russia, despite all the risks attendant on such a course of action. He had earlier been menaced by those of the war party who wanted to undertake hostilities without delay before the opening of the Russian railways in North-East Asia had its effect on Russian troop movements to the area. But his personal influence and that of the peace party, associated with his name, had held things in check for some time. It is arguable that, if the Russians had given the slightest evidence of a willingness to compromise (say) by offering to withdraw from Korea, the Japanese peace party might have had its way and war might have been avoided. As it was, the war party triumphed and the peace party withdrew its opposition to war. By its war with Russia, Japan made important 'imperialist' gains in the field of railways and territory.[4] For present purposes, however, the point that needs to be made is that the Russo-Japanese War did not follow on automatically or inevitably from the Sino-Japanese War of ten years earlier. In fact, there was a substantial discontinuity and considerable reluctance to risk a war with Russia.

It is possible to interpret the events leading up to the Russo-Japanese War from a different standpoint. One of the aspects of the Russo-Japanese War was that Japan had something of an international mission. It was one of the open-door powers, having subscribed to the doctrines put forward by John Hay, the American Secretary of State, in 1899. While Russia, Germany and France were reluctant subscribers to this doctrine, Japan was enthusiastic and bound itself without question to the side of the United States and Britain in the open-door camp between 1900 and 1904. In 1900 China was engulfed by the Boxer disturbances. In their aftermath, Russia, in defence of its growing railway empire there, placed Manchuria under occupation by military forces in retaliation for tearing up its railway tracks. No European power was prepared to dislodge the Russians. In the end the task was left to the Japanese. Thus, when Japan made war on Russia in 1904, it was not solely for its own interests but also for the broader interests of the open-door powers. The United States President, Theodore Roosevelt, told Germany and France rather firmly in 1904 that they should not interfere in the war between Russia and Japan. His remarks are close to being approval of Japan's course of action in fighting the Russians.[5]

This does not mean that others encouraged Japan to make war on Russia. Indeed, both Britain and the United States were careful to avoid giving Japan too much encouragement in case they too were forced at a later stage in the war to intervene. But Japan could claim that Britain and the United States smiled on its enterprise. Nor are we suggesting that Japan attacked Russia purely under the influence of international pressure at the time. It had, in addition, expansionist intentions in Korea and Manchuria of its own so it was by no means pure altruism. But in 1904 Japan was conscious of having international backing for its actions.

Over the next fifteen years Japan's expansion on the Asian continent was neither welcomed nor condemned in international circles. When Japan successfully invaded Qingdao/Jiaozhou in 1914, this suited the Allies in the First World War and they saluted it as an Allied victory. When Japan sent the preponderant force into Siberia in 1918, its action was welcomed by Britain and France and accepted, though not welcomed, by the United States. So Japan could claim to have some international support for some of its continental adventures.

The first major international challenge to Japan's expansion of the 1910s occurred at the time of the Washington Conference of 1921–2. That conference has sometimes been called 'Japan's Versailles'. There is considerable support for that phrase in so far as it was an occasion on which Japan's expansion in China since 1914 came up for international scrutiny. The treaties which emerged from the conference laid down that: the Anglo-Japanese Alliance would shortly be brought to an end; the territorial integrity of China was reaffirmed; and a formula was adopted for limiting the size of Japan's navy by restricting the building of battleships.[6] In addition, Japan's spokesman announced that it would pull its forces out of Siberia during 1922. From the point of view of Japan, the treaties were a mixed blessing. On the one hand, in the eyes of Japan's army and navy, they were a humiliating defeat at the hands of 'an Anglo-American common front' in whose existence they firmly believed. On the other, to Japan's politicians of the day, they had the advantage of limiting the budget for naval building which made up such a high proportion of the budget and cutting the cost of maintaining an expeditionary force in North-East Asia. Following this, Japan's chief delegate to the Washington Conference, Admiral Katō Tomosaburō, was appointed Prime Minister in June 1922 and served until August of the following year. This seemed to be a symbolic acceptance of the settlement with which Katō had been associated. It seemed to represent a triumph of internationalism in Japan and a victory for what the Japanese call the 'Washington system'. If the Washington treaties were 'Japan's Versailles', could it be said that the 1920s were 'Japan's Weimar period'? To be sure, historians have been able to trace the rumblings of nationalist and expansionist forces in Japan in that decade. But they were probably unrepresentative of the mainstream of political thinking and public sentiment. Japan, in the main, accepted the restrictions which had been imposed on it by international pressure.

The 1920s were for Japan a liberal decade when internationalist groups held sway. There was little open evidence, at least until 1927, of any movement that could be described as 'imperialist' or 'expansionist'. This is clearly shown in Japan's relations with Britain. When Britain in January 1927 asked Japan to join an international force to protect the settlement at Shanghai, Japan refused. When British and Americans shelled Chinese forces two months later because of the Nanjing Incident, the Japanese again abstained. At this phase they were anxious to be seen not to associate with what the Chinese called 'the Anglo-American imperialists'.

The next significant example of 'imperialism' was the Mukden Incident of September 1931 which led to the Manchurian Crisis. One of the major Japanese authors on the subject, S. Ogata, has decribed what took place as 'defiance in Manchuria'. She thereby highlights the action of the Guandong Army, the Japanese frontier force in Manchuria guarding Japanese railway interests there, in stealing a march on the civilian Cabinet which was faced with a *fait accompli*.[7] Since the Chinese appealed to the League of Nations, the Tokyo government was forced (as it was deemed necessary) to defend what had taken place in an international forum. On a number of occasions the civilian Cabinet tried to limit the field of action of the army; but their attempts were, in each case, nullified by the defiance of the army. Finally, the army brought about the establishment of the state of Manchukuo and asked all the powers for recognition of the new state. The Tokyo government which had warned the Guandong Army to be careful over this dangerous course initially refused in March to grant recognition to the 'new state' on the ground that international opinion would not tolerate such a thing. It was not until a change of Cabinet that the question of recognition came up for review; and in September 1932, six months after the request had been made, Japan gave recognition to Manchukuo. During the Manchurian Crisis, the Tokyo Cabinet was generally sensitive to international factors and international opinion, while the army was disinterested. Thus, when at the end of the day, Japan left the League of Nations, the government did so with regret, while the army had all along held that the League was an agent of unnecessary restraint on Japan's actions and should have been discarded sooner.[8]

In sheer terms of square miles of territory occupied, there was no more successful piece of Japanese 'imperialism' than the occupation of South-East Asia and the South Pacific Islands in 1941–2. But even here there were policy options and alternatives which suggest that the drive on Singapore was not inevitable. The most powerful consideration was the dispute between the northern strategy of the army and the southern strategy of the navy. The army was anti-Comintern and anti-Soviet and had traditionally called for consolidation on Manchuria's borders against Soviet strength. The navy had for the first time included Britain among its contemplated enemies (along with the United States) when its leaders had thought it opportune to revise the National Defence Plan of May 1936, though it still ranked low among them.[9] From this point onwards the navy became more and more insistent on a southern strategy, though it did not support the army call for a full-scale alliance with the Germans. It was only in the summer of 1940 that the navy withdrew its opposition to an alliance with the Axis powers and thus cleared the way to the conclusion of the Tripartite Alliance (September). But in the next spring the Foreign Minister, Matsuoka, went to Europe and there concluded a Neutrality Pact with the Soviet Union.[10] Within a month, Germany invaded the Soviet Union. It is arguable that, if it had not been for this Neutrality Pact, Japan might have implemented its northern strategy. As it was, it proceeded gradually to pursue its southern strategy. Enough has been said to indicate that in this case as in the others cited, there were alternative policies available. There was no certainty about the direction of imperialism that was to be pursued and no inevitability about the form which expansion would take.

Judgements about Japan after 1945 have to be different in kind from those for the pre-1945 period. After 1952 documents are not available on which historians can base their judgements. So speculation is possible; but proof is difficult. These words of caution are necessary when one considers the years after the peace settlement of 1951. It is beyond dispute that there has been economic expansion on Japan's part in this period. It is doubtful whether this economic expansion should be identified with 'imperialism' or linked with Japan's search for a Greater East Asia Co-prosperity Sphere in the prewar days. The element of continuity between Japan's prewar and postwar economy is a hotly debated issue. On the one hand, the industrial technology of the 1930s and of the ordnance factories of the war years was available to postwar industrial regeneration. On the other, the destruction of plant by bombing and the reduction of plant by reparations were considerable. So there were countervailing factors at work as Japan embarked on the course of recovery. So far as international trade is concerned, there was not continuity in the sense that it was well into the 1960s before Japan became a major exporting country as it had been in the 1930s. For example, in the case of Britain, it was 1963 before Japan turned the bilateral balance of trade in its favour. Up to that time Britain had enjoyed a favourable trade balance. Moreover, there were marked dissimilarities between post-1952 trade and pre-1937 trade. The most notable features were: that there was for political reasons no major return to the China trade which had been the largest sector of Japan's export trade down to 1937; that American connections which had developed during the occupation period (1945–52) came to dominate the pattern of trade; and that the return to markets in South-East Asia was only gradual due probably to the fact that the countries in that area had been occupied by Japan during wartime. When the market was re-entered, it was overwhelmed; and Prime Minister Tanaka when he visited South-East Asia in 1974 was told very pointedly that his countrymen's trading practices were unacceptable. On his return to Tokyo he called together representatives of the exporters and told them so in no uncertain language. Taken together, these factors tend to suggest that there was not a true continuity and that the postwar period should be treated in a different category.

Nor can it be said that at a political level Japan's growing economic strength has been accompanied by much evidence of a desire for political hegemony in its own region. For most of the 1960s Japan was rightly described as taking a 'low posture' in its foreign policy. In the 1970s under the pressure of the oil and China questions it acted more independently of the United States. It would be a matter of debate whether Japan could even now describe itself as the leading power in the area.

It can be said of some powers that the end of empire does not bring to an end their economic predominance in areas which they had previously occupied. This could hardly be said of Japan. The core of its empire (Taiwan, Korea and Manchuria to quote them in order of conquest) had been under Japanese rule for several decades. After 1945 they became bitterly critical of Japan. The outlying parts of the Co-prosperity Sphere had short-lived occupations. They were held only until the surrender in 1945 or (as some would argue) not very effectively after 1943 when Japan lost command of the seas between its home islands and its empire. Japan is, of course, an important economic force in South-East Asia today but this is not the result of pre-1945 connections.[11]

New circumstances beget new techniques. The endeavours which Japan has made in South-East Asia since the 1960s might be described loosely as 'an informal trade empire'. This description may be acceptable as a category of scholarly analysis. It would not be readily understood by the Japanese for whom the term 'imperialism' (*teikokushugi*) is taboo and a thing of the past. At a government level, this was the message underlying the Fukuda Doctrine, announced by Prime Minister Fukuda during the course of a tour of South-East Asian countries in 1977.[12]

In this brief sketch it has not been possible to dwell on the extremely complicated story of Japanese imperialism in anything like the detail which that unique story merits. I have at most commented on some of the more significant peaks and troughs on the chart of Japan's expansion in the period down to 1945, with a short postscript on some aspects of the problem since then. In response to revisionist interpretations, I have served up the rather fuddy-duddy view that Japanese imperialism was based on military initiatives and actions. While, therefore, Japan's experience was in some measure unique, it is not entirely out of line with European theories of imperialism.

Notes: Chapter 7

1 *Shidehara Kijūrō* [Biography of Shidehara] (Tokyo, 1955), p. 499.
2 The original phrase 'Kasumigaseki to Miyakezaka' comes from *Shidehara Kijūrō*, p. 497; I. H. Nish, *Japanese Foreign Policy, 1869–1942: From Kasumigaseki to Miyakezaka* (London, 1977).
3 I. H. Nish, *The Origins of the Russo-Japanese War* (London, 1985), pp. 116–24.
4 Tsunoda Jun, *Manshū Mondai to Kokubō Hōshin* [The Manchurian question and national defence policy] (Tokyo, 1967), ch. 2. Also S. Okamoto, *The Japanese Oligarchy and the Russo-Japanese War* (London, 1970), and J. A. White, *The Diplomacy of the Russo-Japanese War* (Princeton, NJ, 1964).
5 'As soon as this war broke out, I notified Germany and France . . . that, in the event of a combination against Japan to try to do what Russia, Germany and France did to her in 1894 [sic!], I should promptly side with Japan and proceed to whatever length was necessary on her behalf.' Theodore Roosevelt to Cecil Spring-Rice, 24 July 1905, quoted in T. Dennett, *Roosevelt and the Russo-Japanese War* (New York, 1925), p. 2.
6 On the Washington Conference see A. Iriye, *After Imperialism: The Search for a New Order in the Far East, 1921–1931* (Cambridge, Mass., 1965), pp. 16–22.
7 S. Ogata, *Defiance in Manchuria, 1931–32* (Berkeley, Calif., 1964).
8 On the Japanese army during the crisis see M. R. Peattie, *Ishiwara Kanji and Japan's Confrontation with the West* (Princeton, NJ, 1975). On Manchuria, the best account is Kobayashi Hideo, *Daitōa Kyōeikoku no Keisei to Hōkai* (Rise and fall of the Greater East Asia Co-prosperity Sphere] (Tokyo, 1975), pp. 42–4.
9 Ikeda Kiyoshi, 'Japanese strategy and the Pacific War, 1941–5', in I. H. Nish (ed.), *Anglo-Japanese Alienation, 1919–52* (Cambridge, 1982), pp. 125–7.
10 Kobayashi, *Daitōa Kyōeikoku*, pp. 329–41. Also Oka Yoshitake, *Konoe Fumimaro: A Political Biography* (Tokyo, 1983), pp. 97–101.
11 For tables showing the export share of selected Japanese goods in overseas markets, see R. Sinha, *Japan's Options for the 1980's* (London, 1982), pp. 45–50.
12 I. H. Nish, 'Regaining confidence: Japan after the loss of empire', *Journal of Contemporary History*, vol. 15 (1980), pp. 181–95.

8 Imperialism and Revisionism in Interwar Germany

HARTMUT POGGE VON STRANDMANN

> Germany is a furiously 'expansive universe'.
> (Sir Eric Phipps, 28 March 1936)

If it is accepted that there are continuities between Germany's expansionist drive before 1914, its war aims of the First World War and those of the Second World War, then the twenty interwar years need to be analysed to see how German ambitions were kept alive after the defeat of 1918.[1] Such an analysis may also be useful for following the development of German imperialism in the twentieth century.[2] In this context it would be of particular interest to find out how Germany's first democracy coped with the unfulfilled aspirations of German society. The Weimar Republic suffered under the stigma of defeat and had to exist with peace terms which were intended especially to wreck the German Empire's bid for world power.[3] Wilhelmine Germany lost its colonies and its fleet. Any hopes of renewed drives into the East and plans for realizing *Mitteleuropa* were cut short by the breaking up of the Habsburg Empire and the creation of the so-called successor states in Eastern Europe. The strength of the army was substantially reduced and the victors hoped that the spirit of militarism had been broken. A large amount of German property abroad was sequestered and business lost out in world markets. In comparison with the terms of the peace treaty the territorial losses were less important for the reduction of Germany's role as a world power. However, they did increase the general feeling of resentment in the Weimar Republic.

Within Germany the political situation had changed after the revolution of 1918, but many sectors of German society refused to accept Germany's reduced power position. The unwillingness to come to terms with a smaller Reich found its expression in continuous political efforts to revise the peace terms, with the ultimate aim of abrogating the treaty as a crucial step on the path to restoring Germany as a full world power.[4] The widespread acceptance of revisionism as a political goal in the Weimar Republic highlighted the transitory character of Germany's first democracy and thus emphasized the problem of compatibility between democracy and imperialist ambitions. It was widely held that national aggrandizement could only be realized by a 'strong state', not a party democracy. Thus the desire for a 'strong state' reduced the Weimar Republic to a provisional institution.

It was realized during the Weimar Republic that the beginnings of national power ambitions were to be found in Bismarck's Germany.

However, because of the craving for a 'strong state', the similarities between a rising German Empire in the nineteenth century and the longing for a restoration of German power in the twentieth century tended to be overlooked. The acquisition of German colonies under Bismarck and colonial revisionism after 1918 are good examples of the similarity of power ambitions even under different political circumstances. The demand for colonies by a number of political groups after 1871 was very similar to the demand for a return of the colonies after 1918 by similar groups. However, neither the fulfilment of the colonial demands in the nineteenth century nor the hypothetical success of colonial revisionism after 1918 would have satisfied Germany's ambitions. It was not content with the number of colonies it possessed and its continuous efforts to gain more only helped to increase international instability after 1890 and contributed strongly to Anglo-German tensions. In the same way Germany's colonial revisionism after 1918 improved neither international stability nor Anglo-German relations. The German arguments for acquiring colonies in the first place and for demanding their return later on were sufficiently similar to create a certain link between prewar imperialism and postwar colonial revisionism.

There is, however, another dimension. Before 1914 Germany was dissatisfied with the size of its colonial empire. A simple return of its former colonies would not have satisfied the ambition for a considerable extension of its colonial possessions.[5] An article by Maximilian Harden, the editor of the influential periodical *Die Zukunft* and conservative critic of the Wilhelmine establishment, in which he pleaded for a greater Germany in 1904, could also have been published after 1918.[6] When referring to Bismarck's famous speech of 1871 in which the Chancellor tried to calm down international concern about the emergence of an empire in central Europe by calling Germany a 'satiated' power, Harden stated:

> But we are not 'satiated'. We need fertile land, we need large, open areas which could buy our goods at decent prices. This has become necessary since large industrial complexes have developed in the heat of a green house and since the living standard of our nation has risen considerably compared with previous times. Otherwise we shall be so 'dwarfed' that we become a second Belgium.

Harden did not mention emigration as a reason for colonies nor did he regard it as essential to be a colonial power in order to ensure a supply of raw materials. In this respect he was influenced by his friend Walther Rathenau, an influential industrialist and banker. Rathenau belonged to the electro-technical industry and that sector was more interested in co-operating with public institutions, in selling goods and in organizing markets, whereas heavy industry saw an advantage in having colonies if they were a secure source of raw materials. It follows from this division that it was mainly the light-industrial sector which supported the idea of informal empires and therefore something which could be called 'horizontal' expansion without direct political control. Heavy industry, on the other hand, could only sell well if economic development was in the hands of

Europeans who would also guarantee the safe extraction of raw materials. Thus heavy industry favoured, first, the existence of formal administration and, secondly, something which could be defined as 'vertical' expansion. The distinction between the two industrial sectors became more important in the interwar period when Germany was looking for new spheres of influence.

So far it has been argued that there was a certain identity between prewar imperialism and postwar revisionism. Consequently, the interpretations used for explaining prewar imperialism should be used for the postwar period as well. However, some crucial differences have to be borne in mind. After 1871 Germany emerged as a victorious and rising power. After 1918 it was defeated and tried to regain its lost position. It could be argued tht German imperialism before 1914 was characterized by a growing self-consciousness and the general conviction that great powers had a right to expand. This had very little to do with geographical situation, but was based on the assumption that economic power ought to have an equivalent political and territorial power. The press justified Germany's claim for a place in the sun by referring to its growing population, its economic strength and its status as a great power. The same arguments for expansion were repeated after 1918, but they did not have the same ring of confidence about them. Revision of the Versailles Peace Treaty and the return of the colonies were the features of several propaganda campaigns at a time which was otherwise marked by economic and political crises which had no parallel in either Bismarckian or Wilhelmine Germany. Socially defensive arguments or social imperialist tactics were not mentioned. It is interesting to note that in the revisionist debate no reference was made to any prewar crises, instability, or weakness. Whatever the structural difficulties of Wilhelmine Germany may have been they did not leave any impact on the revisionist discussion or influenced the desire to restore Germany to its prewar position in the first instance. Revisionism did not aim at a preservation of any status quo whether in foreign or domestic politics. In fact it was hoped that revisionist successes would lead to an abolition of democracy at home and change the situation in Europe.

Revisionism was not an end in itself but a slogan behind which various dreams for a greater Germany could be hidden. The term concealed the fact that a successful revisionism would lead to the realization of further power ambitions because the mere restoration of Germany's prewar position would not be regarded as sufficient. The accomplishment of revisionism was to be only the first phase of further German expansion. Thus one difference between prewar imperialism and postwar revisionism was political expediency, the other being a lack of national self-confidence in admitting to unashamed aims. This attitude may have influenced historiography which, on the whole, let the discussion of imperialism end in 1914. Neither the First World War not the continuation of postwar colonialism were, outside the socialist camp, interpreted from an imperialist point of view.[7] Therefore nationalist historians even missed the chance of brandishing British and French postwar imperialism. The takeover of German colonies and the expropriation of German property and concessions was not labelled as 'imperialist'. As Germany wanted to rejoin the other imperialist nations the chance for championing an anti-imperialist course was not taken up. Even the fact that Germany was the first major state to experience decolonization, albeit in an enforced form, was not used in any way against the continued existence of colonial empires. The colonial myth persisted and it was hoped that Germany would rejoin the 'colonial concert'.[8] Overseas colonies were still regarded as a necessary attribute for empires. In this context it is noteworthy that the Weimar Republic retained the term 'empire' as a name for the democratic state.

The war itself and the German war aims were discussed within a defensive context. The stance of German politics before the war was considered to be defensive as well. Even military offensives were defined as defensive in character. This attitude, which was motivated by attempts to free Germany from the stigma of having started the war, overshadowed the widespread dissatisfaction with the territorial status quo and the power position overseas as well as in Europe before 1914. Thus Germany was not a 'satiated' power. The war was regarded as the last chance to fulfil the ambitions for a 'Greater Germany', be it on the Continent or overseas. The defeat of 1918 stopped Germany in midflight, so to speak. The dream of a 'Greater Germany' was temporarily shattered and the bitter disappointment at the unfulfilled aspirations explained the rejection of the defeat, the legend of a 'stab-in-the-back' and the development of revisionism. Although a return to the *status quo ante bellum* might have appeared as the aim of revisionism, it would have meant a return to the state of dissatisfaction. Thus Germany would have resumed its prewar policies which led it to start the war. During the war Germany tried to gain a greater power base. Consequently post-Versailles revisionism expressed only the first step on the path to further expansion, but the term was sufficiently vague for the ultimate intentions not to be made obvious. Thus the possibility of revisionism made the Weimar Republic partially acceptable.[9]

Revisionism was not restricted to a bid for the return of the former German colonies and a greater slice of the colonial cake. It included the recovery of the territorial losses as well as expansion into the East, the rebuilding of Germany's military power and the regaining of its financial and industrial strength, in short, restoration to the status of a great power if not a world power. The final aim was to become a type of superpower based on a *Grossraum* in Europe and substantially enlarged colonial areas.

For obvious reasons the aims of revisionism could not be discussed with the same publicity as previous imperialist aims had been discussed before 1914 or on occasions during the war. Yet it is surprising to find how much the subject was discussed in public. Of course, during national crises, such as revolutionary threats, right-wing coups, the possibility of the disintegration of the Reich, hyperinflation and the French occupation of the Ruhr, revisionism did not figure prominently in public, but several goals were kept alive because of the propaganda activities of pressure groups. It is not improbable that in the case of colonial revisionism, a demand for the return of the colonies would not have occurred had this not been constantly articulated by various organizations of the colonial movement, most notably by the Colonial Society.

In any case, it was generally realized that the future of the German Empire depended largely upon the strength of the armed forces and the economy. Whereas the economy could be discussed in public, the rebuilding of Germany's military capacity could only be planned clandestinely.[10] However, without a substantial army and navy the success of revisionism depended on diplomacy and economic recovery. As power could not be used, at least for the time being, the existence of the Weimar Republic had to be tolerated. This was made easier because of the broad political consensus about the pursuit of revisionist policies.

In Wilhelmine Germany imperialist policies could be carried out without the active support of the Social Democrats. This was almost impossible after 1918. The broad basis for revisionism was also necessary to gain credibility for revisionism on the international scene.

It has been argued by historians that German imperialism was used as a palliative against domestic crises brought on by social division and economic slumps.[11] This view is based on the assumption that imperialist policies were regarded as risk-free within the international context. But this was not so and a domestic crisis caused by internal divisions ruled out a policy which might lead to international confrontations because of insufficient domestic cohesion. Imperialist policies, on the other hand, were supported by quite a broad section of society. Most contemporaries on the political right did not experience the existing social divisions as a great domestic crisis. They were more inclined to accept them as a fact of life. Imperialism was not seen as an instrument of manipulation. Instead it was regarded as a sign of positive dynamism which would appeal to a large cross-section of the population. The absence of famines, revolutions and wars in central Europe gave the impression of national strength and therefore of relative stability. Thus the nexus between imperialism and social crisis was not one of cause and effect. The separation of imperialism from the notion of crisis makes it plausible to link imperialism with revisionism in the Weimar Republic. Although the latter was riddled with internal crises and both disliked and rejected by a great proportion of the electorate, revisionism found, with its open-ended commitment, widespread support.

However, the success of revisionism in the Weimar Republic did not only depend on the degree of internal consensus. Internal consensus was necessary for a positive reaction among Western governments towards revisionism. And concessions to the German claim for revisionism were not dependent only on pressure from inside Germany. Whatever individual members of Western governments may have thought desirable, it would have been very difficult to override public opinion in Western countries, particularly in France, against concessions to Germany in the 1920s. A case in point was the Western attitudes towards colonial revisionism.

Inside Germany the torch-bearer of colonial revisionism was the Colonial Society. In the 1880s the colonial movement agitated for colonial acquisitions.[12] After 1918 the Colonial Society argued for a return of Germany's former colonies, but did not need to persuade the government.

Most political parties with the exception of the Communists and the Independent Socialists, favoured a return of the colonies. In fact the republican government subsidized the propaganda activities of the society, unlike its predecessors before 1914. Both sides realized that Germany needed muscle in order to put pressure on the Allies for a return of the German colonies. Therefore the Colonial Society regarded rearmament as a vital condition for eventual success.[13]

The society also believed that it would be easier to keep the German public interested if the economy was seen to be thriving, believing that the stronger the state and the economy the greater the chances of colonial revisionism. Initially, this line of political and economic expectation implied that the Colonial Society hoped for a consolidation of the republic, although it became clear later that the notion of a 'strong state' was more associated with an authoritarian government. Thus the colonial movement adapted to the general political trend which had begun to shift to the right away from a state of tolerance toward the republic.

From an organizational point of view, the different colonial societies worked side by side until 1922 when they co-ordinated their efforts and founded the Koloniale Reichsarbeitsgemeinschaft (KORAG – Imperial Colonial Working Association) as their head organization.[14] The aims were the same as before, first a return of the former colonies and then a realization of a German *Mittelafrika*. Initially, the colonial movement comprised 15,000–20,000 members, a figure which grew by about 5,000 during the second half of the 1920s.[15] The leading committees consisted socially of the same groups as in Wilhelmine Germany. They belonged to what might be defined as upper middle class. New members were comprised of former colonial officers.

Despite great efforts on behalf of the colonial movement, it failed to win a mass basis, but it was successful in lobbying parliamentarians who, in turn, were elected to committees of the colonial movement from 1920 onwards.[16] Four years later the KORAG renewed its parliamentary efforts and investigated the attitudes of all parties regarding a return of the former colonies.[17] The German Communist Party's (KPD) position was clear,[18] but the party leadership of the German Social Democratic Party (SPD) and the Bavarian People's Party did not respond at this time. The most active colonial party was the German People's Party (DVP). One of its members, Heinrich Schnee, a former Governor of East Africa, founded an inter-party committee in 1925 in which all parties except the Communists were represented.[19]

Membership of the committee was not the result of party decisions. Instead it was left to the discretion of Reichstag members as to whether they wanted to join. The voluntary aspect was especially designed to circumvent the refusal of the SPD leadership to commit itself fully to the colonial cause. In the early 1920s the SPD had been less keen on a return of the colonies, but had hoped for transfers of colonial mandates to Germany through the League of Nations.[20] This hope turned out to be an illusion, but the party was sufficiently in favour of some form of colonial possessions that it swayed the International Socialist Congress in Lucerne in 1919 and in Brussels in

1928 to support the German colonial claim.[21] This attitude helped the SPD to free itself from the anti-colonial stigma of the Stuttgart Congress of 1907, a development highly welcome among colonial supporters of the right.[22]

The German National People's Party (DNVP) and the German Democratic Party (DDP) asserted the colonial aims most strongly. However, in comparison with the DVP the enthusiasm of the DDP for the colonies seemed to have waned by the end of the 1920s. The demand for a return of the colonies was the second item in the party programme of the DDP.[23] Yet there was a strong section within the party which doubted the value of colonial possessions. It was overruled by a majority which believed that colonies reflected a nation's power and which thought that colonial revisionism was a useful ploy to keep a link to the parties further to the right. Moreover, the Democrats were of the opinion that colonial revisionism was a vote-catcher and had no intention of allowing the right to monopolize the issue.

Until 1927 the Democrats avoided a general discussion about the justification of colonial revisionism. There were also only a few members who were willing to extend the principle of national self-determination to the colonial situation.[24] After 1927 doubts grew among party members about the benefits of the former German colonies to the German economy and foreign policy. This trend was not an expression of scepticism about the value of colonialism in general, but seemed to be an indication of slackening support for colonial revisionism. The renewed campaign for colonies during the early 1930s, which emphasized the economic necessity for economic and political control over areas which could be detached from the world market, found hardly any echo among the Democrats. Obviously they realized that the main reason for this campaign was to keep the issue of colonial revisionism alive during the economic crisis in which the concept of *Mitteleuropa* and the economic penetration of Eastern Europe were becoming attractive goals.

The Catholic Centre Party (Zentrum) also supported colonial revisionism, but its enthusiasm for colonies was less pronounced than among the other non-socialist parties.

In comparison with Wilhelmine Germany, there were only a few great colonial debates in the Reichstag, mostly in connection with foreign political questions. During the debates on the trade treaties with Britain and Belgium, on the ratification of the Locarno Treaties, on Germany's entry into the League of Nations and, finally, on the British plans to unite the East African colonies, the demand for a return of the colonies was most vigorously put. The colonial revisionist consensus among the parties was sufficiently strong to avoid controversies.

Outside the Reichstag colonial revisionism was supported by industry, banking and commerce although there was some scepticism about the usefulness of colonies. Rhenish industrialists increased their efforts in the colonial campaign in an attempt to avoid the impression that revisionism could no longer be justified. In addition it was believed that economic reasons could give colonial revisionism a much greater impetus. Consequently, the Colonial Society was reorganized a few years later.[25]

Colonial revisionism was mainly supported by liberal and conservative groups, but the consensus did also include pressure groups, business circles and the state bureaucracy.[26] There was co-operation among the various organizations and institutions although it was not always well co-ordinated. However, the relationship between the German Foreign Office and the Colonial Society went further and from the beginning of 1919 a division of labour was developed. The Foreign Office subsidized the society in the carrying out of its propaganda activities, while the society supported the Foreign Office in its attempts to broach the colonial issue on every international occasion. The Foreign Office left it largely to the Colonial Society to conduct its propaganda activities and did not interfere in the society's decision to conduct its activities on two platforms, a nationalist one and an economic one. The slogan 'to be patriotic means to be in favour of colonies' had some appeal.[27] Other phrases must have had some effect because they were repeated so often. 'What was German must become German again', or 'never forget, always remember' were also applied to the colonial cause. The prewar argument about national prestige had been replaced by a reference to national honour. Colonial possessions were regarded as essential for Germany's rejuvenation and colonizing was seen as a task which gave a nation a specific purpose. However, the emphasis on national and legal arguments shifted during the second half of the 1920s to economic arguments. The national supply of raw materials and the extension of the national market were underlined as important reasons.

During the depression the economic arguments were adapted to the new situation. Now it was argued that colonial possessions would reduce unemployment, despite the fact that there was unemployment in Britain as well, would save foreign currencies, absorb any surplus population and enlarge Germany's trade zone unaffected by international trade barriers. Economic necessity was the overriding concern, but critics of the campaign pointed to the possibility of international tensions and to the omission of any reference to the reaction of the indigenous population in Africa or Asia. However, not much attention was paid to this criticism and it did not prevent the Colonial Society from finding supporters for its cause. Yet the society was unable to break out of its social confines and win over a much greater section of the population so as to become a mass-based organization.[28]

How did the other side of the originally agreed division of labour between government and colonial movement work? The demand for the return of the colonies was a constant aim of German foreign policy.[29] The colonial question was broached at the international conferences of Spa, Cannes and Genoa, but to no avail. The next initiative was planned for 1924 and comprised several co-ordinated measures.[30] First, the Ministry of Reconstruction inspired Schnee to publish a pamphlet refuting the so-called 'colonial guilt lie'. Then the fortieth anniversary of the annexation of South West Africa in 1884 was made into a public occasion at the Colonial Congress.[31] At the congress the Colonial Society asked for a redistribution of the colonies and wanted Germany to enter the League of Nations only if it were allowed to administer some colonial mandates as well. When the

Dawes Plan was introduced, revisionist demands could be freed from the complexities of the reparation payments.[32] Moreover, the Colonial Department within the Foreign Office was re-founded. Soon afterwards it came forward with a memorandum entitled 'Guidelines for our Colonial Policy'.[33] In this the economic penetration of the former colonies was advocated as the first practical step towards strengthening any revisionist demand. As a precondition for any success it was realized that the Germans must be granted equal status with other nationalities in the colonial territories. The author of the document then thought it would be expedient if more Germans settled in South West Africa. Propaganda activities were to be stepped up and it was hoped that Germany might be handed over a colonial mandate once it had joined the League of Nations. Consequently, the German government provided something like 34 million marks for subsidizing German enterprises in the former colonies and by 1930 the trade volume surpassed that of 1913, although the value dropped because of falling world prices.[34]

Foreign Minister Stresemann, a keen supporter of the colonial idea, tried his utmost to promote the case of colonial revisionism on the diplomatic stage. He was also the first to raise, during the Locarno negotiations, the demand for a return of the colonies in conjunction with the question of revising Germany's eastern borders. His demands were met with strong opposition from Britain and France; so the German Foreign Office had to change tactics.[35] However, in London, colonial revisionism was, as far as can be seen, not properly analysed and the link to other revisionist issues was not understood. It was not clear in London and Paris that every German government was bound to support colonial revisionism and instead of realizing the complexity of the problem in German domestic politics and its inherent dangers, the repeated revisionist demands were turned down.[36] Germany, on the other hand, tried again and again to stir up the colonial question. When it joined the League of Nations and the committee which dealt with colonial mandates, no opportunity was missed to press for something tangible in the colonial field, but to no avail.[37]

The lack of success of German foreign policy in this question gradually led to disillusionment among colonial supporters and subsequently the links between Foreign Office and Colonial Society began to loosen. By 1929 the relationship had reached its first nadir. When Hjalmar Schacht and Ludwig Kastl, the leading official of the Industrial Association, broached the subject of colonial revisionism during the negotiations for the Young Plan in Paris in 1929, it transpired that the initiative was taken without prior approval of the Foreign Office.[38] Their independent action provoked a strong rebuff from London and caused embarrassment in Berlin. It certainly did not improve the relationship between colonial movement and Foreign Office. Despite Stresemann's support for colonial revisionism the problem of settling reparation payments had become more pressing. Yet it was still hoped within official circles that something might be achieved with British support in West Africa or Portuguese Angola. It is not quite clear what brought about the change in the attitude of the Foreign Office. Did the constant British rejection of German demands weaken the resolution of the

German Foreign Office? Did the possibility of expansion into eastern Europe look more promising? Whatever the answer, colonial revisionism seemed to have reached a dead end. The Foreign Office still held out some hope for progress, presumably for domestic reasons, but this was not enough for the Colonial Society and it began to look for alternative political allies who would be willing to promote its cause.[39] Thus, through Ritter von Epp, the Colonial Society turned to the National Socialist Party, without however, severing its links with the German Foreign Office.[40]

While the first feelers were being stretched out to the National Socialists, the Association of German Industry seized the organizational initiative and suggested a merger of all colonial associations which drew financial support from industry.[41] This intended *Gleichschaltung* was not completely successful, but some people with business connections did move into prominent positions. It is not clear whether there was any link between the contacts made with the National Socialist Party and the taking up of positions in the Colonial Society by people with business connections. It seems likely that these moves were unrelated.[42]

Both these efforts must be seen as attempts to halt the downward slide of the colonial question on the list of revisionist priorities. The general discussion of a possible expansion eastwards had gained in attraction at a time when the National Socialists made their electoral breakthrough. In different circumstances a similar shift in emphasis had occurred before 1914, when concern about the position of Germany on the Continent took priority over overseas ambitions and a further expansion of the battle fleet.[43] The National Socialists certainly put the Continental expansion first, in spite of the attempts of the Colonial Society to influence the National Socialist leadership with its own views. The Colonial Society also tried to stem the growing popularity of the concept of economic autarky and of an eastwards expansion.[44]

Whereas Stresemann and Schacht worked for a return of the colonies together with a revision of the eastern boundaries for power political and economic reasons, in Hitler's mind Continental expansion had priority over any overseas interests.[45] Wolfe Schmokel and Klaus Hildebrand have extensively analysed Hitler's position in this respect.[46] According to them, Hitler's world power ambitions centred on expansion into eastern Europe. The experience of the First World War, military thinking in terms of space and the peace treaty of Brest-Litovsk helped to shape Hitler's ideas.[47] The Colonial Society tried to win Hitler over to their programme of colonial revisionism, but he stood by his position which was well known even at that time.[48] As the Colonial Society wished to retain good relations with the National Socialists, it had to adapt and admit that 'the pursuit of colonial aims did not hinder the solution of the eastern problem in any way'.[49] With this formula, co-operation seemed possible. By moving into Hitler's camp, the Colonial Society hoped to win the mass basis which had so far eluded the colonial movement, while the National Socialist German Workers' Party (NSDAP) welcomed the alliance with conservative and liberal forces.[50] Thus, however different the outlook of the colonial movement and the NSDAP may have been, the deepening domestic and international crisis created a revisionist consensus which formed a launching platform for Hitler's militant and radical foreign policy.

However, the arrangement between Hitler and the Colonial Society came into jeopardy when the National Socialist Party leader renounced all colonial claims in an interview with the *Daily Express* in 1931.[51] A new agreement had to be worked out in which the Colonial Society accepted that 'the old German problem of space' had to be solved and that 'the solution of the Eastern Question is the main task of German politics'.[52] At the same time, the Colonial Society hoped that 'the expansion overseas [is] of equal importance'. The NSDAP, on the other hand, did not go along with this reservation and expressed its support for colonial revisionism only as long as expansion into eastern Europe had top priority. As this question then appeared to be settled, Hitler was able to emphasize, in his negotiations with Britain, that there should be 'colonial equality' between the powers.[53] In March 1935 he impressed upon the Foreign Secretary Sir John Simon and Anthony Eden the 'justification' of the German colonial demands.[54] This initiated a process of rethinking in British foreign policy, but ultimately the British position remained unchanged and the German demands were rejected.[55] However, it was realized that if a general agreement with Germany was to be concluded further negotiations about colonial revisionism could not be avoided. In May 1937 Neville Chamberlain agreed to consider colonial concessions provided there was a general agreement with Germany accompanied by peace measures. Between November 1937 and March 1938 Chamberlain developed a plan which did not envisage a return of any colonies. Instead it offered colonial territories at the expense of smaller nations – colonial appeasement in the true sense of the word.[56] There was also a historical precedent for this plan, namely, the Anglo-German Agreement on the potential partition of the Portuguese colonies of 1898.[57] Hitler rejected this plan simply because he preferred a return of the former colonies. Once this plan for colonial appeasement had fallen through, the chances of a colonial agreement diminished rapidly. It is questionable whether they ever really existed.

Hildebrand has put forward the view that Hitler only took up the colonial demands after 1933 in order to strengthen his bargaining position when trying to conclude an alliance with Britain. If the alliance had come about he would have been willing to renounce all colonial and maritime ambitions and use British backing for his drive to the East. However, it is questionable whether this foreign political aspect was as decisive in Hitler's thinking as Hildebrand assumes.[58] It is also not clear whether a colonial renunciation included all colonial ambitions or only some. Furthermore, Hildebrand assigns to Hitler's foreign policy an underlying rationality and coherence which is difficult to trace. Without some rationality, however, the existence of a plan of seven escalating phases, with which Hildebrand interprets Hitler's foreign policy, is doubtful.[59] Hitler seems to have played the colonial card for tactical reasons: to have good relations with the colonial movement when this seemed to be of some use; in order to divert attention from his other expansionist aims; and in order to underline the supposedly peaceful intentions of his politics. Whether his demand for a return of the former colonies was an indication of his drive towards world domination or not remains an open question.[60] The use of the colonies as a tactical ploy in international politics appears to have been exhausted by 1938, and by the time Germany attacked Soviet Russia the activities of the Reichskolonialbund, which had been set up in 1936, were severely curtailed. Eighteen months later, in 1943, all colonial organizations were dissolved and colonial publications ceased. The dream of a colonial overseas empire was at an end.

As far as Britain was concerned, colonial appeasement did not figure prominently and the chances of success for Chamberlain's initiative in March 1938 were rated low.[61] In the Anglo-German negotiations between 1935 and 1938 the colonies had not been referred to all that often. Yet the colonial issue was at times a useful diplomatic testing ground for Germany's ambitions and British reactions.

In looking back over the interwar period it can be said that colonial revisionism raised, from the beginning, false expectations inside Germany. No power was willing to make any concession unless forced to do so. However, colonial revisionism helped to strengthen an atmosphere in Germany in which expansionist ambitions could thrive. The demand for more space could be aired freely under the cover of a 'colonial cloak' until the National Socialist concept of space became predominant. Thus colonial revisionism kept the desire for expansion alive.

For Hitler the colonial demands offered tactical opportunities in domestic and foreign policy, although he himself does not appear to have been very keen on pursuing colonial politics. Instead he, like many of his supporters, favoured the concept of territorial expansion in Europe which was strongly supported by military circles before 1914 and which gained widespread support during the war.[62] As the National Socialist interpretation of territorial conquest was underpinned by the desire to direct German settlers into these areas, it can be defined as a type of vertical expansionism.[63] This term implies settlement and rule in politically and administratively controlled territories. The proximity to military thinking in terms of conquest, subjugation, control and exploitation is obvious, but it could also apply to the intentions of some raw-material extracting companies which were in favour of vertical colonization because of a cheap supply of raw materials secured militarily and politically. Thus military concepts, which were merged with radical *völkisch* aims and were supported by specific industrial interests, formed essential elements of the National Socialist drive for more space.

All three elements also formed a part of the thinking of the colonial movement – a fact which might help to explain why the colonial movement found it relatively easy to reach an agreement with National Socialism. The other attraction for the colonial movement lay in the insistence on military strength which was a necessary precondition for Hitler's approach to politics and his ideas of expansion. It was realized in the colonial movement that ultimately only military force would bring about the desired revisionist results which the Weimar Republic seemed unable to achieve, and which it was hoped Hitler would be able to achieve before it was too late. Therefore the colonial movement tried to convert Hitler to colonial revisionism and when this was unsuccessful it was hoped that the planned expansion on the Continent could co-exist with an overseas oriented expansion. This illusion had eventually to be abandoned when Germany was faced with the realities of a war of conquest in the East.

It could be argued that the emphasis in the revisionist debate on the demand for a return of the colonies tended to neglect the revisionism of the armed forces without whose strength no real pressure could have been exerted. The colonial movement was aware of the need for military strength for successful revisionism. During the war a military group around Erich Ludendorff believed that a further series of wars among the European powers would finally establish one or possibly two superpowers.[64] The chance to belong to the superpowers would depend largely on the gains in territory and power made during the First World War. The peace treaty of Brest-Litovsk enabled military circles to realize the concept of a German-controlled *Grossraum* which was to make Germany economically autarkic and lay the foundations of a superpower. This concept was regarded as superior to that of a German-dominated *Mitteleuropa* because the latter was still centred in the middle of Europe and therefore vulnerable to any military or economic encirclement that might occur in the future. It was considered essential to rule over an area large enough to avoid the danger of becoming a second-class power. The area should be free from foreign interference and in case of war easily defensible. Economically Germany should then be able to run a self-sufficient war economy which could not be throttled by any sea blockade. For these reasons the Ludendorff group interpreted a return to the prewar situation as already a decline of Germany's power position.

The affinity of these concepts to Hitler's own ideas is obvious, but whatever the bridging function the republic fulfilled with regard to the development of National Socialism, the military leaders of the republic were in the first place concerned with territorial revisionism which could be seen as a first step to further expansion. In March 1926 the Reichswehr suggested a revisionist package which included freeing the Saar region and the Rhineland, regaining Upper Silesia and the Polish Corridor, merging with Austria and altering the status of the remaining demilitarized zones.[65] Consequently, military conflicts with France, Belgium and Poland seemed unavoidable. In anticipation of one or several wars, it was considered that Germany needed to rearm, while it was thought desirable that the German Foreign Office should bring about a reduction in French and Polish armaments. Restoring Germany to its former position in Europe was to be the first stage which was to be followed 'much later' by a reconquest of Germany's world-power status. Reducing French armaments and those of its East European allies was one aim which was to make it possible to introduce parity and thus German rearmaments. The ultimate goal was, however, to be the failure of all disarmament negotiations, assuming that Germany could avoid being blamed for this because only then would it be possible to begin with an unlimited rearmament programme.[66] It was therefore not surprising that the Reichswehr insisted that 'disarmament' politics should become Germany's most important political lever. The growing influence of the Reichswehr in the late 1920s and early 1930s was as much a fact as the determination to rearm one way or another was the practicable beginning of revisionism and therefore a bridge to Hitler. While the Reichswehr and Hitler were in broad agreement about the targets of revisionism and expansion, there is little evidence to suggest that the Reichswehr regarded Russia as a target for German expansionism, while Hitler referred to the possibility of conquering 'new space in the East' rather vaguely in his first discussion with army leaders on 3 February 1933.[67] But it was understood at this meeting that once revisionism had been emphasized in domestic politics first, the drive for more space was to be the most important military and political goal.

Despite some qualitative differences between Hitler's expansionist concepts and those held by the army leaders, it has to be stated that they were sufficiently close to complement each other. In 1918 the army had pressed for an eastward extension of German control, but during the Weimar Republic a more moderate group seemed to be in command with reduced aims. Hitler himself had rejected as insufficient the scope of the German prewar expansionist drive as well as the war aims, but revisionism, in general, and the plans of the army, in particular, formed a bridge between Wilhelmine imperialism and Hitler's own version of an eastward expansion.

Hitler's thinking was very akin to the ideas of the military with regard to the methods of extending German rule. As might be expected the notion of an informal empire did not appeal. Instead, any territorial expansion was perceived in terms of new boundaries, flag hoisting, subjugation, direct administration and sending in German settlers. These were the usual attributes of military conquest. But, whereas the military was primarily interested in extending Germany's power base through territorial acquisitions, Hitler adopted these ideas, but added through racialism a new dimension to them. In foreign politics the army-backed revisionism became the launching pad for a radical programme in imperialism. In domestic politics the army insisted on the importance of the revision of the military clauses of the Versailles Peace Treaty. This in itself – 'the fact of the growing military power' – already changed the field of political gravity in Europe during the early 1930s.[68]

Whereas the army and Hitler concentrated on the European continent, the navy was primarily concerned, as in the prewar years, with overseas expansion and the bid for world power. Thus the colonial movement was much closer to the navy than to the army. The navy regarded the colonial movement as the standard bearer for revisionism because it believed that colonial demands would appear more harmless than any naval propaganda for an enlarged navy. Although it was accepted that the power situation had changed 'temporarily', further overseas expansion had not been abandoned.[69] Nevertheless, many naval officers concurred with the view, which originally had gained ground between 1908 and 1913, that the army should be given priority for its budgets and its plans on the European continent. However, the navy was, unlike the army, unwilling to co-operate with Soviet Russia.[70] Relations with Russia were only tolerated as long as export opportunities existed. Otherwise Soviet Russia was regarded as the main enemy. In 1932 the view was widespread among naval officers that war with Soviet Russia was inevitable.[71]

In any case, there were a number of naval officers who challenged the primacy of the army and argued that Germany's economic growth since 1900 demanded an active involvement in world affairs which could only be carried out by a large fleet. Once 'liberation' from the constraints of the Versailles Peace Treaty had been achieved, such a fleet should be built. This view was repeated at the end of 1928 when the first postwar capital ship was constructed. It was regretted then that Germany was unable to compete with Britain, but once 'the chains of Versailles had fallen' it was expected that the present ship-building programme should fit neatly into plans for extending the navy. In direct reference to Bülow's speech of December 1897, it was made clear that Germany would never renounce its claim to a 'place in the sun'. A leading admiral explained this ambition:[72]

> The military power of a nation is the expression of its will for national self-preservation; the navy's task is to ensure that this nation will neither renounce its role in the world nor give up any share in the world's goods. German national existence and national power are dependent on this role.

To his mind, one of the main tasks army and navy were to have during the Weimar Republic was to foster such ideas among the German people. Seen from this angle, the political function of the army and navy was to be that of a special pressure group. If 'politics [was] the practice of power', and if rearmaments and expansionism were national goals, then it was difficult for army and navy officers to reconcile the existing democratic institutions with the tasks they regarded as necessary.[73] Moreover, as armed conflict was regarded as the most effective means for restoring Germany's power position, it was clear in the minds of probably most officers that aggressive revisionism, that is to say, imperialism, and democracy were incompatible.

Whether this attitude towards Weimar was inspired by a feeling of revenge following the defeat of 1918, or whether the mobilization of all possible forces for a renewed attempt to bid for world power was only conceivable, according to military opinion, by a popular-based, military and authoritarian regime, or whether the rejection of Weimar was the consequence of the militarization of society under Weimar, cannot be decided here. But it looks likely that a combination of all three factors influenced military thinking besides the more mundane tasks of defending the country and organizing the armed forces on a very reduced scale after 1919.[74] There is sufficient evidence to suggest that political and military revisionism occupied the minds of many officers more than the tasks of national defence. A relatively large number of memoranda and speeches have survived which support this suggestion. They did not raise much opposition because they fitted into the general revisionist climate and were part of an ongoing political debate. Finally, the transition from the Weimar Republic to National Socialist rule went smoothly because of a consensus with regard to revisionism and expansion. A further indicator of military adaptability to new political situations was exemplified by the navy's change of attitude towards Britain between 1934 and 1938, and its support for world-power aspirations in 1940.[75]

The legitimacy of the army's political intervention in favour of territorial expansion and world power aspirations was never doubted. The arguments for a greater Germany, such as Germany's need for a German-dominated area for food supplies, for reducing overcrowding and gaining military security in the centre of Europe influenced military as well as civil society. But there was another consideration. During the First World War, economic, social and political life was penetrated by military institutions to the point that the military ran the state. All this came to a sudden end in 1918/19, but it left a sphere in civil society which was consciously not relinquished by the military. The boundaries between military and civil society remained undefined to the extent that the military continued to be a strong political factor.

Military circles were largely influenced by revisionism, conquests and ideas of 'vertical' expansion which went hand in hand with visions of a large *Agrarstaat* with an important industrial sector. Although this view was linked to the idea of a formal empire, it did not exclude the notions of informal empire. Yet there was a contrast in method and perspective. Trade treaties, economic penetration, domination of markets, financial as well as industrial control and collaboration with ruling groups, were the instruments of informal empire building. As economic considerations formed the basis of informal empire building, it was not surprising to find the navy more oriented towards planning along economic considerations than the army. Thus it was mainly the navy which believed that Germany had no alternative but to become a world power for economic reasons.[76] Power depended on economic strength which, in turn, depended on an exclusive use of overseas trade. This line of argument was then used to justify colonial revisionism, the need for a big navy and a foreign policy which was mainly concerned with overseas areas. Although these aims were regarded as a function of imperialism it was accepted in naval circles that German ambitions for expansion in eastern Europe were more realistic taking the Reich's future power position into account. Traditional German business interests in eastern Europe and Russia were regarded as the torch bearers for the establishment of Germany's claim to this area as a German sphere of influence. One of the reasons why the navy agreed to this shift of emphasis was, bearing the experience of the First World War in mind, the geopolitical factor. The eastern European markets lay in the vicinity of Germany and any other west European influence there was at a disadvantage in the long run, compared to Germany. Did the geopolitical and economic lines of argument ever meet? Business operations in eastern Europe could not always be justified by a short-term rationale. There would always be companies which defended their activities in eastern Europe by referring to nationalist causes, but the majority believed that once Germany had regained its economic strength it would draw these neighbouring states into the German economic orbit so that a need for formalizing German predominance would not necessarily arise.[77]

However, immediately after the war there was no opportunity for Germany to see any expectations in economic expansion being fulfilled. As in other parts of the world, German investments were taken over and Germany lost about 60 per cent of its investments in this area, or in other words its value of investments sunk to about one-tenth of the prewar level.[78] Moreover, to free themselves from Austrian and German economic predominance, these successor states looked to western Europe and the United States, but these moves did not boost their economic independence.[79] In fact, all that happened was that the financial control centres moved from Vienna and Berlin to London and Paris. Consequently, trade barriers and an unwillingness to let in German investments made relations between Germany and her eastern neighbours difficult. Although German exports should have benefited from the old Austrian tariff of 1906 which was valid after 1919, the rapid depreciation of eastern European currencies effectively protected national markets until the mid-1920s.[80]

This may have deterred German investors, but did not prevent the development of German projects which were linked, to name but a few, to the Dresdner Bank, the Mannesmann group and Hugo Stinnes who tried to acquire leading Czechoslovakian, Hungarian and Austrian metallurgic firms.[81] Some of these plans did not succeed, but after 1925, when the last trade restrictions for Germany fell, it became easier to think in terms of a trade offensive.[82] In addition, German business was now able to raise international loans so that Germany's credit position improved. However, eastern Europe was not considered as a development area. The economies of the successor states were regarded as having complementary characters, a feature which would become more important if the German economy prospered. The official trade policy took account of this situation because the ministerial bureaucracy, the leading economic interest groups and the Berlin representatives of the large industrial firms co-operated. A look at the ministries involved, that is, the Ministry of Economics, the Ministry of Finance, the Ministry of Food and Agriculture and the Foreign Office, could give the impression that the ministries made economic interests serve political purposes, but it could easily have been the other way round.[83] In the event, a consensus between state bureaucracy and economic interests existed as to the potential of eastern Europe as an economic and political hinterland for Germany.[84]

Thus the question of who took the initiative in this respect misses the point of co-operation between economics and politics. A number of German business enterprises operated in eastern Europe before 1914 and formed the basis for the co-operation between economic interests and state bureaucracy. Yet they needed the help of the ministries when they renewed their activities in the successor states. As business activities formed the basis of German interests in eastern Europe it is worthwhile examining some of the German companies there. Recent research into the business operations of IG Farben, the Mannesmann group and the Siemens group in eastern Europe reveal that all three companies pursued different strategies and different aims.[85] Siemens, for example, concentrated on exports rather than direct investments abroad and eastern Europe was no exception.[86] In

1924/5 Siemens-Schuckert recorded 7·7 per cent of its foreign sales to eastern Europe, an amount which rose to 10 per cent in 1929/30. By 1936 the whole of the Siemens group sold 11 per cent of its exports in eastern Europe.[87] The Siemens subsidiary Telefunken, jointly owned with the AEG, by 1927/8 controlled 74 per cent of the Austrian, 65 per cent of the Czechoslovakian, 43 per cent of the Hungarian, 37 per cent of the Polish and 17 per cent of the Yugoslavian market in radios.[88] Osram, the manufacturer of electric bulbs, also jointly owned with the AEG, enjoyed a monopoly position in south-eastern Europe due to cartel agreements with GEC and Philips dividing the European markets among themselves. However Osram also produced bulbs in Czechoslovakia, Greece and Poland.

Despite numerous measures after 1919 which were directed against Austrian and German enterprises, Siemens was able to overcome organizational problems and re-establish its strong position in eastern European markets. Yet Siemens regarded the whole area only as a minor part of further expansion.[89] In following its prewar tradition, Siemens continued to conduct its eastern European operations through Vienna although this may have created resentment. Like most companies in the electro-technical sector Siemens preferred exports to manufacturing aboard, but the group was flexible enough to set up subsidiaries, service companies and even production facilities if this proved necessary. But on the whole industrialization was not in Siemens' interests.

Not all of Siemens' operations were successful. The group was about to obtain a concession from the Romanian government for installing a telephone network when the government with whom Siemens was on good terms was toppled by Prince Carol's *coup d'état* in 1930.[90] Consequently, the concession was granted to ITT as the latter was less 'compromised' by previous close contacts with the former government. This meant that vying for favourable positions with the respective governments was important, but it did not lead to an outright competition with American companies. Instead, allocation agreements which covered large areas replaced the free choice of customers. Due to the international cartel agreements Siemens was able to operate in the states which belonged to the Little Entente as well as those who lost the war in eastern Europe. Siemens was not a promoter of German interests in eastern Europe, nor did the group adopt the 'concept of a far-reaching economic domination over other European nations by means of a trade policy', an aim other companies pursued.[91] Siemens belonged to those enterprises which were more interested in the control of markets and informal political influence. As the group shared a duopoly with the AEG in Germany and bought all its raw materials after 1925 either from German sources or imported them, it was difficult to see how the group would benefit from German political expansion. In fact, Siemens tried to co-operate with British, French and American companies in the area and did not seem to be interested in any aspects of formal rule. Nevertheless, when Germany began to increase its political influence in eastern Europe in the late 1930s and early 1940s, Siemens went along with the new situation. But then eastern Europe was, even after taking the National

Socialist pressure for creating an autarkic *Grosswirtschaftsraum Südosteuropa* into account, of limited value for the group's overall export strategy. Yet the group could not afford to miss an opportunity with considerable development potential on Germany's doorstep.

In the case of IG Farben, the German chemical giant, the interest in eastern Europe was greater than that of Siemens. IG Farben's main customer in eastern Europe in the 1920s was Czechoslovakia, followed by Austria, Hungary and Romania.[92] Like Siemens, IG Farben was able to reconquer its overseas markets after 1925 and become the main chemical exporter, but its leading manager, Carl Duisberg, regarded south-eastern Europe as an area with the potential of becoming an important market in the future.[93] Like the electro-technical group, IG Farben preferred to export its products to manufacturing in east European states. Only after 1938, when it became clear that south-eastern Europe was to become an integral part of the German war economy and part of the envisaged *Grossraum*, did IG Farben change its policy and go over to direct investments in that region. However, exports and cartel arrangements remained the preferred method of operation, whilst capital exports were of secondary importance.[94]

During the world depression, IG Farben, although pursuing an inflexible financial policy in eastern Europe by which it lost some of its customers, helped to develop cash crops such as linseed in Hungary and soya in Bulgaria as well as Romania. The purpose was to enable these states to undertake compensation deals. Apart from these initiatives the group also operated through cartel agreements, especially in Czechoslovakia. Whether it was the aim to control that market, or to prevent the development of an indigenous chemical industry, or to do both, cannot be answered here, but it is difficult to see why IG Farben should have had an interest in welcoming the competition of a local manufacturer.

All this was part of IG Farben's business strategy abroad which was carried out in conjunction with Germany's foreign-trade policy.[95] The cartel agreements had little to do with official trade policy, but it can be assumed that the state bureaucracy was in favour of this strategy. It has been argued recently that the relationship between IG Farben and various ministries and embassies was sufficiently close as to make it possible for the group to influence foreign-trade policy towards south-eastern Europe.[96] It is difficult to prove such influence exactly, but in an atmosphere of co-operation an exchange of information and collaboration during economic negotiations would have been sufficient. The fact of a foreign policy consensus makes the question of who initiated it less relevant. In any case, both sides supported the concept of a *Grossraum*.

At the beginning of the economic depression, Carl Duisberg, the leading figure of IG Farben and for several years president of the German Industrial Association, advocated a return to free trade when he talked about the 'Future of the German Trade Policy'.[97] As a matter of fact, he rejected the idea of free trade between a cluster of small states and instead he preferred larger units. When in 1931 the possibility of a German-Austrian customs union was aired, he welcomed the chance for the 'emergence of a large

Wirtschaftsraum in Central and Eastern Europe'. A few days before Hitler was appointed Chancellor, Duisberg again emphasized the need for a German *Grossraumwirtschaft*.[98] However, he did not belong to those who linked the idea of a *Grossraum* with the concept of autarky. For him, free trade should be established between large and powerful trading blocs. He wanted to enlarge the German economic base so as to enable Germany to compete successfully with the economic powers of the future. Duisberg was not unique in proposing a *Grossraum*, but was important for lifting it into the area of economic planning. Together with the relevant German state bureaucracy, he regarded central and south-eastern Europe as belonging to the German sphere of influence. So far German aspirations had been blocked by British and French politics and capital exports from both countries, but since the world depression and especially since 1934, western influence was rapidly waning in these states, mostly because of the effects of the economic depression.[99]

Whereas Britain and France were mainly involved in capital exports, German industry was either interested in exports, as the two above cases showed, or in setting up multinational firms. A case in point was the Mannesmann group, Germany's leading tube manufacturer. Mannesmann was founded as a multinational concern with a manufacturing subsidiary in Komotau in Bohemia. Together with another plant purchased in 1905, the Österreichische Mannesmannröhrenwerke GmbH reached in 1913 about one-third of the sales of the entire Mannesmann group.[100] After the war the group did not lose its production facilities in the new state of Czechoslovakia, unlike the Mannesmann plants in Britain and Italy. The company saved its plant by several measures. It moved the seat of its Bohemian plant from Vienna to Prague, ceded 15 per cent of its joint-stock capital to the three largest Czechoslovakian banks and invited six Czechoslovakian businessmen to join the board of directors which was eleven strong. Despite this, Czechoslovakian majority decision-making remained in the hands of the five Germans and business strategy was decided in Germany.[101] Thus Mannesmann was able to keep its foothold in central, east and south-eastern Europe. In fact it was able to expand its business activities which were entirely financed by the earnings of Mannesmann-Komotau.

Despite having a German parent company, Mannesmann-Komotau had a sufficiently strong Czech skin to overcome anti-German sentiments in the Balkans. Moreover, the subsidiary expanded so that the Czech complex was called 'a concern within a concern'.[102] This proved very useful for market-oriented direct investments in eastern Europe, and supplied the parent company with valuable foreign currency in the 1930s under the policies of autarky of the National Socialist government. The benefits that the company drew from its multinational status did not prevent the management from going along with the concept of a *Grossraum*. The company welcomed the extension of German control over the Komotau area when that part of Czechoslovakia was annexed in the aftermath of the Munich Agreement.[103] Under these circumstances, the change from an active pursuit of horizontal informal business expansion to a coercive relationship in south-eastern Europe as part of National Socialist foreign policy did not seem to worry the Mannesmann group. As it adapted to new political circumstances after 1918 the group did not find it difficult to seize upon the new opportunities after 1938.

The behaviour of all three companies mentioned here gives the impression that they followed state initiative when, during the world depression, Germany started its trade offensive towards eastern Europe, with the intention of creating an autarkic *Grossraum* in this area.[104] Although industrial firms had kept German interests in south-eastern Europe alive and had provided economic information about the area as well as possibly even some rationale for the later expansion, they did not appear to be the pacemakers for Germany's drive to the south-east. Yet they helped to create a climate in which the transition from informal influence to the setting-up of a *Grossraum* became possible. The emerging consensus between business and state bureaucracy did not go as far as covering every form of expansion. Bilateral trade agreements were considered to be the best way to organize the economic relationship between Germany and its eastern neighbours. A new element emerged when, under Schacht's *Neuer Plan*, the east European economies were to be used for rearmament and eventually for war preparations. Bilateral trade and barter agreements offered considerable advantages to Germany because of the closer political ties which followed from such arrangements and which went beyond certain practical benefits, such as the use of trade-clearing arrangements which allowed Germany to purchase agricultural goods and raw materials in exchange for industrial products without using up any foreign currencies.[105]

In any case, by 1939 the east European economies were drawn into the German orbit and Germany's trade hegemony was in force.[106] That trade was the thin edge of the wedge was not difficult to foresee if National Socialist intentions with regard to the south-east were taken into account. Thus the head of the Hungarian trade delegation summed up the situation in February 1939 when new trade negotiations took place between Germany and Hungary: 'In general the tendency became obvious that Hungary was to be degraded to the level of a raw material base.' Germany laid down the conditions under which the Hungarian economy was to satisfy German demands. What was true for Hungary also applied to the other states in south-eastern Europe. During the war Germany's influence became even stronger and reduced the 'region to the level of sectors of her [Germany's] war economy'.[107] As in the case of Hungary, enforced 'co-operation' became the hallmark of Germany's economic relations with those eastern neighbours whose states continued to exist. To what extent economic considerations served political ones or, in other words, to what extent the trade followed the flag by this stage can be gathered from the expansion of Hermann Göring's economic empire of the Reichswerke into occupied and independent states.[108] The purpose was to serve Germany's war effort and to prepare the ground for the economic and political New Order once the war was over and after British and French capital had been expelled from eastern Europe.

The ideas and elements of Germany's intensified trade policy of the late 1930s had existed beforehand. From 1920 onwards it has been argued in circles of the ministerial bureaucracy that Germany should use its economic strength after its recovery as a political tool for German expansionist ambitions. Economic strength was regarded as a precondition for the existence of a strong state which would ultimately give substance to imperialist plans. In the early Weimar Republic neither a strong economy nor a strong state existed, but the wish to strengthen both underpinned revisionism. However, Germany's means were limited and thus its early revisionist policies did not achieve anything which satisfied the supporters of revisionism. By the late 1920s Germany's position had recovered to some extent and, as in military politics, the Weimar Republic was in a position to pursue a more independent line. Heavy industry pressed the government to make more use of the regained economic strength and hoped to link eastern Europe more closely to Germany. The German Foreign Office, thinking along similar lines, turned against the so-called Briand Plan of February 1930 for an economic and eventually political European union.[109] The plan was designed to confirm Germany's eastern borders and thus undermine revisionism. To counteract French plans for stabilizing the successor states in eastern Europe, Bülow, permanent under secretary in the Foreign Office, argued that Germany must do nothing to hinder its expansion in Europe because 'the possibilities for it lie only in the east and southeast'. And a few days later he advised that any acceptance of the Briand Plan should be made the precondition for revising the peace treaties with a special view to eastern Europe:

> German politics must exert its leverage there [Eastern Europe] because it is there that the possibilities for Germany lie ... the *union with* Austria must be the most urgent task of German diplomacy, for developments in the South East could be influenced and guided in Germany's interests from an Austria belonging to Germany ...[110]

Against Briand's anti-revisionist policy, Germany suggested in March 1931 setting up a customs union with Austria which half a year later had to be dropped because of French and Czech pressure, and the financial crisis in Austria. Like Siemens and IG Farben the German Foreign Office believed that Vienna was still the key to south-eastern Europe. This was also true for the Rhenish Westphalian heavy industry under whose auspices the Mitteleuropäischer Wirtschaftstag (Middle European Economic Association) was reorganized in 1931.[111] But for the heavy industry the customs union with Austria was only the first step towards the foundation of a German-dominated *Mitteleuropa* which would be realized in the near future. To begin with, the leading industrial associations were not involved but had to toe the line eventually because the leading companies exerted sufficient pressure. The takeover of the Mitteleuropäischer Wirtschaftstag, which had been set up in 1925, by heavy industry demonstrated the political weight and the leading position of heavy industry in the German economy. It also indicated the reorientation of German industrial politics away from free trade.

Earlier on, heavy industry took part in the Deutsch-Österreichische

Arbeitsgemeinschaft in Vienna, but found it more useful to take part in an organization which would be completely dominated by heavy industry. Under the impact of the world depression and the planned intensification of revisionism, it seemed opportune to the representatives of heavy industry to break out of the 'growing economic encirclement of Germany' and activate Germany's economic interests in east as well as south-eastern Europe.[112] Thus heavy industry found itself in agreement with the official foreign policy which worked for an horizontal expansion into eastern Europe and which aimed at reorganization and realignment of those economies.[113] Under the National Socialist regime the political and industrial plans needed only to be picked up and intensified. The idea of a German-south-eastern European agrarian cartel, sponsored by heavy industry, was to take shape after 1933. Unlike Siemens and IG Farben which were oriented towards the world market, German heavy industry was more interested in the German domestic market. However, the idea of a *Grossraum* acted as the common denominator for both orientations because behind it stood the common aim for an enlarged economic basis which would benefit Germany's position on the world market and at home.

The differences in the industrial camp were further enhanced by the stance German agriculture took. Rural interests prevented the von Papen and von Schleicher governments from offering preferential treatment to agricultural imports from the Balkans during the German agricultural crisis. The appeal of the NSDAP to the rural voter might have become even stronger. Even after Hitler came to power German agriculture stood in the way of intensified trade with the south eastern European states.[114] It was at this juncture that IG Farben introduced compensation deals with agricultural products. Thus the combine bought Hungarian cereals at high prices, sold them at a loss to third countries and made good the loss by charging high prices for its chemical exports to Hungary.[115] Thus a steep decline in trade was prevented, especially at a time when the economic recovery was threatened due to the overvaluation of the German mark and the imposition of trade barriers in Britain and France. A way out was suggested by the permanent under secretary in the Ministry of Economics, Hans Posse, who persuaded the Cabinet to change Germany's trade pattern and make more use of bilateral agreements.[116] The subsequent attempts to implement autarky revealed the continuous shortage of foodstuffs and made agriculture more amenable to trade with the south-east.

The bilateral trade offensive which had begun during the depression differed from the economic, semi-autonomous activities of the large companies in south-eastern Europe.[117] Now the government was involved directly in fostering economic relations, but without the business activities of the various companies which laid the foundations for the first steps towards an 'informal empire', the transition to intensified activities in that region as well as ultimately to the National Socialist expansionist aims would have been more difficult. Under National Socialist policies the previous horizontal expansion was superseded by a political and, in this sense, vertical move which was to make those economies completely subservient to German needs. The aim was to establish full economic hegemony by trade policies which would then strengthen Germany's foreign political position and later make possible the National Socialist conquests in the east. As H.-J. Schröder has pointed out, one of the reasons why Germany after 1933 was more successful in its efforts in that region than the Weimar Republic was the fact that it was possible to reduce the internal agrarian opposition in Germany to an active trade policy including agricultural products.[118]

The concept of *Grossraum* was taken over by the concept of *Lebensraum* which had a racialist dimension. Although the terms 'autarky' and '*Lebensraum*' were opposed by those who continued to have an interest in world trade, the militarily backed 'strong state', originally desired by business circles as well, took over the revisionist rhetoric and laid down its own aims for German expansion.

As the revisionist consensus of the Weimar Republic, supported by liberal and conservative groups including the Centre Party (Zentrum) and endorsed by the right-wing of the Social Democrats, was synonymous with an open-ended commitment to a future imperialism, it was relatively easy to graft the National Socialist type of expansionism on to existing schemes. However, the plan of military conquests in the east was a far cry from any economically motivated expansionism in south-eastern Europe. Whether the relatively low trade figures – by 1939 only 17·7 per cent of the German trade volume – influenced military thinking and National Socialist planning in such a manner that military conquests appeared to be the only way to provide the war economy with the necessary raw materials and goods as well as the population with sufficient foodstuff, remains unclear.[119] But it looks much more likely that the plan for an eastern expansion was conceived before the effects of the trade figures had sunk in. Ultimately, military conquests were the hallmark of National Socialist imperialism. The dynamic of the system did not allow informal empire building and trade dependencies to develop.

Nevertheless, states of satellite status were tolerated up to a point, without much sovereignty or independence left. To what extent the development of German trade in South America fits into this interpretation of German imperialism will have to be examined elsewhere,[120] but it seems to be closer to horizontal rather than vertical expansion.

As far as vertical expansion was concerned the case of south-eastern Europe was a mixture of conquest and political subjugation. The National Socialist idea of a New Economic Order in eastern Europe had more affinity to vertical than to horizontal expansion. With the exception of Poland and Czechoslovakia the remainder of south-eastern Europe still fitted into a picture of an economically-based *Grossraum* in which Germany held political supremacy.[121] *Lebensraum*, on the other hand, emphasized a different aspect of vertical expansion. It was directed more towards Poland and Russia than the south-east and included racialist considerations, the extermination of east European Jewry and the sending of German settlers.

What had started – at least as far as the literal meaning of the term revisionism goes – as a bid for revising the terms of the Versailles Peace Treaty, ended up as a bid for political and economic hegemony on the

European continent. After the previous bid for a larger empire had failed during the First World War, revisionism became the expression of frustrated power ambitions and demonstrated the latent desire for gaining a larger power basis. Because of the lack of military power the planned renewal of the expansionist campaign was forced to become *attentiste* in character. However, the repetition of an imperialist effort had little chance of success without the existence of a 'strong government', a 'strong economy' and a 'strong military force', a problem which was solved to some extent in the minds of many revisionists after Hitler's seizure of power. Revisionism started as a negation of the postwar situation in Europe and a rejection of the democratic order inside Germany. Once republican revisionism had, in the eyes of the political right, failed to achieve any substantial results, the radical alternatives the National Socialists seemed to supply became attractive. However, the quality of the National Socialist alternative should not be overemphasized. Revisionism provided the common element which linked together the revisionist concepts, ambitions and policies of the Weimar Republic with those of the National Socialist regime. The military bid for a greater Germany during the First World War, the militarization of society in the Weimar Republic and the military character of the National Socialist movement gave the concept of imperialist conquest priority over any other form of expansionism. It was not the nature of a radical alternative which made this type of imperialism acceptable to many Germans; in fact it was its affinity to the various expansionist ambitions during the Weimar Republic. Under the conditions of a 'strong government', 'strong economy' and 'strong military force' projected (*attentiste*) imperialism became reality, which would have been impossible without a dynamized revisionism.

Notes: Chapter 8

1 A section of the present article was published in an extended form in H. Pogge von Strandmann, 'Deutscher Imperialismus nach 1918', in D. Stegmann, B.-J. Wendt and P.-C. Witt (eds), *Deutscher Konservatismus im 19. und 20. Jahrhundert. Festschrift für Fritz Fischer zum 75. Geburtstag* (Bonn, 1983), pp. 281–93. See for a discussion of 'continuity', A. Hillgruber, *Kontinuität und Diskontinuität in der deutschen Aussenpolitik von Bismarck bis Hitler* (Düsseldorf, 1971); F. Fischer, *Der Erste Weltkrieg und das deutsche Geschichtsbild, Beiträge zur Bewältigung eines historischen Tabus* (Düsseldorf, 1977); A. Hillgruber, *Deutsche Grossmacht- und Weltpolitik im 19. und 20. Jahrhundert* (Düsseldorf, 1977); H.-J. Schröder, 'Deutsche Südosteuropapolitik 1929–1936. Zur Kontinuität deutscher Aussenpolitik in der Weltwirtschaftskrise', *Geschichte und Gesellschaft*, vol. 2 (1976), pp. 5–32; K. H. Jarausch, 'From Second to Third Reich. The problem of continuity in German foreign policy', *Central European History*, vol. 12 (1979), pp. 68–82. See also B.-J. Wendt, 'Deutschland in der Mitte Europas. Grundkonstellationen der Geschichte', *Deutsche Studien*, vol. 29 (1981), pp. 251–8.
2 One of the few books which deal with this problem is: L. Dehio, *Deutschland und die Weltpolitik im 20. Jahrhundert*, 3rd edn (Frankfurt-on-Main, 1961).
3 A. Hillgruber, 'Unter dem Schatten von Versailles – Die aussenpolitische Belastung der Weimarer Republik: Realität und Perzeption bei den Deutschen'; and the subsequent discussion in K. D. Erdmann and H. Schulze (eds), *Weimar. Selbstpreisgabe einer Demokratie. Eine Bilanz heute* (Düsseldorf, 1980), pp. 51–80.
4 See for 'revisionism' and its domestic aspects, M. Salewski, 'Das Weimarer Revisionssyn-

Imperialism in Interwar Germany 115

drom', *Aus Politik und Zeitgeschichte. Beilage zur Wochenzeitung Das Parlament*, 12 January 1980, pp. 14–25. See also M. Rothbarth, 'Grenzrevision und Minderheitenpolitik des deutschen Imperialismus. Der Europäische Minderheitenkongress als Instrument imperialistischer deutscher "Revisionsstrategie" 1925–1930, *Jahrbuch für Geschichte*, vol. 24 (1981), pp. 215–40; G. Wollstein, *Vom Weimarer Revisionismus zu Hitler. Das Deutsche Reich und die Grossmächte in der Anfangsphase der nationalsozialistischen Herrschaft in Deutschland* (Bonn, 1973), pp. 14 ff.

5 W. K. Schmokel, *Dream of Empire: German Colonialism 1919–1945* (New Haven, Conn. and London, 1964). The subsequent page numbers refer to the German edition: *Der Traum vom Reich. Der deutsche Kolonialismus zwischen 1919 und 1945* (Gütersloh, 1967). See also K. Hildebrand, *Vom Reich zum Weltreich. Hitler, NSDAP und koloniale Frage 1919–1945* (Munich, 1969); A. Rüger, 'Die kolonialen Bestrebungen des deutschen Imperialismus in Afrika (Vom Ende des ersten Weltkrieges bis zur Locarno-Konferenz)', unpublished MS, Berlin, 1969; idem, 'Der Kolonialrevisionismus der Weimarer Republik' and J. Ballhaus, 'Kolonialziele und -vorbereitungen des faschistischen Regimes 1933–1939' – both articles in H. Stoecker (ed.), *Drang nach Afrika. Die koloniale Expansionspolitik und Herrschaft des deutschen Imperialismus in Afrika von den Anfängen bis zum Ende des Zweiten Weltkrieges* (East Berlin, 1977), pp. 243–314; A. Rüger, 'Die kolonialen Bestrebungen der imperialistischen deutschen Bourgeoisie und ihre Reaktion auf Forderungen nach Freiheit für Afrika 1917–1933', *Jahrbuch für Geschichte*, vol. 24 (1981), pp. 241–82.

6 H. D. Hellige (ed.), *Walther Rathenau, Maximilian Harden. Briefwechsel* (Munich and Heidelberg, 1983), p. 139.

7 See note 5 above.

8 A small minority of so-called colonial experts watched with concern the Pan-African Congress of 1919 in Paris and the National Congress of British West Africa of 1920 in Accra. A leading German colonial politician, Albert Hahl, believed in 1923 that the struggle for independence in Africa would start soon and that Germany's chances for colonial territories would grow as the colonial powers would need to call upon Germany for assistance. See Rüger, 'Die kolonialen Bestrebungen', p. 247.

9 Salewski in his article overlooked the links between prewar imperialism and revisionism as well as the expansionist consequences of revisionism. See Salewski, 'Das Weimarer Revisionssyndrom', p. 18. It is to be regretted that Salewski did not discuss colonial revisionism.

10 Typical for the former are Stresemann's speeches of autumn 1925: 'The last method which leaves us as a great power is our economic power and it is that we have to use to make foreign policy' (22 November 1925). In his second speech he pointed out that Germany's chance was to 'use economics to solve political questions' (14 December 1925). H. A. Turner, 'Eine Rede Stresemanns über seine Locarnopolitik', *Vierteljahreshefte für Zeitgeschichte*, vol. 15 (1967), p. 434. See also Schröder, 'Deutsche Südosteuropapolitik', p. 7.

11 See for a sympathetic summary of this view with a reference to further literature, W. J. Mommsen, *Theories of Imperialism* (London, 1981), pp. 93 ff.

12 K. Klauss, 'Die Deutsche Kolonialgesellschaft und die deutsche Kolonialpolitik – von den Anfängen bis 1895', PhD diss., Berlin, 1966; H.-U. Wehler, *Bismarck und der Imperialismus* (Cologne and Berlin, 1969), pp. 139–68.

13 Hildebrand, *Vom Reich zum Weltreich*, p. 69.

14 Schmokel, *Der Traum vom Reich*, pp. 19–20; Hildebrand, *Vom Reich zum Weltreich*, p. 58.

15 Hildebrand, *Vom Reich zum Weltreich*, pp. 53–4, and 96; Schmokel, *Der Traum vom Reich*, p. 23.

16 Hildebrand, *Vom Reich zum Weltreich*, p. 57.

17 ibid., p. 58.

18 See now Rüger, 'Die kolonialen Bestrebungen', pp. 254 ff.

19 Hildebrand, *Vom Reich zum Weltreich*, pp. 59–60; Rüger, 'Der Kolonialrevisionismus', pp. 253 ff., pp. 261–2.

20 ibid., pp. 253–4. See also the resolution of the Görlitz Party Congress of 1921.

21 Schmokel, *Der Traum vom Reich*, pp. 25–6.

22 *Internationaler Sozialisten-Kongress zu Stuttgart 1907* (Berlin, 1907), pp. 84–5; *Protokoll über die Verhandlungen des Parteitages der SPD zu Essen* (Berlin, 1907), p. 132.

23 J. C. Hess, *'Das ganze Deutschland soll es sein'. Demokratischer Nationalismus in der Weimarer Republik am Beispiel der Demokratischen Partei* (Stuttgart, 1978), p. 113.
24 Rüger, 'Die kolonialen Bestrebungen', pp. 244, 260 ff., 272 ff.
25 ibid., p. 280.
26 Rüger, 'Der Kolonialrevisionismus', pp. 249–50; Hildebrand, *Vom Reich zum Weltreich*, p. 53.
27 Nationalist propaganda was also used by the League of Colonial Friends which was founded in 1922 to win over members of the trade unions to colonial revisionism. The league had about 15,000 members in 1924 and was subsidized by the Colonial Society which itself received the money from the Foreign Office. The fund had been made available by the Ministry of Finance and was outside the control of the Reichstag. See Rüger, 'Die kolonialen Bestrebungen', pp. 268–9.
28 At a meeting of the KORAG on 28 January 1929 the chairman of the colonial section of the German Agricultural Association complained that not enough colonial propaganda was being produced so that 'only 1 per cent of the German people showed an interest in the colonial question'. Rüger, 'Die kolonialen Bestrebungen', pp. 278–9. Half a year earlier the Colonial Society published a colonial programme at the International Press Fair in Cologne. The slogan 'Raum ohne Volk und Volk ohne Raum' [space without people and people without space] was used for a display of maps. ibid., p. 273.
29 Rüger, 'Der Kolonialrevisionismus', p. 254; idem, 'Die kolonialen Bestrebungen', p. 244.
30 The head of the colonial department in the Ministry of Reconstruction, Meyer-Gerhard, tried to co-ordinate the campaign from the summer of 1923 onwards (Rüger, 'Die kolonialen Bestrebungen', pp. 248 ff). The Ministry of Finance subsidized the campaign and the first instalments came to 241,000 gold marks of which 15,000 gold marks were to be used for the translation and distribution of Schnee's pamphlet in which he argued against the so-called 'colonial guilt lie'.
31 ibid., pp. 249 ff.
32 Hildebrand, *Vom Reich zum Weltreich*, pp. 66–7.
33 Rüger, 'Der Kolonialrevisionismus', p. 260. The document was approved of by Stresemann on 10 November 1924.
34 ibid., p. 264.
35 ibid., pp. 262–3; L. S. Amery, *The German Colonial Claim* (London and Edinburgh, 1939), pp. 122–3.
36 A. E. Ekoko, 'The British attitude towards Germany's colonial irredentism in Africa in the inter-war years', *Journal of Contemporary History*, vol. 14 (1979), p. 289. See also Public Record Office London, FO 371/11304, memo. of 20 August 1926.
37 Even the argument that the re-establishment of German colonies might divert German revanchism did not leave much of an impression.
38 Rüger, 'Der Kolonialrevisionismus', p. 270; Hildebrand, *Vom Reich zum Weltreich*, pp. 129 ff. Earlier on Richard von Kühlmann had visited the British ambassador in Paris, Sir William Tyrell, in order to renew the negotiations, broken off in 1914, about the partition of the Portuguese colonies. In his article (see note 54 below) A. Crozier did not realize who inspired Kühlmann to his trip. According to Hildebrand it was Schacht. See also Rüger, 'Die kolonialen Bestrebungen', p. 275.
39 Hildebrand, *Vom Reich zum Weltreich*, p. 130.
40 Rüger, 'Der Kolonialrevisionismus', p. 270.
41 Rüger, 'Die kolonialen Bestrebungen', pp. 280–1.
42 Rüger, 'Der Kolonialrevisionismus', pp. 270–5.
43 H. Pogge von Strandmann, 'Nationale Verbände zwischen Weltpolitik und Kontinentalpolitik', in H. Schottelius and W. Deist (eds), *Marine und Marinepolitik 1871–1914*, 2nd edn (Düsseldorf, 1981), pp. 301, 309.
44 D. Petzina, *Autarkiepolitik im Dritten Reich. Der nationalsozialistische Vierjahresplan* (Stuttgart, 1968), pp. 19 ff.
45 Schmokel, *Der Traum vom Reich*, p. 88; H. Schacht, *The End of Reparations, the Economic Consequences of the World War* (Glasgow, 1931).
46 Schmokel, *Der Traum vom Reich*, ch. 4; Hildebrand, *Vom Reich zum Weltreich*, pp. 70–88, 212–13. See also Hildebrand, *The Foreign Policy of the Third Reich* (London, 1973).
47 A. Hillgruber, *Deutschlands Rolle in der Vorgeschichte der beiden Weltkriege* (Göttingen,

1967), p. 65; A. Kuhn, *Hitlers aussenpolitisches Programm* (Stuttgart, 1970), pp. 99–104. See also the summary by J. Hiden, 'National Socialism and foreign policy 1919–1933', in P. D. Stachura (ed.), *The Nazi Machtergreifung* (London, 1983), pp. 146–61.
48 There is not enough evidence to suggest that Hitler wanted, as Kuhn alleges, a recovery of Germany's overseas colonies before 1923. Kuhn, *Hitlers aussenpolitisches Programm*, pp. 96–9.
49 Hildebrand, *Vom Reich zum Weltreich*, p. 174.
50 Hillgruber, 'Unter dem Schatten von Versailles', p. 65.
51 Hildebrand, *Vom Reich zum Weltreich*, pp. 176, 214.
52 ibid., p. 225.
53 Ekoko, 'The British attitude', p. 290; Hildebrand, *Vom Reich zum Weltreich*, pp. 301–14.
54 Hildebrand, *Vom Reich zum Weltreich*, pp. 362–3, 470–1; A. Crozier, 'Imperial decline and the colonial question in Anglo-German Relations 1919–1939', *European Studies Review*, vol. 11 (1981), p. 227.
55 Crozier, 'Imperial decline and the colonial question', pp. 228 ff.; Hildebrand, *Vom Reich zum Weltreich*, pp. 293–305, 752–65.
56 Crozier, 'Imperial decline and the colonial question', pp. 230–3; W. R. Louis, 'Colonial appeasement 1936–1938', *Revue Belge de Philologie et d'Histoire*, vol. 49 (1971), pp. 1175–91.
57 P. M. Kennedy, *The Rise of the Anglo-German Antagonism 1860–1914* (London, 1980), pp. 235–6.
58 Hildebrand, *Vom Reich zum Weltreich*, pp. 261–2, 270.
59 Hiden, 'National Socialism and foreign policy', pp. 152–3. See also B.-J. Wendt's review of Hildebrand's book in *Historische Zeitschrift*, vol. 213 (1971), pp. 204–8.
60 H. Gollwitzer, *Geschichte des weltpolitischen Denkens*, Vol. 2 (Göttingen, 1982), p. 545; D. Aigner, 'Hitler und die Weltherrschaft', in M. Funke (ed.), *Hitler, Deutschland und die Mächte. Materialien zur Aussenpolitik des Dritten Reiches* (Düsseldorf, 1976), pp. 58–69; A. Hillgruber, 'England's place in Hitler's plans for world domination', *Journal of Contemporary History*, vol. 9 (1974), pp. 5–22. See also the review article, M. Michaelis, 'World power status or world domination?' *Historical Journal*, vol. 15 (1972), pp. 331–60.
61 M. Cowling, *The Impact of Hitler. British Politics and British Policy 1933–1940* (Cambridge, 1975); G. Schmidt, *England in der Krise. Grundzüge und Grundlagen der britischen Appeasement-Politik (1930–1937)* (Opladen, 1981), pp. 283 ff.
62 Hiden, 'National Socialism and foreign policy', p. 149.
63 Hiden emphasizes Hitler's efforts to put forward a radical alternative in foreign policy after 1929 (ibid., pp. 155, 158).
64 Hillgruber, *Deutschlands Rolle*, p. 61.
65 M. Messerschmidt, 'Aussenpolitik und Kriegsvorbereitung', in W. Deist et al. (eds), *Ursachen und Voraussetzungen der Deutschen Kriegspolitik. Das Deutsche Reich und der Zweite Weltkrieg* (Stuttgart, 1979), p. 549.
66 ibid., pp. 550 ff. See also R. Wohlfeil, *Heer und Republik* (Frankfurt-on-Main, 1970), pp. 196 ff.
67 Messerschmidt, 'Aussenpolitik und Kriegsvorbereitung', pp. 553–4.
68 M. Geyer, 'Militär, Rüstung und Aussenpolitik – Aspekte militärischer Revisionspolitik in der Zwischenkriegszeit', in Funke (ed.), *Hitler, Deutschland und die Mächte*, p. 240.
69 G. Schreiber, 'Reichsmarine, Revisionismus und Weltmachtstreben', in K. J. Müller and E. Opitz (eds), *Militär und Militarismus in der Weimarer Republik* (Düsseldorf, 1978), p. 159.
70 ibid., pp. 162, 173.
71 ibid.
72 ibid., p. 170, Boehm's talk about 'war tasks of the navy' in January 1929.
73 ibid., p. 168.
74 ibid., p. 176.
75 ibid., p. 191, Müller's contribution to the discussion.
76 ibid., p. 168.
77 See for the German policy towards south-eastern Europe, R. Frommelt, *Paneuropa oder Mitteleuropa. Einigungsbestrebungen im Kalkül deutscher Wirtschaft und Politik 1925–1933* (Stuttgart, 1977); W. Schumann (ed.), *Griff nach Südosteuropa* (Berlin, 1973); D. Stegmann, ' "Mitteleuropa" 1925–1934. Zum Problem der Kontinuität deutscher

Aussenhandelspolitik von Stresemann bis Hitler', in D. Stegmann, B.-J. Wendt and P.-C. Witt (eds), *Industrielle Gesellschaft und politisches System. Beiträge zur politischen Sozialgeschichte. Festschrift für Fritz Fischer* (Bonn, 1978), pp. 203–21; H. Sundhaussen, 'Die Weltwirtschaftskrise im Donau-Balkan-Raum und ihre Bedeutung für den Wandel der deutschen Aussenpolitik unter Brüning', in W. Benz and H. Graml (eds), *Aspekte deutscher Aussenpolitik im 20. Jahrhundert. Aufsätze Hans Rothfels zum Gedächtnis* (Stuttgart, 1976), pp. 121–64; Schröder, 'Deutsche Südosteuropapolitik' and idem, 'Die deutsche Südosteuropapolitik und die Reaktion der angelsächsischen Mächte 1929–1933/34', in J. Becker and K. Hildebrand (eds), *Internationale Beziehungen in der Weltwirtschaftskrise 1929–1933* (Munich, 1980), pp. 343–60. See also D. E. Kaiser, *Economic Diplomacy and the Origins of the Second World War. Germany, Britain, France and Eastern Europe 1930–1939* (Princeton, NJ, 1980), pp. 3–16.

78 I. T. Berend and G. Ranki, *Economic Development in East-Central Europe in the 19th and 20th Centuries* (New York and London, 1974), p. 231.

79 R. Okey, *Eastern Europe 1740–1980: Feudalism to Communism* (London, 1982). In 1928 60 per cent of Polish capital was foreign, including 40 per cent in industry. The figures for Hungary were 50 per cent and 25 per cent respectively. In the Balkans, Okey claims, 50–70 per cent of the economy was financed from abroad (ibid., p. 167). See also B.-J. Wendt, 'England und der deutsche "Drang nach Südosten". Kapitalbeziehungen und Warenverkehr in Südosteuropa zwischen den Weltkriegen', in I. Geiss and B.-J. Wendt (eds), *Deutschland in der Weltpolitik des 19. und 20. Jahrhunderts*, 2nd edn (Düsseldorf, 1974), pp. 483–512. See also M. L. Recker, *England und der Donauraum 1919–1929* (Stuttgart, 1976); A. Teichova and P. L. Cottrell, 'Industrial structures in west and east central Europe during the inter-war period', in idem (eds), *International Business and Central Europe 1918–1929* (New York, 1983), pp. 31–55.

80 Berend and Ranki, *Economic Development*, p. 203.

81 ibid., p. 232.

82 Stegmann, '"Mitteleuropa" 1925–1934', p. 204.

83 ibid., pp. 204–5. See also Schröder, 'Die deutsche Südosteuropapolitik und die Reaktion', pp. 344–5.

84 G. Schmidt has recently discussed these aspects in 'Dissolving international politics?' in idem (ed.), *Konstellationen internationaler Politik 1924–1932. Politische und wirtschaftliche Faktoren in den Beziehungen zwischen Westeuropa und den Vereinigten Staaten* (Bochum, 1983), pp. 355–8 and detected as a general trend the 'politicization of economic questions', but it seems to be the other way round because economics have become the determinant factor in international relations.

85 See Teichova and Cottrell (eds), *International Business and Central Europe*.

86 H. Schröter, 'Siemens and central and south-east Europe between two world wars', in ibid., pp. 173 ff.

87 ibid., p. 173.

88 ibid., p. 174.

89 ibid., p. 177.

90 ibid., p. 183.

91 ibid., p. 188. According to Schröter, Siemens operated outside the sphere of the Mitteleuropäischer Wirtschaftstag.

92 See for the following, V. Schröter, 'The IG Farbenindustrie AG in central and south-east Europe 1926–38', in ibid., p. 148.

93 ibid., p. 149.

94 ibid., p. 161.

95 ibid., pp. 155–6 and pp. 161 ff. See also Wendt, 'England und der deutsche "Drang nach Südosten"', pp. 495–6, and the two articles by H. Radandt, 'Die IG-Farbenindustrie AG in Süosteuropa bis 1938', in *Jahrbuch für Wirtschaftsgeschichte*, 1966, pt 3, pp. 146–95 and idem., 'Die IG-Farbenindustrie AG und Südosteuropa 1938 bis zum Ende des Zweiten Weltkrieges', in *Jahrbuch für Wirtschaftsgeschichte*, 1967, pt 1, pp. 77–146. In 1931 IG Farben sold 12·5 per cent of its total exports to central and south-eastern Europe, in 1932 it was 14·6 per cent and in 1933 15·2 per cent. This increase was achieved against its falling exports which dropped from 534·6 million marks in 1931 to 452·0 million marks in 1933. See V. Schröter, 'The IG Farbenindustrie', p. 149.

96 V. Schröter, 'The IG Farbenindustrie', pp. 155–62. See also H. Pohl's commentary, ibid., p. 205.
97 H. J. Flechtner, *Carl Duisberg. Vom Chemiker zum Wirtschaftsführer* (Düsseldorf, 1959), p. 376.
98 ibid., p. 378. See also W. Treue, 'Die deutschen Unternehmer in der Weltwirtschaftskrise 1928 bis 1933', in W. Conze and H. Raupach (eds), *Die Staats- und Wirtschaftskrise des Deutschen Reiches 1929/33* (Stuttgart, 1967), pp. 117 ff.
99 See Wendt, 'England und der deutsche "Drang nach Südosten"'. In the first half of 1933 German trade with Romania and Hungary nearly came to a complete standstill because Germany did help these countries financially. IG Farben, on the other hand, became a commerical agent for these states in order to unfreeze its credits there. See Kaiser, *Economic Diplomacy*, pp. 70 ff. A little earlier the German governments under Brüning, von Papen and von Schleicher had engaged in delaying tactics in order to solve the agricultural crisis in south-eastern Europe so as to exacerbate the situation so that ultimately the dependency on Germany would grow. See Schröder, 'Die deutsche Südosteuropapolitik und die Reaktion', pp. 359 f.
100 See for the following, A. Teichova, 'The Mannesmann concern in east central Europe in the interwar period', in idem and Cottrell (eds), *International Business and Central Europe*, p. 105.
101 ibid., pp. 121 ff.
102 ibid., p. 123.
103 ibid., p. 132.
104 This is supported by the remarks of Treviranus to the German Foreign Office on 24 June 1930 (Schröder, 'Deutsche Südosteuropapolitik', p. 7).
105 ibid., pp. 26 ff; Berend and Ranki, *Economic Development*, p. 267; H.-E. Volkmann, 'Die NS-Wirtschaft in Vorbereitung des Krieges', in Deist *et al.* (eds), *Ursachen und Voraussetzungen*, pp. 264–77.
106 See for a combination of economic *Grossraum* considerations with the requirements of a war economy, Deist *et al* (eds), *Ursachen und Voraussetzungen*, pp. 339–47. Trade statistics show how much this was the case. Between 1937 and 1939 the Bulgarian share of its exports to Germany rose from 43·1 to 71·1 per cent, the Hungarian from 24·1 to 52·4 per cent, the Romanian from 19·2 to 43·1 per cent and the Yugoslavian from 27·7 to 45·9 per cent. Imports from Germany grew proportionately from 54·8 to 69·5 per cent in Bulgaria, from 26·2 to 52·5 per cent in Hungary, from 28·9 to 56·9 per cent in Romania and from 32·4 to 53·2 per cent in Yugoslavia. See Berend and Ranki, *Economic Development*, p. 282.
107 ibid., p. 284 for both quotations.
108 See R. J. Overy, 'Göring's "Multi-national Empire"', in Teichova and Cottrell (eds), *International Business and Central Europe*, pp. 269, 277, 283.
109 Kaiser, *Economic Diplomacy*, p. 15. See also here in general Frommelt, *Paneuropa oder Mitteleuropa*.
110 Kaiser, *Economic Diplomacy*, p. 16.
111 ibid., p. 23; Frommelt, *Paneuropa oder Mitteleuropa*, pp. 85–93.
112 ibid., p. 89.
113 ibid., p. 96.
114 Schröder, 'Deutsche Südosteuropapolitik', p. 24.
115 Kaiser, *Economic Diplomacy*, pp. 70 ff.
116 ibid., pp. 73 ff.
117 It is interesting to note that Germany's growing hegemonial position in south-eastern Europe was achieved without substantial transfers of capital or state loans. Schröder, 'Deutsche Südosteuropapolitik', p. 29.
118 ibid., p. 31.
119 Kaiser, *Economic Diplomacy*, p. 165.
120 See for this R. Pommerin, *Das Dritte Reich und Lateinamerika* (Düsseldorf, 1977).
121 M. Messerschmidt, 'Aussenpolitik und Kriegsvorbereitung', in Deist *et al.* (eds), *Ursachen und Voraussetzungen*, pp. 675 ff.

Part Two

The Legacy of Empire: Some Regional Studies

9 Imperialism and State Formation in Africa: Nigeria and Chad

ALBERT WIRZ

In discussions of imperialism the perspective from the centre has for obvious reasons been predominant. At the same time most attention has been given to economic matters. In this chapter I shall try to look at the problem from the periphery. Furthermore, the analysis will focus on political and institutional matters. One of my main metaphors, however, is taken from economic history. It is my contention that the notion of a product cycle as developed by economists analysing the growth and investment behaviour of business corporations is a valid explanatory device for an interpretation of the process of state formation associated with the history of imperialism.

I am aware of the philosophical problems of a cyclical metaphor if used for historical processes. Without entering into epistemological details, let me just stress the partial opposition of such a notion to models of linear progress so prevalent among social scientists writing about colonialism, *vide* the theory of modernization. On the other hand, it is striking, to say the very least, that cyclical models are quite common in economic theory. As to whether this is evidence of greater realism on the part of economists, I would not like to say.

Clearly, imperialism was, above all, an economic process leading to the incorporation of hitherto external economies into the capitalist world economy as dependent peripheries.[1] Yet imperialism had important political corollaries as well. Indeed, imperialism was once conceived as being conterminous with colonialism and political domination. But as Marxist scholars pointed out long ago, colonialism was but an entr'acte in the spectacle of capitalist penetration of the world. And since J. Gallagher and R. Robinson have published their seminal article on 'The imperialism of free trade' even conservative historians have become accustomed to the idea of an underlying continuity between informal and formal imperialism.[2]

One might even argue that the outcome of this process of capitalist penetration would not have been very different in economic terms if the European powers had refrained from colonial conquest and political domination. In one respect, however, colonialism was crucial: colonial domination set the stage for the establishment of nation-states in areas where, before colonial intervention, other patterns of political organization had prevailed, ranging from stateless societies to chiefdoms, proto-feudal kingdoms and large-scale empires. Today this variety has gone, and we are confronted with a world made up almost entirely of nation-states or, at least would-be nation-states and this, no doubt, as a result of colonial state formation.

Before looking at this process in more detail, some general aspects of imperialist expansion should be pointed out. First of all, it appears that imperialism followed a cyclical course closely resembling the product-cycle model.[3] According to this model, American corporations generate new products and procedures in response to the high-income market of the United States. As innovators they enjoy monopolistic advantages as long as competitors are barred entry to the market. But this does not last long because monopolistic profits induce others to set up competition as soon as possible, the monopoly thereby giving way to an oligopoly. During the initial period the corporations produce mainly for the home market. Later they introduce their products abroad through exports. And when these export markets are also threatened by competition or by political interference, for example, the erection of tariff barriers to shut out imports, then the corporations will go one step further and establish overseas manufacturing subsidiaries in an attempt to prolong their oligopolistic advantages.

The decision to go for direct investment overseas is usually made easier by the fact that by the time the step is taken the technology of production has settled down sufficiently to be transferable to a foreign facility without considerable cost to the firm concerned. In other words, the technology involved has already become obsolete to a certain extent. Full ownership of subsidiaries is preferred, at least initially, but it is neither a *sine qua non* for the investment nor is it sacrosanct. On the contrary, local participation is conceded if local business partners accept the vertical division of labour within the corporation and so long as they service interest and debt payments. In the long run the loss of oligopolistic advantages seems inevitable. When this happens, the enterprise may slough off the product, or it may try to create new oligopolistic advantages by making changes in the product, or it may make efforts to defend its market share by moving to a very much lower-cost production site, as Raymond Vernon has put it.[4]

Political entities such as states are obviously much more complex in their internal structure and in their behaviour than business corporations. Nevertheless, the analogies between the two are more striking than the differences, particularly where politicians tend to equate the success of private enterprise with the general welfare of the nation. This attitude is no doubt typical for politicians in modern nation-states. Representatives of labour, it is true, usually prescribe different solutions for political problems than politicians representing the interests of capital, but the differences between the two sets of politicians are differences in degree rather than differences in kind. While the latter, as a rule, opt for private ownership, the former have a clear preference for public ownership or state capitalism, but neither can propose an alternative to an ever-growing economy. Consequently, in the heyday of colonialism socialists criticized the form colonial domination had taken, but they accepted colonialism as a modernizing force. They criticized exploitation and colonial dictatorship, but they subscribed to the notion of the 'white man's burden'. And not even the most outspoken critics of colonial rule have ever seriously considered adapting European ways to those of the colonized as a viable alternative to changing the world according to European values.

If we then take the product-cycle model and apply it to the political sphere, we realize that the creation of colonies at the end of the nineteenth century was but a response to oligopolistic competition among the foremost European powers (and the United States). At the beginning of the century Britain had enjoyed monopolistic advantages as a result of its lead in industrial development, and as a consequence it could content itself with informal imperialism. But in the course of the nineteenth century other European powers and the United States were able to catch up and contest Britain's pre-eminence, thereby setting off the scramble for colonies in general and for Africa in particular. This notorious scramble for Africa was similar to direct investment overseas in that it was an attempt to prolong or to create oligopolistic advantages in both international affairs and economics by the setting up of colonies overseas. The individual colonies did not have to be meaningful units in business terms (the same is true for some overseas subsidiaries of transnational corporations); what mattered was the profitability of the colonial empire as a whole. In this respect even Chad, for all its remoteness and lack of easily exploitable resources, could make a marginal contribution, linking French West Africa and French Equatorial Africa. Nigeria, on the other hand, was a major asset to the British Empire even in strictly business terms.

Manufacturing subsidiaries overseas are dependent on technology transferred from the centre where most, if not all, research and development facilities are concentrated. Similarly, the creation of colonial states involved the transfer of administrative procedures or technology from Europe to Africa. European government techniques of the day were hardly more appropriate to the needs of African colonies than capital-intensive manufacturing technology is to the needs of an underdeveloped economy with an overabundance of cheap but unqualified labour. But unlike manufacturers of high-technology goods, whose production costs represent only a fraction of the sale price, administrators all over the world have to cope with high production costs. Therefore, the colonial rulers were more or less compelled to adapt themselves to prevailing conditions in Africa. This tendency was strongest where capital investment was smallest, that is, in trading colonies. Like traders who also opt for strategies of adaptation, colonial administrators followed the easiest path and fell back on technology they had already outgrown at home. They set up administrative states based on a web of collaboration with indigenous oligarchies and marked by structural pluralism.

The decision to use local collaborating groups as mediators has led Ronald Robinson to argue that colonial rule was less a function of European society than of indigenous politics.[5] This statement points to the heart of the matter, but it overlooks the very real power differential between ruler and ruled, between Europeans and Africans which had the consequence that European values came to dominate the political discourse.

Non-European values and norms, even where preserved by colonial policy, were relegated to an inferior position and were held in contempt. Furthermore, Robinson's statement does not take account of the fact that the actual government techniques used were hardly those of indigenous cultures but techniques transferred from Europe, although rather obsolete ones.

Another parallel between direct investment overseas and colonial rule can be seen in the fact that both have fostered the growth of new classes and that both have created new opportunities for social advancement while at the same time killing off local competition. In due course both generated new tensions and new hostilities. In this respect, it is noteworthy that the most outspoken criticism came from within those groups which the process of foreign intervention had helped to create in the first place. In the sphere of business the most outspoken critics were the local businessmen who, initially performing roles complementary to those of the foreign firms, tried to become competitors. In the realm of politics the most notable attacks came from the members of the new class of petty-bourgeois clerks, civil servants and teachers who wanted to have a greater share in the affairs of their countries. The final stage of the product cycle or of colonial rule is reached when the foreign enterprise and the foreign administration can no longer claim any cost advantages over their local and foreign imitators.

It is well known that the point at which costs outweighed benefits was reached sooner in trading colonies, such as Nigeria and Chad, than in settler or mining colonies. In trading colonies foreign investment was restricted to commerce and banking, the number of European residents was rather small and the political system was less coercive than in settler colonies or in colonies with mining industries marked by heavy and long-term expatriate investment in production. Furthermore, in trading colonies the transfer of power was achieved mainly by negotiation.

As a result, devolution there culminated in what we might appropriately call conservative decolonization, because the heirs to colonial rule did not question – in the short term at least – the vertical division of labour created during the period of formal imperialism. In the settler and mining colonies, on the other hand, events tended to take a more bellicose turn, especially where settlers resisted any effective power-sharing with the black majority, thereby setting off a process of radicalization on the part of their African competitors. Wherever this happened, decolonization, when finally achieved, was usually radical in intent if not in content. Finally, decolonization was inevitable not least because the United States and the Soviet Union had moved to the forefront of international affairs as a result of two world wars.

At the same time, economic and political aggregation – others might call it development – in the industrial countries as a whole had reached a higher level than ever before. While transnational corporations came to dominate the economic scene, transcending all political boundaries, by accepting the Treaty of Rome (1957) European statesmen opted for integration in Europe in an attempt to overcome the parochialism inherent in a world of nation-states. This decision did not generate the hoped-for results in the short term; in fact the integrationists among European politicians have had to contend with strong countervailing forces ever since. Nevertheless, the Treaty of Rome marked the beginning of a new era in European politics. The process of decolonization, on the other hand, led to the creation of a new array of would-be nation-states in the Third World. As far as French Africa is concerned, this was tantamount to Balkanization as the existing colonial federations were split up in the process.

By spreading the nation-state all over the world, decolonization no doubt marks the triumph of this particular model of political organization. Yet it came at a time when the model was already being called into question in Europe. If conservative decolonization can be interpreted as an attempt by the colonial powers to adapt as best they could to competition from within and without their respective empires, the better to preserve their oligopolistic advantages in an ever-changing world system, then the beginning of nation-building policies associated with the process of decolonization is but another instance illustrating the rule that technologies transferred to the peripheries are essentially obsolete ones. And it is the contention of this chapter that the transfer of the nation-state model, or more particularly the difficulties associated with its implementation in Africa, is one of the means for securing domination and dependency beyond independence into the period of post-imperialism. This dependency was masterminded less by foreign imperialists than theories of neo-colonialism would have us believe. But, even though it is partly self-imposed and partly of structural origin, this continuing dependency has been very real none the less.

Nigeria and Chad are two cases in point.[6] Besides the fact that both are trading colonies, these two countries seem not to have much in common at first sight. Nigeria with its 90–100 million people is not only the most populous country in Africa, it is also well endowed with natural resources and at least the coastal regions have been in commercial exchange with Europe since the beginning of modern times. Chad, on the other hand, has a small population (4 million), is very poorly endowed and European economic penetration began only after colonial conquest. As a consequence, the French in Chad could not rely on market forces for the *mise en valeur* of their colony as the British were able to do in Nigeria. Hence the widespread use of coercion and force in Chad. And if Nigeria was one of the main props of the British Empire, Chad was but a backwater in the French one.

Nevertheless, the two countries also present striking similarities. First of all, the boundaries of both colonial states enclosed a multitude of societies with different cultures, some of which had been on friendly terms in precolonial times, while others had been enemies, and some had had no contact at all. Even though the Europeans did not care much for historical traditions when carving up Africa, in the internal structuring of their colonies they had to adapt themselves. But adaptation to what? The guiding principles for this endeavour were shaped as much by preconceptions about Africa as by the constraints imposed by a lack of funds and personnel for a thoroughgoing administrative penetration of the colonies. According to the contemporary European understanding of Africa, the normal African political unit was the tribe with an autocratic chief at its head. Segmentary societies with diffuse authority systems, such as the Igbo in Nigeria and the Sara in Chad, were misinterpreted as examples of primitive anarchy.

Hence the colonial masters set out to discover or to create tribal chiefs and to incorporate them as mediators in the administrative structure of the colonial state. The British called this procedure indirect rule. Its tenets were succinctly summarized by Governor Clifford in 1920 when he declared: 'It is the consistent policy of the Government of Nigeria to maintain and support the local tribal institutions and the indigenous forms of government ... which are to be regarded as the natural expression of [African] political genius ... ' And pointing to the future he added: 'I am entirely convinced of the right, for example of the people of Egbaland ... of any of the great Emirates of the North ... to maintain that each one of them is, in a very real sense, a nation. It is the task of the Government of Nigeria to build up and fortify these national institutions.'[7] The idea of forging one homogenous nation in Nigeria was anathema to him, not least because he thought that it would violate the right of self-determination of each nation. We might therefore consider Governor Clifford as one of the first ethno-nationalists in Nigeria.

The French in neighbouring Chad advocated opposite goals in their statements of principle. But confronted with day-to-day government in the colony, they adopted a strategy called 'politique de grands turbans' which was quite similar to the indirect rule of the British, except for the fact that the British transferred more power to their local allies than the French ever did. This procedure was efficient because it satisfied the former opponents of colonial rule and because it secured law and order at a very low price indeed to the Europeans.

At the same time, however, this policy deepened historical cleavages. It also fostered autocratic rule and, most important, it institutionalized ethnic compartmentalizations for the authorities in charge tried to make the local administrative units ethnically as homogeneous as possible. In hierarchical societies, such as those in the caliphate of Sokoto (Northern Nigeria) or the Sahelian states in Chad and to a lesser extent also in the Yoruba kingdoms of Western Nigeria, the changes involved were rather minor. They consisted mainly in the splitting up of large-scale polities into their constituent parts. In hitherto stateless societies such as the Igbo or the Sara, however, this policy marked the beginning of a truly new order. It imposed a territorial grid on public affairs, it enlarged the scale of communities, and it introduced new elements of social stratification. But nowhere did it foster democratic procedures in public life. On the contrary, many checks and balances which had existed in pre-colonial society to safeguard the balance between rulers and the ruled were either suppressed or lingered on in empty forms.

The practice of colonial administration not only contradicted the contemporary assumption that colonization was equivalent to political modernization in the European sense, it also created a very real gap between periphery and centre, or between town and country in the colonies. For as far as the central government machinery was concerned, the Europeans *did* transfer up-to-date government technology to their colonies by creating administrative structures based on modern bureaucratic norms and by creating the nuclei of parliamentary systems (the Legislative Council). But in the central state apparatus all executive positions were monopolized by Europeans who thought of themselves as representatives of a superior race. The rulers constituted a racially defined endogamous caste. Thus, contrary to all promises of the colonial discourse, status in the colonial society remained essentially ascribed. Africans might acquire all the knowledge that colonial and European schools could provide, but until decolonization set off a process of Africanization they were restricted to inferior positions. The political alliance between colonial rulers and rural notables also barred them from positions of power at the rural periphery.

These contradictions did not cause much of a problem in Chad because Western schooling there got off the ground only after the Second World War. Thus, there was no large Western-educated Chadian élite before the achievement of formal independence. In Nigeria, however, unequal access to positions of power had been a major political issue since the beginning of the century, because here the formation of a small but highly educated and very articulate urban élite predated colonial conquest. Yet in both Chad and Nigeria, the colonial state, when looked at from the perspective of the Africans, was less a modern state than a polity which was ethnically segmented at the base as well as at the top. In other words, colonial administrative penetration culminated in the creation of administrative states marked by cultural and structural pluralism.[8]

While this structural pluralism alone was likely to cause trouble once the foreign rulers had left the countries, the situation was rendered even more serious by social change as initiated by colonial rule. The forces of social change may not have been very strong during the colonial period, at least in Chad. But even where they were limited, they made a lasting impact because instead of neutralizing the ethnic cleavages which were institutionalized by administrative practice, they enhanced them by adding a class character. A look at economic penetration will illustrate this.

Although the capitalist mode of production has become dominant in all African countries as a result of colonial rule, the economic structure of these countries has remained very heterogeneous. Capitalist penetration was restricted to more or less limited core areas: the new urban centres and the regions with notable export production. In Nigeria three core areas emerged: the cocoa belt in the West with its centre in Lagos, the palm-oil regions in the East, and the peanut and cotton areas in the North centred on Kano and Kaduna, together with the associated tin-mining complex on the plateau of Jos. Foreign capital gravitated to these economic core areas. But what is most striking is the fact that these economic core areas were located in what we might call the homelands of the three biggest ethnic groups in Nigeria: the Yoruba, the Igbo and the Hausa. Production of cocoa was mainly in the hands of Yoruba peasant farmers, while peanut and cotton cultivation was undertaken by Northern Hausa men. In Chad, cotton was the single most important staple crop. It was mainly produced under a system of forced cultivation by Sara people living in the southernmost parts of the country.

Some authors think that these peasant farmers formed a rural proletariat. In my opinion this classification is inappropriate as long as the individual producers own their means of production. And it is one of the most salient characteristics of colonial rule in trading colonies that it safeguards traditional forms of landownership, thereby preserving the main prop of the kinship system. Sara Berry has shown that even in the Nigerian cocoa belt, for all the social differentiation and land accumulation that took place in the twentieth century, kinship is still the most important means of mobilizing and allocating resources, whether land or labour.[9] Indigenous ways of life altered even less in those peripheral areas outside the scope of colonial investors which served essentially as reserves of wage labour for the core areas. There, the communal values of pre-colonial Africa were kept alive and were ultimately only marginally touched by colonial penetration. Rural communities became tributaries of towns and the colonial state, but they safeguarded their identities and much of their systemic autonomy. Therefore, even at the end of colonial rule, a good part of the rural population was not yet dependent on the colonial state, while the state could not do without peasants' and herdsmen's labour and the revenue collected from them.

Social differentiation along regional and therefore ethnic lines was further enhanced by colonial educational policies which had as contradictory an impact as the economic *mise en valeur*. What investment was made in education was concentrated in the core areas of economic penetration. Schooling was mainly left to Christian missionaries. Hence economic penetration, educational expansion and Christianization often went hand in hand. In Nigeria, the Yoruba were among the first to gain access to Western education because the missionary efforts in their country reach back to the middle of the nineteenth century. As a result of this educational advantage, the Yoruba came also to dominate the African petty bourgeoisie before the Igbo ascendancy after the Second World War. In Chad, the Sara Mbaye of Logone Province enjoyed a similar headstart over their neighbours, although the gap was much smaller and of more recent origin. The close connection between schooling and missionary enterprise hampered the diffusion of Western education in the Islamic parts of both colonies, thereby adding a new dimension to the cultural difference between Muslim and non-Muslim and widening the social distance between North and South in the two countries.

This section on education would be incomplete if no mention were made of colonial language policies. It was the consistent policy of most missionary societies to teach and to preach in the vernacular. The British colonial government shared this preoccupation with indigenous languages and did all it could to further their teaching. It even entrenched Hausa as an administrative language for the whole of Northern Nigeria. The French, on the other hand, promoted their own national language to the detriment of all other languages. It is significant, however, that during decolonization, when the French came to fear the political impact of Arabism and Nasserism on the people of Northern Chad, they changed their attitude slightly and established a Franco-Arab college in Abéche in an attempt to counter these destabilizing influences.

In Nigeria the widespread use of vernacular languages provided a vehicle for cultural mobilization and for the emergence of larger ethnic identities which later were to form the basis for the development of competing ethno-nationalist movements. Certainly, ethnicity, as such, is not a colonial invention. But even where ethnic identities had pre-colonial roots, they were reshaped by colonialism which also gave them a new significance.[10] The Hausa, for example, had already shared a common culture, common religious affiliation (Islam) and common political affiliation (as subjects of the caliphate of Sokoto), which had made some of them at least aware of common interests as well. Nevertheless, their identity before colonial conquest was related to the smaller entities of locality, emirate and Islamic brotherhood. And it was only when confronted with competition from ethnic groups from the South that the Hausa began to identify themselves with their larger language group. The common identity of the Yoruba was less rooted in the pre-colonial past. At that time, the relevant solidarity groups were formed around lineage and kingdom. However, the Yoruba shared a belief in a common origin extending back into the mythical past. They thought of themselves as children of Oduduwa. Hence the Yoruba quest for a common consciousness could be presented as the rediscovery of something that had already existed at an earlier time. No such thing could be said of the Igbo for whom lineage and village community had been the only relevant reference groups prior to colonial conquest. They acquired a common self-awareness only in the course of colonial penetration. The same is true of the Sara people in Chad where French language policy hampered the rise of ethnicity without being able to prevent developments reminiscent of those in Nigeria.

Colonial ethnicity was primarily an urban phenomenon, in Chad as well as in Nigeria. It was in the centres of colonial penetration that members of different ethnic groups came into contact with each other. To better enable them both to weather the hardships of life in the competitive economies of the colonial cities and to keep in contact with home, some of the migrants gathered along communal lines and formed voluntary societies, such as the Obolo Clan Improvement Society in Lagos. This coming together assumed greater importance because most of the migrants hoped to return home eventually. They were villagers in towns rather than real townspeople, hence the lasting importance of communal values and communal ties. But, at the same time, social boundaries were steadily changing. Already in the late 1930s some of these voluntary associations started to form federations in Nigeria on the basis of a common language. In Chad, parallel developments took place. But as a consequence of the backwardness of the territory in terms of economic development and urbanization, they started much later and never reached the organizational level which existed in Nigeria before decolonization began.

Decolonization was the period when the Europeans lost their oligopolistic advantages on the international level, but also in the colonies where new competitors emerged. Colonial rulers responded to this challenge by creating a new alliance with the emerging African petty bourgeoisie without entirely abandoning their older allies among the rural notables.[11]

This was coupled with the creation of a parliamentary system and the introduction of electoral processes. Together they led to the politicization of ethnicity, especially in Nigeria where ethnic associations had already become a prominent feature of public life in the towns. As a result, politics in Nigeria came to be dominated more and more by ethnic considerations. Up until the Second World War Nigerian nationalism had still been unitarian in its aims, as had most of the early anticolonialist nationalist movements. But this unitarian outlook did not last. The process of decolonization had hardly begun with the enactment of the Richards Constitution (1946), when most of Nigeria's nationalists discovered ethnicity as a powerful political weapon and resorted to a strategy of ethnic mobilization, turning inter-party competition into inter-ethnic rivalry. The Nigerian historian, E. A. Ayandele, therefore calls the leaders of the anticolonial struggle 'windsowers', assigning to them the responsibility for the political decay which set in soon after independence and which rushed the country into one of the most brutal wars Africa had ever known.[12] And no doubt he is right.

But why this radical shift? First, one has to keep in mind that the politically most relevant boundaries – those dividing Nigeria into three regions – were delimited in such a way as to create a rough correspondence between language groups and political entities. Thus, Hausa speakers formed a majority in Northern Nigeria, while the Yoruba were in the majority in the West and the Igbo in the East. The salience of this was further enhanced by the British strategy of decolonization which favoured the regionalization of power and politics. To the British, devolution of power in the regions was a necessary first step before the transfer of power could take place on the national level, and before independence was to be granted.

Secondly, the leadership of the nationalist struggle was dominated by members of the emerging urban middle classes. Their rise to power, which was equivalent to social advancement, was dependent on winning the electoral support of the rural population. The nationalists may have been the ones most directly affected by racial discrimination, yet as town dwellers they also profited the most from colonialism and, as traders and civil servants, they were even agents of foreign penetration. Although they themselves may have hailed from peasant families, their social position put them in a more or less antagonistic economic relationship to the peasantry. This socio-economic cleavage between town and country is reflected in the fact – related by Obafemi Awolowo, one of the most prominent nationalist politicians – that the Yoruba farmers put less faith in the intellectuals, in the traders and in the African civil servants residing in towns, eating European food, driving expensive cars and testifying by their whole life-style that they had separated themselves from African peasant culture, than they did in British colonial administrators or in their own *obas* (chiefs).[13]

In this last respect the situation in Western Nigeria differed quite markedly from that prevalent in Southern Chad. Here, the forced cotton cultivation administered by colonial chiefs with hardly any traditional legitimation for exacting so heavy a tribute from the local population had driven the peasants to hate their immediate superiors. But it would be a mistake to deduce from this a general resentment of chiefly rule in rural Africa at the end of the colonial period. On the other hand, neither was the Chadian situation unique. Even in Northern Nigeria there were signs of growing rural radicalism, making the British fear peasant revolts during the 1950s.

The Yoruba peasants' assessment of the situation was confirmed as soon as Nigerian nationalists had assumed positions of authority. Once in power, the nationalists tried to fulfil their promises of 'a life more abundant' by embarking on an ambitious and costly programme of infrastructural investments. Yet this policy was heavily biased in favour of the towns while the rural areas were denied social services essential for rural development, although the necessary funds were mainly generated by peasant farmers. After Independence, the unequal allocation of funds and the corresponding neglect of the rural majority went on unimpeded, widening the gap between rural and urban incomes, increasing rural underemployment and the desire to migrate to the cities in search of a better standard of living.[14]

Ethnic and communal mobilization helped to mask or to transcend these very real cleavages between different social groups and between town and country. The peasants, for all their scepticism, were extremely receptive to ethno-nationalist messages, as these political ideas seemed to derive directly from the values of village society. As pointed out above, in the rural areas the kinship system with its strongly redistributive features still operated. Ethno-nationalist ideology consciously appealed to communal values. In short, civil society as depicted by the ethno-nationalists appeared as an extension of village society beyond the borders of the village.

This procedure was by no means restricted to African nationalism. On the contrary, the political discourse of European nationalism also revolves around notions of community and presents the nation as an extended kinship system, although capitalist penetration associated with the rise of nationalism has in fact undermined these communal structures. A parenthetical reference may be made here to a headline in a British Sunday paper during the war over the Falkland Islands (Malvinas) in 1982 which suggested that 'blood is thicker than oceans'.[15] Developments in Africa at the end of the Second World War differed from those in Europe only to the extent that capitalist penetration was still much less advanced than, for example, in nineteenth-century Europe while, at the same time, the hold of foreign interests over African economies was so strong that the newly emerging African bourgeoisies enjoyed little autonomy. Furthermore, suffrage in Africa was universal almost from the beginning of decolonization; at least it preceded the spread of mass education.

But, in spite of these peculiarities of the African situation, it would be wrong to differentiate African ethnic nationalism conceptually from nationalism in Europe, as is done by those who still speak of tribalism in Africa although tribes have vanished with capitalist penetration. And it would be equally misleading to take the colonial territory as the sole and only viable national entity and to disqualify all non-unitarian nationalist movements as mere expressions of regionalism or subnationalism. African successor states are not fully integrated nation-states, but neither are they states without nations as is widely assumed. Rather, they are multinational states.

The Nigerian constitution, as elaborated by the British in conjunction with their competitors, tried to take this heterogeneity into account by setting down a federalist framework. Even the most unrelenting critics of the nation-state ideology, such as the French Africa historian turned *régionaliste*, Yves Person, see federalism as an appropriate means of accommodating different ethnic groups and cultures within one political system. Hence he praises the British with some strictures, it is true, while condemning the 'unitarian folly of French ideology'.[16] However, if examined more closely, the Nigeria of 1960 hardly seems a state which acknowledged the value of cultural pluralism. Rather, it seems, the Nigerian federation was an aggregate of three would-be nation-states of very unequal size, vying with each other for ascendancy. And as unitarianism coupled with an inclination towards authoritarianism (the regions being *de facto* one-party states), multiple minority problems emerged. These problems became more acute as those holding power in the three regions tried to exploit their neighbours' minority problems to extend their own political influence beyond the home region, while at the same time disregarding minority fears in the area under their own jurisdiction.

The minority fears were, by and large, an expression of power deprivation on the part of several fractions of the new classes hoping to inherit the former colonial rulers' positions. As a consequence their charges reflected those the nationalists had raised in their struggle against British colonial tutelage. And likewise redress was sought in further fission by demanding the creation of more states within Nigeria. Secession as attempted in Biafra was but the most extreme form of this strategy which repeated the nationalists' quest for the 'political kingdom'. This strategy is also reminiscent of conflict resolution in segmentary societies where political development is tantamount to a process of fission and fusion. Fission, or segmentation, has the advantage of safeguarding the underlying social structures of the societies concerned, but it does not remove any of the root causes of the conflicts. The same can be said of conservative decolonization and of the process of creating new states within the Nigerian federation. Both have left untouched internal and external dependency structures, hence a tendency to further instability. Incidentally, the number of demands for new states has been increasing since the Nigerian legislators set a precedent by creating the Midwest Region in 1963 and since the military governments of Yakubu Gowon and Murtala Mohammed increased the total number of states to twelve (1967) and nineteen (1976).

Even though Chad seems to have followed an entirely different course – Chad is a paradigm for the failure of unitarian nationalism in Africa – its experiences are not too far removed from those of its mighty neighbour to the west. Quite obviously, appeals to ethnic solidarity never played as prominent a role in Chadian politics during decolonization as they did in Nigeria. Nevertheless, ethnic solidarity was important for the outcome of elections in Chad, political alignments closely following ethnic lines. And the capture of power by Sara politicians resulted in the allocation of the lion's share of public resources to the Southern core area. On the other hand, the strict unitarian outlook professed by Chadian nationalists also testifies to the overwhelming influence of the French and the corresponding lack of autonomy of Africans caught in the web of European idcologies. Chadian nationalists may have been rebels against the colonial order, but their rebellion was conducted with ideological weapons provided by the French.

We may add, parenthetically, that even the recourse to traditional values (deference towards the elders, the centrality of religion in public affairs), institutions (chiefs) and rituals (Yondo initiation) taken by President Tombalbaye in the early 1970s in order to underpin his exercise of power, and which he called authenticity, was justified by his panegyrists with speeches reminiscent of French revolutionary discourses. On the other hand, the one time Frolinat leader, Hissein Habré, presented himself at the beginning of his political career as an African Mao Zedong only to fall back on a strategy of communal mobilization when, back in Ndjamena in 1979, he was finally in a position to take up the power struggle with the then-President, General Felix Malloum.

All these examples are instances illustrating, first, the prevalence of the arithmetic of power over ideological commitments in African politics in the years before and after independence and, secondly, the continuing dependence of the first generation of African politicians in the era of post-imperialism on metropolitan political models and intellectual modes, whether these were suited to the needs of their respective countries or not. Colonialism, then, had created not only dependent economies, but also dependent polities and dependent minds, too. The predominance of metropolitan models was more pronounced in Chad, because there the power differential between metropolitan power and periphery was particularly great. In any case, the Chadian heirs to colonial rule aspired to become, or at least to appear, more French than the French, as is illustrated by, among other things, the administrative reform undertaken immediately after Independence. Henceforth, the Chadian state was to be remodelled along the lines of the French prefectorial system. Of course, the ideal of French centralized administration with its corollary of limited popular participation at the local level was never really implemented, because it was thoroughly inappropriate for a weak state like Chad. But it was considered to be equivalent to modernity by its architects.

It is significant that instead of looking for new solutions, the Chadian authorities, not to forget their numerous French advisers, chose administrative mimesis although they might have known that, as a result of this procedure, law and reality would necessarily contradict each other, thereby increasing the opportunity for authoritarianism and even despotism on the part of the territorial administration. And this is exactly what happened. The Chadian civil servants taking over from the French repeated the mistakes that the French had made at the beginning of the century, resorting to the indiscriminate use of violence whenever conflicts emerged between themselves and the independent-minded peasants and herdsmen. Thus, they set the stage for those peasant revolts in Central and Northern Chad which in 1965 triggered off an internal war that still has not come to an end.

The instability in Chad and in Nigeria has caused tremendous hardship.

Besides that, it has had the effect of tying down human resources and it has blocked the way for finding really appropriate means to fight the ever-increasing problems of underdevelopment. To put it a different way, the preoccupation with the scramble for power has safeguarded the economic structures inherited from colonialism. Furthermore, the resulting instability has closely tied the two countries to their respective metropolitan powers, because their governments were in dire need of allies. In the case of Nigeria, the tremendous windfall profits accruing from the exploitation of its mineral wealth have acted as a powerful counterweight. But it was only after the end of the civil war that the Nigerian government could really profit politically from this state of affairs. The partial indigenization of trade and industry and the radicalization of foreign affairs in the wake of Biafra's surrender testify to this new-found strength. The new constitution of 1979, however, has deceived all those who had hoped that the radicalism displayed in foreign affairs might spill over into internal affairs.[17]

Chad, lacking similar resources, has fared much worse. Not only have the colonially created state structures in Chad tumbled down, the country has almost lost its sovereignty. Chad once again fell under French *de facto* tutelage in 1969/70, and this was ten years later superseded by that of its immediate African neighbours. Today the country is once again a plaything of competing foreign interests, as it had been at the end of the nineteenth century. At that time, France was fighting Rabeh, a Sudanese *conquistador*, in a struggle for hegemony in the area, while Senussites infiltrated the country from the North. In Chad, then, history has turned full circle. The international configuration, however, has changed perceptibly in the meantime, making the Chadian situation even more desperate than it was a century ago, though surprisingly enough, the present international situation is not without parallels to that of a hundred years ago, both being B-phases in the long-term dynamics of capitalist development.[18]

To summarize the main points: states such as Nigeria and Chad created under colonial rule are one of the main legacies of imperialism on the African continent, the salience of the problems of continuing economic underdevelopment notwithstanding. Imperialist expansion into Africa, its corollary of colonial state formation and the eventual devolution of power to African politicians with the final granting of independence followed a more or less cyclical course, closely resembling the product cycle which economists have identified as one of the main factors underlying the spread of multinational corporations. In both instances, the dynamics of the process are essentially determined by the constraints, as well as the opportunities, of oligopolistic competition in the capitalist world system, the creation of colonies by European nation-states being equivalent to the setting up of manufacturing subsidiaries by multinational companies.

Not surprisingly, the requirements of the centre and, more particularly, the world views of the historical actors coming from the centre, remain dominant in both cases, despite the fact that the colonial rulers always had to rely on political alliances with indigenous élites. But just as business corporations usually transfer rather obsolete manufacturing technology when going overseas, the colonial rulers tended to transfer administrative technologies and political models already obsolete or just about to become so. As a result, colonial states such as Nigeria and Chad were administrative states marked by structural pluralism and an institutional set-up favouring authoritarian trends instead of political modernization, although the colonial discourse pretended that colonial rule was meant to further the latter. Later, in the process leading to conservative decolonization, an attempt was made to transform the colonial states into modern nation-states. This came at a time when that particular model of political organization was already being called into question in Europe, not to mention its utter unsuitability for the specific circumstances of the heterogeneous African societies clustered together within the colonial boundaries.

The heirs to colonial rule were usually well aware of the many deficiencies of the political and administrative structures bequeathed to them by the respective colonial powers. But having themselves adopted many European values, being essentially imitators turned competitors, and finding themselves in a more or less antagonistic position *vis-à-vis* the rural majority, the anticolonial nationalists were hardly able to break with the colonial past. Rather they chose, if indeed it was a choice, mimesis on their way to power. Mimesis meant unitarian nationalism in Chad and federalism in Nigeria, in accordance with the differing administrative and political traditions of France and Britain. However, the two political strategies differed less than one might think at first sight because even in Nigeria, despite its federalist constitution, there was ample room for authoritarian centralism in the constituent parts of the federation. As a result, the political consequences of decolonization were rather similar in the two countries, with minority problems emerging and political decay setting in soon after the constraints of colonial rule were removed. The political autonomy of the heirs to colonial rule was thereby further reduced, making them ever more ready for renewed collaboration with all those inside and outside their respective countries who were willing to support them financially, politically, or morally, in words or deeds.

Notes: Chapter 9

1 I. Wallerstein, 'Three stages of African involvement in the world economy', in P. C. W. Gutkind and I. Wallerstein (eds), *The Political Economy of Contemporary Africa* (London, 1976), pp. 30–57.
2 J. Gallagher and R. Robinson, 'The imperialism of free trade', *Economic History Review*, vol. 6 (1953), pp. 1–15.
3 R. Vernon, *Sovereignty at Bay. The Multinational Spread of U.S. Enterprises* (London, 1971).
4 Ibid., p. 77.
5 R. Robinson, 'Non-European foundations of European imperialism: sketch for a theory of collaboration', in R. Owen and B. Sutcliffe (eds), *Studies in the Theory of Imperialism* (London, 1972), pp. 117–42.
6 For historical details see A. Wirz, *Krieg in Afrika. Die nachkolonialen Konflikte in Nigeria, Sudan, Tschad und Kongo* (Wiesbaden, 1982), chs 1 and 3.
7 Quoted in J. S. Coleman, *Nigeria: Background to Nationalism* (Berkeley, Calif., 1958), pp. 193–4.

8   On the problems of cultural and structural pluralism see L. Kuper and M. G. Smith (eds), *Pluralism in Africa* (London, 1971).
9   S. Berry, *Cocoa, Custom and Socio-economic Change in Rural Western Nigeria* (Oxford, 1975).
10 For a general, perceptive treatment of these questions see C. Young, *The Politics of Pluralism* (London, 1976).
11 R. Robinson, 'Andrew Cohen and the transfer of power in tropical Africa, 1940–1951', in W. H. Morris-Jones and G. Fischer (eds), *Decolonisation and After: The British and French Experience* (London, 1980), pp. 50–72.
12 E. A. Ayandele, *The Educated Elite in Nigerian Society* (Ibadan, 1974); not very different is the judgement of O. Nnoli, *Ethnic Politics in Nigeria* (Enugu, 1978).
13 O. Awolowo, *Path to Nigerian Freedom* (London, 1947), p. 32.
14 See D. Olatunbosun, *Nigeria's Neglected Rural Majority* (Ibadan, 1976).
15 P. Worsthorne, 'Blood is thicker than oceans', *Sunday Telegraph*, 23 May 1982.
16 Y. Person, 'Contre l'état-nation', *Pluriel*, no. 8 (1976), pp. 49–65; idem, 'L'état-nation et l'Afrique', *Le Mois en Afrique*, vol. 16, nos 190–1 (1981), pp. 27–35; idem, 'L'idéologie de l'état-nation et sa contestation', *Les Temps modernes*, no. 422 (1981), pp. 455–76.
17 To cite but one of the critics of the new constitution, Y. B. Usman, *For the Liberation of Nigeria* (London, 1979).
18 See *Review*, vol. 7, no. 4 (Spring 1984): special issue on 'Long Waves in History'.

10 The Legacy of the British-Indian Empire in Independent India

DIETMAR ROTHERMUND

Studies of imperialism mostly deal with the dynamics of the rise and fall of empires. The receiving end, the countries subjected to imperial control, gets less attention and the history of the imperial impact on such countries is written either from the point of view of the imperial power, or in terms of the nationalist reaction to it. Imperialism as a transactional phenomenon has been neglected so far. Imperial systems are complex entities: they are more than the sum of their parts as long as they last and leave strange legacies when they disappear. In this chapter I shall attempt to deal with a legacy of this kind by discussing the specific case of British India. But, first, a flashback into the more distant past is required in order to show that the imperial heritage was in itself a hybrid product. The British-Indian empire was not simply a British empire in India; it owed a great deal to the preceding Mogul empire especially with regard to the administrative tradition which will be discussed in the first section of this chapter. Subsequent sections will be devoted to the army, the legal system, agrarian relations, education, the economy and foreign affairs.

Imperial Bureaucracy: An Instrument of Rational Rule?

Max Weber has taught us to look at bureaucracy as a manifestation of rational rule. He has also highlighted the limitations of bureaucratic rule as well as the inescapable effects of its operation which make it so resistant and perennial. He refers to the bureaucratic machine as a 'mind objectified', a well-knit structure of human bondage which controls all relevant actions in terms of defined rules.[1] In India we can trace this objectification by following two converging lines: the revenue system of the Moguls and the 'covenanted service' of the East India Company.

Mogul finance depended to a large extent on the extraction of a substantial land revenue. This was mostly spent on the maintenance of a large army. The hierarchy of the imperial service (*mansabdars*) was defined in terms of military ranks; the salary of the respective officer and the amount to be collected under his jurisdiction were related to his rank. The actual bookkeeping and the collection of the revenue were entrusted to a host of scribes who did not belong to the imperial service. The members of that service often prided themselves on being ignorant of the art of bookkeeping and stressed their military valour. In this way, they were even more dependent on the knowledge of the scribes. The whole system was one of bureaucracy by proxy, but it was based on a very rational scheme: an imperial hierarchy related to an allocation of revenue assignments which had 'congealed' at the time of Akbar. This was more or less faithfully copied by Akbar's successors and even by those regional rulers who finally defied Mogul authority in the eighteenth century.[2]

In the meantime, the East India Company had entrenched itself on India's maritime periphery in numerous factories staffed by members of a 'covenanted service' who were appointed under a system of open patronage by the directors of the company in London. The 'covenant' was an instrument for the protection of the company's interests. On entering this service as a 'writer', the young employee had to deposit an amount of money which exceeded several annual salaries. He was obviously expected to add to this meagre salary by making money on the side; but if, by doing this, he damaged the interests of the company, he was liable to forfeit his deposit. As long as the company was engaged only in commercial activities, this system worked very well and ensured steady recruitment of reliable and resourceful employees. But when the company emerged as a territorial power and received large revenue assignments from the Great Mogul whose power was declining, new responsibilities had to be shouldered by the 'covenanted servants' and the nature of the covenant eventually changed. Initially, the company continued the old system of bureaucracy by proxy but, finally, it decided to fill the crucial posts at district headquarters with 'covenanted servants' who were granted high salaries and given strict injunctions against corruption.[3]

The replacement of the imperial service of the Moguls with the erstwhile bookkeepers of the company implied a major change. The military hierarchy was succeeded by a 'civil' service. The collection of revenue and the maintenance of troops were completely separated. The British governor-general soon emerged as a ruler who was much more powerful than any previous Indian ruler. The extraction of revenue and the maintenance of law and order by a highly privileged but disciplined and transferable 'covenanted service' was the foundation of the new British-Indian empire. This service, later called the Indian Civil Service, remained the 'steel frame'[4] of the empire throughout, and after Independence was achieved it was taken over by the new Indian government and renamed the Indian Administration Service. The first Indian Home Minister, Vallabhbhai Patel, deliberately opted for this conservation of the imperial heritage and asserted that the country had to be kept together by a 'ring of service'[5] – a paraphrase of Lloyd George's 'steel frame'.

The special feature of this service is that it is a cadre of carefully selected 'generalists' who are expected to handle a variety of tasks in the course of a career which involves several transfers from district assignments to positions in a state government or at the centre, as well as managerial duties in public-sector enterprises.[6] Selection by means of a highly competitive examination after a good college education had already been established as a norm in the mid-nineteenth century.[7]

The service continues to attract the brightest candidates who could do well in an academic career, but prefer to affix the prestigious 'IAS' to their names rather than to end up as professors with a much lower salary and status. The few people who have resigned from the service in order to return to an academic career are regarded as saints who have renounced the world.

In independent India the pressures of politics have caught up with the civil servant who is often tempted to break the rules in order to please his political bosses. The usual conflict between the civil servant and the politician arises when the civil servant wants to maintain the norm of his profession and the politician wants favours for his protégés, or some other deviation from the rules. The politician is used to verbal orders and requests; the civil servant must reduce every essential point to writing and can be held responsible for whatever he has signed. A recent study shows that in many such conflicts the civil servants have resisted much pressure and have even risked transfer or premature retirement.[8] Their privileges are still fairly well protected and thus the risks are limited and they can afford to face the wrath of a politician. This certainly acts as a check on arbitrary decisions and provides stability for the system. But, of course, it may also impede quick and unbureaucratic responses to problems of development.

The large-scale involvement of the civil service in developmental activities is one of the negative aspects of the imperial heritage. The prestige of the service is so great that its senior members have been entrusted with all kinds of managerial tasks in the public sector where entrepreneurial qualities are required which by their very nature are different from those associated with a reliable bureaucrat. Similarly, it was wrong to burden the almighty district officers, who still have the time-honoured title 'collector', with the job of acting as dispensers of development funds. Such tasks should have been entrusted to a genuine agency for community development. But initial attempts of this kind have failed and the Block Development Officer has turned into a minor replica of the 'collector'.[9]

The proper role of the civil servant is to act as an umpire and to see that the rules of the game are kept; if he is asked to play the game himself, he is forced to overstep the limits which define his role. The imperial heritage of a prestigious civil service has thus been both an asset and a liability to independent India – an asset wherever the service has been employed in a way consonant with its nature, and a liability where it has been asked to perform functions which it cannot fulfil.

The Indian Army: From Imperial Mercenaries to a National Force

Whereas the civil service has been faced with all kinds of pressures in independent India, the Indian Army has so far retained the limited and therefore professionally effective role which is part of the British heritage. The roots of this army go back to the East India Company's troops, but also to the traditions of the Royal Army. The company's troops were mercenaries well trained by British officers. India was conquered by Indian soldiers under British command at the expense of the Indian taxpayer. Royal troops dispatched from England were rarely used and it was only after the Mutiny of 1857 that the colonial rulers felt the need to station more British troops in India. Nevertheless, the many imperial expeditions of the late nineteenth century, including interventions in distant Africa, relied heavily on Indian soldiers.[10] Finally, millions of Indians fought for the British in two world wars, an experience which was of great importance for the growth of the Indian Army. Initially, the British were very reluctant to entrust the command of their Indian troops to Indian officers. The imperial tradition demanded that orders should come from the British, while the Indians had to obey. It was only the pressing need of the Second World War and the sudden expansion of the Indian Army that forced the British to grant commission to more and more Indian officers so that by the end of that war there were enough experienced Indian officers of various ranks for the transfer of command to be effected very smoothly when the British left India.[11]

The rise of an Indian corps of army officers acted as an antidote to, rather than a catalyst for, nationalist domination of the armed forces while the British had earlier feared that Indian officers could not be trusted because they might join hands with the freedom movement. Subhas Chandra Bose's Indian National Army attracted only very few Indian officers, however. After the war, the British made the mistake of putting some of these officers on trial in order to demonstrate that they regarded them as traitors. This proved to be counterproductive, as it gave rise to a wave of national sympathy for the accused.[12] However, most of their erstwhile colleagues in the British Indian Army had no sympathy for them and none of the officers of the Indian National Army were later able to make a mark in independent India. The new Indian Army was led by those who had remained loyal to the British, or rather, to the British ideal of a non-political army that serves the established authority.

The relative stability of the Indian political system has enabled the army to maintain this non-political position and its professional integrity. In Pakistan and Bangladesh which initially shared the same tradition, the military has seized power because the political systems concerned did not have sufficient stability of their own. In both these countries, military rulers have tried to get back to normality by becoming civilian presidents. But once the precedent of a military coup had been set, there was no guarantee against more or less successful repetitions which would further destabilize the political system. International tensions and the arms race contributed to this destabilization, in that the army which would quite naturally lobby for up-to-date hardware was also in control of the government, which has to sanction its acquisition.[13]

It may sound paradoxical, but it is mainly due to the fact that India experienced a long freedom struggle which did not involve the army that it could evolve a political system which could survive without the army taking over power. If Subhas Chandra Bose had succeeded in his attempt to attract most of the British Indian Army to his Indian National Army in his valiant fight for India's freedom as he saw it, the officers of that army might well have become his political heirs. The present Indian Army, on the other hand, has successfully achieved the transition from an army of colonial mercenaries to a national force because it remained outside the arena of political conflict and has thus remained above reproach.

The Continuity of the Legal System

The most lasting impact of British rule in India was made in the field of law. British jurisdiction in India had two separate roots. Initially, the Supreme Court established in Calcutta was confined in its jurisdiction to Europeans settled there; it was not concerned with Indians. As Diwan of Bengal, the East India Company became responsible for the Diwani Adalat, the civil and fiscal jurisdiction, whereas penal law was administered by the nawab's judges. Diwani law was not Islamic like the penal code, it was a kind of customary law which had evolved in India. The intrusion of British legal concepts into this sphere was thus not impeded by adherence to religious sanctions.[14] In Britain, the law had in the course of time become a powerful instrument for the protection of the creditor against fraudulent debtors. Fees and fines helped to finance the expansion of this jurisdiction, and the same system was now applied to India. The courts added to the revenue of the state and did not burden the budget. Litigants flocked to these courts, as they had learned how to use the new law to their advantage. Legal procedure, rather informal under earlier regimes, was reorganized: everything had to be recorded in writing and the due process of law had to be observed meticulously. The knowledge of precedent and procedure could not be mastered by the litigant who needed a lawyer to guide him. The legal profession prospered as British jurisdiction expanded. Educated Indians found this career very attractive and long before they could aspire to higher positions in the civil service or in the army, they could become judges of a High Court. In this way, they became very much attached to the new legal tradition and guarded it as if it were their own national heritage. Actually, this new legal system which reflected the conditions of an advanced bourgeois society was not very well suited to the conditions prevailing in India with its large population of illiterate peasants. The expansion of credit which occurred when the new legal system was established did not contribute to investments for the improvement of agriculture. Clever moneylenders who knew how to use a mortgage to keep their debtors in permanent bondage reaped the greatest benefits under this new dispensation. Freedom of contract which was the hallmark of the British legal system was based on the assumption that the contracting parties were equals, but there was no such equality between the peasant who put his thumb print under a bond which he could not read and the moneylender who kept him in servitude by procuring ex-parte decrees from the court or foreclosing his mortgage.[15] The British were finally forced to legislate for the protection of indebted peasants and for the control of rents paid by tenants. But in doing this they were very careful not to go too far as they did not want to damage their land revenue system which depended on the availability of credit and the observance of contractual obligations. Unlike earlier rulers who simply imposed their revenue demand, the British adhered to the idea that revenue 'settlement' implied that the revenue payer entered into a contract with the government.[16] In effect, this 'liberal' construction was far more severe than any despotic impositions. While earlier rulers relaxed the collection of their revenue whenever political or climatic conditions did not permit the realization of the full demand, the British rigorously auctioned the land of a revenue defaulter, regardless of the circumstances which had caused him to break his 'contract'. However, while there was such a rigorous law of land sale there was no legal definition of the revenue demand which was left entirely to executive discretion and could not be inquired into by a court of law. In this respect, the revenue assessment remained an imposition.[17]

In the field of penal law the introduction of British standards, which were supposed to be more 'humane' than the Islamic penal code of their predecessors, also led to much more rigorous jurisdiction. Mutilation of thieves horrified the British, while they were quite ready to inflict capital punishment for forgery and other crimes which had never led to such dire consequences under Islamic law. Moreover, Islamic law had such elaborate rules of evidence that it was often difficult to convict the accused. Thus while it appeared to be more brutal, it was in fact more lenient than the new law introduced by the British.[18]

'Law and order' – the motto of British rule in India – was efficiently maintained in this way. British jurisdiction, as we have seen, was much more rigorous than that of previous regimes. Its chief virtue was not humane leniency but rather the establishment of a due process of law with all the formal ritual of the law suit, and the right of appeal to the greatly respected justices of the High Court. When the British deviated from this pattern by passing emergency legislation for the suppression of the national movement after the First World War, the Indians summed up this legislation in a short formula: 'No lawyer, no law suit, no appeal'.[19] The awareness of the due process of law was deeply ingrained and the British never made use of this emergency legislation.[20] Although British-Indian Law had in the course of time become an entity of its own which was in many respects much more well-defined than British Law at home, it was nevertheless constantly in touch with the British legal tradition. There was an important institutional link which helped to preserve this tradition. The highest court of appeal for British India was the Privy Council in London.[21] The judgements and the *obiter dicta* of the learned members of that council provided the guidelines of British-Indian jurisdiction. After independence was achieved, this link was broken and in many instances Indian jurists preferred to turn to the American Supreme Court for leading cases which established important precedents.[22] But the tradition of that court is, of course, also derived from the common British heritage.

One reason for this Indian interest in the American Supreme Court is the fact that India has a written constitution which includes a bill of rights and is in this respect similar to the American Constitution. With the exception of this bill of rights which was a heritage of the Indian freedom movement, the constitution corresponds to the Government of India Act of 1935, the most voluminous Act ever passed by the British Parliament.[23] The rather unique federation which was established by this Act has remained one of the most important bequests of imperial rule. This federalism is designed to support a strong central government, because it was meant to preserve the viceroy's position when the devolution of power took the shape of 'provincial autonomy'. The viceregal tradition is still strong in New Delhi. The continuity of the legal system and the persistence of this viceregal tradition are closely related: the rule of law is supported by a system of government which was originally designed to maintain imperial supremacy.

The Empire and the Rich Peasant

The stability of the Indian political system rests on the social base of the upper strata of the peasantry. This social base is another element of the imperial heritage, because it was constructed by the British with a view to preserving their rule over this vast agrarian country. Unlike many other countries of the Third World, whose governments have a rather narrow or precarious social base, India is fortunate in this respect. This does not mean that India is blessed with an egalitarian social structure and with a universal prevalence of social justice. On the contrary, the distribution of land and income is very unequal,[24] but the absentee landlord who is both politically and economically useless has been eliminated, and the rich peasant who wields influence in the village and determines what is going on in the countryside has emerged as the mainstay of the political system. This social change was not the result of a sudden revolution; it took a long time to evolve under British rule. Initially, the British had relied on the feudal lords and intermediaries of their predecessors. These lords combined functions of local authority with revenue collection. They were surrounded by armed retainers and, whenever the central power was weak, they kept a large share of the agricultural surplus for themselves and ruled like kings over a couple of villages. The British deprived them of all their powers, but converted them into landlords according to their legal traditions.[25] As landlords and owners of private property they enjoyed the expansion of credit and in due course their estates became encumbered.[26] They were tempted to increase the rents of their tenants, and the British who believed in market forces and saw landlord and tenant as freely contracting parties did not intervene for a long time until they were faced with so much agrarian tension that they feared peasant rebellions might shake the foundations of their empire. The measures which they then adopted were aimed at forestalling this political challenge; they were not meant to lead to an agrarian reform in the economic sense of the term. All these measures curtailed the rights of the landlords and enhanced the rights of their immediate tenants while subtenants and sharecroppers remained unprotected and could be exploited even more directly and efficiently by the chief tenants.[27]

In the course of constitutional reforms the British took care to enlarge the rather limited franchise to include these beneficiaries of their agrarian measures. Property classifications were designed to include these upper strata of the peasantry in the electorate.[28] High agricultural prices which had prevailed ever since the First World War had greatly benefited these rich peasants, but revenue and rent had not kept pace with the rise in prices because the assessment of revenue and rent increases were restricted by long-term settlements. Thus the British could hope to find solid political support among the rich peasants, whereas the Indian National Congress led by urban middle-class lawyers would be left high and dry in the enlarged rural electoral arena. But then the Great Depression slashed agricultural prices and the peasants were faced with rent or revenue demands which now proved to be a great burden. In this way, the peasantry was driven into the arms of the National Congress which suddenly acquired a substantial rural base, whereas the British and their loyalist campfollowers were left high and dry. This crucial transition in the 1930s was of great importance for the political development of independent India.[29] The social base which the National Congress acquired in this way gave it a solid foundation but also set limits to its economic programme.[30] Any measure which went against the vested interests of the rich peasantry was bound to fail. This social base which the British had constructed for themselves and had then lost to the National Congress proved to be one of the most enduring elements of the imperial heritage.

Education: the Dilemma of the Colonial Mind

Another element of the foundation of British rule in India which, finally, was of doubtful value to them was the system of education which they introduced in order to get adequate personnel for their administration.[31] The system did not only breed obedient civil servants who were content to work in the lower echelons of that service, but it also produced ambitious intellectuals and seditious lawyers who quoted with verve the liberal political philosophy which they had studied in their colleges. In this way, the education introduced by the British had a liberating influence, but it also produced that peculiar hybrid variety of intellectual life – the colonial mind. The standards of intellectual achievement were set in terms of alien ideas. If the educated Indian looked at the problems of his life and his country, he saw them as reflected by the prism of the education which he had received. If he came to know about the traditions of his country at all, it was through the work of Western indologists writing in English – a fact which explains the enormous popularity of Max Müller in India, whereas Müller is hardly remembered in his own country.[32] Moreover, the system of education did not encourage independent thinking, but the faithful reproduction of the material prescribed in the syllabus. The successful candidate compartmentalized and memorized the knowledge which was transmitted in this way. He neutralized the impact of this knowledge because he could learn by heart without his heart being touched by what he learned. With few exceptions the teachers who taught him were products of the same system; they dictated notes which helped to pass exams. In the interest of objectivity the students were examined in a strictly impersonal way. 'Paper setters' of another college would formulate the questions to be answered by the candidates and the papers would be sent elsewhere. This led to a high degree of standardization of conventional knowledge and discouraged critical analysis which might deviate from the expected pattern. The University of London had served as a model for the Indian educational system and by means of 'affiliation' the university rules and regulations were extended to the smallest college in a provincial town. The result of this standardization was in many ways very striking. Everybody with a college degree in India would have more or less the same standard of knowledge. He would have read the same texts as his colleague at the other end of India. A large but qualitatively rather limited universe of discourse was established in this way. Earlier cultural traditions in India had always been regional in their most explicit manifestations. This new tradition encompassed the whole of British India and did not lend itself to regional articulation. It was only when the regional languages of India developed a modern prose style under the impact of English literature, that this articulation received a new lease of life.

The national universe of discourse which emerged as a result of the expansion of the British educational system in India provided a challenge to the colonial mind. The constraints of this universe of discourse were noticed by perceptive intellectuals. The quest for a national past and a new national identity preoccupied them; a tradition of national solidarity had to be established.[33] The arrogance of the alien rulers who denigrated the Indian past and claimed that they had shown the light of civilization to India prompted Indian scholars to rehabilitate Indian history.[34] In doing this they sometimes overshot the mark, for instance when they tried to trace the roots of republican democracy in ancient India or when they wished to project the image of Greater India, an India which had established colonies overseas much earlier than Great Britain.[35] These reflections of the colonial mind are by now no longer of great consequence, but another colonial paradigm, which juxtaposed the spirituality of India and the materialism of the West, is still very much in evidence even today. It was originally emphasized in order to explain India's subjection to foreign rule as a result of its otherworldly interests and the neglect of material profit and political power, which were pursued so energetically by the British. When the ancient Indian book on statecraft, Kautilya's *Arthashastra*, was rediscovered at the beginning of this century, the colonial mind eagerly drew upon this example of India's sophistication in this field.[36] Many intellectuals would not hesitate to praise India's spirituality and the worldly wisdom of the *Arthashastra* in the same breath as long as they could score a point against the British. The constant dilemma of the colonial mind was the dependence on, and the rejection of, the British impact. Many statements which appear to be inconsistent if taken at face value, make sense when they are interpreted in terms of this dilemma.

The end of British rule should have resolved this dilemma of the colonial mind, but the pattern of defensive reasoning survived the end of direct domination. The perpetuation of the system of education which does not encourage independent thinking has contributed to this survival of the colonial mind. Individual thinkers may be able to emancipate themselves from this prevailing pattern, but they will find it difficult to influence others who are still caught on the horns of the dilemma.

The Contradictions of the Mixed Economy

The puzzle of the colonial mind is not the only instance of the contradictions inherent in the British heritage in India. The mixed economy which was established under the Five-Year Plans in independent India can actually be traced back to the tangled skein of colonial economic development.[37] British rule had kept India in a stage of underdevelopment for a long time. An advanced bourgeois state had enveloped a vast agrarian country, exploiting its resources and using it as a captive market for its industrial products. Indigenous industrialization could not take place under these circumstances; it was only when the First World War interrupted British-dominated 'free trade' that India could achieve some modest industrial progress.[38] The further course of development under 'imperial preference' and the exceptional conditions created by the Second World War contributed to a limited and fragmented industrialization of India. Genuine competitive capitalism never had a chance in India; monopolies grew up in the niches which were left to the Indians by the British system.[39] And yet the few Indian industrialists who got ahead in this way had to be respected by Indian nationalists who deplored India's industrial backwardness and welcomed everybody who made a contribution to industrial progress as a champion of the national cause.

The Second World War created a peculiar situation. The expansion of industrial capacity was stopped as no investment goods could be imported and India could not yet produce its own investment goods. At the same time, the demand for India's industrial production was greatly enhanced in the course of the war; prices rose and the industrialists made windfall profits.[40] Their plans for postwar reconstruction and investment coincided with those of the nationalists who were inspired by socialist ideas. The industrialists wanted large-scale investments by the state in infrastructure and basic industries, while they wanted to be free to invest their resources in those industries which promised quick returns.[41] The planners of the Indian National Congress led by Jawaharlal Nehru wanted large-scale investment by the state in a public sector of the economy because they wanted to prevent a domination of Indian industry by private monopolies, but they were prepared to leave some scope for a private sector in some fields which did not lead to a control of the 'commanding heights' of the economy by the capitalists.[42] In practice, these two different approaches to a mixed economy dovetailed and the contradictions became apparent only at a later stage. Initially, the national planners could take pride in the fact that they seemed to have harnessed the resources of the capitalists by clearly defining the activities open to the private sector and reserving the 'commanding heights' for the public sector. But, in fact, the industrialists

The Legacy of the British-Indian Empire

took full advantage of this situation by investing in production which would guarantee quick growth and good returns, while the state had to foot the bill for heavy investment that did not yield quick profits.[43] In other words, both planners and industrialists could feel that they had got the better of each other. The mixed economy seemed to be an ideal solution, a harmonious symbiosis of private and state capitalism. It was only after some time that the planners noticed that the 'commanding heights' of the economy were not so high after all and that the capitalists had prospered much more than the public sector which was mostly in the red. The performance of the public sector was no encouragement to those who would like to put an end to the mixed economy by expropriating the capitalists; on the other hand, the idea of surrendering to monopoly capitalism by selling out the public sector was too repulsive to all those nurtured in Nehru's school of thought. This means that the mixed economy has come to stay, although it may no longer be regarded as an ideal symbiosis but rather as a truce between forces that cannot afford to do away with each other. In fact, the mixed economy was a truce from the very beginning, as this analysis has shown. This truce was originally arrived at under the impact of the Second World War when the government emerged as the largest customer of Indian industry and also had to interfere with the agricultural market in order to tackle a large-scale food-supply crisis. An imperial government which had earlier adopted a *laissez-faire* policy because it served its interests best and was cheap and expedient, was compelled to embark on an interventionist course by wartime pressures.[44] The instruments of planning and administration were bequeathed to India as part of the imperial legacy, a fact which has been forgotten by those who attribute the rise of economic planning in India purely to Indian initiatives. Without an administrative machinery geared to interventionism such initiatives would have remained abstract intellectual exercises. Of course, as long as imperial rule lasted these instruments were used merely for the narrow aims of the war effort and national reconstruction could be conceived of only in an independent India, but the basic pattern – including the truce mentioned earlier – was established during the war.

The Imperial Heritage in External Affairs

British India was greatly expanded by several imperial proconsuls who annexed surrounding territories. The Indian National Congress had condemned this policy even at its first session in 1885,[45] and when Nehru took office as the first Indian Prime Minister, much of this imperial heritage had been relinquished by the prior separation of Burma and the partition of India, so that apart from the imperial presence in Tibet and some disputed borders between India and China there was no obvious problem for independent India. The outpost in Tibet was soon abolished and Nehru felt that he could live in peace with China.[46] He thus had a free hand for his global mission of anti-imperialism, for which he tried to use the Indian case as a precedent for the liberation of all nations still under colonial rule. The rapid progress of decolonization and India's conflict with China changed this scene. India's global mission was terminated and its regional problems claimed a higher priority. The successful defence of Indian territory against Pakistan in 1965 and the liberation of Bangladesh in 1971 established India's regional hegemony which, of course, has aroused the fears and resentments of India's smaller neighbours. Whether it likes it or not, India has emerged as the major heir of the British-Indian empire. Its hegemony in this region is inevitable, but in the present world of nation-states this hegemony can no longer be maintained by 'expeditions' and annexations of the British type in the heyday of the 'forward policy'. Being firmly attached to the idea of the nation-state because of its long freedom struggle against imperial rule, India will not pursue such a policy. It will respect the national integrity of its neighbours. It will only intervene when the national integrity of the respective neighbour is in doubt, as in the case of the liberation of Bangladesh, which no longer wanted to be East Pakistan. As far as Pakistan is concerned, which was a creation of the departing British, India's attitude will depend on the attitude of the Pakistanis to their state. If they present themselves as an integrated nation-state, India will have every reason to support the integrity and stability of Pakistan, because this stability is in its own national interest. However, if Pakistan is torn by internal strife and offers an opening for superpower intervention in the region, India may be drawn into a conflict.[47] The problem of Pakistan is that it has not yet found an adequate base of territorial nationality, and relies on the 'Two-Nation Theory' propounded by Jinnah, which implies the existence of a Hindu nation and a Muslim nation, but does not define the Muslim nation in territorial terms.[48] This theory has been controverted by the secession of Bangladesh, but it has not been replaced by a viable alternative. Instead the present regime in Pakistan is projecting the ideology of an Islamic state in order to establish its legitimacy.[49] However, this does not solve the problem of territorial nationality, which cannot be adequately defined in Islamic terms because Islam is a universal religion which does not recognize national boundaries, but accepts any state as given. Similarly, national self-determination is not a concept which can claim the support of Islam, nor could the right of resistance or secession be derived from Islamic injunctions. But if, on the contrary, the principles of the Islamic state are invoked in order to suppress movements of national self-determination, India as a secular nation-state would not be in sympathy with such a policy, though it may refrain from intervention for reasons of practical politics.

The Soviet invasion of Afghanistan has put Pakistan into the limelight of world politics and has revived a Curzonian scenario of Russian imperial expansion in South Asia, which must be counteracted by a vigorous 'frontier' policy.[50] In the interests of a common defence of the subcontinent, India should join hands with Pakistan and forget about old disputes caused by the partition. But for India it is difficult to return to Lord Curzon's design, because the course of events after the achievement of Independence had taught India to look upon the Soviet Union and on Afghanistan as friends, and to regard Pakistan as an enemy. The Soviet invasion of Afghanistan has deeply disturbed India, but it could not suddenly reverse its previous policy. For a long time the national interests of India and the Soviet Union had appeared to coincide.[51] Due to strained relations with Pakistan's Western allies, India's reliance on Soviet armament supplies had also grown in recent decades. At present, India seems to be aiming if not at a restoration of non-alignment in its pristine purity, then at least at equidistance as far as the superpowers are concerned. India may finally establish better relations both with Pakistan and China and thus contain further Soviet intervention in Asian affairs. This would be an unexpected fulfilment of Curzon's plans who was, of course, concerned with the security of Asia not for its own sake but in the interest of the British-Indian empire. The departing British greatly delayed this course of events by the partition of India, and it is only due to the Soviet invasion of Afghanistan that old scenarios regain new importance, though in an entirely different context.

Notes: Chapter 10

1. M. Weber, *Economy and Society* (Berkeley, Cal., 1978), p. 1402.
2. For an analysis of Akbar's revenue system see I. Habib, *The Agrarian System of Mughal India, 1556–1707* (Bombay, 1963); for the subsequent period see I. Prasad, *India in the Eighteenth Century* (Allahabad, 1973).
3. For a detailed description of the evolution of the 'covenanted service' see A. K. Ghosal, *Civil Service in India under the East India Company* (Calcutta, 1944).
4. The expression 'steel frame' was used by Prime Minister David Lloyd George in a speech with which he wanted to attract more British recruits for the Indian civil service at a time when there was a lack of candidates and the rapid Indianization of the service was still considered undesirable. See R. Symonds, *The British and their Successors in the New States* (London, 1966), p. 40.
5. Patel referred to the 'ring of service' in the *Constituent Assembly Debates* (Vol. 10, p. 51): 'This Constitution is meant to be worked by a ring of Service which will keep the country intact.'
6. A vivid account of the experiences of members of the Indian administrative service based on reports of a sample of retired officers is given by J. K. Ray, *Administrators in a Mixed Polity* (New Delhi, 1981).
7. Symonds, *The British and their Successors*, pp. 44 ff.
8. Ray, *Administrators*, pp. 89 ff.
9. For a critique of the administration of development programmes, see R. N. Maharaj, 'The impact of state policy on agriculture', in D. Rothermund et al. (eds), *Urban Growth and Rural Stagnation* (New Delhi, 1981), pp. 179–260.
10. For a survey of British military policy in India and its budgetary implications see W. Simon, *Die britische Militärpolitik in Indien und ihre Auswirkungen auf den britisch-indischen Finanzhaushalt, 1878–1910* (Wiesbaden, 1974).
11. For the role of the Indian Army in the Second World War see J. Voigt, *Indien im Zweiten Weltkrieg* (Stuttgart, 1978), pp. 71 ff.
12. ibid., pp. 297 ff.
13. D. Rothermund, 'Pakistans Beziehungen zu Indien und Afghanistan', *Vierteljahresberichte (Forschungsinstitut der Friedrich-Ebert-Stiftung)*, no. 87 (March 1982), pp. 29–36.
14. On the introduction of British law and jurisdiction in India see M. V. Jain, *Outline of Indian Legal History* (Bombay, 1972).
15. D. Rothermund, *Government, Landlord and Peasant in India: Agrarian Relations under British Rule, 1865–1935* (Wiesbaden, 1978), p. 17.
16. ibid., pp. 33–4.
17. ibid., p. 46.
18. A recent study of this contrast between British and Islamic Law is J. Fisch, *Cheap Lives and Dear Limbs* (Wiesbaden, 1983).

152   Imperialism and After

19 *British Parliamentary Papers, Vol. 4 (1920): Punjab Disturbances* (Gujranwala Report).
20 D. Rothermund, *Die politische Willensbildung in Indien, 1900–1960* (Wiesbaden, 1965), pp. 80 ff.
21 Rothermund, *Government, Landlord and Peasant*, p. 55.
22 For references to the relevance of the US Supreme Court for Indian constitutional law see H. M. Seervai, *Constitutional Law of India*, 3 vols, 2nd edn (Bombay, 1975–9): Vol. 1, pp. 58–9, 511–12, Vol. 2, pp. 1170, 1577, Vol. 3, pp. 1618–19, 1795–6.
23 Rothermund, *Politische Willensbildung*, p. 214.
24 D. Rothermund, 'Impediments to "development from below" in India's economic history', *Asian and African Studies (Annual of the Israel Oriental Society)*, vol. 6 (1970), pp. 47–73.
25 Rothermund, *Government, Landlord and Peasant*, p. 214.
26 For a detailed case study of encumbered estates see D. C. Wadhwa, 'Zamindars in debts', in D. Rothermund and D. C. Wadhwa (eds), *Zamindars, Mines and Peasants* (New Delhi, 1978), pp. 131–63.
27 Rothermund, *Government, Landlord and Peasant*, pp. 86 ff.
28 ibid., pp. 123, 144, 186–7.
29 D. Rothermund, 'Die Interferenz von Agrarpreissturz und Befreiungskampf in Indien', in D. Rothermund (ed.), *Die Peripherie in der Weltwirtschaftskrise: Afrika, Asien und Lateinamerika 1929–1939* (Paderborn, 1982), pp. 127–43.
30 Rothermund, *Government, Landlord and Peasant*, pp. 189 ff.
31 Symonds, *The British and their Successors*, pp. 44 ff.
32 D. Rothermund, 'Max Müller and India's quest for a national past', *Dialogue 1972/73* (Bombay: Max Müller Bhavan, 1973), pp. 53–61.
33 D. Rothermund, 'Traditionalism and national solidarity in India', in R. J. Moore (ed.), *Tradition and Politics in South Asia* (New Delhi, 1979), pp. 191–7.
34 D. Rothermund, 'Indiens Verhältnis zu seiner Geschichte', *Indo Asia*, vol. 17, no. 1 (January 1975), pp. 41–50.
35 For an important example of this kind of historiography see R. C. Majumdar, *Ancient Indian Colonies in the Far East* (Calcutta, 1927).
36 For a study of the impact made by the rediscovery of the *Arthashastra* see J. Voigt, 'Nationalist interpretations of Arthaśāstra in Indian historical writing', in S. N. Mukherjee (ed.), *The Movement for National Freedom in India* (Oxford, 1966), pp. 46–66.
37 For an early plan which was aimed at a reversal of colonial stagnation along capitalist lines but with vigorous participation of the state see M. Visvesvaraya, *Planned Economy for India*, 2nd edn (Bangalore, 1936).
38 For an analysis of industrial investment and development see A. Bagchi, *Private Investment in India 1900–1939* (Cambridge, 1972); also R. Ray, *Industrialization in India: Growth and Conflict in the Private Corporate Sector, 1914–1947* (New Delhi, 1979).
39 N. K. Chandra, 'Monopoly capital, private corporate sector and the Indian economy: a study in relative growth, 1931–1976', in A. Bagchi and N. Banerjee (eds), *Change and Choice in Indian Industry* (Calcutta, 1981), pp. 329–81, espec. p. 375.
40 The cotton textile industry, for instance, registered the following increase in profits: 1939 = 100, 1941 = 316, 1943 = 640. See H. Fukazawa, 'Cotton mill industry', in V. B. Singh (ed.), *The Economic History of India, 1857–1956* (New Delhi, 1965), p. 253.
41 Some leading Indian industrialists, including G. D. Birla and J. R. D. Tata, published the so-called 'Bombay Plan'. See G. D. Birla *et al.*, *A Plan of Economic Development for India* (Bombay, 1944).
42 For a study of the first Five-Year Plans and Nehru's economic policy see W. Malenbaum, *Prospects for Indian Development* (London, 1962).
43 For an analysis of the contradictions between the public and the private sectors see A. Bagchi, 'Reinforcing and offsetting constraints in Indian industry', in Bagchi and Banerjee (eds), *Change and Choice in Indian Industry*, pp. 50–51.
44 For a detailed discussion of the evolution of economic planning in India under the impact of the Second World War, see D. Rothermund, 'Die Anfänge der indischen Wirtschaftsplanung im Zweiten Weltkrieg', in P. Hablützel *et al.* (eds), *Dritte Welt: Historische Prägung und politische Herausforderung. Festschrift für Rudolf von Albertini* (Wiesbaden, 1983), pp. 81–93.
45 A resolution was passed at this first National Congress depreciating the British annexa-

tion of Upper Burma, another resolution was aimed at a reduction of the growing military expenditure. See *Proceedings of the First Indian National Congress* (Bombay, 1885).
46 For an assessment of Nehru's foreign policy in the context of Afro-Asian solidarity and non-alignment see G. H. Jansen, *Afro-Asia and Nonalignment* (London, 1966).
47 For an evaluation of the relations between India and Pakistan see Rothermund, 'Pakistans Beziehungen'.
48 The problem of Pakistani attitudes towards territorial nationalism is discussed by D. Khalid, 'Pakistan's Islamic ideology in the secular nation state', in D. Rothermund (ed.), *Islam in Southern Asia* (Wiesbaden, 1975), pp. 46–7, 86–7.
49 Rothermund, 'Pakistans Beziehungen', p. 32.
50 For an analysis of Curzon's frontier policy see S. Gopal, *British Policy in India, 1858–1905* (Cambridge, 1965), pp. 228 ff.
51 D. Rothermund, *Indien und die Sowjetunion* (Tübingen, 1968), pp. 100–1.

11 Continuities and Discontinuities in Indo-British Economic Relations: British Multinational Corporations in India, 1920–1970

B. R. TOMLINSON

Recent work on the economic history of India in the twentieth century has tended to devalue the significance of the coming of independence in 1947 as a great divide. On the one hand, it is clear that close economic links between Britain and India continued well after the end of formal rule. Although crude concepts of neo-colonialism are inappropriate for the analysis of this continuing relationship, it is striking that in the 1950s India was Britain's best customer for iron and steel products, aircraft and parts, various types of machinery and electrical goods, and was among the top three importers of British chemicals, ships, textile machinery and general categories of electrical and non-electrical machinery. As late as 1963 India and Pakistan combined were the fifth largest recipient of the overseas investment of British companies (excluding banking, oil and insurance), and the fourth largest supplier of British corporate income from abroad.[1]

Such evidence of continuing economic ties is significant enough. What is perhaps more important is an emerging consensus of analysis of modern India which sees the main structure of the political economy of the post-independence decades as the logical culmination of pre-1947 events. The crucial period here is that from the early 1920s to the late 1960s, with 1947 as a minor hiccup in the process. Over these fifty years or so the managers of the Indian economy can be seen to be grappling with, and to be constrained by, a set of underlying structural problems. The most important of these include a high rate of population growth, a low rate of agricultural growth (caused largely by the failure of productivity in the absence of technological change), an absence of adequate investment in infrastructure, problems of revenue-raising without regressive taxation, an absence of demand stimulation for wage goods, and endemic foreign-exchange constraints (leading to major crises in the early 1920s, early 1930s, late 1940s, mid-1950s and late 1960s). Agricultural output probably grew less fast than population before Independence and not much faster than population, at best, afterwards (at least until the introduction of new technology at the end of our period); the proportion of the total labour force employed in large-scale industry failed to grow significantly throughout the period. Although after Independence the Indian government adopted a deliberate policy of planning for industrial growth based around public-sector enterprises, and was in receipt of large sources of external funds in the shape of the sterling balances and international aid programmes, these inputs have not given birth to the ability, or the will, to break free of fundamental constraints.[2]

In these conditions the middle years of the twentieth century saw the emergence of a particular type of economy in India in which both industry and agriculture depended for growth on subsidized inputs, and in which the resources available for subsidization were never sufficient. With both rural and urban sectors operating in the interstices of lines drawn by resource scarcity and distributional inequality, economic opportunity became determined by links between the economic and political systems. After 1947 especially, as government's role in the economic system has increased, the Indian state has been forced or seduced (with various degrees of willingness) into a mutually supportive alliance with dominant groups in towns and countryside to ensure political and social stability at the cost of structural stagnation. Most analysts of this process have focused on the symbiotic relationship between the state, the 'rich peasants' (or rurally dominant groups) and the 'industrial bourgeoisie' of the private corporate sector. This relationship has not always been stable, especially since the interests of rural and urban magnates (known collectively as the 'national bourgeoisie') have often come into conflict with each other and since both are potential rivals for a limited amount of resources, and from this instability have grown many of the tensions and crises of recent events in India.[3] This analysis of the contemporary class structure has also recently been employed by historians in an attempt to reveal its origins in the Gandhian nationalist movement of 1917–47.[4]

External forces are usually given some role to play in the creation and sustaining of this political-economic structure, although not usually a decisive one. Foreign governments, and international capital, are seen as one powerful set of interests with which the Indian state and its allies have had to contend, but one whose influence can only be understood as part of a complex, almost pluralistic, bargaining process within the dominant élite. Even so, the analysis of such forces tends to be reductionist, and to assume that causality and change comes about solely as the result of public policy, either inside or outside India. This approach inevitably distorts the complexities of the interplay between foreign capital and the national economy, with foreign capital seen as homogenous and as acting as an aggregate force. The aim of this chapter is to illustrate more clearly the dynamics and constraints that underlay the working of foreign firms in India over the whole of the late-colonial and early-Independence periods. It will do so by investigating the fortunes of a sample of British multinational companies (MNCs), firms which were in the forefront of the move to direct foreign investment (DFI) and which were involved, even before Independence, in the establishment of manufacturing subsidiaries in India. By highlighting the history of one particular set of institutions that made up the economic structure of modern India in the middle years of the twentieth century we can, perhaps, throw more light on the broader problems of the period and on the continuities and discontinuities of the Indo-British economic relationship that emerged after imperialism.

Tracing the activities of British-based MNCs in our period is complicated by acute conceptual and data-gathering problems. Poor coverage and definitional confusions make it very hard to arrive at precise figures for the extent of British DFI in India before the 1950s. But the available material does strongly suggest that such investment had its origins well before Independence – in 1947 perhaps half of British private foreign investment in manufacturing in India was direct investment in the subsidiaries of British-based companies. A survey of 41 British subsidiary companies that had at least Rs500,000 (£40,000) worth of share capital by 1950 reveals that a number of British-based MNCs had certainly become well established in India by then. More than three-quarters of these firms were intended to be manufacturing companies; of these 75 per cent were in production by 1950. The sectoral breakdown and the timing of this investment is interesting. Of the 32 manufacturing companies, 25 were in new industries (4 in electrical engineering and equipment, 1 in building materials, 4 in machinery, machine tools and metal manufactures, 5 in food, tobacco and household goods, 4 in industrial chemicals and pharmaceuticals, 2 in railway equipment, 1 in rubber goods and 4 in paints and varnish). Of the total 41 companies, 3 were set up (or acquired by foreign interests) before 1920, 6 in the 1920s, 21 in the 1930s, 2 between 1939 and 1947 and 9 between 1947 and 1950.[5] Looking backwards from the end of our period the historical base of British DFI in India is striking. Of 123 British subsidiary companies operating in India in the early 1970s, 24 had been established before 1930, 28 between 1930 and 1945, 34 between 1946 and 1955, 23 between 1956 and 1965 and 9 between 1966 and 1975 (with 5 unknown); of the 20 British subsidiaries with assets of more than Rs100 million in 1975, 13 had been established before 1945, 5 between 1946 and 1955 and 2 between 1956 and 1965.[6] By the early 1970s 28 major British MNCs had subsidiary firms ranking among the top 200 Indian companies; of these 16 had established an Indian subsidiary with a capital of over Rs500,000 by 1950, and only 2 had not established a subsidiary company of any size by that date.[7]

The pattern of British DFI in India had clear parallels elsewhere. The move away from simple imports to the establishment of manufacturing subsidiaries in India broadly fits the pattern seen in British relations with the Dominions, beginning in the 1920s with a peak in the 1950s and a relative decline from the mid-1960s as British firms turned their attention to European markets. One comparative estimate based on the number of manufacturing affiliates established by British MNCs reveals that India received about 4 per cent of the total in the 1920s, about 8 per cent from 1930–45, 6 per cent in the late 1940s, a peak of 11 per cent in the early 1950s, falling back to around 5 per cent for the years down to 1965 and then tailing away to less than 2 per cent by 1970.[8] It is striking that it was the early post-

Independence years that saw the greatest flurry of British DFI in India; in 1958 the percentage of such investment that had been made in India was only slightly lower than that in the whole of Europe (7·4 per cent to India, 8·4 per cent to Europe), while by 1971 the proportion was much smaller (4·6 per cent to India, 17·6 per cent to Europe).[9]

Theoretical approaches to the study of MNCs have recently been drawn together into an 'eclectic' theory which stresses the importance of 'internalization' in bringing about successful DFI.[10] Internalization is defined as the creation of vertical or horizontal integration in production and sales by controlled rather than market channels. The major incentives to this type of activity are to avoid the disadvantages, or capitalize on the advantages, of imperfections in external mechanisms for resource allocation. Where markets are perfectly competitive the co-ordinating of interdependent activities through the market could not be improved upon; once imperfections arise, or can be created, however, internalization becomes possible and desirable. The major market imperfections that are important here include problems of securing an adequate size of operations, lack of interdependent systems in local areas that can provide needed services at acceptable costs, and public-authority fiats (notably tariffs, quotas and other restrictions on imports) which can distort market prices and encourage or necessitate internalized activities. The ownership advantages accruing to MNCs, therefore, arise not only from exclusive possession of certain assets but also from the ability to internalize their use to protect themselves against the failures of markets or government fiat. Using this approach the growth of MNCs can be linked to other trends – notably increased vertical and horizontal integration of firms and increased diversification of markets and products. All these factors tend to increase the advantages of internalization and so encourage the spread of DFI rather than simple exports or licensing or royalty agreements.

In investigating the history of particular British MNCs in India it is important to distinguish two main categories of enterprise.[11] The first is what may be termed the 'private' sector – firms which manufactured consumer or intermediate goods intended for private customers; the second is the 'public' sector – firms whose main interest in India was in selling goods to the government especially, before 1947, the suppliers and equippers of the state-owned railway network.

For the private sector defensive reasons for investment decisions are usually stressed. A classic case here is that of Lever Brothers. As David Fieldhouse has pointed out in his *Unilever Overseas*: 'The history of Lever Brothers' activities in India underline the truth that a European industrial enterprise is unlikely to give thought to direct productive investment overseas so long as it has a satisfactory and expanding export market in any particular country.'[12] For Lever Brothers the threat that emerged in the early 1920s, and again in the early 1930s, was that of revenue tariffs which would, it was feared, give local producers of soap and hydrogenated vegetable oils the opportunity to undercut imports. A more extreme example of the effects of tariffs was that of the Swedish Match Company (not a British firm, but one on which good information is available). Swedish Match reacted to the imposition of a protective duty on the Indian match industry in 1922 by founding the Western India Match Company, with the initially highly defensive aim of preventing a new Indian match industry from exporting to other markets supplied by the parent firm. Until 1928 Swedish interests pushed hard for the Indian tariff to be reduced so that imports could replace local manufacture; only reluctantly did the parent firm accept that the Indian market would have to be supplied by subsidiary production.[13] A further problem for a number of British manufacturers in the Indian market in the interwar years was that of Japanese competition. Since Japanese exports could often undercut British goods in India, even after the adoption of full imperial preference in 1932, and since the Japanese refused to join any of the international cartels of the 1930s, local manufacture in India, however inefficient, could enable the parent firm to retain a foothold in the market thanks to local tariff rates. The decision by Courtaulds to set up a small (and eventually unsuccessful) factory in India may have been influenced by such considerations.[14]

Many of the same factors applied to the public-sector firms as well, with the proviso that the key issue here was not tariffs so much as government stores purchase policies. From the mid-1920s onwards the government of India began to buy its stores by rupee tender, accepting goods of adequate quality rather than the best available, and building in small preferences for local manufacturers. The result of these changes can be seen in the history of the Guest, Keen and Nettlefold (GKN) subsidiary, Guest, Keen, Williams (GKW) which was established in 1931 to manufacture dog-spikes for the Indian railways. When the rupee tender system had first been introduced in the 1920s, GKN had appointed an expatriate managing agency house as its agent, but still could not compete with Belgian rivals that benefited from the new stores rules. Even local manufacture could not undercut the Belgians in a free market; only the preference available to goods of Indian origin enabled GKW to win back the market.[15] The establishment of the Westinghouse Brake & Signal Company's subsidiary, Saxby & Farmer (India) Ltd, to manufacture railway-signalling equipment was prompted by the same motives.

Not all decisions to invest in India were quite as defensive as this, however. For some companies an Indian subsidiary could be a way of exploiting a new market that could not be supplied by exports, or that had grown too large to be supplied satisfactorily in this way. For companies making products that were expensive or impossible to ship in bulk – such as Metal Box's tin containers, Turner & Newall's asbestos sheets or British Oxygen's industrial gasses – a move to local manufacture was a reaction to an expanding market. For a number of paint firms too – Goodlass Wall and Blundell Permoglaze among them – local manufacture was the best way of exploiting increased market opportunities irrespective of tariffs or other obstructions to imports; the same was true for Crompton Parkinson, manufacturers of electrical equipment. For Lever Brothers' vegetable-oil interests the growth of the market in the 1930s was a positive embarrassment since the increase in demand gave dealers effective control over prices and so Lever Brothers were unable to take advantage of efficient production techniques to increase their market share by lowering prices. Even in the public sector some firms switched from trade to investment for genuinely expansionary reasons. A good example here is the case of Braithwaites (manufacturers of bridges, jetties and steel structures), whose Indian operations began with the competitive edge derived from a new technique of screw piling and expanded into workshops and small foundries to service their increasing local business.

It is impossible at present to establish any simple relationship between the growth of the parent firm and direct investment in India, either taking growth as dynamic expansion or as the establishment of defensive oligopoly.[16] However it is striking that a number of British firms that were successful in the Indian processed-food industry were those that had been in the lead in the marketing 'brand-name revolution' at home. Companies such as Brooke Bond and Britannia Biscuits (a subsidiary of Associated Biscuits) prospered in India thanks to standardized production and integrated marketing techniques. Brooke Bond, for example, was the first company to supply the Indian domestic market with branded and widely distributed packaged tea. The Metal Box subsidiary was established to supply containers for British firms operating in this way in the Indian market.[17] The success of ICI's penetration of the Indian market was due, in part, to the establishment of the largest single sales network of any firm in the subcontinent, with 1,500 depots, 15,000 distributors and a staff of 2,500 by the mid-1930s. In its early years in India ICI operated as much by providing skilled marketing expertise as by importing or manufacturing chemicals. By contrast, the sluggish performance of Lever's soap business in India in the 1920s was partly the result of an unfortunate decision to rely initially on an unsound expatriate group (Boulton Brothers) to handle the Indian end, and partly the consequence of Lord Lever's idiosyncratic views on business organization which resulted in the three main producing companies – Lever Brothers, Crossfields and Gossages – each maintaining their own competing marketing networks (the alternative of an integrated system being known disparagingly as 'scrambled eggs').

The expansion of dynamic firms in Britain to a position of market dominance clearly had a positive result in terms of overseas expansion in some instances. Thus British Oxygen became involved in India as a result of taking over three small producers of liquid gasses in the late 1920s, each of which had a small investment in India. By integrating and expanding these operations the parent firm was able to increase its sales of liquid oxygen in India six-fold between 1935 and 1945 (helped, of course, by the expansion of demand during the Second World War), while reducing the price by 50 per cent. The same process lay behind Turner & Newall's entry into the Indian market in the 1930s. Having taken over a small company with some export business and a rudimentary sales and servicing organization in India (Bell's United Asbestos) in 1929, Turner & Newall used this as the foundation for expansion, setting up three factories manufacturing asbestos cement products between 1934 and 1939 to feed demand created by the Indian urban construction boom of those years. It is harder to find clear examples of direct investment in India as the result of the creation of new oligopolistic structures in Britain, but the case of steel tubes gives some idea of what could happen. The steel-tube manufacturers Stewarts & Lloyds were prepared to invest in a small pioneer manufacturing plant in India in 1935 (the Indian Tube Company) because the market-sharing and price-fixing agreement they had made with their main domestic rivals, Tube Investments, protected them from possible competition from British exports. When Stewarts & Lloyds were considering expanding their Indian operation in 1945 by allowing the Tata Iron & Steel Company to inject capital in return for a majority shareholding, the only difficulty about conceding control was whether the Tata directors would abide by the agreement with Tube Investments.[18] When Tube Investments, in turn, came to attack the Indian market in the late 1940s it concentrated on the subsidiary manufacture of bicycles.

The approach of war in the late 1930s acted as a further stimulus to some British companies to establish local manufacturing plants to supply markets that might soon be cut off from British shipping. The war itself resulted in a considerable expansion in demand for industrial products. In addition, the problems of the Indian war effort forced the colonial government to intervene in the local economy and to monitor foreign-exchange expenditure and capital issues more closely. After 1945 economic and political difficulties prompted a number of new entrants into DFI in manufacturing, but again defensive considerations were not the only motivation. Some firms had been attracted to India during the war by the colonial government's need for military supplies, and stayed on thereafter to get the most out of their investment. A good example of this process is the case of the Chloride Electrical Storage Company, which was committed to a large Indian factory as part of the war effort by 1944, even though that factory did not begin production until after 1947.

In making their initial investment in subsidiary manufacturing in India most British MNCs tried to avoid diluting their control over such operations. Almost all the major subsidiaries in the early years were owned 100 per cent by the parent firm and their activities were internalized within the group as far as possible. One striking, and at first sight surprising, fact is how few of the MNCs used the services of long-established British expatriate companies in the Indian market. The managing agency houses prided themselves on their knowledge of local conditions; many of them acted as sales representatives for British importers in a wide range of goods. Yet while a few MNCs did go into alliance with an expatriate firm, pooling capital and giving the local firm a say in the running of manufacturing or marketing organizations, the norm was for the MNC to provide its own managerial and manufacturing staff. There is some evidence to suggest that a number of the new British firms regarded the managing agency houses as inadequate for their requirements. Perhaps for this reason several of them, including Metal Box and Associated Biscuits, used the ICI marketing organization for their products before setting up their own sales networks. Clearly, if the advantage of the MNCs lies in their ability to internalize market imperfections then the creation of integrated manufacturing and marketing organizations is a sign of dynamism among British companies setting up in India in the interwar period. It is tempting to assume that those companies which were content to rely on the expatriate sector for management skills (notably Goodlass Wall, Pinchin Johnson and Crompton Parkinson) were less effective than some of their fellows, but the data at present are too limited for any rigid comparisons to be made.

The early entry and vigorous performance of British MNCs in India was a feature of Indo-British economic ties in the late-colonial and early Independence years. But in the late 1960s British DFI in India appeared to be suffering from a number of constraints which impaired its relative and absolute performance. By then British DFI in India was more concentrated in fewer, larger firms than was the case generally. A survey of the geographical spread of the affiliates of UK companies in the late 1960s indicates that the Indian subcontinent was the only area of the world in which the fall in the number of large affiliates established before the mid-1960s was not cancelled out by the growth of smaller affiliates of new enterprises.[19] Various pieces of data give the impression that British DFI in India from the 1920s to the 1960s was closely linked to a wave of activity by a relatively small number of firms, most of which rose to prominence in the home economy in the 1930s and 1940s and many of which performed poorly worldwide during the 1960s. Comparative data on major British MNCs between 1953 and 1973 reveal that a number of companies heavily involved in India failed to grow as fast as the norm – Brooke Bond, ICI, Vickers, Turner & Newall, Tube Investments, Hawker Siddeley and Babcock & Wilcox among them. Other companies with extensive Indian interests, such as Guest, Keen & Nettlefold, British Oxygen, Metal Box and Dunlop, did no more than hold their own in relative growth in this period. Of the British MNCs that grew fastest in the 1950s and 1960s, those that increased their capital by a factor of 9 or more, only Glaxo and General Electric had major investments in India in the 1950s.[20]

It is hard to pinpoint the source of these constraints with any accuracy, especially since they could well lie outside India. Certainly investment in India remained relatively profitable; according to the *Reddaway Report* pre-tax profits of British MNCs in India in 1955–64 were 120 per cent of the world average, and post-tax profits were only just lower than the world average.[21] Although depressed conditions have stunted the expansion of the private corporate sector in India since the late 1960s foreign firms seem, on the whole, to have performed better than have local ones. Government actions to control the activities of foreign firms may have made life more difficult for certain companies, but it is not clear how significant this factor has been in limiting growth overall.[22] Within India, two types of problem may have been especially important. The first is that demand for industrial goods has remained limited and skewed, and a mass market even for basic consumer goods has not yet emerged. One estimate suggests that in the 1960s 20 per cent of the population was buying 50 per cent of industrial production.[23] The second set of problems concerns the inadequacy, or peculiarity, of institutional networks within the Indian economy. Despite the initial rejection of local partnerships by most MNCs before 1950, the trend towards joint-ventures subsequently was dramatic. In 1971, 10 per cent of total joint-ventures established by British MNCs were in India, whereas only 4 per cent of the total subsidiaries of British companies were there. The proportion of joint-ventures to total subsidiaries of 20 per cent in India was equalled only in the case of Portugal.[24] This search for local collaboration was not simply the result of implicit or explicit host-government pressure. According to one survey of the reasons that British MNCs gave for setting up joint-ventures in India down to 1967, the need for a local partner to provide facilities and resources was far and away the most important motive.[25] This evidence suggests that MNC activities in India may have been significantly different from those elsewhere because particular conditions in India made it less suitable as a base for 'pure' MNC activity. If one of the strengths of MNCs is their ability to internalize imperfections then it may be that by the 1960s companies in India were faced by imperfections that were too large to be coped with in that way.

Past accounts of the history of British MNCs in India have stressed political change as the major causal factor.[26] The main focus of inquiry has been on the coming of independence and the desire of the national government to stimulate local, self-reliant industrialization. The restrictions that have been imposed on imports since 1947 are usually seen as providing the major stimulus to direct investment and the story of relations between MNCs and the Indian economy is often told simply in terms of the confusions of policy and the failures of its implementation. These arguments could be pushed back to cover the late colonial period as well, with public authority fiats again providing the major stimulus to DFI, and with this aspect of government policy being viewed as a reaction to a larger set of political and economic problems. The switch of colonial economic policy after the First World War away from free trade and *laissez-faire*, as represented by revenue tariffs, 'discriminating protection' and rupee tenders for stores, for example, was clearly, in part, a reaction to the political need for decentralization (which threw central government on to customs duties for its revenue), and the desire to meet political pressures for industrial development and agricultural protection.[27] The evidence sketched out in the body of this chapter, however, makes it possible to suggest that these obvious political changes were perhaps less important than a number of underlying, yet more elusive, economic problems which determined the actions of MNCs and colonial and national governments.

It is now clear that developments in the form and function of British capital and enterprise in India in the middle decades of the twentieth century must be related to structural changes in the local and international economies, rather than to simple alterations in the system of political management that were mapped by the decline and fall of the British Raj and the emergence of a national government linked to specific class interests. In the interwar period new markets for new types of goods were being opened up in India. The staple consumer goods of the advanced economies – processed foods, tobacco goods, toiletries and pharmaceuticals – found an increased demand just as the old consumer imports (such as textiles) were undergoing terminal decline. At the same time, a new range of intermediate and capital goods were required to supply the spurt of import-substituting industrialization in textiles, construction goods, metal manufacturers, and so on, and to equip the government for its military and developmental efforts after 1939. The successful companies that manufactured such goods in Britain may well have been particularly suited to multinational operations, preferring to integrate production with distribution and to establish overseas subsidiaries rather than hire the services of local agents. Running parallel to these changes in domestic economic organization were a number of new factors in the international economy that underpinned and reinforced local circumstances. The crucial period here was the decade from the late 1920s to the late 1930s which saw the paralysis of the old colonial economy based on the export of raw materials and processed agricultural products and the import of finished consumer goods. The colonial government's attempt to combat the effect of declining agricultural prices by protecting the domestic market for wheat, rice and oil-seeds sapped still further the international competitiveness of Indian primary produce. The bullion exports of the 1930s prevented any major foreign-exchange crisis after 1931, but only so long as exchange costs were kept down by encouraging local manufacture. By the 1930s India had ceased to be a net supplier of goods to the outside world. There trends continued, and were strengthened, during the Second World War and after Independence.

In these circumstances successful early entry into the Indian market by British MNCs seems to have depended on a complex mix of economic opportunities and appropriate strategies and structures. Reviewing the history of a number of such firms from the 1920s to the 1960s leaves a strong impression that we are witnessing a distinct, discrete, wave of business activity with a clear beginning and, perhaps, a clear end. The operations of these firms seem to have resulted from a specific set of stimuli and responses in the British, Indian and international economies in the decades before and after 1947. Many of the firms that had established subsidiary manufacturing companies in India by 1950 were exploiting a new product or a fresh technique and were internalizing market imperfections to exploit these ownership advantages by the creation of multinational enterprises. But by the late 1960s the further expansion of these firms, and the encouragement of large numbers of followers, were being constrained as these bridgeable gaps in market imperfections closed and as fewer new ones were opened. It may well be that by the 1970s Indian corporations had acquired the internalizing skills of the first wave of MNCs and so were able to compete with them effectively and to take on an even wider range of integrated activities, while entry into new fields required an ability to overcome much larger imperfections that was beyond the reach of anyone except the public sector.

The activities of British MNCs in India in this period represent something of a special case. Large-scale entry of subsidiary manufacturing plant aimed at the domestic market and without significant local collaboration is rare in the history of relations between international capital and contemporary Third World economies, especially in a wide range of consumer and intermediate goods. Despite the Indian government's avowed aim from 1948

164 *Imperialism and After*

onwards of discouraging majority control of subsidiaries by foreign capital, and despite the creation of licensing policies designed to limit the impact of subsidiary companies on the Indian economy, British firms suffered few effective constraints on this type of activity until the Foreign Exchange Regulation (Amendment) Act of 1973.[28] Yet by the late 1960s the economic links between Britain and India were becoming increasingly marginal. In 1969–71 British exports and imports to and from India represented less than 2 per cent of total trade; bilateral trade between the two countries as a proportion of their total trade had by then fallen to between one-half and one-third of the 1949 figure.[29] Within Britain the 1970s were a consistently difficult time for many established companies with the phenomenon of high inflation and low or negative growth taking a heavy toll. Within India, too, this decade saw an intensification of the political turmoil and economic stagnation that had begun with the 'crisis of planning' in the mid-1960s, continued through the political upheavals of 1969 and culminated in the Emergency and its aftermath. Some recent commentators on the Indian political economy of these years, indeed, have argued that there has been a fundamental change in the relationship between the state and dominant classes leading to the emergence of Bonapartism in some accounts, and the rise of a new 'intermediate class' in others.[30] In these circumstances it is hardly surprising that the pattern of multinational firms' involvement in the Indian economy has changed considerably, with increasing stress on short-term operations involving limited commitment to the running of direct subsidiaries. The trend has been, rather, towards licensing and royalty agreements, often with public-sector enterprises, to maximize rent on technologically sophisticated manufacturing processes without a large input of capital or management. Only 2 per cent of the new manufacturing subsidiaries established by British MNCs between 1965 and 1970 were in India; the increase in value of British direct capital holdings in India rose by only 11 per cent between 1962 and 1971, as against 145 per cent overall and 25 per cent in Asia as a whole.[31] Almost half the local firms registered by the Indian government as British subsidiary companies in 1975 (59 out of 123) had ceased to be listed as such in 1980.[32] Whatever the reasons, it is striking that thirty-five years after the transfer of power British MNCs have switched decisively from formal to informal techniques in their operations within the Indian economy.

Notes: Chapter 11

1 Central Office of Information, *Economic Co-operation between India and the United Kingdom* (London, 1961), pp. 6–7; *Board of Trade Journal*, 15 November 1965, pp. 1080, 1086. On the pattern of Indo-British links overall in this period see M. Lipton and J. Firn, *The Erosion of a Relationship: Britain and India since 1960* (London, 1975).
2 For an introduction to the Indian economy since 1947 see P. Chaudhuri, *The Indian Economy* (London, 1978); S. L. Shetty, 'Structural regression in the Indian economy since the mid-sixties', *Economic and Political Weekly*, vol. 13 (1978), pp. 185–244; A. Vaidyanathan, 'The Indian economy since independence (1947–70)', in D. Kumar (ed.), *The Cambridge Economic History of India*, Vol. 2 (Cambridge, 1983), pp. 947–1026.

Multinational Corporations in India 165

3   See F. Frankel, *India's Political Economy, 1947–77* (Princeton, NJ, 1978) and the excellent short summary in J. Harriss, 'Indian industrialisation and the state', in *South Asian Research Paper 1: The State in South Asia* (Norwich, 1983), pp. 1–33.
4   On the problem of the colonial state and class formation see D. A. Washbrook, 'Law, state and agrarian society in colonial India', *Modern Asian Studies*, vol. 15 (1981), pp. 649–721.
5   B. R. Tomlinson, 'Foreign private investment in India, 1920–1950', *Modern Asian Studies*, vol. 12 (1978), pp. 655–77.
6   Calculated from data in Government of India, Department of Company Affairs, *Directory of Joint-Stock Companies in India* (New Delhi, 1975).
7   The list of 200 companies is in Lipton and Firn, *The Erosion of a Relationship*, table 6.13.
8   T. Houston and J. H. Dunning, *U.K. Industry Abroad* (London, 1976), table 5.2.
9   Lipton and Firn, *The Erosion of a Relationship*, table 6.6.; Houston and Dunning, *U.K. Industry Abroad*, table 5.2.
10 The following paragraph is based on J. H. Dunning, *International Production and the Multinational Enterprise* (London, 1981), ch. 2.
11 Much of the information used in compiling the case studies on which the following account is based cannot be documented. Data on firms for which no source is given have been supplied as private information in interviews, correspondence, unpublished company histories, etc.
12 D. K. Fieldhouse, *Unilever Overseas: The Anatomy of a Multinational 1895–1965* (London, 1978), p. 148. The information on Unilever used in the rest of this article is drawn from this source.
13 H. Modig, *Swedish Match Interests in British India during the Interwar Years* (Stockholm, 1979).
14 D. C. Coleman, *Courtaulds: An Economic and Social History*, Vol. 2 (Oxford, 1969), chs 10 and 12.
15 Tomlinson, 'Foreign private investment', p. 670.
16 On the background to industrial concentration in Britain in this period see L. Hannah, 'Strategy and structure in the manufacturing sector', in idem (ed.), *Management Strategy and Business Development* (London, 1976), pp. 184–202. There is considerable debate about whether British MNCs acted as dynamically as theory, and the American experience, would suggest. For the 'pessimist' view see A. D. Chandler, 'The growth of the transnational industrial firm in the U.S. and the U.K.: a comparative analysis', *Economic History Review*, vol. 33 (1980), pp. 396–410, and idem, 'Changing perspectives on investment by British manufacturing multinationals', *Journal of International Business Studies* (Fall–Winter 1976), pp. 15–27. For a more optimistic account see G. Jones, 'The expansion of British multinational manufacturing, 1880–1939', in T. Inoue and A. Okochi (eds), *Overseas Business Activities* (Tokyo, 1983) and, on recent developments, M. Panic, 'International direct investment in conditions of structural disequilibrium: the U.K. experience since the 1960s', in J. Black and J. H. Dunning (eds), *International Capital Movements* (London, 1982), pp. 140–71.
17 W. D. Reader, *Metal Box: A History* (London, 1976), ch. 2.
18 'Notes on the history of Stewarts & Lloyds – overseas companies, 23 July 1946', Stewarts & Lloyds Papers 1791/23; Minutes of meeting of directors of Stewarts & Lloyds Ltd, 27 February 1945, Stewarts & Lloyds Minute Book 14/T. HQ/SEC 065 C1 B3: BSC Eastern Midlands Regional Record Centre, Irthlingborough.
19 Lipton and Firn, *The Erosion of a Relationship*, table 6.14.
20 Houston and Dunning, *U.K. Industry Abroad*, pp. 158–9.
21 W. Reddaway et al., *Effects of U.K. Direct Investment Overseas: Final Report* (Cambridge, 1968), table IV.5.
22 Fieldhouse's study of Hindustan Lever, for example, concludes that it was general economic problems associated with the stagnation of the local economy, rather than explicit government pressure or discrimination, that was the most severe constraint on Unilever's expansion in India (see Fieldhouse, *Unilever Overseas*, p. 228). An official committee of inquiry concluded in 1969 that foreign firms had not been systematically discriminated against by licensing policy. See Government of India, Department of Industrial Development, *Report of the Industrial Licensing Policy Enquiry Committee: Main Report* (Dutt Committee) (New Delhi, 1969), pp. 123–38.

166   Imperialism and After

23 M. Barratt Brown, *The Economics of Imperialism* (Harmondsworth, Middx, 1974), p. 322.
24 Houston and Dunning, *U.K. Industry Abroad*, pp. 187–8.
25 J. W. C. Tomlinson, *The Joint-Venture Process in International Business: India and Pakistan* (London, 1970), pp. 26–7.
26 The classic study, M. Kidron, *Foreign Investments in India* (Oxford, 1965), illustrates this approach.
27 On the economic policy and problems of the colonial government see B. R. Tomlinson, *The Political Economy of the Raj, 1914–47* (London, 1979).
28 See A. Dasgupta and N. Sengupta, *Government and Business in India*, rev. edn (Calcutta, 1981), ch. 9.
29 Lipton and Firn, *The Erosion of a Relationship*, table 2.4.
30 See, for example, A. Sen, *The State, Industrialisation and Class Formation in India* (London, 1982) and P. S. Jha, *The Political Economy of Stagnation* (New York, 1980).
31 J. W. Vaupel and J. P. Curham, *The World's Multinational Enterprises* (Boston, Mass., 1973), table 1.17.3; Lipton and Firn, *The Erosion of a Relationship*, table 6.5.
32 *Directory of Joint-Stock Companies in India*, 1975 and ibid., 1980.

12 Imperialist Domination in Vietnam and Cambodia: A Long-Term View
DIETER BRÖTEL

This chapter analyses different forms of, and motives for, imperialist domination in Vietnam and Cambodia, ranging from the early European influences of the seventeenth and eighteenth centuries up to the Vietnamese invasion of Kampuchea. It is based on an attempt to combine aspects of 'periphery-oriented' theories of imperialism with economic explanations. When studying French colonial expansion, it is especially important to take into account not only causative factors arising from the metropolitan economy, and from European politics, but also the peripheral undertow (for instance: a turbulent frontier; the collaboration of indigenous élites; or sub-imperialist aspirations and activities).[1] If we take as our model the interaction of unequal societies,[2] we can grasp the continuity together with the discontinuity of imperialist domination. Interaction between the crisis in the Vietnamese social system (that is, the power struggles which took place between three feudal families in a country divided into two after the collapse of the Lê Dynasty) and the intermingling of trade and missions, can be considered the decisive factor in the penetration of the eighteenth and nineteenth centuries.

In 1659-60 the Pope entrusted the Far Eastern missions to French missionaries. They were to play a decisive part in the long prehistory of French intervention. There was a close connection between missions, trade and politics. French missionaries stimulated interest in a commitment overseas. They supplied news and information and devised commercial projects. This conflation of mission and business was typical of French missionary endeavours. It was apparent especially in the influence of the Société des Missions Etrangères on Colbert's foundation of the Compagnie des Indes Orientales in 1664.[3] It is significant that merchants showed no interest in the Compagnie, and the raising of capital proved arduous. Political pressure had to be brought to bear on officials and dignitaries to subscribe.

The structural crisis of the French Compagnie des Indes Orientales at the beginning of the seventeenth century together with Dutch encroachment in the Indian Ocean at the same time, precipitated the collapse of French trade with the Far East. It also led to the ruin of the French trading station established at Pho-Hien (Tonkin) in 1680. In the course of the Tây-Son uprising against despotic rule in the South, the director of the Cochin-China mission supported Nguyen Anh by helping to supply arms and by bringing some deserters – naval officers and French colonial troops – to

Cochin-China. Pigneau de Béhaine tried to find support for an expedition in government and missionary circles. It was suggested that help for Nguyen-Anh would ensure a lasting French commitment and an official recognition of Christianity in Cochin-China. Corresponding ideas were expressed in the Versailles Agreement (28 November 1787), but the government did not send an expedition.

Historians agree that protection of the missions was the primary motive for the territorial occupation of Cochin-China (1858–62). At first French economic interests were of only marginal significance. During the joint Franco-British expedition against China, the possibilities of trade with China were realized in metropolitan trading circles. They envisaged Saigon's development into a reconsignment centre. However, it cannot be said that annexation was primarily the product of economic imperialism, even if we take into account the demand for raw silk by industry in the Lyons area. This demand began to increase after 1852/3.[4] By 1864 a new foreign bureaucracy was definitively involved in the domestic affairs of Cochin-China.[5] This involvement arose from the early colonial administrators' belief in a 'mission civilisatrice', a rationale of military security in case of uprisings, and the ultimately decisive withdrawal of the mandarinate directly after the occupation, which left a political vacuum.

What were the decisive forces behind the foundation of the French protectorate in Annam and Tonkin? The occupation of Cochin-China led to local problems in safeguarding and possibly extending French rule. Apart from the extension of influence to Cambodia, the Mekong River Expedition (1866–8) was important in this context. The result of the expedition – the Mekong proved unnavigable – diverted attention to the Red River as a route for political and commercial penetration of South-West China and Laos. Frenchmen in the colony of Cochin-China, not metropolitan circles, were the driving force behind the genesis of this expedition. In the trading centre in Cholon, known as the *bazar chinois*, Francis Garnier developed plans to channel products from Laos and South-West China to Cochin-China. The intention was to allow Saigon to become a major distribution centre for South-East Asia. Governors Charner and de la Grandière effectively put the fully-worked-out idea of the Mekong expedition to the Ministry for Naval Affairs. The informal expansion, originally conceived in Cochin-China as an answer to local problems, was finally sanctioned by government circles in Paris.[6] These expansionist efforts were pioneered by a colonial adventurer, Garnier, and found increasing support in the Saigon administration. They resulted in a system of informal control which was established in the 1874 agreement between France and the Emperor Tu Duc. On the one hand, this agreement indicated the limits of metropolitan readiness to intervene and, on the other, it satisfied at least the minimal demands of the French expatriates in Cochin-China.[7]

The transition to formal rule in the 1880s may be explained, first, as a reaction to a series of local problems which could not be solved by informal methods on the basis of the 1874 agreement; secondly, in terms of subimperialist agitation and projects closely interwoven with the political and commercial interests of France itself; and, thirdly, by the demand of economic circles for privileged access to new markets, against a background of recession and increasingly intense international competition.

The free access of French trade to Yunnan postulated in the 1874 agreement was blocked by unrest in Tonkin. Hué and Peking decided on a common policy of non-collaboration; Vietnam called on China for help in resisting French penetration. China itself prepared for the eventual military defence of its suzerainty. The limits of the French consuls' jurisdiction were inadequately defined in the 1874 agreement. This led to an undermining of French supremacy. The Foreign and Naval Ministries reacted by preparing for intervention with the aim of consolidating French powers of jurisdiction by establishing a protectorate in Annam and Tonkin. Simultaneously, plans for annexation were devised in politico-military and commercial circles in Cochin-China in order to provide opportunities for trade in Tonkin and Yunnan. The governor and the *député colonial* energetically recommended these plans to the Paris authorities.

Within a decade, peripheral speculation grew to almost 'national' proportions. Intending to satisfy claims for financial indemnities by obtaining mining concessions, a mining syndicate called for the occupation of the whole of Tonkin. Private interests were rationalized as national interests, and the occupation was presented as a crusade which would use the restoration of the Lê Dynasty as a means to liberate a Tonkinese population supposedly oppressed by the mandarins.[8] Mining speculation influenced the stage-by-stage intervention prepared for by various Cabinets. As aims became grander, more radical means were considered. A policy of limited aims and informal control was finally replaced by a strategy of territorial occupation of all Tonkin, despite the growing resistance of Vietnam and China.[9] This decision also brought the prospect of coal-mining in Tonkin into the calculation. The coal deposits at Hon Gay and Ke Bao were geologically surveyed for the first time by an expert from the Ecole des Mines in 1881/2. Developments after the turn of the century were to confirm that profitable exploitation of the Asian market was possible. These expectations kindled further mining speculation. In contrast to the extremist demands of some newspapers, until the end of 1882, commercial pressure groups restricted themselves to requests for political control of the Red River Delta in order to secure favourable conditions for peaceful trading. The establishment of colonial companies dates essentially from the final phase of colonial expansion. At the beginning, however, the involvement of the republican middle class which had come to power in 1880, and especially of the Gambettan Union Républicaine, with business circles, exercised a fundamental influence on the process of decision-making.

Though structural imperfections in the French social and economic system as a whole (such as a basically Malthusian situation and an inadequate fusion of industrial and banking capital) provided a poor socio-economic foundation for an aggressive form of imperialism, the aspirations of regional and sectoral economic interests should not be overlooked. Thus, after the failure of the Freycinet Plan during a structural and cyclical crisis, Loire heavy industry responded with preparations for a syndicate. In spring 1886 these preparations resulted in the foundation of a nationwide

China consortium of heavy industry under the leadership of the Comptoir d'Escompte de Paris.[10] The Ferry government answered the demands of heavy industry by inserting vague railway clauses into treaties between France and China. Representatives of trade and industry advocated a penetration of Tonkin (leaving aside the issue of the mines) not so much because of the specific economic importance of the region, but more because of competition with other industrial nations for the political and commercial opening and exploitation of China. Rising silk imports to the Lyons regions from China, especially after 1875, are one example of a sectoral interest that formed a constant element in the history of French imperialism in East and South-East Asia. Lyons's interest in the acquisition of Tonkin was based on the hope of obtaining raw silk there and, in the long run, of developing a market for mixed fabrics.[11] Finally, in the complex motivational structure of French 'preclusive imperialism' in Vietnam, the claim to great power status, advanced for reasons of foreign and domestic political prestige, cannot be separated from economic factors.

French experience with indigenous collaboration differed in the central and northern parts of Vietnam. In Cochin-China, after 1862, local uprisings and the withdrawal of the traditional officials – the mandarins – from the administration of the country accelerated the advent of direct rule. Following a similar pattern, the colonial power reacted to the general uprising of 1885 with progressive intervention in the internal affairs of Vietnam. In the end this led to a system of direct administration. The maxim 'divide and rule!' governed the protectorate agreements of 1883 and 1884, which introduced three different systems into Vietnam. Cochin-China became a colony; Annam was given the status of a protectorate with relative administrative autonomy; an effective protectorate was decreed for Tonkin as a preliminary step towards direct rule – with a view to exclusive control of its mineral resources.

Annamese officials engaged in armed resistance – supported by the populace – against a group of collaborationist mandarins at the Hué court who were prepared to tolerate territorial fragmentation and creeping annexation.[12] The rebellion of the literati ruined French plans for formal maintenance of the traditional institutions of emperor and mandarinate. In Annam the colonial power intervened right down to district level. A collaborationist party consisting of members of the royal family and high-ranking mandarins clustered round the French-supported emperor, Dong Khanh. In the decade after 1887 they facilitated the gradual consolidation of French rule in Annam.[13] The circumscription of the mandarinate's power in Tonkin had its radical aspects; to a considerable extent the mandarinate was not recognized by the French as a governing body and a traditional and legitimate ruling class with a firm basis of authority. The French largely saw the mandarinate as a mere administrative system. In Tonkin a policy of 'local collaboration'[14] and military pressure made it possible to crush the resistance of the Can-Vuong movement and of Chinese guerrilla units, and to 'pacify' North Tonkin. North Tonkin was brought under control by 1897 with the aid of collaborationist measures (replacement of the 'militia' concept by the traditional village self-defence system; winning over the mandarins and village notables; support for the autonomy of ethnic minorities; Franco-Chinese border agreements). Conscription in military districts also played a part in the subjection of Tonkin.

The Union Indo-Chinoise was established in 1887. At first it comprised the colony of Cochin-China and the protectorates of Annam, Tonkin and Cambodia. In 1893 it was extended to include the protectorate of Laos. With the Union, France created an 'artificial colonial administrative unit'.[15] The fictitious nature of the protectorate idea was finally exposed by the centralized administration for which Governor-General Paul Doumer (1897–1902) was responsible. Doumer removed the regent (Kinh Luoc, who had been appointed at Tonkin in 1887 as supreme administrator under French supervision), and henceforth the mandarinate was directly subordinate to French residents. Doumer's organizational structure was based on direct rule. In essentials, this remained the basis of the French colonial system until 1945.

The political map of Indo-China in the pre-colonial phase was characterized by a 'dual vassalage' of the Kingdom of Cambodia (belonging to an 'Indianized' civilization) to its expanding neighbours Siam and Vietnam. Whereas Cambodia in the eighteenth century was no more than a vassal-state of Siam, in the first half of the nineteenth century it experienced phases of Vietnamese occupation during the protracted conflict between Vietnam and Siam. Finally in 1846, with Ang Duong's accession to the throne, Siam's influence was acknowledged as preponderant.[16] Trade and Christian mission played subordinate roles in French penetration. Local factors resulting from the French presence in Cochin-China were of paramount importance. Military intervention was intended to preclude unrest and uprisings on the 'turbulent frontier', and to prevent Vietnamese resistance groups from retreating into Cambodian territory. It was also designed to check Siamese expansion which was thought to have been incited by the British. In the first decade of 'informal control' established in 1863, the exercise of French power was limited to the suppression of uprisings. In contrast to Cochin-China, lack of personnel dictated a policy of non-interference in internal affairs. The administration early toyed with the idea of putting the compliant Sisowat on the throne, in order to break King Norodom's resistance to growing French influence. The first civil government in Cochin-China under Le Myre de Vilers (1879–83) increased the pressure. Cambodia was to be annexed by *de facto* control of its institutions and by officially supported immigration from Vietnam.

In 1884 a treaty was exacted which provided for the appointment of French residents to control the Cambodian provincial administration. It also made provision for a civil list, the abolition of slavery and the introduction of private landholding. The general resident was accorded direct access to the king and was granted chairmanship of the Council of Ministers. A general uprising against growing French influence at court and against attempts to enforce strict control of the provinces compelled the colonial power to make concessions, at least for the time being. The decisive turning-point came with the virtual deposition of the sick Norodom in 1897. Executive power was transferred to the Council of Ministers under the chairmanship of the general resident. Henceforth the king could appoint and dismiss officials only at the suggestion of the Council of Ministers and with the counter-signature of the general resident.[17] Yet the destruction of the monarchy never went as far as in Vietnam. There the imperial institution was stripped of its divine power and continued to exist only in a purely formal sense. The Cambodian monarch, by contrast, remained a symbol of tradition. He represented the continuity of the state and was the 'veritable religious leader of the country'.[18]

Already during Norodom's lifetime intransigent ministers and governors had been removed from office. With Sisowat an era of obliging collaboration began. With a few exceptions the high officeholders who came to terms with the new rulers were members of the traditional Cambodian élite, which had been closely linked with the court for generations through service and appointment. After 1897 the colonial administration was consolidated into an increased number of residencies, each comprising several provinces. They supervised the collection of taxes and the overall activities of provincial governors. On the whole, the theory of 'dual power' was revealed as fictitious, because decisive *de facto* power lay with the resident. It was impossible for a genuinely Cambodian state to develop. The social mobility which (theoretically at least) existed before 1897 disappeared. The local administration became the domain of sons of high officials or rich businessmen, whereas Vietnamese monopolized the colonial administration.[19] The general budget devised by Doumer was greatly to the disadvantage of Cambodia. By means of a high tax levy, the Khmer empire provided additional funds for government projects which usually favoured French companies in Vietnam.

The integration of the Indo-Chinese economy into the capitalist world market turned the periphery into a complement of the metropolitan economy. On the one hand, agricultural and mineral products were exported; on the other, manufactured goods were imported from France. Through taxation, a colonial land policy and the introduction of forced labour, the colonial administration mobilized local economic resources with the purpose of providing conditions which would attract foreign investments.[20] The public financing of infrastructural projects was intended to persuade metropolitan capitalists to abandon their initial reluctance to invest. The colonial administration supported private investment with tax incentives, financial aid and low-interest loans. Other measures in this policy of outwardly oriented colonial development included restrictions on investment from other countries and colonial protectionism. Customs assimilation (Loi Méline, 1892) restricted imports of consumer goods as far as possible to supplies from the metropolis. The customs law of 1928 raised tariffs against cheap imports from the United States, China and especially Japan.[21] Colonial subordination was clearly apparent, for example, in the long-term emphasis on the interests of Lyons. Having abandoned its nineteenth-century free-trade policy, Lyons opposed any liberalization of imports to Indo-China between the two wars. When hopes of obtaining Indo-Chinese raw silk were not fulfilled, the intention was that the Indo-Chinese market for French textile imports should receive customs protection against Japanese competition.[22]

Generally speaking, until the First World War commercial capital took precedence over industrial capital: a few French trading companies dominated commercial relations with the Far Eastern empire. Of all French capital exports in 1914, which amounted to 4,500 million francs, the overseas territories' share was 10 per cent.[23] In 1918 capital investment in Indo-China, according to Robequain, amounted to some 500 million francs,[24] whereas Marseille reports public investments of 425 million francs against private investments totalling 230 million francs.[25] It is important to note the dominant share of public investment. Relatively modest private investments were made in Vietnam initially in the spheres of coal, zinc and tin-mining. The first rubber plantations were established in the 1890s. Apart from the Distilleries Françaises, sugar refineries, cement works, glass factories, saw mills, match and paper factories were established to meet local demands. A cotton mill founded in Hanoi in 1894 was the starting-point for a textile industry.[26]

Unlike that in Vietnam, the colonial administration in Cambodia undertook only minimal infrastructural measures.[27] Given that only 23 *établissements de colons* were registered between 1897 and 1920 one cannot speak of real colonization having taken place. The First World War was a turning-point. Metropolitan investments now replaced undercapitalized family enterprises. An economic gap opened between Cambodia and Cochin-China. In 1908 a total of 5·5 million francs was invested in Cambodia as against 56 million in Cochin-China. The concentration of private investment in Vietnam can partly be attributed to the policy of the government. After the war, investment in the *terres rouges* in 1919–20 was a prelude to the subsequent establishment of large rubber plantations. But even during the interwar period, Cambodia functioned as a hinterland of Saigon.[28] The export products of this agrarian country – paddy rice, pepper, cattle, dried fish, raw cotton – had lasting problems to contend with because the market was inadequately diversified. Until the formation of the Comptoir de l'Industrie Cotonnière, the establishment of cotton mills in Cambodia got nowhere because of resistance from metropolitan interests and from cotton firms based in Tonkin.[29]

Between the two world wars, the level of investment in the French colonial empire as a whole increased more than fourfold. For the colonial empire in 1940 Marseille gives a figure of 17,500 million gold francs out of total French capital exports amounting to about 40,000 million.[30] The percentage increase of the empire's share in the external portfolio from 10 per cent in 1914 to nearly 45 per cent in 1940 underlines the significance of the colonial empire as the lifebuoy of French capitalism. On the basis of the value of the franc in 1940, Indo-China received private investment of 39,000 million francs and government investment of 14,000 million, totalling 53,000 million and equivalent to 3,800 million gold francs. A look at the geographical distribution of total French colonial investment reveals that Indo-China's share between 1914 and 1940 was relatively constant at just over 40 per cent.[31] As Table 12.1 demonstrates, between 1914 and 1940 Indo-China's share of public investment remained all but constant, while that of West Africa declined slightly but still remained a little higher than that of Indo-China.

Table 12.1 *Geographical Distribution of French Investment in the Colonial Empire* (in per cent)

	Public		Private	
	1914	1940	1914	1940
Indo-China	36·2	38·0	54·6	46·1
West Africa	45·7	39·0	24·8	32·6
Madagascar	8·9	10·0		13·5
Other colonies	9·2	13·0	20·6	7·8
	100	100	100	100

Source: J. Marseille: 'L'investissement français dans l'empire colonial: l'enquête du gouvernement de Vichy (1943)', Revue historique, no. 512 (1974), p. 419.

In 1914 private investment showed a clear emphasis in favour of Indo-China, though the attractiveness of West Africa grew markedly until 1940. This shift to Africa increased after 1945 against a background of change in the overall political situation. Not only in Indo-China, but also on a broader front, the state used public investment to prepare the way for private capital.

Much of the private investment in the empire was made between 1919 and 1930. The devaluation of the franc and the expansion of the world market after 1924 helped business circles to appreciate the value of the colonies as suppliers of raw materials. During the boom phase between 1924 and the onset of the Great Depression, private investors gave special preference to rubber plantations, mines and rice cultivation. In general, no radical shift from one sector to another was noticeable. The share of mines and industry in private investment rose from a total of 19·2 per cent in 1914 to 32·5 per cent in 1940. If the interwar period as a whole was the heyday of *banques d'affaires*, in the colonies, too, a financial oligarchy emerged from the concentration and centralization of metropolitan capital. The Banque de l'Indochine made vast profits and took over a number of rival financial enterprises. By promoting business ventures, joint investment and absorbing bankrupt firms during the depression years, the bank rose to a position of *de facto* monopoly in the mining and railway sectors as well as in plantation agriculture and trade.[32] Three financial groups controlled 85 per cent of private investment. The other two were the Rivaud Group which dominated the enclave sector of rubber plantations, and the Rothschild-de Wendel Group which occupied a strong position in mining (zinc and tungsten) and electricity generation.[33]

Strike movements and agrarian unrest – for example, the Nghe-Tinh Rebellion, peasant uprisings in Cochin-China, in Nghe-An, and so on – in 1930–2 threatened the colonial status of Vietnam. This structural crisis of colonial rule coincided with the world economic crisis. One of the principal effects of the depression was to step up the growth of large landed properties. The level of investments made in the boom phase of 1924–9 caused the government to intervene. It thereby helped to strengthen the big colonial companies. The long-term social and political consequences were momentous. On the one hand, the consolidated power of the big French companies upset the upper stratum of Vietnamese society; on the other, the gulf grew deeper between the major Vietnamese landlords (who enjoyed preferential treatment by the colonial administrators), and the lower rural strata of tenant farmers, small cultivators and agricultural labourers. The flight to the countryside furthered a political convergence between poor peasants and workers. The fact that the economic crisis and the emergence of the Communist Party occurred at the same time is politically significant. However, there is no question of strict causal determination of the one by the other.[34]

Vietnamese nationalism in its second stage was supported by the rise of new urban strata. It had two different answers to the reality of colonialism. The political orientation of the well-to-do, Francophile, urban middle class ranged from reformist nationalism to open collaboration. A radical, lower-middle-class variant of urban nationalism, on the other hand, rejected any kind of co-operation with the French. The upper-middle-class reformists wanted appropriate representation in the Colonial Council and Vietnamese access to positions in the administration. They criticized the position hitherto enjoyed by Chinese in business. This moderate constitutionalist version of nationalism did not call for a French withdrawal but for Canadian-style Dominion status with indigenous participation in governmental power.[35] A similar solution was advocated by the Democratic Party. By contrast, the largely Tonkin-based Vietnamese Nationalist Party, with its lower-middle-class roots, advanced the idea of a national revolution: the colonial regime would be removed by force and a democratic republic would be proclaimed. As a whole, urban nationalism was split ideologically and organizationally fragmented. It also neglected the countryside. During the 1930s its moderate elements with their taste for collaboration lost a good deal of influence within the national movement.

Though socialists and the majority of *radicaux* in France followed the British model in advocating gradual decolonization and a movement towards self-government, nevertheless after 1930 a policy of 'colonial restoration' predominated.[36] Many Frenchmen in Hanoi and Paris recognized the extent of disarray within the colonial regime. They interpreted communism as a manifestation of radical patriotism, and connected it with the agrarian crisis and growing impoverishment. They were also aware of the crisis of the Vietnamese village community, the excesses of landlordism and the extent of peasant indebtedness. Still, French colonial policy failed to respond in a constructive way and clung to its attitude of immobilism. Communism was to be dealt a mortal blow by a combination of unremitting repression and limited concessions to moderate nationalists. Hence, in 1932–3 the state apparatus was strengthened rather than political reform introduced. The colonial regime relied more than ever before on the support of village dignitaries and the mandarinate. Any kind of agrarian reform was ruled out, lest landlord support of the regime should be forfeited. The social crisis persisted and the Communist Party eventually overtook its reformist opponents, mainly as a result of urban mass campaigns, but also by making an initial impression in rural areas. By 1936 it had achieved political hegemony in the Vietnamese national movement. Between 1931 and 1936 the gulf between the national movement and the colonial regime had widened, and the national reformists and supporters of Franco-Annamite collaboration had lost ground.

In France, the Popular Front government abandoned the socialist positions of 1930. It combined the approaches of colonial administrators and business circles into a coherent colonial strategy whose key terms were *économie interne, économie complexe* and *paysannat*.[37] In the debate in colonial circles on the organization of an imperial economy, the Popular Front adopted the complementary thesis: the colonial economy was an extension of the metropolitan economy. It rejected the industrialization of Indo-China called for by colonial experts; that is, it rejected the extension of the domestic market in Indo-China, the abolition of customs assimilation and the state-sponsored construction of a peripheral economy that would compete with that of the metropolis.[38] In view of the pressure exerted by metropolitan business circles and of the tendency towards pauperization visible among the Vietnamese peasantry, the government concentrated on supporting agriculture.

Even the Popular Front came to terms with the traditional élites and pursued a judicious policy of revaluation of the Nguyen Dynasty and, at the same time, an uncompromising attitude towards the Marxist intelligentsia. The Indo-China policy of the late 1930s from André Tardieu through Léon Blum to the Vichy government shows that the desire to safeguard imperial continuity outweighed demands for a withdrawal from the overseas empire. The governments of the Union Nationale had categorically ruled out decolonization for the future; after 1936 a revision of the political constitution of the colonial empire was no longer rejected on grounds of principle; it was, however, put off until the distant future.[39]

After the outbreak of the Sino-Japanese War in 1937 and of the Second World War two years later, France aimed mainly to preserve its Asian empire unharmed until the cessation of hostilities. In regard to Japan, the governor-general and the Vichy regime veered between neutrality and collaboration. A *modus vivendi* allowed Japan to station troops in Indo-China which, in turn, profited economically, particularly through the Banque de l'Indochine, from the Greater East Asia Co-prosperity Sphere which the Japanese tried to establish. Put on the defensive by the welcome given to Japan's brand of Pan-Asianism by some sections of the Indo-Chinese population, the Decoux regime tried to ensure the continuation of French rule by granting superficial concessions: federalism and a 'policy of consideration and respect'.[40] In view of Roosevelt's notion of 'trusteeship' and the Guomindang's plans to extend Chinese influence to Indo-China in the event of a Japanese defeat, de Gaulle and the Resistance believed that they could restore full French sovereignty only by active participation alongside the Allies in the liberation of Indo-China. For de Gaulle, legitimate title and military and political presence took priority over a policy of colonial reform.[41] There was no question of any specific strategy of decolonization. Instead the general advocated an extension of the 'freedoms' already granted to Indo-China. In this sense, it is possible to discern a liberalization of political status from the December declaration of 1943 to the declaration of the provisional government of 25 March 1945, which finally acknowledged the administrative and economic autonomy of the Indo-Chinese Federation within the framework of the Union Française.

Indo-China thus exchanged its colonial status for a *statut d'état* – though, of course, with a continuing French presence.[42] Since, however, the Japanese *coup de force* of 9 March 1945 had already disposed of French sovereignty, French policy ignored the political facts in Indo-China. On the basis of a broadly based united front including 'patriotic landlords', the 'national bourgeoisie' and urban and rural communist groups,[43] the Viet Minh demanded unity as well as independence. Against that, retention by the metropolitan power of five units within the federation suggested a form of colonial separatism for Cochin-China.[44] Recent research shows that there seems to have been a conflict of aims in the Gaullist camp. Laurentie, Jean Sainteny and Léon Pignon were probably prepared to accept the results of the August Revolution – the proclamation of the Democratic Republic of Vietnam and the existence of a united Vietnam under Viet Minh leadership from 19 August to 22 September 1945 – and, furthermore, to concede both national unity and independence in an agreement to be sought with Vietnam.[45] De Gaulle rejected this and planned to restore the Nguyen Dynasty in the person of Prince Vinh San – the ex-Emperor Duy Than who had been exiled in 1916. This last solution also implied a compromise with nationalism, since in a political testament the prince had called for the unity of the three parts of Vietnam (the 'three *Ky*') and for 'indépendance à terme'.[46]

The strategy of integration was also pursued from 1946 onwards by the coalition governments in which Georges Bidault's Mouvement Républicain Populaire (MRP) played a key role. The agreement of 6 March 1948 did not as yet guarantee full independence, even though Vietnam was accorded the prospect of separate statehood with a right to its own government, parliament, army and financial sovereignty within the framework of the Union Française.[47] The need for the MRP to accommodate, for reasons of electoral politics, the Rassemblement du Peuple Français (RPF) which in public at least took an uncompromising view of colonial questions, was a significant factor in shaping French Indo-China policy. Nevertheless, it was essentially an ideological consensus of all groups from the Communists to the Gaullists which, in 1946–7, prevented an agreement on the basis of the Viet Minh's demands.[48] Against the advice of experts on South-East Asia (for example, Jean Sainteny and Paul Mus) a chance was missed of introducing a change in colonial Indo-China at the Conference of Fontainebleau in 1946. This would have meant a shift towards a form of informal rule relying on the economic association of an independent Vietnam with the French bloc. Instead, the autonomy strategy which was also supported by the Socialists prevailed.[49] In the final analysis, influential economic circles, the lobby of French Indo-China expatriates and the colonial administration were responsible for High Commissioner d'Argenlieu's proclamation of Cochin-China as a separate state under French control. This was part of a policy of forcibly defending the colonial *status quo ante*.

The approval of all parties in 1946 for a solution within the framework of the Union Française reflected both the tradition of assimilation and, in terms of social psychology, a desire to compensate for the outcome of the Second World War. The re-establishment of the colonial empire would surely underpin France's claim to be a major power. There was also a widespread belief that only colonial economic resources could help the mother country to recover from the war. Anti-communism played only a subordinate role in 1946–7. Thereafter, however, the MRP and the Vietnamese clergy came under the influence of the Vatican and of *missions étrangères*, and talks with Ho Chi Minh were avoided. Strikes at home, the start of the Cold War, and the victory of the Communists in China in 1949 resulted in a continuation of the colonial war under the ideological banner of a struggle of the 'free' world against communism. The 'Bao Dai solution' was adopted as a moderately nationalist alternative to Ho Chi Minh. It was mainly supported by the MRP and involved the gradual transfer of the internal administration into Vietnamese hands, especially after 1952–3, and the simultaneous building-up of a Vietnamese army with increasing financial aid from the United States.

After the start of what turned out to be the final Viet Minh offensive, Mendèsisme, an informal political group, abandoned this neo-colonialist compromise centred around the Union Française, even though it had previously joined the MRP and the Socialists in accepting it. Pierre Mendès-France and his associates called for the acceptance of a neutral, independent Vietnam if it was unavoidable and, above all, for an end to the colonial war. They thereby drew the political consequences of the growing conviction in economic circles that the costly war in Indo-China had become an unbearable financial burden on French capitalism.

As late as in spring 1947 French businessmen had expected favourable economic developments in Vietnam. At that juncture, a desire to recover a firm hold on the Vietnamese economy was characteristic both of the French administration and of business circles.[50] New companies were founded;[51] the reconstruction and modernization plan drawn up in 1947 provided for investments of 1,000 to 1,500 million piastres for Indo-China within a period of ten years. Although the war and the vigorous resistance put up by Ho Chi Minh's Democratic Republic of Vietnam (DRV) restricted the scope of their activities, colonial companies carried on. Rice merchants, for example, were badly affected by the crisis: rice exports in 1951 had fallen back to 21 per cent of the 1939 export figure. Others fared better. The Cochin-China coal and rubber companies had ensured the protection of their mines and plantations by expeditionary forces; in spite of a downwards trend, their production remained considerable. The artificially stabilized piastre contributed, in spite of slack business for some firms, to a rise in the profits of the major colonial companies after 1946. The profits of forty-five French Indo-China companies rose between 1946 and 1951 from 542 million to 10,101 million francs.[52]

Military setbacks against the Viet Minh and a growing pessimism with regard to political prospects caused an exodus of French capital after 1948.[53] The Banque de l'Indochine paved the way with its strategy of geographically spreading the risk. In 1948 it opened subsidiaries in Jeddah, San

Vietnam and Cambodia 179

Francisco and Port Vila, bought shares of banks in the United States and Latin America, and invested in French African territories. The migration of capital and the increasing orientation towards Africa were results of the following developments:

(1) Companies whose production units were situated in DRV-controlled areas (tin and zinc mines) stopped production;
(2) colonial companies ceased trading;
(3) after their property had been damaged by military action companies did not resume production and invested in other territories of the Union Française;
(4) the rubber companies intensified production without taking tree exhaustion into account, and used their huge profits to finance new plantations in West Africa.[54]

Mendèsisme assessed this development realistically. It called for a concentration of French energies on Europe and Africa under a policy of *euro-africano-centrisme*.[55] The aims of this basically anti-communist policy were social reforms in France and a major military role for France to be played in the planned European Defence Community. According to Mendès-France, *la sale guerre* was indirectly to the advantage of the Communist Party. The colonial withdrawal to Africa shows that Mendèsisme was not fundamentally critical of neo-colonialism, but only of its geographical emphasis.

A policy of discrimination against non-French capital meant that American investment played no part at all in Indo-China before 1940. In the initial stage of enforced decolonization (1946–7), American exploratory activities indicated some interest in succeeding French imperialism in the direct exploitation of Indo-China. American private companies and members of the diplomatic corps co-operated in investigating the economic resources of Indo-China, and especially tin and phosphate deposits in the northern areas of Tonkin. Members of the board of directors of a major French raw-materials company, the Société des Phosphates d'Extrême-Orient, had connections with American financial and industrial capital. Both before and directly after the Second World War, the United States received increasing quantities of natural rubber from Indo-China. Between 1946 and 1950 these supplies accounted for 98 per cent of total American imports of natural rubber. However, after 1948 Indo-China's balance of trade with the United States went into the red. American exports now entered not only Indo-China but the entire South-East Asian market.

These facts provide a limited measure of support for the thesis of a connection between a deficit in strategic raw materials and global political involvement, proposed in revisionist interpretations of American foreign policy.[56] However, the penetration of French colonial trade by American capital did not reach considerable levels, either directly or indirectly, by means of dummy firms.[57] The American 'commercial import programme' covered South Vietnam's external trade deficit and kept inflation within tolerable limits, but as the result of an artificially produced demand it led to congestion of the consumer-goods market. There was no industrial development and there were no long-term investments, all the more since Diem and his mandarins opposed American economic principles by relying on state enterprises.[58] In colonial Indo-China, France established the primary bases of limited economic growth, but any industrialization worthy of the name had foundered because of the resistance of established metropolitan interests. American commitment intensified the underdevelopment left behind by colonialism. The result was the prototype of a dependent economy.

Strategic factors and factors relating to world politics determined American commitment after 1950. After the Second World War the United States established a network of military bases in Asia. After the outbreak of the Korean War this was secured by a series of 'security agreements'.[59] Until the outbreak of that war, Washington's foreign-policy élite had had only a vague understanding of the nature and associations with Moscow of the communist rebellions in Indonesia and Burma in 1948, and in Malaysia and the Philippines in 1948–9. The defeat of the Guomindang in China (1949) and the Korean crisis removed any remaining doubts. The revolutionary movements were now seen as threats to the South-East Asian region with Moscow and Peking pulling the strings. The containment policy advocated at that time in Europe offered a basis from which the Vietnamese liberation movement could be seen as the advance-guard of a supposedly monolithic Chinese-Soviet bloc. Hence Washington overlooked the nationalist elements of the Vietnamese struggle for independence. Yet, we cannot speak in general of any material aid from Moscow and Peking, at least before 1953, that went beyond propaganda support.[60] Although American policy tried to avoid identification with French colonialism and forced Paris to make concessions to Vietnamese nationalism, this position was neutralized by a fundamental anti-communism. After 1950–1, Washington feared that a defeat in Vietnam would destroy the balance of the bipolar system, block Western access to an economically and strategically important region and weaken France – of basic importance to Western European security.

Alongside the geostrategical doctrine of the primacy of Europe, and the concept of *Realpolitik*, the ideology of anti-communism was one of the three essential components of American understanding of its own national interests. Domestic political developments strengthened this anti-communism. McCarthyism produced a veritable anti-communist hysteria, charging the Democrats with betraying vital American interests by maintaining an inadequate military commitment and allowing the Communists to win in China.[61]

These factors explain the massive economic, technical and military support for the French colonial war which started with the Truman–Acheson administration and was continued by the Eisenhower government. In 1954 that conflict was more than 70 per cent financed by the United States.[62] The Judd Mission's report confirmed various pronouncements by Dulles about the key position of Indo-China for the strategic and economic stability of South-East Asia:

The area of Indochina is immensely wealthy in rice, rubber, coal and iron ore. Its position makes it a strategic key to the rest of South East Asia. If Indochina should fall, Thailand and Burma would be in extreme danger, Malaya, Singapore and even Indonesia would become more vulnerable to the Communist power-drive ... Communism would then be in an exceptional position to complete its perversion of the political and social revolution that is spreading through Asia ... The communists must be prevented from achieving their objectives in Indochina.[63]

This train of thought was also echoed in Eisenhower's domino theory. Here the President and his Foreign Minister, as well as Vice-President Nixon, put special emphasis on Malayan raw materials. The differing social, political and economic conditions in South-East Asian countries were ignored in the superficial domino theory. It suggested a link between an all-embracing American global strategy and Vietnam.[64] The containment elements of the domino theory stressed the possible effects on Japan of a chain reaction as the result of a 'loss' of Indo-China. Eisenhower and Dulles saw free access to South-East Asian markets as a precondition of Japanese industrial growth; as a military and industrial base, Japan was considered to occupy a key position in the containment of the Soviet Union and China.[65] Identifiable material interests, expressed as such, were originally at the forefront of American intervention but, with military escalation, they were overtaken by ideologically, socially and politically motivated goals.

The Eisenhower administration found support for its policies in the doctrine of massive retaliation and gave absolute precedence to confrontation with the Soviet Union. It did not have much to say about the Third World. Global considerations made the Kennedy administration change the American approach to social-revolutionary movements in the Third World. In 1960 national liberation movements in Algeria, the Congo and Vietnam threatened the status quo. In 1954, after the Geneva Conference, the reactionary, Catholic, militantly anti-communist Diem regime had been introduced with the aim of 'reconstructing the South'.[66] After about 1960 its repressive police-state methods and growing non-communist, and especially Buddhist, resistance to it posed the threat of the regime's collapse. The Kennedy government accepted the principle of the 'containment' policy without testing it: that is, that a non-communist South Vietnam was vital to American global interests. The ground was prepared for later military escalation.[67]

The Kennedy administration interpreted developments in Asia and Africa from the perspective of its 'nation-building' programme, which advised Third World countries to imitate capitalist development in the American mould. Walt W. Rostow's *The Stages of Economic Growth* (1960) analysed historical phases of economic growth, from 'take-off' to 'sustained growth', and seemed to forecast probable successive stages of development for developing countries. Rostow and the Kennedy administration reacted to developments at the periphery in the light of this prognosis. Across the world the American model of capitalist evolution had to be defended against the onslaught of social-revolutionary movements. Vietnam became the test case for the global containment of anti-capitalist revolutionary movements. The goal of intervention in Vietnam was to ensure the creation of a 'sufficiently self-reliant anti-communist bastion'; it worked along the lines of an 'integrated and systematic military-political-economic-strategic counter-insurgency-concept'.[68]

Fear that foreign policy would be misinterpreted as weak prevented the insight that the United States was 'overcommitted' throughout the world and stood in the way of any new definition of national interests. Instead the credibility of American deterrence had to be demonstrated by a transition from a policy of massive nuclear retaliation to one of 'flexible response'.[69] The decision in favour of 'counter-insurgency' was also influenced by a highly superficial form of thinking in historical analogies. This extended from Acheson via Dulles to Rusk, and equated the danger of Soviet expansion with the threat of German expansion before 1940.

In the course of the conflict in Indo-China the United States sought neither territorial gains nor *direct* economic advantages – as has been emphasized by the 'stalemate machine' school of thought.[70] The decisive motives were psychological and ideological. They were manifestations of social values, especially of the 'business creed' that politics had to provide favourable conditions worldwide for growth-oriented investment. The New Frontier's general line, expressed in Rostow's notion of modernization, was astonishingly similar to later ideas of the revisionist school in historiography. It associated global strategies with the social structures and economic interests of the United States. With hindsight, however, the absolute or relative dependence on markets for raw materials is questionable.[71] Counter-insurgency imperialism used both massive military intervention and techniques of indirect domination (the Diem regime; President Nixon's programme of 'Vietnamization', and so on). America's Indo-Chinese policy finally broke down with the communist conquest of South Vietnam and Cambodia in the spring of 1975 and of Laos by the end of the same year.[72]

By way of a postscript, we may ask if there are any traces of continuing imperialism in Indo-China after American withdrawal and the reunification of Vietnam.

The superimposition of three patterns of conflict – Vietnam *v.* Kampuchea, China *v.* Vietnam and the strategic triangle of the United States, the Soviet Union and China – produced an explosive situation. Local and regional conflict escalated into a military confrontation involving the great powers. Initially local friction between Vietnam and Kampuchea turned into a 'homemade proxy war' between China and the Soviet Union.[73] Both Cambodia and Vietnam had – and still have – to rely on outsiders to implement their interests. The Soviet Union supported the Vietnamese invasion in order to get a foothold in South-East Asia both politically and militarily, and to contain Chinese influence in the Indo-Chinese peninsula. China, however, committed itself on the side of 'Democratic Kampuchea' in order to prevent Vietnam from taking a leading role with the Soviet Union in the background.

Vietnam and Cambodia 183

The colonial legacy must be seen as having a decisive influence among a variety of factors most of which had local roots. Animosities, border conflicts and socio-cultural antagonisms extending over generations burdened both Vietnamese-Cambodian and Sino-Vietnamese relations. From the Vietnamese colonization of the Mekong Delta in the seventeenth and eighteenth centuries right up to the 1978–9 invasion, the search for rice and agricultural land has been a constant factor in Vietnamese expansion. Whereas Cambodia was almost wholly controlled by the Vietnamese provincial administrative system from 1830 onwards, the colonial administration's support of Vietnamese immigration into Cambodia and the appointment of Vietnamese to subordinate posts in the colonial administration presented the possibility of long-term conflict.[74] The non-recognition of colonial borders both by Sihanouk and by Pol Pot later resulted in several armed frontier conflicts.[75]

As against the independent revolutionary strategy of the Communist Party of Kampuchea (founded 1960), the Vietnamese claimed to have waged the anti-colonial war of liberation in Indo-China, to have offered the decisive resistance to American intervention, and thereby to enjoy 'special relationships' with Kampuchea and Laos.[76] From the Kampuchean viewpoint, this was tantamount to an Indo-Chinese federation dominated by Vietnam. Different starting-points and stages of development in the two communist movements gave rise to ideological differences in what each saw as the way to socialism. The Vietnamese conceived their revolutionary united front policy in a classical colonial situation, whereas the Cambodian communists proclaimed armed class war against a neo-colonial, but nationalist regime.

Sino-Vietnamese relations were clouded not only by historical conflicts, but also by disputed frontiers, as well as by China's claim to control of the South China Sea. Considerations of security and the regional balance of power persuaded China to unite with 'Democratic Kampuchea' against an 'Asiatic Cuba', and to offer a strategic counterweight to a Vietnam-centred regional system supported by the Soviet Union.[77]

The example of Indo-China illustrates the capacity of the 'excentric theory of imperialism': it can accommodate the whole range of imperial domination from pre-colonial penetration to the unsuccessful attempts of the United States, using the informal methods of a regime based on collaboration as well as direct military intervention, to destroy Vietnamese efforts for emancipation, and to impose on the country a concept of modernization based on Western models. The victory of the Vietnamese Revolution, however, by no means seems to have banished the danger of imperialist domination in South-East Asia. Although the situation of stalemate in which both superpowers find themselves strategically prevents any recourse being taken to classical imperialistic activities, 'proxy war' can be interpreted as a new variation of sub-imperialism. All three levels of conflict described above reveal elements of informal imperialism, at least in a formal analysis. While Vietnam attempts to realize traditional hegemonial objectives by combining techniques of collaboration with military occupation, China repeatedly resorts to 'punitive expeditions', simultaneously supporting anti-Vietnamese resistance movements. Ultimately, by supplying military and technical aid, the superpowers are keeping their clients in position to maintain a regional balance of power which suits the superpowers' global interests.

Notes: Chapter 12

This chapter was translated by John Cumming and Angela Davies.

1 D. K. Fieldhouse, *Economics and Empire 1830–1914* (London, 1973), pp. 76 ff., 460 ff.; R. Robinson, 'Non-European foundations of European imperialism: sketch for a theory of collaboration', in R. Owen and B. Sutcliffe (eds), *Studies in the Theory of Imperialism* (London, 1972), pp. 117–40; J. Galbraith, 'The "Turbulent Frontier" as a factor in British expansion', *Comparative Studies in Society and History*, vol. 2 (1959), pp. 150–68; W. J. Mommsen, *Theories of Imperialism* (London, 1981), pp. 100 ff.
2 See Chapter 18 by Ronald Robinson in this volume.
3 N.-D. Lê, *Les Mission-Etrangères et la pénétration française au Viêt-Nam* (Paris, 1975), pp. 14 ff.; J. Buttinger, *Vietnam: A Political History* (New York, 1968), pp. 55 ff. On the development of the French East India Company see D. Rothermund, *Europa und Asien im Zeitalter des Merkantilismus* (Darmstadt, 1978), pp. 125 ff.; L. T. Khôi, *3000 Jahre Vietnam* (Munich, 1969), pp. 243–4; J.-R. Clementin, 'Le comportement politique des institutions catholiques au Vietnam', in J. Chesneaux *et al.* (eds), *Tradition et révolution au Vietnam* (Paris, 1971), pp. 109–10.
4 Fieldhouse, *Economics and Empire*, pp. 199–203; M. E. Osborne, *The French Presence in Cochinchina and Cambodia: Rule and Response (1859–1905)* (London, 1969), pp. 26 ff.
5 ibid., pp. 35, 54–5, 63, 75.
6 G. Taboulet, 'Le voyage d'exploration du Mékong (1866–1868): Doudart de Lagrée et Francis Garnier', *Revue française d'histoire d'outre-mer*, vol. 206 (1970), pp. 5–90; J. Valette, 'L'expédition du Mékong (1866–1868) à travers les témoignages de quelques-uns de ses membres', *Revue historique*, no. 502 (1972), pp. 347–74; idem, 'Origines et enseignements de l'expédition du Mékong', *Bulletin de la Société d'Histoire Moderne*, vol. 14 (1968), pp. 7–12. In contrast to Taboulet, Valette places greater emphasis on the decision-making process in Paris. Financial circles such as the Crédit Foncier, were made aware of the problem of Vietnam by Garnier's publications. Garnier's links with financial and, in particular, trading circles have still to be carefully examined.
7 D. Brötel, *Französischer Imperialismus in Vietnam. Die koloniale Expansion und die Errichtung des Protektorats Annam-Tongking* (Freiburg im Breisgau, 1971), pp. 15 ff.
8 See ibid., pp. 28 ff., 41 ff., 339; C.-R. Ageron, *France coloniale ou parti colonial?* (Paris, 1978), pp. 104 ff.
9 Brötel, *Französischer Imperialismus*, pp. 102 ff., 119–20; C. Fourniau, 'L'évolution de l'affaire du Tonkin: la genèse; le drame tonkinois (mai-décembre 1983), de la mort de Rivière à la prise de Sontay', *Revue historique*, no. 500 (1971), pp. 395–6, 400 ff.
10 On the French implantation in the China market see D. Brötel, 'Frankreichs ökonomische Penetration auf dem China-Markt, 1885–1895', in P. Hablützel *et al.* (eds), *Dritte Welt: Historische Prägung und politische Herausforderung. Festschrift für Rudolf von Albertini* (Wiesbaden, 1983), pp. 30–56. As regards the social and economic system see G. Ziebura, 'Interne Faktoren des französischen Hochimperialismus 1871–1914', in W. J. Mommsen (ed.), *Der moderne Imperialismus* (Stuttgart, 1971), pp. 88 ff., 101 ff.
11 J. Laffey, 'Les racines de l'impérialisme français en Extrême-Orient: à propos des thèses de J.-F. Cady', in J. Bouvier and R. Girault (eds), *L'impérialisme français d'avant 1914* (Paris, 1976), pp. 15–37; Brötel, *Französischer Imperialismus*, pp. 253 ff., 313–14.
12 T. Q. Vu, *Die vietnamesische Gesellschaft im Wandel. Kolonialismus und gesellschaftliche Entwicklung in Vietnam* (Wiesbaden, 1978), pp. 136 ff., 148 ff.; D. G. Marr, *Vietnamese Anticolonialism* (London, 1971), pp. 43, 46; Fourniau, 'L'évolution de l'affaire du Tonkin', p. 391; idem, 'Les traditions de la lutte nationale au Vietnam: l'insurrection des lettrés (1885–1895)', in Chesneaux *et al.* (eds), *Tradition et révolution au Vietnam*,

pp. 98–9; J. Chesneaux, 'Stages in the development of the Vietnam national movement, 1862–1945', *Past and Present*, no. 7 (1955), pp. 63–75.
13   Marr, *Vietnamese Anticolonialism*, pp. 49, 52, 60.
14   J. K. Munholland, '"Collaboration strategy" and the French pacification of Tonkin, 1885–1897', *Historical Journal*, vol. 24 (1981), pp. 629–50.
15   R. von Albertini, *European Colonial Rule 1880–1940* (Westport, Conn. and London, 1982), pp. 193–4. See also B. Eli, 'Paul Doumer in Indochina 1897–1902. Verwaltungsreformen, Eisenbahnen, Chinapolitik', PhD diss., Heidelberg, 1967, pp. 7, 22 ff., 36 ff.
16   Osborne, *The French Presence*, pp. 9–10.
17   A. Forest, *La Cambodge et la colonisation française. Histoire d'une colonisation sans heurts (1897–1920)* (Paris, 1980), p. 63.
18   ibid., p. 79.
19   ibid., pp. 80 ff., 97 ff., 112.
20   M. J. Murray, *The Development of Capitalism in Colonial Indochina, 1870–1940* (Berkeley, Calif., 1980), pp. 45 ff., espec. 60–1, 90–1.
21   ibid., pp. 166–7, 196 ff.; von Albertini, *European Colonial Rule*, p. 215.
22   J. Laffey, 'Lyonnais imperialism in the Far East', *Modern Asian Studies*, vol. 10 (1976), pp. 225–48.
23   J. Bouvier and R. Girault, 'Avant-propos', in idem (eds), *L'impérialisme français d'avant 1914*, p. 9; R. Cameron, *La France et le développement économique de l'Europe 1800–1914* (Paris, 1971), p. 380; Ziebura, 'Interne Faktoren', p. 113.
24   French Capital Invested in Indochina 1888–1917:

	million gold francs
industry, mining	249
transportation	128
commerce	75
agriculture	40
total	492

Sources: C. Robequain, *The Economic Development of French Indo-China* (London, 1944), p. 161; Murray, *The Development of Capitalism*, p. 110.
25   J. Marseille, 'L'investissement français dans l'empire colonial: l'enquête du gouvernement de Vichy (1943)', *Revue historique*, no. 512 (1974), p. 415.
26   von Albertini, *European Colonial Rule*, p. 210. On the development of the rubber and mining sectors, see also D. J. Tate, *The Making of Modern Southeast Asia*, Vol. 2 (Oxford, 1980), pp. 322 ff.
27   The construction of roads was primarily dictated by military and ideological considerations. Doumer's plan for a railway connection between Saigon and Phnom Penh had to be dropped. See Forest, *La Cambodge*, pp. 252–3.
28   ibid., pp. 261–2, 265–6.
29   ibid., pp. 308–9.
30   Marseille, 'L'investissement français', pp. 417–18.
31   ibid., p. 418.
32   See for details Murray, *The Development of Capitalism*, pp. 146–9.
33   P.-R. Féray, *Le Viêt-Nam au XXe siècle* (Paris, 1979), p. 50; J. Chesneaux, *Geschichte Vietnams* (East Berlin, 1963), p. 233; Tate, *The Making of Modern Southeast Asia*, Vol. 2, pp. 323, 327.
34   P. Brocheux, 'Crise économique et société en Indochine française', *Revue française d'histoire d'outre mer*, vol. 63 (1976), pp. 656, 661 ff. On the question of rebellion and repression see D. G. Marr, *Vietnamese Tradition on Trial, 1920–1945* (Berkeley, Calif. and Los Angeles, Calif., 1981), pp. 377 ff.
35   W. J. Duiker, *The Rise of Nationalism in Vietnam, 1900–1941* (Ithaca, NY, and London, 1976), p. 138.
36   D. Hémery, 'Aux origines des guerres d'indépendance vietnamiennes: pouvoir colonial et phénomène communiste en Indochine avant la Seconde Guerre Mondiale', *Le*

Mouvement social, vol. 10 (1977), p. 9.
37 ibid., pp. 21 ff.
38 ibid., pp. 22–3.
39 ibid., pp. 32–3.
40 Vu, *Die vietnamesische Gesellschaft*, pp. 336–7. On overall French policy in this phase: G. Haas, 'Französisch-Indochina zwischen den Mächten 1940–1945', PhD diss., Berlin, 1970; G. Pilleul (ed.), *De Gaulle et l'Indochine 1940–1946* (Paris, 1982), p. 79.
41 Pilleul (ed.), *De Gaulle et l'Indochine*, pp. 10, 13, 126, 133.
42 The federation was given a governor-general, who was assisted by an elected assembly with advisory authority. Customs assimilation was abolished. See ibid., pp. 13–14, 186, 190, 241.
43 For the development of the united front policy see Duiker, *The Rise of Nationalism*, pp. 234 ff., 275 ff.; Marr, *Vietnamese Tradition*, pp. 387 ff.
44 Pilleul (ed.), *De Gaulle et l'Indochine*, pp. 142, 186, 202.
45 ibid., pp. 14–15. On the August Revolution see Marr, *Vietnamese Tradition*, pp. 408 ff.
46 Marr, *Vietnamese Tradition*, pp. 15, 30–1, 175 ff. The prince was killed in a plane crash.
47 J. Buttinger, *Rückblick auf Vietnam* (Klagenfurt, 1976), pp. 12 ff.; Vu, *Die vietnamesische Gesellschaft*, pp. 360 ff.
48 E. Irving, *The First Indochina War: French and American Policy 1945–1954* (London, 1975), pp. 149–50; T. Smith, 'The French colonial consensus and people's war, 1946–1958', in idem (ed.), *The End of the European Empire: Decolonization after World War II* (London, 1975), pp. 103, 105 ff.
49 Irving, *The First Indochina War*, pp. 31 ff.; R. F. Turner, *Vietnamese Communism: Its Origins and Development* (Stanford, Calif., 1975), p. 61; D. Lancaster, *The Emancipation of French Indochina* (London, 1961), p. 160.
50 H. Lanoue, 'L'emprise économique des Etats-Unis sur l'Indochine avant 1950', in Chesneaux *et al.* (eds), *Tradition et révolution au Vietnam*, pp. 299–300.
51 For example, the Société des Phosphates d'Extrême-Orient with a capital of 10 million piastres (= 170 million francs).
52 Chesneaux, *Geschichte Vietnams*, pp. 327–8.
53 In contrast to Lanoue who assumes a flight of capital from Indochina, Chesneaux rejects the thesis of an exodus, pointing to the fact that as late as 1954 French investments in Vietnam were estimated at 26,000 million piastres.
54 Lanoue, 'L'emprise économique', pp. 301–2. On the conduct of the rubber companies see also Murray, *The Development of Capitalism*, pp. 268 ff.
55 A. Ruscio, 'Le mendèsisme et l'Indochine', *Revue d'histoire moderne et contemporaine*, vol. 29 (1982), p. 326 ff.
56 G. Kolko, *Hintergründe der US-Aussenpolitik* (Frankfurt-on-Main, 1969), pp. 65 ff.
57 Chesneaux, *Geschichte Vietnams*, pp. 328–9.
58 G. C. Herring, *America's Longest War: The United States and Vietnam, 1950–1975* (New York, 1979), pp. 59 ff.
59 In 1945 American military bases were established in Japan, Okinawa, Korea and the central Pacific, and in 1947 in the Philippines.
60 Material aid from Peking started in 1953. See P. M. Kattenburg, *The Vietnam Trauma in American Foreign Policy, 1945–1975*, 2nd edn (New Brunswick, NJ, 1982), pp. 14–15, 21, 42.
61 ibid., pp. 37 ff.; D. Ellsberg, *Ich erkläre den Krieg. Vietnam – Der Mechanismus einer militärischen Eskalation* (Munich, 1973), pp. 82 ff., 191–2.
62 M. Gurtov, *The First Vietnam Crisis: Chinese Communist Strategy and United States Involvement, 1953–1954* (New York, 1967), pp. 22 ff.
63 ibid., p. 26.
64 Kattenburg, *The Vietnam Trauma*, pp. 43–4; Kolko, *Hintergründe der US-Aussenpolitik*, p. 100; Buttinger, *Rückblick auf Vietnam*, pp. 162–3. On the policy of the Eisenhower administration see A. D. The, *Die Vietnampolitik der USA von der Johnson- zur Nixon-Kissinger-Doktrin oder die Neuorientierung der amerikanischen Aussenpolitik* (Frankfurt-on-Main, 1979), pp. 95–6; J. Lacouture and P. Devillers, *La Fin d'une guerre. Indochine 1954* (Paris, 1960), pp. 76, 103, 172.
65 W. LaFeber, *America, Russia, and the Cold War*, 4th edn (New York, 1980), pp. 110–11; H. Magdoff, *The Age of Imperialism: The Economics of U.S. Foreign Policy* (New York,

Vietnam and Cambodia 187

1969), p. 53. For a critique of this interpretation see R. W. Tucker, *The Radical Left and American Foreign Policy*, 2nd edn (Baltimore, Md, 1972), pp. 116–17.

66 On the Diem regime see Lacouture and Devillers, *La Fin d'une guerre*, pp. 297 ff.; P. Devillers, 'La lutte pour la réunification du Vietnam entre 1954 et 1961', in Chesneaux *et al.* (eds), *Tradition et révolution au Vietnam*, pp. 329–55; Buttinger, *Vietnam*, pp. 384 ff.; J. P. Harrison, *The Endless War: Fifty Years of Struggle in Vietnam* (New York and London, 1982), pp. 207–39.

67 Herring, *America's Longest War*, p. 74.

68 J. L. Gaddis, *Strategies of Containment* (New York, 1982), pp. 74–5. On W. W. Rostow's role see ibid., pp. 200 ff.

69 ibid., pp. 209 ff.; L. Freedman, *The Evolution of Nuclear Strategy* (London, 1981), pp. 285–6. For the view that Kennedy's decision was taken under pressure from Republican politicians see S. Pelz, 'John F. Kennedy's 1961 Vietnam War decisions', *Journal of Strategic Studies*, vol. 4 (1981), pp. 357, 362–3, 380.

70 Tucker, *The Radical Left*, pp. 118 ff.

71 On the final phase of the war, see Harrison, *The Endless War*, pp. 266–95.

72 W. P. Elliott (ed.), *The Third Indochina Conflict* (Boulder, Col., 1981), p. 15; P. Schier, 'Der Konflikt zwischen der Sozialistischen Republik Vietnam und dem Demokratischen Kampuchea und seine Ursachen', in W. Draguhn and P. Schier (eds), *Indochina. Der permanente Konflikt?* (Hamburg, 1981), p. 78.

73 See the very detailed account in Forest, *La Cambodge*, pp. 433 ff.

74 On border issues see Schier, 'Der Konflikt zwischen der Sozialistischen Republik Vietnam', pp. 83 ff.; M. Kreile, 'Kambodscha', in D. Nohlen and F. Nuscheler (eds), *Handbuch der Dritten Welt*, Vol. 7, 2nd edn (Hamburg, 1983), p. 358.

75 According to Heder, the ideological conflict as regards the aims and strategies of revolution were of principal importance, border problems taking second place. S. P. Heder, 'The Kampuchean–Vietnamese conflict', in Elliott (ed.), *The Third Indochina Conflict*, pp. 21, 34 ff.

76 R. Machetzki, 'Politik der VR China gegenüber Indochina unter besonderer Berücksichtigung des chinesisch-vietnamesischen Konflikts', in Draguhn and Schier (eds), *Indochina*, pp. 157 ff.

77 B. Garrett, 'The strategic triangle and the Indochina crisis', in Elliott (ed.), *The Third Indochina Conflict*, pp. 200, 201–2, 206–7.

Part Three

Imperialism and the World Economy

13 Historical Roots of Economic Underdevelopment: Myths and Realities

PAUL BAIROCH

It is obvious that economic underdevelopment, like any other specific economic condition, has historical roots. The underlying question in this chapter is to what extent two centuries of intense economic relations between the European world and what has become the Third World, have had negative repercussions for the economic structures of the Third World today. A subsidiary but no less important question is what contribution these economic relations made to the 'success story' of Western development. To answer these questions is not a simple task, not least because many preconceptions have to be countered.

The real economic and social drama with which the Third World is confronted today helps to explain, even if it cannot justify, certain extreme positions taken by some intellectuals of both less developed and industrialized countries. One of the most dangerous of these is subscribing to the myth that the development of the West can only be explained in terms of colonialism and imperialism. This implies, erroneously, that a level of economic development close to that achieved by the Western world cannot be achieved without colonial expansion.

This chapter is divided into five sections. In the first I shall investigate to what extent a gap in economic development existed between the two major economic 'groups' before the industrial revolution. I shall then move on to the question of the nature of European colonization before the industrial revolution. The third section will deal with the constraints of traditional colonization. It will show that far-reaching economic relations between colonies and the metropolises were only possible after the profound changes brought about by the industrial revolution. The fourth section brings us to the heart of the issue: the myths and realities of colonization and economic underdevelopment. Finally, I shall look at the other side of the story: the myths and realities of colonization and economic development in the West.

International Economic Disparities before the Industrial Revolution

Disparities in standards of living are not only a characteristic of the post-industrial revolution era. What was new about the industrial revolution was that the range of standards of living increased considerably. This was achieved more by extending the upper than by depressing the lower part of the range. As far as individual countries are concerned the upper level was probably increased by some 1,600–1,800 per cent, whereas the lower level decreased (if at all) by no more than 10–20 per cent. Indeed, if we disregard a certain number of small countries with exceptional resources, it appears that differences in international income levels were very limited before the industrial revolution. The gap between the poorest and the richest countries was probably in the range of only 1·0 to 1·6. If we compare larger economic entities, such as Western Europe or China, the difference was even smaller, in the order of 1·0 to 1·3 or less. Within the framework of a traditional economy, a favourable natural resource endowment generally led to a rapid increase in population which, in turn, resulted in a new equilibrium with a lower level of resources per capita.

It seems likely that differences in income levels were more important at the micro-regional level, defined as a country or region with a population of less than 2 million, than at the international level. Indeed, high per capita income levels could only derive from exceptional factors, and it is most unlikely that such factors existed throughout a large region. Such factors include both natural elements such as fertile land, rich subsoil or a favourable geographical location, and factors resulting from human activities such as industrial specialization or, even more importantly for that period, commercial activity. In general, commercial activity led to a situation in which a small country took over commercial activities for a much larger region.

Within specific micro-regions the value added of each industrial worker did not exceed that of an agricultural worker by more than 100 per cent. Regional disparities in agricultural productivity, resulting from both natural factors and differences in agricultural technology were more important, but probably did not exceed a ratio of 1·0 to 3·0. This suggests that if we exclude small micro-regions specializing in international trade (for example, the Italian republics before the sixteenth century) the greatest difference in average regional income would not exceed a ratio of 1·0 to 3·0.

For the purposes of this chapter, incomes will be measured by real per capita gross national product (GNP) at market prices. This does not imply that GNP is a perfect yardstick; it is not only an inadequate measure of economic levels, it is an even less adequate indicator of living conditions. National accounting takes external costs of growth into consideration only imperfectly, if at all. The same is true of such important elements in living conditions as climate and the urban and rural environment. But at the present stage of research into alternative indicators, and especially as far as historical data are concerned, real per capita GNP remains the least questionable single indicator of income levels.

In a previous paper I tried to estimate the greatest spread of national per capita income before the industrial revolution.[1] I used six different approaches which all provided convergent results. Table 13.1 shows GNP per capita figures for thirteen countries at a stage of development preceding or close to that of traditional societies. Those figures were arrived at by applying the available series of historical data showing the growth of per

Table 13.1 *Real GNP per capita for Selected Countries at a Stage of Development Close to that of Traditional Societies* (in 1960 US dollars and prices)

	Coefficient used to correct 1960 data[a]	GNP per capita Periods	GNP per capita Data
COUNTRIES NOW DEVELOPED			
Great Britain	1·30	1700	160–200
United States	1·00	1710	200–260
France	1·15	1781–90	170–200
Russia	1·14[b]	1860	160–200
Sweden	1·20	1860	190–230
Japan	1·75	1885	160–200
COUNTRIES NOW LESS DEVELOPED			
Egypt	2·10	1887	170–210
Ghana	1·70	1891	90–150
India	2·80	1900	130–160
Iran	1·75	1900	140–220
Jamaica	1·30	1832	240–280
Mexico	1·60	1900	150–190
Philippines	1·70	1902	170–210

Source: P. Bairoch, 'Ecarts internationaux des niveaux de vie avant la révolution industrielle', *Annales, ESC*, vol. 34 (1979), pp. 145–71.

[a] To correct the 1970 GNP data expressed in local prices (converted at the prevailing rate of exchange) into 1960 US dollars and prices.
[b] Correction not only for price differences, but also for the translation of net material product into GNP.

capita GNP to the corrected 1960 levels of per capita GNP. If we exclude the United States and Jamaica, at that time micro-regions of some 300,000 inhabitants, the spread of income lies between about US$130 and US$200, a gap of 1·0 to 1·5. After taking various other factors into account the probable maximum spread was in the order of 1·0 to 1·4–1·6.

The most significant of the other five approaches used was the determination of the minimum cost of living, expressed in current prices, of countries which, in the first half of the nineteenth century, had already achieved an average standard of living higher than those of the richest countries (but not micro-regions) in the framework of traditional societies. Comparing the minimum cost of living with the average level of consumption per capita provides an excellent indicator of the extreme spread of income before the industrial revolution. The data were assembled and the computation was made for four countries; the result was a probable spread of 1·0 to 1·5–1·7.

The other four approaches and the results they provided in terms of the probable range of income are as follows: situation of European countries at the beginning of the nineteenth century in terms of real GNP per capita: 1·0 to 1·4–1·6; long-term (for more than two or three centuries) evolution of real wages in traditional societies: 1·0 to 1·4–1·6; per capita income of

European cities in the sixteenth and seventeenth centuries (the GNP was provided by an indicator method):[2] 1·0 to 1·5–1·7; contemporary views of national inequalities as assessed by seventeenth- and eighteenth-century pioneers of national accounting: 1·0 to 1·3–1·5.

Thus, it is possible to conclude that before the industrial revolution, the income gap between the poorest and the richest country was certainly smaller than a ratio of 1·0 to 2·0, and probably in the order of only 1·0 to 1·5. In terms of 1960 US dollars and prices, the lowest level for traditional countries lay around 130 to 150, the highest around 190 to 240.[3] This does not take into account primitive societies, the poorest of which probably had an 'income level' some 30 per cent below the poorest traditional country at a stage beyond that of the neolithic revolution. Obviously, primitive societies existed (and may still exist) that were richer than very poor traditional societies.

Where did Europe stand within this limited range of inequalities of income at the end of the seventeenth century? The end of the seventeenth century or the beginning of the eighteenth is a period when the Western world had not yet been affected by the industrial revolution which was just starting in England. It was also a time in which the great civilizations in Asia had not yet entered a period of 'traditional' decline. At this moment of world history, it is very likely that the average standard of living of Europe taken as a whole was equal to, or a little lower than, that of the 'rest of the world'. This was due largely to the relatively high level achieved by the Chinese civilization and the importance of this society in the 'rest of the world' (some 34–38 per cent), and to the low level achieved by Russia which represented a significant proportion of Europe (some 24–28 per cent).

If a similar comparison around the thirteenth century could be made it is likely that the position of Europe was relatively more negative, and even more so around the eleventh century. It should not be assumed from the low level of inequality that there was no evolution. And in the case of the traditional societies, evolution was not a unilinear process. This was also true of technical levels. In this respect comparisons are easier and therefore it is certain that from 600–700 until somewhere between 1620–40 and 1700–20, the most advanced civilization in Asia was ahead of the most advanced civilization in Europe. However, it is probable that the differences in technological levels did not lead to similar differences in standards of living until the industrial revolution. In traditional societies such factors as natural resources in terms of quality and quantity of farmland could largely balance technological factors. The same was also largely true of traditional forms of colonization or of imperialism.

European Colonization before the Industrial Revolution: One of Several?

Even if colonization is defined in terms of the main negative aspects of European colonization the European case has numerous historical prece-

Historical Roots of Underdevelopment 195

dents. The following three elements summarize the major negative aspects of European (or other forms) of colonization:

(1) An attempt to impose (by persuasion, or by force, or by a combination of the two) the civilization of the metropolis on the inhabitants of colonies; the term civilization here includes religion and language.
(2) The introduction of a set of rules that subordinates the economic interest of the colonies to that of the metropolis.
(3) Discrimination based on race, origin, or religion against the inhabitants of the colonies and in favour of those of the metropolis.

Even if the history of non-European colonization remains largely to be written, there is no doubt that it has a number of elements in common with that undertaken by Europe from the sixteenth to the twentieth centuries. To mention just a few: the Egyptian Empire, five centuries (from the sixteenth century to the eleventh century BC); the Persian Empire, three centuries (from the seventh century to the fourth century BC); the Roman Empire, four centuries (from the first century BC to the fourth century AD). Further away from Europe at least the Chinese Empire, the Mongolian Empire and those of pre-Columbian America have to be mentioned. Coming closer to the contemporary period, one should not forget the Arab and Ottoman empires which colonized parts of Europe during a much longer period than that in which Europe colonized the Middle East. The fact that all these empires did not expand beyond their actual size is not attributable to a lack of colonial appetite, but to the military and economic constraints of that period which put a certain limit to the extent of an imperial system.

The picture of a colonization process was, and still is, radically different depending on the side from which it is viewed. For example, the expansion of the Muslim or Christian cultures can be considered either as the progress of civilization or as colonization, depending on the cultural background of the observer. Historically speaking, many contributions to the wide spectrum of civilization are after-effects of colonizations; this, however, was not a one-way process, since in many cases the metropolis also gained from its colonies. There is, however, a possibility that the negative aspects of European colonization before the industrial revolution were more severe than those of most of the other traditional colonization processes; a possibility, but not a certainty, since the compilation of balance sheets in this field is made difficult by the almost total lack of studies on the effects of non-European colonization as against a profusion of studies on European colonization. This profusion implies *ipso facto* a wide range of points of view ranging from underestimation to overestimation of the negative aspects.

The Constraints of Traditional Colonization

As we have mentioned above, the extent of traditional colonization was limited not by lack of will but by economic and military constraints. We shall attempt to demonstrate these constraints, focusing mainly on the economic ones. These are found in a type of colonization based on economic exploitation, rather than on settlement, and will help to explain the exceptional nature of colonialism after the industrial revolution.

Traditional Europe, like any other traditional pre-industrial society, could have only limited economic relations with its colonies, and therefore could have (or needed) only a relatively limited colonial empire. 'Traditional' Europe implies a low standard of living and a level of per capita consumption close to that of the colonies. This standard of living and level of consumption, in turn, implied that products from the colonies (tropical goods and luxury manufactured goods) could represent only a very small fraction of total consumption. On the basis of various indications, we have estimated that the consumption of these goods represented at least 2 per cent of total consumption (or of per capita consumption) and at most 10 per cent; the most likely figure is some 4–6 per cent.

Let us assume, to simplify the problem, that all 'colonial goods' imported into European countries came from their own colonies. The size of these colonies was then determined by two conflicting constraints: colonies could not be too small, otherwise the amount of 'exports' would have placed too heavy a burden on the local economy, and would therefore have endangered the economic and social equilibrium. On the other hand, they could not be too large, otherwise the economic (and military) costs of controlling them would have been too high.

Taking into account the very high transport costs, the generous profits of the middlemen and the relative parity of income between Europe and its colonies, it can be assumed that if European imports from the colonies represented 4–6 per cent of per capita consumption, it would have represented 2–3 per cent of the per capita production of the colonies if these had been the same size as Europe. This is obviously too low a rate of colonial extraction in view of the constraints presented above. A more normal figure would be in the region of 15–25 per cent.[4] This means that traditional Europe could have found all the 'colonial goods' it needed in an exploitative empire whose total population represented some 8–20 per cent of that of Europe.

The actual figure for the relative importance of the European empire was indeed close to that deduced above. Around 1700 (see Table 13.2) the population of all the European colonies represented some 8–15 per cent of the population of Europe. The situation began to change rapidly at the end of the eighteenth century with the British penetration of India. But at that stage, Britain was no longer a traditional society. Around 1800 it produced an amount of iron that represented some 40–50 per cent of that of the entire world in 1700, and this with a population of only 1 per cent of that of the world. With only about 35 per cent of its labour force in agriculture Britain could feed its entire population, a situation that continental Europe reached only after the Second World War.

Table 13.2 *Comparison of the Population of Europe[a] and its Colonies* (in millions)

	Europe	European colonies	Colonies compared to Europe (in per cent)
1700	140	16	11
1750	160	22	14
1800	207	120	58
1830	242	240	100
1860	294	270–680[b]	92–252
1900	414	490–960[b]	118–232
1913	481	530–1030[b]	110–214

Sources: Author's estimates and computations.
Note: The population figures for the colonies are only approximate. The margin of error is about 40% for 1700 and 1750; 30% for 1800; 20% for 1830 and 1860; and 10% for 1900 and 1913 (the margin of error for the European population is about 10% for 1700 and 1750; 5% for 1800; and below 4% after 1800.)

[a] Including Russia.
[b] The first figure excludes China, the second includes it.

Colonization and Economic Underdevelopment: Myths and Realities

Let us consider myths and realities. Unfortunately, the realities are very numerous and very negative. Two centuries of modern colonization resulted in many unfavourable structural changes in those regions which now form the Third World. The negative structural elements that characterized the Third World after the period of direct imperialism include a low level of industrialization, strong specialization of export crops, and the beginnings of a demographic inflation. All these and some other negative aspects are undoubtedly the legacy of modern colonization. Let us begin with these realities and then follow with some myths.

(1) *The Reality of the De-Industrialization Process*
The reality in this case is a very conclusive one, even if more research is needed to establish with some precision the exact degree of de-industrialization reached by various countries. In case A was it 85 or 95 per cent, and in case B was it 50 or 70 per cent?

Case A could be India which, however, is not the most extreme case. There is no doubt that the massive influx of British-manufactured goods from 1813 onwards led to a massive de-industrialization of India. Let us take the case of the Indian textile industry (in traditional societies textiles represented some 65–75 per cent of total industrial activity). During the centuries preceding the nineteenth, Indian textiles and especially its calicoes were highly prized in Europe. More important is that during the eighteenth century calicoes, together with other manufactured textile goods, represented some 60–70 per cent of India's total exports.[5] As long as the East India Company had a monopoly of trade, very few English wool textiles and no English cotton textiles were imported into India. As soon as the monopoly disappeared (in 1813) the influx of English textiles into India increased remarkably. About 1 million yards of cotton cloth were imported in 1814; 13 million around 1820; 51 million around 1830; 995 million around 1870 and 2,050 million around 1890.[6]

This influx is certainly due to the enormous progress made by the English spinning industry as a result of technological innovations. By 1830 the productivity of an English spinning worker using modern equipment was 300–400 times higher than that of an Indian artisan.[7] The same comparison could also be made with European artisans, even though there were differences because of tariff policies. While Europe (and the United States) as a rule either totally prohibited the import of yarn and of manufactured cotton, or imposed duties ranging from 30–80 per cent, British textile goods could enter the Indian market with no duties at all. And when for fiscal reasons the British government in India introduced modest import duties (3–10 per cent) on those imports, as a result of 'legitimate' protests by British manufacturers, local producers were subjected to a tax of the same magnitude, in order to put the two types of production in the 'same position'.[8]

It is easy to understand the causes of the local Indian textile industry's rapid disappearance under such circumstances. The difficulty of establishing a modern textile industry in the second half of the nineteenth century is obvious. Imports probably covered 55–75 per cent of total textile consumption. The only debate that is possible is about the precise extent of this process of de-industrialization. Around 1870–80, were local industry and artisans able to provide 25 or 45 per cent of the local textile consumption? The same question can be put of the iron industry: around 1890–1900 did it produce 1 or 5 per cent of local consumption?

The process was quite similar in the rest of Asia except for China. Here local industry was better able to survive and also to reconstruct itself, because the influx started later, because there was a larger degree of local autonomy and also because of the sheer size of the country. But greater resistance did not imply a victory. In the Chinese case the question mark is around the 60 per cent level: around 1890 did local Chinese textiles provide 50 or 70 per cent of local consumption?

The African story is similar to the Asian one, except that the starting-point was generally lower. The Latin American story is rather different, since in this case modern colonization succeeded three centuries of traditional colonization. Another difference is that while most of Asia was in the process of being colonized in the first years of the nineteenth century, Latin America became almost totally independent. This political independence is not negligible in explaining the fact that around 1913 Latin America, with only 7 per cent of the Third World population, had 21 per cent of Third World cotton-spinning spindles.

Incidentally, it is worth emphasizing that Latin America only has a small share of the population of the Third World, since often problems specific to this continent are taken as a general model of the Third World. In 1800 Latin America had less than 3 per cent of the total Third World population. This means that the success or failure of Latin America had little influence on the total evolution of the Third World.

Historical Roots of Underdevelopment 199

Table 13.3 Third World Manufacturing Production (Level on the Basis of UK of 1900 = 100)

	Total production Level	In per cent of world production	Per capita production Level	In per cent of world production
1750	93	73·0	7	100
1800	99	67·7	6	100
1860	83	36·6	4	57
1913	70	7·5	2	10
1938	122	7·2	4	13
1953	200	6·5	5	10
1980	1323	12·0	17	17

Source: P. Bairoch, 'International industrialization levels from 1750 to 1980', Journal of European Economic History, vol. 11 (1982), pp. 269–332.
Note: The degree of rounding off of the figures does not imply a correspondingly low margin of error.

The global impact of the de-industrialization process is demonstrated in Table 13.3 which shows the probable evolution of Third World manufacturing from 1750 to 1980. The figures in the table refer to both traditional and modern industry. If we restrict the data to modern industry, in 1913 the Third World would account for only 1–2 per cent rather than 7–8 per cent of world manufacturing production.

To what extent did political independence change the picture? In this case the change is radical since one of the first economic objectives of almost all the newly independent Third World countries was industrialization. Clearly to a very large degree this was a success story. Between 1950 and 1983 manufacturing production has multiplied by more than 8 times. This is equivalent to a yearly growth rate of more than 6 per cent in total terms or of 3·5 per cent in per capita terms. It represents a rate of growth more than twice (in total terms) that of the developed world during its first century of industrialization (about 50 per cent more rapid again in per capita terms).

Apart from the high cost of this industrialization in terms of mismanagement and even more in terms of depriving the vital agricultural sector of much-needed investments, it should be noted that the industrialization of the Third World has at least three weaknesses. The first one concerns regional inequalities. Most of the manufacturing is concentrated in six countries: Brazil, Mexico, Taiwan, Singapore, South Korea and Hong Kong. According to our calculations and estimates these six countries provided about 25 to 29 per cent of the manufacturing production of the Third World in 1953 and by 1980 were contributing 66–70 per cent. These six countries have a total population which is only 11 per cent of that of the Third World market economies.

The other two points which must be raised are the growing multinationalization of manufacturing industry in the Third World and the specialization in traditional sectors. Whereas the proportion of the total manufacturing output of the developed countries produced abroad in factories owned by multinational companies was about 11 per cent in 1973, in the market economies of the Third World the proportion was between 28 and 31 per cent (33–36 per cent in Latin America and 16–19 per cent in Asia). As regards specialization in the traditional sectors, in 1973 the Third World provided 10 per cent of world manufacturing production, but the proportion was nearly 50 per cent in the case of cotton yarn, as against 1–2 per cent for artificial fibres. In the same way, the share of the Third World in the world chemical industry, in advanced electronics and in aerospace industries was less than 3 per cent.[9]

(2) *The Reality of a Strong Expansion of Export Crops*
Exports of tropical goods to Europe began long before the industrial revolution. Pepper and silk trade between Asia and Europe began more than 2,000 years ago (some claim 5,000 years ago). This type of trade increased in volume after the sixteenth century when direct contact between the two continents was established. Total imports of spices, for example (coming almost entirely from Asia), can be estimated at 2,400 tons around 1500 and at 6,500 to 8,500 tons around 1700.[10] An even greater expansion took place in European sugar imports. In the fifteenth century sugar in Europe was a highly luxurious product. At that time in England sugar was 29 times more expensive than butter, already an expensive product; by the end of the sixteenth century this had been reduced to 5 times.[11] (Today in Europe sugar is about 6–10 times cheaper than butter; or in relative terms some 200 times cheaper than around 1400.) Total imports of sugar into Europe around 1500 were in the region of only a few tons.[12] By 1700 this had increased to about 70,000–90,000 tons and in terms of volume sugar probably represented some 75 per cent of the total imports of agricultural products from non-temperate regions. The total quantity of those goods around 1700 amounted to about 100,000–120,000 tons. In the years preceding the First World War the volume of exports of agricultural products from the Third World had reached some 18,500,000 tons or about 16·5 kg per capita compared to some 0·2 kg around 1700.[13] In terms of per capita volume of exports, the peak was probably reached at the end of the 1920s (but with a figure only slightly above that of the period before 1914). Around 1980 the figure was close to 12 kg; the increase in population having been more rapid than the exports of these agricultural products. However, and this is important in view of the limited opportunities for land expansion, in terms of total volume around 1970 (an absolute peak) these exports were twice as high as before the First World War.

To what extent has political independence led to a change in the prevailing trend? In this case the impact is rather limited. The main factor influencing the pace of development of this type of export is the demand of developed countries, especially for food products. By the early 1950s (and in some cases even in the late 1930s), the per capita consumption of many tropical products had reached a level not far from the peak in a large number of important countries (see Table 13.4).

Table 13.4 *Evolution of the Apparent Consumption per capita of some Tropical Agricultural Products (selected countries; in kg per capita; five-year annual average)*

	1830	1860	1910	1927	1936	1953	1979[a]
Cocoa							
France	0·02	0·12	0·62	0·89	1·02	1·03	1·80
Germany[b]	(0·01)	0·17	0·66	1·14	1·21	1·49	3·10
Great Britain	0·01	0·07	0·52	1·23	1·96	2·16	2·10
United States	—	—	0·59	1·44	1·89	1·67	1·20
Coffee							
France	0·30	0·91	2·76	3·99	4·40	3·83	5·25
Germany[b]	(0·50)	1·42	2·67	1·86	1·90	1·61	5·85
Great Britain	0·40	0·55	0·29	0·35	0·28	0·62	1·89
United States	—	0·30	4·40	5·34	5·86	7·27	5·03
Tea							
France	0·003	0·01	0·03	0·04	0·03	0·03	0·12
Germany[b]	—	0·02	0·06	0·08	0·07	0·08	0·14
Great Britain	0·57	1·20	2·85	4·14	4·38	4·40	3·43
United States	—	0·36	0·45	0·35	0·29	0·30	0·37

Sources: *Annuaire statistique de la France 1933* (Paris, 1934) and *1938* (Paris, 1939); G. Sundbarg, *Aperçus statistiques internationaux* (Stockholm, 1908); United Nations, *Yearbook of International Trade Statistics*, issues 1954 (New York, 1955) and 1980 (New York, 1981); various collections of national statistical data.
[a] Three-year annual average.
[b] For 1953 and 1979 West Germany only.

This saturation of demand is one of the reasons leading to an evolution of prices which is unfavourable compared with the nineteenth century. We shall come back to this problem when discussing the myth of the secular deterioration of the terms of trade.

(3) *The Reality of the Demographic Inflation*
Until the industrial revolution, the long-term increase in population was very small. Around 1700 the world population was some 600–820 million, compared with 230–400 million in AD 0. If one takes the higher limit in 1700 and the lower one in AD 0, this implies a yearly growth rate of 0·07 per cent. However, since the trend has not been a uniform one, the highest yearly increase in a medium- or long-term period (thirty to sixty years) in the case of a non-recovering situation[14] in a country of average size, has been much higher, but not more than 0·6 to 0·8 per cent per year. During the nineteenth century, as a direct result of colonization, in some colonies the population increased at a rate unknown in traditional societies. This was notably the case in Java whose population increased from 9·6–28·7 million between 1850 and 1900 (a yearly growth of 2·2 per cent). Such rates were exceptional and may well be overestimated, but in many cases during

the second half of the nineteenth century 1 per cent was exceeded, for example in Latin America and in Egypt.

The real problem, however, began in the twentieth century. For the Third World taken as a whole, the population increased at a yearly rate of 1·1 per cent between 1920 and 1950. And 1920 was far from being a low starting-point: the population was then some 60 per cent higher than it had been around 1800 which, in turn, was some 40 per cent higher than it had been around 1700. Except for most Latin American and some black African countries this development led to a rather high ratio of population to agricultural land by the early 1950s. Since this time the situation has seriously deteriorated. Between 1950 and 1980 agricultural land increased by some 20 per cent, while total population increased by 95 per cent and the agricultural labour force by about 60 per cent.

(4) *The Reality of the Creation of a Huge Income Gap and the Probability of a Decrease in the Standard of Living*

Let us begin with the second aspect, stopping at around 1950. The crucial question is to see if the average standard of living of the population of the Third World was lower around 1950 than two centuries before. It is far from being an easy question. We have limited data for a few countries which enable us to assess the long-term evolution in the area. In the case of India, we have two sets of independent comparisons between the standard of living at the time of Akbar (turn of the seventeenth century), the 1930s and the 1960s. According to one estimate, real urban wages decreased by 60–80 per cent; according to the other, by 30–40 per cent.[15] On the other hand, the average level of consumption of the Third World around 1950 was so low that there is a strong suspicion that things could only have been better before. Around 1950 the per capita consumption of cereals was some 190 kg.[16] In traditional Europe (in the eighteenth century) the figure was well above 250 kg, probably around 300 kg. It is very likely that per capita consumption of cereals in traditional non-European societies before colonization stood somewhere between the Third World level of 1950 and the traditional European level. It is also likely that per capita consumption of meat (and fish) in traditional European societies was higher than that of the average Third World country around 1950.[17]

For manufactured goods, the picture is less negative. As far as production is concerned, we have seen (Table 13.3) that per capita production around 1950 was some 30–40 per cent lower than around 1750. However, in 1950 the Third World was, as it is today, a net importer of manufactured goods. On the basis of the available statistical data (which are far from perfect) we have estimated that net imports of manufactured goods represented some 80–120 per cent of local production, so that the per capita consumption of manufactured goods around 1950 was some 20–50 per cent higher than around 1750. In view of the relative importance of the two classes of consumption (food and manufacturing) the higher level of manufacturing cannot offset the lower level of food.

Again, here as in all the other aspects, these are average data, each continent and each country having its own pattern. As a general rule, the

Table 13.5 *Evolution of GNP Per Capita (in 1960 US dollars and prices)*

	Developed countries		Third World				
	Average	More developed	Average	Less developed	Africa	Latin America	Asia
1750	182	230	188	130	133	250	199
1800	196	240	188	130	132	245	196
1860	324	580	176	130	130	260	179
1900	540	1070	175	130	131	312	171
1913	662	1350	191	130	140	356	184
1938	856	1570	202	135	158	404	183
1950	1054	2480	203	140	183	468	172
1973	2537	4030	342	145	282	701	301
1980[a]	3000	4250	380	150	285	766	337

Sources: P. Bairoch, 'The main trends in national income disparities since the industrial revolution', in P. Bairoch and M. Lévy-Leboyer (eds), *Disparities in Economic Development since the Industrial Revolution* (London, 1981), pp. 3–17; P. Bairoch, 'World Gross National Product, 1750–1985' (forthcoming).
Note: The degree of rounding off of the figures does not imply a correspondingly low margin of error.
[a] Preliminary figures.

decline in per capita income has been confined mainly to Asia, while for Latin America the likelihood is an increase (due largely to the temperate parts of this continent). It is likely that an increase has also occurred in Black Africa, but the starting level was low. Such estimates involve a large number of what could be called 'guesstimates' and the figures we have arrived at can be found in Table 13.5.

Even allowing for a margin of error of 20 per cent in the data for the less developed countries, and a margin of error of 10 per cent in the data for the developed countries, the increasing gap between average incomes is evident. Around 1750 the average per capita GNP of the future Third World was either 30 per cent above that of Europe (including Russia) or 20 per cent below that of Europe (excluding Russia). The most probable situation is that what was to become the Third World had a standard of living some 5–10 per cent above that of Europe. While the future Third World saw a decline in its average income during the nineteenth century, in the developed countries per capita GNP increased by some 260 per cent between 1750 and 1913, leading to a gap between the average per capita GNP of those two regions in the order of 1 to 3–4.[18] Despite the two world wars and the Depression, the average GNP of the developed world increased by 60 per cent between 1913 and 1950, while the average GNP of the Third World increased by only 3–10 per cent, bringing the gap to 1 to 4·5–6·0.

The three and a half decades since the end of the Second World War have been exceptional in terms of economic growth. In the developed world between 1946 and 1981, the increase in per capita GNP was as large as during the twenty preceding decades. The pace of economic growth also changed drastically in the Third World. Between 1950 and 1980, if we accept the United Nations figures, per capita GNP increased by some 130 per cent. According to our own estimates (Table 13.5), the increase was in the order of only (sic) 90 per cent. In the developed world, this increase was 180 per cent. Thus, at best, this led to a 40 per cent increase in the gap between the two regions.

The more positive evolution of income in the Third World (compared to the pre-1950 period) raises two questions. To what extent is this a statistical fallacy; if it is not, to what extent can this be attributed to political independence?

A statistical fallacy? What is certain is that the 'official' figures are too high. Kuznets has shown that if the statistical biases are removed for the period 1954–8 to 1964–8 the growth rate of per capita GNP was only 1·06 per cent, instead of 2·21 per cent. On the other hand, he concludes that for the developed countries, the growth rate was underestimated; the figure should be over 4·0 per cent rather than 3·38 per cent.[19] If we accept Kuznets's corrections and if we postulate that the same correction applies to the entire period from 1950 to 1980, the real increase of per capita GNP in the Third World would then be about 60–65 per cent, instead of 130 per cent.

Despite the fact that in our estimate we retained a 90 per cent increase, it cannot be ruled out that even an 80 per cent increase is an overestimate. The fact that leads us to believe this is that per capita consumption of food has increased by only around 30–35 per cent. To simplify the problem, let us concentrate on the so-called developing market countries, that is, the non-communist Third World. Per capita consumption of cereals for 1948–52 was about 180 kg; by 1980 this had increased by 33 per cent to 240 kg[20] and it is also likely that this increase had been somewhat overestimated. Per capita production has, according to 'official' figures, increased by 24 per cent from 172 kg around 1950 to 214 kg around 1980, and it is likely that the underestimation was more important around 1950 than around 1980. The possible growth of consumption of other foodstuffs may have brought the total real increase in per capita food consumption to around 35 per cent; for cereals, the real increase is probably in the region of 25–30 per cent.

In Europe in the first half of the nineteenth century, an increase of 10 per cent in per capita consumption of cereals was usually accompanied by an increase of 15–17 per cent in per capita GNP. If the same relationship existed in the Third World, this would mean an increase of per capita GNP of 40–50 per cent. Clearly the demand elasticity of cereals must be lower now in the Third World than in Europe in the first half of the nineteenth century, mainly in response to the demonstration effects that lead to an over-consumption (in relation to real income) of manufactured goods. But even taking this into account, as well as the low level of food consumption around 1950 and the low prices of cereal imports, it is very unlikely that a 25–30 per cent increase in consumption of cereals was accompanied by an increase in GNP of more than 60–80 per cent.

But even if we assume a 60–80 per cent increase in GNP per capita, this still marks a break with the preceding period. Can this be attributed to poli-

Historical Roots of Underdevelopment 205

tical change? To a certain degree it can, since this more rapid economic growth is due, in part, to rapid industrialization which, in turn, can be linked to political independence. On the other hand, this acceleration of industrial as well as agricultural growth can be attributed to the impact of new technologies originating from the developed world. It must be admitted that at the present state of knowledge, it is impossible to estimate the exact magnitude of the positive changes due to political independence

Having presented the main realities of the negative effects of colonization on the economic development of the Third World, let us move on to the myths. The main myth is the one related to the long-term deterioration of the terms of trade of exports from less developed countries. Less important is the myth that exports of tropical agricultural products are the main cause of food imports.

(5) *The Myth of the Long-Term Deterioration of the Terms of Trade of Third World Exports*

The origins of this myth which is gradually fading can be clearly established. It can be traced, first, to a United Nations study: *Relative Prices of Exports and Imports of Underdeveloped Countries* (New York, 1949). This study in fact only repeated the results of an earlier and famous League of Nations study of 1945, *Industrialization and Foreign Trade* (Geneva, 1945). The findings of the secretariat of the League of Nations were popularized by Raul Prebisch's works on the deterioration of the terms of trade.[21] According to the secretariat, between the last quarter of the nineteenth century and the eve of the Second World War, or more precisely between 1876–80 and 1936–8, there had been a 43 per cent reduction in the price of primary products compared with the price of manufactured products. Since Third World exports are made up almost entirely of primary products and Third World imports almost totally of manufactured goods, the conclusion from a deterioration of the terms of trade of primary products to that of Third World exports is a legitimate one.

The first bias in this estimate is related to the choice of the final phase, that is, 1936–8. The Depression was a very untypical period, especially for the evolution of prices. If we compare 1876–80 to 1926–9, the deterioration in the terms of trade of primary products is reduced to 20 per cent. This, however, is only a minor aspect. On the evidence of the information available on productivity changes in various sectors, it is almost impossible to accept a price evolution in which primary goods experienced a price decrease relative to manufactured goods. The major outcome of the first two centuries of the industrial revolution was a very rapid increase in the productivity of manufacturing; twice as rapid as that of the other sectors.

The chief bias in the League of Nations world trade price indices is that they use British prices only, and that some three-quarters of the prices used in the British indices are import prices. So, in fact, what is measured is not only the price of the products but also, and mainly, the transport costs that fell very considerably during this period. Since those import prices are more numerous for primary products, and since for those products transport costs are of particular significance, this involves a major distortion of the prevailing trend. Another bias derives from the fact that British export prices of manufactures increased more rapidly during that period than those of the rest of the developed world (this was one of the major causes of the depression in Britain in the 1920s). Indeed, during the 1960s and 1970s, whenever a specific study was carried out on the nineteenth-century evolution of the terms of trade either of an individual less developed country or for a particular primary product,[22] the results were generally 'contrary to the general case ... here we have an improvement of the terms of trade of ...'.

Using better international export prices, we deduced that between the 1870s and the 1926–9 period, the terms of trade for primary products relative to manufactured goods improved by some 10–25 per cent, instead of worsening by about 20 per cent as had been calculated by the League of Nations. (It should be mentioned that the League of Nations never presented those figures as valid indices for measuring international terms of trade.) On the other hand, we have assembled a set of over fifty individual export prices of primary goods exported from less developed countries. This study is not yet completed, but the preliminary results confirm that the terms of trade improved during the nineteenth century and up to the end of the 1920s.

The fact that the terms of trade, or in more precise and 'technical' terms the net barter terms of trade of less developed countries have improved, does not mean that this is necessarily a positive development. It would have been so if this had been accompanied by a rise in wages and in other incomes as has happened in the developed countries. While the real wages of primary-goods producers in the Third World remained stagnant between the 1870s and the 1920s the real wages of the producers of manufactured goods in the developed world increased by some 100–160 per cent in the same period. This implies that in 1926–9 an average Third World worker could buy with his average wage 10–25 per cent more manufactured goods than his grandparents could around 1875, while an average worker in the developed world could buy with his average wage 80–130 per cent more primary goods originating from the Third World than had been possible for his grandparents. In more technical terms, this means that the factorial terms of trade for primary goods from the Third World declined.

The story for the net barter terms of trade is very different for the 1950s, and this is the main reason why the myth of long-term deterioration was so easily accepted: economic history is too often neglected in the training of economists and still more so in that of political scientists.[23] From the early 1950s until 1961–2, there was a real deterioration in the terms of trade of primary products, and even more so of those primary products exported by the less developed countries (see Table 13.6). Since the 1960s a stabilization of those terms of trade has taken place. But in view of the previous prevailing trends this stabilization can be regarded as a negative evolution. Since 1979 the sharp increase in oil prices has led to a dramatic deterioration in the terms of trade for non-oil exporters. But this case can be regarded as a cyclical phenomenon. The real problem thus lies in the negative evolution of the 1950s.

Table 13.6 *Recent Evolution of the Terms of Trade* (1963 = 100)

	Developing market economy countries			Developed market economy countries
	Major oil exporters	Other	All countries	
1938	—	—	80	99
1948	—	—	95	95
1950–4	—	—	111	91
1960–4	101	101	101	101
1965–9	90	105	94	102
1970	89	112	97	104
1971	103	107	99	103
1972	100	107	98	104
1973	110	109	105	103
1974	272	110	172	91
1975	270	101	163	94
1976	286	99	167	93
1977	286	108	173	92
1978	257	100	159	94
1979	308	92	170	91
1980	462	88	215	85
1981	541	81	230	83
1982	532	86	222	85
1983	476	80	211	86

Sources: United Nations, *Yearbook of International Trade Statistics*, various issues (New York); United Nations, *Handbook of International Trade and Development Statistics 1983* (New York, 1983).

The paradox is that the beginning of this negative evolution of the barter terms of trade coincided with the wave of political independence. The causes of this evolution can only be briefly sketched here. Among the factors that explain this change in the long-term trend we should include the slowdown in demand for a large range of primary goods, combined with an increase in supply, the development of synthetic products, measures to restrict the imports of some tropical goods (internal taxes), technological progress that has reduced the input coefficients of raw materials in manufacturing industry and, last but not least, what is called the Singer–Prebisch thesis. This thesis suggests that due to weaker organization, the unequal relationship between the developed and the underdeveloped worlds leads to a situation where, in the case of primary products, the gains in productivity are translated into a decline in prices, while in the case of manufactures, those gains are translated into higher salaries and profits. The irony is that, to a certain extent, independence could mean a freer hand for buying purchasing companies to press for lower prices since, in such a case, the local social situation has no effect on the developed country.

Finally, another explanation of this new evolution is conceivable, but it has not yet been tested. Since the 1940s in the United States and the 1950s in Western Europe, there has been a complete reversal of the relative rates of increase of productivity in agriculture and manufacturing. From those years until today, productivity has increased almost twice as fast in agriculture as in manufacturing industry, resulting in a deterioration in the barter terms of trade of temperate agricultural products. If during the past thirty years the rate of increase of productivity of tropical agriculture has been more rapid than that of manufacturing, this could explain, at least in part, if not totally, the post-1950 evolution of terms of trade.

(6) *The Myth of Exports of Tropical Agricultural Products being the Main Cause of Food Imports*

As we have seen, the rapid expansion of export crops is a reality. Furthermore, it is certain that in many countries this development had numerous negative social and economic consequences for the local society. In some cases, this involved a reduction of indigenous food supplies leading to the regular import of cereals. However, in view of the decline in prices of cereals during the nineteenth century (and more specifically during its second half) there was a general improvement in the terms of trade of tropical agricultural products as compared with temperate cereals. Furthermore, those imports seemed rather limited until after the 1960s. The real increase in imports of cereals took place in the 1970s. The net imports of all cereals in the developing market economies (excluding Argentina) which amounted to 15 million tons yearly for the 1958–62 period reached 24 million for 1968–72 and 63 million for 1978–82.

The problem here is to assess what share of total net import of food could be produced on the land taken up by tropical agricultural products grown for export. We restricted our calculation to the developing market countries (excluding Argentina) and to the period around 1980 (five- or three-year annual averages). For each tropical non-food product[24] we calculated the share of production exported, and this share was related to the total area cultivated with this product. We then calculated the total amount of non-food imports (converting meat and dairy products into cereal equivalents), also taking into account the positive trade balance of sugar and oilseeds (and oil). The amount of land devoted to exported non-food crops can be estimated to cover some 18–20 million hectares. The total amount of net import of food around 1980 can be estimated at 69–73 million tons of cereals equivalent. If the land devoted to export crops had been entirely used for cereals, and if we assume that the average yield of this land is similar to that of the total cereals area (some 1·4 tons per hectare), the conclusion is that it could have produced some 34–41 per cent of the total food deficit. These percentages are probably on the high side, since close to a third of the land involved is devoted to rubber production and it is very unlikely that this sort of land would have been able to produce the average yield of cereals. The same question mark applies to the area used for the cultivation of coffee. A more plausible overall figure would therefore be around 25–35 per cent. This is not an insignificant proportion, but it cannot be considered as the main cause of the high level of food imports. The main cause of the food deficit is the rapid population increase leading to high pressure on land combined with the very rapid urbanization process. This

Historical Roots of Underdevelopment

produces a situation in which additional demand for food from urban populations generally leads to an increase in imports, since most big cities are located on, or near, the coast.

Colonization and the Economic Development of Industrialized Countries: Myths and Realities

To what extent has the colonization process furthered the development of the Western world? The predominant myth is that the West owes much of its economic development to colonization. This idea is mainly based on three arguments: the developed world depended for its industrialization on raw materials from the Third World; the Third World was an important outlet for the manufacturing output of the West; colonial profits played a major role in financing the first stages of the industrial revolution. Although they are incorrect in general terms, they nevertheless do have a certain basis in reality which explains their widespread acceptance.

(1) *The Myth of a Western Industrialization Process Based on Raw Materials Originating from the Third World*

Around 1973 some 33 per cent of the commercial energy used by the Western developed countries came from the Third World; for Western Europe this share was as high as 61 per cent. In the case of some metals the developed Western countries obtained as much as 100 per cent of their supplies from Third World countries; globally (in terms of volume) for all the metals this was over the 50 per cent mark. But all this is a fairly recent phenomenon. Until the early 1920s the developed world produced more oil than it consumed and in 1913 had a sizeable export surplus in energy. As late as in the immediate post-1945 period the developed countries (even the Western developed countries) were almost totally self-sufficient in their energy consumption.

On the eve of the First World War when the developed world had a volume of manufacturing production that in global terms was 6–8 times higher than that of the entire world around 1750, and when their per capita manufacturing production was already 7–9 times higher than that of the world in 1750, some 99 per cent of metals used by the developed countries' industries came from the developed world; 90 per cent of its textile fibres and 100 per cent of its energy had the same origin. In terms of the volume of all raw materials, the degree of local autonomy was over 99 per cent,[25] and the excess of net coal and oil exports represented a volume about 5 times bigger than the net imports of the rest of the raw materials. The situation in terms of value was a little different since the values of most of the ores are higher than those of energy and most values of textiles are higher than those of ores. Also the share of imports was much higher for more costly metals, such as copper, than for the cheap ones, such as iron.[26] In terms of value, the self-sufficiency of the developed countries in raw materials was in the vicinity of 96–98 per cent around 1913. It is obvious that if the problem is looked at from the other side, the picture seems very different.

In most of the Third World countries almost 100 per cent of the raw materials produced were exported to the developed countries. But, even taking this view, raw materials should not be equated with primary goods. If indeed during the nineteenth century primary goods represented more than 90 per cent of exports from the Third World, raw materials only represented a quarter of total exports.[27]

This self-sufficiency in raw materials increased during most of the nineteenth century; after 1913 it declined gradually. But even at the end of the 1930s the self-sufficiency of the developed countries in raw materials was around 96–97 per cent in terms of volume and some 93–96 per cent in terms of value.[28] As late as 1953 the developed Western countries produced 95 per cent of their own commercial energy consumption.[29] And around 1953 the per capita level of industrialization of the West was some 22 times higher than that of the starting-point of modern development, the global industrial production some 85 times higher. So, if in fact from 1955 onwards the dependence on raw materials from the Third World is a reality, before that period it is an almost total myth. The developed countries were able to reach a very high level of industrialization on the basis of local raw materials and the exploitation of their local labour forces.

(2) *The Myth of the Important Role of Colonial Outlets for Western Industries*

There has been no period in the history of the developed countries when the outlet provided by colonies or by the entire Third World was a very important one for the industries of the West. In this case, the myth probably has its origin in the fact that for the majority of the Third World countries, from the beginning of the nineteenth century until recently (and in many cases until today), almost all the manufactured products consumed locally came from the developed countries. We shall return to this question later in this section. But, first of all, let us look at the facts.

The first of those facts is the modest role played by trade with the Third World in general. Even if we limit ourselves to Europe, which had more relations with the Third World than the rest of the developed countries, we can see that during the period from 1800 to 1938, only 18 per cent of total exports went to the Third World[30] and, of those, only half went to colonies, which means that only 9 per cent of total European exports went to the colonial empires. If we include the other developed countries, all those percentages should be reduced by one point. Since during this period total exports represented some 8–9 per cent of the GNP of the developed countries, it follows that exports to the Third World represented only 1·3–1·7 per cent of the total volume of the production of the developed countries and exports to the colonies only 0·6–0·9 per cent. Obviously, these figures, like any average figures, mask some specific facts, in this case regional and product differences. The main regional exception was Great Britain. For this country, exports to the Third World represented some 40 per cent of its total exports (during the period 1800 to 1938). This fact is probably one of the foundations of the myth. Furthermore, the share of exports in GNP was greater for Great Britain than for the average of the developed countries:

some 12 to 13 per cent. Exports to the Third World represented some 5·0 per cent of UK total production.

There were also differences on the sectoral level. The main exports to the Third World being manufactures, the proportion of manufactured goods exported by developed countries to the Third World was higher than their proportion of total production. For the period between 1899 and 1938, it can be estimated from Maizels's data[31] that 26–32 per cent of total export of manufacturers went to the Third World (compared with 20 per cent for total exports). For the same period, the share of exports in total manufacturing may be estimated at around 20–25 per cent. This implies that between 1899 and 1938 roughly 5–8 per cent of the total manufacturing production was exported to the Third World.

Data are insufficient to calculate comparable percentages for the nineteenth century. I tried to approach the problem in my recent study on the levels of industrialization.[32] By cumulating annual production, I calculated the total volume of production in these two regions, that is, the developed world and the Third World. I also estimated the total domestic volume of the consumption of manufactured products in the Third World on the basis of various hypotheses about the growth of per capita consumption. It can be assumed that the difference between the estimated volume of consumption and the estimated volume of indigenous production was made up by imports from the advanced countries. In view of the declining living standards of the populations of the Third World, it seemed unduly optimistic to assume that the per capita consumption of manufactured goods would have remained stable; an extremely pessimistic hypothesis allows for a fall of 30 per cent. Leaving aside the two extreme hypotheses and allowing for a margin of error in the data, the present approach would suggest that 6–14 per cent (with a mean average of around 10 per cent) of the manufactured goods produced in the developed countries were exported to the Third World during the nineteenth century.

This would seem to suggest that the damage caused to Third World industries by colonization did not in fact have a correspondingly massive positive effect on the developed countries. Taken as a whole, access to the markets of the Third World was no more than a subordinate stimulus to the industries of the developed countries. We must, however, also examine national peculiarities. Certainly, in the case of Great Britain the relative contribution of the markets of the Third World countries was at least 2 times greater than for the average of the industrial countries. As far as textiles in general are concerned, some 35 per cent of British production was exported to the Third World at the turn of this century. For cotton textiles this proportion was even higher: some 67 per cent.[33] But, even in this case, the contribution of the markets of the Third World came only after five or six decades of modern industrial development. On the other hand, it is obvious that even a marginal additional outlet may have a sizeable influence on the profitability of a particular industrial sector. However, we should also remember that access to such outlets might have certain negative repercussions: for example, since they were 'easy' markets they did not encourage innovation and technological change. Although Great Britain illustrates this very well, this explanation is not sufficient to explain the loss of vitality in British industry which was already evident between 1880 and 1890.

(3) *The Myth of the Role of Colonialism in the Outbreak of the Industrial Revolution*

This myth specifically concerns Britain. We should not forget that not only was this the first country to experience the industrial revolution, but it was also for five to eight decades the only one touched by it.

It is difficult to defend the position which assigns colonialism an important role in the birth of the British industrial revolution. Britain began to be influenced by the industrial revolution and the agricultural revolution which was a major part of it, as early as around 1680–1700. The pace of development accelerated between 1700 and 1750. Yet, in the first half of the eighteenth century the colonial domain of Britain was very limited. The most important part of it was North America and even here it was not until the Treaty of Paris of 1763 which transferred Canada and Louisiana to the British Empire, that Britain's American possessions assumed any real significance. Around 1720 the British empire in North America had a total population of 0·5 million, most of whom lived under conditions of autarky. The total population of the colonies scattered over India (Bombay, Madras, and so on) and in Africa (Accra, Sierra Leone, Cape Coast, and so on) did not exceed 0·3 million, and the West Indies (mainly Jamaica and Barbados) were only slightly more important with a total population of less than 0·4 million. This made a total of some 1 million inhabitants. At the same time the Portuguese and Spanish empires together had more than 10 million inhabitants.

Even more important is the fact that an analysis of the colonial export markets of Britain during the crucial first phases of the industrial revolution shows that their role was a very negligible one. In an earlier paper[34] I tried to assess the role of total foreign trade in the first stage of the British industrial revolution. This stage can be delimited as the period between 1720 and 1780–90. Before 1720, even if things had already begun to change, the economy was still a traditional one, but after 1780 Britain could no longer be considered a traditional society. The process of development had by then certainly passed the point of no return. For the whole of the British economy all foreign markets absorbed only 4–8 per cent of the total demand during those six to seven decades. In terms of the additional demand (which is probably a better indicator) foreign additional markets absorbed only 5–9 per cent of the total additional demand. During this period trade with non-European countries represented some 33–39 per cent of total British trade, so that the contribution of the future less developed countries could have absorbed at most 3–4 per cent of total additional demand.

For the two most important industrial sectors, textiles and iron, the contribution of foreign markets was more important but not decisive. For the iron industry additional foreign markets absorbed 18 per cent of additional production (11 per cent of total production). For the wool textile industry foreign markets declined in relative terms, but for the new cotton industry, which was the first to be mechanized, between 1760 and 1790 foreign markets absorbed some 10–15 per cent of total production and 15–20 per cent of additional production. Here again, Third World markets represented less than 40 per cent of total foreign markets and can therefore have absorbed only 6–8 per cent of the additional production of iron and cotton industries (4–5 per cent of total production).

In the same study I also estimated the relative contribution to total investment of total profits derived from international trade in the preceding centuries. I concluded that investments derived from commercial profits had probably not provided more than 6–8 per cent of total investment. This concerns profit from all international trade. More recently Patrick O'Brien made a similar but more elaborated set of estimates to show the contribution of commercial relations with the Third World for Britain between 1489 and 1789. Here are his main conclusions:

> What this exercise in counterfactual history suggests is that if the British economy had been excluded from trade with the periphery gross annual investment expenditures would have fallen by not more than 7 per cent. All biases in these calculations (which refer to decades after the onset of the Industrial Revolution) run in favour of the hypothesis that this commerce provided a large share of the reinvestible surplus; and Britain, to reiterate the point, traded with other continents on a far larger scale than other European countries. There is, moreover, no evidence in the admittedly poor data now available that 'average' rates of profit earned on capital in commerce with the periphery were 'supernormal'. Over wide areas of tropical trades competition between the merchants of several maritime powers operated to hold prices of commodities and the returns to capital below monopolistic levels. And the significance of the periphery cannot be inflated much beyond its share in the national product by reference to externalities or to imports, described as decisive for the growth of the core. Trade in tropical produce gave rise to far greater opportunities for consumption than possibilities for production, and the view that American bullion was indispensable for economic progress in Western Europe is almost certainly untenable.[35]

This very limited impact of colonialism on the first stages of the industrial revolution does not imply that the same was true for the entire nineteenth century in Britain. Beginning with the period from 1820 to 1830 colonial markets provided a very important outlet for British manufactured goods, and this went on for some decades.

Conclusion

The most important conclusion is the tragic irony of the historical impact of colonization on economic development. While there is no doubt that a large number of structurally negative features of the process of economic underdevelopment have historical roots going back directly to European

214 Imperialism and After

colonization, colonization has probably contributed very little, if at all, to the success story of the economic development of the West. There is not necessarily a link between the advantages to one partner and the disadvantages to the other in certain types of economic relations. This is a tragic but also an optimistic conclusion. If the developed world owed its development to the exploitation of the Third World, it would imply the great risk that development is not possible (or at least is very difficult) without such exploitation.

Since this chapter was written in one of the richest and most developed countries, it is worth mentioning that if Switzerland's chances of becoming a developed country had been discussed in the eighteenth century, few observers would have predicted much economic development. Switzerland had, at that time, many of the characteristics which today identify those countries of the Third World with the lowest chances of economic development: no raw materials, no access to the sea, limited availability of good agricultural land, a negative migration balance, and so on.

Yes, ... but around 1760–80 the population density on Switzerland's agricultural land was much lower than that in most Asian countries today, where 75 per cent of the Third World population is concentrated. There were probably no more than about 65 persons per 100 hectares of agricultural land at that time in Switzerland (only about 40 in Britain) compared to around 370 persons in India today (950 in Bangladesh). Even allowing for the climatic difference (using a very rough and optimistic corrective factor which assumes that – excluding technological elements – Asia's land can produce twice as much as that of Europe) it still means a 1–3 difference between Switzerland and India, and a 1–12 difference between Britain and Bangladesh. And what is even more important, between 1780 and 1850 Switzerland's population increased by 50–55 per cent, while the population of the Third World in the absence of catastrophes will increase by 140–160 per cent between 1980 and 2050.

Notes: Chapter 13

1. P. Bairoch, 'Ecarts internationaux des niveaux de vie avant la révolution industrielle', *Annales, ESC*, vol. 34 (1979), pp. 145–71.
2. P. Bairoch, 'Estimations du revenu national dans les sociétés occidentales préindustrielles et au XIXe siècle', *Revue économique*, vol. 28 (1977), pp. 177–208.
3. To convert the 1960 US dollars and prices to those of 1983, the figures should be multiplied by 3·4.
4. The share of exports to GNP of the Third World at the beginning of this century was 15–17 per cent. This implies that for some of those countries it was above 20 per cent.
5. K. N. Chaudhuri, *The Trading World of Asia and the English East India Company, 1660–1760* (Cambridge, 1978).
6. M. Desai, 'Demand for cotton textiles in nineteenth-century India', *Indian Economic and Social History Review*, vol. 8 (1971), pp. 337–61.
7. Derived from H. Carling, *The Spinning Mule* (Newton Abbot, Devon, 1970).
8. After 1919, however, a more balanced policy will be implemented.
9. P. Bairoch, 'Industria', in *Enciclopedia Einaudi*, vol. 7 (Turin, 1979), pp. 313–52.
10. C. H. Wake, 'The changing pattern of European pepper and spice imports, 1400–1700', *Journal of European Economic History*, vol. 8 (1979), pp. 361–403, espec. 392–5.
11. P. H. Lyle, 'The sugar industry', *Journal of the Royal Statistical Society*, vol. 63 (1950), pp. 531–43.

Historical Roots of Underdevelopment 215

12 Sugar was used in Europe before the sixteenth century mainly as a drug. See E. O. Lippmann, *Geschichte des Zuckers* (Berlin, 1929), espec. ch. 9, pp. 324–99.
13 P. Bairoch *et al.*, *La Production des produits tropicaux* (forthcoming).
14 By this is meant periods following exceptionally sharp increase in population due to epidemics, famines and wars.
15 R. Mukerjee, *Economic History of India 1600–1800* (Allahabad, 1967); A. V. Desai, 'Population and standard of living in Akbar's time', *Indian Economic and Social History Review*, vol. 9 (1972), pp. 43–62.
16 Per capita production was around 185 kg. Those production and consumption figures exclude Argentina.
17 Meat consumption around 1950 was in the range of 6–8kg (per year and per capita) for Asia and 30–40kg for Latin America and below 20kg for Africa, making an average of some 10–12kg for the entire Third World. For traditional Europe the figure was probably above 35kg. But it is also likely that in this respect traditional Europe had a higher consumption than the average of the rest of traditional societies.
18 These figures are corrected for the differences in the local purchasing power of the various currencies; in terms of monetary average GNP per capita, the gap is even more important.
19 S. Kuznets, 'Problems in comparing recent growth rates for developed and less developed countries', *Economic Development and Cultural Change*, vol. 20 (1972), pp. 185–209.
20 As for the previous figures, Argentina excluded.
21 R. Prebisch, *The Economic Development of Latin America and its Principal Problems* (New York, 1950).
22 Among those see B. M. Bhatia, 'Terms of trade and economic development. A case study of India 1861–1939', *Indian Economic Journal*, vol. 14 (1969), pp. 414–33; A. Montesano, 'Il movimenti dei prezzi in Giaponne dal 1878 at 1958', *Giornale degli economisti e annali economia* (1967); E. R. Owen, *Cotton and the Egyptian Economy, 1820–1914. A Study in Trade and Development* (Oxford, 1969). T. Morgan, 'The long-run terms of trade between agricultural and manufacturing', *Economic Development and Cultural Change*, vol. 8 (1959), pp. 1–23. See also J. Spraos, 'The statistical debate on the net barter terms of trade between primary commodities and manufactures', *Economic Journal*, vol. 90 (1980), pp. 107–28 and P. Bairoch, *The Economic Development of the Third World since 1900* (London, 1975), ch. 6.
23 Another reason lies in the fact that the only important tropical product for which the price evolution has been a more negative one is sugar, a major export item of Latin America. The more negative evolution of sugar is due to the rapid rise of beet sugar production in Europe. Beet sugar in 1900 represented more than 60 per cent of total sugar production and the volume of beet sugar in 1900 was at least ten times higher than total world sugar production in 1800 (then 100 per cent cane sugar).
24 In this case, non-food meant all agricultural products excepting cereals, sugar, oilseeds (see below), which implies that in the 'non-food' such tropical products (which are in fact edible) as fruit, cacao, coffee, and so on have been included.
25 If we include a large range of industries that always use very local raw materials, the share would be even higher. Examples of this type of industry are building materials (bricks, tiles, cement), glass, pottery, and so on.
26 High transport costs prevented the international trade of low-cost products.
27 The (weighted) average shares of the main products exported from the Third World during the 1815–1914 period were the following (in per cent of total, excluding non distributed):

Raw materials	27·9
for textile industries	16·9
for metal industries	2·3
energy products	0·9
Other non-food products	4·9
Food products	48·2
Manufactured goods	9·1
Other	9·9
Opium	2·8
gold and silver	3·8

See also P. Bairoch and B. Etemad, *Commodity Structure of Third World Exports, 1830–1937* (Geneva, 1985).
28 Excluding very locally based raw-material industries, see above.
29 For total energy consumption the share was even higher, since non-commercial energy was almost 100 per cent locally produced.
30 P. Bairoch, *Commerce extérieur et développement économique de l'Europe au XIXe siècle* (Paris, 1976); idem, 'The geographical structure and trade balance of European foreign trade from 1800 to 1970', *Journal of European Economic History*, vol. 3 (1974), pp. 557–608.
31 A. Maizels, *Industrial Growth and World Trade* (Cambridge, 1965).
32 P. Bairoch, 'International industrialization levels from 1750 to 1980', *Journal of European Economic History*, vol. 11 (1982), pp. 269–332.
33 Derived from P. Deane and W. A. Cole, *British Economic Growth, 1688–1959* (Cambridge, 1967); Maizels, *Industrial Growth*; W. Schlote, *Entwicklung und Strukturwandlungen des englischen Aussenhandels von 1700 bis zur Gegenwart* (Jena, 1938).
34 P. Bairoch, 'Commerce international et genèse de la révolution industrielle anglaise', *Annales, ESC*, vol. 28 (1973), pp. 541–71.
35 P. O'Brien, 'European economic development: the contribution of the periphery', *Economic History Review*, vol. 35 (1982), pp. 1–18, here p. 17.

14 The Third World in the International Economy

J. FORBES MUNRO

Is there 'imperialism' after empire? Have the relationships between the advanced industrial economies and the less developed or Third World economies since the Second World War been so unequal and one-sided that, despite the break-up of the old colonial empires, the term remains appropriate? Have the United States and the Soviet Union merely stepped in to acquire 'informal' empires in areas abandoned by the former European colonial powers? Such interesting and deceptively simple questions receive little attention in the standard accounts of the recent history of the international economy. Perhaps surprisingly, in the light of so much nationalist and Marxist literature which sees nothing but 'imperialism' in the post-colonial world, most general surveys of the international economic order since 1949 either ignore the phenomenon of 'imperialism' altogether, or assume that it has passed away with decolonization.[1] The reasons for such lack of interest are not difficult to find. Other than in Leninist formulations which equate 'imperialism' with capitalism, almost to the point of tautology, the concept tends to be seen to pertain more to the sphere of politics and diplomacy – to the relationships between states – than to the sphere of economics. Those who study the international economy use different paradigms. They tend to think first and foremost in terms of the structure and operations of markets – the exchange of commodities and currencies, movements of technology and organization of production, and the development of institutions, more especially transnational ones, which facilitate intercontinental trade and payments. They usually accept the state system as a given, and assume a rough equality between states. Concepts of power, influence and control which are the staples of the political scientist or diplomatic historian seldom enter their theories or models.

Paul Bairoch's contribution[2] falls into that particular mould. His vision is of a world divided into two kinds of states – those which are constitutionally independent and those which are the formal colonies or possessions of others – and into two conditions, the developed and the less developed. Such a framework of neat dichotomies, however, elides the ambiguities and misses the marginal cases which challenge the explanatory powers of history and the social sciences alike. Just as his categories of 'developed' and 'less developed' are essentially static, based upon late-twentieth-century patterns, and take no account of national economies which historically may be said to have shifted from one to the other, so too, the lack of recognition of a possible 'informal' empire means that the debate as to whether influence and control is exercised over the Third World by means other than formal sovereignty, including economic measures, is not entered into. But if the potential for a contemporary 'imperialism' is not explicitly addressed, his attempt to clarify and quantify certain long-run trends in world economic history raises issues which are relevant to the theme of the present volume.

Three chronological divisions lurk within Paul Bairoch's sweep through modern times. The first deals with the pre-industrial world of approximately between 1500 and 1750, when European states first acquired colonial possessions overseas. Such formal imperialism, however, contributed only marginally to the economic growth of Europe, a point which has been made even more forcefully by Patrick O'Brien, using some of Bairoch's earlier results.[3] This is a useful and salutary corrective to the rather simple 'Third Worldism', explaining Europe's early modern growth by reference to exploitation of overseas areas, which has been around from Eric Williams and John Strachey to André Gunder Frank and beyond. However, Bairoch and O'Brien are possibly guilty of sins of omission in failing to consider the impact of early modern imperialism on weaker societies – whether Amerindians devastated by Old World diseases and reduced to debt peonage, Africans subjected to the Atlantic slave trade, or the inhabitants of the Spice Islands whose production and trade was seized and controlled by the Dutch. The 'historical roots of underdevelopment' surely lie in colonial endeavours which, while perhaps helping to generate economic growth only in Europe's Atlantic fringes, had destructive and distorting effects on economic activity and material life in certain specific locations outside Europe.

The second period is the age of industrialization and extensive 'imperialism' between 1750 and 1950, when most of the rest of the world becomes subject to the European state system. There was a growth in exports of manufactures from Europe to the Third World, which caused a decline of handicraft industries in the latter. The corresponding increase in trade in primary products was mainly in agricultural commodities, for the 'developed world' was largely self-sufficient in energy and most minerals. No long-run deterioration occurred in the net barter terms of trade of the primary producers (in so far as they can be measured), but per capita incomes in the Third World as a whole declined as a result of negative growth in Asia. Despite such an apparently major impact of the industrial core on the non-industrial periphery, it is argued that trade with the Third World had little relevance for European industrial growth, except perhaps in the case of Britain.

Students of Europe's overseas expansion and relations would undoubtedly wish to question aspects of Professor Bairoch's approach to this period. Aside from specific points of detail – it is no longer so certain, for example, that Java experienced a 2·5 per cent per annum rate of population growth in the nineteenth century[4] – a whole range of methodological problems relate to the application of national income accounting techniques to territories which, in the eighteenth and nineteenth centuries, were in no sense integrated national economies, or even market economies,[5] and where data deficiencies are so acute as to undermine confidence in even the most informed 'guesstimates'. How much trust, for example, can be placed on the claim that around the end of the eighteenth or the beginning of the nineteenth century 'the average standard of living of Europe taken as a whole was equal to, or a little lower than, that of the "rest of the world"'? Especially when it transpires that there is a large margin of error in such calculations which often undermines any meaningful generalization. Furthermore, the diversity of historical conditions in what we currently define as the Third World was such that aggregate measures of its economic growth would seem to have little practical utility in scholarship. China, in particular, deserves to be distinguished from the rest of Asia, as well as from Latin America and Africa – while within Europe the distinctions between Russia and the rest have significant historical weight.

The large issues about this period concern the effects of the core on the periphery. Accepting, as indeed we must, that the industrialization of the inner core – other than in the particular case of Britain – owed little or nothing to overseas expansion, the problem remains as to whether the incorporation of what are today's less developed countries into the international economy, 1750–1950, explains the fact that, according to Bairoch, 'the future Third World saw a decline in its average income during the nineteenth century.' Was such an absolute, and not just relative, impoverishment a consequence of the industrialization and 'imperialism' of the more advanced economies? On closer examination, the problem begins to lose some of its more universal characteristics. The Third World as a whole, it transpires, did *not* experience a fall in levels of per capita income, for data in Bairoch's Table 13.5 reveal no long-run, albeit some short-run, income decline in the Americas and Africa between 1750 and 1950. The problem, it seems, was essentially an Asian one.

Without a more detailed knowledge of how Paul Bairoch arrived at his figures for Asian GNP per capita – so much depends, of course, on whether the 1750 or 1800 levels are correct – it is difficult to pass informed judgement on the alleged impoverishment of Asia. Presumably the two largest population areas, China and the Indian subcontinent, are responsible for the greater part of the national income figure. As for India, it must be observed that its supposed 'de-industrialization' under British rule has possibly been exaggerated by nationalist historiography, while India's participation in the world economy, it must be remembered, had compensatory income- and employment-generating effects.[6] Furthermore, changes in the foreign-trade sector were perhaps relatively unimportant in what was a large agrarian economy, one in which the value of foreign trade was probably never much more than 10 per cent of any notional GNP, even at its maximum around 1900–14. Demography and agricultural productivity were, and are, the key factors in levels of income and wealth, and in the absence of really reliable data on these variables, historians of British India are uncertain about the direction of long-run trends in per capita incomes.[7]

If the Indian case lends little, or at best ambiguous, support to the idea of a real decline in Asian material prosperity and living standards, the qualitative evidence from China points more strongly in that direction. China's fall from grace, from the high point of economic and technological achievement under the Song dynasty to the poverty and disorder of the early twentieth century, has, of course, been recognized by historians and explanations have been offered, most notably by Mark Elvin.[8] But if China can be accepted as a real example of a decline in average incomes, we must still ask – was this caused by negative effects from international trade and investment? It is noticeable that, apart from Frances Moulder's unconvincing attempt to fit China into a Wallerstein-type world system,[9] most economic historians stress factors domestic to China rather than the impact of Western industrialization and 'imperialism'. During the nineteenth century that influence was confined to the enclaves of the treaty ports and their immediate hinterlands,[10] and it was only in the early twentieth century, with railway construction, that the greater part of China could be said to have been integrated into the international economy. Until then, at least, China was subject primarily to its own internal dynamics and statics. China was not just like the rest of the Third World, and cannot be taken as being synonymous with it. China's demographic trajectory, for example, was rather different. In 1500 population density on the land in China was already some 20 per cent higher than in India or Europe; by 1800, after a phase of extremely rapid demographic growth, population densities were twice as great as in South Asia or Europe. China then experienced a mid-nineteenth-century Malthusian crisis on a scale unsurpassed in any other part of the world at any time between 1700 and 1950.[11] Explanations of the long-run impoverishment of China, at least before the early nineteenth century, must, it seems, rest more on what was happening, or alternatively not happening, within the Chinese economy and polity than on their relationship with the industrializing West.

To suggest a need for greater refinement in Paul Bairoch's analysis, to allow for the differences between the various parts of the non-industrial world, both in their internal characteristics and in the timing and nature of their incorporation into the international economy – in short, to question the utility of something called 'the future Third World' as a coherent historical category – is not to assert the opposite of his general conclusion. If the 'Third World as a whole' did not unambiguously experience absolute economic decline between, say, the late eighteenth century and the First World War, no more did it experience any dramatic economic advance. Outside China, the general trend was probably one of rising per capita incomes, but the rate of increase was, of course, much slower than in the industrializing economies. Furthermore, the broad pattern obscures the hesitant and fragile nature of much of the growth which occurred in specific Latin American, African, or Asian countries, where short bursts of economic progress could equally well alternate with periods of stagnation or decline. If participation in international trade was not an unmitigated disaster for many less developed economies (Africa and the slave trade perhaps apart), neither did it open the door to increased per capita output by more than a very little. The ambiguity of such a situation is what renders discussion of the causes of international disparities in levels of economic development such a complex and contentious area of scholarship.

What was the role of 'imperialism' in the emergence of the gap between rich and poor? Paul Bairoch does not raise the question, and a review of the extensive debate which has occurred, far less any attempt to adjudicate between the different positions adopted, is beyond the scope of this chapter. At one level, it is difficult to absolve the colonial powers wholly from the charge that they contributed in some measure to the relatively slow growth of the less developed economies under their authority. Whatever gains to income accrued from their introduction of modern infrastructure, their promotion of foreign trade and the rise of export production, their policies gave less emphasis than they might have done to the improvement of food-crop productivity and the development of manufacturing industry. On the other hand, it remains uncertain whether, in the absence of colonial rule, indigenous states would have been any more successful in achieving economic modernization. How many potential Meiji Japan's were there in the rest of Asia, Africa, or the Caribbean? The effects of 'informal imperialism', where such may be said to have existed, are even more ambivalent. If foreign trade and investment produced comparatively slow growth and sectorally unbalanced development, did the bottlenecks and barriers lie in the external relationship or within the local economy, society and government? On such questions little common ground has yet emerged among historians.

Finally, Bairoch deals with the world after 1950, a time of decolonization and the end of formal empire. He demonstrates, with the authority of better data, that the less developed countries as a group experienced a more widespread and more rapid economic growth than before. Should this be taken as evidence that formal empire retarded economic development prior to 1950 and that political independence was the key to improved standards of living, including average levels of food consumption? No such conclusion can be drawn, if only because some newly independent countries, like Burma or East Pakistan/Bangladesh, did poorly in growth terms. There would appear to be two principal explanations for the better average less developed country (LDC) performance after 1950 – first, the revival of China under its Communist government, which gave the economy effective central management after so many decades of weak government and, secondly, the rapid growth of the international economy as a whole, between the end of the Second World War and the crises of the mid-1970s, which imparted a stimulus to most LDCs. Averages, however, can be misleading, and a prominent feature of the period is the differential pattern of growth rates between LDCs. The poorest countries, principally in South Asia and Tropical Africa, were generally the slowest growing with per capita rates of less than 2 per cent per annum, so that the real increases in levels of income were pitifully small. Another group with higher per capita incomes to begin with, mainly in Latin America and South-East Asia, did rather better in growth terms, while yet a third group, comprising the smaller oil-exporting economies, secured a rapid advance in per capita incomes.[12] Just as there was no single, homogeneous Third World before 1950, so, too, after that date the dissimilarities between the world's poorer economies are as striking as any commonality.

Differential growth on the margins of the international economy was associated with shifts in patterns of world trade. In certain respects, the industrialized economies of the inner core turned inwards on themselves, trading more with each other than with the primary producers. Much of the increase in world trade during the 1960s and early 1970s came from the exchange of manufactured goods between high-income economies. Thanks to significant increases in the productivity of their agricultural sectors, to which the EEC's Common Agricultural Policy made a dubious contribution, the developed market economies as a group became not just self-sufficient in, but net exporters of, basic foodstuffs. At the same time, there was a slowing down of inner-core demand for tropical agricultural produce (more so in the traditional groceries, such as sugar or tea, than the green groceries, that is, fresh or tinned fruit and vegetables) which, together with the development of synthetic substitutes for certain agricultural raw materials, resulted in some deterioration in LDC terms of trade between 1950 and the early 1960s. But while interdependence between core and margin was weakening in the exchange of manufactures for agricultural commodities, the growth of Western demand for energy and certain minerals created new lines of core dependence on specific LDCs, an erosion of self-sufficiency for which the West, and even more so the non-oil LDCs, would pay dearly after 1973.

Such changes in global trading patterns, along with a rise in the manufacturing capacity of a number of LDCs, took place in a post-colonial world, and seem to indicate a movement away from the simple complementary relationship between industrial and primary-producing economies of the classical period of formal 'imperialism'. Where, if anywhere, does 'imperialism' relate to the post-colonial world as seen by the economic historian? Leadership of the international economy in the nineteenth century rested with Britain, a role it assumed in manufacturing production and its growing reliance on external trade and investment. It became the largest supplier of manufactures, finance and transport services to the peripheral economies, and served as the crucial hinge between many of them and the rest of the inner core.[13] In this context, Gallagher and Robinson claimed to discover a British 'informal imperialism' in Latin America, the Middle East and the Far East, a claim which has not, however, passed without challenge and controversy.[14] After an interregnum between the two world wars, leadership of the international economy passed to the United States, so that from Bretton Woods to the early 1970s, world trade and settlements operated on a dollar standard. Did this mean that the mantle of British 'imperialism' also passed to the United States? Was decolonization by Britain and other European powers replaced by a greatly enlarged sphere of American 'informal imperialism' in the Third World?

American antagonism towards what was perceived as the neo-mercantilism of European empires was clearly a prime force behind post-1949 decolonization,[15] and American statesmen and businessmen undoubtedly saw the ideal postwar international economy in terms very close to the liberal, free-trade system which had operated in the mid-nineteenth century. The use of military power, foreign aid and overseas investment to create and defend such a system has lent itself to analyses of American foreign relations as 'imperialist'.[16] However, to see the United States' world role in the 1950s and 1960s as a re-creation of Britain's 'free-trade imperialism' of the 1850s and 1860s may be to misread history. Centre–periphery relationships have altered between the two periods. The American economy, for example, is much more self-sufficient than the British one was, with foreign trade representing only about 7 per cent of GNP in the early 1970s, and it is relatively less important as a market, and clearing house for Third World commodities than nineteenth-century Britain. Nor (apart from oil) is American capital so extensively involved in financing and managing the production, exchange and transport of Third World commodities as British capital was in its period of hegemony. In short, there has been a greater degree of multilateralness in trade and finance in the post-1945 world which diffuses both the content of, and perceptions about, American dominance of the international economy.

Some support for this proposition comes from the emergence of concern about North–South conflicts of interest, supplanting to some extent the Cold War rhetoric of East–West conflict in which charges of American and Soviet 'imperialism' abound. For the majority of LDCs, the key issue has come to be the structural dislocation within the international economy, dividing the inner core (including the industrialized socialist economies) from the rest. In the debates about the impact of transnational firms on Third World development, in the discussions which have been conducted in and through UNCTAD about the protectionism of the industrialized countries against the products of the newly industrializing and about the need to create and finance buffer stocks of primary commodities, in the charges of bias against LDCs in the policies of the International Monetary Fund, and in the growth of a demand for a New International Economic Order, are embedded general problems of core–margin relations. Thus, older ideas about 'imperialism' can seem an irrelevance or a distraction in identifying and resolving these.

Notes: Chapter 14

1 A. G. Kenwood and A. L. Lougheed, *The Growth of the International Economy 1820–1980* (London, 1983), pp. 249–325; W. Ashworth, *A Short History of the International Economy since 1850* (London, 1975), ch. 10; W. M. Scammell, *The International Economy since 1945* (London, 1980).
2 See Chapter 13 by Paul Bairoch in this volume.
3 P. O'Brien, 'European economic development: the contribution of the periphery', *Economic History Review*, vol. 35 (1982), pp. 1–18.
4 B. Peper, 'Population growth in Java in the 19th century', *Population Studies*, vol. 24 (1970), pp. 71–84.
5 For an early discussion of such issues, see S. H. Frankel, *The Economic Impact on Underdeveloped Societies* (Oxford, 1953), pp. 29–55.
6 N. Charlesworth, *British Rule and the Indian Economy, 1800–1914* (London, 1982), pp. 32–5; K. N. Chaudhuri, 'India's international economy in the nineteenth century: an historical survey', *Modern Asian Studies*, vol. 2 (1968), pp. 31–58.
7 M. D. Morris *et al.*, *The Indian Economy in the Nineteenth Century: A Symposium* (New Delhi, 1969).

224 Imperialism and After

8   M. Elvin, *The Pattern of the Chinese Past* (London, 1973), pp. 203–319.
9   F. V. Moulder, *Japan, China, and the Modern World Economy: Toward a Reinterpretation of East Asian Development, ca. 1600 to ca. 1918* (Cambridge, 1977).
10 R. Murphey, 'The treaty ports and China's modernization', in M. Elvin and G. W. Skinner (eds), *The Chinese City between Two Worlds* (Stanford, Calif., 1974), pp. 17–72; idem, *The Outsiders: The Western Experience in India and China* (Ann Arbor, Mich., 1977).
11 For the demographic data on which these points are based, see C. McEdvey and R. Jones, *Atlas of World Population History* (Harmondsworth, Middx, 1978).
12 World Bank, *World Bank Atlas 1981* (Washington DC, 1982).
13 S. B. Saul, *Studies in British Overseas Trade* (Liverpool, 1960); M. de Cecco, *Money and Empire: The International Gold Standard, 1890–1914* (London, 1974); Kenwood and Lougheed, *The Growth of the International Economy*, pp. 21–173; C. P. Kindleberger's *The World in Depression, 1929–1939* (London, 1973), although concerned with the interwar years, makes some incisive comments on the role of the British economy as an equilibriating centre for the international economy before 1914 (pp. 291–308).
14 J. Gallagher and R. Robinson, 'The imperialism of free trade, 1815–1914', *Economic History Review*, vol. 6 (1953), pp. 1–15; D. C. M. Platt, 'Further objections to an "imperialism of free trade", 1830–1860', *Economic History Review*, vol. 27 (1973), pp. 77–91; W. R. Louis (ed.), *Imperialism: The Robinson and Gallagher Controversy* (New York, 1976); P. J. Cain, *Economic Foundations of British Overseas Expansion, 1815–1914* (London, 1980).
15 W. R. Louis, *Imperialism at Bay, 1941–1945: The United States and the Decolonization of the British Empire* (Oxford, 1977).
16 M. Hudson, *Super Imperialism: The Economic Strategy of American Empire* (New York, 1972); V. G. Kiernan, *America: The New Imperialism* (London, 1978); H. Jaguaribe, 'The new inter-imperial system', in K. W. Deutsch *et al.*, *Problems of World Modeling* (Cambridge, Mass., 1977).

15 'A New Imperial System'? The Role of the Multinational Corporations Reconsidered

DAVID FIELDHOUSE

A multinational company (alias multinational corporation, transnational enterprise and many other synonyms, but hereafter referred to as MNC) can be defined as a firm which owns or controls income-generating assets in more than one country. The substance has existed for more than a century, but it was only twenty-five years ago that it was given a special name within the framework of foreign direct investment (FDI) and so became a defined concept. Paternity in name and concept can be disputed, principally between the French economist, Maurice Byé, who gave a paper called 'La Grande Unité Interritoriale' in 1957[1] and David E. Lilienthal, one-time head of the Tennessee Valley Authority and, after 1955, chief executive of the Development and Resources Corporation of New York who, in 1960, gave and published a paper under the title 'The Multinational Corporation'. Two years later Lilienthal claimed in his journal that 'so far as I know, my talk ... was the first time that the word had been used; I rather think that I coined it ...'[2]

It does not matter much who gave the thing a name. The significant point is that, once it was christened, the MNC assumed an autonomous existence as a special category of capitalist organization and was seized on by intellectuals and publicists of many types as a convenient pole on which to raise their particular flags. In this, of course, the MNC resembled 'imperialism', once the word came into vogue in the later nineteenth century,[3] though with this difference. It might be possible to house all books of any significance written on the theory of imperialism since, say, 1900 on one short shelf. The literature on MNCs is now so large that books are published as guides to the bibliography.[4] An historian of European overseas expansion can hope only to know a selection of those works that he can understand (that is, not in the shorthand of the mathematical economists) and which bear on the questions the historian thinks important.

There are many such questions, but this chapter concentrates on one only: is the MNC an affront to the sovereignty of the Third World, a form of imperialism after empire and a cause of 'underdevelopment'? I do not claim to answer it, merely to summarize the issues and to suggest a broad line of approach.

The Multinational as 'A New Imperial System' in the Third World

The most important question concerning the modern MNC is why its character and activities should be regarded as a special problem. At one level, of course, the MNC is liable to the same criticism as any capitalist enterprise: that it exists to extract surplus value and thus exploit the proletariat. Its two special features are that, in common with all forms of FDI, it operates across national frontiers and that control is retained by one global centre. It might, therefore, have been expected that the first and main attack on MNCs would have come from Marxists; yet this was one dog that did not bark until there was a chorus into which it could join. It is always difficult to explain why something did not happen. The probable explanation is that, while Marx provided ample leads in his comments on concentration of the means of production and, in the *Communist Manifesto*, remarked that 'in place of the old local and national seclusion and self-sufficiency, we have intercourse in every direction, universal interdependence of nations . . .';[5] and though Rudolf Hilferding's concept of 'finance capital' included the fact of FDI as distinct from portfolio investment,[6] Lenin and later Marxist–Leninists chose not to distinguish between different forms of capitalist enterprise that collectively constituted what they called 'imperialism'. Thus it was not until 1968 that those two stalwart New England Marxists, Baran and Sweezy, included in their book *Monopoly Capital*, a direct Marxist appreciation of MNCs.[7] Ironically, this stemmed from their reading an article in the Wall Street journal, *Business Week*, for 20 April 1963. Following *Business Week* (which in turn was merely elaborating Lilienthal's paper) they took Standard Oil (NJ) as their model of an MNC, noting with surprise that it really was a world-wide enterprise and that, far from exporting capital in the way finance capital was supposed to do, its post-1945 expansion had been financed almost entirely by its overseas earnings. Moreover, they realized that since 1945 sales and profits of American overseas subsidiaries had been rising faster than those in the United States. Clearly, the MNC needed special analysis; but this led Baran and Sweezy only to the somewhat naïve conclusion that the main reason why the United States opposed the growth of socialism in the Third World was that this would restrict further opportunities for expanding FDI, despite the fact that socialist states, being industrialized, were the best trading partners.

Baran and Sweezy did not, then, pursue the matter further. They were, in fact, merely getting on to a bandwagon that had been set in motion the previous year by J.-J. Servan-Schreiber, a Frenchman whose *American Challenge* is conventionally taken to have been the first widely noticed rationalization of the impact of American industrial investment on post-1945 Europe.[8] His central argument was that American corporations had seen the opportunity presented first by postwar reconstruction and the shortage of dollars which inhibited normal imports, then by the integration of the market following the Treaty of Rome in 1958. They had moved into Europe on a very large scale, concentrating mainly in the more technologically advanced industries, in which they now had a commanding lead, using the products of their research and development facilities (R&D) at home to make money abroad. Paradoxically, 90 per cent of this 'investment' had been raised by loans and government grants within Europe. But the most important fact was that Europe stood in danger of becoming dependent on the United States not only for its most sophisticated industries but, more serious, for the technology that made them possible. Europe would thus be condemned to remain in perpetuity on the second rung of a five-rung ladder, as an 'advanced industrial' economy below the five 'post-industrial' states – the United States, Canada, Japan and Sweden. The solution was not to exclude American investment but for Europe to compete more effectively through a genuine federation, including Britain, state support for R&D, specialization by major European corporations in advanced products and improved technical education.

Servan-Schreiber's book aroused much interest and may have helped to trigger off widespread investigation into the character of MNCs (a term, incidentally, which he did not use). Probably his most influential concept was that of an emerging 'hierarchy' of countries in different stages of technological development which might, because of the unprecedented advantage then possessed by American companies, become ossified. This challenged the then conventional assumption that all economies were on the same escalator which would bear them from poverty to affluence. It is uncertain whether this idea was his own creation; but there is no doubt that within a year or two this became the key element in two quite different strands of radical thinking on MNCs and Third World development. On the one hand, some of the Latin American dependency theorists who, as a group, had hitherto shown no great interest in MNCs, now quickly built them into their existing concept of 'underdevelopment'.[9] This was frankly derivative and is not worth discussing here. Much more important and influential was the work of S. H. Hymer whose seminal ideas, published between 1970 and 1972, are central to the modern debate over the role of the MNC in less developed countries.

Hymer accurately reflects the way in which assessments of the MNC became increasingly hostile after about 1960. His PhD dissertation, completed at MIT in 1960 but not published until 1976,[10] was widely read in typescript and seems to have been the origin of the argument that the primary function of FDI was to exploit control of overseas investment to obtain a monopoly rent. Yet in 1960 Hymer was not an unqualified critic of MNCs; his position was that of a conventional North American liberal (he was a Canadian) who believed in an anti-trust approach to large enterprises of all types in order to counter monopoly and promote competition within a competitive economy. By the later 1960s, however, he had become a Marxist; and it was from this standpoint that he developed a more radical critique of the MNC in a series of articles which were subsequently collected and published after his accidental death (1974) in 1979.[11]

Hymer's central message was that, although MNCs might increase the world's wealth through their efficient use of resources, the benefits would go mainly to the countries in which the MNCs were based, while the rest of the world paid the price of their monopoly profits. The result would be an hierarchical world order as corporations developed a complex division of labour within individual firms and throughout the international economy. Two quotations summarize his views on these points.

> The process of capital accumulation has become more and more specialized through time. As the corporation evolved, it developed an elaborate system of internal division of labor, able to absorb and apply both the physical sciences and the social sciences to business activity on a scale which could not be imagined in earlier years. At the same time, it developed a higher brain to command its very large concentration of wealth. This gave it the power to invest on a much larger scale and with a much wider time-horizon than the smaller, less developed firms that preceded it. The modern multidivisional corporation is thus a far cry from the Marshallian firm in both its vision and its strength. The Marshallian capitalist ruled his factory from an office on the second floor. At the turn of the century, the president of a large national corporation was lodged in a higher building, say on the seventh floor, with wider perspectives and greater power. In the giant corporation of today, managers rule from the tops of skyscrapers; on a clear day, they can almost see the world.

> A regime of multinational corporations would tend to produce a hierarchical division of labor between geographical regions corresponding to the vertical division of labor within the firm. It would tend to centralize high-level decision-making occupations in a few key cities in the advanced countries, surrounded by a number of regional sub-capitals, and confine the rest of the world to lower levels of activity and income, that is, to the status of towns and villages in a New Imperial System. Income, status, authority, and consumption patterns would radiate out from these centers along a declining curve, and the existing pattern of inequality and dependency would be perpetuated. The pattern would be complex, just as the structure of the corporation is complex, but the basic relationship between different countries would be one of superior and subordinate, head office and branch plant.[12]

This was an interesting echo of Lenin's 'division of the world'.[13] Hymer's preferred alternative was a 'polycentric' system in which technology would be disseminated horizontally and concentration would take place within a single state, carried through by 'a public institution that organises one or a few industries across one region'.[14] Moreover, Hymer believed that, despite the apparent strength of the MNC, its foundations were weak and could not be sustained indefinitely. This led him to the suggestion (in 1971) that 'one could easily argue that the age of the Multinational Corporation is at its end rather than at its beginning'.[15]

These ideas form the starting point of most recent assessments of the impact of the MNC on host countries in which it has subsidiaries under its effective control.[16] The essence of Hymer's concept of an international hierarchy was that the interests of its lower echelons must be subordinated to those of the highest level: that is, subsidiaries exist only to serve the shareholders in the parent company at the top of the pyramid; so that, when a conflict of interest arises, the interests of the base will necessarily be sacrificed to those of the apex. Without this assumption the debate over the role of the MNC would be merely technical, concerned with its motivation, organization and profitability. By contrast, most of the literature since about 1970 has turned on two different issues. First, whether there is a necessary conflict of interest between MNCs and host countries. Secondly, whether the specific methods adopted by MNCs in particular countries are to the disadvantage of their hosts, even if the MNC performed a generally useful role; and if so, what measures the host should adopt to minimize or reduce these disadvantages.

It is important to recognize that these issues are not necessarily related. That is, we could take the view that FDI may, in principle, be in the best interests of host countries, while accepting that particular corporations, types of enterprise, or the way in which they operate may be disadvantageous to the host. I propose very briefly to outline the standard arguments on both these issues. To simplify, I shall concentrate on two of the four generally accepted types of MNC: those that manufacture in host countries for international markets ('off-shore' enterprises) and those that manufacture for the host market. That is not to ignore the importance of enterprises which specialize in the extraction of minerals and petroleum or in production of agricultural commodities. These are central to the debate over the MNC and will be considered in the conclusion. But most of the modern literature tends to assume, rightly, that these are now historic phenomena, rapidly losing their importance as host countries nationalize oil supplies, mines and plantations. The central issue in the debate over the MNC turns on its industrial investments, now the largest single element in FDI and its dynamic sector. Let us consider first the general theoretical arguments for and against direct investment in manufacturing from the standpoint of host countries, then some evidence of their actual effects.

It is conventional to discuss the effects of MNCs under two heads: the 'direct' economic effect on the host country and 'externalities' or side-effects. The direct economic effect of establishing a manufacturing subsidiary of an MNC should consist of an increase in the real income of the host country resulting from the import of capital, skills and technology which would otherwise not be available. Provided the total increase of the income of the host government (through taxes) and of the society (through higher incomes or cheaper goods) exceeds the amount accruing to the owners of the MNC as profits, we would expect the direct economic effect to be favourable. Only if the profits made by the MNC are, in effect, provided by the host government in the form of subsidies (direct, by remission of taxes or through public investment in the infrastructure made solely to attract or facilitate the MNC's operations); or, alternatively, if the level of effective protection is so high that the subsidiary adds no value (because the goods it makes could be bought more cheaply on world markets) should there fail to be a net direct benefit to the host economy.

The list of actual or potential indirect benefits is much longer and can, in fact, be cut to taste. Let us take the relatively simple example of FDI in a developed economy. In his pioneering survey of American direct investment in Britain, published in 1958, J. H. Dunning singled out the following indirect benefits.[17] The general effect on British industrial development was good because of the diffusion of imported skills and the creation of close links with the more dynamic American economy. The impact of this imported efficiency was both vertical (affecting British suppliers of American firms 'upstream' and consumers of American products 'downstream' of the subsidiary), and horizontal, affecting many other parts of the British economy. American firms set higher standards of pay and conditions, which had a valuable demonstration effect on British labour and employers. Some American factories were set up in development areas. Although these caused some strain on the supply of skilled labour, this was not a general or serious problem. Finally, American firms had a directly measurable effect on the British balance of payments. Partly because they were geared to exporting to established markets for their products, American firms had an excellent export record and, in 1954, accounted for 12 per cent of total British manufacturing exports. In that year the net balance of payments effect was plus £231 million.[18] In addition, Britain was saved an unmeasurable quantity of dollars through the import-substituting effect of American industries in Britain.

Dunning therefore sums up the direct and indirect benefits of American FDI to Britain before 1958 in terms of the law of comparative costs. Just as, under Ricardo's law of comparative advantage, and in a free trade world, any two countries could trade to their mutual advantage provided each concentrated on those products in which it had a relative (though not necessarily absolute) advantage, so in the modern age of protection and economic management, American FDI in Britain enabled each country to use its respective assets more effectively than either could have done in isolation. In his own words,

> For what in essence has happened is that the principles behind the law have been extended to cover the different *stages of the manufacturing process* as well as the specialization of *products*. Generalizing, we might say that the U.K. *vis-à-vis* the U.S. has a *relative* advantage in the discovery of new ideas and pure manufacturing costs, whilst the U.S. has a *relative* advantage in the application of ideas up to the stage of actual manufacturing – and sometimes in their post-manufacturing commercialization. This means that the close association between the two countries occasioned by international investment of the kind described in this book is of mutual benefit.[19]

There could be no clearer statement of both the theoretical and actual benefits of FDI in a developed country: Servan-Schreiber's clarion call nine years later was a false alarm, since the Continent had benefited as much as Britain, and in much the same ways, from the activities of American MNCs. Moreover, the United States had long since lost the monopoly of advanced technology it had briefly held in the 1940s and was no longer the only large-scale foreign investor: by 1978 Western Europe's accumulated stock of FDI had almost caught up with that of the United States. Clearly, what had been sauce for the goose was now sauce for the gander. Europe had nothing to fear from the United States because it could play the same game.

The question that is central to the study of the multinational in the Third World is whether the same holds true there as in developed countries. On any principle of comparative costs or comparative advantage it ought, of course, to do so. The main reason for wondering whether it does is that for less developed countries (LDCs) FDI is a one-way, not a two-way process: they are almost entirely recipients of foreign investment, not investors. Defined as 'underdeveloped' countries, they do not, for the most part, possess the technology, capital, or know-how which might enable them to reverse roles. Their governments may not have the sophistication (or, perhaps, as dependency theorists commonly argue, the patriotism and concern for public welfare) which is expected of Western governments and which might enable them to judge whether the cost of providing conditions attractive to MNCs will outweigh the 'direct' economic benefits their countries might obtain. Above all, the indirect effects may be very different because the host country may not be able to respond to the stimulus of foreign enterprise in the way expected in developed countries. Thus, even if Dunning's law of comparative costs holds good at a purely economic level, there may be other non-economic considerations specific to LDCs which outweigh the direct benefits provided by MNCs.

This, indeed, is the basic assertion made by a large number of critics of MNCs who do not seriously question their utility in the developed world but argue, from very diverse standpoints, that they are of dubious benefit to LDCs. To adopt Sanjay Lall's typology,[20] there are three common ways of looking at the deficiencies of the MNC in poor countries: that of the 'nationalists', who accept the potential benefits of FDI but have reservations about certain aspects of it; the *dependencia* approach, which (according to Lall) cannot be incorporated into any formal economic analysis; and that of some Marxists, who deny all possibility that an MNC can convey any benefits on host countries.[21] All three are interesting; but, since most criticism of MNCs falls under the first head, let us consider the reservations made by Lall himself and Paul Streeten from a 'nationalist' standpoint.[22]

Their starting-point is the dual proposition that the proper criterion for assessing the role of MNCs in LDCs must be social welfare in the broadest sense; but also that there is no possibility of making a final objective judgement on their welfare implications.[23] The reasons are limited information on many aspects of MNC activities, unmeasurable 'externalities', different economic theories of development, differing value judgements on 'welfare' and wide contrasts in defining 'alternative situations'. Nevertheless, conventional assessments of the costs and benefits of MNCs which use these difficulties as a ground for mere agnosticism are vulnerable to the accusation of circularity. Thus, if we accept the neo-classical Paretian welfare paradigm, which assumes a basic harmony of interests in society, the ability of individuals to know and pursue their own interests and the neutrality of the state, which pursues a 'national' interest, then MNCs are bound to be in the best interests of a host country because they satisfy individual preferences in the market and provide technology, marketing, management skills and other externalities. Adverse effects can simply be blamed on to the policies of the host government: transfer prices within MNCs alone lie to some extent beyond state control. Thus, to obtain any grip on the subject, we must look for limitations in this basic welfare critique.

Lall and Streeten point to four possible defects in welfare theory as it relates to MNCs. It makes no distinction between 'wants' on ethical or social grounds: that is, consumer preference may not be the ultimate criterion of welfare. Wants may not be genuine but learnt. Income distribution is excluded. The state may not be neutral, rather reflecting class or group control of state power in its own interests. It is therefore necessary to analyse the role of MNCs on the assumption that, even if they raised national income at 'undistorted prices', 'it would not follow that economic welfare in the host country is increased, unless a number of other conditions are also satisfied'.[24]

This means that we have to go beyond the actual activities of MNCs into a normative assessment of 'desirable' forms of social and economic development in LDCs. Or, to put it bluntly, the standard of assessment must be what conduces most to the sort of society the critic would like to see. For Lall and Streeten, as for most 'nationalist' critics of MNCs, this would seem to be one in which the needs of the poor majority take precedence over the wants of the relatively affluent minority, so that the character and distribution of the benefits provided by MNCs are more important as a measure of their contribution to 'growth' than undifferentiated figures of per capita or national income, which conceal the distribution of advantages.

Once this is conceded, it is possible to construct a quite different critique of the desirability of MNCs, in which the test is whether some alternative source of a desired good would make a greater contribution to social welfare, as defined above. Lall and Streeten therefore survey the various benefits conventionally ascribed to MNCs under three main heads, in each case emphasizing concomitant costs and alternative policies.

(1) *Capital*

MNCs have preferential access to the capital market and their investment may stimulate further aid from foreign governments. But, in fact, MNCs bring in very little capital, which might benefit the host's foreign-exchange position, instead reinvesting local profits and raising funds in the host country. This is desirable in so far as the MNC raises equity capital, since it reduces the 'rent' and the foreign-exchange costs of servicing the investment; but less good if it uses local loan capital, since this diverts local savings from other activities. Thus the main capital import consists of machinery, know-how, patents, and so on; and here the danger is that these things, coming as part of a 'package', may be over-priced. Thus the role of MNCs as a source of capital is far from simple. Each case must stand alone and there may be better ways for a LDC to acquire these capital assets than through an MNC.

(2) Organization and Management
In this field the superiority of an MNC is undoubted, both as an efficient user of resources and as a demonstrator of sound business methods in countries where corporate 'management' is a novelty. Yet, once again, there may be hidden costs, seen from a 'nationalist' or 'welfare' position.

First, as Hymer argued, the price of accepting a MNC may be subordination as a 'branch-plant' in an hierarchical world system, which means dependence.

Secondly, there is transfer-pricing within MNCs, which Lall and Streeten define as follows.

> The problem arises from the fact that transfer prices, being under the control of the firm concerned, can be put at levels which differ from prices which would obtain in 'arms-length' transactions, and so can be manipulated to shift profits clandestinely from one area of operations to another. If the different units of a MNC behaved like independent firms, clearly the problem would not arise. However, given the growing extent of intra-firm trade, it is the *centralization of authority* and the growth of a *global business strategy* that creates fears on the part of governments (both host and home) that they are losing legitimate tax revenue.[25]

Obviously the host government can and should attempt to monitor such transactions so as to ensure that profits declared reflect actual profits made. But there are technical difficulties in doing so, particularly for LDCs with comparatively weak bureaucracies; and transfer-pricing remains one of the most suspect aspects of MNCs.

Thirdly, the very efficiency of an MNC may have an adverse effect on domestic entrepreneurship in the host country. If all the dynamic and technically advanced sectors of the LDC's economy pass into the hands of foreign firms, this may check economic development by reducing the rate of capital accumulation. But this, in fact, is very unlikely. It would happen only in any of three hypothetical cases: first, if the MNC made no higher profits than local men and repatriated a proportion of these profits, by contrast with local capitalists, if these are assumed to reinvest all their retained profits at home; secondly, if subsidiaries were made to pay more for technology than local entrepreneurs could have paid for the same thing on an open market; and, thirdly, if the MNCs created an oligopolistic market structure, as contrasted with an assumed competitive market if local capitalists had it entirely to themselves.

These are potentially disadvantageous economic consequences of the organizational superiority of the MNC. But other, non-economic, costs may also have weight in a nationalistic welfare balance sheet. National ownership of the means of production may be intrinsically desirable. MNCs may adversely affect social, cultural and political values. Patterns of development may be distorted, local élites reinforced and the road to 'socialist' change blocked. The inclusion of such criteria in almost any 'nationalist' or 'radical' critique of the MNC is significant. However valid, they are necessarily subjective and incompatible with economic assessment of the value of MNCs to development countries.

(3) *Technology*

Lall and Streeten define this as 'the human ability to handle the means of production and innovation, the production of new technology'.[26] Technology, rather than capital, is now usually taken to be the main contribution made by MNCs to LDCs and, while not disputing this in principle, they consider that two questions have to be asked in each case. First, could the same benefits have been obtained by the LDC except through the medium of a multinational so that some of the associated costs could have been avoided: for example, by licensing indigenous producers? Secondly, and characteristic of the 'radical' critique, are the technologies imported by MNCs 'appropriate' to the circumstances of LDCs? For example, are they excessively capital-intensive and do they serve the desires of an élite rather than the 'basic needs' of the masses? Such questions, of course, reflect normative assumptions: there are 'optimal' patterns of production which are 'appropriate' to the special circumstances of LDCs and should therefore be preferred on welfare criteria. The same applies to another MNC speciality, marketing skills. However valuable these may be in stimulating an internal market and domestic production, MNC advertising may create 'unsuitable' tastes, inducing the starving to spend their money on Coca Cola rather than on milk.

To sum up, the common denominator of such reservations is that the apparent economic benefits of the types of industrial activity normally associated with MNCs may be outweighed for LDCs either by the economic costs included in the 'package' in which they are imported or, alternatively, by the fact that they are 'inappropriate' by other, non-economic criteria. In either case, the standard answer is that it is up to the host government to decide and to control. But on this also most radical critics of MNCs tend to question whether the state in most LDCs can match up to its assigned role. If not, if it is too weak or class-dominated, if its officials are too ignorant or corrupt to promote 'suitable' policies, then sovereignty becomes no defence against the MNC. So, ultimately, our assessment of the probable and potential impact of MNCs on host countries must turn on how effectively the host state performs its role as maker of policy and defender of the 'national interest'. Let us, therefore, finally consider the capacity of the nation-state to use and control the potential of the MNC and whether the multinational constitutes a form of economic imperialism after the end of formal empire.

State Sovereignty and the Multinational

It is only when one poses these questions that the fundamental difficulty of studying MNCs becomes fully evident. Unless one is an unqualified believer in dependency theory, or a neo-Marxist of the sort denounced by Warren and Emmanuel – both of whom reject the possibility that a non-socialist state could wish, let alone be competent, to subordinate class or sectoral interests to those of the society as a whole – there is no possibility of providing a definite answer. This is not to be evasive: there are two sound reasons for agnosticism.

First, there is very little hard information on the operations of MNCs. Their operations can be studied at two levels: the general and the specific. Most published information is general, based on surveys of a very large number of firms and their activities in host countries.[27] So far as it goes, such information is valuable as the basis for making general statements concerning both the source and distribution of FDI by country of origin and investment and as between the several hundred largest MNCs. It also throws light on methods of entry into host countries, the extent of local equity holding, output, profitability according to published accounts, receipts from royalties and fees, expenditure on R&D and on the contribution to export earnings.[28] Such information makes possible broad statements indicating the importance of the economic role of the MNC in the modern world economy; but it has two obvious limitations. It gives no insight into the motivation and internal operations of individual corporations or the attitudes and policies of host governments; and, consequentially, it cannot provide the evidence by which we might assess the 'welfare' implications of FDI as we have defined it. The first need can only be met by detailed research on particular corporations with deliberate emphasis on the issues raised by theorists.[29]

But even if the flow of specific information increases greatly (and both large corporations and host governments are commonly very reluctant to allow their inner secrets to be revealed) there is a second reason why no comprehensive answer could be given on the compatibility of the MNC and the welfare of host countries. Each corporation and each country is a special case. Individual examples can neither prove nor disprove general propositions. Thus no general theory of the MNC and its relationship with the sovereign state can be drawn up. At most I can suggest some broad propositions that seem to be reasonably consistent with the facts of the case in the 1980s. Let me, therefore, attempt a broad answer to the main question posed in this chapter: what is the role of the MNC in the world economy? Is it a key weapon in the armoury of a new informal imperialism?

The fundamental point is that while the public image of the MNC in the Third World has remained virtually static for over two decades, the reality has changed and is changing very fast. In the 1950s, when the alarm bells started to ring, the common assumption was that most MNCs were American-owned, expressing the United States' postwar economic and political hegemony throughout the world; and that most of these enterprises extracted oil or minerals, or ran plantations. Neither assumption was valid then, and they have become almost entirely untrue three decades later. Western Europe has now achieved rough parity with the United States as the source of FDI; and in the Third World the focus of MNC activity has shifted decisively from 'exploitation' of 'irreplaceable' reserves of oil and minerals or growing tropical crops to investment in manufacturing for re-export or for local consumption. This structural change is reflected in the critical literature: where once Standard Oil and United Fruit were the villains, now it is the multitude of industrial companies who are accused of debauching indigenous tastes and extracting Baran's 'surplus' through excessive profits and the abuse of transfer prices, royalty payments, and so on. My argument is that the change in the functions of the multinational has significantly affected its relationship with the sovereign state in which it operates; and that, even if accusations of 'imperialism' might have been to some extent justified in a Third World context in the past, they are much less relevant in the present.

The most legitimate criticism of MNCs has always been that their very function was to make competition imperfect, distorting the economic process and obtaining a 'monopoly rent' by internalizing the market. This makes them agents of a new mercantilism, which has historically tended towards some form of imperialism. Is this, indeed, their common aim and, if so, why can private firms frustrate market forces in this way?

First, the question of intention. There are a number of alternative theoretical explanations of why large business firms should wish to establish overseas subsidiaries, and all assume that they do so to obtain a higher overall profit by 'internalizing' their total operations than they might do by using some alternative strategy. Their reasons, however, vary according to the nature of their activities and the environment in which they operate; and the main contrast is between the extractive and utility companies, on the one hand, and those which manufacture in host countries on the other.

The salient fact about the utility, oil, mineral and agricultural corporations is that, by and large, they grew in a more or less free-trade environment: that is, the things they dealt in were seldom subject to protective duties, quantity controls (except in wartime), or tariffs. These firms engaged in production and trade in commodities for many reasons, but most did so either to achieve vertical integration within a single firm, or to sell to third parties on the international market. In both cases, however, and also in that of public utilities, one of their primary aims was to erect some form of monopoly as a defence against the risks of a competitive free-trade market. Oil companies, primarily concerned with refining and marketing, nevertheless bought leases of oil deposits so that they could control the price of their raw material and balance supplies from low- and high-cost areas within their global operations. Mineral firms and agricultural producers were both notorious for using monopoly, monopsony, cartels, rings, and so on, to force down the price paid to host governments, peasant producers, and so on, and conversely to force up the price they could charge to consumers.

Thus MNCs of this type attempted to create some form of monopoly in a free-trade environment as their best means of maximizing profits. As an important by-product, they tended also to be 'imperialistic'. Because their activities commonly depended on concessions (for oil, mines, plantations) or, if they were engaged in trade, on satisfactory access to the producers of their commodity, relations with host governments were of crucial importance. And because much of their business was done with the relatively weak states of Latin America and the Middle East and with the early post-colonial states of Africa and Asia, they commonly achieved a position approaching dominance over their hosts: hence the concept of United Fruit's 'banana republics' and the near-sovereignty of Standard Oil or Anglo-Iranian in some parts of the Middle East. In this sense it was characteristic of MNCs engaged in the commodity trade, and some in public utilities (ITT, for example) that they established 'informal empires' as a response to the need to establish monopoly as the basis of profitability in a competitive environment.

Exactly the opposite is generally true of the modern manufacturing multinationals. They are, by their nature, interested in freedom of trade outside their protected home base. They do not need physical control over their markets. Above all, they normally engage in manufacture in other countries as a direct response to some form of obstruction in the market, which either threatens an established export trade or offers opportunities for higher profit through some form and degree of monopoly in a previously competitive market. The chronology of FDI in manufacturing shows this to be universally true. The timing of the great spate of direct industrial investment, which started in the 1920s in Britain after the McKenna duties of the First World War, and from the 1950s in most LDCs as they adopted severe protectionism along with their new independence constitutions, shows that (with probably the sole exception of post-1950 American 'off-shore' industries in South-East Asia) the manufacturing multinational was conjured up by protectionist governments. The effect was a double distortion of the market. 'Effective protection' raised domestic prices above international prices, so creating for the first time a market that might be profitable for modern industry, despite the restricted demand and high production costs of the Third World countries. For their part, the multinationals, compelled or tempted by protectionism to jump the tariff wall, further distorted the market by exploiting the opportunities provided by their monopoly of technology and know-how. Thus, as Hymer argued as early as 1960, it was indeed imperfections in the market that attracted MNCs to undertake overseas manufacturing; but in the Third World these imperfections were created by the protectionist state.

If, then, the power held by the MNCs in the Third World is in any sense 'a New Imperial System' (or perhaps a 'third colonial occupation')[30] then it must be said that the gates were opened from the inside. But we must not beg this question. Empire means the imposition of external authority, the transfer of the power to make final decisions to a central metropolis. Hymer's concept of a world hierarchy assumed that senior corporate executives in Manhattan could determine what happened in Manchester, Bombay, or Nairobi; that the power of the great corporations was greater than that of small or even middling states. Is this really so, or is his New Imperial System merely a fable?

Paradoxically, there was more substance in Hymer's vision in the past than when he saw it and there is still less in the 1980s. His prototypes were the big utility and extractive corporations. These, as we have seen, were a special case. They needed power to achieve their objectives and were able to hold it because of the weakness of many of the states (including some colonies) in which they operated. They were, indeed, states within states, largely autonomous, latter-day feudal barons, able to bargain, even dictate, because of the importance of their activities to the host states. It was precisely because they were so powerful that the new sovereign states found it essential, whenever they had the power, to destroy them: in many countries effective decolonization consisted in the nationalization of telecommunications, oil wells and copper mines.

It is entirely different with the modern, manufacturing multinational. Its very presence in the host country reflects local policy decisions: it is a genie summoned to serve protectionism. It depends for its profit on the continuance of that policy. It has little power because, in most cases, the only sanction it could impose on a hostile state would be to stop production; and, since this is seldom for export, the economic consequences for the host would be negligible. Physically, moreover, a factory bears no resemblance to a large mine or plantation. It is in no sense autonomous or remote, not a city-state. It is easy to starve out by simply refusing licences for essential inputs. Indeed, virtually the only threat the modern manufacturing multinational can make to its host government is that unreasonable treatment may inhibit further foreign investment or technological transfer. The threat is real but seldom compelling. A determined state will normally act as it wishes and risk the consequences.

My conclusion, therefore, is that in so far as there is a latent tension between the power of the MNC and that of the sovereign host state, it is the state that now holds most of the cards and can determine the rules of the game. At the macro-economic level it can adjust its policies in such a way that it is no longer possible for MNCs to make 'excessive' profits or attractive for them to import factors of production. At the administrative level, it is always possible to use anti-trust laws against excessive concentration, to impose quotas, limit prices, above all to insist on a minimal level of local participation in the equity and of nationals in employment. Nationalization is a rare last resort simply because experience shows that very large foreign corporations will normally accept the bid from the very small states.

Yet we must end on a note of caution. I have argued that the modern multinational chief executive in Hymer's allegorical skyscraper is not the ruler of an informal overseas empire. The humblest LDC is in no danger from the power of a multinational which is engaged in manufacturing and technology transfer. But there are other, more subtle dangers. The main danger of the modern MNC to the LDC lies not in its power but in two much less dramatic qualities: its superior cunning and its apparent harmlessness. The cunning of an MNC is one aspect of its managerial efficiency and its ability to take a global view of its interests. Without it an MNC could not operate successfully in Third World states with their jungle of regulations. The problem is to draw the line between cunning and dishonesty as, for example, represented by abuse of transfer-pricing; and much of the substance in criticisms made by 'nationalist' and 'radical' critics of MNC behaviour amounts to the accusation that this line has been crossed. Lall's study of the pharmaceutical industry supports the general prejudice that this is commonly the most guilty type of multinational.[31] Yet, while such practices may cause loss to LDCs, they are unlikely to cause disaster. The real danger lies rather in the seductiveness of the industrial MNC. The benefits a foreign corporation can offer to a poor, non-industrial state are extremely attractive: an instant, advanced factory at little or no immediate cost with payments due only when, and if, the subsidiary flourishes. It is not surprising that during the optimistic 'development' decades before the mid-1970s so many LDCs welcomed manufacturing corporations with open arms and failed to see the long-term risks they were running.

The analogy with much of the borrowing in which many Latin American and Islamic states in the Mediterranean indulged during the nineteenth century is obvious and the dangers equally great: on the economic side a growing and ultimately intolerable strain on foreign-exchange earnings to pay for imported inputs and to meet the cost of repatriated profits, and so on; more generally, a host of social and political problems at home as the alien presence makes itself felt. In the later twentieth century the result will not be the formal imperialism of a Dual Control or a protectorate; but a number of LDCs have now learnt that excessive foreign investment, if coupled with inappropriate economic and social management, may lead to virtual bankruptcy, dictation by the World Bank or the IMF and possibly domestic revolution. Sovereignty, in fact, may be proof against the multinational, but it carries no guarantee against lack of wisdom; and the essential message of the 'national' or 'radical' critic of the MNC to developing countries should be *caveat emptor*. It may, therefore, be appropriate to end with a similar warning given by Edith Penrose a quarter of a century ago, when the study of multinationals was in its infancy, against the seductive attraction of FDI to a state anxious to industrialize quickly and cheaply.

One suspects that for some countries there may be a basic incompatibility between the economic objectives of fostering very rapid industrial development and at the same time promoting domestic full employment at all times regardless of the state of foreign balance, and the acceptance of an unlimited, unknown and uncontrollable foreign liability.[32]

Notes: Chapter 15

1 'L'autofinancement de la Grande Unité Interritoriale et les dimensions de son plan', *Revue d'économie politique*, vol. 67 (1957), pp. 269–312, published in English as 'Self-financed multiterritorial units and their time horizon', *International Economic Papers No. 8* (London, 1958).
2 D. E. Lilienthal, *The Harvest Years 1959–63* (New York, 1971), p. 313.
3 See R. Koebner and H. D. Schmidt, *Imperialism: The Story and Significance of a Political Word, 1840–1960* (Cambridge, 1965).
4 See, for example, S. Lall, *Private Foreign Manufacturing Investment and Multinational Corporations: An Annotated Bibliography* (New York, 1975).
5 Quoted in D. Fernbach (ed.), *The Revolutions of 1848* (Harmondsworth, Middx, 1973), p. 71.
6 R. Hilferding, *Das Finanzkapital* (Vienna, 1910).
7 P. Baran and P. M. Sweezy, *Monopoly Capital* (Harmondsworth, Middx, 1968), pp. 191–201.

8. J.-J. Servan-Schreiber, *Le Défi américain* (Paris, 1967); English translation: *The American Challenge* (Harmondsworth, Middx, 1969).
9. For a convenient survey, see P. J. O'Brien, 'A critique of Latin American theories of dependency', in I. Oxaal *et al.* (eds), *Beyond the Sociology of Development* (London, 1975), pp. 7–27.
10. S. H. Hymer, *The International Operations of National Firms: A Study of Direct Foreign Investment* (Cambridge, Mass., 1976).
11. idem, *The Multinational Corporation. A Radical Approach* (Cambridge, 1979).
12. ibid., pp. 43, 157–8. This argument owed much to A. D. Chandler's work, notably his *Strategy and Structure* (New York, 1961).
13. For Lenin's concept of the vertical division of the world see W. I. Lenin, *Imperialism: The Highest State of Capitalism* (London, 1948), pp. 108–9.
14. Hymer, *The Multinational Corporation*, pp. 163–4.
15. ibid., p. 72.
16. 'Control' is usually taken to mean at least 25 per cent of the equity of a subsidiary company. In practice most MNCs have more than that. But power to take decisions is more important and MNCs normally insist on full managerial control, whatever their equity holding. Even so, dilution of the equity affects the distribution of profits, commonly resulting in larger dividend distributions at the expense of reinvestment.
17. See J. H. Dunning, *American Investment in British Manufacturing Industry* (London, 1958), ch. 10.
18. ibid., p. 292.
19. ibid., p. 320; italics in original.
20. See S. Lall, *Developing Countries in the International Economy* (London, 1981), pp. 53–67.
21. Not all Marxists, however. Bill Warren's *Imperialism: Pioneer of Capitalism* (London, 1980) shocked the orthodox by arguing that 'private foreign investment in the LDCs is economically beneficial irrespective of measures of government control' (p. 176). See also A. Emmanuel, *Appropriate or Underdeveloped Technology?* (Chichester, Sussex, 1982).
22. See S. Lall and P. Streeten, *Foreign Investment, Transnationals and Developing Countries* (London, 1977). The following general analysis is based on ch. 3.
23. ibid., p. 47.
24. ibid., p. 53.
25. ibid., p. 59; italics in original. TNC = transnational company.
26. ibid., p. 64.
27. In addition to works mentioned above, the United Nations Centre on Transnational Corporations published a large amount of statistical and other material on MNCs.
28. See, for example, United Nations, *Multinational Corporations in World Development* (New York, 1973) which gives data on all these matters down to 1971.
29. D. K. Fieldhouse, *Unilever Overseas* (London, 1980) is an example of this approach. Another recent critical study is A. E. Harvey, *The Rio Tinto Company* (Penzance, Cornwall, 1981).
30. For the concept of the 'second occupation' see D. A. Low and A. Smith (eds), *History of East Africa*, Vol. 3, ch. 1, by Low and J. Lonsdale.
31. See S. Lall, *The Multinational Corporation* (London, 1980), chs 7–9 for a detailed analysis of the pharmaceutical industry and how these problems may be tackled by LDCs.
32. E. Penrose, *The Growth of Firms* (London, 1971), p. 79.

16 Multinational Corporations in World System Perspective

VOLKER BORNSCHIER

The modern multinational corporation (MNC) that has spread all over the world, especially since the end of the Second World War, has had a profound impact on the structure and development of the capitalist world economy. One approach to the analysis of problems connected with MNCs is to view them in the perspective of world system development.

The modern world system can be regarded as being composed of three subsystems, that is, the world economy, the world politico-military system and the world socio-cultural system. During the gradual evolution of the modern world system, the politico-military system has generally had a certain primacy over the emerging world economy. Core actors normally subordinated others by force and thereby very often turned them into peripheries. Nevertheless, as the world economy expanded, it became increasingly institutionalized and the orientation of actors shifted from economically motivated behaviour to economic behaviour. At least during certain periods, the consequence was that the relative weight of the politico-military system declined in favour of world economy forces. Pure world economy forces, however, still need to be supported by extraeconomic factors: either by political and military force, or by a normative consensus. This applies to the functioning of the world system as a whole as well as to the structuring of relations between core and periphery.

Until the Second World War, diffusion of the socio-cultural values of the core only occurred on a rather limited scale. Since the war, however, the core culture has massively penetrated the periphery and superimposed itself on indigenous socio-cultural systems. For the first time in history, ideas and values concerning economic development and political egalitarianism are being shared by members of vastly differing cultures. In the postwar period, capitalist development is no longer primarily the result of various forms of coerced labour. Whereas in the past, development on the pattern set by the core was only promoted by modernizing élites or counter-élites, in the contemporary world cultural diffusion has mobilized wider segments of world population.

The shift from politico-military to socio-cultural support of world economy forces has had profound effects on the way in which the core asserts control over the periphery. An economic integration of the periphery that is mainly based on the politico-military sphere, in other words, that involves formal colonialism and dependent states, usually leads to centralized and politically structured relations between core and periphery. By contrast, an integration which derives its chief support from the sociocultural system by means of the diffusion of shared values leads to less-centralized patterns of control that are also more internalized and more anonymous. The modern MNC is a result of this change in the world system. Like its predecessor, the new mode of global integration is not immune to crises. Economic control by the core of the periphery can only be succesfully maintained as long as shared values exercise their integrating power. It is doubtful whether this is still the case. From the late 1960s onwards, a gap has opened in the less developed countries (LDCs) between rising aspirations and slow or even non-existent material progress for the masses, causing widespread disenchantment with the supreme value of 'development'. The MNCs have been playing an important role in the development strategies of Third World countries. Since these strategies have increasingly led to economic and social dualism and the marginalization of the majority of the people at the periphery, the MNCs have also come under attack. They are now facing unprecedented risks.

There has been considerable discussion as to whether and how the spread of MNCs, especially manufacturing MNCs, has changed the core–periphery structure of the world economy. My own assessment is somewhat different from the view expressed by David Fieldhouse.[1] As I see it, the growing role of MNCs has contributed to the stabilization of core–periphery structures and has tended to ossify them more than was the case under the previous system of international trade. This is true in spite of industrialization in many LDCs. The operations of MNCs imply an internalization of economic relationships which were in the past regarded as international. This is due to the MNCs' internal division of labour across countries. Hence, we should regard MNCs not only as *a* new feature of the world economy, but as *the* emerging new organizational form of that system in recent decades. This view follows Stephen Hymer's well-known arguments.[2] Through its internal division of labour the MNC connects the various levels of the spatial-economic hierarchy of the world. This organizational predominance of the core corporation in the postwar period is mirrored in the core–periphery structure of the world economy.

The 'classic' relations of economic dependence were characterized by the core specializing in the export of finished goods and the periphery specializing in the export of a few raw materials to a small number of core countries. In the course of dependent industrialization at the periphery, this structure has gradually been supplemented by a new form of economic dependence. The new hierarchy is being superimposed on the still existing 'classic' one. Its main feature is a world-wide division of labour between core and periphery in the secondary and tertiary sectors. The core specializes in the supply of capital and technology, in the manufacture of the most advanced and sophisticated industrial products and in the provision of elaborate services (embodying much human capital). The periphery is engaged in standardized and routinized production, destined either for the domestic or for the world market. This change has not come about through pure market forces. The industrialization which has occurred in several peripheral countries has to some extent been sponsored by the peripheral state. To put it in more general terms: a certain amount of state power at the periphery is a prerequisite for industrialization and the spread of industrial MNCs. Decolonization has made possible dependent industrialization.

It is essential for any sound analysis of the role of MNCs accurately to assess their quantitative position in LDCs. First of all, caution is advisable in drawing conclusions from figures about foreign direct investment which cover longer periods of time. Figures may, for example, be deceptive if they represent book values. Moreover, stocks are quite different at different points of time. This applies to sectoral location as well as to organizational forms. Secondly, it would be misleading to conclude that MNCs have become less important for LDCs since the First World War. Today the share of LDCs in foreign direct investment is clearly higher than their share in world Gross National Product (GNP). It follows that on average LDCs are no less penetrated by MNCs than are core countries. They were penetrated to a greater extent in the past, but the difference has shrunk in recent decades. The importance of foreign companies within the industrial sectors of LDCs is demonstrated by figures giving the proportion of the largest industrial enterprises in peripheral countries made up by subsidiaries of the MNCs. Figures which we have for Argentina, Brazil, Colombia, India, Mexico and Pakistan indicate that around 1970, more than 50 per cent of the 100 largest industrial enterprises in those countries were controlled by MNCs.[3]

Fieldhouse's observations of a 'shift in investment from the "developing" to the "developed" countries' may become true for the future if economic and political obstacles restrict investments in LDCs. But it does not apply to the decades after the Second World War. Instead of becoming less important in sheer quantitative terms, MNCs have increased their weight in the economy of the typical LDC. For an illustration we can point to Argentina which is by no means one of the LDCs with the highest degree of penetration. In 1955 MNCs controlled 18 per cent of Argentina's total industrial output. By 1972 this figure had risen to 31 per cent.[4] During that period the share of MNCs in industrial employment constantly remained as low as 11 per cent. This is evidence of another problem connected with MNC-controlled industrialization.

It has been suggested by Fieldhouse and others that MNCs are open to the same criticisms as any other capitalist enterprise and that there is no reason for a special controversy over MNCs. This rather underrates the characteristics and significance of MNCs. They are huge organizations with considerable control over economic resources; they are not just business firms, but the most complex and most highly developed organizations in world capitalism, operating in the most important branches and the most highly concentrated sectors of the economy. Mexico is a case in point. In the 1970s MNCs controlled about 35 per cent of Mexican industry. Industries with a high level of concentration (concentration ratios of more than 75) had a foreign share of 71 per cent, whereas less-concentrated industries (ratios below 25) had a share of only 13 per cent.[5] Brazil in 1968 was another example. All of those industrial branches (eleven out of nineteen) which showed an above-average concentration ratio were dominated by MNCs. In these branches three out of four leading firms were in foreign hands. Today this tendency is likely to be even more pronounced. To sum up the argument: MNCs mean big business and monopoly, if this term is used in a broad and generic sense. It is therefore understandable that they have aroused much debate. They are not merely the 'typical, average firm' we know from economic textbooks.

In discussing the question of how MNCs operate in developing countries we have again to be wary of naïve misconceptions. While it is useful to analyse, as David Fieldhouse does, areas of conflict between host countries and MNCs, we must be very precise in defining the interests of a 'host country'. One of the important contributions of the *dependencia* school of thought was to point to the harmony of interests between foreign capital and indigenous 'bridgeheads' within a penetrated country. This convergence or identity of interests is primarily economic, but not exclusively so. It is constituted by societal factors and involves processes of class formation and political organization which can partly be seen as responses to the impingement of the world economy. There is plenty of empirical evidence for the thesis that penetration by MNCs is accompanied by unequal development within the 'host country' in favour of a comparatively small proportion of its total population. This privileged segment usually includes the labour aristocracy employed by MNCs, by local big business and by the state. We may conclude that a form of industrialization which relies heavily on MNCs and tolerates growing inequality is not one to satisfy the needs of the majority of the people in LDCs. If we only look at the interests of host countries as defined by their ruling élites, we easily lose sight of this fundamental problem.

An assessment of the role of MNCs in economic development should also take two other aspects into consideration: the effect of monopoly on development and the spatial-economic hierarchy in a world economy governed by MNCs. The role of monopoly in development has been convincingly discussed in an excellent book by Meir Merhav.[6] He arrives at the conclusion that, due to monopoly, tendencies towards stagnation appear at an early stage of industrial growth in an underdeveloped country. After an initial spurt, monopolization is likely to stunt further development. As a result of the redistributive character of MNC business within the spatial-economic hierarchy of the world economy, MNCs show little inclination to invest monopolistic profits in the host country, especially when the unequal distribution of income had led to market saturation at the periphery. Although LDCs provide substantial marginal profitability for MNCs, they do not offer attractive opportunities for diversification.

MNCs have various means of extracting resources from penetrated countries: profits, management fees and the transfer of goods and services. These exchanges completely by-pass the market. In general, intermediate goods and intellectual property (such as patents) are overpriced to the disadvantage of the LDCs. This does not necessarily stem from an intention on the part of the MNC to exploit the penetrated country. Rather, it follows from the logic of MNC operation in an unequal world. According to this logic, subsidiaries have to contribute to overall costs even if these costs do not arise within the subsidiary in question. The tasks of central management, innovation and lobbying are located in those countries where the MNCs maintain their headquarters, with obvious effects on occupational structure. By means of transfers to the headquarters, the customers of MNCs in peripheral countries pay for the organizational superstructure of MNC business without receiving corresponding employment benefits.

Finally, research on MNCs includes a whole tradition of cross-national studies which examine the impact of MNC penetration on *overall* development. Two main conclusions emerge from this line of investigation.[7] First, MNC penetration is, as a rule, accompanied by high personal income inequality in LDCs. Secondly, whereas fresh MNC investment increases GNP per capita in the short term, in the long term the level of MNC penetration itself has the effect of lowering the subsequent growth rate of GNP per capita. Given that there is a large amount of empirical evidence to support these conclusions, it is difficult to argue that MNCs have no impact on development in LDCs.

David Fieldhouse is right in suggesting that the post-colonial world economy whose hallmark is the predominance of MNCs has little to do with imperialism in the narrow sense of the word. There is no imperialism after empire, because any meaningful definition of that term must take into account the prominent role of political control. From a world system perspective, the control of the core over the periphery has been the constant feature of world system development. But this control has appeared in different forms during different historical epochs. As I have tried to show, it is possible to analyse the period since the end of the Second World War without drawing misleading terminological analogies with earlier times. But what are the prospects for the future? Is there likely to be 'imperialism' *after* the multinationals?

I have pointed to the shift from political and military force to sociocultural consensus which has taken place in the extra-economic underpinning of the world economy. This shift was characteristic for the earlier part of the postwar era. As the hopes and aspirations of the majority of people in the Third World are being increasingly frustrated, the sociocultural consensus is shaken. The question arises as to whether a shift back to more centralized and politically structured relations between core and periphery is likely to take place and, if so, what forms such a shift may assume. MNCs have come under increasing attack in many LDCs, and their position has been weakened by many instances of expropriation of their property. Financial controls, which have conspicuously increased in importance during recent years, may also be seen as a device that is open to more centralized and political controls.[8] However, at the beginning of the 1980s, world trade and exports from LDCs are on the decline, and it is doubtful whether many heavily indebted LDCs will ever be able to repay their debts. Under such circumstances, we may well question whether the financial system allows much control in the future.

Given the enhanced power of the peripheral state and the stagnation of the world economy, a reasonable prognosis suggests that the economic

246 Imperialism and After

links between core and periphery will become weaker – at least for an intermediate period. A large-scale return to the classical methods of politico-military control is, therefore, rather unlikely. Unfortunately, this does not automatically imply a more peaceful world. On the contrary, force as a substitute for consensus – both within countries and in relations between them – will probably play a prominent role in the years to come.

Notes: Chapter 16

1. See Chapter 15 by David Fieldhouse in this volume. My commentary is based on the original version of his paper, read at the conference in Bad Homburg (1982). The published version does not contain the detailed figures that were presented in the original paper.
2. S. Hymer, 'The multinational corporation and the law of uneven development', in J. N. Bhagwati (ed.), *Economics and the World Order* (New York, 1972), pp. 113–40.
3. V. Bornschier, 'Multinational corporations and economic growth: a cross-national test of the decapitalization thesis', *Journal of Development Economics*, vol. 7 (1980), pp. 191–210, here p. 194.
4. United Nations Economic and Social Council, *Transnational Corporations in World Development: A Re-examination* (New York, 1978), p. 270.
5. ibid., p. 61; Bornschier, 'Multinational corporations', p. 194.
6. M. Merhav, *Technological Dependence, Monopoly and Growth* (Oxford, 1969).
7. V. Bornschier *et al.*, 'Cross-national evidence of the effects of foreign investment and aid on economic growth and inequality: a survey of findings and a reanalysis', *American Journal of Sociology*, vol. 84 (1978), p. 651–83; idem, 'Auslandskapital, Wirtschaftswachstum und Ungleichheit: Überblick über die Evidenzen und Realanalyse', in V. Bornschier *et al.*, *Multinationale Konzerne, Wirtschaftspolitik und nationale Entwicklung im Weltsystem* (Frankfurt-on-Main, 1980), pp. 149–92; V. Bornschier, 'Dependent industrialization in the world economy: some comments and results concerning a recent debate', *Journal of Conflict Resolution*, vol. 25 (1981), pp. 371–400; V. Bornschier and C. Chase-Dunn, *Transnational Corporations and Underdevelopment* (New York, 1985).
8. V. Bornschier, 'The world economy and the world system: structure, dependence and change', *International Social Science Journal*, vol. 34 (1982), pp. 38–59.

17 The Newly Industrializing Countries of East Asia: Imperialist Continuity or a Case of Catching Up?

ULRICH MENZEL

The Problem

In recent years the theoretical discussion about development has been enhanced by the concept of 'newly industrializing countries' or *Schwellenländer*.[1] The term is applied to those countries which approximate to the profile of industrial societies by virtue of their increasing per capita income, their industrial growth rates, the proportion of exports made up by finished products, or social indicators of development, such as average life expectancy, literacy levels, distribution of income, the proportion of the workforce engaged in non-agricultural work, and so on. However, no generally accepted definition of the term has so far been found, which has meant that the different check lists of characteristics proposed and the series of countries which result bear the stamp of the particular approach of the writer concerned. Nevertheless, every list does, at least, have in common the countries of Hong Kong, Singapore, Taiwan and South Korea, and even though the explanations offered may vary, there is agreement that the countries involved are all those which have experienced spectacular industrialization over the past twenty years.[2] Although the debate has been less concerned with them, this also applies to North Korea and the three north-eastern provinces of the People's Republic of China (PRC), formerly Manchuria – both areas which would certainly fulfil most of the criteria of newly industrializing countries. Even if it is conceded that special conditions apply to the two city-states of Hong Kong and Singapore, such as the absence of an agrarian question and the importance of their role as centres of international finance and services, it remains a startling fact that in the East Asian region there is a conspicuous concentration of newly industrializing countries. In addition to the general problem of explaining the phenomenon of newly industrializing countries in the first place, there is thus the specific problem of explaining why this phenomenon is encountered in such a concentrated form in East Asia. This is a particularly difficult problem because we are dealing with countries which have very different social systems and very different development strategies. On the one hand, countries like South Korea and Taiwan can be taken as case models of intensive integration into world markets and wide scope given to private enterprise leading to industrialization. On the other hand, in the case of North Korea and what used to be Manchuria the exact opposite can be argued – that is, a considerable separation from world markets, substituted for by the use of domestic resources and abilities ('trust in self-reliance') and state-run economic planning. It is no accident that North and South Korea are both taken as 'model cases' of catching-up in their respective contexts.[3]

This particular problem can be formulated even more starkly if the neighbouring countries of the region are included for the purpose of contrast. Here there are both socialist societies (Vietnam and Laos) and capitalist ones (the Association of South East Asian Nations – ASEAN countries); there are countries which are closely integrated into world markets (Indonesia) and those which are largely isolated from them (Burma). In neither case is it possible to detect comparable industrializing processes. The existence of a market or planned economy, of an associative or dissociative strategy thus does not of itself offer an adequate explanation for the level of development achieved. What all these countries do, however, have in common is a past which was colonial and a present which has brought (apart from those in the socialist camp) a degree of export specialization and penetration by multinational corporations (MNCs); both are phenomena which are generally regarded by proponents of critical development theories as significant causes of development blockages and progressive underdevelopment.

In the light of the observations made, the following theoretical problems can be raised.

(1) How can the phenomenon of the newly industrializing countries be explained? Most writers on the subject tend to put forward one of three positions. Neo-classical authors see the explanation as lying, first, in the orientation of these countries towards the world market on the basis of those factors of production which are available and, secondly, in the exploitation of comparative international advantages, backed up by an appropriate economic policy.[4] In view of their lack of natural resources, their abundance of relatively skilled labour, their low wage-levels, shortage of capital and small domestic markets, specialization in the production of labour-intensive, light industrial goods for export is seen as the obvious strategy and the only one likely to be successful. The factors of production needed, which were not initially available within the country, were imported. The success achieved in industrializing can thus be ascribed essentially to a combination of labour-intensive finishing of imported raw materials and semi-finished products with the international competitive advantage gained as a result of lower unit labour costs. According to this line of argument, there is a clear historical break with the colonial past.

By contrast, advocates of dependency theory – or the theory of peripheral capitalism – fundamentally reject the view that the strategy outlined here can lead to a country catching up in any valid sense.[5] Industrialization in the Third World and, in particular, in East Asia is, on this view, purely the expression of shifts in the international division of labour. This division no longer merely involves – as hitherto – the exchange of raw materials for finished products, but also the exchange of finished products differing with regard to the intensity of the various factors of production going into their manufacture. As a result of increasing wage costs and environmental restrictions in the industrialized countries, finishing processes, which are labour intensive and particularly polluting, are shifted to the Third World only for the products then to be re-exported back into those countries. The agents of this process are, in the main, multinational corporations which are in the best position to exploit the international advantages of different locations. However, as only semi-manufacturing is involved, largely concentrated in special economic zones with special legal status (industrial estates or Free Production Zones), the sole result is industrial enclaves which are as little integrated into the domestic economy as were the older plantations and mines. The result is a distorted form of industrialization which can be cut back once more if the international climate changes or shifts to other countries. This simply leads to economies that are peripherally capitalist rather than to coherent and self-sustaining economies, such as those in the industrial countries. The formal dependency of the old colonial areas has, it is argued, simply been replaced by informal dependency, constituted by an asymmetrical international division of labour, the activities of MNCs and, in some cases, the economic and political influence of international organizations, such as the World Bank. This interpretation, therefore, rests on a belief in historical continuity with the colonial past.

By contrast, a third position, which leans towards the orthodox Marxist camp, rejects any fundamental distinction between peripheral and metropolitan capitalism. In contrast to the famous Leninist thesis, this argument maintains that capitalism is a long way from having exhausted its potential. On the contrary, the newly industrializing countries are, in fact, seen as the visible expression of the incipient capitalization of the Third World. In the 1850s Marx saw positive aspects to British rule in India, since he thought it would destroy the basis of Asiatic despotism. In a similar way imperialism and neo-imperialism and, above all, the MNCs are seen as having a historically progressive character in that they result in capitalism being introduced into the Third World. This position, therefore, also emphasizes historical continuity, but – in contrast to the position outlined earlier – welcomes it.[6]

(2) The theoretical controversy about newly industrializing countries raises a second, more fundamental question. Are these countries evidence of a process of continuing modernization à la Rostow and Lerner,[7] now spreading into former colonial territories? Does this mean that the thesis put forward by dependency theorists, which fundamentally questions the possibility of underdeveloped countries catching up, has been refuted? The theorists of modernization and stages of growth have to face the question of why it is that other parts of the Third World are continuing to experience economic stagnation or progressive pauperization with no sign of political modernization in the sense of developing Western-style democracies. On the other hand, proponents of the dependency theory are confronted with the epistemological question of how many exceptions a theory which, after

all, claims to have universal application can bear, before it can be regarded as disproved. Wallerstein's extension of the original paradigm by the term 'semi-periphery',[8] which he regards as an essential element of the modern world system, must surely be considered as an attempt to rescue the old theorem while, at the same time, incorporating the results of recent discussions.

The question which has to be put to all the explanatory attempts and global theories mentioned here is why the phenomenon of the newly industrializing countries is concentrated in East Asia, in particular. After all, cheap labour, export orientation, imports of capital and the influence of the MNCs can be observed throughout the Third World without them leading in any other region to comparable growth rates and to effective industrialization.

(3) This brings us to the central question under discussion here: to what extent is it possible to detect special conditions for East Asia which are either completely or largely absent elsewhere and which could therefore throw light on to the question of imperialist continuity or discontinuity? One of the special conditions is undoubtedly the fact that in the case of South Korea and Taiwan (but also North Korea and Manchuria) we are dealing with the core of the former Japanese Empire – the part which from 1895 onwards experienced the longest and most intensive phase of Japanese rule. By contrast, the neighbouring regions, largely identical with the present-day ASEAN countries have a European or American colonial past and only experienced Japanese rule for a short time after 1941.

The second special condition is the fact that since early 1945 the East Asian region has been a major arena of East–West conflict. What were the consequences for the client states of the intense involvement of the two superpowers in the area? To what extent is the global conflict of the two systems, which since the 1960s has shifted from the military to the economic level, a significant factor in creating new dependencies, leading the superpowers to provide substantial outlays of capital and expert advice and thus creating a significant impetus for development?[9] In this context, Japan's more recent involvement in its old sphere of influence can be interpreted as its assumption – with American support – of the role of a proxy, in order to ease the economic burden of the United States.

Finally, the newly industrializing countries of East Asia all share a high level of education, a population which is strongly motivated to achieve and be upwardly mobile, a 'strong state' in Myrdal's sense of the word, and an effective bureaucracy – all of which can be traced back to a common Confucian heritage. Although this aspect will not be further discussed here in more detail, it is none the less essential for an assessment of the overall scenario. We shall now examine some of the questions posed here in connection with the concrete example of South Korea, with occasional reference to the other cases.

The Special Nature of Japanese Imperialism

How typical was Japanese imperialism in the phase from 1895 to 1945 compared with the much longer-standing expansion of the classical imperialist powers? In the third quarter of the nineteenth century Japan was itself the target of imperialism; from 1854 it had been forced to accept unequal treaties and was only able to avoid the fate of its Chinese neighbour by harnessing domestic political resources in the course of the Meiji restoration and because of its isolated and economically less-interesting geopolitical position.[10] Compared with the other industrialized countries, it was a latecomer, suffering the additional handicap of possessing limited raw materials; until the turn of the century it had to fight on two fronts: on the one hand, against the areas which it believed to be necessary to secure a raw-material base for industrialization and, on the other hand, against the established great powers, which distrusted newcomers or were its rivals for those areas still open to colonization. This particular pattern explains two features of Japanese imperialism. First, military expansion always preceded economic exploitation (trade followed the flag) and, secondly, unlike the other colonial powers, Japan did not limit itself merely to the extraction of plunder, to commercial penetration or, at most, the development of marginal enclaves: instead, it made great efforts to force the dependent areas systematically to pay their way. Although private activity and private profit were sought in the colonies, they were increasingly tied in with the long-term development plans of state-organized 'joint ventures', in which either the army or enterprises partly or wholly run by the state acted as partners to the *zaibatsu*. It is only in this light that the purposeful, rapid and effective modernization of agriculture and the industrialization of the dependent areas is understandable: competition among private companies was largely excluded.

In Korea,[11] after the installation of the governor-general in 1910, a basic administrative and political framework was established by building up the civil service and a police system. Nation-wide cadastral and land surveys, which were completed by 1918, represented the first steps in establishing a capitalist legal framework for agriculture and were the basis for a long-term plan to increase rice production. The Japanese state was represented by the Oriental Development Company, which later extended its activities to Manchuria, North China and Mongolia. Alongside the traditional Korean landlords it became the largest landowner in the country. Although the planned settlement of Japanese peasants met with only limited success and Korean tenants had to be called on instead, investment in agriculture, used for extending arable land from 4·5 million to 5 million hectares (1938), for irrigation schemes and commercial fertilizer production reached considerable proportions. Between 1910 and 1935 rice production increased from 25 million to 32 million hectolitres; by 1940 it stood at 39 million; meanwhile rice exports went up from 4 million (1915/16) to 14 million hectolitres (1930/36). Since the extra production was exported to Japan the living conditions of the indigenous population did not undergo any improvement. On the contrary, as Japanese domestic supplies began to improve in the 1930s and Japanese producers came under competitive pressure from Korean and Taiwanese rice imports, further measures for raising productivity in Korea were stopped. From then on, a rise in exports could only be achieved at the cost of domestic consumption and this led to a rapid deterioration in the supply of rice and a move to lower-quality grains.

In mining the first step was a systematic geological survey. By 1923 this had led to the discovery of 115 types of minerals and clays. Industrialization proper, especially in heavy industry, did not develop until the 1930s when Japan experienced a new industrial boom, which required increased imports of raw materials (for example, coal and iron ore). In addition, Japan's armaments programme in the 1930s brought a demand for large quantities of both light and heavy metals for use in aircraft and armour plating as well as for chemical products, and Korea was in a position to supply them. Between 1929 and 1940 industrial production in Korea increased in value from 350 million to 1,800 million yen. As much as 55 per cent came from heavy industry and 37 per cent alone from the chemical industry (artificial fertilizer and explosives). Around 1940 the contribution made by the agricultural sector towards the GNP had already been overtaken by mining and manufacturing industry, although it had been nearly 90 per cent in 1910 and was as high as 67 per cent in 1933.

This development was made possible by the previous establishment of an infrastructure which, in colonial terms, was astonishingly good. Up to 1940, 5,670 km of railway line were built in Korea (in Manchuria the existing length was roughly doubled), running largely from north to south and thus creating links between Manchuria and the South Korean ports, which helped the transportation of goods to Japan. In addition, there were roads, harbours, communication networks and the hydroelectric power stations built in Northern Korea, to supply Manchuria with energy.

After the great protest demonstrations against Japanese rule early in 1919, which were partly encouraged by the October Revolution and Wilson's Fourteen Points, the Japanese introduced a relatively 'liberal' regime in the 1920s. It was only with the conversion of the Korean economy to the requirements of armament production at the start of the 1930s that repression was stepped up. All forms of political and journalistic activity by Koreans were banned and the attempt to 'Japanize' the Koreans sometimes led to hysterical excesses: not only was Japanese made the official language but the Koreans were forced to accept Japanese names and were even forbidden to speak Korean within the family. Even though mass immigration from Japan did not materialize, the colonial power did practise a full-blooded apartheid policy which involved reserving nearly every responsible position for the Japanese. The result of this harsh political repression and the declining living conditions during the 1930s was mass emigration. In addition to about 700,000 Korean forced labourers in the mines and armament factories of Japan there were some 3·3 million Koreans who emigrated to Manchuria, China, Siberia and Japan, as against a domestic population of 25 million.

While the Korean economy was largely geared to the production and export of agricultural and mineral raw materials and heavy industrial intermediate products, the industrialization of Manchukuo after 1933 had its accent on heavy industry.[12] It included the development of iron-ore and coal mining, smelting, metal-working and motor and vehicle engineering into an integrated system. Manchukuo, for its part, delivered machines to North China and Korea. The projected settlement of Japanese farmers into largely desert regions failed because heavy demand for soldiers and armament workers limited the number of potential settlers. There was, in addition, little desire on the part of the Japanese farmers to emigrate to Manchukuo.

In Taiwan[13] Japanese activity concentrated on the establishment of an infrastructure, primarily in agriculture, where rice and sugar were cultivated to meet Japanese needs. In North China the Japanese occupation lasted the shortest and investment activity was correspondingly slight; here the main products were textile raw materials, such as wool and cotton and, in addition, coal.

The yen bloc, which reached a peak of effectiveness in the years 1940–2, required all its members to comply with a long-term plan, dictated by the needs of the war economy. The aim was to achieve a large degree of self-sufficiency for the bloc as a whole, based on an internal division of labour. Japan, with few raw materials of its own, directed this division of labour to suit its own needs. It housed both manufacturing industry and the decision-making centres. In addition to forced labour Korea supplied rice from the South and coal, iron-ore and non-ferrous metals from the North. The only manufacturing industries located there were energy-intensive chemical factories and metal works. These were designed to harness the plentiful hydro-electric power of the North. Manchukuo's contribution consisted in supplying soya and wool, heavy-industrial raw materials and selected machine and vehicle products. North China supplied mainly the coal, wool and cotton on which the Japanese textile industry was dependent. The main products which the yen bloc needed partly to import in order to make up for shortages were oil, rubber and cotton. The United States continued to be the most important supplier of these items until the extension of Japanese rule to the South.

The whole system was backed up by a dense network of railway lines, harbours and shipping connections (although the final link in the chain – that with Japan itself – was in fact vulnerable, as the later course of the war clearly showed). Exports and imports from the three dependent areas were almost exclusively tailored to the needs of the yen bloc with Japan at its centre. It was only the imperial centre which enjoyed trading relations with third countries.

If we draw up a balance sheet of the effect of Japanese colonialism on the dependent areas, it has to be pointed out that, although growth rates were impressive, the one-sided and specialized development of the dependent economies meant that no area was viable on its own, since the input–output relationship with Japan or other members of the yen bloc was indispensable for the working of the system. Furthermore, thanks to the apartheid regulations the educative effect on the indigenous labour force was probably limited, since skilled positions in management and engineering were largely occupied by the Japanese. Nevertheless, it should be stressed that in the changed political circumstances after 1945 it was possible for the railways, ports, mines, and so on, which had been built in the interests of Japan to be transformed into positive assets for the Koreans and Chinese. Since then they have had at their disposal an industrial and, indeed, heavy industrial capacity unique in the Third World, and which in Manchuria and Northern Korea has been a major factor to the present day. The development of agriculture was also an untypical colonial experience in that Japanese interests concentrated on rice, soya, wool and cotton, in other words, on staple foods and textile raw materials, which – then as now – formed the basis for satisfying the needs of the indigenous population. The balance sheet would have looked quite different if Japan had turned Taiwan into a second Cuba and had only cultivated sugar for sale in the world market. In the light of the Japanese legacy neither the linking of Taiwan's development in the 1950s with agriculture and processing of agricultural products for export nor the further expansion of heavy industry in North Korea and Manchuria appears at all coincidental. The particular development strategy adopted in each region after 1945 thus clearly shows evidence of continuity with the colonial era.

East Asia as an Arena of East–West Conflict

The development of East Asia into an arena of the East–West conflict[14] was an almost inevitable result of the course of the Pacific War. Originally the war had been a conflict between the aspiring great power of Japan and the already established great power of the United States over hegemony in the Pacific area. Japan, as an industrial latecomer and the economically weaker state, sought to establish political and economic security by setting up an economic sphere reserved exclusively for its own use. From its standpoint as an economically superior power, the United States sought to maintain the policy of informal penetration which had been explicitly formulated in the open-door doctrine of 1899.

The war had turned in favour of the United States after the Battle of Midway in the summer of 1942; nevertheless, tough Japanese resistance on the Pacific Islands had made it clear that an occupation of the Japanese mainland could not be achieved without considerable loss of American lives. The adoption of the strategy of deploying, as far as possible, material rather than human resources to wage the war, depended on the military support of the Soviet Union, politically undesirable though this was. The price for Soviet entry into the Asian war – laid down in the secret annex to the Yalta Agreement – involved the return to the Soviet Union of territories and rights in Manchuria which until 1905 had belonged to tsarist Russia. A Soviet advance would also threaten to bring Korea into the Soviet sphere of influence. The Soviet Union would thus become a major power in East Asia. China, whose agreement was supposed to be obtained retroactively by a Sino-Soviet treaty, became the victim of the separate deals done by the superpowers. As a result, the role of Japan *after* the war was already moving into the centre of internal American discussions during the war itself; this was reinforced by the fact that it was still unclear which party would ultimately gain control in China. It was already possible to envisage the vacuum in China being filled not by the Americans' ally, Chiang Kai-shek, but by Mao Zedong allied to the Soviet Union. As early as the end of 1943 this prospect had led to consideration of the future role of Japan and of a possible *rapprochement* between the two enemies. The problem was that a vanquished Japan would be weak, not only militarily, but – without the yen block – economically as well. Logically, therefore, it would not only have to be given reconstruction aid but it also had to be given a place in the American conception of a worldwide liberal economic order; there it would be able to obtain raw materials and sell its finished products.

The successful completion of the atom bomb tests in June 1945 meant a fundamental change in the political parameters of East Asia.[15] By dropping the bomb the United States was able to force the Japanese to capitulate quickly. What is more, the United States could now dispense with Soviet support. On the other hand, by invading Manchuria one week before the Japanese surrender, the Soviet Union succeeded in gaining a strategic advantage. Negotiations between the great powers led to the provisional compromise of partitioning Korea along the 38th parallel. The geographical front-line of the East–West conflict and the future zones of influence in East Asia were thus fixed within the space of a week.

The United States signed the cease-fire without any Soviet participation and, despite British presence, was able *de facto* to occupy Japan independently and thus determine its future. The Soviet Union occupied Manchuria and Korea as far as the demarcation line, thus regaining the position which the tsars had lost in 1905.

The question of who was responsible for the subsequent escalation of the East–West conflict has sparked off a lively debate between conservative and revisionist historians.[16] What seems to be clear is that the United States did initially decide against a long-term military presence in Korea and did, in fact, try to implement a substantial degree of demilitarization, democratization and the dissolution of *zaibatsu* in Japan. However, as early as May 1947, the decision was taken that no reparations should be paid and no dismantlement undertaken. In April 1948 the break-up of the *zaibatsu* was stopped. Nevertheless, in 1948 both Soviet and American troops carried out the agreement to withdraw from Korea. When the civil war in China flared up again it became clear that a communist victory was likely (although the Soviet Union supported the Guomindang almost to the last). This, combined with the outbreak of the Korean war, in which the Korean communists tried to take the national question into their own hands after the south had been militarily exposed by American withdrawal, finally resulted in a re-formulation of the Americans' East Asian policy. On 27 June 1950 Truman made the decision to intervene militarily in Korea under cover of the UN, to support France in its colonial war in Vietnam and to dispatch the Seventh Fleet into the Straits of Taiwan in order to prevent an invasion by the People's Liberation Army. This decision established military parameters in East Asia which have remained effective up to the present day. On 8 September 1951 the Peace Treaty with Japan was signed in San Francisco on the same day as an American–Japanese military pact, in the face of Soviet protests and strong opposition in Asia. Similar military pacts with South Korea on 1 September 1954 and with Taiwan on 2 December 1954 formed the basis both for a continued American military presence in East Asia and a massive programme of military and financial aid for both countries. The Soviet Union signed similar agreements with China and North Korea.[17]

The Implementation of the Export Strategy

In summer 1953, after a large number of casualties on both sides, the Korean War was halted when a cease-fire was signed largely re-establishing the territorial *status quo ante*. Nevertheless, the war had resulted in the South, at least, becoming massively dependent, financially and militarily, on its protector. As a result, the sovereignty regained in 1948 was once more called into question. Not only did American troops remain stationed in the country, but the South Korean army was now built up and equipped with American aid. In addition, the United States deployed substantial resources in order to keep the country economically viable. In this way some $US 7,000 million in military aid and some $US 4,500 million in economic aid flowed into the country from 1945. Between 1953 and 1960 aid and deliveries of goods amounted to an average of 10 per cent of the South Korean GNP.[18]

Thanks to these contributions it was possible to rebuild those former Japanese factories which had been destroyed in the war and, later on, mostly nationalized, so that by 1957 the economic level existing at the height of the colonial period had been approximately regained. However, at the same time, the policy of import substitution of basic consumer goods began to exhaust its potential. After 1958 the growth rate went down rapidly and in 1960 was about minus 2 per cent (per capita) in real terms. The proportion of the GNP provided by manufacturing industry stagnated at a level of about 12 per cent, with the per capita income lying below $US 100. This made Korea one of the poorest countries in the world. In view of these trends American advisers became increasingly sceptical about the future prospects of a strategy of import substitution alone, which in other countries, too, had clearly led up a blind alley.

The government of Syngman Rhee now came into sharp conflict with the American government.[19] Whereas Rhee wanted to use American aid to initiate grass-roots industrialization on the Japanese model – in other words, to enter the second phase of import substitution – the American government was pressing him to open up the Korean economy to world markets. There were several arguments behind this. First, in the 1950s growth rates in North Korea were higher than in the South which, for reasons of ideological rivalry, was unacceptable. Secondly, by orientating industrialization more towards exports, it was hoped that a renewed burst of growth could be created which would make it possible to set South Korea on its own feet and so provide relief for the American budget. Thirdly, the opening-up of the Korean economy would also benefit the Japanese economy, an aspect which had long been a global aim of American foreign policy. The lever with which South Korea was to be forced into the economic direction favoured by the United States was a considerable reduction in financial aid.

The American strategy met with opposition from Rhee, whose main goals were political. For him, a crucial need to maintain a distance from Japan was almost as important a priority as reunification. Although a crude thesis of American wire-pulling may perhaps be difficult to substantiate it remains true that the economic crisis of the late 1950s developed in 1960/1 into a political crisis which was finally solved wholly on American terms. Latent opposition to the authoritarian Rhee regime erupted on 19 April 1960 into a student uprising. Because the American forces remained inactive Rhee was forced to resign on 27 April 1960. The elections which followed produced a majority for the Democratic party, which elected Chang Myŏn as President. Although early in September 1960 the new government moved towards the Americans by promising economic reforms and efforts to normalize relations with Japan, the United States made no effort to prevent the putsch of 16 May 1961 of about 250 army officers under the leadership of Park Chung Hee. The immediate occasion was a reunification movement which started gaining momentum from November 1960, and which had already collected 5 million signatures calling for the neutralization of both Koreas under a UN guarantee. In early May a large reunification conference was announced for the end of the month. It was the prospect that neutralization might replace economic integration into the West and the orientation towards Japan which provides the motive for the American troops failing to prevent the putsch. At any rate, Park's military junta, consisting of officers who had already served in the Japanese Army and who had been trained in Japanese military academies, appeared to be the best guarantee for the fulfilment of American interests. Park's main argument in favour of his so-called 'revolution' was, in fact, based on economic necessity.

While anti-communism continued to be used to legitimize political repression and the militarization of society, competition between the two systems now shifted to the economic sphere. The first measure was the announcement, in January 1962, of a Five-Year Plan which, because it still reflected Rhee's ideas for wide-ranging industrialization, immediately came in for American criticism.

The new rulers faced economic difficulties from their very first year in office; 1963 and 1964 then saw bad harvest failures and the government was forced – after tough negotiations with the United States – to start a stabilization programme in order to obtain urgently needed American grain deliveries. Not until 1965 is it possible to speak of a turning-point in the foreign and economic policy of South Korea.[20] As far as foreign policy was concerned, the United States continued to increase the pressure on South Korea to normalize its relations with Japan and to allow Japanese capital access to the South Korean economy. It was their increasing involvement in Vietnam which made the Americans attempt to ease their financial burden in the rest of Asia by obtaining direct or indirect participation from their allies. For this reason it was intended that South Korea, like Taiwan, would become economically viable and initiate the kind of export-based industrialization which offered the only chance of success. The process was to be financed, increasingly, by Japanese capital – a development which meant that not only were Japanese wishes being directly accommodated but that Japan was given the opportunity of acting as a proxy power in line with American political and economic goals. At the same time, the United States was interested in South Korea taking direct part in the Vietnam War. For this participation it paid compensation, which Korea was able to use towards financing its industrialization. The Japanese became interested in the South Korean (and Taiwanese) economy as the economic upturn in Japan in the 1960s began to produce a shortage of labour. The outcome was a rise in wages which it was hoped to counteract by shifting labour-intensive industries into low-wage countries, notably the conveniently placed neighbouring countries of South Korea and Taiwan. Although political opposition in both countries, originating in the colonial past, admittedly represented a barrier, it was overcome by American mediation. The Park regime, consisting as it did of former collaborators, was Japan's most suitable partner in South Korea.

In June and July 1965 several agreements were signed which, at first sight, seemed to solve all the problems. On 22 June 1965 a normalization treaty with Japan was concluded and – in the face of strong opposition in Parliament – approved. As a direct consequence the Japanese committed themselves to capital aid to the tune of $US 800 million of which $US 300 million was in the form of a grant (practically a form of reparations), $US 200 million in that of a public loan and $US 300 million in that of a private loan. At the same time, an International Monetary Fund (IMF) stand-by credit and other commercial credits were agreed upon. Additional agreements (including one with Taiwan) set up Free Production Zones and allowed direct Japanese investment in South Korea. On 29 July 1965 Park agreed to an American request to send South Korean troops to Vietnam. In October they were dispatched. From 1966 to 1973 there were 50,000 Korean troops in action in Vietnam, bringing American payments to South Korea of $US 1,000 million. South Korea's economic policy was taken under the wing of American economic advisers and consistent export-based industrialization was initiated. The second Five-Year Plan (1967–71) and all the later plans were largely the result of the work of American experts. Up to 1980, long-term loans and direct investment amounting to some $US 19,000 million flowed from the United States, Japan and the World Bank into the country.

There followed a period of rapid growth.[21] After about 1965 it was mainly based on manufacturing industries (and export industries, in particular), while agriculture was relatively neglected. Agricultural prices were even undervalued in order to guarantee low living costs and low wages. Between 1962 and 1982 the GNP grew on average by 8·3 per cent per year and manufacturing output by 16 per cent. This went hand in hand with a considerable shift in the sectors contributing to GNP and in occupational structure, as well as with a rapid process of urbanization. The contribution to the GNP from the secondary sector was as high as 43·7 per cent by 1982, while that of the primary sector had sunk to 18·0 per cent. The income per capita in 1982 was some $US 1,670. What is significant is that no halt was made at the labour-intensive phase of export-based industrialization; instead, the 1970s saw a shift towards industries which produce higher-value consumer goods (electronic goods for entertainment and cars) or production goods (ships, steel, artificial fertilizers and cement). At the same time, the internal integration of the economy was increased by the utilization of linkages arising from the export sectors.

If the officially propagated version or the comments of numerous international business journals are to be believed, there can be no doubt about the success of a development strategy which clearly takes its inspiration from the Japanese model. Nevertheless, there are a number of reasons for recommending a degree of scepticism:

(1) The intensive export drive has not succeeded in preventing imports from rising even more steeply, since as well as requiring imports of necessary capital goods, these exports have led to large imports of raw materials and semi-finished products. The value of the products exported is therefore considerably less than their volume. In particular, the disproportionate increase in the cost of oil (needed for the energy and fibre industry) is having a more and more devastating effect.

(2) The consistently negative balance of trade and the high level of foreign loans has led to considerable and growing levels of indebtedness.

(3) Korea's export strategy is coming under increasing pressure from two sides. Growing protectionism among major customers, as expressed, for example, in the world textile agreement or in subsidies to shipbuilding industries, is putting the strategy at risk; so, too, is increasing competition from other low-wage countries, such as that coming in recent years from the People's Republic of China which can offer even lower wages at a comparable level of labour productivity.

(4) Many of the industries which were ambitiously set up and planned – in the car and shipbuilding industries, in particular – have been forced by the world recession to work below capacity and hence at high unit costs. Just how precarious it is for an economy to be oriented purely towards world markets was shown dramatically when the reopening of the Suez Canal led to the collapse of the world market for supertankers, a sector which South Korea had specialized in.

(5) Social, regional and sectoral disparities seem to be increasing rather than decreasing since agricultural growth, albeit remarkable in international terms, is well below that of industry.

(6) While real wages and agricultural incomes have risen, the rise is slow in comparison with the growth rate of the economy as a whole. Considering the industrial potential which has already been realized, this could well constrain any further broadening of the domestic market.

(7) However, the most significant objection is that the overall scenario points towards an increasing potential for social conflict. The undoubted success achieved in industrializing is in stark contrast to the small benefit accruing to the mass of the population, all the more so since the regime's

ideology of modernization has set up a high level of expectation which has only been slightly satisfied. In addition, the level of education among all groups, which is disproportionately high, even in comparison with the level of economic development, increases the ability of the opposition to mobilize sectors of the population. The most serious aspect is probably the striking contrast between the development of the economy, on the one hand, and the lack of political and trade union participation on the other. A system which is formally presidential and parliamentary and the existence of 'yellow' trade unions cannot disguise the fact that low wages laid down by the government, a long working day, virtually non-existent legal protection at work, the prohibition of strikes and independent trade unions are precisely what gives Korea its substantial local advantage for export industries. Relaxing the repressive political system would unsettle the export strategy on the domestic side. Official accounts and favourable investigations from abroad, especially by the World Bank, naturally justify this system as a regrettable but indispensable political precondition for the economic success since the 1960s.

Conclusion

In drawing up a balance sheet of the role of imperialism and neo-imperialism in East Asia, the starting-point should perhaps be the observation made at the beginning: if Japan's projected Greater East Asia Co-prosperity Sphere is divided into an inner circle, consisting of the areas subjugated up to 1932, and an outer circle of those conquered up to 1942, it becomes clear that basically only the inner circle (North and South Korea, Manchuria and Taiwan) displays the features of newly industrializing countries – in so far as it is possible to disregard the two city-states. By contrast, the outer circle – essentially identical with Eastern and Southern China and the present-day ASEAN countries – still shows many signs of underdevelopment.

The special form of Japanese imperialism described here has meant that the inner circle has experienced a far-reaching impetus to modernize, which – notwithstanding its negative aspects – it was possible to convert into development potential after the end of Japanese colonial rule. This impetus was partly or totally absent in the outer circle because formal Japanese rule either lasted only a short time or else tended to be in the nature of plundering rather than systematic colonization. In those countries, European colonialism remained the decisive force leading only to partial modernization based on enclaves.

Social upheavals in China and Korea led to capital as well as entrepreneurial and professional élites fleeing to the non-socialist parts of their respective countries. This is probably part of the explanation for the success stories of Hong Kong and Singapore. Taiwan and South Korea's exposed positions between East and West and the global interests of the superpowers resulted in a concentration of international capital and advisory agencies – a major precondition for financing and implementing the export strategies of the two countries.

In conclusion, therefore, both countries, to a large degree, owe their present positions as newly industrializing countries to a two-fold external intervention. In contrast to other countries of the Third World, they have been able to seize the chance presented by national independence and the gain of resources from the industrialized countries. These cases demonstrate therefore that, in principle, it is possible for former colonies to catch up and that restricted political sovereignty and high capital imports should not be equated *per se* with blockages to development.

Even though this does not mean that the dependency theory has been refuted *in toto*, these cases do show that its claim to provide a universally valid explanation for the causes of development and underdevelopment can no longer necessarily be maintained.[22] In East Asia, at least, the international situation was such that it appeared to be in the interest of the metropolitan power to allow Korea and Taiwan to catch up. The traditional system of both countries proved to be strong and effective enough to keep the possible negative consequences of the new informal penetration within bounds and to exploit the opportunities offered by a strategy for developing the domestic economy based on the world market. However, since these special conditions are hardly to be found anywhere else in the Third World it is not possible to conclude that the East Asian newly industrializing countries are initiating a worldwide trend. We are not looking here at the tip of the iceberg, but at the iceberg itself.

Notes: Chapter 17

This chapter was translated by Robert Knight.
1 See S. Borner, 'Die Schwellenländer. Vorhut auf der Entwicklungsleiter oder wirtschaftliche Sonderfälle?', *Wirtschaft und Recht*, vol. 33 (1981), pp. 70–85; C. I. Bradford, 'The newly industrializing countries in global perspective', *New International Realities*, vol. 5 (1980), pp. 6–15; A. Edwards, *The New Industrial Countries and their Impact on Western Manufacturing*, 2 vols (London, 1979); Klaus Esser and Jürgen Wiemann, *Schwerpunktländer in der Dritten Welt. Konsequenzen für die Südbeziehungen der Bundesrepublik Deutschland* (Berlin, 1981); Organization for Economic Co-operation and Development (OECD), *The Impact of Newly Industrializing Countries on Production and Trade in Manufactures* (Paris, 1979); L. Turner *et al.*, *Living with the Newly Industrializing Countries* (London, 1980); S. Woolcock, 'The newly industrializing countries, trade, and adjustment in the OECD economies', *Intereconomics*, vol. 16 (1981), pp. 13–18; C. Bergmann, *Schwellenländer: Kriterien und Konzepte* (Munich, 1983).
2 E. K. Y. Chen, *Hyper-growth in Asian Economies: A Comparative Study of Hong Kong, Japan, Korea, Singapore and Taiwan* (New York, 1979); R. Hofheinz and K. E. Calder, *The Eastasia Edge* (New York, 1982).
3 On North Korea see R. Juttka-Reisse, *Agrarpolitik und Kimilsungismus in der Demokratischen Volksrepublik Korea* (Meisenheim, 1979); E. Brun and J. Hersh, *Socialist Korea: A Case Study in the Strategy of Economic Development* (New York, 1976). On South Korea see J. C. H. Fei and G. Ranis, 'A model of growth and employment in the open dualistic economy: the case of Korea and Taiwan', *Journal of Development Studies*, vol. 11 (1975), pp. 32–63; *Korea: The Miracle of the Han River* (London, 1977); L. L. Wade and B. S. Kim, *Economic Development of South Korea: The Political Economy of Success* (New York, 1978).
4 B. Balassa, *The Newly Industrializing Countries in the World Economy* (New York, 1981); J. B. Donges and L. Müller-Ohlsen, *Aussenwirtschaftsstrategien und Industrialisierung in Entwicklungsländern* (Tübingen, 1978). With special regard to South Korea see

C. R. Frank et al., *Foreign Trade Regimes and Economic Development: South Korea* (New York, 1975); L. E. Westphal, 'The Republic of Korea's experience with export-led industrial development', *World Development*, vol. 6 (1978), pp. 347–82.

5 V. Fröbel et al., *Die neue internationale Arbeitsteilung. Strukturelle Arbeitslosigkeit in den Industrieländern und die Industrialisierung der Entwicklungsländer* (Reinbek, 1977); H. U. Luther, *Südkorea: (K)ein Modell für die Dritte Welt? Wachstumsdiktatur und abhängige Entwicklung* (Munich, 1981); H. H. Sunoo, 'Economic development and foreign control in South Korea', *Journal of Contemporary Asia*, vol. 8 (1978), pp. 322–39; J. Halliday, 'Recession, revolution and metropolis–periphery relations in East Asia', ibid., vol. 7 (1977), pp. 347–63; D. Long, 'Repression and development in the periphery: South Korea', *Bulletin of Concerned Asian Scholars*, vol. 9 (1977), pp. 26–41; H. Gates, 'Dependency and the part-time proletariat in Taiwan', *Modern China*, vol. 5 (1979), pp. 205–46.

6 See especially, B. Warren, *Imperialism: Pioneer of Capitalism* (London, 1980). On Korea see N. Harris, 'The Asian boom economies and the "impossibility" of national economic development', *International Socialism*, no. 3 (1978/9), pp. 1–16.

7 W. W. Rostow, *The World Economy: History and Prospect* (London, 1978); D. Lerner, *The Passing of Traditional Society* (Glencoe, Ill., 1958). For a critique of modernization theory see H.-U. Wehler, *Modernisierungstheorie und Geschichte* (Göttingen, 1975).

8 I. Wallerstein, *The Capitalist World-Economy: Essays* (Cambridge, 1979); J. Blaschke (ed.), *Perspektiven des Weltsystems. Materialien zu Immanuel Wallerstein, 'Das moderne Weltsystem'* (Frankfurt-on-Main, 1983).

9 For a more comprehensive discussion see U. Menzel, 'Konflikte im internationalen System und nachholende Entwicklung in Ostasien', *Verfassung und Recht in Übersee*, vol. 16 (1983), pp. 351–64; idem, 'Schwellenländer und internationales System', *Internationales Asienforum*, vol. 14 (1983), pp. 149–73.

10 See F. V. Moulder, *Japan, China, and the Modern World Economy: Toward a Reinterpretation of East Asian Development, ca. 1600 to ca. 1918* (Cambridge, 1977); J. Halliday, *A Political History of Japanese Capitalism* (New York, 1975).

11 G. Wontroba and U. Menzel, *Stagnation und Unterentwicklung in Korea. Von der Yi-Dynastie zur Peripherisierung unter japanischer Kolonialherrschaft* (Meisenheim, 1978); Sang-Chul Suh, *Growth and Structural Changes in the Korean Economy, 1910–1940* (Cambridge, Mass., 1978); Sung-Jo Park, *Die Wirtschaftsbeziehungen zwischen Japan und Korea 1910–1968* (Wiesbaden, 1969). Among earlier works which are still outstanding, see A. J. Grajdanzev, *Modern Korea* (New York, 1944).

12 E. B. Schumpeter (ed.), *The Industrialization of Japan and Manchukuo, 1930–1940* (New York, 1940); Kungtu C. Sun, *The Economic Development of Manchuria in the First Half of the Twentieth Century* (Cambridge, Mass., 1969); K. Chao, *The Economic Development of Manchuria: The Rise of a Frontier Economy* (Ann Arbor, Mich., 1983).

13 S. P. S. Ho, *The Economic Development of Taiwan, 1860–1970* (New Haven, Conn., 1978).

14 Y. Nagai and A. Iriye (eds), *The Origins of the Cold War in Asia* (New York, 1977); A. Iriye, *Power and Culture: The Japanese–American War, 1941–1945* (Cambridge, Mass., 1981). For a comprehensive review of recent scholarship on the war in the Far East see B. Martin, 'Japan und der Krieg in Ostasien. Kommentierter Bericht über das Schrifttum', *Historische Zeitschrift*, special issue no. 8 (1980), pp. 79–220.

15 See G. Alperowitz, *Atomic Diplomacy: Hiroshima and Potsdam* (New York, 1965).

16 F. Baldwin (ed.), *Without Parallel: The American–Korean Relationship since 1945* (New York, 1974); B. Cumings, *The Origins of the Korean War: Liberation and the Emergence of Separate Regimes, 1945–1947* (Princeton, NJ, 1981).

17 U. Menzel, *Theorie und Praxis des chinesischen Entwicklungsmodells. Ein Beitrag zum Konzept autozentrierter Entwicklung* (Opladen, 1978), pp. 245 ff.; J. Sang-hoon Chung, *The North Korean Economy: Structure and Development* (Stanford, Calif., 1974).

18 For a good overall account, see E. S. Mason et al., *The Economic and Social Modernization of the Republic of Korea* (Cambridge, Mass., 1980); U. Menzel, *In der Nachfolge Europas – Autozentrierte Entwicklung in den ostasiatischen Schwellenländern Südkorea und Taiwan* (Munich, 1985).

19 Tae-hwan Kwak et al., (eds), *U.S.–Korean Relations, 1882–1982* (Seoul, 1982); Hak-

chung Choo, *Effects of the Vietnam War and the Normalization of the Korean–Japanese Relations on Korean Economic Development in the 1960s* (Seoul, 1972).

20 For a similar argument, see H. P. Bix, 'Regional integration: Japan and South Korea in America's Asian policy', in Baldwin (ed.), *Without Parallel*, pp. 179–232. See also J. Halliday and G. McCormack, *Japanese Imperialism Today: Co-prosperity in Greater East Asia* (New York, 1973), p. 135.

21 P. Hasan, *Korea: Problems and Issues in a Rapidly Growing Economy* (Baltimore, Md, 1976).

22 In a similar vein, see R. Luedde-Neurath, 'Export orientation in South Korea: how helpful is dependency thinking to its analysis?' *IDS Bulletin*, vol. 12 (1980), pp. 48–53; A. H. Amsden, 'Taiwan's economic history: a case of étatisme and a challenge to dependency theory', *Modern China*, vol. 5 (1979), pp. 341–79. See also U. Menzel, 'Der Differenzierungsprozess in der Dritten Welt und seine Konsequenzen für den Nord-Süd-Konflikt und die Entwicklungstheorie', *Politische Vierteljahresschrift*, vol. 24 (1983), pp. 31–59.

Part Four

Towards a General Theory of Imperialism

18 The Excentric Idea of Imperialism, with or without Empire

RONALD ROBINSON

For the historian, the paradox of imperialism after empire raises questions that are not usually asked, perhaps because they are too difficult to answer. If, for instance, imperialism goes on after the fall of Europe's colonial empires, which types have survived and which are new? Even more intriguing – is what is called imperialism today more or less the same thing as that of the colonial era, or has a beast of a different species emerged from a new habitat of Cold War and the World Bank? And if so, does it bulk larger or smaller in international affairs than it once did? In the light of the continuities and discontinuities, it may be that ideas of 'capitalist' or 'free-trade imperialism' apply *a fortiori* to the post-colonial age; or it may be that the old imperial formulæ are now out of date.

To define the term is the difficulty, of course, and as the historian has to describe imperialism through time in experimental hypotheses, this trenches on general theory. Theory, at present, is in disarray, even for the colonial period. Until it can be reformed, post-colonial issues can hardly be formulated comparatively. Out of the confusion meanwhile, theory for the post-colonial period runs to notions of economic 'dependency' that often refer more to Utopia than history. Ideally, as Wolfgang Mommsen has suggested, a revised theory is required for our times, to specify in historical depth 'the circumstances in which economic relations between unequally developed states can be regarded as imperialistic, and how far the international capitalist system contains latent or manifest imperial tendencies'.[1]

The manifestations of imperialism in the industrial era are easy to see in colonization, imperial rule and 'dollar' and 'gunboat diplomacy', whereby a stronger state subjects weaker societies to its own purposes. It involves the exertion of power to impose subsidiary alliance, paramount influence or colonial control. Conversely, economic superiority is exploited in order to maximize power. An unfavourable transfer of resources is implied, by way of distorting economic exchanges, extracting financial or military dividends, or conscripting land and labour. Beyond that, some form of social integration with the stronger country is evident, which tends to insert its beliefs and institutions into the weaker society. What is not so manifest is the precise nature of these processes and where, over broad margins, they merge into 'normal' international relations.

Several contentious roads might be taken in quest of a revised theory to resolve these problems, but in this chapter the writer sets out merely to explore one of them. After mapping the latest approach to a definition for the high imperial age along 'excentric' lines, he reflects on some implications for the post-colonial era.

I

The excentric idea[2] begins by considering certain defects in previous theories, and ends in moving out of their Eurocentric perspectives. For all their intellectual brilliance, it has to be admitted that the classic authorities looked at imperialism from a curiously oblique angle. Theorists from Ricardo to Marx were chiefly concerned as to whether capitalism in Europe could survive without colonies, arguing from first principles of its domestic growth.[3] And they continued to find their map of imperialism in Europe, from Hobson and Schumpeter to Hilferding and Lenin. Debating whether its political economy was imperialistic or not, they referred by the way to the scrambles for Africa and Asia before 1914. Though some identified imperialism with the economics of capitalism,[4] and others blamed the politics of militant nationalism,[5] their specifically imperial theory amounted to little more than deducing a prime cause from a critique of maldistributed wealth or power in Europe. Prewar definitions were thus not so much about imperialism, in the modern sense, as about Caesarean forces in the domestic state. It was imperialism in one continent that came into focus, rather than the intercontinental process, and so far as the rest of the world entered into the picture it appeared as an extension of Europe. On assumptions taken from an obsolete cosmography, the process came to be defined almost entirely in terms of metropolitan drives projecting on passive peripheries.

This formula succeeded famously in defining expansive forces inside Europe, whether the economic thrust for markets and investment, or the strategic imperative to protect them against rivals in world politics. But imperialism was more than those metropolitan components. It was but part of Europe's total expansion. Without taking account of the workings at the other end of the process, it is hard to see why expansion required imperial intervention in some countries but not in others, why it took different forms from time to time, or why, eventually, empires fell. Doctrines which neglect the interplay of imperialism in Europe with nationalism (or the lack of it) in other regions, are unlikely to take us far with imperialism after empire.

Because they defined imperialism only in part, Eurocentric concepts do not work well historically, even for the colonial period. It would be a gullible historiography that could see imperial frontiers coextending with those of capitalist economy in the nineteenth century. From the colonial revolutions in North and South America onwards, imperial intervention declined progressively in the European-colonized world, where economy expanded most, while advancing spectacularly in Africa and Asia, where relatively little trade or capital followed the flag.[6] Of these annexations, India alone provided a major field for European industry, yet the imperial horse had arrived there long before the finance capitalist's cart. This empire had been conquered in the mercantilist age for its land revenues and armies, which also generated hegemony over inter-Asiatic trade from the Red Sea to the Yangzi River. The wealth and power required, moreover, had not been projected substantially from Europe, but was extracted from Asia. Where, then, is the true metropolis of these empires to be found? The asymmetry between the imperial and economic arms of expansion is even more remarkable in tropical Africa, where colonies of almost supreme irrelevance to the expanding economy were taken, only to be given up three-quarters of a century later, when their economic value was at its greatest.[7] The incongruities suggest that imperialism was by no means a necessary function of the spread of capitalism.

Neither was it a single projection of nationalist strategy from the European balance of power, though strategic rivalry had much to do with the partition of other regions. With few exceptions, the various interests of rival European states in the Ottoman and Qing empires, or tropical Africa had coexisted for decades without requiring imperial occupation. So far, evidently, their competing ambitions could as easily work to preserve as to invade the integrity of foreign states and, more often than not, the outcome depended on conditions outside rather than inside Europe. It was when indigenous regimes tottered that rivalry sharpened, and partition came from the imbroglio of interests in local crises which drove the powers to stake them round with territorial claims. The chief partitioners had no serious intention of colonizing their new acquisitions. Giving empire a much lower priority than Eurocentric theory supposed, they looked first to their security in Europe, or the world at large and, when all the compensatory diplomacy was done, they had accommodated each other's major interests in dividing continents on maps.[8] All the powers, even the French, agreed in the end that it would be absurd to fight a European war for the sake of more colonies in Africa or Asia. Such marginal improvisations do not look like necessary functions of militarism, the balance of power, or the highest stage of capitalism in Europe.

The idea of metropolis acting on impotent peripheries clearly leaves much imperial geography and chronology of the nineteenth and twentieth centuries unexplained. Admittedly, the concept fits some cases, sometimes. For instance, centre and periphery are one, in effect, where an imperial state such as Russia extends internal control and colonization across its own borders. Metropolitan government and society also projected the planting of European colonists overseas in the initial stages. The idea suits the principle if not the achievement of mercantilist empire, in which metropolitan territorial control went hand in hand with centralized commercial monopoly. Power exerted from Europe was clearly required to integrate new areas into imperial systems at the outset. But central coercion alone will not account for their proliferation. The power of Europe was always relative to the countervailing strength of national or proto-national organization on the peripheries; it was also relative to the weight of a divided Europe in different regional power balances. The rise of the British raj, for example, waited on the decline of the Mogul Empire; but all the forces in Europe proved not enough to turn China into another India, or suppress the rise of the United States or Japan. By the 1850s, the 'Great Republic' dominated the Americas; by the 1890s, supremacy in the Far East was divided among Asian and American as well as European states; by 1914, Australasia and South Africa had joined Canada as allies of the Commonwealth rather than subjects of the empire. In region after region, the imperial centre dispersed to the peripheries in the face of nationalism and maturing colonial economies. Transfers of power were as common in some areas during the so-called age of imperialism[9] as they became in others during the age of decolonization. At some stage in the process, metropolitan empire-building translated into autonomous state-making and economic growth on the periphery. It is reasonable to think that, long before, imperialism had proceeded by combining with local interests and affiliating with local institutions. By the same logic which sees empires projected by structural change in Europe, it must be admitted that they were also projected by structural change at the other end of the process. The proportionate contribution of periphery and metropolis varied with time and place over an exceedingly wide range.

There is another reason to doubt that the forces of imperialism were concentrated entirely in the metropolis. The imperial effort of Europe was insufficient in itself to have generated the immense extension of empire and international economy that occurred. If the bulk of the power required for oriental empire was drawn from Asia, and but a fraction of the capital developing the Western world was exported from the European *bourses*,[10] perhaps the metropolis of imperialism was not altogether where Eurocentric theorists found it? If its true position could be fixed, the ultimate enigma of how imperialism tended to metropolize peripheries and peripheralize metropolises might fade away.

II

With these issues in mind, the excentric idea broadens the perspective of previous notions to bring the missing extra-European factor into play. Borrowing from the practice of imperialists, rather than social theory, the idea assumes the principles which informed the largest of European empires. In extent, at least, the British Empire has as good a claim as any to be regarded as the norm, though extensive qualification is necessary on behalf of other empires. But, if each had its unique formation in the beginning, they all more or less conformed to the British model in the end.

It is assumed, first, that the imperialists were not in the business of exporting surplus wealth and power out of Europe. Imperialism, as they saw it, was a question of deploying quantities, comparatively insignificant in European terms, to places where they would signify relatively greatly, for maximum returns at least risk and cost. In investing a little, they expected other continents to contribute much. The chances of squandering or multiplying the national strength depended on it. On this principle normally, the metropolitan power to be deployed would suffice to manipulate, but not to abolish, the indigenous politics of other countries. Secondly, to be worthwhile, empire of any kind had to be 'on the cheap'. The costs and benefits of imperial policy were calculated on input–output ratios. By this reckoning, thirdly, empires had to be founded to a greater or lesser extent on indigenous organizations and built out of local resources in the countries imperialized. Finally, enough of their leaders had to be attracted or conscripted into transferring the necessary resources and allegiances, if such feats were to be accomplished profitably. Unless the weightier part could be cajoled to co-operate, or at least acquiesce, trade could not be promoted, *imperium* upheld or xenophobic reaction contained cheaply. Imperial cost-benefits depended on finding local intermediaries who would be pliable without being ineffective, and this depended, in turn, on the nature of their social organization and its ability to undergo change without foreign control.[11]

To the imperialists at least, imperialism was not simply something that Europe did to other countries, but also something they were persuaded or compelled to do to themselves. For good or ill, it was designed to gather strength from unequal economic partnerships and political alliances with sub-imperial contractors in other parts of the world. Who could harness pre-industrial societies to Europe's expansive demands? Accordingly, excentric theory suggests, imperialism has to be redefined to include the various collaborative systems which connected its European and extra-European components, and transformed imperial inputs into multiplied indigenous outputs. And the excentricity of the notion is found in this: when imperialism is looked at as an inter-continental process, its true metropolis appears neither at the centre nor on the periphery, but in their changing relativities.

These relationships might run from commodity and financial markets in Paris, London, or Berlin to unequal bargains with overseas merchants and producers; they might extend from European chanceries and conference tables to 'unequal' treaties and colonial regimes imposed on overseas politicians; and ancient, or modern nationalities might resist and make things more equal. But the imperial sum of all these relativities, excentric theory argues, is registered locally in the collaborative system. Any significant shift in the balance of wealth and power at international, metropolitan, or local level affecting an area of formal or informal empire, required a corresponding shift in collaborative terms. Consequently, the nature of imperialism in any particular country is shown in the balance of terms struck between the imperialists and their local contractors from time to time. Contracts are seen to be more or less imperialistic, in so far as the imperial state used power to extract resources, and economic superiority was used to establish control. Both the extent of imperial intervention and its economic relativity are indicated in the inequity of more or less forced, more or less mutually profitable partnerships. Conversely, the inequities tended to equalize with higher resistance, as countries revived or acquired national organization. As a result, the relativity of imperialism to proto- and modern nationalism can also be measured in the changing balance of collaborative equations.

During the late imperial age, while Europe's lead over other regions in state-making, technology and world markets was probably at its longest, intermediaries were easily recruited on exorbitant terms. Imperial coercion, however, often proved expensive, and the terms on offer still decided the chances of collaboration or resistance. The greater the European military effort committed to a system, the less mediators were needed, but the less they were employed, the more imperial balance sheets were overdrawn. On the other hand, the greater the economic resources committed, the more attractive commercial partnerships with Europe became and the less imperial coercion was required. Whereas imperialists preferred to rely on collaborators of one sort or another, rather than go to the expense of doing things themselves, collaborators usually had no alternative but to settle with the intruders as best they could before their rivals did so. Their bargaining position, however, was not always quite as hopeless as it might seem. Two sets of local contracts were involved in working collaboration – one between European agents and their intermediaries, the other, between the intermediaries and their own people. When imperialists demanded more from their sub-contractors than their people would tolerate, contracts could not be delivered and the system became unstable. Each set of arrangements had to be acceptable in terms of the other if they were to be carried into effect. A system of this kind implied a degree of mutual support, a recognition of overlapping interests, an element of mutual exploitation. Hence the collaborative equations which reflected all these considerations, show the imperial input–output ratios and cost-benefits on both sides of the bargain.

In the light of these relativities, imperial chronology and cartography become more easily understandable. At the outset, the proportion of effective resisters to mediators decided the possibility of European penetration by informal means. In many instances, the breakdown of informal collaboration in a local crisis led to an imperial takeover. During the ensuing formal phase the choice of collaborators determined the organization and depth of colonial administration, which institutionalized the indigenous political and economic affiliations upholding its authority. And, at last, when nationalists succeeded in detaching enough mediators from colonial regimes into a united front of non-cooperation, their rulers either chose to leave or were compelled to go. They had run out of collaborators, which fixed the time for the transfer of colonial power. Since the anti-colonialists had triumphed by inverting the previous alliances, their succeeding party governments carried a kind of mirror image of colonial collaboration into the early years of independence. Evidently structural connections and disconnections at both ends of the process governed the scope and penetrative depth of European imperialism. According to their relativities European expansion did not take imperial form in many countries, but in others has ranged from informal paramountcy to colonial rule and, eventually, back to external influence.

The excentric idea therefore contains two basic theorems: one is that European imperialism generated its main force through linking and exploiting relative inequalities in local and regional balances of wealth and power, which determined its input–output ratios, cost-benefits and its role in economic and strategic expansion. The other is that the imperial sum of all these structural relativities is encapsulated in the changing terms for local collaboration. These indigenous linkages, it is suggested, comprise the only field of study in which the so-called metropolitan and peripheral elements come together. Consequently, the nature and extent of imperialism, with or without empire, can only be defined in terms of local collaborative systems at the point of impact.

More than a theoretic construct, the unequal reciprocities on which they ran were specified in countless commercial concessions, international treaties and colonial constitutions. As each society required a special set of linkages, each tended to generate a special kind of imperialism. The relativities involved fall into patterns so various as to imply as many different kinds of imperialism as the number of countries imperialized. Such an approach has a particular advantage over Eurocentric notions for the present object. As the unified field for studying degrees of informal imperialism at its frontiers with normal international relations, collaboration theory provides a measure for the post-colonial era.

III

Almost by definition, the technique of collaborating élites was the essence of Europe's informal empires. For the most part, countries integrated in this way into imperial systems were, as yet, too unified or internationally controversial to be bundled under colonial rule. Nor was this the objective. In principle, their 'progressive' classes were to be attracted into economic partnership with the world's banker and workshop, while the imperial state exerted external suasion on their governing élites to reform their institutions for the link-up with imperial systems and international economy. Here, imperialism modulated into subtler influences – technical aid, diplomatic pressure, the dangled loan and subsidiary alliance, reinforced occasionally with blockade, bombardment, or expedition. By such means informal policy aimed at reorientating indigenous structures along lines that would produce imperial influence internally, with the growth of trade and investment, but with minimal imperial effort. Though informal imperialists operated some of the levers, the real motor of the process lay largely out of their control, in the meshing of autonomous private enterprises with the internal politics of quasi-autonomous governments.

The extraordinary flexibility of these informal linkages during the century before 1914 may be indicated in two historical models. The first exemplifies the working of informal empire in those parts of the world colonized by Europeans, which helps explain why colonial rule contracted in these areas as the economy expanded. The second shows why informal empire in Asia and Africa tended to modulate into colonial rule, with relatively little economic growth.

As the home of the first industrial revolution, Britain inevitably practised the richest variety of free-trade imperialism, which was put into high gear whenever a regional power balance offered the chance of combining with the right collaborators. European colonists and ex-colonists were its best prospects. Ironically, they were also nationalists struggling to be free. Thus in the 1820s, Canning and Castlereagh cast the colonial revolutionaries of Latin America for this role, seeking to redress the regional balance in the Americas against the United States, and that of Europe in favour of Britain. By shielding the rebels against their erstwhile Spanish and Portuguese rulers with naval supremacy, London planned to demolish their eroded economic monopolies and constuct a new informal sway out of the ruins of old formal empires. The contracts were let out to the liberated merchant classes of Argentina, Brazil, Chile, Mexico and Colombia, on terms of reciprocal *laisser-faire*: free access to London's capital and commodity markets, in return for free imports of British manufactures and diplomatic or naval co-operation.[12] There were several false starts, when *portēno* regimes failed to sell these terms to producers in the backlands. Defaults on government loans frequently interrupted the connecting flows of capital and trade, provoking Latin American embargoes and British naval intervention sporadically. But from the 1860s onwards, as railways and steamships developed Latin American economies in ways that complemented the British, informal linkages took hold. By 1913 the City of London had invested several hundred million pounds sterling in what had become long since a major supplier of food and raw materials, a significant importer of British manufactures. Increasingly, local capital formation and the coming of American and German enterprise diversified and internationalized the economic networks which the British had established, with a corresponding decline in their political influence. But then, their achievement of informal empire in Latin America had always owed much more to mutually attractive business transactions than to the interference of the imperial state. That is what free-trade imperialism was designed to do. As a country's links with international economy tightened, imperial intervention slackened. And for a good reason: once a local economy became sufficiently dependent on foreign trade and capital, the classes who profited could normally be relied upon to work in local politics to stabilize the collaborative system by themselves.[13] At a later stage of unification, they would go further and realign it entirely to their national advantage. In the United States, for example, though British business had turned the 'Cotton South' into a branch of informal empire, it was impossible to stop American industrialization, or prevent the industrialized sections absorbing the South into a nationalized continental economy behind protective tariffs. The political and economic strength of the country stood in the way.

The decline of direct imperial action in the most flourishing members of the British informal empire was matched by the grant of democratic self-government to those regions of formal empire sufficiently developed to receive it. In British North America and Australasia, the collaboration of imperialists with nationalists won its most remarkable successes. After rebellions in Canada and discontents in the southern continent, direct control from Downing Street rusted into disuse from the 1850s onwards. Yet, the elected nationalistic governments of these colonies still co-operated loyally with the empire. Its yoke was light, but the economic enticements were compelling and the strategic protection which empire provided against foreign interference was needed. Up to 1914 the Australasian Dominions had no alternative to the mother country as an export market, investor of long-term capital and protector. This was also true of the Canadian Confederation, if for a different reason. Though the Canadians had an alternative protector and economic ally next door in the United States, and traded substantially there, they relied as nationalists on the imperial connection to save their independence from their powerful neighbour. The French Canadians were no exception. For this reason Canadian governments excluded American capital so far as possible, built their railways with British loans and, forestalling the north-westward expansion of the United States, they extended Canadian territorial nationality from the Atlantic to the Pacific.[14] Under these conditions, proliferating economic connections with Britain in Canada and Australia and New Zealand provided superior substitutes for colonial rule. The export–import sector tended to govern the economic growth of these colonies in line with the needs of British industry, while loans from London to their governments had as much to do with their loyalty as their prosperity. It is not surprising that bankers in Montreal or Toronto, wheat farmers of the Canadian prairies, wool merchants in Sydney or Melbourne and pastoral barons of the Australian outback took their politics from the export–import sector, where their bread was buttered. What is surprising is that, by and large, colonial politicians and colonial labour did the same. But then, government revenue depended largely on external trade duties; British capital, though small in proportion to local capital invested, was vital for railways and public works to set local capital and labour working, and so colonial politics were to a great extent 'railway politics'.[15] Iron roads and other public-loan investments meant employment for the farmer and town-worker alike, and supplied the patronage which often won elections. Consequently, whatever their anti-imperial rhetoric, populist politicians and their radical followings were as susceptible to the allure of the imperial connection as capitalists, and equally eager to embark on sub-imperial expansion along railways bringing sub-continents into the orbit of 'Greater Britain'. Whether the terms for co-operation were so unequal as to justify the description of 'capitalist imperialism' is questionable. But in these cases, where racial and cultural affinities were strong and regional relativities favourable, there were sufficient economic inputs from Britain to be converted comparatively smoothly into imperial collaboration, through the local democratic politics of self-governing nationalism. Here, the relativities of informal empire also worked constructively. By 1919 these countries had taken off into virtual economic, as well as political, independence.

At the same time, the Union of South Africa was not far behind them, but this was the exceptional case in which collaboration between British imperialists and European colonial nationalists had broken down. Up to 1895 the self-governing Cape Dutch majority leaders had co-operated economically and politically with the English-speaking minority of the export–import sector. Once again, railways figured largely in the contracts which drew the Afrikaner farmers of Cape Province and the Orange Free

State into imperial partnership. This long-standing system of British sway over two self-governing colonies and two quasi-independent republics, however, was overturned in the flood of British and foreign capital into the gold mines of the Witwatersrand. At a stroke, the key to economic and political supremacy over the sub-continent, including the rapidly expanding export–import sector, had been transferred to the *trekboer* leaders of the Transvaal Republic, the most anti-imperialistic of the four local states. British attempts to recapture it in the Jameson Raid fiasco and the Boer War completed the collapse of the imperial collaborative system. It was left to the defeated leaders of the Afrikaner nationalist reaction which followed, to put it together again in the Union of 1909. In effect, a sudden inrush of largely British economic inputs into what had been a subsistence sector had released the export–import sector's grip on the politics of a Balkanized sub-continent.[16] Since the financiers of London, out for the main chance, were inadvertently responsible for shattering this British informal empire, the imperial loyalty of capital of any nationality should not be taken for granted.

These successes of British free-trade imperialism in European-settled parts of the world were attained under special conditions, which reflect on post-colonial 'dependency' theory. In these countries, clearly, the export–import sector tended to govern the speed and direction of economic growth, according to the needs of the British industrial economy, and inclined their domestic politics in favour of British strategy. To that extent, collaborative terms were unequal, although nowhere except in Utopia is it laid down that every country should be industrialized equally at the same time. During the first three-quarters of the nineteenth century, and to a lesser extent up to 1914, British merchants dominated trade outside Europe just as the Royal Navy, however precariously, dominated the oceans, while the City of London was the main exporter of long-term capital. These quasi-monopolistic conditions were vital for the success of British informal collaborative systems in self-governing colonies and independent states. So long as they had no alternative buyer, supplier or protector they were in principle free to choose, but in practice they had no choice of foreign collaborators for the time being. Even so, terms arranged voluntarily between private sectors or mediated by local governments, which had to be justified to local producers and electorates, would not have been agreed if they had not been mutually profitable, however unequally. As alternative foreign partners appeared, and colonial political economy matured, terms tended to equalize and informal empire-building modulated into national state-making.

The connecting links of imperialism in Asia and Africa belong to an entirely different category. In the informal phase of this model, the Europeans tried to lever indigenous regimes into line with their various imperial strategies from outside, hoping to modernize their institutions through commerce and subsidiary alliance. So in the 1830s, the French found a modernizing collaborator in the Egyptian khedive, Muhammad Ali, training his army and navy to such effect that he invaded Syria and Arabia in the joint cause. And so, Palmerston in 1839, with an eye to keeping French and

The Excentric Idea of Imperialism 277

Russian influence off the India routes, brought his navy to rescue the Commander of the Faithful in Constantinople from his over-mighty Egyptian subject, but on one condition: government monopolies were abolished and free trade allowed throughout the Ottoman satrapies.[17] During the next two decades, the Son of Heaven in Peking was driven to do the same.[18] From the Oxus to the Niger and to the Yellow River ancient empires, along with countless sultanates and chiefdoms, were cajoled into opening their doors to the international economy. Later, in return for trading credit, loans, or under the muzzles of high-velocity guns, they were to be pressed into reforming their 'antiquated' institutions in enlightened ways, calculated to bring their 'productive classes' into power as collaborators. By such means some useful economic connections with West African trading states were formed, though the Bible and legitimate trade had little penetrative effect. Some more important commercial links were forged with Chinese compradors or Levantine business classes in the Ottoman domains.[19] Here, Europeans with the aid of their consuls obtained railway concessions, or land and mineral rights, while 'advisers' were attached to indigenous administrations. But, for all the reforms decreed at Constantinople in 1839 and 1876,[20] and in China as late as 1898,[21] they were smothered in traditionalist reaction. Modernity was still to seek. In these polymorphic societies, the institutional barriers to Europeanization proved intractable.

As a result, informal imperialists found the scope for proliferating collaborative connections narrowly restricted. In the great empires of Asia, their comprador partners were shut up in cosmopolitan export–import enclaves, which had little systemic influence over their military or bureaucratic governments, and little effective leverage on indigenous economy. Compared with those in European-colonized areas, these sectors had a low generative capacity either for economic growth or imperial influence. In China, for instance, British merchants, unable to discover the expected millions of customers for Lancashire cotton, had to content themselves with annexing part of the domestic riverine traffic.[22] Moreover, in the Mediterranean and, to a less extent the Chinese cases, the strategic interests of too many great powers were involved. A rise in the influence of any one of them tended to be countered by a combination of the rest. Informal empire, which had to proceed normally by international agreement, was thus to a great extent internationalized in the form of alien enclaves, inserted and sustained internationally, under extra-territorial consular jurisdiction. There was of course one exception. By reforming their state to divert the forces of imperialism to the tasks of national strengthening, Japanese collaborators from 1869 onwards did what otherwise only European colonists and ex-colonists seemed able to accomplish.[23]

Unable to make headway with economic levers in the private sector elsewhere in Asia and North Africa, the Europeans found their chief mediators in ruling oligarchies and traditional élites. Hence, the European economic inputs, which might have gone to economic development, tended to be diverted to the making of political influence and alliances for purposes of imperial power strategy. So Palmerston, building up British influence at Constantinople with loans and naval support, contrived to throw back

Russian pressure with the aid of the Turkish army from the Eastern Mediterranean, the North–West frontier of India and the Persian Gulf in the 'Great game of Asia'. Similarly, France strove for paramountcy over the Muslim states of North Africa against other powers for the sake of national security at home.[24] Although the Qing Empire rejected loans and railways so long as it was able, the Ottoman and North African Empires were more accommodating. Pledging their revenues, they borrowed too much from Europe and spent too little on productive projects. One by one in the 1860s and 1870s they were bankrupted. Their pledged revenues came under the administration of international debt commissioners sent by the Concert and capitalists of Europe, and their independence was at an end. Under the strain of fiscal reform, repayment and the unpopularity of foreign controls, these rulers lost the authority to contain anti-foreign disturbances or outright rebellions. The imperialists in this way had driven their collaborators into playing for too high stakes with too few cards. Local crises of this type overturned informal systems in much of Asia and Africa, and as they did so the imperialists had to choose between scrapping their interests, or taking over the government and reconstructing collaboration from inside.

Thereafter, in the formal phase of the model for Asia and Africa, terms altered dramatically in some respects, though not in others. By partition treaties and other arrangements the European powers had given each other a free hand to deal with their respective colonies and spheres of influence. A kind of imperial collective security system was thus built into the European Concert for the twentieth century, which proved an indispensable condition for the survival of colonial empires, without unacceptable risks to national security or intolerable demands on the European taxpayer. More immediately, this meant that the colonial ruler had a monopoly of his subjects' international relations. And as they had no alternative external protector, to that extent terms for collaboration turned against them. Meanwhile, colonial equations depended much more on other considerations: on how far the imperial state invested its own power in colonial administration, or relied on its indigenous alliances; on what was demanded of subjects and what powers of unified resistance they could muster.

Like those of informal imperialism, the relativities involved in colonial empire during the nineteenth and twentieth centuries cover a remarkably wide range. The proportionate contribution of metropolis and periphery varied from place to place, as did the role of colonial government in expanding imperial economy and strategy. At one end of the scale, proconsuls backed with sufficient metropolitan force demolished indigenous structures for the time being and, with little need of collaborators, save for a Europeanized cadre of subordinate officials and sergeants, imposed the most exorbitant terms on colonial subjects.[25] Such conditions prevailed for example in the early Belgian[26] and French Congo, or in British Southern Rhodesia.[27] In cases of this kind, virtually absolute colonial rule was exerted to conscript local military forces, or to expropriate land and labour for the European settler or capitalist concessionaire. Coercive territorial control established an unquestionable European monopoly of a colony's political economy, and resulted in classic examples of economic imperialism.

These cases, however, were the exception rather than the rule. Over most of the range, colonial linkages, especially for the British, took the form of 'over' or 'indirect' rule. Once primary resistance had been overcome, the object here was to build empire without calling on metropolitan resources, except in emergency. Pro-consuls, with enough reserve support to manipulate but not to suppress indigenous politics, were left to cajole the substance of colonial authority out of their subjects. According to this principle of minimum metropolitan input for maximum indigenous output, colonial administration consisted of a tiny tophamper of European officials working through local states and other institutions. Under such conditions, collaborators were essential. If the pro-consuls were to avoid rebellion and keep control, the terms offered would have to be calculated sensitively. Hence the means of production were normally left in the hands of subjects, with rulers doing what they could by way of taxes and loans to connect indigenous economies with the private European-controlled export–import sector. But since economic inputs usually remained relatively small, colonial rule had to be sustained chiefly through indigenous political affiliations.

The British raj in India may be seen as the paradigm of an extraordinary mixture of military and indirect types of colonialism. Beginning with a tiny European military input which multiplied in alliances with the troops of rival Indian states, an immense indigenous army was assembled which completed the military occupation of the sub-continent and backed up its civilian administration thenceforward. A divided India thus conquered itself for the empire, paid for it, and provided sepoy forces sufficient to arm imperial strategy throughout the East. Unlike the Congo, as a rule, the sword was not used to expropriate indigenous land and labour. Rather, this was to be exploited through reform of the fisc inherited from the Moguls. One-third of India was ruled indirectly through the medium of princely states, and from 1919 to 1939 the local and provincial administration was increasingly shared with other collaborators representing communal élites or political parties.[28] Another clear example of relatively small imperial military inputs producing enormous indigenous outputs is that of the French, who by the First World War were mobilizing from their African dependencies a significant proportion of the forces required to defend the metropole itself.[29]

At the other extreme of the colonial range stands British indirect rule in Malaya or West Africa. Where India's rulers had a quarter of a million bayonets at their back, the district officer in West Africa was lucky if he could call up a single company. With but puny European inputs he had more to give. Indigenous chiefs had to be left to govern their people locally much as they had done in pre-colonial times. Terms for this sort of over-rule involved discouraging or excluding of European concessionaires, and as a rule Africans retained economic and political control of production and supply, while British merchants provided credit and marketed the exports. As a result, colonial indirect rule up to 1939 tended to preserve traditional structures and limit itself to the tasks of supervising local indigenous authorities and keeping the peace for free trade. Once primary resistance had been overcome, the colonial terms of Anglo-African co-operation here differed remarkably little from those of the pre-colonial era on the West African coast. A handful of pro-consuls manufactured a precarious authority out of manipulating indigenous political processes.[30]

Colonialism through collaboration depended fundamentally on proconsuls keeping a monopoly of central arbitration among divided subject communities. Administrative patronage might be distributed to one group and taken away from another, but always so as to draw the weightier part of the indigenous leaders into co-operation and make sure that none of them became overmighty enough to challenge the colonial regime. In India the indigenous political arenas were urban and provincial.[31] In tropical Africa they were ethnic and local, and over and between these divisions the central rulers rang the changes on bargains with maharajas and zemindars, sultans, emirs and chiefs. These permutations constituted the true genius of indirect colonial administration, and in the more or less unequal contracts with its intermediaries the degree of imperialism in colonialism may be defined. The intermediaries, for their part, competed for official patronage on behalf of their followings against other factions and communities, or to exploit their opportunities in the modern sector. The less the pro-consuls demanded of their mediators in the way of reform, the safer they were; and the more they tried to develop societies into modern, secular shapes, the harder it became to solve collaborative equations. So long as traditional local and provincial heads kept hold of the peasantry in defiance of nationalist agitators from the schools and towns, the pro-consuls could easily keep control. But as soon as nationalist organization had succeeded in transcending local and provincial divisions, had united an urban élite with peasant discontents and reached for central power, the terms for collaboration swung progressively against the rulers. To keep control of a colony required more and more power-sharing, or else an ever-increasing metropolitan effort. Either way, costs and risks soon outweighed the dividends of colonialism until it became no longer worth while.

IV

And so, retreating in some places, advancing in others, imperialism sprawled its roving variances from Latin America to Australia, from China to Africa, changing degree and shape between formality and informality with endless flexibility. But did the various cases have anything in common? They all show the same international connections at work to a greater or lesser degree imperialistically. The linkages connecting the European and extra-European components obviously fall under three heads: first, the exchanges of European commodity and financial markets with preindustrial economies. A great part of these were transacted in the normal way of international business from private sector to private sector. Had they taken place in the best of all possible worlds of voluntary transfers untainted by imperialism, presumably they would still have pulled weaker economies into export–import complementarity, and influenced their politics in its favour. Again, the bulk of the capital transferred was invested by the European private shareholder in the bonds of autonomous or independent governments which, though dependent on one or two suppliers of long-term capital, were normally free to reject excessively onerous terms. Other things being equal, from a purely economic standpoint, any imperialistic effect of these exchanges must have been due more to the weakness and folly of borrowing governments than to the imperial conspiracies of the lenders. There was, however, in any case one such effect. Borrowers anxious to keep their loan status with European stock exchanges were wise to make their financial and economic policies conform to their creditors' requirements. Although capital transfers of this kind have been seen as intrinsically imperialistic by definition, they do not appear to deviate that much from normal international business practice today.

Power exerted by the imperial state which initiated the second set of imperial linkages, obviously distorted and exploited the unequal economic exchanges more or less imperialistically, though these were substantially out of its control. British imperial intervention, especially during the first three-quarters of the nineteenth century, acted as the auxiliary of expanding economy, breaking autarkic regimes open to European private enterprise, imposing free trade, promoting structural reform wherever necessary. By informal means if possible, by formal means if necessary, imperialism integrated new regions into international capitalist economy, providing local *pax* and strategic protection. But, increasingly after the 1850s European statesmen were just as much concerned to bring economic expansion into the service of imperial strategy as they were to serve economic expansion with imperial power. For instance, they encouraged or guaranteed a relatively small number of large loans intended to extract monopolistic concessions of economic resources from borrowing states and create such strong influence over their rulers as to turn their governments into instruments of imperial strategy. This was the case, for example, of the French Suez Canal Company, the Russian Chinese Eastern and German Baghdad railway concessions. It was even more so with Indian railway loans which, guaranteed on Indian tax revenues, tightened the imperial military grip on the sub-continent with bands of steel, at the same time binding its primary producers into the British industrial economy. For the rulers of states under informal influence, however, loan contracts were not so unequal when the lines built served to bring their own realms more tightly under centralized control. The endless debate as to whether imperialism is economically or politically motivated seems ultimately futile. It is clearly a reciprocal process whereby the banker and merchant exploited empire for maximum profit while the pro-consul exploited their business transactions for maximum imperial power. Over and above that, it was designed to extract its strength from other countries. Whether by subordinating alliance or colonial conscription, the military and financial resources of other states were absorbed into the imperial system, and so it mobilized and demonstrated its world power.

But, for all the initiating force of the metropolitan components in these economic and power relations, they produced such vastly different imperial effects in different countries as to suggest that imperial wealth and power were generated substantially through the third set of linkages which ran from top to bottom of local political economies. In the last analysis, imperialism gathered its forces from the local collaborative systems which translated European economic and power inputs into multiplied indigenous outputs. The character of local collaboration and resistance, the extent of national unification, decided the balance of inequalities and so the degree of imperialism involved.

According to the excentric view, therefore, the transfers of resources necessary for making formal and informal empire may be defined theoretically in terms of the international contracts required to mobilize these resources and redistribute their cost-benefits in the imperialists' favour. Bargains were more or less mutually agreeable or imposed unilaterally according to how far local economic and political markets tended towards, or were rigged in favour of, imperial oligopoly. Terms for formal and informal collaboration alike varied with the ratio between European inputs of wealth and power and the countervailing economic strength and nationalist opposition encountered, and they swung more or less unequally according to whether the weaker country had an alternative European protector and supplier, or not.[32]

The contracts which governed the rise and fall of Europe's colonial empires show these principles at work most clearly, for here inequalities achieved through monopoly were at their highest. The first contract was signed at international level in the European conventions which insulated a colony from interference by other great powers and gave the rulers a monopoly of its international relations. The second was dictated at metropolitan level, requiring pro-consuls to build empire out of local resources with minimal European aid. The third is found at local level in the collaborative arrangements which extracted a colonial administration's recurrent costs, provided its subordinate authorities and, in many instances, placed large armies at the disposal of the imperial state without expense to the metropole, and helped to defend it in Europe and the world at large. At local level, the colonial rulers' monopoly tended to be, but was not necessarily, economic. Above all, it was that of central arbiter in local politics between factions and communities that had yet to achieve a national organization. Except under these conditions, formal empires were likely to prove unprofitable. Without monopolies at local and international levels, costs rose swiftly out of all proportion to benefits, and in the breaking of these monopolies the colonial empires eventually fell.

A change of terms at one level involved a corresponding alteration of contracts on the others, and cost-benefits were redistributed accordingly throughout the system. At metropolitan level, the tolerances varied with the financial and military cost of colonial upkeep, the supposed economic benefit, and the balance of imperial and anti-imperial sentiment. The commitment of men and money in the metropolitan contract affected the colonial administrator's bargaining power with resisting subjects, and the degree of colonial resistance, in turn, tested metropolitan willingness to coerce or concede. At local level, the problems for rulers was one of how much power to share with subjects in exchange for their co-operation; for the subjects, the question was how much non-cooperation would elicit the maximum share of power. Between the two extremes, the outcome depended not only on the metropolitan commitment, but also on the depth of colonial intervention in peasant affairs: the demands for development, land, labour, taxes, and the resistance thus provoked. In this way, the existence of colonial empire depended on the possibilities of translating its contracts on one level into terms acceptable on the others.

After 1940 the task became more and more intractable, and the model went into reverse. As the weight of Europe in regional power balances dwindled, its collective security for colonial empire disappeared. Rhetorically at least, the Americans called for a swift approach to colonial self-determination, which encouraged nationalists in the colonies to demand the same. The imperialists' monopoly of their colonies' international relations was at an end.[33] At the same time, in South and South-East Asia national organization, which the British had suppressed in India and the Japanese had promoted in Indo-China, Burma and Indonesia during the war, emerged strongly enough to break the imperial monopoly of central arbitration in local politics. To keep control now required either a virtual concession of power or a prohibitive metropolitan military effort which, in India and Burma at least, the war-weary British public under the Labour government could not tolerate. They transferred power precipitately, or resigned from retrieving it, in fear of impending anarchy and civil war. In the Indian case, it was the local contract for continuation that could not be translated into metropolitan and international terms any longer.[34]

In the transfers of colonial power in tropical Africa, however, it was an improved metropolitan contract designed in the light of new international conditions, that could not be translated eventually into colonial terms. In 1947 nationalist organization had barely begun in British tropical African colonies; the monopoly of central arbitration appeared to be intact, although economic discontent with inflation and shortages left over from wartime mobilization was seething. Alarmed at a riot in the Gold Coast, the British began to prepare their colonies for democratic self-government, and introduced the ballot box in West Africa on the theory that liberal concessions would prolong colonial rule. In any event, after India and Palestine, the British electorate, and doubtless the Americans, also wanted no more colonial troubles. The attempt to democratize colonial government gradually from below swiftly manufactured popular national movements, and after breaking their own monopoly of central colonial politics, the imperialists could not have stopped the transfer of power had they wished to do so. Hence a metropolitan 'new deal' in local collaboration for purposes of developing the colonies economically was translated into terms of political independence. Considering international circumstances and

British opinion, it appeared that nationalism would accomplish the purposes of imperialism by cheaper, and far more effective, means.[35] Thus the colonial state which had come into existence by manipulating, reforming and unifying indigenous economic and political structures, was inevitably nationalized through its own dynamic. The excentric idea in this way attempts to extend imperial theory from the rise to the fall of colonialism through the reversal of a single model.

V

Coming at last to the possibilities of imperialism after empire in theory,[36] it seems reasonable to conclude that the model of formal imperialism is irrelevant to the post-colonial era, at least for the time being. There is, of course, Afghanistan, but it is not likely that it has been occupied for the sake of empire on the cheap. Until the great powers agree on new partitions, which is a possibility, the conditions for creating the international and local monopolies required for the unequal contracts of colonial empire do not exist. Nor do the great powers, which are now so much greater than they were, have any need of the comparatively insignificant increments of wealth and power to be extracted from colonial empire. They may yet embark upon it involuntarily as the Europeans often did, but if they do, the cost-benefits will look ridiculous. And, since the word 'imperialism' is associated in theory with formal empire, a more precise definition of whatever is still going on in the post-colonial era is required.

Those historians who doubt the existence of an 'imperialism' of free trade may be wrong as to the nineteenth century but right as regards the years since 1950. How far is the model of informal imperialism suggested above relevant to the postwar years? One of its essential elements was the use of gunboats to open countries for free trade, to enforce loan repayments and protect European merchants and concessions. Although gunboat diplomacy goes on, it is no longer required, as it once was, to integrate new regions into the international economy; but it may still be needed to integrate the 'Southern' regions into the Eastern socialist or the Western economy.

The use of foreign loans and military aid to weak states in return for commercial concessions and political alliance – another element in the informal model – obviously goes on manifold. On the other hand, the virtual European world monopoly of overseas trade and investment that once made foreign free-trade contracts so imperialistic in effect has, perhaps, no parallel today. It could be argued that since there is competition in the foreign-aid market, weak states have a choice of creditors and foreign alliances, and even non-alignment; and this is true. The grossly unequal contracts of the old monopolistic type of informal imperialism no longer apply. Nor are the political and potentially imperialistic dividends as sure or as enduring. It could be argued that foreign aid represents a genuine transfer of resources for purposes of constructing the economy of the recipient country, not for extracting wealth from it. Again, many weak states have their own internal resources of capital, and so are less dependent than they were in the nineteenth century. It is said that, in competing to give aid, the great powers have embarked on a struggle for the hearts and minds, not the economic resources, of the 'South'. At bottom, however, that was exactly what the imperialism of free trade was all about.

On the other hand, a good case for defining foreign aid as a type of informal imperialism can be made. In spite of the competition, the United States is by far the largest capital exporter. Without its contributions, the international aid agencies would be much the poorer; in the case of large development loans, the Western alliance negotiates with weak states in consortia; almost all loans have explicit economic and implicit political conditions attached; and they are normally intended to create collaboration in the domestic politics, foreign and economic policy of the recipients. Weak states can choose between the West, or the East, whose conditions are equally stringent and whose objects are the same.

Like the foreign loans of Europe to the Ottoman Empire and North Africa, aid is accompanied by financial, technical and military advisers, and since its scale dwarfs that of the nineteenth century, it tends to influence and corrupt administration and politics in weak countries to a correspondingly greater extent. One other comparison with the age of imperialism may be made. Then, the channels of international investment normally proceeded from the private investor through European stock exchanges to overseas governments in search of private profit; now, the bulk of the international transfers pass from donor government to recipient government. Hence, the opportunities for using foreign investment for purposes of informal imperialism have increased enormously. A considerable proposition, however, is also transferred by multinational companies who presumably do so in the old-fashioned way. In so far as the international capitalist system can be identified with the Western alliance, it appears to show manifest imperialistic tendencies of an informal type. The same could be said of its world rivals. If this thesis holds good, it may well be that new scrambles for the South are now in process in sporadic fashion, though much more marginally perhaps than the old ones.

The great powers, nevertheless, have had comparatively little success in intervening directly in the affairs of weak states by means of military coercion or economic sanctions compared with powers of smaller stature with a comparatively strong position in the various regional balances of power. This suggests that the lack of accommodation between American, Soviet and Chinese strategies ensures that none of them dominate the regional balances as effectively as the European Concert once did. It also suggests that in spite of vast nuclear inequality, the technological gap between strong and weak states in conventional capabilities, like the institutional gap in national organization, has narrowed compared with disparities between Europe and the South in the imperial age. The reduction of these inequalities, together with political independence, have increased the costs and risks of direct foreign intervention enormously. By the same token, the bargaining position of weak states in international relations generally has greatly improved. On the other hand, it could be argued that the successful interventions of such states as Israel, South Africa, Vietnam and Cuba, if not those of India, are cases of sub-imperialism.

Existing theories of imperialism for the post-colonial period have fundamental defects from a historical point of view, particularly those of neo-colonialism and the imperialism of the international capitalist economy. They all assume the continuation of imperialism from the colonial period; and thereby, they imply that it is of the same kind. The assumptions are interesting; but in projecting the classical theories which were designed to explain the rise of European empire into the post-colonial era, they take no account of the fall of colonial empire or the triumphs of colonial nationalism.

Any revised theory of imperialism must incorporate a theory of the colonial state with a theory of colonial nationalism, and so account for the coming of independence. Only then can it be extended into the post-colonial period. The excentric hypothesis suggested above is one of the first attempts to approach this task.

The basic idea is simple. Imperialism is conceived in terms of the play of international economic and political markets in which degrees of monopoly and competition in relations at world, metropolitan and local levels decide its necessity and profitability. In an integrating world containing gross inequalities of wealth and power, comparatively weak societies need the help of a 'big brother' for their domestic economic development and external protection, even if they do not want one. During the classic age of imperialism, the powers of Europe were able to work the international balance in conjunction with the expanding economy to ensure that every little brother had only one 'big brother'; and so long as little brother collaborated, the big brother could take over his domestic affairs and foreign relations, where it was profitable or necessary to do so. Imperialism was a relatively marginal activity of Europe's competing national business and state systems in the world at large; but from the standpoint of little brother, it involved colonial state-building in some form or other, which eventually projected his countervailing national organization, and his takeover of the colonial states.

Little brother was able to do this during sweeping changes in the international balance of wealth and power and, as a result, he now has a choice of several big brothers. He is usually in a better position to exploit his choices in the world's economic and political markets. These are still dominated by even more powerful systems of expansion; but the South is much more marginal to the continental systems of East and West than it was to the old European world system. Big brothers have relatively less need to exploit little brothers than formerly. The competition between big brothers, moreover, means that independent little brothers' affairs are no longer at the disposal of the effective national monopolies that made the old imperialism profitable, except at unacceptable risk and cost.

These fundamental alterations in the bargaining position of weaker societies as compared with the colonial era, suggest certain conclusions. First, if nationalism is indeed the continuation of imperialism by other means, it is imperialism of an altogether different species. A continuation of the previous beast in the revolutionized habitat seems unlikely. Secondly, the competing world systems of the post-colonial era tend to consolidate the political and economic independence of weak states, rather than undermine it, because where one expanding world system aims at destabilizing its independence, there is usually a competing world system striving to stabilize it. To fail in consolidating little brother's national organization and economic growth opens the way for the other side. Thirdly, it is said that the international capitalist economy has developed an imperialism of its own, and this is true, both in the use of the transfer of resources for purposes of informal imperialism, and in the sense of 'World Bank imperialism', of proliferating the principles and institutions of good capitalist management into little brother's organization. But there is enormous resistance, not to say inertia; and very few, if any, economic planners of either East or West have succeeded for long in dictating his policies or controlling his independence for foreign purposes. Many little brothers are not so little any more, many big brothers are not so big any more, and so, though it survives, this type of informal imperialism is usually very expensive, and its dividends, except in stabilizing independence, highly problematical.

Fourthly, what is much more significant is that this kind of economic imperialism can no longer be exploited as an instrument of any one national world strategy. In this sense, the expanding international economy has become detached from the expansive power strategies of rival world systems, whereas in the comparatively monopolistic European world system of the colonial era, national expanding economies more often than not served the purpose of extending national world power. Lastly, from the standpoint of the South, it must be obvious that the element of imperialism in their international relations has diminished out of all recognition in comparison with the colonial era.

Notes: Chapter 18

1 W. J. Mommsen, *Theories of Imperialism* (London, 1981), pp. 144–5.
2 Earlier formulations of this idea are given in J. Gallagher and R. Robinson, 'The imperialism of free trade, 1815–1914', *Economic History Review*, vol. 6 (1953), pp. 1–15, and R. Robinson, 'Non-European foundations of European imperialism: sketch for a theory of collaboration', in R. Owen and B. Sutcliffe (eds), *Studies in the Theory of Imperialism* (London, 1972), pp. 117–40. The historiographical setting of the notion is suggested in R. Robinson, 'Oxford in imperial historiography', in F. Madden and D. K. Fieldhouse (eds), *Oxford and the Idea of Commonwealth* (London, 1982), pp. 30–48.
3 See B. Semmel, *The Rise of Free Trade Imperialism: Classical Political Economy, the Empire of Free Trade and Imperialism, 1750–1850* (Cambridge, 1970); M. Barratt Brown, *The Economics of Imperialism* (Harmondsworth, Middx, 1974).
4 See J. A. Hobson, *Imperialism: A Study* (London, 1902); R. Hilferding, *Das Finanzkapital. Eine Studie über die jüngste Entwicklung des Kapitalismus* (Vienna, 1910); V. I. Lenin, *Imperialism, the Highest Stage of Capitalism* (London, 1916); G. W. F. Hallgarten, *Imperialismus vor 1914*, 2nd edn (Munich, 1963).
5 See J. A. Schumpeter, 'Zur Soziologie der Imperialismen', *Archiv für Sozialwissenschaft und Sozialpolitik*, vol. 46 (1918/19), pp. 1–39, 275–310; W. L. Langer, *The Diplomacy of Imperialism* (New York, 1935).

288 Imperialism and After

6   D. K. Fieldhouse, *Economics and Empire 1830–1914* (London, 1973).
7   See R. Robinson, 'Andrew Cohen and the transfer of power in tropical Africa, 1940–51', in W. H. Morris-Jones and G. Fischer (eds), *Decolonisation and After: The British and French Experience* (London, 1980), pp. 50–72.
8   R. Robinson and J. Gallagher, 'The partition of Africa', in F. H. Hinsley (ed.), *New Cambridge Modern History*, Vol. 11 (Cambridge, 1962), pp. 593–640.
9   See J. M. Ward, *Colonial Self-Government: The British Experience, 1759–1856* (London, 1976); G. Martin, *The Durham Report and British Policy* (Cambridge, 1972); A. G. Doughty (ed.), *The Elgin–Grey Papers* (Ottowa, 1937); P. Burroughs, 'The determinants of colonial self-government', *Journal of Imperial and Commonwealth History*, vol. 6 (1978), pp. 314–29.
10 See D. C. M. Platt, 'The imperialism of free trade: some reservations', *Economic History Review*, vol. 21 (1968), pp. 296–306; idem, 'Further objections to an "imperialism of free trade"', *Economic History Review*, vol. 26 (1973), pp. 77–91; idem, 'The national economy and British imperial expansion before 1914', *Journal of Imperial and Commonwealth History*, vol. 2 (1973), pp. 3–14.
11 See R. Robinson, 'European imperialism and indigenous reactions in British West Africa, 1880–1914', in H. L. Wesseling (ed.), *Expansion and Reaction* (Leiden, 1978), pp. 141–63.
12 See C. K. Webster, *Britain and the Independence of Latin America, 1812–1830: Select Documents* (Oxford, 1938); H. S. Ferns, *Britain and Argentina in the Nineteenth Century* (Oxford, 1960); D. C. M. Platt, *Finance, Trade and Politics in British Foreign Policy, 1815–1914* (Oxford, 1968); idem, *Latin America and British Trade, 1806–1914* (London, 1972).
13 See H. Blakemore, *British Nitrates and Chilean Politics, 1886–1896: Balmaceda and North* (London, 1974); P. Winn, 'British informal empire in Uruguay in the nineteenth century', *Past and Present*, no. 73 (1976), pp. 100–26; W. M. Mathew, 'The imperialism of free trade: Peru, 1820–70', *Economic History Review*, vol. 21 (1968), pp. 562–79; R. Graham, *Britain and the Onset of Modernization in Brazil, 1850–1914* (Cambridge, 1968); D. C. M. Platt (ed.), *Business Imperialism 1840–1930: An Inquiry Based on British Experience in Latin America* (Oxford, 1977).
14 See D. Roman, 'The contribution of imperial guarantees for colonial railway loans to the consolidation of British North America, 1847–65' (Oxford D. Phil. thesis, 1978); K. E. Wilburn, 'The climax of railway competition in South Africa, 1870–1899' (Oxford D. Phil. thesis, 1982).
15 ibid.
16 ibid.
17 See V. J. Puryear, *International Economics and Diplomacy in the Near East: A Study of British Commercial Policy in the Levant, 1834–53* (Stanford, Calif., 1935); Palmerston to Archland, 22 January 1841, quoted in C. K. Webster, *The Foreign Policy of Lord Palmerston* (London, 1951), Vol. 2, p. 751; H. C. Bell, *Lord Palmerston* (London, 1936), p. xiv.
18 M. Greenberg, *British Merchants and the Opening of China, 1800–42* (Cambridge, 1951); N. A. Pelcovits, *Old China Hands and the Foreign Office* (New York, 1948).
19 See R. Owen, *Cotton and the Egyptian Economy, 1820–1914* (Oxford, 1969); D. S. Landes, *Bankers and Pashas: International Finance and Economic Imperialism in Egypt* (London, 1958).
20 R. H. Davison, *Reform in the Ottoman Empire, 1839–76* (Princeton, NJ, 1963); W. R. Polk and R. L. Chambers, *Beginnings of Modernisation in the Middle East: The Nineteenth Century* (Chicago, 1968); O. Köymen, 'The advent and consequences of Free Trade in the Ottoman Empire', *Etudes Balkaniques*, vol. 7 (1971), pp. 47–55.
21 Teng Ssu-yü and John K. Fairbank (comps), *China's Response to the West, a Documentary Survey, 1839–1923* (Cambridge, Mass., 1954), p. 5.
22 See C. F. Remer, *Foreign Investments in China* (New York, 1933); R. F. Dernberger, 'The role of the foreigner in China's economic development, 1840–1949', in D. H. Perkins (ed.), *China's Modern Economy in Historical Perspective* (Stanford, Calif., 1975), pp. 19–48; D. McLean, 'Commerce, finance and British diplomatic support in China, 1885–6', *Economic History Review*, vol. 26 (1973), pp. 464–76.
23 W. G. Beasley, *Great Britain and the Opening of Japan, 1834–58* (London, 1951); A. M.

Craig, *Chōshū in the Meiji Restoration* (Princeton, NJ, 1961); J. K. Fairbank *et al.*, *East Asia: The Modern Transformation* (Cambridge, Mass., 1965).

24 See J. Ganiage, *L'Expansion coloniale de la France: les origines du protectorat Français en Tunisie* (Paris, 1959); C. Martin, *Histoire de l'Algérie Française* (Paris, 1963); J.-L. Miège, *Le Maroc et l'Europe* (Paris, 1961–3).

25 A. S. Kanya-Forstner, *The French Conquest of the Western Sudan: A Study in French Military Imperialism* (Cambridge, 1969); T. C. Weiskel, *French Colonial Rule and the Baule Peoples: Resistance and Collaboration, 1889–1911* (Oxford, 1980); J. Iliffe, *A Modern History of Tanganyika* (Cambridge, 1979).

26 See R. Slade, *King Leopold's Congo* (London, 1962); R. Anstey, *King Leopold's Legacy: The Congo under Belgian Rule* (Oxford, 1966); J. Stengers, 'La Belgique et la Congo, politique coloniale et decolonisation', in *Histoire de la Belgique Contemporaine, 1940–70* (Brussels, 1974).

27 J. S. Galbraith, 'Origins of the British South Africa Company', in J. E. Flint and G. Williams (eds), *Perspectives of Empire* (London, 1973), pp. 148–71; T. Ranger, *Revolt in Southern Rhodesia, 1896–7* (Manchester, 1967); R. Robinson and J. Gallagher, with A. Denny, *Africa and the Victorians: The Official Mind of Imperialism* (London, 1961), pp. 234–53.

28 J. Gallagher, G. Johnson and A. Seal (eds), *Locality, Province and Nation: Essays on Indian Politics, 1870–1940* (Cambridge, 1973); C. Baker, G. Johnson and A. Seal, *Power, Profit and Politics* (Cambridge, 1981); A. Seal, *The Emergence of Indian Nationalism* (Cambridge, 1968); B. R. Tomlinson, 'India and the British Empire, 1880–1935', *Indian Economic and Social History Review*, vol. 12 (1975), pp. 339–81.

29 A. Clayton, 'The French military in Africa', Oxford Commonwealth History Seminar paper.

30 See A. H. M. Kirk-Greene, *Principles of Native Administration in Nigeria: Select Documents, 1900–47* (Oxford, 1965); M. Perham, *Native Administration in Nigeria* (Oxford, 1937); D. Kimble, *A Political History of Ghana, 1850–1928* (Oxford, 1963). For examples elsewhere, see D. A. Low, *Buganda and British Over-rule* (Oxford, 1960); G. Bakheit, 'British administration and Sudanese nationalism' (Cambridge PhD thesis, 1966); C. D. Cowan, *Nineteenth-Century Malaya: The Origins of British Political Control* (London, 1961).

31 See note 28 above.

32 See as a case study: J. Osterhammel, 'Imperialism in transition: British business and the Chinese authorities, 1931–37', *China Quarterly*, no. 98 (June 1984), pp. 260–86.

33 W. R. Louis, *Imperialism at Bay: The United States and the Decolonization of the British Empire, 1941–45* (Oxford, 1977); idem, *The British Empire in the Middle East: Arab Nationalism, the United States and Postwar Imperialism, 1945–51* (Oxford, 1984).

34 D. Rothermund, 'Constitutionalist reform versus nationalist agitation in India, 1900–1950', *Journal of Asian Studies*, vol. 21 (1961/2), pp. 505–22; R. J. Moore, *The Crisis of Indian Unity, 1917–1940* (Oxford, 1974); B. R. Tomlinson, *The Indian National Congress and the Raj: The Penultimate Phase, 1929–42* (London, 1976); N. Mansergh, with E. Lumby and P. Moon (eds), *Constitutional Relations between Britain and India: The Transfer of Power* (London, 1970 ff.), 12 vols to date.

35 See Robinson, 'Andrew Cohen'; W. R. Louis and R. Robinson, 'The United States and the end of British Empire in tropical Africa, 1941–1951', in P. Gifford and W. R. Louis (eds), *The Transfer of Power in Africa: Decolonization 1940–1960* (New Haven, Conn. and London, 1982), pp. 31–55.

36 The author acknowledges his debt for several points in the last section to Professor Hedley Bull's paper given to the Oxford Commonwealth History Seminar in 1980.

19 Semi-Colonialism and Informal Empire in Twentieth-Century China: Towards a Framework of Analysis

JÜRGEN OSTERHAMMEL

Historians studying colonialism in a comparative perspective would be well advised not to neglect modern East Asia. The case of Japanese-dominated Manchuria from 1931 to 1945 provides an almost unique example of large-scale industrial development under colonial rule,[1] whereas the British Crown Colony of Hong Kong embodies a special type of 'peripheral capitalism' flourishing under a free-trade regime.[2] The eighteen provinces that form China proper were, of course, never subjected to alien domination. China by and large maintained its own currencies, conducted its own foreign affairs and received recognition as a sovereign member of the international community. It was even elevated to the rank of one of the four 'big policemen' in Franklin D. Roosevelt's vision of the postwar global order.[3] Unlike the average colonized people which, according to David Fieldhouse, 'lost whatever collective identity it might previously have possessed',[4] the overwhelming majority of the Chinese held on to their time-honoured little traditions, while the 'modern' élites, however eagerly they embraced Western ways of life and thought, never abandoned their native language and a cultural frame of reference which remained genuinely Chinese.

Still, China provides a most variegated assortment of historical phenomena which have been subsumed under the heading of 'imperialism' by writers of widely differing theoretical persuasions:[5]

- foreign territorial enclaves, other than colonies, beyond the jurisdiction and effective control of the Chinese government (leased territories, concessions, settlements);
- extraterritoriality and consular jurisdiction which placed nationals of the treaty powers out of reach of Chinese law throughout the country;
- sizeable expatriate communities maintaining their own socio-cultural infrastructures;
- discrimination, often with a racist tinge, against the local population in areas of foreign settlement;
- foreign naval forces plying freely in China's coastal and inland waters;

Informal Empire in China 291

- foreign troops stationed in the national capital and guarding other major concentrations of foreign property;
- repeated forcible intervention in Chinese domestic affairs ranging from the casual deployment of a gunboat to underscore a point made by foreign diplomacy to war-like 'punitive' expeditions;
- the most atrocious war for colonial subjugation fought in modern history (1937–45);
- infringements upon the ability of the Chinese government to implement economic and financial policies of its own (absence of tariff autonomy until 1930, monopoly clauses in the treaties, and so on);
- far-reaching control over foreign trade by expatriate business houses;
- direct foreign investments in mining, manufacturing, transport, public utilities, and so on, in some cases leading to foreign domination of particular sectors and branches of the indigenous economy;
- operations of transnational corporations via their own subsidiaries;
- control by foreign banks over vital foreign-exchange transactions;
- large-scale loans, given under conditions unfavourable to China, many of which were never applied to productive uses and whose repayment constituted a drain on national wealth;
- massive indemnity obligations imposed as a result of China's military defeats;
- *de facto* foreign control over some of the most important revenue-collecting agencies (maritime customs, salt administration);
- railway construction with foreign capital, according to foreign plans and under foreign technical supervision;
- foreign railway property on Chinese soil (Chinese Eastern Railway, South Manchurian Railway, Yunnan Railway);
- a pattern of foreign trade whereby agricultural and mineral products were exchanged for manufactured goods (mainly consumer goods);
- sporadic dislocation and destruction of indigenous handicraft production and rural industries through imports of manufactured goods and marketing of the output of foreign factories located in the Chinese treaty ports;
- development of export-oriented sectors highly dependent on the vicissitudes of overseas demand (tea, silk, soya beans, tungsten, antimony, tin, and so on);
- emergence of indigenous collaborating élites ('comprador bourgeoisie', puppet regimes in the 1930s and 1940s);
- disruption of the local socio-cultural fabric by the proselytizing activities of foreign missionaries;
- institutions of higher education funded and run by foreigners (mainly missionaries);
- presence of foreign military and economic advisers in positions which allowed them to influence the Chinese government and put pressure on it;
- large-scale emigration of surplus labour, often suffering exploitation in metropolitan (United States) and peripheral (South-East Asian, Latin American) economies.

Theories

Some of these individual aspects have been carefully studied, others remain virtually unresearched. Generally speaking, work on imperialism and China falls into two distinct categories. On the one hand, scholars have devoted much attention to China as an object of great power politics. The guiding questions have been: What were the subjective motives of policy-makers and the objective driving forces in the metropolitan countries (or rather, a particular metropolitan country) that spurred them on to the path of expansion to the Far East? What inter-power rivalries resulted in the East Asian region and how were they resolved? How did the powers acquire their possessions, privileges and interests in China and how did they attempt (more or less successfully) to assert political, economic and cultural influence and control? While the Chinese side has by no means been neglected, its behaviour has mainly been discussed in terms of the Chinese 'response to the West' which tends to be seen as determined by the cultural traditions of 'Confucian' China. Only recently have attempts been made to break away from the action-response paradigm and to link the various levels of interaction between China and the imperialist powers.[6]

On the other hand, historians and social scientists have addressed themselves to the effects of China's piecemeal incorporation into the modern world system on the country's socio-economic structures. The principal concern has been with the reasons for China's decline into relative economic backwardness during the nineteenth and twentieth centuries. It is now widely accepted that China, as late as in the second half of the eighteenth century, 'stood out as a prosperous looking giant among the multitude of premodern societies',[7] well endowed with many of the natural and human resources that economists have identified as prerequisites of sustained economic growth. Why then, by the early twentieth century, should it be a poor and manifestly underdeveloped country?[8] Most of the answers given so far[9] emphasize intrinsic impediments to economic development and social change, but at least for the time since the Opium War (1839–42) nearly all of them in some way also take account of extrinsic influences. Broadly speaking, the current debate is dominated by three basic lines of argument.

(1) The *oppression argument*,[10] mainly expounded by Marxists in China and elsewhere,[11] but also stock-in-trade of Chinese non-Marxist nationalism since Sun Yat-sen advanced his view of China as a 'hypo-colony',[12] has lately received fresh support from dependency and world system theorists.[13] Roughly, it runs like this: imperialist intrusion unbalanced the traditional economy and stifled its inherent developmental potentials (on the nature of which the authors disagree); genuine capitalism was not allowed to unfold; the Chinese state was weakened to the extent that it could not behave in a Gerschenkronian manner, that is, take the lead in economic development; the Chinese economy was partially reshaped to suit the needs of the metropolitan economies; a lopsided or even dualistic structure emerged with a foreign-dominated modern sector existing alongside a stagnant traditional sector that was not only exploited to provide

cheap export commodities, but was also penetrated and partly ruined by foreign manufactured goods. The class structure of Chinese society was deformed with a nascent bourgeoisie vacillating uneasily between 'national' and 'comprador' attitudes. Imperialism allied itself with indigenous landlord, merchant and usury capital and, in general, propped up the most backward and oppressive elements in Chinese society.

(2) Directly pitted against the oppressionists' denunciation of imperialism is the *modernization argument*. It had its heyday in the 1960s and early 1970s.[14] Although none of the writers associated with this argument would deny some deleterious effects of imperialism – such as wounding China's national pride – they generally believe that the 'input' of Western capital, Western technology and, above all, Western values was necessary, perhaps historically inevitable and at any rate beneficial to China. Late traditional China had reached a stage where a highly efficient but technologically stagnant economy was operating under increasingly severe demographic constraints, unable to achieve on its own strength a breakthrough into sustained growth. The Chinese had to be awakened from their slumber and imbued with the virtues of a dynamic West. The major problem with this argument is that it is very difficult to speak of thorough-going modernization during the century of intense involvement with the industrializing countries. To this, modernization theorists offer two answers. According to the cruder version, progress towards modernity was largely wiped out by 'extraneous' forces such as war and revolution; China allegedly was on the brink of a great leap forward when war broke out in July 1937.[15] According to the more refined version, it was all a matter of missed opportunities: had China possessed a vigorous and enlightened leadership comparable to that of Meiji Japan, it might have taken modernization into its own hands. As it was, however, the West offered a challenge which the Chinese élites failed to take up.[16]

(3) The *marginality argument*, a fairly recent addition to the debate, derives from an insight into the dilemmas of the modernization school of thought. Its exponents claim that foreign observers have allowed themselves either to be hoodwinked by the noisy lamentations of Chinese nationalists or to be deluded by an inflated and over-optimistic idea of the West's modernizing achievements at the periphery. By arguing that imperialism made no significant impact on China proper, the marginalists leave the debate between oppressionists and modernizationists suspended in mid-air. If the effects of imperialism were slight or even negligible, the entire issue is much reduced in importance and attention turns to the question of why China managed so successfully to withstand foreign advances.[17] It is fascinating to see how one and the same historical phenomenon is adduced to support mutually exclusive readings of the evidence. The treaty ports have always been regarded by adherents of the oppressionist argument as the commanding heights of imperialist invasion, as funnels for goods and capital and as bridgeheads of metropolitan capitalism.[18] The marginalists turn this interpretation upside down. The existence of the treaty port system, the very confinement of foreign influence to selected areas, proves to them that China succeeded in throwing up dikes against the

imperialist tide. As Albert Feuerwerker concludes, 'very little of China was drawn into the pattern of development set by the Western-dominated treaty ports. The tenacity of the traditional economy and society, which reflected strength and integration within the constraints of the indigenous technology, that is, "development", left no vacuum for the foreigners to fill.'[19] One of the attractive features of the marginalist argument is its insistence on the uniqueness of China's historical experience – before 1949 and since. No attempt is made here to fit China into universal modernization patterns, nor to squeeze it into the moulds of Frankian or Wallersteinian global theory. Yet, the marginalist view is marred by a somewhat restricted understanding of imperialism and by its lack of answers to the questions of why such a supposedly highly sophisticated traditional society failed so signally to provide for the livelihood of a large part of its population, and why the Chinese since the turn of the century should have responded with a fierce, anti-imperialistic nationalism.[20]

At the present stage, the debate about the effects of imperialism on China cannot be expected to yield generally accepted results. One obvious methodological reason is that the contentious issues are bound up with value judgements which are unlikely to be brought into harmony by plain logic and scrupulous handling of the historical record. A second reason is that we simply do not know enough about the foreign presence in China. Much current theorizing merely consists in rearranging a limited number of facts and figures, sometimes culled from a handful of well-established secondary works, in the light of preconceived theories. As long as the authors of theoretical treatises do not claim to do more than suggest some general thoughts from which testable hypotheses can be derived, their efforts are helpful and welcome. If, however, they allow their works to be read as substantive answers to one of the most intriguing questions in modern history, many of them expose themselves to methodological criticism on at least four counts.

First, quite a number of contributions, mostly from the oppression and modernization schools of thought, are flawed by fallacious analogies. It is true, for example, that a significant amount of foreign capital was invested in mining in China proper. Yet, the foreign-dominated part of Chinese coal mining was by no means 'extraverted' toward the world market, while those mining sectors that were (tin, antimony, tungsten) had hardly any foreign capital invested in them. This has been widely misunderstood because it does not fit into the familiar pattern of mineral-exporting economies found elsewhere in the Third World. The inclination to dip into modern Chinese history and emerge with the results that theory has led one to expect has blinded some observers to the fact that, as Ulrich Menzel has pointed out, 'the penetration of China during the 19th and 20th centuries followed a pattern different from that of most other countries in the Third World'.[21]

Secondly, only very few authors take note of the diversity which characterized the foreign presence in, and the foreign impact on, China. Hence, hardly any interpretative work is as comprehensive as it purports to be. Rhoads Murphey, for instance, in his brilliant presentation of the marginalist argument, has a few pages on the relationship between foreign and native banks,[22] but is surprisingly reticent about the entire issue of foreign loans and indemnities which had a considerable influence on Chinese domestic finance and, consequently, on the stability and capability of the peripheral state.[23] Frances Moulder, advocating the oppression argument in a Wallersteinian guise, neglects, among other things, the spatial dimension of market penetration and the organization of Chinese domestic commerce, both of which would have alerted her to powerful impediments to penetration.[24]

Thirdly, a weak spot of much of the interpretative literature on imperialism in China is the failure to spell out specific connections between individual pieces of evidence. Arguments of the *post hoc ergo propter hoc* type abound, and temporal coincidence is often taken to indicate causation. Such cavalier treatment of explanatory problems pervades all lines of argument, but the oppressionist school is particularly susceptible to it. There is, indeed, abundant evidence of China's poverty and backwardness, of economic exploitation and political repression, of industrial stagnation and agrarian collapse. There is also, in spite of marginalist disclaimers, the fact of a very considerable foreign presence in China during the first half of the twentieth century. Yet, causal connections – or non-connections – between these two sets of data are more often than not asserted rather than proven. What remains to be shown is *where, when, how* and to what *effect* did *which* extraneous forces impinge upon the indigenous socio-economic system? Through what *mechanisms* were world market influences transmitted to the Chinese economy, and so on? The way to answer such questions would be, as Peter Robb has argued with regard to India, 'first to examine individual cases, asking in particular whether impediments were extrinsic or intrinsic, and second to assess the function and importance of each individual case to overall economic performance'.[25]

Fourthly, very few attempts have been made to link 'metropolis-oriented' to 'periphery-oriented' approaches. The imperialism of the diplomatic historians seems to be worlds apart from that of the sociologists and economic historians. While the former usually limit themselves to vague references to economic interests as perceived by policy-makers in chancelleries and foreign offices, the latter tend to treat politics and diplomacy as a given framework with some structural influences (effects of the treaty system) but hardly any operational ones on economy and society at the periphery.

Models

In order to avoid these pitfalls and deficiencies, conceptualizing work should be devoted to the elaboration of models on an intermediate level of abstraction between empirical research and grand theory. Such models – a model being 'a more or less schematic conceptional representation of a complex system'[26] – would

- help to identify the elements that made up the foreign establishment in China and to establish hypothetical connections between them;
- help to pinpoint areas on the Chinese side where an impact of extrinsic forces could be expected, and to establish hypothetical cause-and-effect relationships;
- serve the heuristic task of loosely structuring a field of study so as to provide a flexible framework for detailed research;
- like James N. Rosenau's 'pre-theories' of international relations, allow for a 'preliminary processing' of empirical material;[27]
- be open to be modified by the results of empirical investigation;
- be primarily descriptive, but would indicate crucial connections between factors that might be suitable for explanatory treatment;
- use categories wide enough to be applicable to historical cases basically similar to that of China (especially 'semi-colonies' like Persia, Siam, or the Ottoman Empire), thus preparing the ground for comparative analysis.

The classic theories of imperialism offer the notion of 'semi-colonialism', a label that has been applied to China ever since without much regard for its potential theoretical implications. For Lenin, semi-colonialism is not a clearly defined mode of imperialist control, but a 'transitional form'[28] on the way towards outright colonial takeover. Semi-colonialism, in this sense, is a somewhat deficient colonialism, short of overt political domination but, under certain circumstances, opening outlets for metropolitan capital which might exceed those provided by straightforward colonies.[29] In discussing the prospects for China, J. A. Hobson went into more speculative detail than Lenin. In one of several scenarios, he anticipated a *joint* invasion of China by the financiers of the great powers.[30] Writing at a time when China seemed to be on the brink of partition, Hobson prophetically envisaged the possibility of a co-operative *mise en valeur* of China's resources under conditions of formal sovereignty. Semi-colonialism in this sense would be an enduring state of affairs rather than a prelude to colonialization. Hobson, however, was more concerned with the repercussions of informal control over the periphery on the metropolitan countries than with its effects on the target areas.

Chinese Marxism adopted the Leninist term, but gave it a different twist. During the 'debate on Chinese social history' in the 1930s[31] it was made an integral part of a comprehensive theory of China's 'semi-feudal semi-colonial society'. The theory tried to make sense of a historical process in which 'feudalism' obviously disintegrated, but no significant transition to capitalism took place. A feudal system was penetrated, but not superseded, by colonialism, thus giving rise to a hybrid social formation that had not been anticipated by classical historical materialism. In a sustained attempt at original analysis, the economist Wang Yanan elaborated a kind of Chinese dependency theory which has so far not been duly appreciated by theorists in the West.[32] Wang neither used a crude impact-response model, nor did he set out from an analysis of individual sectors of the Chinese economy. Instead, he focused on the central categories of classical political economy – commodity value, price, capital, interest, profit, wage and rent – and attempted to trace their form under conditions of a traditional economy partly invaded by world market forces. His work, the fibre of which is oppressionist, is, of course, riddled with problems of attributing causes to effects. Yet, within the context of our present discussion, it is important to be aware of two of Wang's major contributions. First, he rejects the notion of a neatly demarcated 'foreign' or 'modern' sector, pointing instead to the numerous linkages that existed between foreign and domestic elements, to their tight concatenation and their frequent merging together.[33] Secondly, he takes up in a systematic way an argument widespread in the 1930s and 1940s: not only was indigenous collaboration essential for informal political control by the great powers to be successful, it was also a necessary concomitant of economic penetration. Indigenous collaboration is not just perceived as a type of political behaviour resulting from deliberate choice,[34] but as a structural element of China's interaction with the advanced capitalist countries. It is thus part of the very definition of a 'semi-feudal semi-colonial society'. The interests of its ruling classes – the big landlords, compradors and bureaucrats – are not in every instance necessarily identical with those of the foreigners, but these classes still base their political power and economic prosperity on imperialism.[35]

Next to Marxist reflections on 'semi-colonialism', the other significant stepping stone towards a model of China's interaction with the advanced capitalist countries is the concept of 'informal empire'. It owes much of its appeal to its inherent ambiguity. At least two readings of it are possible. According to the first one, informal empire, or rather informal imperialism, marks a mode of expansion: free trade plus the more or less forcible opening up of secluded agrarian societies. In this sense, the notion lies at the heart of Ronald Robinson's and John Gallagher's famous continuity thesis.[36] In other words, it is part of an evolutionary model of imperialism. The second reading, towards which Ronald Robinson himself seems to shift in his most recent contributions,[37] emphasizes informal empire – as opposed to formal empire – as an ideal type, that is, as a conceptual tool of, potentially, universal applicability. It thus describes a specific manner of exercising superiority in asymmetrical relationships between societies or nations.

Following Robinson and building upon his suggestions, some basic features of the ideal type of informal empire can be discerned:

(1) A power differential exists between two countries[38] and is exploited by the stronger country (henceforth S) in pursuit of its own real or perceived interests in the weaker country (henceforth W).
(2) S avoids direct rule over W, but possesses effective veto power over its domestic policy-making, intervening against any attempt to infringe upon its real or perceived interests in that particular country.
(3) S has the capability to impose basic guidelines for foreign-policy orientation on W, ideally including it in asymmetrical alliances which are controlled by the hegemonial centre.
(4) S maintains some sort of military establishment in W and/or is in a

position to bring influence to bear on *W*'s armed forces (through military aid, advisers, and so on).
(5) Nationals of *S* maintain a substantial economic establishment in *W*, consisting of various types of businesses ranging from agency houses to subsidiaries of multinational corporations.
(6) Foreign actors are monopolistically or quasi-monopolistically entrenched in those sectors of *W*'s economy that show above-average rates of growth; the basic economic decisions concerning the allocation of resources in these sectors are taken by foreigners.
(7) Public finance in *W* is to a significant extent controlled by foreign private and/or government banks; this control may be used to enforce political compliance.
(8) *W* is a net recipient of capital (business and portfolio investment).
(9) *S*'s hold over the inferior nation is supported by the collaboration of indigenous rulers and comprador groups; 'big brother' reserves the right to intervene in struggles for power, supporting contenders of his choice.
(10) Indigenous collaborators partly or completely share a common 'cosmology' with the political and economic élites of the superior nation.

Admittedly, this is a fairly restrictive definition of informal empire as an ideal type, and historians and theorists of international relations should consider carefully whether or not all of the ten conditions suggested above are of equal importance and have to be met for any one individual case to be classified as a concrete manifestation of informal empire. It may well be that the ten conditions can be understood as constituting a sliding scale which would allow special features of particular historic cases to be pinpointed and contrasted with similar or related ones. It may also be possible to arrive at a sub-typology of various forms of informal empire. In any case, an ideal type does not claim to describe empirical reality; rather it is a heuristic instrument constructed with the deliberate intention of representing as precisely as possible those aspects of empirical phenomena which seem to be the most significant in the light of the analyst's intention. Therefore, informal empire as defined above will be encountered in a pure and complete form only under exceptional circumstances. What is of interest to the historian is the degree of approximation towards the ideal type which can be detected through a careful examination of the empirical evidence in any individual case.

So far, this discussion has concentrated on the relationship between two countries or nations within a dyadic structure characterized by fundamental asymmetries. To this vertical dimension must be added the horizontal one. From the perspective of the theory of imperialism the emphasis falls on *informal*, and the basic contrast is that with formal empire. Yet, from the point of view of the theory of international relations, 'imperial' relationships must be distinguished from other types of asymmetry, above all from hegemonial structures.[39] In what sense is it justifiable to speak of informal *empire*? Part of the answer seems to lie in the idea of economic dependency, defined mainly in terms of the locus of decision-making. As Peter

Winn has written, reflecting on the case of Uruguay in the nineteenth century, informal empire means 'the integration of a peripheral area into the economy of an industrial power in a relationship of dependence, one in which the strategic decisions governing the direction and rate of growth of the "informal colony" are made by the imperial power and governed by its own interests'.[40] Ronald Robinson's idea of 'unequal contracts' which secure monopolies of political and economic decision-making points in the same direction. To this, a second condition should be added: informal empire should be viewed not only in functional, but also in institutional terms. It involves the existence in the peripheral area of a foreign establishment, a 'bridgehead' in Johan Galtung's term,[41] consisting of a differentiated system of business firms *and* political-military agencies (the proconsul-type of diplomat, a naval squadron, troops or police forces under foreign command, and so on) capable of translating potential superiority into effective influence and control. In contrast to theories of dependency and unequal development, which are chiefly concerned with structures, the concept of informal empire, having grown from historiographical concerns, gives equal weight to actors. The 'men on the spot', so often adduced in explaining imperial takeovers, should not be omitted from an analysis of the actual working of empire, formal and informal alike.

There are numerous cases that are suitable to illustrate the theoretical ideas outlined so far. That of China can, at this particular point, be approached in two different ways.

First, the ideal type of informal empire can be confronted with reality as it presents itself to the historian, the degree of approximation of reality to the various features of the ideal type can be assessed and the question answered whether or not it is possible to apply the concept of 'informal empire' to the historical phenomenon under consideration. Proceeding in this way, Britten Dean, for instance, has argued that there was no British informal empire in China before 1870,[42] while David McLean and Peter J. Cain claim there was one in the two decades leading up to the First World War.[43] Secondly, it is possible to take up the suggestion made earlier and build a model on an intermediate level of abstraction that takes important features from the ideal type of informal empire but, at the same time, already incorporates basic characteristics of the Chinese situation. The purpose of such a model is heuristic; it is partly a research programme, partly a general framework that helps to interconnect results of empirical research in a systematic way. It will be open to interpretation in the light of several 'grand theories'.

Informal Empire in Modern China: Sketch of a Model

The history of imperialism in China spans the eleven decades from the Opium War to the elimination of Western influence in 1949/50. It was a story that began with the imposition of the treaty system,[44] went through a phase of slow commercial and missionary encroachment, accelerated after 1895 with a multinational invasion, peaked in Japan's war of conquest and ended in an uneasy entanglement of the antagonists in a civil war with the two remaining world powers which were increasingly locked in global conflict. Within this history, the twenty years between the collapse of the monarchy in 1911 and Japan's take-over of the north-eastern provinces in 1931 marked the high point of foreign informal influence.[45]

In spite of frequent inter-power tensions, until the Manchurian Crisis of 1931/2, imperialism in China was fundamentally a co-operative venture. Most-favoured nation treatment spread the benefits of foreign acquisitions evenly among the treaty powers; financiers banded together in banking consortia; the International Settlement at Shanghai – the linchpin of the foreign establishment – was ruled by a cosmopolitan merchant oligarchy; intervention in Chinese domestic affairs was often undertaken jointly by the Diplomatic Body in Peking. Above all, the powers were unanimous in warding off Chinese resistance and Chinese nationalist aspirations, as happened in the Eight-Power Expedition against the Yihetuan (the 'Boxers') in 1900/1, at the Versailles Peace Conference in 1919, at the Washington Conference of 1921/2 and at the Peking Tariff Conference of 1926. Informal empires of the major powers coexisted within the borders of an unpartitioned China and were by no means as neatly delimited as the various agreements about spheres of interest seemed to suggest. Thus, a strong case can be made for grouping together, for analytical purposes, the various metropolitan countries into one 'centre' confronting an equally undifferentiated 'periphery'. Yet, China was an enormously variegated country in terms of social conditions and economic development even before extrinsic forces imposed some kind of 'structural heterogeneity'[46] on to it. On the other hand, each of the major imperialist countries was goaded into expansion by specific driving forces at a specific time following a specific schedule and using a specific mixture of methods of building its position of influence and domination. Though they frequently overlapped and interacted, the various foreign establishments displayed characteristic features of their own. After the First World War Britain and Japan were the only powers possessing formal colonies (Hong Kong, Taiwan), while Germany and the Soviet Union did not even enjoy the privileges accruing from the unequal treaties (above all extraterritoriality). France, the United States and Britain maintained a strong missionary presence, something totally absent from the Japanese set-up and almost absent from the Russian one even before the Revolution. Japan and France were in possession and control of substantial railways, while some of the other powers merely had a tenuous financial hold over Chinese lines. These and other factors can be taken together to form 'profiles of interest' for each nation having a stake in China.[47]

China being primarily important as a market for manufactured goods and as a source of primary commodities, economic interests, as a rule, took priority over strategic or cultural interests. Consequently, we can assume the existence of a *business system* to be the core of each of the major national foreign establishments. It comprised the firms operating in the China market from their own offices in the treaty ports. A business system can be perceived in four analytical dimensions:

(1) The sectoral dimension. It refers to the sectoral distribution of foreign investment. In the 1920s and early 1930s, for example, Britain and Japan maintained widely diversified business systems in China which included banking, export–import, manufacturing, mining, shipping and public utilities in areas of foreign settlement. By contrast, the United States and Germany – in the early 1930s the most dynamic trading nations in China – had geared their business investments almost exclusively to the requirements of commerce, with transport, manufacturing and mining ranking low. At the other end of the spectrum, France maintained an investment profile with a marked colouring of pre-1914 financial imperialism. While in 1931 it contributed only 5·8 per cent of the business investments in China (including Manchuria) and while the share of the entire French Empire in China's foreign trade was in 1936 no higher than 5·6 per cent, France held some 23 per cent of China's foreign loan obligations, all of which had been contracted before 1914.[48]

(2) The institutional dimension. This covers the types of enterprises involved and invites the application of the business historian's analytical tools. Some issues are of particular interest: the fate of the nineteenth-century agency houses, the growth of large multi-sector China firms (Jardine, Matheson & Company, Butterfield & Swire), the role of multinational corporations since the turn of the century (Standard Oil, Asiatic Petroleum, British-American Tobacco Corporation, Imperial Chemical Industries, Unilever, I. G. Farben, Siemens, the Japanese *zaibatsu*, and so on), the function of foreign banks in relation to the financing of trade and industry, the political leverage of different types of companies (largely dependent upon their standing in metropolitan politics and the efficiency of pressure groups), and so on.

(3) The spatial dimension. 'Oppressionists' claim to detect foreign economic activities almost everywhere, and 'marginalists' see them confined to an irrelevant fringe. But the actual geographical distribution of the various business systems is far from clear. At what places were foreign firms represented and how strongly in terms of staff and fixed assets? How important were the individual treaty ports for the operation of foreign enterprise? Which factors determined the location of business interests? The geography of penetration has still largely to be written.

(4) The diachronic dimension. Each business system had its own history of quantitative growth and qualitative change. The history of the British business system in China, for example, can roughly be divided into two major periods. Up to the 1890s the agency houses, the earliest form of British private enterprise in the Far East, underwent a process of functional differentiation: functions such as finance and insurance, that had originally been within the scope of a bigger agency house, were taken over by specialist institutions such as banks and insurance companies. During the same period the gradual opening of the interior provinces to foreign trade gave rise to foreign shipping companies, while the growth of Shanghai and a few other large treaty ports created a demand for services which public utility companies stepped in to satisfy. From the mid-1890s onwards, three new elements were incorporated into the British business system: factories, coal

mines and subsidiaries of multinational corporations.[49] By 1914, the system was complete as far as its basic pattern was concerned. Thereafter, no new element was added and growth took place largely within a given institutional framework. By contrast, Japanese expansion followed a different timetable. Japanese cotton manufacturing in China, for example, became prominent only after the end of the First World War, at first in Shanghai and Qingdao and by the mid-1930s attaining industrial hegemony in the Tianjin area, too.

Not all forms of commercial representation constitute a business system. The Belgians were heavily involved in railway financing and the Czechs in the arms trade; the Norwegians had a stake in Chinese shipping and the Italians in silk exports. But none of these countries maintained anything like a *system* of business interests in China, if by a system we mean an entity whose elements are more frequently engaged in relations with each other than with elements outside the system. In the British case, the system was integrated on three levels. First, there was a network of interlocking business transactions: coal of the semi-British Kailan Mining Administration in Hebei Province was shipped southwards in British vessels to be burnt in the furnaces of the Shanghai Power Company (British until 1930) which, in turn, sold electricity to British cotton mills and the British tramway company in Shanghai, and so on.[50] Secondly, British firms operated under British law, profited from the existence of British-controlled territories and enjoyed, in principle, though not always in practice, the active or tacit support of HM government. Thirdly, British firms in China organized themselves into interest groups and chambers of commerce. Socio-cultural affinity among the communities of expatriate Britons on the China coast was accompanied by a common representation of interests. In this sense of triple integration through the market, through imperial politics and through the articulation of interests, only Britain, Japan, France, the United States, Russia (before 1917) and Germany (except during the 1920s) can be said to have possessed business systems in China during the period from 1895 to 1937.

Relations between foreign business systems must be assessed in terms of competition and co-operation. In some cases, most notably that of the Western oil companies, which sold kerosene and gasolene to Chinese customers, cross-national co-operation amounted to an oligopolistic grip on the market. This became apparent during the Cantonese 'kerosene war' of 1933/4 when the companies used their combined economic strength to defeat an attempt by the province's government to exclude them from business in the south.[51] Market-sharing agreements existed, for example, between German and British chemical corporations. In other areas rivalry was tense. Thus in the early 1930s British companies faced stiff competition from Japan in the markets for sugar and cotton goods and from Germany in machines and railway equipment.

Foreign business systems have backward linkages to the world market and the respective metropolitan economy. This is a well-trodden path and it may suffice to make two preliminary points. First, international trade with East Asia, from the time of the shipments of Peruvian silver in exchange for luxuries demanded in Europe, has frequently followed a triangular or an even more complicated pattern. Hence, the analysis has to allow for cases other than that of simple bilateral exchange. Secondly, and partly resulting from this, a nation's trade *with* China, as documented in its foreign-trade statistics, is not identical with the commercial activities *in* China of that nation's business system. Up to the end of our period the major part of China's foreign trade was mediated through foreign firms, especially the internationally connected British, German and American houses. Although statistical corroboration is hard to find, circumstantial evidence suggests that at times the amount of foreign trade with third countries handled by British firms in Hong Kong and in the treaty ports at least equalled that of their transactions with the mother country.

Forward linkages from the foreign business systems to the indigenous socio-economic environment are to be analysed in terms of penetration. The notion is a tricky one, as it has frequently been used in a sloppy and undefined way to denote all sorts of foreign economic activities in a peripheral country, thereby glossing over significant differences. It does make a difference, for example, whether a market is supplied with imported goods through independent indigenous trading networks or through foreign-controlled distribution systems. In the latter case the chances for foreign firms to define the parameters of exchange are likely to be considerably higher. The term 'penetration' is sorely in need of theoretical precision and it should eventually be possible to distinguish between degrees and alternative patterns of penetration. There were, for example, three such patterns in the marketing of imported goods and of goods that originated in foreign factories and mines on Chinese territory:

(1) *Treaty port trade*. The goods were already taken up in the larger treaty ports by Chinese merchants who distributed them 'up-country' through their own sales networks. The foreign importers in the treaty ports typically acted upon orders taken from Chinese wholesalers, thus being hardly more than purchasing agents for Chinese merchants.[52]

(2) *Up-country distribution*. A number of big foreign companies maintained their own sales organizations, mainly for oil products, cigarettes, sugar, dyes and chemical fertilizers. Though these networks adapted to existing commercial channels rather than replaced them, they still gave the foreign company a much stronger influence on prices and quantities in local markets than would have been possible with treaty port trade.[53]

(3) *Government trade*. Chinese governments bought arms, railway equipment and machinery for state-run factories. Much of this business was not entirely private on the foreign side; it often involved loans to the Chinese government or at least guaranteed export credits. This type of trade was likely to carry a strong political accent.[54]

It is important to note the difference between penetration and dependency on the world market. While, for instance, the British business system did not significantly penetrate into Chinese export production, apart from the processing of eggs and tong oil,[55] through monopolistic purchasing arrangements it exercised a large measure of control over prices paid to the indigenous producers, as was the case with tea and tungsten (prior to the establishment of a government monopoly in 1936).[56] Another crucial element of outward dependency which cannot easily be conceptualized in terms of market penetration is the incorporation of a peripheral economy into international flows of bullion and money. China's main problem was its silver currency which remained one of the decisive influences on domestic economic conditions right up to the introduction, with British assistance, of a managed currency in November 1935.[57]

One special, but none the less significant form of penetration must not be obscured by a preoccupation with exogenous forces thrusting into the Chinese economy. It may be called, for want of a better term, symbiotic penetration. A foreign company establishes itself in the China market, building on an initial input of imported capital and technology. It then uses – or exploits – local factors of production (labour, land, raw materials). The output is then mainly marketed in the host country, and profits are partly ploughed back into local reinvestment. The classic case in China was the British-American Tobacco Corporation, whose Chinese subsidiary grew into the biggest capitalist organization on Chinese soil.[58] The two big Sino-British coal-mining companies (Kailan Mining Administration and Pekin Syndicate) operated in a similar fashion. All of them possessed fairly tenuous links with exterior markets, but interacted closely with the indigenous economic environment.

The actual degree of penetration of a particular market results from a combination of three groups of factors: push factors, pull factors and resisting factors. Market resistance refers to structural impediments to penetration. It is a very complex and difficult category and its real underpinnings have so far been little studied and less understood. If we knew how market resistance worked in practice we would be close to comprehending why China perennially failed to live up to the expectations of those who indulged in Utopian fantasies of 'the world's largest undeveloped market'. Some of the factors involved are: the inaccessibility of many parts of the country; the limited purchasing power of the rural masses; the tenacity of traditional patterns of consumer behaviour; the partial self-sufficiency of the Chinese economy; the continuing availability of substitutes for imported goods; the efficiency of traditional trading and transportation networks, and so on. While these factors would be classified as 'traditional' by modernization theorists, a certain amount of 'modern' market resistance should not be overlooked. The rise of modern Chinese banking in limited rivalry with foreign banks is the outstanding example, but in the 1920s and 1930s Western firms also met competition from modern Chinese industry in the markets for cigarettes, machinery and chemicals.[59]

A second form of resistance was official resistance, a term preferable to 'economic nationalism' since it is more formal and less ideologically charged. Official resistance to foreign encroachment runs through modern Chinese history from the introduction of the Canton system in the eighteenth century to the expropriation of foreign firms after 1949. In a sense, the Communists took up and radicalized a tradition that included not only Commissioner Lin Zexu's failed attempt to eradicate the opium trade, and the rights recovery movements of the late Qing period, but also the

Nanjing government's effort, between 1928 and 1937, to reassert a limited measure of Chinese control over the modern sector of the economy, even if this endeavour was motivated as much by the selfish interests of 'bureaucratic capitalists' as by a genuine commitment to the liberation of the country.[60] The Communists could also build on another tradition, that of popular resistance. While 'official resistance' refers to actions undertaken by those in possession of state power, with control over the instruments at the disposal of a sovereign government (legislation, taxation, military coercion), 'popular resistance' is carried out by private citizens, the people (*min*) or the masses (*qunzhong*) in Chinese parlance. 'Traditional' resistance movements, defined as 'the forcible, instinctive attempt of an unmodified traditional structure to extrude a foreign body'[61] were typical of the nineteenth century. They ranged from the Sanyuanli Incident of 1841 through hundreds of 'missionary cases' during the second half of the century to the Boxer Rebellion which had been smouldering under the surface since about 1895 and broke out in 1899.[62] After the defeat of the Boxers and China's brutal punishment at the hands of the powers, the boycott and the strike became the principal weapons of Chinese popular anti-imperialism. The anti-American boycott of 1905 was followed by the May Fourth Movement of 1919, the May Thirtieth Movement of 1925 and the Hong Kong–Canton General Strike of 1925–6, the anti-Japanese boycott of 1931–4 and the December Ninth Movement of 1935.[63] After the Anti-Japanese War, in itself an instance of popular resistance on a massive scale,[64] student protests were aimed at American policy in China.[65]

Some of these movements were tacitly or overtly encouraged and supported by office-holders, popular resistance thus overlapping with official resistance. Most of them were not purely anti-imperialistic, but also directed against those members of China's ruling circles who, in the eyes of the protesters, failed to stand up to the foreigners or even openly collaborated with them, thus smoothing the way for penetration.

Since Ronald Robinson's and Johan Galtung's pioneering articles, it has become commonplace to regard 'indigenous collaboration' as a basic constituent of formal colonial rule and informal semi-colonial influence.[66] As was mentioned earlier, Chinese authors were aware of its significance from at least the 1920s onwards. It is helpful to distinguish between two levels on which collaboration occurred. Penetration was facilitated by comprador mechanisms of various kinds which were all the more important in China since Westerners – and to a lesser degree the Japanese – took a long time to get accustomed to a civilization which was much more alien and inscrutable than, for instance, the Latin American countries where Western informal empires had been established. These mechanisms not only included the institution of the compradore in the narrow definition of the term (a Chinese of good standing and a knowledge of Western languages commissioned by a foreign firm to look after its dealings with Chinese customers), but also a number of other arrangements on the market level, such as joint Sino-foreign ventures with foreigners in effective control, foreign firms camouflaged as Chinese enterprises, co-operation between foreign banks and the so-called 'native banks' (*qianzhuang*), the recruitment of labour through Chinese contractors, and so on.[67] It must be pointed out that these comprador mechanisms were ambiguous from a foreign point of view. On the one hand, they were indispensable for gaining a foothold in the Chinese economy, on the other, they kept the foreigner away from the primary markets for goods and services. In some cases, he might even be at the mercy of his comprador, while in others – British American Tobacco's involvement in tobacco cultivation is a case in point[68] – compradors were instrumental in carrying foreign penetration far into the domestic economy. Given this inherent ambiguity, comprador mechanisms were essential for linking foreign business systems with the indigenous economic environment. Even after the eclipse of the classical comprador during the 1920s they continued to exist under various names.[69] Collaboration remained a necessity for imperialism throughout its history in China.

Whereas comprador mechanisms were operative on the level of market penetration, official collaboration led to the surrender of control over national resources in exchange for political, military and, above all, financial support from foreign governments and business interests. Again, this notion covers a very broad range of actions and attitudes. Only rarely did official collaboration reach the extreme of puppet-like submission to a foreign power. The role played by Emperor Puyi *alias* Kangde, in Manchukuo after 1932 is a good illustration of such a stance.[70] In most cases, as Ronald Robinson has argued,[71] collaboration involved 'bargaining' and often the Chinese used the threat of resistance to push up the price demanded for collaborative services. To what extent this was possible depended, of course, on the power gap between Chinese and foreigners at any given moment. Wang Jingwei's ill-fated government set up in Japanese-occupied Nanjing in March 1940 found itself in a position vastly different from that of Prince Gong and the other advocates of the 'cooperative policy' of the 1860s or the Guomindang in the early and mid-1930s. A second factor determining the proportions of collaboration and resistance within the behaviour of Chinese leaders towards foreigners was the availability of alternative sources of support. As Ernest P. Young has demonstrated with regard to the early Republic, the quest for foreign, and especially Japanese, assistance was, in many cases, a desperate last resort 'when other routes seemed closed or ineffective'.[72] Thirdly, the benefits deriving from collaboration could be partly or wholly offset by a loss of political legitimacy in the eyes of domestic public opinion. Chinese ruling circles were aware of this dilemma to a greater or lesser extent, especially after the emergence of mass nationalism during the May Fourth Movement of 1919. The Guomindang after 1928 tried to paper it over with a nationalistic and neo-traditionalist ideology, without however solving the problem, apart from the early years of the war against Japan. Chinese Marxists for a long time attempted to allocate certain types of political behaviour to specific social classes. But it has recently been doubted by eminent Chinese historians whether the line between a patriotic 'national bourgeoisie' and a treacherous 'comprador bourgeoisie' can be drawn as neatly as orthodoxy would have it.[73]

So far, the model has been built around economic interests. We must now try to fit in the political dimension. The system of 'unequal treaties' had been completed by the end of the nineteenth century, but it continued to be in force for Britain, the United States, France and a number of less important countries until the 1940s. The contents of the treaties have been described in most textbooks on modern Chinese history, but very few of them mention how the system worked in practice. The model must, therefore, allow for an analysis of the function of legal privilege. There are strong indications, for example, that its importance was declining in the early twentieth century. German trade in China prospered from the mid-1920s onwards, although German interests at that time were no longer protected by extraterritoriality.[74] The big foreign companies which penetrated the market far beyond the treaty ports increasingly preferred informal arrangements with the Chinese on local, provincial and even central government level to formal invocation of the treaties.[75]

The 'flag' took the lead over trade in times of heightened foreign aggressiveness towards China. During the quieter periods in between, however, the political-military establishment was largely concerned with the protection of existing interests. Three dimensions are worth analysing:

(1) Antagonism and co-operation between the diplomatic and military representatives of the major powers 'on the spot' (partly, but not totally a reflection of alignments on the wider international stage).

(2) The relationship between diplomacy and enterprise in the imperial centre (influence of commercial pressure groups on parliaments, Cabinets and foreign offices) and at the periphery (between consuls and diplomats, on the one hand, and the expatriate business communities on the other).[76]

(3) The behaviour of official representatives towards the indigenous environment, to be conceptualized in terms of mechanisms of intervention (gunboat diplomacy, 'advice' to Chinese governments, 'good offices' employed for the benefit of foreign business interests, and so on). The efficacy of the various means of intervention has to be assessed for each individual case, with the possible result that long-term trends become discernible (such as the decline of gunboat diplomacy since the early 1920s).

An analysis along these lines will reveal a complicated interplay of numerous factors. The political-military establishment not only carried out orders from its home government, but frequently took matters into its own hands. In some cases (the takeover of Manchuria by the Japanese Guandong Army in 1931/2 being the most notorious), this amounted to fully fledged 'sub-imperialism'. In others, forceful diplomats like Sir Rutherford Alcock, Sir John Jordan or, on the American side, William W. Rockhill, left a strong imprint on the China policies of their respective countries. Within the political-military establishment the diplomats and the soldiers did not always share the same opinion. The main structural cleavage, however, existed between the diplomats and the expatriate communities of the treaty ports which time and again clamoured for tough action against what were, in their view, unruly and devious natives. Behind the scenes, imperialism at the periphery rarely functioned as an integrated machine, even though the colonized and semi-colonized had some justification for regarding it as such.

The model, as outlined above, aims to provide a structural framework for an analysis of the actual working of imperialism at the periphery. It assumes the existence at the periphery of a bifurcated foreign establishment, consisting of a business segment and a political-military segment for each of the major foreign powers concerned. This foreign establishment mediates between the indigenous environment on the one hand, and the international environment on the other.

Several limitations as well as further potentials of the model should be borne in mind. First, it does not conceptualize the sources, motives and modes of imperial expansion, but the operations of foreign actors who are already entrenched at the periphery. Secondly, it is essentially static and allows, above all, the taking of 'snapshots' of a political-social-economic configuration at any given moment. It can, however, easily be dynamized in two related ways. The categories 'penetration', 'intervention' and 'resistance' are interactionist rather than structural; in other words, they refer to processes that occur within given institutional set-ups and may, in turn, modify them. Moreover, a business system evolves in time and the same may be said of a political-military establishment. Thirdly, the model refers to 'semi-colonial' conditions where a metropolitan country exerts power and influence within an asymmetrical relationship, but does not assume outright domination and formal sovereignty over the peripheral country. It might, however, be possible to modify the model to make it applicable to formal colonialism. Presumably, the concept of 'intervention' would have to be substituted by that of 'foreign rule' and the category of 'administrative penetration' incorporated alongside 'economic penetration'. The latter would then be the mode of operation of the colonial business system, the former that of the colonial state. Also, under colonial conditions, the coexistence of several national political-military establishments would have to be ruled out. Semi-colonies can – but need not – have more than one colonial master, formal colonies by definition have only one. Fourthly, the model does not take account of a foreign cultural and, in particular, missionary presence. This element, however, may be added as a third component to the foreign establishment. Fifthly, the model has been chiefly designed to fit the case of China from the full development of the unequal treaty system up to the national 'liberation', as the Chinese call it, in 1949. Nevertheless, its categories are broad enough to be applied, with some modifications, to parallel historical phenomena such as semi-colonial Latin America, Persia, or the Ottoman Empire. Modification can consist of deleting certain elements or adding new ones. For example, legal privileges as accruing from 'unequal' treaties continued to exist in China until 1943, whereas they had been removed in most of the Latin American countries by 1850. Modification can also mean an intrinsic refinement of the analytical categories themselves. Thus, to give but one example, the category of 'intervention' can be broken down into a typology which would account not only for the various forms of action taken by a peripheral political-military establishment, but also for direct intervention from the imperial centre; the deployment of naval and air-borne 'task forces' is a highly pertinent example. In any case, a flexible application of the model to comparable historical configurations might result in an empirically based theory of informal empire that would encompass differentiations in time and space and would, in the final analysis, relate various forms of expansion and reaction to different types of peripheral societies, on the one hand, and to the overall evolution of the global political and economic system on the other.

Conclusion

This chapter started out from a seemingly simple and straightforward historical problem: that of making sense of the diversity of individual phenomena which, on the face of it, characterized imperialism in China before 1949. The various grand theories, ranging from world system to modernization approaches, were found wanting since none of them succeeds in grasping the systematic nature of imperialism as it operated at the periphery. Being mainly interested in developing broad explanations of imperial impact – in itself a perfectly legitimate enterprise – they nevertheless lack descriptive adequacy. The concept of informal empire, understood not as part of an evolutionary theory of imperialism, but as an ideal type of potentially universal applicability, is less well suited to dealing with general explanatory problems, while possessing a higher degree of descriptive power. An ideal type is a construct that brings out as sharply as possible those features of the empirical world that are considered significant in the light of a specific analytical purpose. It cannot be directly 'applied' to reality. In order to bridge the gap between the highly abstract ideal type and the mass of data unearthed by historical research, a model was suggested which structures rather than interprets the historical evidence and thus provides a guide and framework for detailed research. Interpretation appears at the other end of this epistemological strategy. It is there that the big guns of grand theory can be fired.

Notes: Chapter 19

1 See R. H. Myers, *The Japanese Economic Development of Manchuria, 1932 to 1945* (New York, 1980); K. C. Sun, with the assistance of R. W. Huenemann, *The Economic Development of Manchuria in the First Half of the Twentieth Century* (Cambridge, Mass., 1969).
2 E. Cooper, 'Karl Marx's other island: the evolution of peripheral capitalism in Hong Kong', *Bulletin of Concerned Asian Scholars*, vol. 14 (1982), pp. 25–31. There is no satisfactory overall account of Hong Kong's economic history. For the time being see T. N. Chiu, *The Port of Hong Kong: A Survey of its Development* (Hong Kong, 1973).
3 C. Thorne, *Allies of a Kind: The United States, Britain and the War against Japan, 1941–1945* (London, 1978), pp. 175–6.
4 D. K. Fieldhouse, *Colonialism 1870–1945: An Introduction* (London, 1981), p. 12.
5 Much information on imperialism in China can be obtained from vols 10 to 12 of *The Cambridge History of China* (1978–83), espec. A. Feuerwerker, 'The foreign presence in China', in J. K. Fairbank (ed.), *The Cambridge History of China*, Vol. 12, pt 1 (Cambridge, 1983), pp. 128–207. A wide-ranging introduction is J. Ch'en, *China and the West: Society and Culture 1815–1937* (London, 1979). Still useful as a concise survey is the book

by a member of the British Consular Service: Sir Eric Teichman, *Affairs of China: A Survey of the Recent History and Present Circumstances of the Republic of China* (London, 1938).
6   See, for example, Michael H. Hunt's impressive *The Making of a Special Relationship: The United States and China to 1911* (New York, 1983).
7   G. Rozman et al., *The Modernization of China* (New York and London, 1981), p. 141.
8   On the comparative economic position of China see I. Adelman and C. T. Morris, 'A typology of poverty in 1850', *Economic Development and Cultural Change*, vol. 25, supplement (1977), pp. 314–43, espec. 331–2, 335–40: A. Maddison, 'A comparison of levels of GDP per capita in developed and developing countries, 1700–1980', *Journal of Economic History*, vol. 43 (1983), pp. 27–41; P. Bairoch, 'International industrialization levels from 1750 to 1980', *Journal of European Economic History*, vol. 11 (1982), pp. 269–333, espec. 281, 283–4, 292–6, 302–4; also Chapters 13 and 14 by Paul Bairoch and J. Forbes Munro in this volume.
9   For a stimulating discussion see R. H. Myers, 'Society and economy in modern China: some historical interpretations', *Bulletin of the Institute of Modern History Academia Sinica*, vol. 11 (1982), pp. 197–224.
10 The term is borrowed from Hou Chi-ming, 'The oppression argument on foreign investment in China, 1895–1937', *Journal of Asian Studies*, vol. 20 (1960/1), pp. 435–48.
11 The *locus classicus* is Mao Tse-tung [Mao Zedong], 'The Chinese revolution and the Chinese Communist Party', in *Selected Works of Mao Tse-tung*, Vol. 2 (Peking, 1978), pp. 309 ff. See also Ma Yinchu, 'Bupingdeng tiaoyue yu wo guo jingji shang zhi yingxiang' [The impact of the unequal treaties on the Chinese economy], in *Ma Yinchu yanjiang ji* [Collection of Ma Yinchu's lectures], Vol. 3 (Peking, 1926), pp. 100–9; Qi Shufen, *Jingji qinlüe xia zhi Zhongguo* [China under economic aggression] (Shanghai, 1925), pp. 49 ff.; Zhou Gucheng, *Zhongguo shehui zhi xianzhuang* [The present social structure in China] (Shanghai, 1933), pp. 117 ff.; Shi Fuliang, *Zhongguo xiandai jingji shi* [Contemporary Chinese economic history] (Shanghai, 1932), pp. 1–14 and *passim*. A recent restatement is A. K. Bagchi, *The Political Economy of Underdevelopment* (Cambridge, 1982), pp. 94–111. See also J. Esherick, 'Harvard on China: the apologetics of imperialism', *Bulletin of Concerned Asian Scholars*, vol. 4 (1972), pp. 9–16, and for the opposite view, A. J. Nathan, 'Imperialism's effects on China', ibid., pp. 3–8.
12 In his second lecture on the Principle of Nationality, given on 3 February 1924: *Sun Zhongshan xuanji* [Selected works of Sun Yat-sen], Vol. 2 (Peking, 1956), p. 607. For a brief survey of Sun Yat-sen's view on imperialism see Liao Kuang-sheng, 'Dr. Sun Yat-sen and the nationalist policy of anti-imperialism', *Chu Hai Journal*, vol. 13 (1982), pp. 198–209. See also Ku Hung-ting, 'The emergence of the Kuomintang's anti-imperialism', *Journal of Oriental Studies*, vol. 16 (1978), pp. 87–97; Huang E'hui, 'Xinhai Geming hou Sun Zhongshan fan di sixiang de fazhan' [The development of Sun Yat-sen's anti-imperialist thinking after the Revolution of 1911], *Zhongshan Daxue xuebao* [Journal of Sun Yat-sen University, Canton], 1979, no. 4, pp. 33–42.
13 F. V. Moulder, *Japan, China, and the Modern World Economy: Toward a Reinterpretation of East Asian Development, ca. 1600 to ca. 1918* (Cambridge, 1977); V. D. Lippit, 'The development of underdevelopment in China', *Modern China*, vol. 4 (1978), pp. 251–328.
14 Hou Chi-ming, *Foreign Investment and Economic Development in China, 1840–1937* (Cambridge, Mass., 1965); M. Elvin, *The Pattern of the Chinese Past* (London, 1973), pp. 312–16; R. F. Dernberger, 'The role of the foreigner in China's economic development, 1840–1949', in D. H. Perkins (ed.), *China's Modern Economy in Historical Perspective* (Stanford, Calif., 1975), pp. 19–48. More recently, Mah Feng-hwa, 'External influence and Chinese economic development: a re-examination', in Hou Chi-ming and Yu Tzong-shian (eds), *Modern Chinese Economic History* (Taibei, 1979), pp. 273–98. Rozman et al., *The Modernization of China*, occupies an intermediate position between the modernization and marginality arguments. For a critical discussion see J. Osterhammel, 'Modernisierungstheorie und die Transformation Chinas 1800–1949. Kritische Überlegungen zur historischen Soziologie', *Saeculum*, vol. 35 (1984), pp. 31–72.
15 A. N. Young, *China's Nation-Building Effort, 1927–1937: The Financial and Economic Record* (Stanford, Calif., 1971).
16 This is the central thesis in Rozman et al., *The Modernization of China*, pp. 255, 343–4.

Informal Empire in China 311

See also D. H. Perkins, 'Government as an obstacle to industrialization: the case of nineteenth-century China', *Journal of Economic History*, vol. 27 (1967), pp. 478–92, espec. 491.
17 R. Murphey, 'The treaty ports and China's modernization', in M. Elvin and G. W. Skinner (eds), *The Chinese City between Two Worlds* (Stanford, Calif., 1974), pp. 17–72; idem, *The Outsiders: The Western Experience in India and China* (Ann Arbor, Mich., 1977); S. R. Brown, 'The partially opened door: limitation on economic change in China in the 1860s', *Modern Asian Studies*, vol. 12 (1978), pp. 177–92; idem, 'The transfer of technology to China in the nineteenth century: the role of direct foreign investment', *Journal of Economic History*, vol. 39 (1979), pp. 181–9. For an interpretation of maritime China as a 'minor tradition' see J. K. Fairbank, 'Maritime and continental in China's history', in idem (ed.), *The Cambridge History of China*, Vol. 12, pp. 1–27.
18 For example, Fei Hsiao-t'ung, *China's Gentry: Essays in Rural–Urban Relations* (Chicago, 1953), pp. 104–7.
19 A. Feuerwerker, 'Characteristics of the Chinese economic model specific to the Chinese environment', in R. F. Dernberger (ed.), *China's Development Experience in Comparative Perspective* (Cambridge, Mass., 1980), pp. 289–90.
20 On its origins and principal themes see M. C. Wright, 'Introduction: the rising tide of change', in idem (ed.), *China in Revolution: The First Phase, 1900–1913* (New Haven, Conn. and London, 1968), pp. 3–23.
21 U. Menzel, *Theorie und Praxis des chinesischen Entwicklungsmodells. Ein Beitrag zum Konzept autozentrierter Entwicklung* (Opladen, 1978), p. 635.
22 Murphey, *The Outsiders*, pp. 180–2, 187–8.
23 Research on finance imperialism in China is still in its infancy. Recent studies include R. A. Dayer, *Bankers and Diplomats in China 1917–1925: The Anglo-American Relationship* (London, 1981); F. H. H. King (ed.), *Eastern Banking: Essays on the History of the Hongkong and Shanghai Banking Corporation* (London, 1983); R. Quested, *The Russo-Chinese Bank: A Multi-National Financial Base of Tsarism in China* (Birmingham, 1977); G. Kurgan-van Hentenryk, *Léopold II et les groupes financiers belges en Chine: la politique royale et ses prolongements (1895– 1914)* (Brussels, 1972); idem, 'Un aspect de l'exportation des capitaux en Chine; les entreprises franco-belges, 1896–1914', in M. Lévy-Leboyer (ed.), *La Position internationale de la France* (Paris, 1977), pp. 203–13; A. B. Chan, 'The consortium system in Republican China, 1912–1913', *Journal of European Economic History*, vol. 6 (1977), pp. 597–640. K. C. Chan, 'British policy in the reorganization loan to China 1912–13', *Modern Asian Studies*, vol. 5 (1971), pp. 355–72; Xia Liangcai, 'Guoji yinhangtuan he Xinhai Geming' [International banking groups and the Revolution of 1911], *Jindai shi yanjiu* [Research on modern history] 1982, no. 1, pp. 188–215. Most of these and other studies deal with the foreigners' perspective; there is hardly anything on the effects of foreign financial operations on China's domestic finance.
24 Moulder, *Japan, China, and the Modern World Economy*. Murphey *The Outsiders*, (chs 7 and 9) is, in turn, particularly good on commercial organization.
25 P. Robb, 'British rule and Indian "improvement"', *Economic History Review*, vol. 34 (1981), p. 520.
26 M. Bunge, *Scientific Research*, Vol. 1: *The Search for System* (Berlin and Heidelberg, 1967), p. 470. Similarly the historian Peter Burke: 'Let us define a "model" in simple terms as an intellectual construct which simplifies reality in order to emphasise the recurrent, the constant and the typical, which it presents in the form of clusters of traits or attributes' (*Sociology and History* [London, 1980], p. 35). The philosophical and logical complexities of the concept of 'model' may be disregarded for the present limited purpose.
27 J. N. Rosenau, *The Scientific Study of Foreign Policy*, rev. edn (London and New York, 1980), pp. 123–4.
28 V. I. Lenin, 'Imperialism, the highest stage of capitalism', in idem, *Collected Works*, Vol. 22 (Moscow, 1964), p. 259.
29 See also W. J. Mommsen, *Der europäische Imperialismus. Aufsätze und Abhandlungen* (Göttingen, 1979), pp. 91 ff.
30 J. A. Hobson, *Imperialism: A Study*, 2nd edn (London, 1905), pp. 310–14. See also P. J. Cain, 'International trade and economic development in the work of J. A. Hobson before 1914', *History of Political Economy*, vol. 11 (1979), pp. 412–14; N. Etherington, 'Reconsidering theories of imperialism', *History and Theory*, vol. 21 (1982), pp. 23–4; H. Bley,

'Hobsons Prognosen zur Entwicklung des Imperialismus in Südafrika und China. Prognosenanalyse als Beitrag zur Theoriediskussion', in J. Radkau and I. Geiss (eds), *Imperialismus im 20. Jahrhundert. Gedenkschrift für George W. F. Hallgarten* (Munich, 1976), pp. 43–69.

31 See A. Dirlik, *Revolution and History: The Origins of Marxist Historiography in China, 1919–1937* (Berkeley, Calif., 1978), pp. 58 ff. Ye Guisheng and Liu Maolin, 'Zhongguo shehui shi lunzhan yu Makesizhuyi lishixue de xingcheng' [The debate on Chinese social history and the emergence of Marxist historiography in China], *Zhongguo shi yanjiu* [Research on Chinese history] 1983, no. 1, pp. 3–16.

32 Wang Yanan, *Zhongguo banfengjian banzhimindi jingji xingtai yanjiu* [Studies on the semifeudal-semicolonial economic formation in China], reprint of the 1957 edn (Peking, 1980). The first version of the book was published in 1946.

33 See, for example, Wang's discussion of the relationship between foreign and indigenous capital, ibid., pp. 123–6.

34 Hu Sheng, *Imperialism and Chinese Politics* (Peking, 1981), also puts strong emphasis on collaboration, but keeps closer to a conspiratorial interpretation than does Wang Yanan.

35 Wang Yanan, *Zhongguo banfengjian*, pp. 1–3. For an intellectual biography of Wang see Chen Kejian and Gan Minzhong, 'Wang Yanan jingji sixiang chutan' [Wang Yanan's economic thought], *Xiamen Daxue xuebao* [Journal of Amoy University], 1981, no. 1, pp. 1–11, no. 2, pp. 50–62, no. 3, pp. 94–102.

36 For a survey of the thesis and the debate about it see W. R. Louis, 'Robinson and Gallagher and their critics', in idem (ed.), *Imperialism: The Robinson and Gallagher Controversy* (New York and London, 1976), pp. 2–51.

37 See his Chapter 18 in this volume.

38 It is advisable to speak of countries, not of nations, since the process of nation-building on the weaker actor's side need not necessarily be completed.

39 See E.-O. Czempiel, *Internationale Politik. Ein Konfliktmodel* (Paderborn, 1981), pp. 189–90.

40 P. Winn, 'British informal empire in Uruguay in the nineteenth century', *Past and Present*, vol. 73 (1976), p. 126.

41 J. Galtung, 'A structural theory of imperialism', *Journal of Peace Research*, vol. 8 (1971), pp. 81–118.

42 B. Dean, 'British informal empire: the case of China', *Journal of Commonwealth and Comparative Politics*, vol. 14 (1976), pp. 75–7.

43 D. McLean, 'Finance and "informal empire" before the First World War', *Economic History Review*, vol. 29 (1976), pp. 291–3; P. J. Cain, *Economic Foundations of British Overseas Expansion 1815–1914* (London, 1980), pp. 61–3.

44 For contrasting views on the treaty system see J. K. Fairbank, 'The creation of the treaty system', in idem (ed.), *The Cambridge History of China*, Vol. 10, pt 1 (Cambridge, 1978), pp. 213–63, and Tan Chung, 'The unequal treaty system: infrastructure of irresponsible imperialism', *China Report*, vol. 17, no. 5 (September–October 1981), pp. 3–33.

45 A. Feuerwerker, *The Foreign Establishment in China in the Early Twentieth Century* (Ann Arbor, Mich., 1976), p. ix. Similarly Fairbank ('Maritime and continental', p. 2): 'Truly, the early republic was moved by foreign influences that were almost as pervasive as the Japanese invasion was to become after 1931.'

46 See A. Córdova, *Strukturelle Heterogenität und wirtschaftliches Wachstum* (Frankfurt-on-Main, 1973). The concept is applied to China by Menzel, *Theorie und Praxis*, pp. 178 ff.

47 See J. Osterhammel, *Britischer Imperialismus im Fernen Osten. Strukturen der Durchdringung und einheimischer Widerstand auf dem chinesischen Markt 1932–1937* (Bochum, 1983), pp. 30–1.

48 Chinese Maritime Customs, *The Trade of China, 1936*, Vol. 1 (Shanghai, 1937), p. 55; R. Lévy et al., *French Interests and Politics in the Far East* (New York, 1941), p. 27.

49 A certain number of foreign factories were illegally established already before 1895 when the Treaty of Shimonoseki legalized foreign industry in the treaty ports. Most of the coal mines were joint Sino-foreign enterprises with the foreigners, as a rule, being in effective control.

50 These were, of course, no closed national circuits: the Kailan Mining Administration sold their coal also to the Japanese; the Shanghai Power Company supplied electricity to the entire International Settlement and beyond.

51 See I. H. Anderson, Jr, *The Standard Vacuum Oil Company and United States East Asian Policy, 1933–1941* (Princeton, NJ, 1975), pp. 42–9; Osterhammel, *Britischer Imperialismus*, pp. 323–7.
52 The typical case is that of cotton goods. See Department of Overseas Trade, *Report of the Cotton Mission to the Far East* (London, 1931), pp. 61 ff.; H. D. Fong, *Cotton Industry and Trade in China*, Vol. 1 (Tianjin, 1932), pp. 262 ff.
53 See the excellent case study by S. Cochran, *Big Business in China: Sino-Foreign Rivalry in the Cigarette Industry, 1890–1930* (Cambridge, Mass., 1980), pp. 27–35, 130–4. On distribution networks for oil, sugar and fertilizers see Osterhammel, *Britischer Imperialismus*, pp. 141–82.
54 On the arms trade see A. B. Chan, *Arming the Chinese: The Western Armaments Trade in Warlord China, 1920–1928* (Vancouver, 1982).
55 Wang Chi-tung, *Eggs Industry in China* (Tianjin and Shanghai, 1937), pp. 21–2; Zhu Meiyu, *Zhongguo tongyouye* [China's tong oil industry] (Shanghai, 1939), pp. 78 ff.
56 Osterhammel, *Britischer Imperialismus*, pp. 187–96, 337–43.
57 Chang Hsin-pao, *Commissioner Lin and the Opium War* (Cambridge, Mass., 1964), pp. 39–46; Lin Manhong, 'Dui wai huilü changqi xiadie Qing-mo guoji maoyi yu wujia zhi yingxiang' [The depreciation of silver and its effects on foreign trade and prices in late Qing China], *Jiaoyu yu yanjiu* [Education and research], no. 1 (February 1979), pp. 147–76; Liao Bao-seing, *Die Bedeutung des Silberproblems für die Entwicklung der chinesischen Währungsverhältnisse* (Berlin, 1939); M. B. Russell, 'American silver policy and China', PhD thesis, University of Illinois, 1972. The problem reaches far back beyond the imperialist era and lends itself to treatment in the *longue durée*. See M. Cartier, 'Les importations de métaux monétaires en Chine: essai sur la conjoncture chinoise', *Annales, ESC*, vol. 36 (1981), pp. 454–66; W. S. Atwell, 'International bullion flows and the Chinese economy, circa 1530–1650', *Past and Present*, no. 95 (1982), pp. 68–90.
58 See Cochran, *Big Business*, passim.
59 ibid., chs 3, 5 and 6; T. G. Rawski, *China's Transition to Industrialism: Producer Goods and Economic Development in the Twentieth Century* (Ann Arbor, Mich. and Folkestone, Kent, 1980), ch. 1.
60 On the 'bargains' between the Nanjing government and foreign firms see J. Osterhammel, 'Imperialism in transition: British business and the Chinese authorities, 1931–37', *China Quarterly*, no. 98 (June 1984), pp. 260–86.
61 E. Stokes, 'Traditional resistance movements and Afro-Asian nationalism', *Past and Present*, no. 48 (1970), p. 104.
62 F. Wakeman, Jr, *Strangers at the Gate: Social Disorder in South China, 1839–61* (Berkeley, Calif. and Los Angeles, Calif., 1966); P. A. Cohen, 'Christian missions and their impact to 1900', in Fairbank (ed.), *The Cambridge History of China*, Vol. 10, pp. 569–73; V. Purcell, *The Boxer Uprising: A Background Study* (Cambridge, 1963); W. J. Duiker, *Cultures in Collision: The Boxer Rebellion* (San Rafael, Calif. and London, 1978).
63 Hunt, *The Making of a Special Relationship*, pp. 233–47; J. T. Chen, *The May Fourth Movement in Shanghai* (Leiden, 1971); R. W. Rigby, *The May 30 Movement: Events and Themes* (Canberra, 1980); N. R. Clifford, *Shanghai, 1925: Urban Nationalism and the Defense of Foreign Privilege* (Ann Arbor, Mich., 1979); J. Israel, *Student Nationalism in China, 1927–1937* (Stanford, Calif., 1966), ch. 5; C. F. Remer, *A Study of Chinese Boycotts* (Baltimore, Md, 1933) chs 12–14; D. A. Jordan, 'China's vulnerability to Japanese imperialism: the anti-Japanese boycott of 1931–1932', in F. G. Chan (ed.), *China at the Crossroads: Nationalists and Communists, 1927–1949* (Boulder, Col., 1980), pp. 91–123.
64 This should, however, not obscure the usually less than heroic everyday arrangements of people under Japanese rule. See L. E. Eastman, 'Facets of an ambivalent relationship: smuggling, puppets, and atrocities during the war, 1937–1945', in A. Iriye (ed.), *The Chinese and the Japanese. Essays in Political and Cultural Interactions* (Princeton, NJ, 1980), pp. 275–303.
65 S. Pepper, *Civil War in China: The Political Struggle, 1945–1949* (Berkeley, Calif. and Los Angeles, Calif., 1978), pp. 52–8, 72–8.
66 R. Robinson, 'Non-European foundations of European imperialism: sketch for a theory of collaboration', in R. Owen and B. Sutcliffe (eds), *Studies in the Theory of Imperialism* (London, 1972), pp. 117–40; Galtung, 'A structural theory of imperialism', cit. at n. 41; idem, '"A structural theory of imperialism" – ten years later', *Millenium*, vol. 9 (1981),

pp. 181–96. Interesting discussion papers are M. H. Hunt, 'Resistance and collaboration in the American Empire, 1898–1903: an overview', *Pacific Historical Review*, vol. 48 (1979), pp. 467–71; J. Suret-Canale, '"Résistance" et "collaboration" en Afrique noire coloniale", in J. Vansina *et al., Etudes africaines: offertes à Henri Brunschwig* (Paris, 1982), pp. 319–31.

67 Hao Yen-p'ing, *The Comprador in Nineteenth-Century China: Bridge between East and West* (Cambridge, Mass., 1970); Nie Baozhang, *Zhongguo maiban zichan jieji de fasheng* [The emergence of the compradore bourgeoisie in China] (Peking, 1979); A. L. McElderry, *Shanghai Old-Style Banks (Ch'ien-Chuang), 1800–1935* (Ann Arbor, Mich., 1976), pp. 21 ff.; C. T. Smith, 'Compradores of the Hongkong Bank', in King (ed.), *Eastern Banking*, pp. 93–111; T. Wright, '"A method of evading management" – contract labor in Chinese coal mines before 1937', *Comparative Studies in Society and History*, vol. 23 (1981), pp. 656–78.

68 See Chen Han-seng, *Industrial Capital and the Chinese Peasants: A Study of the Livelihood of Chinese Tobacco Cultivators* (Shanghai, 1939), pp. 9–15, 26–32.

69 One example is the transformation of compradores into 'Chinese managers' with roughly the same functions. See Osterhammel, *Britischer Imperialismus*, pp. 228–35.

70 J. H. Boyle, *China and Japan at War, 1937–1945: The Politics of Collaboration* (Stanford, Calif., 1972), p. 10.

71 Robinson, 'Non-European foundations', espec. p. 123.

72 E. P. Young, 'Chinese leaders and Japanese aid in the early republic', in Iriye (ed.), *The Chinese and the Japanese*, p. 138.

73 For example, Wang Jingyu, 'The birth of the Chinese bourgeoisie', *Social Sciences in China*, vol. 3 (1982), pp. 220–40.

74 See L. E. Glaim, 'Sino-German relations, 1919–1925: German diplomatic, economic and cultural re-entry into China after World War I', PhD thesis, Washington State University, 1973, pp. 98–102, 107–15; W. C. Kirby, 'Developmental aid or neo-imperialism? German industry in China (1928–1937)', in B. Martin (ed.), *Die deutsche Beraterschaft in China 1927–1938. Militär, Wirtschaft, Aussenpolitik* (Düsseldorf, 1981), pp. 201–15; W. C. Kirby, *Germany and Republican China* (Stanford, Calif., 1984), pp. 23 ff., 77 ff.

75 See Osterhammel, 'Imperialism in transition', pp. 282–4.

76 See, as examples of this approach, N. A. Pelcovits, *Old China Hands and the Foreign Office* (New York, 1948); S. L. Endicott, *Diplomacy and Enterprise: British China Policy 1933–1937* (Manchester, 1975).

20 Conflict and Convergence in Development Theory

COLIN LEYS

After the Second World War the academic establishments of the Western imperial powers perceived the problem of development as one of fitting the colonies for independent statehood within the 'free' world. 'Development' of the colonies meant (explicitly or tacitly) capitalist development. However, as Sunkel has pointed out, in the intellectual climate of the Cold War historical materialism was excluded from the discourse of development in the West (and, indeed, from that in the Soviet Union as well);[1] Marx's analysis of the historical conditions in which capitalist production arose and spread in Europe was ignored. Development in the colonies or ex-colonies was theorized in terms of the need to supply a series of 'factors' that were presupposed both in the neo-classical and the Keynesian models of growth.

However, the development which took place under the aegis of these ideas (summed up in the theory of 'modernization' and the 'diffusion' of capital and skills through 'aid' and 'private overseas investment') failed to ameliorate mass poverty and tended to heighten inequality and increase social tensions, resulting in a series of crises throughout the Third World. These crises threatened to strengthen socialist forces, and culminated in a large number of repressive, and mostly parasitic and inefficient, military regimes.

One reaction to this was to abandon the liberal and democratic presuppositions of earlier development theory and accept that inequality, unemployment, conflict and authoritarianism are 'the inevitable consequences of the transition to capitalist development, the price to be paid in order to achieve development'.[2] The best-known theoretician of this reaction was Huntington.[3] It is explicitly upheld today by American officials such as Mrs Kirkpatrick and Mr Enders, and implicitly accepted by many of those concerned with development in Washington and other Western capitals. The other reaction was to accept – often rather eclectically – the theses of the dependency school.

The dependency school accepted the concept of development implied in the postwar orthodoxy but asserted that so far from being promoted by aid and trade it was prevented from occurring in the ex-colonies by the prior development of capitalism in the 'metropoles'. The 'periphery' economies had been structured to be suppliers of primary products and importers of manufactures, the 'surplus' generated at the periphery was transferred to the centre by MNCs, and a range of political, commercial and cultural relations reinforced both these mechanisms. Moreover, a class structure was created at the periphery – comprador classes deploying authoritarian state powers, and politically weak and backward peasant majorities – which 'internalized' these external relations of dependence.

What unites dependency theorists is the view that the historical circumstances of the insertion of the colonial and ex-colonial countries into the capitalist world economy structured their positions in that economy in ways which decisively influenced their subsequent development. While this development was capitalist it was subordinate to the needs of capital in the imperial metropoles. But in considering the dependency school it is necessary to distinguish between several variants. A strong version, developed most notably by A. G. Frank, stressed the appropriation to the metropoles of surplus produced at the periphery, and argued that so long as this subordination lasted development at the periphery would remain 'blocked'.[4] A weaker version, associated with F. H. Cardoso but common to most Latin American dependency theorists, holds that capitalist development may occur in a particular peripheral country such as Brazil, where conditions make investment attractive for international capital, but that this 'associated-dependent development' remains qualitatively different from development in the metropoles. It is by implication less benign (for example, resting on repression) and is seen as lacking its own internal dynamic – it depends on foreign capital, technology and markets. In its most cautious version, this is not so much a theory as an 'approach' which simply stresses the historical experience of each peripheral society, the implications of, and especially its relations with, the imperial centre, for its development prospects, while recognizing that these implications may be very different for different countries.[5]

The dependency school, in turn, was subjected to criticism from both the right and the left. The latter is particularly interesting. Although dependency theory had been influenced by Marxism, and its radical versions used Marxist terminology, a more theoretically rigorous Marxist critique showed that the core concepts of dependency theory were largely *inversions* of the concepts of bourgeois developmentalism.

We can distinguish two phases of the Marxist critique; in the first phase, the Marxist critics broadly accepted that the problem was one of stagnation of output and lack of structural change in the ex-colonial economies, but rejected the *dependentistas* conceptualization and explanation of this. In the second phase, the critics, responding (like Cardoso and other Latin American *dependentistas*) to the growth of industry in Brazil and the other newly industrializing countries or NICs, questioned the definition of the problem as one of stagnation.

Both sets of critics agree that the modern condition of the ex-colonies is not due to capitalist exploitation. In Kay's words, the problem is that 'capital created underdevelopment not because it exploited the underdeveloped world, but because it did not exploit it enough'.[6] They have suffered not so much from the 'looting of their surplus' (important though this may have been in some cases) but from the failure of capital to create conditions in which the peoples of these ex-colonies produced enough surplus value to loot. Capitalism has created a world market in which all commodities

Development Theory 317

exchange at approximately the values imparted to them by the average productivity of the most productive producers, but has not reorganized production at the periphery to make workers there equally productive. But, in the view of these theorists, nothing in the logic of capital, or in the interests of the metropolitan bourgeoisie, dictates that capital should *not* do this at the periphery; if it has not, it is because conditions at the periphery make it less profitable to do so there.

Those Marxists who agreed with Frank and other early *dependentistas* that the problem was to explain the lack of capital accumulation at the periphery had to provide alternative explanations. Thus Laclau suggested that the reason was initially that forms of forced labour inherited from pre-capitalist colonialism permitted capital to offset a falling rate of profit in Europe by investing constant capital (equipment, raw materials) in the colonies and ex-colonies, but only in minimal proportions in relation to variable capital (labour); whereas subsequent advances in productivity in Europe made it no longer necessary to invest significantly in the periphery at all.[7] Emmanuel, with reference to the present day, argued that mass-consumption markets were now the decisive determinant of the location of productive capital; MNCs would always invest in San Francisco, not in Calcutta.[8] Kay, writing with the West African experience primarily in mind, argued that the reason for capital's avoidance of the ex-colonies was rather that the prior impact of merchant capital had been to extract surplus value without reorganizing production – above all, without separating the producers from their means of production, the soil – while, at the same time, extracting their exiguous surpluses more and more ruthlessly as industrial capital increasingly cut into merchant capital's own share of total surplus.[9] This led to social dislocation, the dominance of purely trading classes, and the preservation of individualized landholding but on an increasingly fragmented basis; this prevented agricultural productivity from increasing but also slowed down the appearance of a workforce fully dependent on wage labour – conditions highly unfavourable for the location of industrial capital. More generally, Brenner argued that the 'class structure of production', in the ex-colonies was the reason why capital did not go there from the metropoles; profits could be made in exports and in luxury production for the local market but not in the local production of mass-produced industrial goods because there was no significant free-wage labour force and no significant domestic class of capital.[10]

A second phase of Marxist critics, especially those who started out from an historical analysis of the global division of labour, agreed that if capital was not accumulated at the periphery it was for reasons internal to the periphery, but insisted that such reasons were *not* always present; in other words, some accumulation of capital was taking place, most obviously in the NICs but also, at an earlier stage and on a smaller scale, in many other countries and regions of the periphery. Examples include the work of Warren, Cowen, Swainson, Leys, Marcussen and Torp, and Lipietz.[11]

In recognizing the fact of capitalist growth in particular parts of the periphery this group of Marxist theorists coincided with those *dependentistas* who had acknowledged the same phenomenon and who rejected the simplistic view that 'dependence' entailed economic stagnation. The Marxists, however, were more inclined to see these cases as part of a process which could be expected to lead in some places to capitalist development *sans phrase*, whereas the *dependentistas* remained sceptical of its long-term capacity to serve as the basis for genuine national independence, and called it 'dependent capitalist development'.

One of the latter group of Marxist critics of dependency, Bill Warren, carried the argument to a new limit by arguing that imperialism had not only *not* acted to block development in the ex-colonies; on the contrary, it had imposed capitalist relations of production on them with the result that, however painfully and unevenly, a rapid expansion of capitalist production was now occurring in the Third World generally, carrying in its train the formation of the working class which would, as Marx had foreseen, eventually take control of the vastly expanded forces of production and reorganize them on socialist principles.

As Seers and Lipietz pointed out, Warren's position appeared close to that of the neo-classical developmentalists and the theorists of modernization.[12] His posthumous book *Imperialism: Pioneer of Capitalism* argues, first, that capitalist development is occurring *throughout* the Third World, rather than at particular poles of accumulation within it, with corresponding areas of stagnation and even decline; secondly, it is presented as a process accelerating as a result of an immanent logic of capitalism; and, thirdly, it is presented as 'progressive', in the historical sense of offering a way (and in Warren's view, the only way historically available in the actual circumstances of the Third World today) of harnessing social co-operation to the dynamics of continuously expanded production.[13] Its means are 'anarchic, chaotic, unplanned, sometimes brutal, but nevertheless vigorous'.[14]

And even those Marxists who do not share Warren's universalism also exhibit some tendency to converge with the earlier diffusionist and modernization perspective. For instance, all of them have stressed, as against the dependency school, that the obstacles to development are more 'internal' than 'external', especially in the shape of pre-capitalist social relations of production, class structures and dominant class cultures, a view which has something in common with the thinking of early 'modernization' writers such as McLelland, Shils and Lerner.

Even Warren's critic, Lipietz, seems less distant from the thinking of bourgeois developmentalism than he evidently imagines. He puts forward a typology of 'regimes of accumulation', each having the 'cohesion' necessary for sustaining at least a period of capitalist growth – for example, low wage 'export-substituting' economies with small markets (such as Singapore), low-wage economies with large internal markets (such as Brazil), low-wage economies close to high-wage markets (such as Spain, Portugal and Poland), and so on.[15] The combination of circumstances which makes possible the pursuit of each of an appropriate development strategy in each case – particular capacities of the state and dominant classes, for example – and which Lipietz indicates by the term 'cohesion', seems to function in his account very much as the notions of 'political development' and 'modernization' did in the work of, for example, David Apter or Myron Weiner.[16]

The reason for Lipietz's bitter criticism of Warren was that from similar intellectual premises to his own Warren appeared to arrive at a political position that was overtly pro-imperialist, because he saw imperialism as the pioneer of capitalism and capitalism as historically progressive. As Munck has observed, Warren's basic political position was more sophisticated than his critics have sometimes appreciated; in his polemic against 'dependency' he made a number of extreme statements that are not entailed by his general framework. Warren's position was that of the Lenin of *The Development of Capitalism in Russia*, who, as Warren pointed out, attacked the Narodniks (or 'populists') for wanting to arrest the development of capitalism while *also* attacking capitalism for the 'misery' it brought to the masses.[17] In his own book, however, Warren only attacked the latter-day Narodniks (that is, the *dependentistas*), and Lipietz quite justifiably criticizes him for this.[18]

Even those Marxists who do not go as far as Warren, however, are apt to exhibit a distinct degree of political passivity. For them, socialism requires a massive expansion of the productive forces, and they see capitalist development as the historical option most likely to develop the productive forces, however inadequately and at whatever social cost; and they do not see, in many cases, any social forces capable of undertaking an equally effective non-capitalist development path. This is especially true of Marxists studying Africa, where the process of dissolution of the 'natural economy' is generally least advanced.

This judgement, however, leaves Marxism in a politically untenable position. Dependency theory identifies the multinational companies, the imperialist states which support them, and their local capitalist collaborators, as enemies of the ordinary people, which implies a programme of popular revolutionary struggle against imperialism and for socialism. This, however, appears Utopian to many Marxists, in the same way that in 1850 most of the German members of the Communist League seemed Utopian to Marx, when they wanted to fight immediately for a workers' victory and he told them that it would take 'fifteen, twenty or fifty years of civil war' before conditions would be ready for the workers to take power in their own interest.[19] But whereas Marx was convinced that such conditions *were developing* in Germany, most contemporary Marxists do not share Warren's conviction that they are developing throughout the Third World. Marx himself seems to have faced the same dilemma later on in relation to Russia, not being sure even in 1881 that the Narodniks were wrong to oppose the advance of capitalism. As Palma notes, however, he does not seem to have doubted that capitalist development was *possible* there, and eighteen years later (in 1899) Lenin showed that it was occurring rapidly.[20] Whereas today, Marxists must often doubt whether any particular country created in the process of decolonization can ever be expected to become the locus of a significant process of capital accumulation. On the other hand, not wishing to adopt Utopian positions, they often fail to indicate what workers, farmers, students, or anyone else could do instead: they are, as Beckman has remarked, 'embarassingly weak in inspiring useful political analysis'.[21] As a result in Africa it is dependency theory which has won general acceptance among politically conscious people, whereas a 'Marxism' that appears to support capitalist development has little attraction.[22] 'Dependency theory' may have abandoned what was scientific in classical Marxism, but contemporary Marxism often seems to have abandoned what was revolutionary.

The degree of theoretical and political convergence that thus appears to have occurred, between Marxist critics of dependency and the bourgeois developmentalists whom dependency theory was developed to attack, should not be exaggerated, but it is significant enough to provoke some reflection. In the case of Warren and apologists of imperialism such as Rostow (the comparison drawn by Lipietz), it seems partly due to exaggerations in Warren's text which go beyond the requirements of his theoretical position, and which he might well have qualified had he lived to revise it himself. The general convergence of Marxist theorists with neo-classical theorists may also be attributed, in part, to some shared conceptual roots, notably in the labour theory of value: they are in agreement that development consists ultimately in the expansion of the productive forces through raising the productivity of labour, and they share a (sometimes tacit) belief in progress culminating in the emancipation of labour (debased, in the case of Rostow, into the idea of 'high mass *consumption*'). Many dependency theorists, by contrast, show a marked ambivalence towards this conception of development, and are inclined to define 'development' in terms of changes in the 'quality of life' (mortality or literacy rates, for example), and especially changes in the distribution of income and wealth, at existing or only modestly increased levels of output. Also, from a shared starting-point in the analysis of the logic of the process of capital accumulation, both 'development economists' and Marxists are sceptical about arguments which explain development or the lack of it by the 'mentality' or place of residence of the *owners* of capital ('domestic' *v.* 'metropolitan', and so on): hence their shared inclination to give priority to 'internal' determinants of the low-rate of capital accumulation at the periphery, whereas dependency theorists attribute prime importance to the fact that the ownership of industrial capital is concentrated in the metropoles.

Yet, by any reckoning, the theoretical differences between Marxism and neo-classical (or Keynesian) conceptions of development should be very great, above all in the centrality of history in Marxism, as opposed to static analysis, and in Marxism's conception of the social totality as a dynamic unity and as a field of contradictions, as opposed to the separation of economics from the social whole and analysis in terms of the concept of equilibrium, so characteristic of neo-classical economics; not to mention Marxism's radical commitment to the proletariat and against its exploiters. The fact that 'Marxist' development theory seems to have converged to any significant extent towards orthodox developmentalism, both conceptually and politically, needs a more particular explanation.

The first reason, in my view, is a persistent tendency of Marxist treatments of capitalism in the epoch of imperialism to lapse into economistic, functionalist and positivist generalizations. There is a tendency to ascribe an unrealistic efficacy to the 'logic' or 'needs' of capital, independently of historically given political and social conditions, and to seek simple and universal causal relations between the accumulation process and world events. Lenin's treatment of imperialism is a case in point: while he correctly considered it a much broader phenomenon than the drive for territorial empire, he wrongly sought to establish a general 'cause' of it. This attempt was misguided; there are no general determinants of the international politics of large-scale capitals and their states, as their needs and interests constantly develop and change. Similarly, contemporary Marxist (or 'Marxisant') discourse has tended to seek general relationships between the logic or needs of capital (or capitalism) in general, and accumulation at the periphery. Frank originally saw these needs as requiring underdevelopment at the periphery. Warren saw them as requiring, and now producing, capital accumulation everywhere.

Whereas it is surely clear by now that (1) the logic of capital accumulation has had very different implications for accumulation at the periphery at different periods (as Brewer has cogently pointed out);[23] (2) the question of whether a particular country experiences a process of domestic capital accumulation at any given period is a social, cultural and political question, as much as a question of its natural resources, strategic location, population size, and so on. The 'natural laws of capitalist production'[24] operate on every country that is incorporated in the world market, but no particular national future can be read off from this, especially for small countries whose frontiers are the result of highly arbitrary colonization and decolonization processes. If 'the country that is more developed industrially only shows, to the less developed, the image of its own future',[25] it must be remembered that Britain showed to Germany (the comparison Marx had in mind in this famous passage) not just Manchester and the Midlands, but also the Scottish 'deer forests' (that is, vast regions of the 'development of underdevelopment') and the oppressed and stagnant home colony of Roman Catholic Ireland. It is by making political and other contradictions which operate to determine the fate of particular countries or regions within the capitalist world market central to its analysis that historical materialism should differentiate itself radically from the approaches of the neo-classical developmentalists. And it is significant, in this regard, that Cardoso and Faletto, in their 1979 Preface to the English edition of their book, *Dependency and Development in Latin America*, present a conception of 'dependency' analysis which not only rejects any stagnationist theory but is also strongly Marxist both in its language and its formulation of the problem, while fully retaining the emphasis on historical political, class and ideological dimensions that the dependency school has always stressed. It is this convergence which deserves attention and development; that is, between a dependency approach stripped of any residue of bourgeois nationalism, and a Marxism freed from abstract economism.

Secondly, the political 'Menshevism' (that is, waiting to let capitalism develop first) of much 'Marxist' theory shows the need to shed the positivist conception of socialism inherited from the Marxism of the Second International: that is, socialism conceived of as a sort of inheritance of the productive forces raised to the level of abundance by capitalism, and guaranteed by the fact that the great majority of the population have become wage-earners. This image, too, often lies behind the otherwise correct Marxist critique of the Utopianism of dependency thinkers who call for 'socialist revolution' as the only alternative to capitalist underdevelopment. The question must be asked whether it is any more Utopian to call for socialism (in some sense of the term) based on peasants' and workers' struggles in, say, Zambia, than it is to suppose that capitalism will establish the classical 'preconditions' for socialism there. At a time when reductionist and economistic conceptions of socialism (that is, as a social form emerging more or less spontaneously from the final crisis of capitalism) are being increasingly replaced by more activist and 'populist' conceptions in the advanced capitalist countries, it is essential for Marxism to shed this 'Menshevik' residue in relation to the Third World. To say this is not to abandon the view that the 'emancipation of labour' (through raising productivity) is necessary for any viable form of socialism, or to deny that success in national popular struggles often depends on the outcome of struggles elsewhere. But the need for a non-reductionist, immediate political analysis that is, as Beckman says, *useful* for popular action, is inescapable.

Third, and relatedly, it is necessary to disentangle the concept of imperialism from the concept of capitalism. The prevailing failure to do this is a legacy of Lenin's reduction of imperialism to capitalism by defining the former as a stage of the latter. Not only was his characterization of this stage faulty in detail and in general (that is, it was not the 'highest' stage of capitalism), but this procedure left no room for the autonomy of politics from economics. Imperialism needs to be defined as the international politics of international capital (or the international class struggle of the international bourgeoisie), largely conducted by the states of the advanced capitalist countries and international agencies controlled by them (though not to be *identified* with the actions of such states and agencies): it is *registered in* all aspects of international relations (trade, aid, culture, and so on). It has its own logics and dynamics (military, financial, and so on) and it is primarily concerned with the political rather than the economic interests of capital, its most obvious expression being the policing of the Third World by the reinforcement of reliable regimes and the destabilization of unreliable ones.

The rationality of imperialism, defined in this way, flows from the interests of international capital in general, but is not identical with it: it can coincide or conflict with the economic interests of individual capitals and even of capital in general, in particular situations. By the same token imperialism's interest in the capitalist development of particular countries or areas at a given moment varies. It is concerned with control and with strategic issues, not development; it has required, for example, massive unproductive expenditure on the Falkland Islands, and the prevention of potentially lucrative trade with, and investment in, Cuba. There is no invariant or necessary relation between imperialism and the process of capital accumulation in any particular part of the periphery.

It follows from this that even if you think capitalist development is possible or occurring in a given country, this does not entail any sympathy for

Development Theory 323

imperialism, as Warren seemed to think; it is not necessarily the pioneer of capitalism. Conversely, it is not necessarily the enemy of capital accumulation at the periphery, as Beckman, among others, has argued.[26] The links between the political strategy and programmes of international capital, and the capitalist development process, are complex and specific, not simple and general.

Recognizing this is necessary for a useful theory of development, which must distinguish between at least three separate dimensions of struggle in the Third World: against capitalist exploitation and oppression, for the development of the working class and a transition to socialism; against capitalist underdevelopment, for a transition to a, no doubt different, socialism based on the social forces formed by the specific conditions of underdevelopment and the struggles to which it gives rise; and against imperialism, which has no simple or general relationship with the process of capital accumulation at any given point in the 'periphery', but does consistently oppose the popular right of self-determination.

Notes: Chapter 20

1 O. Sunkel, 'The development of development thinking', in J. Villamil (ed.), *Transnational Capitalism and National Development* (Brighton, Sussex, 1979), pp. 21–3. On modernization see also J. Valenzuela and A. Valenzuela, 'Modernisation and dependence', in ibid., pp. 31–65.
2 Sunkel, 'The development', p. 26.
3 *Political Order in Changing Societies* (New Haven, Conn., 1969). For a discussion and references to critiques see C. Leys, 'Samuel Huntington and the end of classical modernisation theory', in H. Alavi and T. Shanin (eds), *Introduction to the Sociology of 'Developing Societies'* (London, 1982), pp. 332–49.
4 Notably in his famous *Capitalism and Underdevelopment in Latin America* (New York, 1969).
5 See espec. F. H. Cardoso and E. Faletto, *Dependency and Development in Latin America* (Berkeley, Calif., Los Angeles and London, 1979), espec. pp. vii–xxv and 149–216.
6 G. B. Kay, *Development and Underdevelopment: A Marxist Analysis* (London, 1975), p. x.
7 E. Laclau, *Politics and Ideology in Marxist Theory: Capitalism, Fascism, Populism* (London, 1977), pp. 37–41.
8 A. Emmanuel, 'Myths of development versus myths of underdevelopment', *New Left Review*, no. 85 (1974), p. 75.
9 Kay, *Development and Underdevelopment*, ch. 5.
10 R. Brenner, 'The origins of capitalist development: a critique of neo-Smithian Marxism', *New Left Review*, no. 104 (1977), pp. 84–5.
11 B. Warren, 'Imperialism and capitalist industrialisation', *New Left Review*, no. 81 (1973), pp. 3–44, and idem, *Imperialism: Pioneer of Capitalism* (London, 1980); a selection of M. P. Cowen's seminal papers is appended to his 'The British state and agrarian accumulation in Kenya', in M. Fransman (ed.), *Industry and Accumulation in Africa* (London, 1982), pp. 142–69; N. Swainson, 'The rise of a national bourgeoisie in Kenya', *Review of African Political Economy*, vol. 8 (1977), pp. 39–55, and idem, *The Development of Corporate Capitalism in Kenya* (London, 1980); C. Leys, 'Capital accumulation, class formation and dependency: the significance of the Kenyan case', in R. Miliband and J. Saville (eds), *Socialist Register 1978* (London, 1978), pp. 241–66; H. S. Marcussen and J. Torp, *Internationalisation of Capital: Prospects for the Third World* (London, 1982); A. Lipietz, 'Towards global Fordism?', *New Left Review*, no. 132 (1982), pp. 33–47.
12 D. Seers, *The Congruence of Marxism and Other Neo-Classical Doctrines*, Institute of

Development Studies Discussion Paper No. 136 (Brighton, Sussex, 1978). See also A. H. M. Hoogvelt, *The Sociology of Developing Countries* (London, 1976), pp. 78 ff.; and A. Lipietz, 'Marx or Rostow?', *New Left Review*, no. 132 (1982), pp. 48–58.
13 Warren, *Imperialism*, ch. 2, espec. pp. 17–18.
14 ibid., p. 223.
15 Lipietz, 'Towards global Fordism?'.
16 D. A. Apter, *The Politics of Modernization* (Chicago, 1965); M. Weiner (ed.), *Modernization: The Dynamics of Growth* (New York, 1966).
17 R. Munck, 'Imperialism and dependency: recent debates and old dead-ends', in R. H. Chilcote (ed.), *Dependency and Marxism* (London, 1981), pp. 169, and 38, n. 65.
18 It also seems rather likely that had Warren lived to complete his book, its political thrust would have been somewhat more nuanced. Lipietz's interpretations of Warren, moreover, are sometimes questionable. It is something to point out that Warren does not attack capitalism; another to say that he finds it 'legitimate' ('Marx or Rostow?', cit. at n. 12 above, p. 56). Moreover, Lipietz's own positions are not self-evidently superior. For example, Warren is castigated for assuming that the 'dissolution of particular natural ties' by peripheral capitalism universally gives rise to 'a higher level of social, economic and cultural cohesion' on the basis of which manufacturing capitalism can develop; on the contrary, Lipietz says, the way this 'now develops on the periphery . . . [he cites 'Saigon's brothel economy] . . . endows it [the periphery, presumably] with precisely that significance which distinguishes a centre from a periphery' (p. 57). But Lipietz does not state what this significance is, let alone suggest what alternative kinds of 'cohesion' may be available.
19 K. Marx, 'Minutes of the Central Committee meeting of 15 September 1850', in D. Fernbach (ed.), *The Revolutions of 1848* (Harmondsworth, Middx, 1973), p. 341.
20 G. Palma, 'Dependency theory: a critical overview', in D. Seers (ed.), *Dependency Theory: A Critical Reassessment* (London, 1981), p. 31.
21 B. Beckman, 'Imperialism and the national bourgeoisie', *Review of African Political Economy*, vol. 22 (1981), p. 10.
22 ibid.
23 A. Brewer, *Marxist Theories of Imperialism* (London, 1980), pp. 23–4.
24 The expression is from Marx's preface to the 1st edn of *Das Kapital*. See K. Marx, *Capital*, Vol. 1 (Harmondsworth, Middx, 1976), p. 91.
25 ibid.
26 The argument leads to difficulties because the relation is ambivalent. See Beckman, 'Imperialism', cit. at n. 22 above, pp. 18–19.

21 Theories of Imperialism in Perspective

ANTHONY BREWER

A theory of imperialism must explain how a few European countries came to rule most of the world, and also why their empires collapsed so suddenly in the period after the Second World War. This question cannot be discussed in narrowly political and diplomatic terms. The expansion of empire was inextricably bound up with the development of capitalism in Europe and its spread throughout the rest of the world, and also with the emergence of very large and very long-lasting economic inequalities between 'centre' and 'periphery' (to use a convenient shorthand).

It is pointless to debate whether or not imperialism can be explained in 'economic' terms. To argue that imperialism had nothing to do with the economic dynamic of the centres of capitalism would be absurd. It would be equally absurd to suggest that every specific act of annexation, every twist and turn of colonial policy, was directly motivated by the hope of immediate economic gain. To counterpose 'economic' and 'non-economic' explanations is unhelpful; what has to be done is to trace out the interconnections between economic and political development and to explain the particular forms of economic and political domination which have come into existence in different regions at different times. In short, what is needed is a theory of the (capitalist) world system. Such a theory does not yet exist, and it will not be easy to construct.

Capitalism

Capitalism is a system in which privately owned firms employ workers and sell their products on the market. In such a system there are very powerful incentives for capitalists to reinvest profits in new and better equipment and to seek out more efficient methods of production, new and more attractive products, new markets, cheaper sources of supply, and so on. An innovator who succeeds (many fail) can escape the direct pressures of competition for a time, until others catch up, and can make abnormally large profits. Those who fall behind find that they have higher costs or less marketable products than their competitors, and they are soon driven out of business. Capitalism therefore tends to produce cumulative economic development.

The historical record unequivocally supports this theory. No preceding form of economic organization has displayed anything remotely comparable to the dynamism of capitalism. There are, of course, incentives for economic advance in other systems (if more is produced, there is more to go round), but the incentives are relatively weak, the obstacles to change are much stronger, and the results have been puny by comparison. (How socialism rates on this count is a thorny question, which can be passed over here.) Europe's economic lead, the foundation of the expansion of European power, can be explained by the historical fact that a fully capitalist economic system first emerged in Europe.

The outward thrust of capitalism is also easy to explain. The emerging disparity of economic development between capitalist and non-capitalist areas meant that relative prices differed, which created opportunities for profitable trade. Capitalist enterprises seek out opportunities for trade just as they seek out new methods of production, and for the same reasons. Those who find cheaper sources of supply will undercut those who lag behind. Development at the centre and expansion into the periphery were, and still are, part of the same process. This is not to say that capitalism needed a periphery or that development would have been impossible without external trade (though it would have been slower), but given the opportunities, it was inevitable that they would be seized, and equally inevitable that traders would look to their home governments for support.

The argument presented above rests heavily on the competitive process as an explanation of capitalist development and expansion. Many theories of imperialism, by contrast, emphasize monopoly. The important point is that the concepts of 'monopoly' and 'competition' can be defined in a variety of ways, and are not necessarily mutually exclusive. 'Perfect' competition, much discussed in economics textbooks, is a situation in which individual buyers and sellers are so numerous that they have no control at all (as individuals) over the market price, which is set by the impersonal workings of the market. 'Pure' monopoly, by contrast, is a case where a single firm faces no competition from sellers of the same or similar products, and no threat of competition from new entrants into its line of business, so it can set whatever price it likes. These concepts have some uses in economic theory, but neither bears much relation to reality.

In practice, most firms have some degree of control over the markets they sell in, some degree of monopoly power, but these partial monopolies are under constant threat from new competitors (perhaps firms which are already established in other lines of business), from new products and new methods of production. The analysis of pricing in imperfectly competitive markets is difficult, but need not be discussed here. The point is that the competitive pressures to innovate and to expand are undiminished, while a certain degree of monopoly may actually increase firms' capacity to commit resources to new ventures. It is no paradox to say that a monopolist has to compete vigorously in order to remain a monopolist.

It is also important to distinguish between the mercantile monopolies characteristic of the early stages of capitalist development, and the large firms of today. In early capitalism, markets were small, transport costs were high and production was largely carried out by small firms and by independent artisans and peasants. Long-distance trade was restricted to items of high value, and was very risky though potentially very profitable. The mercantile monopolies of this era controlled trade, not production (except incidentally), and played a central role in the early stages of European imperial expansion. The large firms of today are based on large-scale production, and depend on large markets and large-scale trade; they are the opposite of mercantile monopolies in almost every respect, and the two must not be confused.

Mercantile monopolies were swept aside in the centre countries and on the main arteries of trade, as capitalism developed, but they retained their hold for a very long time in much of the periphery, where they often operated in close association with colonial administrations. They very probably contributed to blocking or delaying economic development, since it threatened their interests. In particular, as traders, they had an interest in blocking any diversification of production via import substitution. Modern multinational companies, by contrast, can act as a means of transmitting technology into underdeveloped regions by setting up branch plants, either for the local market or for export.

Theories of Imperialism

The classical Marxist theory of imperialism was constructed in the first quarter of this century, mainly by Hilferding and Bukharin, and popularized by Lenin.[1] The main aim of these writers was not to explain the development of colonial empires, but to account for the build-up of aggressive nationalism which culminated in the First World War. They should not be criticized for Eurocentrism; war was the most urgent problem of their time, and the causes of war were to be found in Europe.

The basic theory runs as follows. Competition weeds out small firms, leaving fewer and fewer large firms. At a certain stage, reached in about 1900 in the main capitalist centres, monopolistic cartels and trusts began to form, under the leadership of the banks. At this stage, the world market was still too large and diversified to be monopolized effectively, so nascent national monopolies turned to the state for protection against foreign competitors in their home markets, and for support abroad. Competition was not eliminated; rather it was transferred to the political and military arena, in the form of competition between 'state capitalist trusts', linking government, banks and industry. Inter-imperialist rivalry and war was the result. This is a coherent and well-constructed theory, yielding striking conclusions from rather a simple basic model, as a good theory should. Its main prediction has, however, been falsified by events. Since 1945, inter-imperialist rivalry has declined almost to vanishing point (unless you count East–West rivalry, which would be equally damaging to the theory, since Russia ought not, in classical Marxist terms, to be imperialist). Where was the flaw? The most important, perhaps, was the failure of the classical Marxists to recognize the extent to which large firms were infiltrating each other's home markets by international investment. To put it simply, multinationals have no incentive to back one state against another when they are well entrenched in both.

It should be noted that the classical Marxist theory had little to say about the mechanics of imperial expansion. It provides little help in the detailed analysis of colonial policy, and empirical evidence about colonial policy can do little to either support or disprove it. It is not, in modern terms, a theory of imperialism at all. In any case, most Marxists have abandoned the substance of the classical Marxist theory of imperialism, even though they may conceal it by working in a few dutiful references to Lenin. Its place has been taken by a rather loose body of theory which I shall call 'dependency' theory.[2]

The focus of dependency theory is on the relation between advanced and underdeveloped countries, centre and periphery. In this view, the prospects of any given national economy depend primarily on its position in the world economy, and the unequal structure of the world economy works to perpetuate itself by blocking, or at least limiting, development in the periphery.

The mechanisms involved are not wholly clear, since different members of the school tell different stories, but some common themes emerge. 'Surplus' is extracted from the periphery, through biased terms of trade or through the direct repatriation of profits to the centre, starving the periphery of investment funds. The economic structures of the periphery also retard development because markets are narrow, because local producers face crushing competition from established rivals in the centre, and because the periphery exports primary products, which are said to have limited prospects of growth.

There is some truth to all of these arguments, but they are not conclusive. The basic problem is that dependency theorists seem to think of the world economy as a zero-game, in which the centre's gain is necessarily the periphery's loss. It is, however, perfectly possible for both to gain (which is not to say that they always do).

The empirical evidence suggests that the world is more complex and more subject to change than dependency theory suggests. First, the gap between centre and periphery, which widened in the nineteenth century, now shows signs of closing, albeit slowly. Growth rates of output in the periphery are considerably higher than those in the centre, though higher population growth offsets the beneficial effect on average incomes, and many people in underdeveloped countries have yet to gain any significant benefits at all from growth. Secondly, the experience of different countries is very varied. In every period of the history of the world capitalist system some countries have been rising in relative terms, and others falling back. What is needed is a theory which can explain the differences between periods and countries.

The difference between the nineteenth and the later twentieth centuries may be because many countries have attained national independence, and can look to their own state to protect their interests. Alternatively, it may be because wages have risen faster in the centre than in the periphery, so that the balance of competitive advantage has switched over, and many labour-intensive activities are now being transferred to the periphery. It is even harder to suggest any useful general explanation for the different records of different countries, though it can be pointed out that successful export-led growth in one place makes it harder for others to follow, by intensifying competition, so that competition with other peripheral areas may be more important than any exploitation by the centre in holding back development. Some areas make the breakthrough, but only some.

Dependency theory does not generally have much to say about direct imperial rule, since the theory originated in Latin America and was designed specifically to explain why 150 years of political independence had not sufficed to bring about development in that region. The thrust of dependency theory is to argue that all peripheral regions are in the same boat, whether they are politically independent or not. Direct political intervention is, on this view, only one of a range of options open to centre states, while local élites commonly have an interest in preserving the status quo without needing to be prompted by outsiders. It may be noted that the 'excentric' theory of imperialism, to be discussed below, would fit in quite well with dependency theory.

The excentric theory of imperialism, presented by Professor Ronald Robinson in Chapter 18 above, has much more limited and specific aims than classical Marxist or dependency theory. As Robinson says, it is not a theory in its own right but an extension of classical theories.

The theory takes as given both the asymmetry of power between centre and periphery (which dependency theory aims to explain) and the outward thrust of the centre. Spheres of influence were established, dividing the world between the imperial powers; we are not told how the division was made, but we are told that there was a tacit agreement between European powers not to interfere with each other's possessions. (Robinson clearly differs from the classical Marxists on this point.)

The question then is why centre states imposed formal imperial rule in some places, and contented themselves with less formal forms of control in others. The centre states are presented as rational, maximizing agents weighing costs against benefits; they made different choices because circumstances and opportunities were different in different peripheral areas (hence 'excentric' theory: theory that stresses conditions in the periphery). The crucial factor was the availability of local collaborators. Where the existing social and economic system was able to accommodate itself to the needs of the centre, where local élites had an interest in collaborating, formal rule was unnecessary. Where local system did not fit in, they were conquered and remade.

Terminology apart, this theory has much in common with some Marxist writings which focus on the 'mode of production'.[3] Where capitalism, or at least commodity production, was well established, central capital could penetrate by economic means with orthodox diplomacy to back it up. Non-commodity producing modes of production, those in which the market was restricted or non-existent, resisted peaceful penetration and were conquered and reshaped.

Excentric theory clearly cannot stand alone, since it is an explanation of forms of political control, and these cannot be divorced from the development of economic, political and social structures in both centre and periphery. It should be noted, in particular, that economic interests in both centre and periphery were shaped by the interaction between the two as well as shaping that interaction. Excentric theory does, however, have much to contribute to a more complete model.

The End of Empire?

The period since the Second World War poses a severe test for any theory of imperialism. Any theory which posits a direct link between the spread of empire and the expansion of the world capitalist economy fails the test, since the collapse of formal empire coincided with the most vigorous burst of economic expansion in the history of capitalism.

One possible explanation of decolonization focuses on the centre, on the shift of power from the old colonial centres to the United States, and on the emergence of the Soviet Union as the focus of an alternative world system. This explains the collapse of the old empires, but leaves the question: why did the United States not step in as a replacement? To say that the Americans were anti-imperialist (that is, that they preferred informal to formal empire) is not an explanation; the aim should be to explain American policy, not merely to describe it. Nor can it be argued that formal empire fell because of the breakdown of the monopoly which each colonial power maintained in the external relations of its possessions. Formal empire was as much a means of maintaining such a monopoly, as a result of it, and the United States was probably in a position to impose a monopoly if it had wanted to do so.

The alternative is to look to the periphery for an explanation. The hypothesis is obvious: social and political changes had raised the costs of maintaining formal empire to a prohibitive level. This change was itself the result of imperialism. The integration of the periphery into the metropolitan capitalist economy involved the creation of a local working class, a nascent capitalist class of traders and subcontractors, and a centralized administrative apparatus staffed by a growing body of functionaries. Formal colonial rule antagonized most of these groups, while independence made it possible to reconstruct an alliance with those who benefited from the economic link with the centre. The root cause of decolonization, then, is to be found in the periphery, though changes at the centre provided the occasion, and no doubt explain why the change came at almost the same time in areas at very different levels of development.

A further factor was the development of multinational companies (companies which have production operations in more than one country). These, while not a new phenomenon, became much more important after the Second World War. Almost all multinationals grew up within a single national economy, are still firmly attached to their base, and look to their home government for support. Nevertheless, their interests are not identical with those of their home country, especially when they shift operations to low-wage areas in the periphery, weakening the home economy. Multinationals frequently prefer to deal with weak governments in the periphery, which they can play off against each other, rather than with relatively inflexible colonial administrations. Multinationals are sometimes accused of acting as agents of their home governments; it would more often be true to accuse the governments of acting on behalf of the corporations.

The collapse of formal empire has left the inequality of wealth and power between centre and periphery almost undiminished. Much the larger part of the world remains integrated into the capitalist world economy, and the United States is clearly the dominant power, though its relative preponderance is declining from the extraordinary levels reached just after the Second World War. There is a tacit agreement among the centre powers (partly formalized in a variety of institutions such as the IMF, GATT, and so on) that the others will accept the leadership of the United States in return for an American undertaking to respect the interests of the others. The United States, for example, works for free trade rather than for special concessions for American firms (sometimes). The United States, then, has a substantial monopoly of policy-making.

The economic, diplomatic and military pressures which can be brought to bear on relatively weak countries are considerable (civil and military aid, access to credit, arms supplies, trade concessions, and so on). Successive American governments have used all of these to reward their allies and to punish those who step out of line. So, of course, does the Soviet Union and so do other countries; it is not that the United States is more malevolent than other countries, but that it is much more powerful. It would be Utopian to expect that the power would not be used.

The main aim of American diplomacy has been to exclude the Russians, to protect capitalist interests, and to maintain as far as possible the freedom of action of multinational firms. Put simply, the aim is to defend capitalism, and this aim finds ready support among dominant groups in capitalist underdeveloped countries. The normal pattern is for the United States to support rightwing or centre governments and to harass any that rebel. Direct intervention is rarely necessary, though the United States has intervened brutally on occasion. This policy is not, of course, always successful.

Whether this profoundly unequal world system is called 'imperialist' or not is a matter of terminology, and it is a waste of time to quarrel over words. It seems to fit Robinson's model of informal imperialism more closely than he himself is willing to concede. That American politicians deny any imperialist intent is, of course, irrelevant. It is the outcome, not the intention, which matters.

According to dependency theory, underdeveloped countries are doomed to remain poor and dependent unless they break away from the capitalist world system, which American policy is designed to prevent them from doing. In this view, the world system remains the same in essentials, continuity outweighs discontinuity, and a new, relatively more effective system of control (informal imperialism or neocolonialism) has been substituted for one which was failing (formal imperialism).

An alternative view derives from Marx's writings on India, and has been restated by Warren.[4] In this view, imperialism served not to defend capitalism, but to implant it in new territories. Capitalist development can then start, and imperialism will fade away, albeit slowly. The end of formal empire was by no means the end of imperialism, but it did mark a crucial change of direction.

Neither argument is wholly satisfactory. Development is taking place in the periphery, so Warren may prove right in the end, but that is little comfort to present generations. Competition between peripheral countries, and the emergence of new centres of power, new 'sub-imperialisms' in the periphery, may well be the most significant features of the coming decades.

Notes: Chapter 21

1 R. Hilferding, *Finance Capital* (London, 1981); N. Bukharin, *Imperialism and World Economy* (London, 1972); V. I. Lenin, 'Imperialism, the highest stage of capitalism' in idem, *Collected Works*, Vol. 22 (Moscow, 1964). See also A. Brewer, *Marxist Theories of Imperialism* (London, 1980), chs 4 and 5.
2 See, for example, A. G. Frank, *Capitalism and Underdevelopment in Latin America* (New York, 1969); idem, *Dependent Accumulation and Underdevelopment* (London, 1978); I. Wallerstein, *The Capitalist World-Economy: Essays* (Cambridge, 1979).
3 See Brewer, *Marxist Theories of Imperialism*, chs 8 and 11.
4 B. Warren, *Imperialism: Pioneer of Capitalism* (London, 1980).

22 The End of Empire and the Continuity of Imperialism
WOLFGANG J. MOMMSEN

Strategies of Imperialist Rule

A recently published study on European imperialism in the nineteenth and twentieth centuries begins with the observation, 'the "age of Imperialism" is over', only to add that 'on the other hand, "imperialism" itself, as a variety of human political and economic behaviour, appears to be quite alive, judging from events in Vietnam and Afghanistan'.[1] Furthermore, it points out that many people hold the view that 'the dissolution of the colonial empires in our own time was simply the end of a phase in the history of imperialism', not of imperialism itself.[2] Apparently there is no easy answer to these questions. There can be little doubt that the ending of formal colonial rule by the Western powers with but few remnants of their former colonial possessions still intact is a crucial cæsura in the history of mankind. This is true equally of the peoples formerly subjected to imperialist control and of the European peoples.

The break-up of the European colonial empires which had been built up in the course of more than four centuries was associated with Europe's loss of hegemony over the globe which had been so noticeable in the eighteenth and nineteenth centuries. Two new superpowers, the United States and, with some delay, the Soviet Union, had stepped in. Their rise to hegemonial status in world affairs, particularly since the Second World War, can well be described as the emergence of two new varieties of informal and, for the most part, indirect imperialism. While there will be disagreement as to whether the hegemony exercised by the United States over much of the Western world since 1945 should be described as imperialism, formal or informal, few people will object to assessing the Soviet bloc as an empire of a new sort, one which displays striking continuities with its tsarist predecessor. Whatever the case, the process of decolonization was intimately connected to the rise of these two antagonistic powers to the world power status which they enjoy today.

The cæsura marked by decolonization and the end of empire, that is to say, the forfeiting of all direct control by the former colonial powers, appears to be a very marked one. But on closer inspection, it evaporates to some extent. The formal granting of independence did not change social reality at the periphery overnight; instead it was merely a stage, though an important one, in the painful and difficult struggle for emancipation in a world still dominated by the West economically, culturally and, at least to some degree, politically, though perhaps no longer to the same extent as before 1940.

This fact becomes all the more apparent if the end of empire is seen against the backcloth of the reality of imperialist rule during the classical age of imperialism. The classical interpretations of imperialist rule which stressed, above all, formal imperialist domination were far too simplistic. None of the imperialist powers ever established a full system of direct rule in their colonial possessions directly comparable to classic European patterns of government; instead, they all relied upon various combinations of formal and informal, direct and indirect rule which could not do without the partly enforced, partly voluntary collaboration of indigenous élites.

According to Robinson and Gallagher's famous definition, European imperialism proceeded according to the paradigm 'informal control if possible, formal rule if necessary'.[3] That is to say, the establishment of imperialist control was a gradual process. Initially it was effected by informal techniques with a minimum of governmental interference, if any at all. The establishment of formal and direct rule was only the ultimate stage in this process of extending imperial control, a stage which from the point of view of the metropolitan society did not necessarily turn out to be the most profitable one. For, as Robinson has so aptly put it, 'if empire could not be had on the cheap, it was not worth having at all'.[4] It has by now been established beyond doubt that there was a continuity of expansion, however slow, at the periphery throughout the nineteenth century, irrespective of what metropolitan governments might say about it, and of whether public opinion was in favour of further imperialist expansion, or, as was the case in the early Victorian period in Britain and elsewhere, against it. In many instances, trade paved the way for the eventual establishment of formal colonial rule, in others it was prepared for by missionary activity, or by a combination of both, whilst in only a relatively small number of cases strategic considerations played a decisive role. It was the rivalry between the European powers which eventually made it necessary to formalize imperialist rule and establish proper bureaucratic administrations by which the usually vast and often thinly populated territories in Asia and Africa could be effectively controlled.

In fact most, if not all, of the imperialist powers found that the co-operation of indigenous élites was not only convenient, but indispensable for the administration of the territories in question. Direct rule, that is, administration without the assistance, however limited, of indigenous élites or social groups with an independent standing in the respective polity, was the exception rather than the rule. Britain is commonly held to have invented and practised widely the strategy of 'indirect rule', whilst France allegedly acted according to the theory of 'assimilation'. In fact, however, all the imperialist powers employed techniques of subsidiary rule in administering their colonial possessions, though in differing ways, which were conditioned by local circumstances and the availability of indigenous governmental systems or collaborative élites suitable for the colonial power's purposes; sometimes these even had to be created artificially. Almost everywhere we find rather colourful and complex combinations of direct or near-direct rule and indirect or subsidiary rule with the assistance of indigenous puppet regimes. The Indian principalities, which were sometimes arranged like a chessboard, provide one example of this. Not surprisingly the European powers often preferred to exercise imperial control in the form of a protectorate, however fictitious this may have been. Often this fiction was maintained right to the very end in the face of actual reality, as was done by Britian in the case of Egypt, and by France in the case of Morocco.

Thus, Robinson and Gallagher's paradigm 'informal control if possible, formal rule if necessary' needs to be supplemented by the formula 'indirect rule wherever possible, direct rule only if unavoidable'. Without relying on indirect or subsidiary forms of rule, it would never have been possible to control, let alone administer, vast territories overseas with only fairly small numbers of white officials and amazingly small military forces, even if indigenous auxiliary forces are taken into account. A variety of factors, including indigenous resistance and the crisis at the periphery, on the one hand, and the growing rivalry between the imperialist powers on the other, eventually made it necessary to turn increasingly to formal and direct rule. This process, amongst other factors, precipitated the final collapse of the colonial empires, since proper territorial administration (including policing and military protection) eventually proved too costly for the mother country and too onerous for the indigenous population, thereby provoking increased resistance from many quarters.

Whilst formally dichotomies, *formal* and *informal empire*, or *direct* and *indirect rule* must in fact be considered complementary forms of imperialist domination; in most cases combinations of these strategies were practised during the classical age of imperialism and, as will be discussed later, in many cases even after the ending of formal colonial rule. Economic penetration, cultural (or religious) predominance, technological superiority, political predominance and, above all, an unheard-of military preponderance, all these factors played a role in establishing imperial control, informal or formal, indirect or direct. Imperialist control was usually effected with the help of comparatively miniscule economic resources from the metropolitan country and a minimum of military force. Herbert Lüthy justifiably pointed to the weakness of the indigenous societies at the periphery in their confrontation with the European invaders.[5] In most cases, only minimal efforts were necessary to crush indigenous resistance to European penetration, while often it was not openly apparent at all. In this way, the imperialist powers established their rule with comparative ease and limited expenditure, both financially and in terms of human effort.

Therefore the view put forward by Ronald Robinson in his contribution to this volume[6] is rather fruitful. Robinson suggests that imperialist rule could be described as a set of 'unequal bargains' between the European imperialist groups and various indigenous groupings on the local level which varied greatly in character according to circumstances and time. These 'unequal bargains' were, for the most part, possible only because of the enormous imbalance in economic, intellectual, military and political power potentials which existed between the two from the start.[7] In general, the indigenous population had no real chance of refusing these bargains, let alone of effectively combating European imperialist penetration, although there were many cases of heroic resistance. It goes without saying that the possibility of recourse to violent action was always an essential element of those bargains; yet often a mere symbolic demonstration of the white man's might sufficed to achieve the submission of the indigenous peoples. Representatives of the metropolitan powers were fully aware of the fact that empire was, in the last resort, based upon the sword.[8] This was an 'unspoken assumption' on both sides. Only an initial powerful display of military might (symbolic or real) on the part of the imperialist intruders made unequal bargains of this kind possible. The experience of totalitarian regimes tells us that usually only a minimum of actual suppression and terror is necessary to force even highly advanced peoples into apparently ready submission. It can be assumed that this was also the case in the imperialistic situation.

However, the fact that power (direct or indirect) played an important part in bringing about these bargains does not invalidate the thesis that they were none the less in a way negotiated. Admittedly, the imperialist 'intruders' were often able to exploit local power rivalries and social divisions within indigenous societies for their own purposes. Furthermore, in many cases military superiority was seen by the indigenous population as a genuine source of legitimacy. They had usually experienced little else but subjection to the arbitrary domination of rulers or castes, often of a different ethnic origin, based only on the 'right of conquest'.[9] Hence, in many cases, the imperialist powers could to some degree successfully 'steal the emperor's clothes'. That is, they could slip into traditional patterns of legitimacy within the indigenous societies and establish themselves at the top of the indigenous ruling system, thereby transferring to themselves the traditional legitimacy in the eyes of the indigenous people. In fact, collaboration and resistance were by no means entirely exclusive phenomena. Rather, they could to some degree coexist, in view of Western society's great superiority over indigenous ones in terms of power and prestige, at least at first sight.

From this point of view, the process of imperialism and its corollary, the so-called process of 'decolonization', can indeed, as Ronald Robinson has suggested, be interpreted as a series of 'unequal bargains' between the imperialist powers or their representatives and indigenous societies about the running of colonial or semi-colonial systems; this usually included a certain degree of participation by the indigenous élites in the running of the administrative or the economic systems, though mostly only at the lowest levels. For a variety of reasons, however, conditions gradually strengthened the position of the indigenous partners. As Western influences of various sorts increasingly penetrated indigenous societies, traditional élites often found it difficult to enter into or maintain collaborationist partnerships of however limited a nature, because they ran the risk of undermining their privileged standing and their traditional prestige within the indigenous society, even though their social position was usually propped up by the imperialist authorities. Indeed, one of the main charges which can be levelled against imperialism was that imperialist rule artificially petrified traditional social structures at the periphery while, at the same time, restricting educational opportunities for the Asian and African intellectual élites and limiting their rise to responsible positions within their own societies. In the long run, however, the gradual rise of Westernized élites could not be halted. They soon began to challenge the authority of the traditional élites and the collaborationist bargains which they had obtained. Gradually they forced the traditional élites either to join forces with them in demanding a better bargain from the colonial administration, or to give way to new nationalist leaders.

The Decline of Empire

Imperialism and empire must be analysed essentially on three planes: first, the processes within Western societies which induced them to embark upon imperialist expansion and empire-building, often on a grand scale; secondly, the dynamics of power and expansion engendered by the international system of powers; thirdly, the indigenous factor, that is, the events at the periphery which often determined the particular methods and the timing of European expansion.

For many decades research focused on the first plane, namely the analysis of the political, economic and social forces at work in the metropolitan countries which provided the impetus for imperialist expansion. Whilst there is still no agreement among scholars about which of these factors was most important there can be no doubt that a combination of political considerations and economic motives was at work. Public opinion rated the potential economic benefits to be reaped from colonial empire enormously highly; those who were supposedly to benefit directly from them, namely the business community, were somewhat more realistic about it and, at times, quite unenthusiastic. The latter usually favoured, and with sound reasons, informal and, if possible, indirect forms of control, as formal control was bound to be associated with considerable public expense for which they in the end would somehow have to pay. There were always economic groups directly interested in the economic opportunities which were opened up by imperialist enterprises, particularly if they were offered a monopolistic position in overseas countries. Often overseas investments did pay handsomely, although the international banks who were in charge of the original arrangements usually fared rather better than the bondholders and creditors who sometimes lost a great deal of money from unsound investments.

On the whole, however, the importance of European overseas expansion for the European economies has been considerably overrated. Whilst the impact of European economic and financial engagement in Third World regions, both in colonies and in semi-colonies as well as in undeveloped, albeit formally sovereign countries, such as those of South Africa was considerable in local terms, from the point of view of the European economies it was none the less marginal. India was perhaps an exception, both because of its importance to the Lancashire cotton industry and its role as a key factor in the development of a multinational system of world trade, as S. B.

Saul has shown in an important study.[10] Even so, economic interests, economic expectations (which usually overstepped reality to a great extent) and nationalist emotions amalgamated into a popular imperialist philosophy which then gained a political momentum of its own. Politicians had to reckon with this whether they liked the idea of further colonial expansion or (as was more often the case) whether they viewed it with considerable scepticism as it would involve the government in ever more complex and unforeseeable entanglements and financial obligations. The colonial empires of the nineteenth and twentieth centuries were in fact far less solidly constructed political edifices than an agitated public aroused by feelings of imperialist grandeur was inclined to assume. Joseph Chamberlain's belated attempts to turn the British Empire into a united economic bloc after the turn of the century and to give it at least the semblance of a federated super-state failed dismally.[11] The French were no more successful, possibly with the exception of Algeria which was eventually declared an integral part of the mother country.

It has already been pointed out that subsidiary and indirect forms of rule were used wherever possible, not only in the British case, where the Dominions gradually established themselves as independent nation-states under the British Crown, but almost everywhere else as well. Whilst imperialist rule did indeed hamper the independent development of indigenous societies and often put a heavy burden on the shoulders of the population, it was far from being exercised effectively. This correlates with the fact that, as a rule, it was not governments which were at the forefront of imperialist expansion. In the first place it was small, interested pressure groups at home, associated with the 'men on the spot' at the periphery, which pressed for the extension of informal or formal control for economic reasons, but also often for idealistic reasons such as those expressed by the missionaries. None the less, governments were invariably involved from the beginning, although only in the role of a potential protection agency. But, as time went on, they were more or less forced into direct engagement and eventually they ended up taking the initiative. As Lord Rosebery put it in 1892, governments were now expected 'to peg out claims for the future', instead of stepping in afterwards, as they had done previously.[12]

Traditionally, however, colonial affairs were not in the forefront of European politics. Although many of the colonial possessions acquired during the eighteenth century changed hands during the course of the European wars of the 1760s, as a rule diplomats did not consider colonial affairs to be of much importance. It was diplomatic custom not to interfere with one another's colonies or, at any rate, there was a tacit agreement that white governments should not collaborate with indigenous populations against their European rivals, although this was occasionally violated to no small degree, as was the case in India during the late-eighteenth- and early-nineteenth-century Franco-British wars. In fact, the principle of non-interference was a necessary condition for the practice of informal or indirect rule.

Until the 1870s the European powers and the United States displayed a considerable degree of willingness to act jointly in overseas matters, such as, for example, in the handling of Ottoman affairs or, later, the Egyptian debt. With the British occupation of Egypt in 1882 this admittedly fragile consensus disintegrated rapidly. At the Berlin West Africa Conference in 1884/5 Bismarck made a final bid for a joint approach by the powers to colonial problems, but to no avail. The 'scramble for Africa' which began in the mid-1880s initiated a process of accelerated land-grabbing throughout the world which marked the age of 'high imperialism'. Only the core of the Ottoman Empire, Persia, China and Siam escaped being formally divided up among the powers, though only because any attempt to do so could have triggered off a major European war. Instead the West resorted to informal economic penetration, supported by a network of arrangements among the business groups most affected and assisted by the exercise of the European powers' 'influence' upon what were, in fact, semi-colonial governments.[13]

The steadily increasing rivalry between the great powers which culminated in the First World War and peaked again in the 1930s with the Japanese and Fascist challenge to the established world system, made the maintenance of empire more and more expensive. International factors meant that it was necessary to exercise a far greater degree of formal and direct control over the colonial territories than had previously been the case. This required the stepping-up of direct rule and the establishment of formal colonial administrations which affected the lives of the indigenous population far more directly than before; thus, the level of local resistance to colonial rule rose. It became more difficult to strike bargains with indigenous élites on terms favourable to the imperial power or its representatives. Since the turn of the century, and most markedly following the First World War, the position of the traditional élites was increasingly challenged by the rise of new Western-educated élites who demanded a proper share in the actual running of their countries.

During the interwar period the Western powers mostly succeeded in fending off the challenge to their rule, as well as to the authority of the traditional collaborating élites, though this required a considerable degree of manœuvrability and certain far-reaching concessions regarding participation by the indigenous population in the running of colonial affairs. On the whole, the task of the colonial administrations had become far more difficult. By then imperialist rule had lost much of its former attraction in the eyes of the populations of Western societies. Their willingness to see taxes being used for the economic development of colonial possessions was limited, all the more so as the interwar period was marked by slow growth, high unemployment and retarded international trade. The old demand that the colonies be turned into profitable ventures became overwhelmingly strong. Thus, tension always existed between those views which pleaded for infrastructural and economic investments at the periphery in view of the long-term economic and political advantages to be derived from them, and the narrow-minded philosophy of *mise en valeur* which refused to put up any public funds for such purposes.

The Second World War put a sudden end to this period of relative tranquillity at the periphery. The colonial empires of the European powers had been experiencing a gradual shift of power towards the new nationalist movements, but they could still be contained with relative ease, even in India where things had gone further than elsewhere. The exigencies of the Second World War changed all this. Initially, the British Empire and also the Union Française showed remarkable solidarity in the face of the threat to the international order posed by Japan and then by the Fascist powers. However, as the Western powers began to demand considerable sacrifices from their colonial peoples, it became inevitable that some political concessions were made as compensation for a joint war effort. The military success of Japan in East and South-East Asia and (though it was far less important) National Socialist agitation among the Indian national movement undermined the prestige of the imperialist powers in the region to a considerable degree. The Japanese occupied not only large tracts of Burma and Malaya, but also the Dutch East Indies and the French possessions in Indo-China. Everywhere they encouraged the formation of anti-Western emancipatory movements, although they were to remain under the tutelage of Japan. However, the new Japanese Empire in the Far East, which operated primarily with formal, but partly also with informal and indirect techniques of control, was not to last, and after 1945 the British, Dutch and French were able to re-install themselves as colonial powers, at least for the time being. But the days of imperial rule were numbered, all the more so as the United States threw considerable political weight behind the policy of a gradual disbanding of empire; it increasingly demanded that formal arrangements be established with indigenous regimes according to Western democratic practice.[14] The influence of the United States and the Soviet Union, both determined antagonists of empire in the traditional sense after 1945, finally tipped the balance in favour of a policy of 'decolonization' which envisaged the fairly early transfer of power to trustworthy indigenous regimes.

However, there is much to be said for the argument that the nationalist movements played a decisive role in this process, not only at this critical juncture, but long before. It was the changing attitudes of the old and new indigenous élites towards colonial rule in interaction with events in the metropolitan societies and developments in the international system which determined not only the methods, but also the timing and the eventual outcome of European imperialist control. Ronald Robinson, John Gallagher and David Fieldhouse have shown convincingly that throughout the nineteenth century 'crises at the periphery' which undermined the local balance of power between the indigenous population and the representatives of the imperialist powers had been a prime factor behind the process of imperialist expansion. Imperial rule, dependent upon 'unequal bargains' with local collaborating élites, was inherently unstable. Imperialist control of local affairs by the metropolitan powers, however informal it might have been, was sooner or later bound to destabilize the standing of the collaborating élites. The need to secure the imperialist position therefore required the gradual intensification of direct control, if not a change in the internal power structure at the local level. But these measures were, in turn, likely to engender new crises. Popular resentment of imperialist rule gradually grew, whilst acceptance of indirect rule was gradually undermined.

The End of Empire

It was, however, the emergence of small élites of nationalist intellectuals which did most to alter the situation at the periphery.[15] The new nationalist movements challenged the traditional strategies of imperialist rule which favoured the traditionalist élites and, at the same time, used tactics of *divide et impera* as far as the diverse indigenous groups were concerned. The new nationalist élites passionately demanded a share in the running of the administration, if not the discontinuation of imperialist rule itself. Initially they could only muster limited support from the population and the imperialist rulers could outmanœuvre them by seeking the co-operation of the more conservative sections of the indigenous societies, such as the rural population in the case of India. But gradually the nationalists became a political force without whose support no 'bargains' of any kind could be sustained.

From this point of view, the policies of gradually preparing colonial territories for self-government, for which, in the British case, the white Dominions provided a kind of pattern (although they had never been dependencies in the full sense), could be seen as a necessary further stage in the development of empire. Only in this way could the limited co-operation of the new nationalist groups within the system of colonial rule, as it had developed since the 1920s, be obtained. The intention to prepare the colonies for self-government was undoubtedly sincere, but it should be realized that during the interwar period and even in the early 1950s the representatives of colonial government still reckoned that the transitional period until the eventual transfer of power would last generations, and it is probably correct to say that without the effects of the Second World War it would indeed have taken considerably longer. In fact, in the early 1950s it became clear that there was no longer any appreciable breathing space for the colonial administrators. The interaction of internal and external factors made it impossible to contain the nationalist movements in the colonial or semi-colonial territories (for instance, Egypt) any longer.

The policy of preparing the colonial dependencies for self-government, which became the catchword soon after the end of the Second World War, was not so much a new departure as the only way to maintain a minimum of imperial control in the future, albeit on a much reduced level. The 'bargains' which had to be struck were no longer as one-sided as they had been in the early days of Western imperialist expansion; the nationalist movements had, in many cases, established firm roots amongst the population and, furthermore, could often count upon a certain amount of moral support, at least from the two professedly anti-imperialist superpowers.

Some of the 'bargains' which, short of the granting of full independence, the Western powers tried to strike under these conditions with the nationalist movements, such as attempts by the French to restore imperial control in Indo-China and by the Dutch to reconquer what was to become Indonesia, failed disastrously. The Dutch refused to give in to Sukarno's rule and eventually resorted to military action, only to find that world opinion, and more particularly that of the United States, was no longer prepared to tolerate the use of force in such matters. The French initially fared somewhat better, inasmuch as they succeeded in reconstructing a collaborationist regime under Bao Dai against the Viet Minh; but all they achieved was to drive the latter firmly and definitely into the Communist camp. The French struggle to regain imperial control in Vietnam was presented to the world as a struggle against communism; to a certain degree this was a self-fulfilling prophecy in that the conflict indeed developed into a major confrontation between the West and the Communist East even though China and the Soviet Union refrained from any direct intervention. The ensuing Vietnam war was perhaps the last genuine imperialist war, but it was fought on false assumptions and on the basis of a partial misjudgement of the real situation. In the end the United States had to pay a bitter price for these misconceptions.

The Transfer of Power

On the whole, the transfer of power to the new nationalist élites which began in 1947, but rapidly took on the proportions of an avalanche, was implemented fairly smoothly. However, nobody (with the possible exception of the Portuguese who took a little longer to realize what was on the cards) wanted to retain full imperial control in their major colonial dependencies any longer than was absolutely necessary. This led to a series of dramatic crises, the most disastrous being the transfer of power in the Belgian Congo in 1960 which led to chaotic conditions in Zaire, as it was henceforth to be called. In the case of Algeria decolonization was achieved only after a bitter struggle, and furthermore it led to a severe crisis of the French political system. In the majority of cases, however, the transfer of power aroused only limited controversy in metropolitan societies, largely because governments acted upon the assumption that the new indigenous regimes would retain existing political and economic ties with the former mother country and that, by and large, business would be carried on as usual.

However, the formal handing over of power to the leaders of the nationalist movements cannot be considered a total watershed as far as imperialist control is concerned. From the African or Asian point of view, it was very often no more than a new 'bargain' struck with those sections of the indigenous élites which had been 'acculturated' to Western values and Western political traditions rather than with the people as a whole. It could be seen as a new sort of 'collaboration' designed to maintain traditional cultural, economic and political ties with the former mother country and, in many cases, it was in fact so.

It was in the interests of the West to have the former colonial peoples take over the political institutions of Western parliamentary government. It was also considered to be in the interests of the new nations to maintain existing economic links with the industrialized world, particularly those with the former mother country; in many cases this may indeed have been the case. But naturally the nature of the relationship with the former imperial power soon became a matter of serious internal dispute, which intensified as the anticipated immediate beneficial effects of independence on the indigenous economy turned out to be a chimera. The heritage of the Western nation-state with its rational bureaucratic administration and the idea of national unity transcending all tribal differences initially benefited the new Westernized intellectual élites, but often at the expense of other indigenous groups less well placed in the post-colonial systems which emerged in the 1960s.

In a variety of cases this final 'bargain', as it were, between the former imperial power and the new nationalist movements did pay off. The new states accepted membership of the British Commonwealth of Nations, or the Union Française, thereby maintaining, at least symbolically, a formal tie with the former metropolitan country. The latter was, therefore, often able to maintain a limited degree of actual influence, however informal it may have been; in addition, membership of these new federations amounted to a guarantee that existing informal economic and cultural links would be maintained and perhaps even intensified.

These new forms of relations between metropolitan and peripheral countries can surely not be considered straight-forwardly 'imperialist', but neither did they represent a clearcut break with the past, particularly if continuing informal links, that is, those of an economic nature, are taken into consideration. Often the granting of independence took place on the unspoken assumption that any substantial violation of the rights of nationals of the former mother country who were to stay in the newly independent state would amount to a breach of this 'contract' which, in turn, would establish the right of intervention by whatever means considered suitable by the former colonial power. Furthermore, it was expected that the new country would remain in the West's political camp. Often co-operation in military affairs and the supply of military technology in the future was considered a necessary corollary.

From the point of view of the non-Westernized sections of the indigenous population it could be argued that the final break with the imperialist past came only much later when the groups who had contracted the 'bargain' marking the granting of independence had gradually been replaced by other, more lowly placed sections of society. In the same vein, parliamentary institutions were either relinquished or reduced to a mere façade behind which new authoritarian power structures emerged. This is exactly what happened in the great majority of cases: there was a takeover by new leaders no longer directly associated with the colonial tradition, who had not been brought up under Western political institutions and under the influence of Western culture. All that remained was the use of sophisticated Western military technology, partly as a source of prestige, partly in order to engage in aggressive policies carried out using imperialist tactics on a regional basis. Sometimes these new regimes, often of a massively dictatorial nature, associated themselves with either the Soviet bloc or other major powers. Hence, formal emancipation from imperialist control of the classical kind at times led straight into an acceptance of the informal imperialist paramountcy of one of the superpowers which presently dominate the international arena.

The transfer of power to the new nationalist élites did constitute a cæsura in the development of relations between the West and the Third World. Yet, as we have described, it is far less marked than is usually assumed. It must be conceded that one key element of imperialist rule was formally abdicated, at least in principle, namely the right to use coercion and, if necessary, military force in the event of flagrant violations of the 'bargains' relating to the transfer of power. In a way the classic paradigm of imperialist rule had changed, it was now to be 'informal control wherever possible, while formal control no longer applies'. But even this was a matter of degree, rather than of clearcut principles. It was in fact only the emergence of a new international system dominated by two rival superpowers, both professedly anti-imperialist, that denied the Western powers the possibility of direct imperialist intervention in formally independent countries in order to maintain informal control, economic or otherwise.

Neither the United States nor the Soviet Union was henceforth prepared to permit direct intervention by third powers in Third World countries to any great extent. In this respect, the Suez crisis of 1956 represented a turning point: British intervention had to be abandoned in the face of joint pressure from the United States and the Soviet Union. Since this juncture, open imperialist interventions based upon historical claims acquired during the age of imperialism have become extremely rare, if not impossible. None the less they do occur, as the cases of Vietnam, Afghanistan, the Falkland Islands and recently the revival of American interventionist policies in Central America demonstrate. But now a legitimation for intervention, perhaps a cry for help by some indigenous group or movement, whether it be engineered or genuine, is usually indispensable. For today, imperialist action is no longer considered morally justified; it cannot be carried out with anything like the self-righteousness which was typical of nineteenth-century imperialism.

Legacies of Empire and Dependency

But can the age of imperialism be considered finally closed (regardless of the fact that some remnants of former colonial rule still linger on) because informal imperialist control, whether it takes economic, cultural, political, or some other form, can no longer be backed up, if necessary by force? This would perhaps be premature. On the economic and, less ostentatiously, on the cultural level 'unequal bargains' are still very much with us and, furthermore, the legacies of older 'unequal bargains' still to a large extent determine the bargaining positions of each side. The legacies of imperialist rule condition the life and prospects of many Third World peoples to no small degree. It would be a mistake, therefore, to discard lightheartedly the argument that the Third World dependency upon the industrialized nations of the world is so firmly rooted that formal imperialist control is no longer required. Social and economic structures, and the educational systems in Third World countries are – it is claimed – so firmly linked to the West that they have to conduct their affairs as if they were still subjected to formal colonial rule. This argument must be taken seriously, all the more so if we take into account the very important role which informal and indirect rule played during the age of classical imperialism, when formal imperialist rule could well be considered to be only the tip of the iceberg.

Let us briefly look into this on two levels. First, we shall consider the relevance of the *legacies* of the imperialist past for the relationship of the less developed countries to the Western countries. Secondly, we shall investigate ways in which Western predominance in the Third World survives informally, particularly on the economic plane or, in the terminology made fashionable by Paul A. Baran, whether there is a continuing, and perhaps even growing *dependency* of the countries of the Third World on the West.

One of the more important legacies of colonial rule is perhaps the modern nation-state as a coherent, political unit which is supposedly the political organization of one nation with a uniform legal order and a centralized administrative system claiming sovereignty for itself in accordance with international law.[16] But the boundaries of these new states, drawn during the age of imperialism, usually cut right across ethnic and cultural boundaries, not to mention declared loyalties. This is particularly true of the African continent. In the Middle East historical tradition was respected to a certain degree, but only inasmuch as the European powers found it convenient to keep the decaying Ottoman Empire alive for more than a century, helping to contain and at times to suppress nationalist independence movements or, at any rate, preferring not to intervene when this happened, as in the case of the Armenians. Perhaps it could be argued that Arab national unity might have been established as early as 1838 if the European powers had not forced Muhammad Ali to respect the rule of the Sultan of Constantinople.

The emergence of the nation-state in the less developed regions of the world was stimulated by the establishment of formal colonial administrations during the last stage of imperialist rule. In many ways the indigenous governments, which took over after independence, inherited what was, at least in principle if not in fact, a Westernized governmental system. With the end of imperialist rule, however, a factor which indirectly benefited the indigenous peoples also disappeared, namely the hegemonial control which, in the British case has so aptly been called *pax Britannica* but which was to some degree effective elsewhere too. It had effectively limited internal strife amongst the indigenous peoples, by the imposition of a legal system of conflict resolution, however inadequate.

However, Albert Wirz has drawn attention to the fact that this sort of imperial legacy was not an undisguised blessing. The colonial practice of playing off different ethnic and social groups against each other in order to strengthen the core position of the colonial authority did nothing to promote a sense of unity and loyalty to a common body politic among the indigenous population; on the contrary, the strategies of imperial rule tended to fragment the indigenous communities even further. At the same time central governments far removed from the people have had little unifying effect upon the indigenous population. The practices of indirect and subsidiary rule kept alive traditional loyalties to social élites whose status was not compatible with the principle of a unified nation-state.[17]

346 *Imperialism and After*

It is not surprising, therefore, that many of the newly created states soon experienced intense internal strife while, in other cases, the political units created during the age of imperialism broke up immediately, as was the case in India and Pakistan. Only during the course of bitter conflicts, repeatedly erupting into devastating wars, could the Third World slowly find its way towards a new, acceptable division of political power. Giovanni Arrighi arrives at essentially the same conclusion; however, he sees this as a 'positive' phenomenon reflecting the shift of power in the relationship between the Third World and the Western countries: 'the new independence of Third World countries is manifested above all in their greater promptitude and capacity to resort to war to regulate their mutual relations and consolidate their fragile national unity'.[18]

The European powers, particularly the British, often liked to flatter themselves by thinking that they had left behind not only the idea of democratic government, but also democratic institutions. In some ways this was real: in Egypt attempts to reorganize the country according to Western constitutional ideas go back at least to Urabi. Usually governments and institutions in former colonial countries which had been granted independence were still very much dominated by those indigenous élites which had already had the say during the later stages of colonial rule, and more often than not the parliamentary institutions were seen as a guarantee of continuing informal Western influence. However, the trend is undoubtedly for Third World countries to deviate from the Western pattern of constitutional government, perhaps only temporarily. This is partly due to the rise to power of new groups which have not experienced colonial influence to the same degree. How long the Western tradition will survive the present period of internal upheaval and transition following the transfer of power is a matter for speculation.

This is even more the case with regard to the socio-economic legacy of imperialism. It has often been argued that the social structures which emerged in most Third World countries were largely determined by the way in which these regions were integrated into the economic system of the former metropolitan country. Indeed, it will be necessary to ask whether the typical social stratification in underdeveloped countries which is characterized by a gross dichotomy between a vast, almost undeveloped, traditional sector and a small Westernized modern sector almost entirely geared to export interests is rooted in the conditions of imperialist rule.

Arguments of this nature serve as a point of departure for those social scientists who emphasize the lopsided nature of the economic relationship between advanced industrial and less developed countries in the post-colonial era. They argue that during the period of classical imperialism the metropolitan societies developed bridgeheads at the periphery, in business and elsewhere, in the form of collaborationist élites who had a direct interest in serving the needs of the metropolitan country and in maintaining economic and political links with it even though these policies ran counter to the interests of the large majority of the indigenous population.[19]

In dogmatic Marxist terms this has been described as a mere reproduction of the metropolitan capitalist system at the periphery. To express it in this way would be rather naïve. But there is much to be said for the argument that the socio-economic structures which emerged were not particularly conducive to balanced economic growth, as they favoured monocultural agrarian production (as in the case of Egypt in the later nineteenth century) or specialized export industries, very often concerned more with the extraction of raw materials than with the production of finished goods. Wherever new industries developed they were geared primarily to export markets and linked to the interests of the metropolitan countries, or otherwise tied up with external rather than internal trade. Hence they remained islands within an otherwise traditional economy, which remained based on mere self-subsistence and engendered no impulses for economic or social change.

To some degree this argument links up with the findings of historians like Ronald Robinson and David Fieldhouse.[20] Indeed, those more or less Europeanized, Western-oriented élites which developed during the later stages of imperial rule or semi-imperial influence usually were, and often still are, far removed from the rest of the peripheral society, both in terms of wealth and cultural outlook.

The colonies of white settlement did not fall outside this pattern. In fact, as Ronald Robinson has put it, the white colonist has always been the 'ideal collaborator'.[21] The white communities living in Asian and African countries often enjoyed a privileged legal status, as for example in Tunisia until 1881, in Egypt up to 1882 or in China right into the 1930s. Until the recent past they naturally played a key role in shaping the fortunes of the countries concerned. Obviously, they were extremely interested in maintaining the old ties with the former metropolitan country.

The classic pattern of colonial rule, namely that administrative as well as commercial affairs were largely run, however informally, by expatriates in conjunction with indigenous élites, did not come to a sudden halt with the formal ending of imperialist domination. Instead, it survived in many varieties with indigenous élites of different origin gradually taking over. Naturally, opinions differ widely as to the true nature of these Westernized élites. To some, they are pioneers of modernization who by importing capital and technology from the West help to advance their own countries economically and intellectually.

Others have described these élites as 'comprador classes' which, because of their vested interest in maintaining 'unequal' commercial connections between peripheries and metropolises, were instrumental in developing a system of 'peripheral capitalism'. While it provided for the well-being of the classes associated with it, this system did not provide any incentive for the economic development of the peripheral country as a whole, as it did not add in any significant way to the purchasing power of the masses of the population. Instead it reinforced traditional class distinctions which had emerged during the period of colonialism. In this way, it has been argued, 'peripheral capitalism' created, and is still creating, self-perpetuating patterns of underdevelopment. Industrialization at the periphery, largely carried on by foreign firms, offered numerous opportunities to reinforce co-operation between metropolitan economic interests and 'comprador classes' at the periphery, and to forge new links with other indigenous groups. With reference to the case of post-colonial Kenya, Colin Leys has concluded that 'the phase of industrialisation at the periphery of the capitalist system does not lead to an autonomous process of capitalist development, but to a further consolidation of underdevelopment'.[22]

It must be pointed out, however, that the situation is far less uniform than many *dependencia* authors seem to believe. Quite a number of former colonial countries, the so-called newly industrializing countries, have successfully broken the mould of peripheral capitalism, whilst others have remained stagnant or experienced further economic decline. This has caused considerable debate among the underdevelopment theorists, Marxist, populist, or otherwise.

It remains a matter for passionate dispute whether or not responsibility for the poverty and economic backwardness of many less developed countries must be laid at the door of imperialism. Some development economists, such as Bairoch,[23] argue that with the integration of the peripheral economies into the international economy during the age of imperialism the, by and large, efficient traditional sectors in the non-European countries were destroyed with lasting negative consequences for their ability ever to attain sustained economic growth. This judgement, as Forbes Munro points out,[24] is perhaps too sweeping. On the whole, Third World countries under colonial rule experienced slow if uneven growth and the impoverishment of large parts of Asia, notably China, during the later eighteenth and nineteenth centuries cannot be considered a direct consequence of imperialism. It is perhaps fair to say that the economic consequences of colonial rule were, on the whole, moderately beneficial to the peripheral countries as they enforced the gradual modernization of the indigenous economies. The foundations for a modern economic infrastructure were laid, however slowly and belatedly, often at a net loss to the European investors.

It could be said that the colonial powers (with the exception of Japan) did too little, and that too late, to develop their possessions economically. Before the First World War it was expected that colonies should be financially self-supporting (though very often they were not), and should not make any claims whatever on the Exchequer of the mother country. Only to a limited extent were public funds ever used for economic development in the modern sense; Joseph Chamberlain wrangled bitterly with the British Treasury to extract small, in present terms infinitesimal, sums for investment in British West Africa. Not until after the First World War did the Western colonial powers initiate programmes of overseas development on a grander scale, though the chief intention was not necessarily to improve the livelihood of the indigenous populations. Even so, the balance of colonial rule may, after all, not have been as bad as is usually assumed nowadays.[25]

On the whole, however, it would appear that it is not possible to make a definite assessment of imperialism's economic effects upon both the metropolitan and the peripheral countries, if only because conditions varied enormously according to time and region. Much is still a matter of conjecture, while other observations will remain controversial for ever.

It may be argued that, in one respect at least, imperialism has left behind a positive legacy, namely in the cultural and scientific fields. In terms of cultural orientation the period of imperialism was also a period of the 'acculturation' of indigenous societies to the Western rationalist tradition, though often by way of indoctrination and political pressure. Certainly, the agents of Western imperialism were convinced that their intellectual traditions would be an unmixed blessing for the indigenous peoples of the Third World; colonization was considered by many to be the bringing of civilization to heathen and backward people throughout the world. Today we are no longer so sure whether Western ideas, the Western life-style and the Western intellectual tradition, let alone Christianity, are the only ways to achieve happiness and a humane life in this world. At least to some degree, modern technology and industry cannot thrive without the rationalist ways of thought developed in the West, but in this particular respect we are perhaps also at a turning-point. The West itself is no longer so sure of the validity of the philosophy of progress which it taught to the rest of the world during the classic age of imperialism.

The value of intellectual Westernization as a secondary spin-off of colonial rule has been challenged, most radically perhaps by Frantz Fanon in his famous book *Les Damnés de la terre*.[26] He pointed to the deep psychological split experienced by intellectuals from Third World nations who had enjoyed a European education and become used to thinking according to Western standards, only to find themselves deeply alienated from their own peoples and cut off from their own cultural heritage. Fanon went so far as to argue that the identity crisis of the Westernized élites of Third World countries could only be healed by recourse to violence against the oppressors. In his view, anti-colonial wars not only helped to create a new culture, but also restored the self-respect of the indigenous intellectual élites. It is doubtful whether this extremist recipe, which was to some extent acted upon during the North African War of Independence, was a rational way out of the dilemma in which the educated élites in many underdeveloped countries found themselves.

Indeed, if imperialism is to be condemned on cultural grounds it should be because during the colonial era too little rather than too much was done for the education of the indigenous intellectual élites. Most Western colonial regimes (perhaps with the exception of the French) were in fact reluctant to extend the benefits of higher education beyond a rather small indigenous élite, as it was feared that this would create a national-revolutionary potential. British colonial practice, in particular, was influenced by the philosophy of indirect rule which did not recommend any large-scale Westernization of the indigenous peoples (although influential men like Macaulay had argued otherwise); instead, it aimed at preserving the traditional institutions and cultures, often of a rather archaic nature, thereby minimizing administrative costs and achieving maximum submissiveness on the part of the population. All in all, with hindsight it is very much an open question whether the system of indirect rule or a policy of ruthless modernization, breaking with traditional customs and, in particular, the often rather crude legal traditions of indigenous societies, was more beneficial in the end.[27]

Of course, in the last resort it all depends on the evaluation of the Western model of modernization. Many rulers of Third World countries ran into trouble because of an all too uncritical adherence to what, until very recent times, was considered the Western path towards modernity. The dramatic revival of Islam as a major intellectual and moral force indicates that there are alternatives which need not necessarily clash with a policy of modernization and economic and social progress according to Western standards of technology and constitutional government.

Continuities of Empire?

It remains for us to return to the question of whether the present relationship between the West and the underdeveloped world must be considered a continuation of imperialism by informal, but even more effective means. There is little doubt that in the economic sphere at least an abundance of 'unequal bargains' still exist in the dealings of the West with less developed countries. On the other hand, some of the arguments of *dependencia* theorists as to why this must be so, have worn thin with the passage of time. Johan Galtung's argument that the economic relationship between the peripheral and the metropolitan countries is necessarily always asymmetrical, if only because the terms of trade always favour the latter,[28] can no longer be maintained as a universal law. Nor is it fully convincing any longer to argue that the collaborationist classes installed at the periphery during the age of imperialism will for ever guarantee the smooth working of the unequal trade relations with the industrialized world. For by now the 'comprador classes' have disappeared or, at any rate, their social composition has so radically changed that the original contention, based upon the continuity of patterns of collaboration supported by joint economic interests of the metropolitan business circles and their partners in the overseas 'bridgeheads', can no longer be sustained to the same degree as a generation ago.

Even Girvan, who cannot be considered a partisan of the West, maintains that by the 1960s the situation *had* changed: 'for once, countries in the Third World are actively controlling the terms of their trade with the industrialised world and the returns they get from the powerful multi-national corporations, instead of the other way round'.[29] Indeed, the alleged asymmetrical trade relationship between underdeveloped and industrialized countries had not consistently worked against the former; recent developments indicate that things do work the other way round as well. And it is doubtful whether the additional argument that the multinational corporations have taken over the role of agents of imperialist exploitation from former governmental agencies, necessarily holds water. For it depends on circumstances whether multinational corporations can exploit their monopolist position in the market or whether their operations can be subjected to governmental control so as to conform with the interests of the society within which they operate.[30] Most less developed countries now welcome the operations of multinationals in their markets subject to specific conditions. It depends, after all, on whether particular political conditions exist which allow the exploitation of monopolist opportunities of one kind or another.

The key problem seems to lie elsewhere. The majority of less developed countries do not suffer primarily from asymmetrical capitalist exploitation and an unrestricted exposure to international capitalist enterprise. Rather, the reverse is true. Their plight is due above all to the fact that their economies are insufficiently integrated into the international economy. They are being marginalized not because of capitalist exploitation by the core countries, but because of sheer neglect. These problems are intensified by the heavy debts which these countries have incurred in their attempts at partial modernization. The servicing of these international loans in many cases exceeds their capability to earn foreign exchange by exporting raw materials, agricultural products and, though less often, finished goods. This sorry state is undoubtedly partly a result of the legacies of imperialism; however, many individual factors come into play, and it is not enough to try to explain it as the result of skilful neo-colonialist strategies on the part of the advanced industrial countries.

However, the modern world-system theory tends to ascribe this state of affairs in many, though not all, of the less developed countries to the working of the capitalist system as such, as it has emerged over the last centuries. Immanuel Wallerstein reconstructs the course of world history as a progressive unfolding of the capitalist world system which, in his view, originated in the sixteenth century.[31] Free-trade imperialism, high imperialism and neo-colonialism (as a new variety of informal imperialism which can do without the coercive instruments of classical imperialism) are merely stages in one evolutionist process which inevitably results in an ever-widening gap between accumulation of wealth in the core countries and deprivation at the periphery.

Wallerstein's theory is to be seen as a radical challenge to the developmentalist theories of the 1950s and 1960s which had optimistically assumed that the Third World would, by and large, follow the developmental patterns of the West, whilst being able to cut short some of the earlier stages in the emergence of the industrial system. According to Wallerstein, in Western history periods of growth and periods of contraction alternate with each other in the sequence of time; none the less, the world system essentially follows a unilinear developmental path which leads to a progressive differentiation of wealth between different regions of the globe according to a matrix of differentiated economic growth. High economic growth is associated with political predominance and consequently a differentiation emerges between core, semi-periphery and periphery, with the proviso that the regional and geographical distribution of wealth and power is subjected to change in time, often conditioned by singular historical circumstances.

For this new school of thought the capitalist world system itself creates inequality, as it were, of necessity. Wallerstein argues that 'it is not possible theoretically for all states to develop simultaneously. The so-called widening gap is not an anomaly, but a continuing basic mechanism of the world economy.'[32] All varieties of imperialism, in the classic meaning of the word, are mere manifestations of the capitalist world system in the different stages of its evolution. Ideally, it is argued, that imperialist coercion of a formal kind was necessary only to open up the markets of underdeveloped countries to Western capitalism, and to establish firm footholds of capitalist enterprise and, in some cases, 'comprador classes' and 'comprador regimes' at the periphery. The unspoken assumption behind this is that capitalism, once established, will force its way through in any case, exploiting the periphery for the benefit of the capitalist classes and perhaps also the bureaucrats and intellectuals associated with them in the peripheral countries. This appears to be a very suggestive model, particularly in a situation in which the traditional vestiges of formal imperialist rule are increasingly receding. It seems to explain the present trend which is characterized by a widening gap between rich and poor countries in the world and offers hope, though of a rather Utopian kind, to those who expect a momentous shift of the core of the system to other geographical regions of the world. Above all, it makes nonsense of all the developmentalist theories of the 1950s and 1960s, put forward by social scientists busy designing shortcuts to industrial development in underdeveloped countries.

Not surprisingly it has, therefore, found considerable support even though it is a matter of considerable controversy whether the starting-point of the 'capitalist world system' ought to be placed in the early sixteenth century, or as most economists would have preferred, in the late eighteenth century. Patrick J. McGowan and Bogdan Kordan have recently put forward an alternative model focusing on the development of the British Empire since the late eighteenth century.[33] But Wallerstein's new approach enjoys considerable popularity, both with Marxists and with *dependencia* theoreticians, such as André Gunder Frank, who recently published a book entitled *World Accumulation, 1492–1789*,[34] in which he argues along similar lines, and even with Johan Galtung *et al.* who, comparing the late Roman Empire with the development of our own times, arrive at rather fatalistic conclusions.[35]

These approaches suffer from a fundamental flaw, namely their generality. They replace the different varieties of imperialist, semi-imperialist, or merely informal control with a rather monolithic, essentially deterministic model which is not particularly suited to providing new insights into the interpretation of classic imperialism or of the mechanisms helping to maintain informal influence in peripheral countries after the ending of formal imperialist control. Nor do they offer a key to the solution of the present relationship between the West and the Third World.

Far more constructive, however controversial, are the arguments of the developmental economists who concentrate on the segmented character of the industrial systems at the periphery which produce goods primarily, if not exclusively, for export and show little or no interest in developing the home market. Multinational companies, whose often dominant position in the market allows them to exact special privileges from the host country, admittedly enter the scene on this particular count. According to this view, they tend to aggravate the given state of affairs, as they are interested primarily in export-oriented production. They are often blamed for contributing significantly to the development of a 'peripheral capitalism' which is hardly, if at all, interested in developing those internal markets of the peripheral country in question which are unsuited to their products; instead, they benefit from cheap labour and, often, from cheap primary products. Hence the role of the multinationals is a subject of much dispute, although it now appears that their role is not necessarily always negative.

It has been argued, furthermore, that the impact of imperialism on the economies of Third World countries was tantamount to the 'deformation of the periphery by destroying the indigenous trades by superior competition'.[36] The peripheral economies were thereby reduced to mere satellites of the core economies and the resulting relationship was essentially imperialistic.[37] 'Autocentric development' can therefore be achieved only by a policy of protection from overseas competition with the help of high tariffs and a gradual restructuring of the peripheral economies which reduces their dependency on the core countries and their superior market position and technological advantage.[38] But be this as it may (and there are indeed many examples of it), could the economies of the less developed countries really be protected from the devastating impact of the new technologies of the West long enough and in such a way as to allow them to maintain viable home industries which, after a period of adaptation, might be able to compete successfully in the international market? It appears to us that it is only Japan which has succeeded in doing so, and only by an extremely rapid adaptation to Western technology, actively assisted by a modern governmental administration; few colonial or semi-colonial territories could have achieved this. Incidentally, the Khedive Ismail attempted to do just this in Egypt in the middle of the nineteenth century, with little success.

It is also controversial whether, as Bairoch for instance has argued, the net balance of colonial rule with regard to economic development has in fact been negative throughout.[39] Although colonial governments as a rule, though by no means always, conducted economic and tariff policies so as to give preferential treatment to the export industries of the imperial metropolis, it cannot be said that colonial government was detrimental to the indigenous economy as such. Undoubtedly, investments in infrastructural matters had to be paid for largely by local taxes, but colonial governments provided security for business and, therefore, often encouraged investment and economic engagements which otherwise might not have been forthcoming, or would have been more costly. Even so, there is some point in the plea for redressing the distortions caused by a long period of almost unmitigated exposure of the indigenous economies to international competition, which by and large was a corollary of colonial or semi-colonial status. The take-off into sustained growth or, as Samir Amin and Dieter Senghaas prefer to argue, 'autocentric development',[40] might well be encouraged by protectionist strategies. This would require a definite end to all forms of influence exerted by Western countries, either directly or indirectly, on decision-making processes in matters of economic policy.

In principle, the former imperialist powers no longer possess any legal right to force Third World countries to pursue economic policies conducive to the interests of their economies and to the economic interests of their nationals resident in those countries. In a way, the outcome of the Suez conflict in 1956 settled this once and for all. But it would be futile to deny that a considerable arsenal of indirect means still exists by which less developed countries can be pressured into adopting economic policies which are in line with the interests of the core economies. Above all, two mechanisms are available: the provision of international loans, either directly or through international organizations like the World Bank and, secondly, the granting of foreign aid. But, apart from particular instances which may operate in different ways, these mechanisms do not always provide effective leverage for a policy which could be called informal imperialism; at least, not of the variety which we associate with the classic notion of imperialist control.

The Rise of New Superpowers

The older varieties of imperialism are universally on the retreat. The heritage of the classic era of imperialism usually favours metropolitan interests, but occasionally things may operate the other way round. The ability of the Western states to exercise direct pressure on Third World countries, for instance via diplomatic or military intervention, has become increasingly limited. But it would be rather naïve to leave things here. Until the end of the Second World War the Western powers enjoyed an undisputed imperialist status in the world. Since then their imperial roles have gradually been superseded by a new world order characterized by the emergence of new rival hegemonial systems dominated by two superpowers, the United States and the Soviet Union.

Both the United States and the Soviet Union were explicitly antiimperialist in origin. The United States, in particular, deriving its very existence from an anti-colonial revolution, has been engaged in seeing that the remnants of older imperialist systems, namely the British Empire, were abolished. It defeated Japan's ambitious attempts to establish a new Far Eastern empire and contributed substantially to bringing down Adolf Hitler's somewhat anachronistic attempt to establish an east-central European empire. The existence of empire was incompatible with its economic interests encompassing the whole globe. But due to a spiralling process of conflict between the West and the Marxist–Leninist bloc, the United States, its professedly anti-imperialist position notwithstanding, in fact gradually embarked upon a course which, though defensive in intention, amounted to the emergence of a new empire of an altogether informal nature. This empire exercised hegemony over a considerable part of the world, thanks to the dominant economic resources, military potential and political position of the United States. This was further strengthened by the development of nuclear weapons which made all the other Western powers in part dependent upon American protection. The United States or, as Raymond Aron so aptly put it, the 'Imperial Republic'[41] succeeded in reestablishing a new world order according to democratic and free-trade principles, generally in line with American economic interests in those parts of the world which were not directly or indirectly subject to Soviet influence. Whether this global hegemony which the United States enjoyed in the two decades following the Second World War should be described as super-imperialism, as many Marxist authors would have it, or as a world system which could count upon the voluntary co-operation of its Western partners, would appear to make little difference. At least from 1945 until 1970 the American position in the world was tantamount to that of an informal imperialist power. This fact is corroborated by the fact that the United States, in pursuit of a policy of containment of Soviet influence, in many instances turned to policies of indirect and sometimes even direct intervention. Or, in peripheral countries, it established control which qualified as imperialist in the traditional sense, even though these interventions were usually motivated by a desire to fend off alleged or real advances by the Communist bloc.

This is true in particular of the policies of the United States in Central America. Even though direct interference here was the exception, the United States used all the indirect means at its disposal – political, economic, military, or other – to establish in power or maintain there such friendly or collaborating regimes in the region as were considered vital for its security. American anti-imperialism as a rule worked for the establishment of regimes in line with Western interests and, if possible, in accordance with Western political standards. If these were not available then 'bargains' were made with rightist élites often all too readily. It should, however, be noted that the increasing rivalry with the Soviet Union had a great deal to do with the revival of regional interventionist policies by the United States; these policies were often carried out with the formal co-operation, or at least the connivance, of its Western allies, especially with the development of the Cold War after 1948.

In the case of the Soviet Union one is undoubtedly justified to speak of the emergence of a new imperialist system or even of a Soviet empire since the end of the Second World War. It comprises the whole of East Central Europe, in so far as it belonged to the Russian sphere of interest which was agreed to by the Western powers as early as at the Yalta Conference. In principle, this empire is largely informal, inasmuch as the socialist peoples' democracies are considered sovereign states, though within certain undefined limits. Clearly, though, they are tied to the Soviet Union by political, economic and military bonds which guarantee the absolute preponderance of the Moscow centre. None of these countries is supposed to leave the 'club' of socialist states, as Hungary found in 1956 and Czechoslovakia in 1968, whilst the Polish case has not been put to the ultimate test. In fact, the collaborationist model of imperialist control proves applicable to this system to an amazing degree. The communist parties, or at least their upper echelons which, in Djilas's term, form a 'new class', have on the whole acted as reliable collaborators. Informal control is exercised with the assistance of those élites which have a vested interest in maintaining the 'special relationship' with the Soviet Union and whose privileged status within their own society depends upon the preservation of the status quo. They also participate in a common 'cosmology' which, according to Galtung, is a typical feature of imperialist systems. It is therefore not surprising to see that the Soviet Empire carries on in the traditions of its tsarist predecessor, although it professedly made a clean break with the latter in the October Revolution.

Anti-imperialist rhetoric notwithstanding, the Soviet Union has done its best to extend its influence among the new nations of the Third World, partly in order to muster support for its struggle for the eventual victory of socialism, or rather to strengthen its position against that of the United States and its European allies. On the whole, attempts at exercising informal control beyond the geopolitical sphere of east-central Europe have been rather unsuccessful as well as fairly costly. In this respect, the maintenance of empire is even more expensive than it was in the early twentieth century.

The secular conflict between the two world systems, both of which consider themselves anti-imperialist, but have none the less in some ways stepped into the place of the older empires, has had a considerable impact on the advanced industrial nations' relationships with the Third World. First, the international constellation which emerged after the 1950s made the maintenance of empire in the traditional sense impossible. None of the other powers, in a way not even the United States or the Soviet Union themselves, were allowed to embark upon avowedly imperialist ventures in the classic style. The United States and the Soviet Union competed with one another to lure the non-committed new nations of the Third World into their own camp; thus they would have nothing to do with imperialist practices of the past, at least not openly. The action by both the United States and the Soviet Union on the occasion of the British intervention in Suez in 1956 which forced the British into immediate and full retreat, can be considered a milestone in this respect.

More importantly, the relative stalemate between the superpowers considerably increased the bargaining power of Third World nations. Grossly 'unequal bargains' were no longer likely, at least not those of the old style. Conditions for international loans were improved and development aid was made available on a scale unthinkable only a few years previously. Furthermore, possibilities of backing up informal influence in peripheral countries by force, if only in extreme exigencies, were greatly reduced, although they did not disappear totally. 'Imperialist' interventions were no longer tolerated; if necessary they had to be legitimized in the eyes of the world as assistance to indigenous governments who had requested help. Furthermore, both the Soviet Union and the United States were careful to engage themselves indirectly rather than directly and always with limited military force in order to avoid a full-scale confrontation which might escalate into a major war.

Paradoxically, the international constellation, whilst curtailing the Western powers' freedom of action *vis-à-vis* the Third World, allowed new regional sub-imperialisms to emerge which would certainly not have been tolerated during the age of classic imperialism. Even remnants of what used to be called the *pax Britannica* no longer exist, and American hegemony has not proved strong enough to prevent regional sub-imperialisms from emerging at the periphery, such as Vietnam's control of Kampuchea, Iraq's attack upon Iran, South Africa's undeclared war against 'rebel forces' in Namibia and, more recently Israel's preventative military offensive in Lebanon.

All in all, it may well be said that the older varieties of imperialism have been on the retreat for many years. It is no longer possible to impose 'unequal bargains' on peripheral peoples in the old way, although the practice does survive to some extent on the economic plane. But this is partly because older empires have been replaced by new forms of political imperialism.

Notes: Chapter 22

1   W. D. Smith, *European Imperialism in the 19th and 20th Centuries* (Chicago, 1982), p. 1.
2   ibid., p. 5.
3   See R. Robinson and J. Gallagher, 'The imperialism of free trade', *Economic History Review*, vol. 6 (1953), p. 13.
4   R. Robinson, 'Non-European foundations of European imperialism: sketch for a theory of collaboration', in R. Owen and B. Sutcliffe (eds), *Studies in the Theory of Imperialism* (London, 1972), p. 120.
5   H. Lüthy, 'Ruhm und Ende der Kolonisation', in idem, *Nach dem Untergang des Abendlandes* (Cologne, 1959), p. 372; see also H. Lüthy, 'Colonization and the making of mankind', *Journal of Economic History*, vol. 21 (1961), pp. 483 ff.
6   See Chapter 18 by Ronald Robinson in this volume.
7   This observation has been taken by David S. Landes as a point of departure for an interpretation of imperialism as the outcome of a fundamental 'disparity of power' between the colonizing powers and the indigenous societies, power being the sum of all the political, economic, technological and cultural resources which constitute the historical driving force behind large social entities. See D. Landes, 'Some thoughts on the nature of economic imperialism', *Journal of Economic History*, vol. 21 (1961), p. 510. See also W. J. Mommsen, *Theories of Imperialism* (London, 1981), pp. 79 ff.
8   See D. A. Low, *Lion Rampant. Essays in the Study of British Imperialism* (London, 1974), pp. 23 ff.
9   ibid., pp. 24-5. See also W. J. Mommsen, 'Pax Britannica. Probleme der Friedenswahrung in der Dritten Welt', in G. Molitor (ed.), *Die Idee des Friedens in der neueren Geschichte* (Düsseldorf, 1985, forthcoming).
10 S. B. Saul, *Studies in British Overseas Trade, 1870–1914* (Liverpool, 1960).
11 On this issue see Wolfgang Mock, *Imperiale Herrschaft und Nationales Interesse. 'Constructive Imperialism' oder Freihandel in Grossbritannien vor dem Ersten Weltkrieg* (Stuttgart, 1982), Veröffentlichungen des Deutschen Historischer Instituts London, Vol. 13.
12 See Lord Rosebery's speech at the Royal Colonial Institute on 1 March 1893, in G. Bennet (ed.), *The Concept of Empire. Burke to Attlee 1774–1914* (London, 1953), p. 310; J. Chamberlain, *Foreign and Colonial Speeches* (London, 1897), p. 114.
13 For an analysis of this type of informal imperialism, with special reference to the Middle East, see W. J. Mommsen, 'Europäischer Finanzimperialismus vor 1914. Ein Beitrag zu einer pluralistischen Theorie des Imperialismus', in idem, *Der europäische Imperialismus. Aufsätze und Abhandlungen* (Göttingen, 1979), pp. 85 ff.
14 W. R. Louis and R. Robinson, 'The United States and the liquidation of the British Empire in tropical Africa, 1941–1951', in P. Gifford and W. R. Louis (eds), *The Transfer of Power in Africa: Decolonization 1940–1960* (New Haven, Conn. and London 1982), pp. 31 ff. See also W. R. Louis, *Imperialism at Bay: The United States and the Decolonization of the British Empire, 1941–1945* (Oxford, 1976).
15 We are indebted here to D. A. Low's masterful analysis: 'The Asian mirror of tropical Africa's independence', in Gifford and Louis (eds), *Transfer of Power*, pp. 1–29, which

describes the initiating role of the nationalist movements on the Indian subcontinent and in Asia generally in this process.
16 See on this point Chapter 9 by Albert Wirz in this volume. See also idem, *Krieg in Afrika. Die nachkolonialen Konflikte in Nigeria, Sudan, Tschad und Kongo* (Wiesbaden, 1982).
17 ibid., espec. pp. 571 ff.
18 G. Arrighi, *The Geometry of Imperialism: The Limits of Hobson's Paradigm* (London, 1978), pp. 99 f.
19 The literature on *dependencia* and underdevelopment has grown to such proportions today that it is impossible to give a proper assessment here of its various tendencies. A good overview may be got from D. Seers (ed.), *Dependency Theory: A Critical Reassessment* (London, 1981); G. Kitching, *Development and Underdevelopment in Historical Perspective: Populism, Nationalism and Industrialisation* (London, 1982) emphasizes the populist strands within this school of thought. See also L. Blussé, H. L. Wesseling and G. D. Winius (eds), *History and Underdevelopment: Essays on Underdevelopment and European Expansion in Asia and Africa* (Leiden, 1980). N. Etherington, *Theories of Imperialism: War Conquest and Capital* (Beckenham, Kent, 1984) is disappointing on this count. For a survey of the main positions see W. J. Mommsen, *Theories of Imperialism*, pp. 113 ff. See also Chapters 20 and 21 in this volume by Colin Leys and Anthony Brewer.
20 This point is also made by Brewer, see above p. 328.
21 Robinson, 'Non-European foundations', pp. 124–5.
22 C. Leys, *Underdevelopment in Kenya: The Political Economy of Neo-Colonialism* (London, 1975), p. 17.
23 See Chapter 13 by Paul Bairoch in this volume.
24 See Chapter 14 by J. Forbes Munro in this volume.
25 See the interesting summary in D. K. Fieldhouse, *Colonialism 1870–1945: An Introduction* (London, 1981), pp. 88 ff.
26 Paris, 1961. English translation: *The Wretched of the Earth* (London, 1965).
27 See the passionate defence of the virtues of indirect rule by Margery Perham in her Reith Lectures 1961, *The Colonial Reckoning* (London, 1961), pp. 56 ff.
28 See J. Galtung, 'A structural theory of imperialism', *Journal of Peace Research*, vol. 8 (1971), pp. 81–116, 173–206.
29 Quoted by Arrighi, *Geometry*, p. 99.
30 See the controversy between David Fieldhouse and Volker Bornschier in Chapters 15 and 16 of this volume.
31 I. Wallerstein, *The Modern World-System. Vol. I: Capitalist Agriculture and the Origins of the European World Economy in the Sixteenth Century* (New York, 1974); idem, *The Modern World-System. Vol. 2: Mercantilism and the Consolidation of the European World Economy, 1600–1750* (New York, 1980); idem, *The Capitalist World Economy* (Cambridge, 1980); idem, *Historical Capitalism* (London, 1983).
32 Wallerstein, *Modern World-System*, Vol. 1, p. 73.
33 P. J. McGowan and B. Kordan, 'Imperialism in world-system perspective', *International Studies Quarterly*, vol. 25 (1981), pp. 43 ff.
34 A. G. Frank, *World Accumulation, 1492–1789* (London, 1978).
35 J. Galtung, T. Heiestad and E. Rudeng, 'On the decline and fall of empires: the Roman Empire and Western imperialism compared', *Review*, vol. 4 (1980), pp. 91–153.
36 H. Eisenhans, 'Grundlage und Entwicklung der kapitalistischen Weltwirtschaft', in D. Senghaas (ed.), *Kapitalistische Weltökonomie. Kontroversen über ihren Ursprung und ihre Entwicklungsdynamik* (Frankfurt-on-Main, 1979), p. 135.
37 See D. Senghaas (ed.), *Imperialismus und strukturelle Gewalt. Analysen über abhängige Reproduktion* (Frankfurt-on-Main, 1972), espec. pp. 17–18, 21.
38 See D. Senghaas, *Von Europa lernen. Entwicklungsgeschichtliche Betrachtungen* (Frankfurt-on-Main, 1982).
39 See Chapter 13 by Paul Bairoch in this volume.
40 S. Amin, *Unequal Development* (New York, 1976); D. Senghaas, 'Vorwort: Elemente einer Theorie des peripheren Kapitalismus', in idem (ed.), *Peripherer Kapitalismus. Analysen über Abhängigkeit und Unterentwicklung* (Frankfurt-on-Main, 1977), pp. 15–31.
41 See R. Aron, *The Imperial Republic: The United States and the World, 1945–1973* (London, 1973).

Notes on Contributors

Paul Bairoch is Professor of Economic History at the University of Geneva. His numerous books include *Le Tiers-monde dans l'impasse*. *Le démarrage économique du 18ᵉ au 20ᵉ siècle* (1971), *Révolution industrielle et sous-développement* (4th edn, 1974), *The Economic Development of the Third World since 1900* (1975), *Commerce extérieur et développement économique de l'Europe au XIXᵉ siècle* (1976), *Urban Unemployment in Developing Countries* (2nd edn, 1976), *Taille des villes, conditions de vie et développement économique* (1977) and *De Jéricho à Mexico. Les villes et l'économie dans l'histoire* (1985). He has edited, with Maurice Lévy-Leboyer, *Disparities in Economic Development since the Industrial Revolution* (1981) and published, with Bouda Etemad, *Commodity Structure of Third World Exports, 1830–1937* (1985).

Volker Bornschier is Assistant Professor of Sociology at the University of Zurich. His publications include *Wachstum, Konzentration und Multinationalisierung von Industrieunternehmen* (1976), *Multinationale Konzerne, Wirtschaftspolitik und nationale Entwicklung im Weltsystem* (1980) and *Transnational Corporations and Underdevelopment*, co-authored by Christopher Chase-Dunn (1985), as well as numerous articles on various problems of social stratification, economic sociology and world system analysis. He is member of the board and president of the World Society Foundation in Zurich.

Anthony Brewer is Senior Lecturer in Economics at the University of Bristol. Among his publications are *Marxist Theories of Imperialism. A Critical Survey* (1980) and *A Guide to Marx' 'Kapital'* (1984).

Dieter Brötel is Professor of History at the Pädagogische Hochschule Ludwigsburg. His major book-length study is *Französischer Imperialismus in Vietnam. Die koloniale Expansion und die Errichtung des Protektorates Annam-Tongking 1880–1885* (1971). His other works include articles on French economic interests in China and in the Malayan Peninsula in the nineteenth century, as well as essays on the teaching of history.

A. E. Campbell is Professor of American History at the University of Birmingham. Among his publications are *Great Britain and the United States, 1895–1903* (1960), *Expansion and Imperialism* (1970), *The USA in World Affairs* (1974) and *The Past as Destiny: American History and American Culture* (1974).

David Fieldhouse is Vere Harmsworth Professor of Imperial and Naval History at the University of Cambridge and Fellow of Jesus College. Among his major books are *Colonial Empires: A Comparative Study from the Eighteenth Century* (new edn, 1982), *The Theory of Capitalist Imperialism* (1967), *Economics and Empire 1830–1914* (1973), *Unilever Overseas: The Anatomy of a Multinational 1895–1965* (1979) and *Colonialism 1870–1945* (1981).

Dietrich Geyer is Professor of East European History at the University of Tübingen. He has written extensively on many aspects of modern Russian history. His more recent publications include *Der russische Imperialismus. Studien über den Zusammenhang von innerer und auswärtiger Politik 1860–1914* (1977), *Die russische Revolution. Historische Probleme und Perspektiven* (4th edn, 1985), *Kautskys russisches Dossier. Deutsche Sozialdemokratie als Treuhänder des russischen Parteivermögens 1910–1915* (1981). He is also editor of *Wirtschaft und Gesellschaft* *im vorrevolutionären Russland* (1975) and of *Osteuropa-Handbuch. Sowjetunion. Aussenpolitik* (3 vols, 1972–6).

Colin Leys is Professor of Political Studies at Queen's University, Kingston (Canada). He has published extensively on problems of the Third World, especially on East and Central Africa. Among his major books are *European Politics in Southern Rhodesia* (new edn, 1982), *Underdevelopment in Kenya: The Political Economy of Neo-Colonialism, 1964–1971* (1975) and *Politics in Britain: An Introduction* (1983).

Bernd Martin is Professor of Modern History at the University of Freiburg im Breisgau. He has published widely on Japanese and European contemporary history. His major studies include *Deutschland und Japan im Zweiten Weltkrieg. Vom Angriff auf Pearl Harbor bis zur deutschen Kapitulation* (1969) and *Friedensinitiativen und Machtpolitik im Zweiten Weltkrieg 1939–1942* (2nd edn, 1976). He has edited *Die deutsche Beraterschaft in China 1927–1938. Militär, Wirtschaft, Aussenpolitik* (1981), *Die Juden als Minderheit in der Geschichte*, with Ernst Schulin, (1981) and, with Alan S. Milward, *Agriculture and Food Supply in World War Two* (1985).

Ulrich Menzel is research fellow at the University of Bremen and lecturer in political science at the University of Frankfurt. Among his books are *Theorie und Praxis des chinesischen Entwicklungsmodells: Ein Beitrag zum Konzept autozentrierter Entwicklung* (1978), *Auswege aus der Abhängigkeit. Die entwicklungspolitische Aktualität Europas* (1985), *In der Nachfolge Europas. Autozentrierte Entwicklung in den ostasiatischen Schwellenländern Südkorea und Taiwan* (1985) and, with Gerd Wontroba, *Stagnation und Unterentwicklung in Korea. Von der Yi-Dynastie zur Peripherisierung unter japanischer Kolonialherrschaft* (1978).

Wolfgang J. Mommsen is Professor of History at the University of Düsseldorf. From 1977 to 1985 he was Director of the German Historical Institute London. He has published extensively on German and European history, on imperialism, on Max Weber and on the history and theory of historiography. Among his more recent books are *The Age of Bureaucracy: Perspectives on the Political Sociology of Max Weber* (1974), *Der europäische Imperialismus. Aufsätze und Abhandlungen* (1979), *Theories of Imperialism* (1980) and *Max Weber and German Politics, 1890–1920* (1984). He is also co-editor of the *Max Weber-Gesamtausgabe* (1984 ff.).

J. Forbes Munro is Senior Lecturer in Economic History at the University of Glasgow and is an editor of the *Journal of African History*. His publications include *Colonial Rule and the Kamba: Social Change in the Kenya Highlands, 1889–1939* (1975), *Africa and the International Economy 1800–1960* (1976) and *Britain in Tropical Africa 1880–1960: Economic Relationships and Impact* (1984).

Ian H. Nish is Professor of International History at the London School of Economics and Political Science. His many books and articles on international and Japanese history include *The Anglo-Japanese Alliance: The Diplomacy of Two Island Empires* (1966), *Alliance in Decline: A Study in Anglo-Japanese Relations 1908–1923* (1972), *Japanese Foreign Policy 1869–1942. Kasumigaseki to Miyakezaka* (1977) and *The Origins of the Russo-Japanese War* (1985). He is also the editor of *Anglo-Japanese Alienation 1919–1952* (1982) and, with Charles Dunn, *European Studies on Japan* (1978).

Jürgen Osterhammel is research fellow at the German Historical Institute London. His major publication to date is *Britischer Imperialismus im Fernen Osten. Strukturen der Durchdringung und einheimischer Widerstand auf dem chinesischen Markt, 1932–1937* (1983).

Hartmut Pogge von Strandmann is Fellow and Praelector of University College, Oxford. He is the editor of *Walther Rathenau, Tagebuch 1907–1922* (1967) of

Notes on Contributors

which a revised and extended translation will be published shortly: *Walther Rathenau. Diaries and Notes*. He is the co-editor, with Roger Bullen and Anthony Polonsky, of the Festschrift for James Joll, *Ideas into Politics* (1984) and joint author, with Imanuel Geiss, of *Die Erforderlichkeit des Unmöglichen* (1965). He has also published *Unternehmenspolitik und Unternehmensführung. Der Dialog zwischen Aufsichtsrat und Vorstand bei Mannesmann* (1978), as well as numerous articles on German imperialism and colonialism, German domestic politics, German-Russian industrial relations in the interwar period and the role of industrial interests in modern German society.

Ronald Robinson is Beit Professor of the History of the British Commonwealth and Fellow of Balliol College, Oxford. He is co-author, with the late John A. Gallagher, of *Africa and the Victorians: The Official Mind of Imperialism* (1961) and of the chapter on the partition of Africa in Vol. 11 of the *New Cambridge Modern History* (1962). Among his seminal articles on the theory of imperialism is 'Non-European foundations of European imperialism' (1972). He has recently been working on the transfer of power in tropical Africa.

Dietmar Rothermund is Professor of History at the South Asia Institute of the University of Heidelberg. His many publications include *Die politische Willensbildung in Indien 1900–1960* (1965), *Grundzüge der indischen Geschichte* (1976), *Europa und Asien im Zeitalter des Merkantilismus* (1978), *Government, Landlord and Peasant in India* (1978), *The Indian Economy under British Rule and Other Essays* (1982), *Indiens wirtschaftliche Entwicklung von der Kolonialherrschaft bis zur Gegenwart* (1985) and, with Hermann Kulke, *Geschichte Indiens* (1982). He has edited *Die Peripherie in der Weltwirtschaftskrise. Afrika, Asien, Lateinamerika 1929–1939* (1982).

Klaus Schwabe is Professor of Modern History at the Technische Hochschule Aachen. His publications include *Wissenschaft und Kriegsmoral. Die deutschen Hochschullehrer und die politischen Grundfragen des Ersten Weltkriegs* (1969), *Woodrow Wilson, Revolutionary Germany and Peacemaking 1918–1919* (1985) and *Woodrow Wilson* (1971). He is also co-editor, with Rolf Reichardt, of *Gerhard Ritter. Ein politischer Historiker in seinen Briefen* (1984), editor of *Die Ruhrkrise 1923* (1984) and the author of numerous articles on German and American history.

Tony Smith is Professor of Political Science at Tufts University, Medford (Mass.). He has published *The French Stake in Algeria, 1945–1962* (1978), *The Pattern of Imperialism: The United States, Great Britain and the Late Industrializing World since 1815* (1981) and, as an editor, *The End of European Empire: Decolonization After World War II* (1975). He is also well known for several articles on the theory of development and underdevelopment. At present he is completing a book on ideology entitled *Thinking like a Communist*.

B. R. Tomlinson teaches economic history at the University of Birmingham. He is the author of *The Indian National Congress and the Raj, 1929–1942. The Penultimate Phase* (1976) and of *The Political Economy of the Raj, 1914–1947: The Economics of Decolonization in India* (1979). He has also published a number of articles on British imperialism in South Asia and on the theory of decolonization.

H. L. Wesseling is Professor of History at the University of Leiden and Director of the Centre for the History of European Expansion. He is the author of *Soldaat en Krijger. Franse opvattingen over leger en Toerlog, 1905–1914* (1969) and of several important articles, notably on French and Dutch colonial history. He is also editor of the series *Comparative Studies in Overseas History* (since 1977).

Albert Wirz is Privatdozent and lecturer in history at the University of Zurich. His major books are *Vom Sklavenhandel zum kolonialen Handel. Wirtschaftsräume und Wirtschaftsformen in Kamerun vor 1914* (1972), *Krieg in Afrika. Die nach-*

kolonialen Konflikte in Nigeria, Sudan, Tschad und Kongo (1982) and *Sklaverei und kapitalistisches Weltsystem* (1984). He has also published several articles on the modern social and economic history of Africa and has contributed chapters on Africa to Rudolf von Albertini's *European Colonial Rule 1880–1940. The Impact of the West on India, South East Asia and Africa* (1982).

Index

Abéche 130
Accra 115n, 212
Acheson, Dean 180, 182
Afghanistan 47, 150–1, 284, 333, 344
Africa 4, 61, 97, 115n, 123–37, 179, 181, 198, 203, 212, 215n, 219–21, 237, 268–9, 273, 276, 278, 280, 283, 319, 334, 342, 345, 347; *see also* East Africa, Horn of Africa, North Africa, South Africa, South West Africa, West Africa
Akbar (Mogul Emperor) 140, 202
Albania 51
Alcock, Sir Rutherford 307
Alexander I (Tsar of Russia) 57
Alexander II (Tsar of Russia) 54
Algeria 23, 37, 187, 338, 342
Allende, Salvador 28, 47
America, *see* Central America, Latin America, North America, Pre-Columbian America, United States of America
Amin, Samir 353
Ang Duong (King of Cambodia) 171
Angola 47, 98
Annam 168–71, 176
Apter, David E. 318
Arabia 276
Arbenz, Jacobo 26
Argentina 208, 243, 274
Armenia 345
Aron, Raymond 16, 354
Arrighi, Giovanni xi, 346
Asia 5, 61, 63, 97, 181, 198, 200, 203, 214, 215n, 218–21, 237, 268–70, 273, 276–8, 334, 342, 347–8; *see also* Central Asia, East Asia, North-east Asia, South Asia, South-east Asia
Atatürk, Mustafa Kemal 57
Australasia 270, 274–5
Australia 69, 72–3, 275, 280
Austria 35, 102, 106–8, 111
Austria-Hungary 54
Awolowo, Obafemi 132
Ayandele, E. A. 132

Bairoch, Paul 6, 217–21, 348, 353
Balaguer, Joaquín 28
Balkans, The 57, 109, 112, 118n
Baltic, The 54, 56
Bangladesh (East Pakistan) 142, 150, 214, 221
Bao Dai (Emperor of Vietnam) 342
Baran, Paul A. 226, 236, 345

Barbados 212
Batistá (y Zaldivar), Fulgencio 27, 47
Bay of Pigs 27
Beard, Charles 13
Beckman, Bjorn 319, 322–3
Belgium 91, 96, 102, 278, 302, 342
Berlin 57, 106, 271, 339
Berry, Sara 130
Bessarabia 54
Biafra 136
Bidault, Georges 177
Bismarck, Otto Fürst von 51, 57, 90–1, 339
Blum, Léon 176
Bombay 212, 237
Bornschier, Volker 7
Bosch, Juan 27–8
Bose, Subhas Chandra 142
Boston 17
Brandt, Willy 24
Brazil 199, 243, 274, 316, 318
Brenner, Robert 317
Brest-Litovsk 99, 102
Bretton Woods 222
Brewer, Anthony 7, 321
Briand, Aristide 111
Brussels 95
Bukhara 61
Bukharin, Nikolaj Ivanovich 327
Bukovina 54
Bulgaria 108, 119n
Burma 73, 149, 153n, 180–1, 221, 248, 283, 340
Byé, Maurice 225
Brötel, Dieter 6
Brüning, Heinrich 119n
Bülow, Bernhard Fürst von 104
Bülow, Bernhard Wilhelm von 111

Cain, Peter J. 299
Calcutta 143, 317
Cambodia (Kampuchea) 167–87, 357
Cambridge 2
Campbell, A. E. 5
Canada 212, 227, 270, 274–5
Cannes 97
Canning, George 274
Canton (Guangzhou) 304–5
Cape Coast 212
Cape Province 275
Cardoso, Fernando Henrique 316, 321
Caribbean, The 39, 221
Carol, Prince (later Carol II, King of Romania) 107

364 Imperialism and After

Carpatho-Ukraine 54
Carranza, Venustiano 19
Carter, Jimmy (James Earl) 47-8
Castlereagh, Viscount (2nd marquis of Londonderry) 274
Castro, Fidel 27, 47
Catherine II (Tsarina of Russia) 54, 57
Caucasus, The 54
Central America 48, 344, 355
Central Asia 54, 57
Chad 123-37
Chamberlain, Joseph 338, 348
Chamberlain, Neville 100-1
Chang Myŏn 257
Charner, Leonard-Victor-Joseph 168
Chesneaux, Jean 186n
Chiang Kai-shek (Jiang Jieshi) 24, 46, 255
Chile 28, 33n, 47, 274
China 5, 7, 17-18, 22, 37, 45-7, 51, 58, 61, 64, 66-8, 70-2, 77-8, 83-6, 88, 149-51, 168-73, 176, 178, 180, 182-3, 192-3, 195, 198, 219-21, 247, 251-6, 259-60, 270, 277, 280, 285, 290-313, 339, 342, 347-8
Cholon 168
Clifford, Sir Hugh Charles 128
Cochin-China 167-71, 173-4, 177-8
Colbert, Jean-Baptiste 167
Colombia 243, 274
Confucius 67
Congo 181, 278-9, 342
Constantinople (Tsargrad) 56, 277
Cowen, M. P. 317
Cuba 17, 19-21, 27, 47, 61, 254, 286, 322
Curzon of Kedleston, Lord 150-1
Czechoslovakia 107-9, 111, 113, 302, 355

D'Argenlieu, Georges Thierry 177
Dawes, Charles G. 98
Dean, Britten 299
Decoux, Jean 176
Denmark 19
Diem, Ngo Dinh 25-6, 181-2
Djilas, Milovan 355
Dominican Republic 27-8
Dong Khanh (Emperor of Vietnam) 170
Doumer, Paul 171-2, 185n
Duisberg, Carl 108-9
Dulles, John Foster 24, 180-2
Dunning, John H. 230-1

East Africa 96
East Asia 254-6, 260-1, 290, 292, 302, 340; see also Far East
East Indies 340
East Prussia 54
Eastern Europe 61, 90, 96, 106, 112
Eden, Sir Anthony 100
Egbaland 128

Egypt 195, 202, 335, 341, 347, 353
Eisenhower, Dwight D. 25, 27, 46-7, 180-1
El Salvador 47
Elvin, Mark 220
Emmanuel, Arghiri 234, 317
Enders, Thomas 315
Epp, Franz Ritter von 99
Estonia 54
Europe 5-7, 9-10, 20-1, 37, 51, 63, 66, 69, 77, 93-4, 102, 105, 125-7, 137, 179-80, 194-8, 200, 202-4, 210, 214, 215n, 218-20, 226-7, 231, 250, 267-4, 276, 278, 281-2, 285-6, 303, 315, 317, 326-7, 333-6, 339, 345-6, 348, 355, 356; see also Eastern Europe, South-eastern Europe, Western Europe

Faletto, Enzo 321
Falkland Islands (Malvinas) 133, 322, 344
Fanon, Frantz 349
Far East 54, 56-7, 61, 167, 222, 270, 292, 301, 340, 354; see also East Asia
Ferry, Jules 170
Feuerwerker, Albert 294
Fieldhouse, David K. xi, 7, 157, 165n, 242-5, 290, 340, 347
Finland 54
Fischer, Georges x
Fontainebleau 177
Formosa, see Taiwan
France 4, 6, 8, 21, 23-5, 33n, 37, 44, 46, 52, 56-7, 67, 85, 92-4, 98, 102, 107, 109, 111-12, 125, 127, 128, 130, 134-7, 167-72, 175-7, 179-80, 255, 269, 276, 278-9, 300-2, 307, 335, 338, 340-3, 349
Frank, André Gunder 218, 294, 316-17, 321, 352
Frederick the Great (King of Prussia) 57
Frederick William III (King of Prussia) 57
Freycinet, Charles-Louis de Saulces de 169
Fukuda, Takeo 88

Gaddafi, Muammar 47
Gallagher, John A. 2-3, 15, 34-5, 123, 222, 297, 334-5, 340
Galtung, Johan 299, 305, 350, 353, 355
Gambetta, Léon 169
Gandhi, Mahatma 155
Garnier, Francis 168, 184n
Gaulle, Charles de 57, 176-7
Geneva 25, 181
Genoa 97
Germany 4, 6, 8, 18-20, 22, 29-30, 36, 50-1, 56-7, 61, 63, 67-9, 72, 75, 85, 87, 90-119, 182, 274, 300-3, 307, 319, 321
Gerschenkron, Alexander 292
Geyer, Dietrich 5
Girvan, Norman 350
Gold Coast 283

Gong, Prince 306
Gorchakov, Alexander Mikhailovich, Prince 57
Gowon, Yakubu 134
Grandière, Pierre-Paul-Marie de la 168
Great Britain 1–2, 4, 6, 8, 21, 23–5, 35, 39, 42, 56, 67–8, 70, 77, 85–8, 91–2, 96–8, 100–1, 105, 107, 109, 112, 125, 128, 132, 134, 137, 139–66, 168, 171, 196–8, 200, 205–6, 210–13, 218–19, 222–3, 227, 230, 237, 249, 255, 269–70, 273–80, 282–4, 299–304, 307, 321, 334–5, 338–41, 343–6, 348–9, 354, 356
Greece 25, 33n, 46, 107
Guantanamo 20
Guatemala 26, 47
Göring, Hermann 110

Habré, Hissein, 135
Habsburg Empire 90
Hahl, Albert 115n
Haiti 18
Hancock, Sir Keith ix, xi, 1
Hanoi 173, 175
Harden, Maximilian 91
Hay, John 18, 52, 85
Hebei 302
Hildebrand, Klaus 99–100, 116n
Hilferding, Rudolf 79, 226, 327
Hirohito (Emperor of Japan) 70
Hirota Kōki 75
Hitler, Adolf 20, 51, 54, 57, 60, 72, 99–103, 109, 114, 117n, 354
Ho Chi Minh 38, 44, 178
Hobson, John A. x, 1–3, 8, 18, 63, 268, 296
Holland (The Netherlands) 2, 4, 8, 23, 36, 167, 340–1
Hon Gay 169
Honduras 39
Hong Kong 7, 199, 247, 260, 290, 300, 303, 305
Hoover, Herbert 20
Horn of Africa 47
Hoshino Naoki 80n
Hué 169–70
Huerta, Victoriano 19
Hull, Cordell 21, 42
Hungary 28, 107–8, 110, 112, 118n, 119n, 355
Huntington, Samuel 315
Hymer, Stephen H. 227–8, 233, 237–8, 242

Iceland 231
India 6, 42, 69, 72–3, 139–66, 197–8, 212, 214, 219–20, 243, 249, 268, 270, 277–81, 282, 286, 295, 331, 334, 337, 340–1, 346
Indian Ocean 167
Indochina 6, 21, 25, 44, 46, 171–4, 176–83, 283, 340–1
Indonesia 2, 44, 180–1, 248

Iran (Persia) 45–7, 61, 195, 296, 308, 339, 357
Iraq 357
Ireland 321
Iriye, Akira 63
Ishii Kikujiro, Viscount 68
Ismail (Khedive of Egypt) 353
Israel 39, 45, 286, 357
Italy 35, 72, 109, 302
Itō Hirobumi 84
Ivan the Terrible (Tsar of Russia) 52, 54
Iwakura Tomomi, Prince 66, 83

Jamaica 193, 212
Japan 4–6, 8, 19–20, 23, 42, 45, 54, 57–8, 61, 63–89, 158, 172, 176–7, 181, 186n, 227, 250–60, 270, 277, 290, 293, 299–302, 305–7, 312n, 339–40, 348, 352, 354
Java 201, 218
Jeddah 178
Jiaozhou 85
Jinnah, Mohammed Ali 150
Johnson, Lyndon B. 24, 27–8, 47
Jos 129
Judd, Walter 180

Kaduna 129
Kampuchea, see Cambodia
Kano 129
Kastl, Ludwig 98
Katō Tomosaburō 86
Kautilya 147
Kay, Geoffrey 316–17
Ke Bao 169
Kennedy, John F. 27, 29, 47, 181
Kenya 348
Keynes, John Maynard 315, 320
Khiva 61
Khomeini, Ayatollah 47
Kinh Luoc 171
Kirkpatrick, Jean 315
Kishi Nobusuke 69, 71, 73–4, 80n
Kissinger, Henry A. 33, 45, 47
Kita Ikki 69, 72
Komotau (Bohemia) 109
Konoe Fumimaro, Count 71–2
Kordan, Bogdan 352
Korea, 5, 7, 24–5, 46, 66–7, 78, 83–5, 88, 180, 186n, 199, 247–8, 250–61
Kuhn, Axel 117n
Kuril Islands 54
Kuznets, Simon 204
Kōtoku Shūsui 8, 63
Kühlmann, Richard von 116n

Laclau, Ernesto 317
Lagos 129, 131
Lall, Sanjay 231–4, 238
Lancashire 277, 337
Lansing, Robert 68

Laos 168, 171, 182–3, 248
Latin America 4, 21, 26, 70, 113, 179, 198, 200, 202, 215n, 219–22, 227, 236, 268, 274, 280, 291, 305, 308, 316, 329
Latvia 54
Laurentie, Henri 177
Lausanne 57
Le Myre de Vilers, Charles-Marie 171
Lebanon 357
Lemberg 54
Lenin, Vladimir Ilich x, 18, 52, 57, 79, 226, 228, 268, 296, 319, 321–2, 328
Lerner, Daniel 249, 318
Leys, Colin xi, 7, 317, 348
Liaodong Peninsula 67, 80n
Libya 47
Lilienthal, David E. 225–6
Lin Zexu 304
Lipietz, Alain 317–20
Liska, George 15
Lithuania 54
Lloyd George, David 140, 151n
Locarno 96, 98
Logone Province 130
Loire region 169
London 106, 140, 144, 271, 274, 276
Louisiana 212
Lucerne 95
Ludendorff, Erich 102
Luther, Martin 51
Lyons 168, 170, 172
Lüthy, Herbert 335

Macaulay, Thomas Babington 349
Madras 212
Maizels, Alfred 211
Malaya 181, 279, 340
Malaysia 180
Malloum, Felix 135
Malthus, Thomas Robert 169, 220
Manchester 237, 321
Manchukuo 86–7, 252–3, 306
Manchuria 5, 20, 61, 67, 69–70, 75, 77, 80n, 84–8, 247–8, 250–5, 260, 290, 300–1, 306–7
Manhattan 237
Mao Zedong 135, 255
Marcussen, H. S. 317
Marseille, Jacques 173
Marshall, Alfred 228
Martin, Bernd 5, 8
Marx, Karl 226, 249, 268, 315, 318–19, 321, 331
Matsuoka Yosuke 87
McCarthy, Joseph 180
McClelland, Charles E. 318
McGowan, Patrick J. 352
McKenna, Reginald 237
McKinley, William 17

McLean, David 299
Mediterranean, The 277–8
Mekong Delta 183
Melbourne 275
Mendès-France, Pierre 178–9
Menzel, Ulrich 7, 294
Merhav, Meir 244
Mexico 19–20, 25, 199, 243, 274
Middle East 195, 222, 236–7, 345
Midlands 321
Midway 254
Mogul Empire 269
Mohammed, Murtala 134
Molotov, Vyacheslav Mikhailovich 57
Mommsen, Wolfgang J. 3, 267
Mongolia 61, 195, 251
Montreal 275
Montreux 57
Morocco 335
Morris-Jones, W. H. x
Moscow 54, 56–7, 180, 355
Moulder, Frances 220, 295
Muhammad Ali (Khedive of Egypt) 276, 345
Mukden (Shenyang) 86
Munck, Ronaldo 319
Munich 109
Munro, J. Forbes 7, 348
Murphey, Rhoads 294
Mus, Paul 177
Myrdal, Gunnar 250
Müller, Max 146

Nairobi 237
Namibia 357
Nanjing 86, 305–6
Napoleon Bonaparte (Emperor of France) 57
Napoleon III (Emperor of France) 57
Ndjamena 135
Near East 56
Nehru, Jawaharlal 148–9
Neto, Agostinho 47
New Caledonia 72
New Delhi 145
New Zealand 72, 275
Ngo Dinh Diem, see Diem
Nguyen Anh (Emperor of Vietnam) 167–8
Nicaragua 47
Nicholas I (Tsar of Russia) 52
Nigeria 123–37
Nish, Ian H. 5
Nixon, Richard M. 14, 25–6, 47, 181–2
Norodom (King of Cambodia) 171–2
North Africa 21, 277–8, 285, 349
North America 212
North-east Asia 84, 86
Norway 302

O'Brien, Patrick 213, 218

Oduduwa 131
Ogata, Sadako 86
Okey, Robin 118n
Orange Free State 275–6
Osterhammel, Jürgen 7
Ottoman Empire 54, 61, 269, 278, 285, 296, 308, 339, 345

Pacific Islands 72, 254
Pakistan 142, 150–1, 154, 243, 346
Palestine 283
Palma, G. 319
Palmerston, Viscount 276–7
Panama Canal 19
Papen, Franz von 112, 119n
Pareto, Vilfredo 231
Paris 18, 98, 106, 115n, 116n, 168, 175, 212, 271
Park Chung Hee 257–8
Patel, Vallabhbhai 140
Peking 70, 169, 180, 277, 300
Penrose, Edith 239
Persia, *see* Iran
Persian Gulf 278
Person, Yves 134
Peru 302
Pescadores, The 67
Peter the Great (Tsar of Russia) 54
Philippines, The 2, 17–18, 21, 34, 44, 46, 73, 180, 186n
Phipps, Sir Eric 90
Pigneau de Béhaine, Pierre-Joseph-Georges 168
Pignon, Léon 177
Pogge von Strandmann, Hartmut xi
Pol Pot 183
Poland 39, 47, 54, 56–7, 102, 107, 113, 118n, 318, 355
Polish Corridor 102
Port Vila 179
Portugal 4, 8, 35, 100, 162, 212, 274, 318, 342
Posse, Hans 112
Prague 109
Prebisch, Raul 205, 207
Pre-Columbian America 195
Puerto Rico 17, 21, 27, 32n
Pusan 66
Puyi, Henry 306

Qingdao 67, 85, 302
Qing Empire 269, 278

Rabeh fadl Allah 136
Rapallo 56–7
Rathenau, Walther 91
Reagan, Ronald 47
Reid (Cabral), Donald 27
Rhee, Syngman 256–7
Rhineland 102

Ricardo, David 230, 268
Richards, Sir Arthur 132
Robb, Peter 295
Robequain, Charles 173
Robinson, Ronald xi, 2–3, 9, 15, 34–6, 38, 78, 123, 125–6, 222, 297, 299, 305–6, 329, 331, 334–6, 340, 347
Rockhill, William W. 307
Roman Empire 195, 352
Romania 54, 107–8, 119n
Rome 126–7, 226
Roosevelt, Franklin D. 20–2, 28, 42, 44, 176, 290
Roosevelt, Theodore 17, 85
Rosebery, 5th earl of 338
Rosenau, James N. 296
Rostow, Walt W. 181–2, 249, 320
Rothermund, Dietmar 6
Ruhr area 93
Rusk, Dean 182
Ryūkyū Islands (Okinawa) 66, 186n

Saar area 102
Sahelian states (Chad) 128
Saigon 25, 168, 173
Saint Petersburg 57, 84
Sainteny, Jean 177
Sakhalin 54
Salewski, Michael 115n
San Francisco 76, 178–9, 255, 317
Santo Domingo 27–8
Sanyuanli 305
Saul, S. B. 337–8
Schacht, Hjalmar 98–9, 110, 116n
Schleicher, Kurt von 112, 119n
Schmokel, Wolfe 99
Schnee, Heinrich 95, 97, 116n
Schröder, Hans-Jürgen 113
Schwabe, Klaus 4, 34–5
Schumpeter, Joseph A. x, 78, 268
Scotland 321
Seers, Dudley 318
Senghaas, Dieter 353
Servan-Schreiber, Jean-Jacques 226, 230
Seton-Watson, Hugh 2
Shandong 68
Shanghai 86, 300–2
Shidehara Kijūrō 83
Shiina Etsusaburo 79
Shils, Edward 318
Shimonoseki 80n, 312n
Siam, *see* Thailand
Siberia 19, 54, 69, 85–6, 252
Sierra Leone 212
Sihanouk, Norodom, Prince 183
Simon, Sir John 100
Singapore 7, 87, 181, 199, 247, 260, 318
Singer, Hans 207

368 *Imperialism and After*

Sisowat (King of Cambodia) 171–2
Smith, Tony 5, 33n
Sokoto (Northern Nigeria) 128, 131
South Africa 270, 274–5, 286, 337, 357
South Asia 220–1, 283
South-east Asia 42, 44, 64, 66, 70, 72–3, 76, 78, 87–8, 168, 170, 180–3, 221, 237, 283, 291, 340
South-eastern Europe 110–11, 113, 119n
South Pacific Islands 87
South West Africa 97–8
Southern Rhodesia 278
Soviet Union (Russia) 2, 4–6, 9–10, 19, 22–4, 27–30, 39, 41, 46–62, 67–8, 70, 72, 84–5, 87, 101, 103–5, 113, 150–1, 180–3, 194, 203, 217, 219, 254–6, 277–8, 285, 300, 302, 319, 327, 330–1, 333, 340, 342, 344, 354–6
Spa 97
Spain 17, 35, 212, 274, 318
Speer, Albert 73
Stalin, Joseph 46, 52–7, 59–60, 72
Stinnes, Hugo 106
Strachey, John 218
Streeten, Paul 231–4
Stresemann, Gustav 98–9, 115n, 116n
Stuttgart 96
Suez 23, 354, 356
Sun Yat-sen 292
Sunkel, Osvaldo 315
Swainson, Nicola 317
Sweden 158, 227
Sweezy, Paul 226
Switzerland 214
Sydney 275
Syria 276

Taiwan 5, 7, 46, 66–7, 78, 88, 199, 247, 250–1, 253–6, 258, 260–1, 300
Tanaka Kakuei 88
Tardieu, André 176
Thailand 171, 181, 296, 339
Thornton, Archibald P. 15
Tianjin 302
Tibet 149
Tocqueville, Alexis de 52
Tokyo 66, 73, 75, 80n, 83, 88
Tombalbaye, Francois (Ngarta) 135
Tomlinson, B. R. 6
Tonkin 167–71, 173, 175, 179
Toronto 275
Torp, J. 317
Transvaal 276
Treviranus, Gottfried 119n
Truman, Harry S. 25, 44, 180, 255
Tu Duc (Emperor of Vietnam) 168
Tunisia 347
Turkey 46, 56–7, 278
Tyrell, Sir William 116n

Ukraine 54
United States of America 2, 4–5, 8–9, 13–48, 51–2, 58, 60–1, 63–4, 67–70, 73–5, 77, 79, 85–8, 106–7, 124–5, 144, 172, 178–83, 193, 198, 207, 213, 217, 219, 222–3, 226–7, 230–1, 235, 237, 250, 253–8, 268, 270, 274–5, 283, 285, 291, 300, 302–3, 305, 307, 330–1, 333, 338, 340–1, 344, 354–6
Upper Silesia 102
Urabi Pasha 346
Uruguay 299

Vatican, The 178
Vernon, Raymond 124
Versailles 56–7, 68, 70, 92, 103–4, 113, 168, 300
Vichy 176
Vienna 106–7, 109, 111
Vietnam 6, 13–14, 17, 24–6, 37–9, 44–7, 52, 167–87, 248, 255, 257–8, 286, 333, 342, 344, 357
Vinh San, Prince (Duy Than) 177
Virgin Islands 19
Vladivostok 54

Wallerstein, Immanuel 220, 250, 294–5, 351–2
Wang Jingwei 306
Wang Yanan 8, 296–7
Warren, Bill, 234, 317–21, 323, 331–2
Washington 26–8, 68, 85, 300, 315
Weber, Max 79, 139
Weiner, Myron 318
West Africa 98, 125, 173–4, 179, 277, 279–80, 283, 317, 339, 348
West Indies 212
Western Europe 24, 192, 207, 209, 213, 230, 235
Williams, Eric 218
Williams, William Appleman 14, 19
Wilson, Woodrow 4, 18–20, 22–3, 25, 28–30, 252
Winn, Peter 298–9
Wirz, Albert 6, 345
Witte, Sergej Yulyevich 61
Witwatersrand 276

Yalta 22, 254, 355
Yokohama 80n
Yoruba Kingdoms (Western Nigeria) 128
Yoshida Shigeru 75
Young, Ernest P. 306
Young, Owen D. 98
Yuan Shikai 68
Yugoslavia 22, 107, 119n
Yunnan 169

Zaire 342
Zambia 322